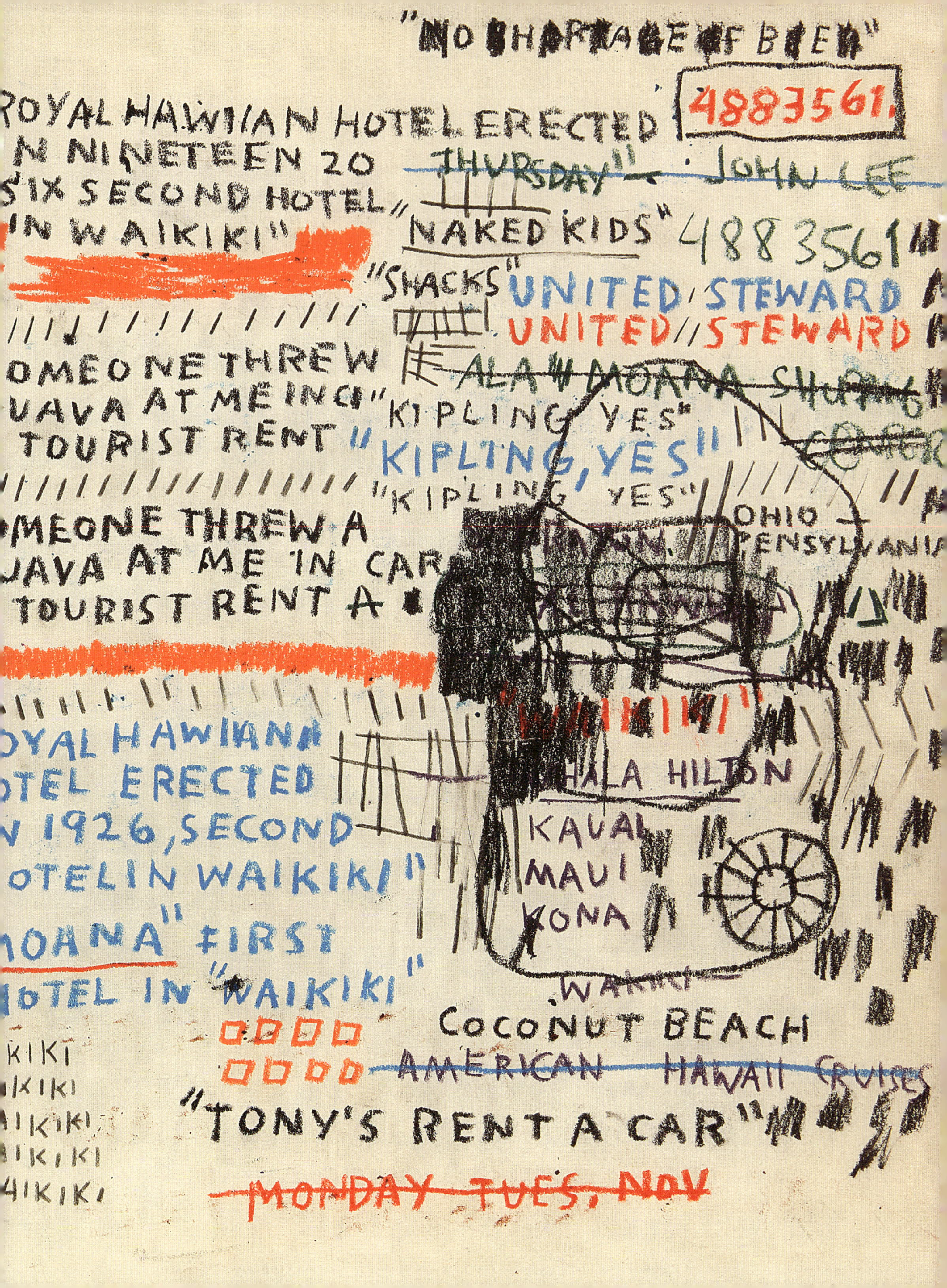
"NO SHORTAGE OF BEER"
4883561.
ROYAL HAWIIAN HOTEL ERECTED
N NINETEEN 20
SIX SECOND HOTEL
IN WAIKIKI"
"THURSDAY"
JOHN LEE
"NAKED KIDS"
4883561
"SHACKS"
UNITED STEWARD
UNITED STEWARD
ALA MOANA
OMEONE THREW
UAVA AT ME INC"
TOURIST RENT "
"KIPLING YES"
"KIPLING, YES"
"KIPLING YES"
OHIO
PENSYLVANIA
MEONE THREW A
UAVA AT ME IN CAR
TOURIST RENT A
"WAIKIKI"
OYAL HAWIANA
OTEL ERECTED
N 1926, SECOND
OTELIN WAIKIKI"
HALA HILTON
KAUAI
MAUI
KONA
OANA" FIRST
OTEL IN "WAIKIKI"
COCONUT BEACH
AMERICAN HAWAII CRUISES
KIKI
IKIKI
IKIKI
IKIKI
IKIKI
"TONY'S RENT A CAR"
MONDAY TUES, NOV

JEAN-MICHEL BASQUIAT:
KING PLEASURE©

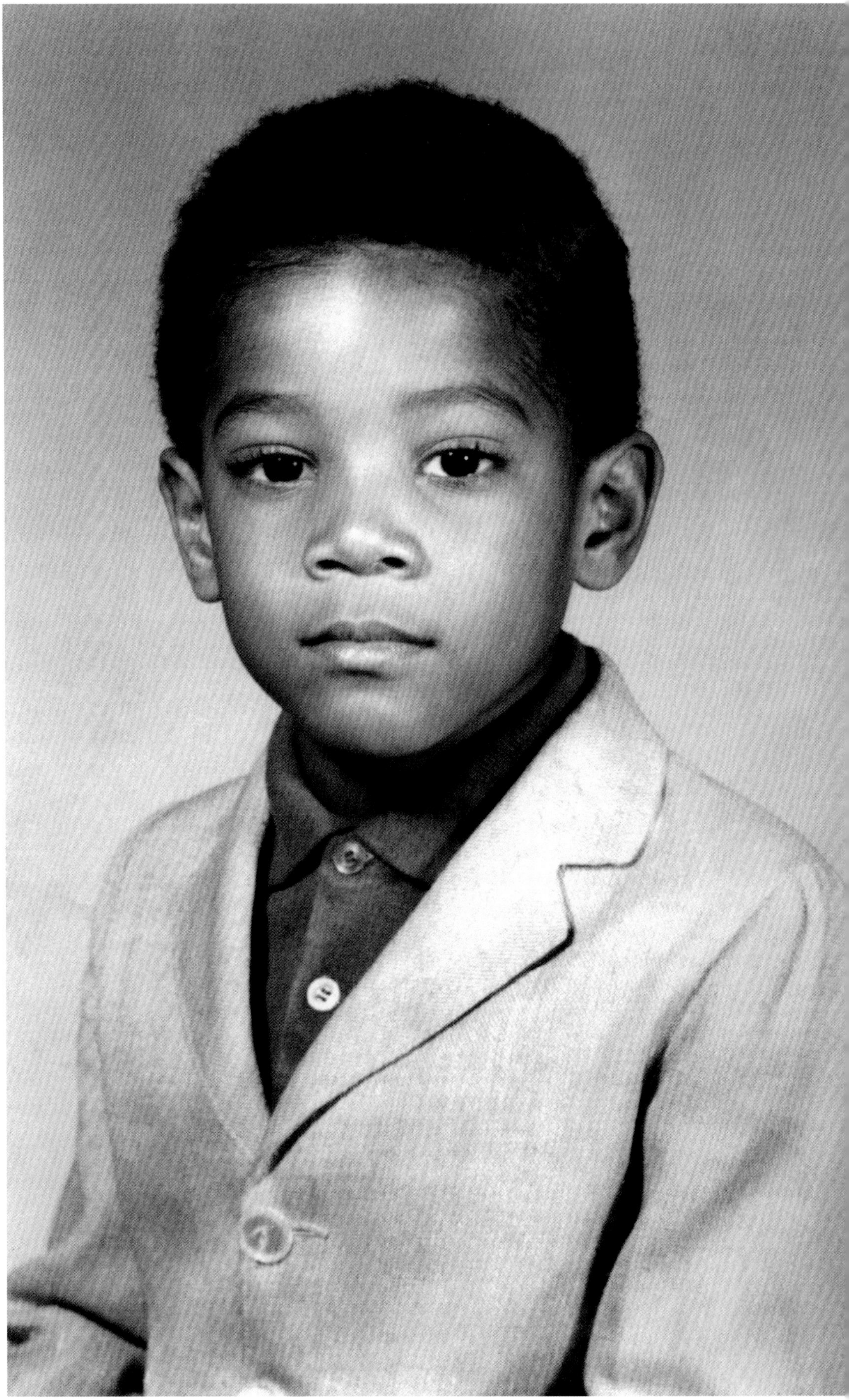

JEAN-MICHEL BASQUIAT: KING PLEASURE©

BY THE FAMILY OF JEAN-MICHEL BASQUIAT

Lisane Basquiat
Jeanine Heriveaux
Nora Fitzpatrick

Rizzoli Electa

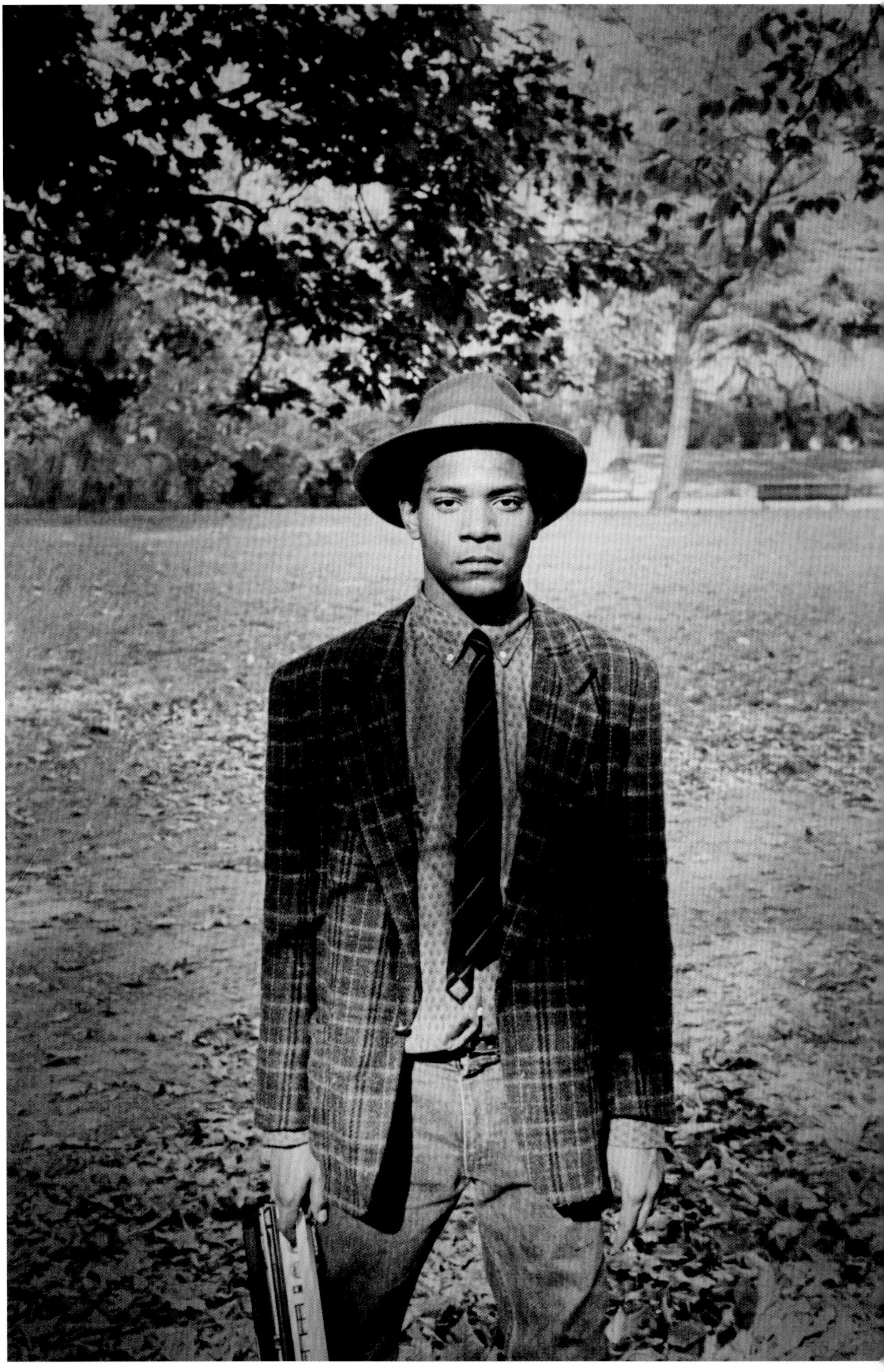

CONTENTS

FOREWORD

The decision to curate an exhibition and write this catalogue devoted to Jean-Michel's artwork from the family's collection did not come easily. The impetus to do this stemmed from conversations we had that his works needed to be seen and not hidden away in a warehouse. This is not meant to be a scholarly exhibition and book on Jean-Michel but a fresh perspective told from our family's point of view. Creating the themes, choosing the works, and revisiting our childhood memories and family stories has been joyful and profoundly healing for my sister Lisane, our stepmother Nora, and me. Carefully going through what he left behind—books, hundreds of VHS movies, his collections of African sculpture, toys, and other objects, and his many sketchbooks and notes—has afforded us an even richer understanding of our brother now as adults. In putting the project together, we have also connected, and reconnected, with so many people who were a part of Jean-Michel's life—it has been such a blessing. JEANINE

What you hold in your hands is a celebration of the life, legacy, and voice of Jean-Michel Basquiat, and I want to open it with a note of gratitude: thank you for seeing him. Our family is humbled and in awe of how impactful our brother's life was and how widely appreciated and loved he is. We are profoundly happy for him.

In the pages that follow, we share an intimate and personal view on our brother Jean-Michel's life that only we as his family can share. Each chapter—replete with photographs, personal effects (from childhood notebooks to the bicycle he used to get around New York City), and the extraordinary drawings and paintings from our family's collection—is the distilled result of countless hours spent poring over all things Jean-Michel. We hope that you enjoy this glimpse into his life's journey as much as we've enjoyed creating it. LISANE

PAGE 4
Jean-Michel Basquiat, Milan, 1986

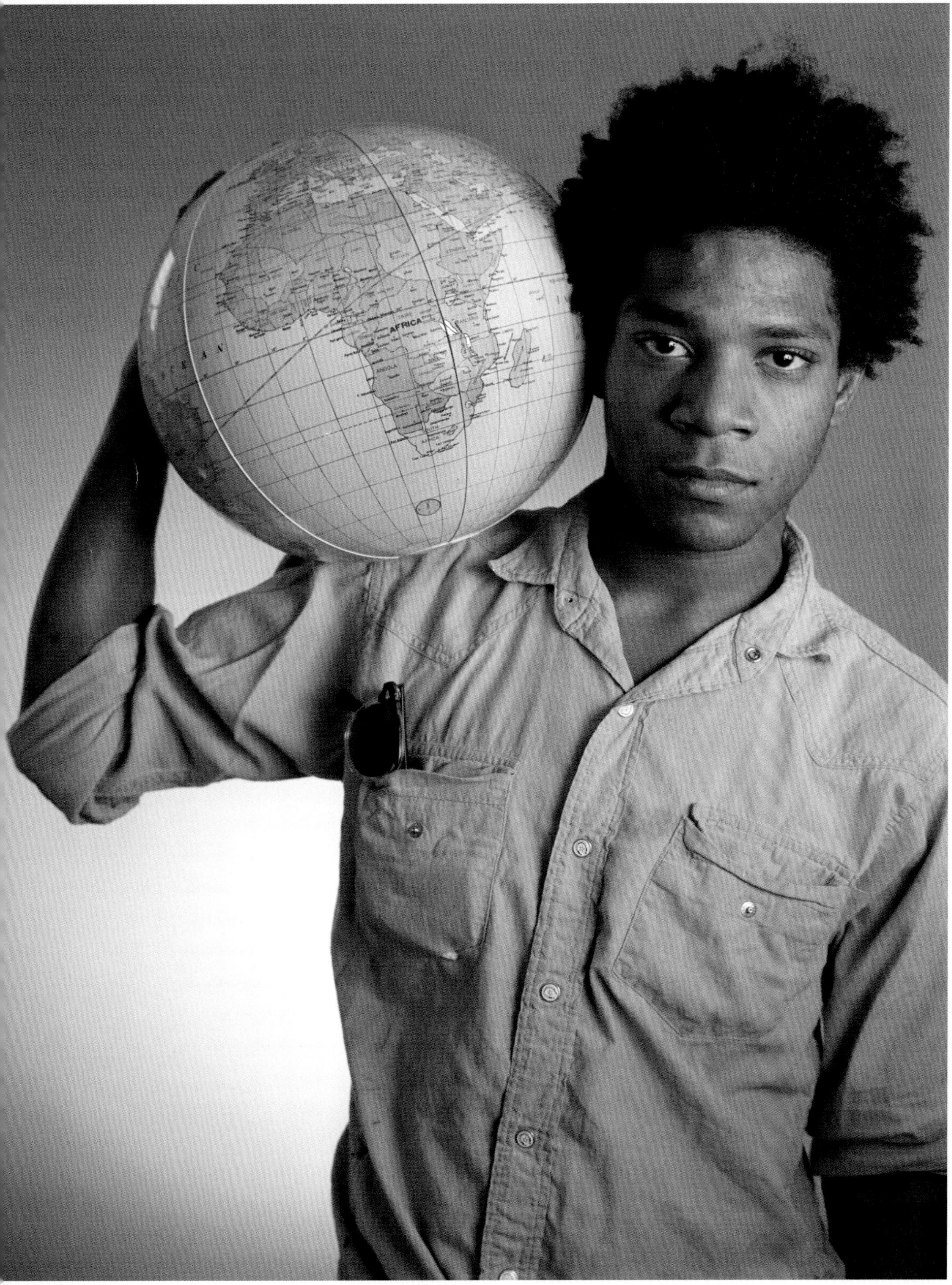

Jean-Michel, May 29, 1984 © CHRISTOPHER MAKOS

Jean-Michel Basquiat was born in Brooklyn on Thursday, December 22, 1960, to a Haitian father and a Brooklyn-born Puerto Rican mother. He entered the world less than two months after Cassius Clay made his professional boxing debut in a six-round decision over Tunney Hunsaker, within weeks of John F. Kennedy being elected president of the United States, and at the height of the Civil Rights Movement. The year 1960 was also referred to as the "Year of Africa," a time of declared independence for seventeen countries across the continent that by year's end had all joined the United Nations, evidence of the increased focus on Pan-Africanism. These are among the many topics that fueled my brother's work.

Jean-Michel always seemed profoundly connected to the myriad influences that informed his identity, from our familial heritage to the popular culture that shaped his generation. From the time he was a child, he was inquisitive and deeply observant—he watched people and their behaviors, and tracked how their beliefs created the world around him. Through his work Jean-Michel challenged us to look at life through a broader lens and encouraged us to aspire to a higher level of consciousness about the world we live in. He sought meaning in everything that surrounded him and, as he himself said, thought not about art but about life. He generously shared what he learned and did so without mincing words. Jean-Michel is and has always been fire. *Fire*.

In bringing together the photographs and other material for this chapter—going through copious photo albums and boxes of mementos from our childhood—I reflected on the time my brother entered the world. Born a year after the tragic loss of my parents' first child, Jean-Michel was their first living child and only son. He was Jeanine's and my protective, rambunctious, and pioneering older brother who paved the path for so much. Jean-Michel was huge energy entering this world. LISANE

1960

Matilde Basquiat with Jean-Michel, Prospect Heights, Brooklyn, 1961. *Look at Jean-Michel looking at us even then.* LISANE

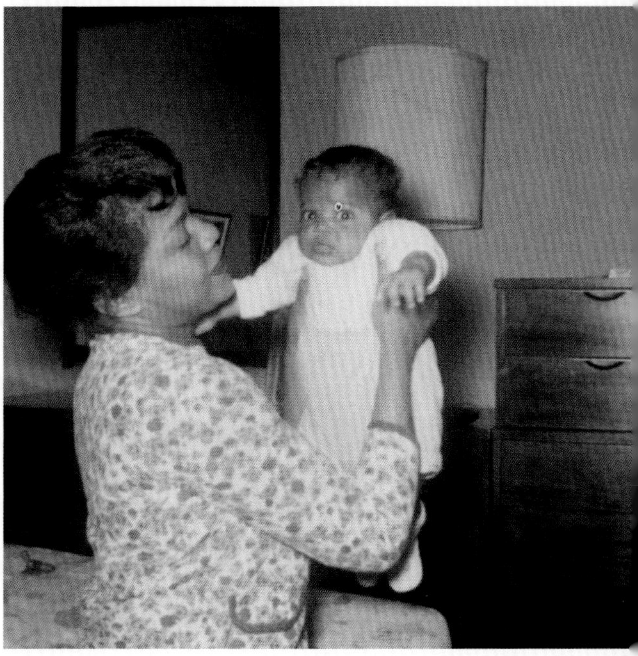

GENESIS

Matilde, our mother, was the second child and only daughter to parents who migrated to the mainland from the Commonwealth of Puerto Rico. Her father, John Andrades Sr., was a longshoreman who made his way to Texas to earn money to send back to his family in Puerto Rico. A Black Puerto Rican man who'd never experienced segregation, he soon left Texas for Philadelphia to live with a cousin who helped him become a Merchant Marine. Matilde's mother, Flora, was sent to Philadelphia by her family to go to nursing school. She and John's family knew each other through a Christian school that Flora's mother owned in Puerto Rico. The couple met in Philadelphia, married, and moved to Brooklyn to start their lives.

John and Flora Andrades had four children in all: my mother and her brothers, John Jr., Reuben [Sr.], and Joseph. The family lived in Bushwick, a working-class neighborhood in the northern part of Brooklyn. LISANE

By the mid 1950s in Haiti, Dr. François "Papa Doc" Duvalier had firmly established his presidential throne with support from the Tontons Macoutes, a special operations unit he created to counter any threat against his regime. The country was in terrorized turmoil as examples were made of alleged political opponents who were held under house arrest, beaten, burned, or who simply disappeared in the middle of the night. One such victim was Yves Basquiat, who at twenty-four was murdered on his way home to his pregnant wife after expressing his disdain for the political environment at the local post office while in conversation with other men.

Soon after the death of his brother and amid the growing violence, Gerard Basquiat, our father, received his mother's blessing to leave Port-au-Prince and the havoc that Papa Doc was wreaking on his country and, in particular, the Haitian elite. He left for what his parents, Cheristine and Leonce Basquiat, hoped would be a better life in New York for their seventeen-year-old son. Gerard's parents, older brother Lesly, and younger sister Marie Carmelle remained in the country until soon after his father Leonce died while the family was under house arrest.

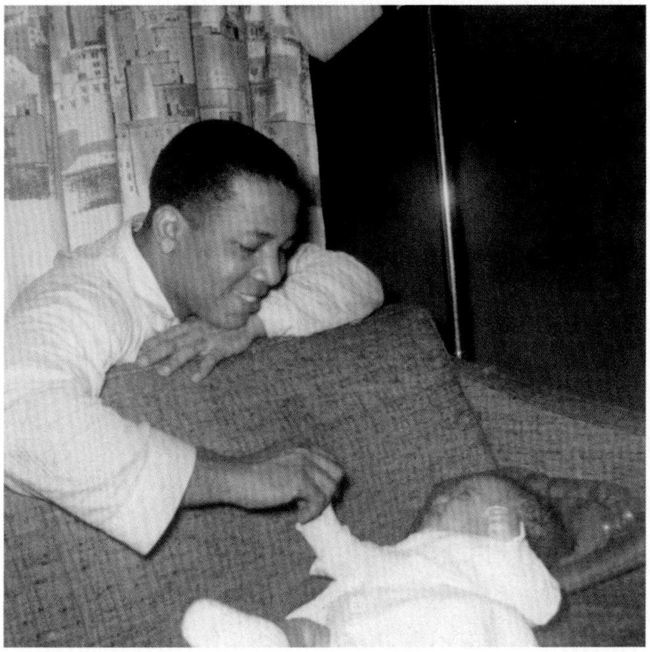

Gerard Basquiat with Jean-Michel, Prospect Heights, Brooklyn, 1961

Gerard arrived in New York in 1955 in the dead of winter and would later (and often) share with his children that he "came to this country with a toothbrush in my pocket, no money, and I couldn't speak or understand English. It was so cold!"

Once here, he connected with other young Haitian men with whom he lived and worked. His first job entailed hauling racks of clothing through the Garment District, work that was easy to do for non-English-speaking immigrants.

Our parents, Gerard and Matilde, met at a local dance hall. My mother attended with her brothers and my father with his friends. They bonded over music and were able to communicate in Spanish. She would help him learn English and navigate the nuances of life in the United States. Ambitious and charismatic, he would provide her the stability that she so desired.

They were married in 1957 and set out with very clear goals in mind. He would attend City College as a night student while working a full-time job in an accounting department by day. My mother would have the primary responsibility of keeping their home. Their first son, Max, was stillborn in 1959; they were devastated. A year later, in 1960, Jean-Michel was born, followed by me in 1964 and Jeanine in 1967. Gerard and Matilde were very determined to live the proverbial American Dream, and Gerard was resolved to "make it in this country." By their mid-twenties, they had purchased their first home on 35th Street in the East Flatbush neighborhood of Brooklyn. LISANE

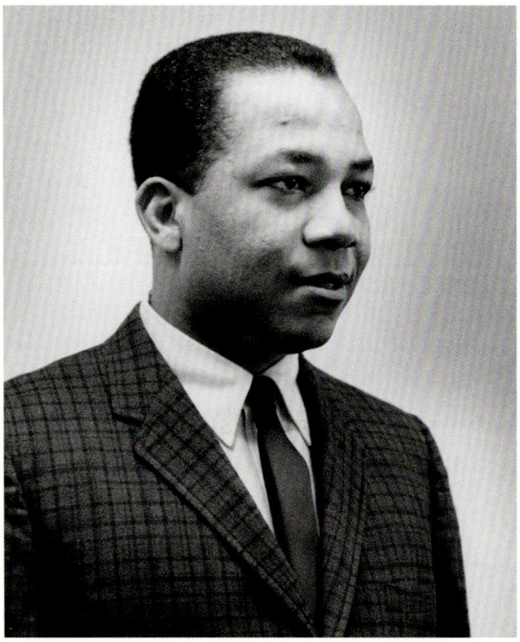

Gerard.
Our father, whom we called "Papa." This became an affectionate nickname of sorts used by friends and family as well. Papa was always so well dressed. LISANE

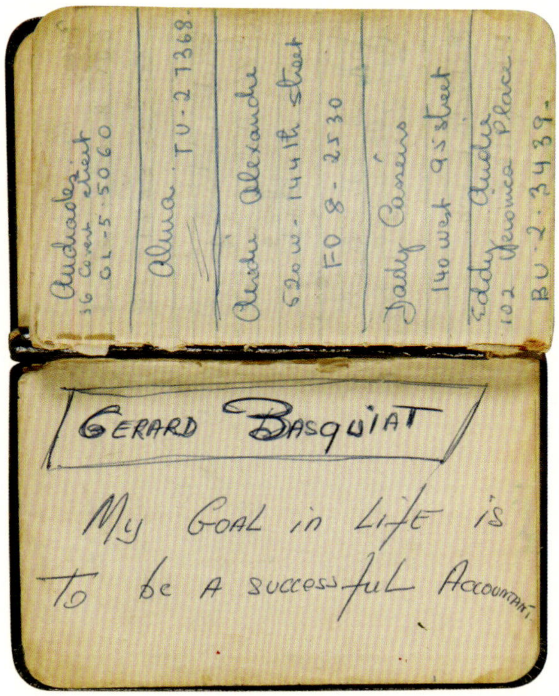

Gerard's address book.
When we were kids, our father shared stories about listening to Haitian radio and hearing about America. As a teen he aspired to come to the United States to become a businessman. JEANINE

Matilde pregnant
with Jean-Michel,
1960

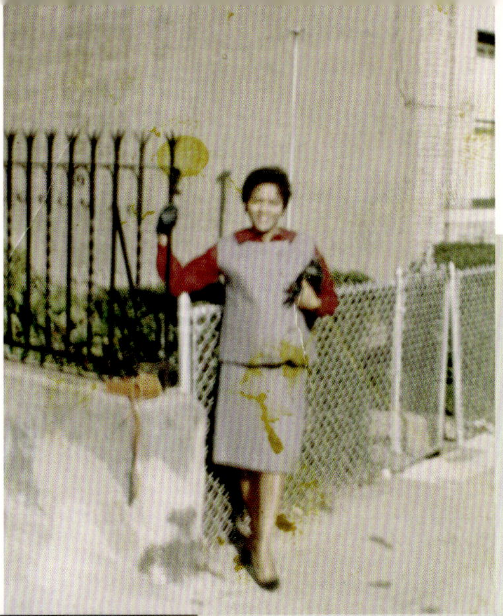

Jean-Michel's birth
announcement,
1960

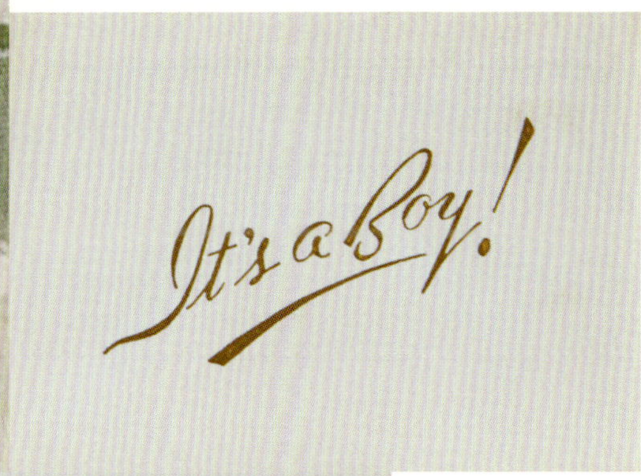

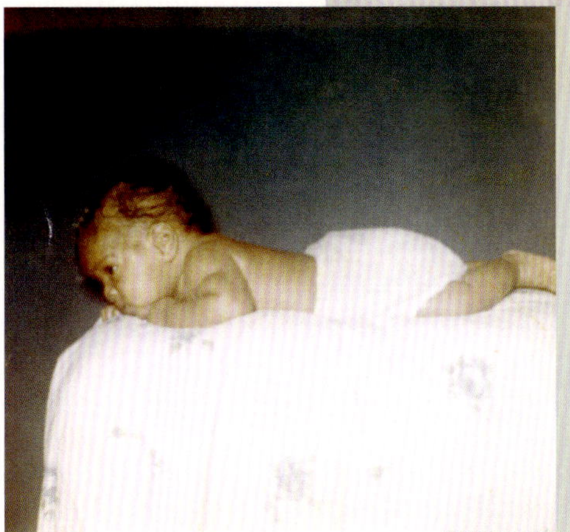

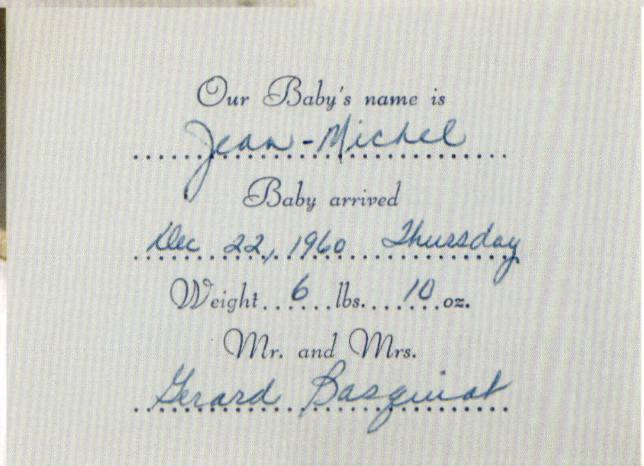

Gerard with
Jean-Michel,
Prospect Heights,
Brooklyn,
March 1961

ABOVE AND RIGHT
Jean-Michel,
Prospect Heights,
Brooklyn, ca. 1961

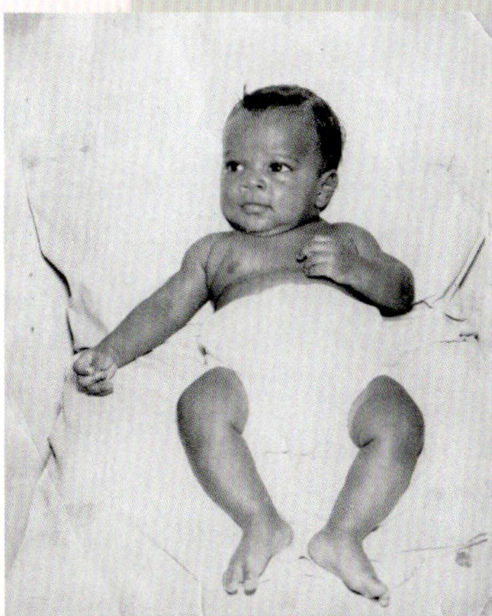

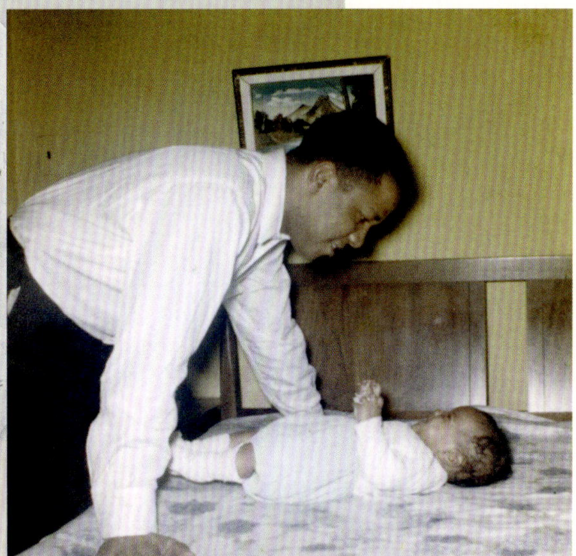

RIGHT
Matilde with
Jean-Michel, Prospect
Heights, Brooklyn,
March 1961

BOTTOM FAR RIGHT
Flora Andrades (the
Basquiat children's
grandmother, whom they
called "Abuelita," an
affectionate way to say
grandmother in Spanish)
with Jean-Michel and his
cousin Reuben Andrades
Jr., in her garden in
Bushwick, Brooklyn, 1961

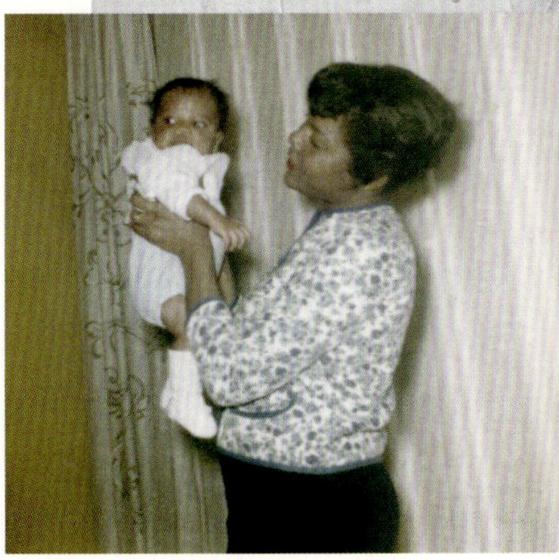

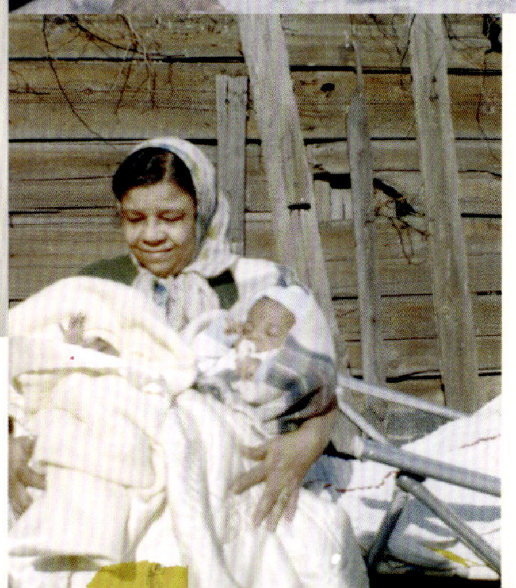

EXTENDED FAMILY

We have a fairly large extended family, particularly on our mother's side. Our maternal uncles had several children: Juan Jr. (Johnny) has two daughters, Hilda and Nita; and Reuben Jr., Ali, Michael, Theresa, and Andrea are the children of Reuben Sr. I was a baby, but in the early years Jean-Michel and Lisane spent quite a bit of time in Bushwick, where they had close relationships with Reuben Sr.'s kids. Jean-Michel and Reuben Jr. were two months apart in age and very close when they were young, most of the time celebrating birthdays together.

Our paternal grandparents Leonce and Cheristine (née Augustin) Basquiat's children were our father Gerard, Lesly, Marie Carmelle, and their half-brother Yves. Yves had a daughter, Katia, and our Aunt Marie Carmelle has four daughters: Patricia, Anna, Maria, and Christine. JEANINE

After leaving Puerto Rico, our maternal grandparents settled their family in Bushwick, Brooklyn, where our mother grew up. Their house was always very lively. Our Uncle Reuben, Aunt Martha, and our cousins lived in their apartment on the top floor. Our grandmother's kitchen was on the ground floor and was center stage. Our grandmother, Abuelita, was very beautiful, quite social, and very animated. She would often entertain her girlfriends from church and we children loved to bear witness to all the conversations and goings-on. She was a fantastic cook, and when Jean-Michel, Jeanine, and I visited we would hang out with our cousins and all hungrily await her rice, beans, and *bacalao*. On Saturday evenings, our grandfather, whom we called Abuelo, and his buddies would hold jam sessions in the basement. We children weren't allowed down there but we would dance around to their congas, guitars, and other instruments, and take turns lying on the ground to watch their performance from the top of the stairs. The men always looked so happy. Looking back on it now, I imagine that it reinforced their connection to each other and to Puerto Rico.

We would visit our mother's family there often, as they were close to where we lived. Bushwick was always teeming with activity—there were lots of kids, block parties, music, and passion. LISANE

Abuelita with Matilde at her graduation from middle school, June 27, 1949

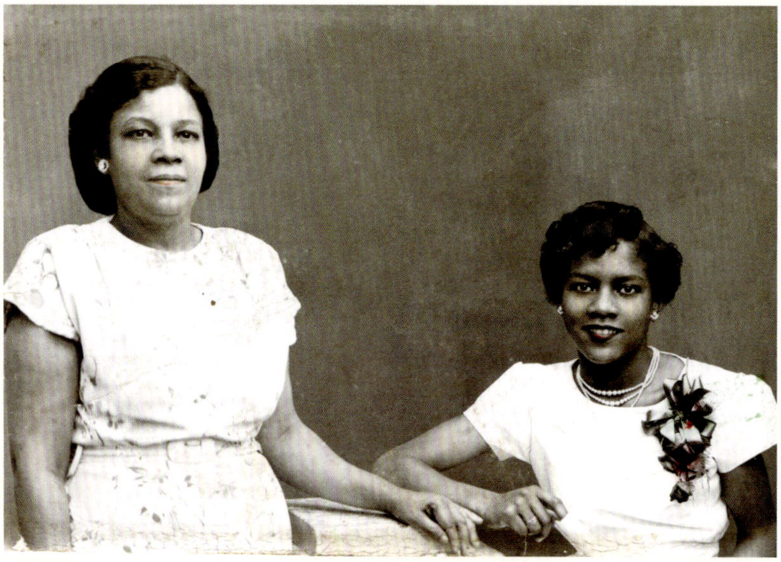

Untitled (No Summer Hot Water Ossning)
Ballpoint pen and crayon on paper
19¼ × 15 in. (48.90 × 38.1 cm).
Jean-Michel always had a strong regard for tribal history and familial connections. This work reads like a Jean-Michel version of a genogram. Some information about the references: "Woody" Worthy was a friend of our father's and he lived in Ossining. "Bongos in the basement" referred to our maternal grandfather and his friends who would have jam sessions in the basement. We would hang out on top of the steps and listen from upstairs. Josie was our maternal uncle. Snooky was a reference to me. Josey was in the army, Johnny served in the navy, and Abuelo, our grandfather, was a Merchant Marine. LISANE

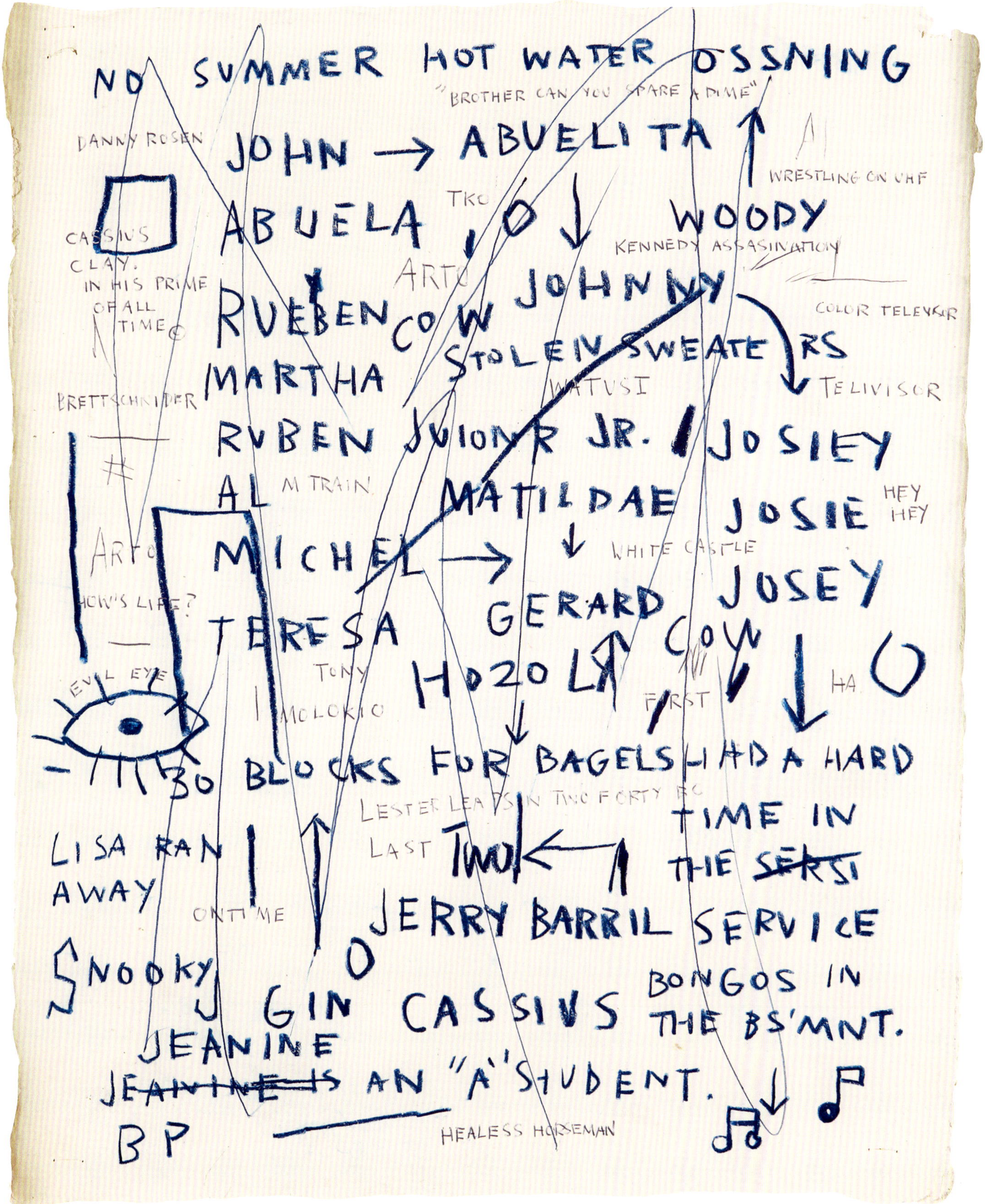
NO SUMMER HOT WATER OSSNING
"BROTHER CAN YOU SPARE A DIME"
DANNY ROSEN
JOHN → ABUELITA
WRESTLING ON UHF
TKO
ABUELA
WOODY
CASSIUS CLAY. IN HIS PRIME OF ALL TIME©
KENNEDY ASSASINATION
ARTO
JOHNNY
RUEBEN COW
COLOR TELEVISOR
STOLEN SWEATERS
MARTHA
WATUSI
TELIVISOR
BRETTSCHNIDER
RUBEN JUIONR JR.
JOSIEY
AL
M TRAIN
MATILDAE
JOSIE
HEY HEY
ARTO
MICHEL →
WHITE CASTLE
JOSEY
HOW'S LIFE?
GERARD
TERESA
COW
EVIL EYE
TONY
H2O
HA
MOLOKIO
FIRST
30 BLOCKS FOR BAGELS
HAD A HARD
LESTER LEAPS IN TWO FORTY FO
TIME IN
LISA RAN AWAY
LAST TWO
THE SERSI
ONTIME
JERRY BARRIL
SERVICE
SNOOKY
GIN
CASSIUS
BONGOS IN THE BS'MNT.
JEANINE
JEANINE IS AN "A" STUDENT.
BP
HEALESS HORSEMAN

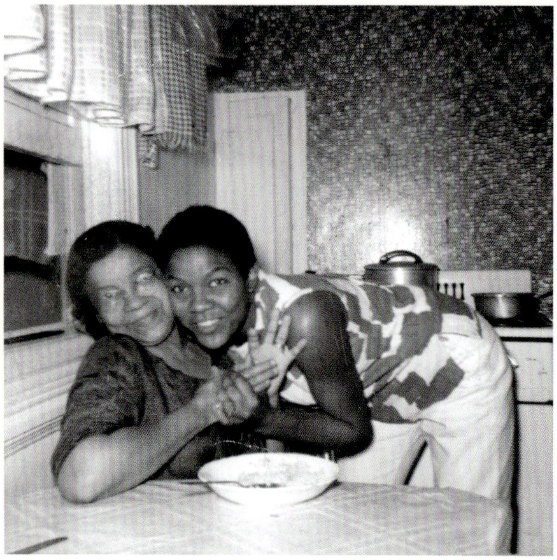

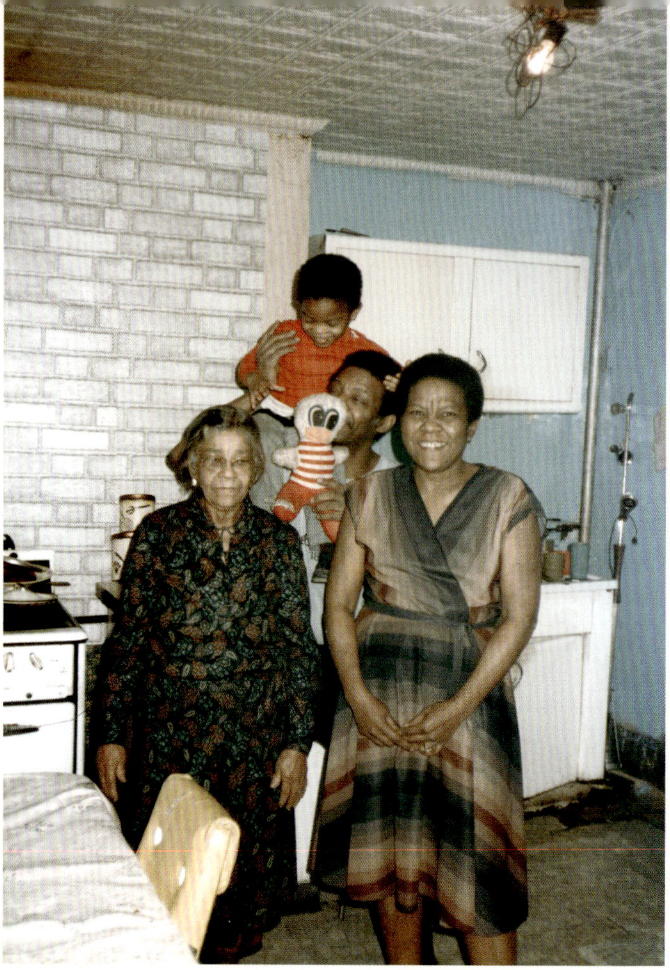

TOP LEFT
Abuelita and Matilde in Bushwick, Brooklyn, ca. 1950. *Our mother Matilde was Abuelita's only daughter. I always loved this photo. It captures the fun in their relationship.* LISANE

TOP RIGHT
Left to right: Abuelita, Joseph Basquiat, Joe Andrades, and Matilde, Bushwick, Brooklyn, ca. 1985

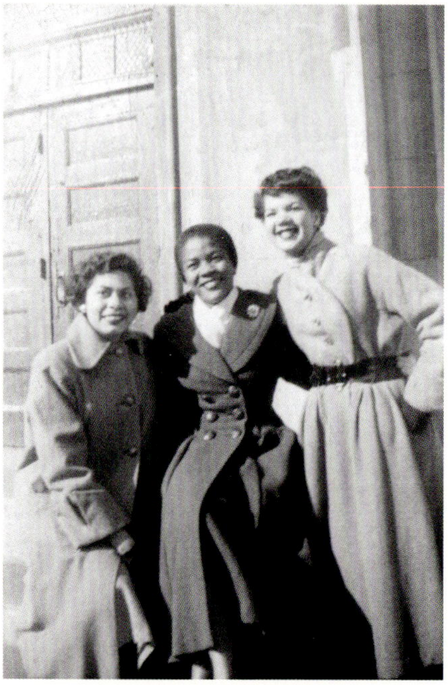

Left to right: Matilde's close friend Virginia, Matilde, and unknown woman. *Virginia and our mother were sister-friends from childhood until our mother passed away in 2008. When we were young, we would all play with Virginia's children. We are still in contact today.* LISANE

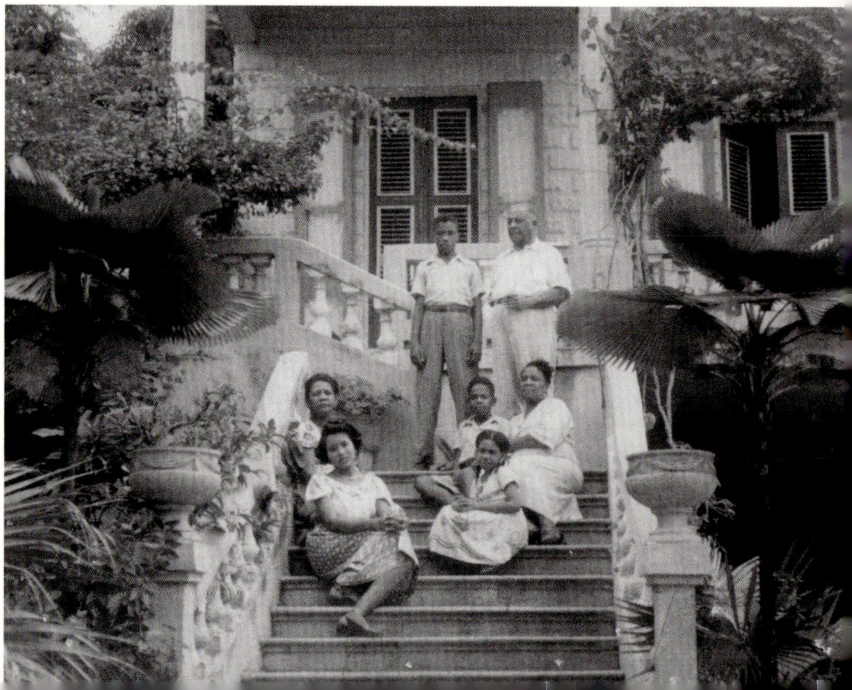

Gerard's family in front of their gingerbread-style home in Turgeau, Port-au-Prince, Haiti, early 1950s. Top row: Gerard, his father Leonce Basquiat. Middle row: Unknown woman, Gerard's brother Lesly, Gerard's mother Cheristine Basquiat. Bottom row: Unknown woman, Gerard's sister Marie Carmelle

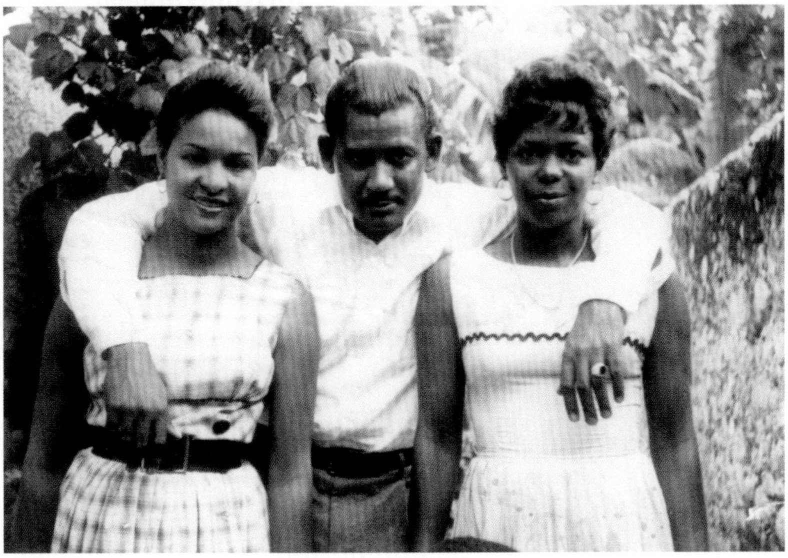

Left to right: Lillie Basquiat (Yves Basquiat's wife), Gerard's half-brother Yves Basquiat, and unknown woman, Haiti, 1950s. *Papa really looked up to Yves and spoke of him very fondly—and often.* LISANE

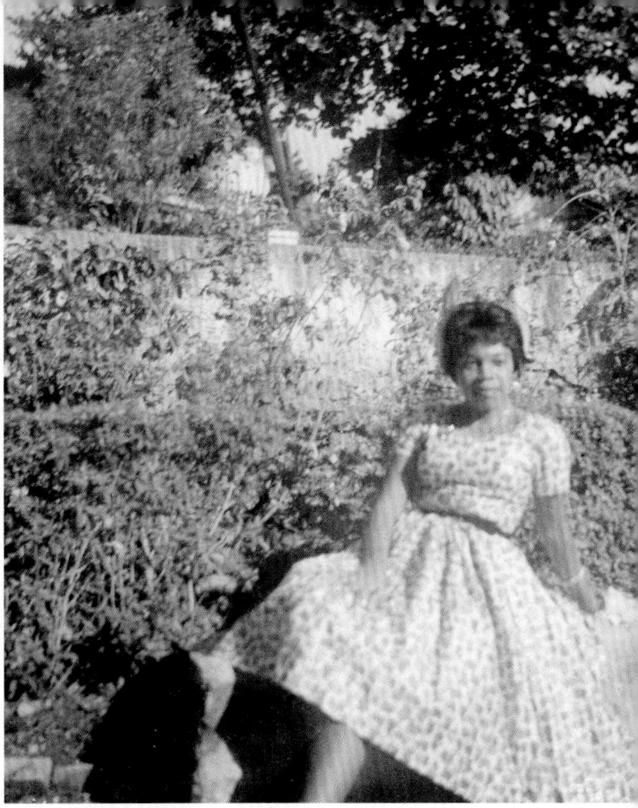

Gerard's sister Marie Carmelle in Haiti

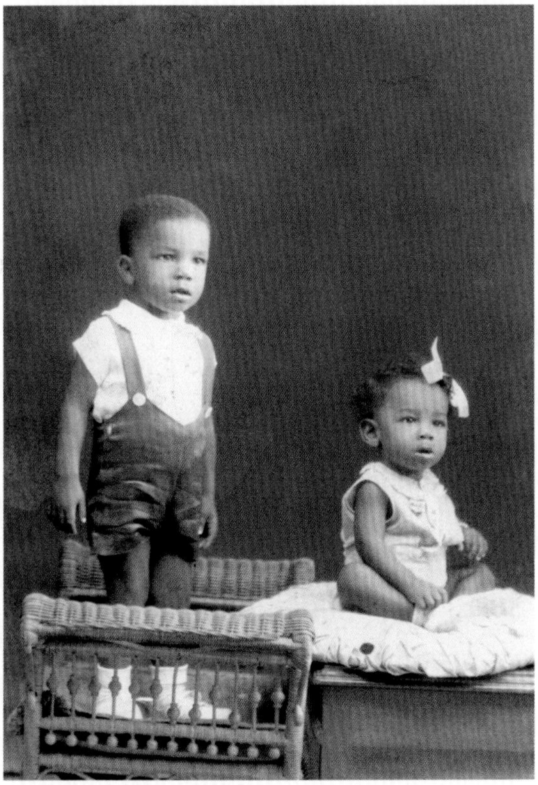

Gerard and his older brother Lesly in Haiti as children

GROWING UP IN HAITI

Cheristine Basquiat, our grandmother, was a very accomplished businesswoman who owned various stores similar to Woolworth's in her local community. The family lived an upper-middle-class life in a suburb of Port-au-Prince. Marie Carmelle, our aunt, recalled for us life in Haiti as they were growing up: going to the movies on Saturdays, getting dressed up and attending fancy dances called *balles*, and spending every summer in a house they rented in the mountains outside of Port-au-Prince in an area called Pétion-Ville. Our grandmother was known to cook big meals for the holidays, and the family sat down and ate together every day.

Those happy days were cut short when François "Papa Doc" Duvalier came into power in the mid-1950s. Families, including ours, were stripped of their homes and businesses. Cheristine and Leonce, our grandfather, were activists and were forced to move the family several times as their homes were taken away. JEANINE

Throughout Jean-Michel's work, there are many references to things we experienced during our childhood in Brooklyn in the 1960s and early 1970s—cartoon characters, TV shows, streetball, hide-and-go-seek, news reports about moon exploration. As kids, we were surrounded by family, great food, amazing music, art, culture, and gorgeous brownstones, all while we watched the adults in our lives trying to figure things out.

In addition to the many family photos and keepsakes—like Jean-Michel's junior membership card to the Brooklyn Museum and his school newsletter featuring his illustrations—we have gathered here a selection of Jean-Michel's artworks and sketchbooks that are reminiscent of our weekends at home growing up, especially Saturday morning cartoons and the light-hearted characters that entertained us. These works convey the essence of Jean-Michel as a young person: his curiosity, playfulness, imagination, and his exploration of fantasy. He was like a roving reporter constantly observing, and his sketchbooks capture his adolescent musings about the world around him. In them I see him beginning to ponder his life and determine a clear delineation between the "mainstream" and how he intended to show up in the world. I see the formation (or perhaps the clarification) of his ideology in the sketchbook page *Upon leaving the "norm"* (page 42), where he depicts a character holding a balloon and sailing above a group of "working class heroes" with the thought bubble "Ho-Hum." LISANE

KINGS COUNTY

THE EARLY DAYS IN FLATBUSH, BROOKLYN

We lived in several neighborhoods in Brooklyn, including Prospect Heights—where our parents lived when Jean-Michel and I were born—and, when we were older, Boerum Hill. But our formative years were spent in East Flatbush where my parents bought a home on East 35th Street.

Our childhood felt very innocent and playful. Looking back now, I realize that we were witnessing gentrification, and that the neighborhood was transitioning while also remaining very much "old Brooklyn." There were block parties, cake baking contests, kids playing in the streets.

Back in those days, the ice cream truck coming around was a very exciting event. We would hear the music from blocks away and would scatter to ask our parents for money so we could be ready before the truck got to our street. One day I was walking away from the ice cream truck very happily eating my ice cream cone. I was so into it that I walked right into a tree—bang! Jean-Michel was laughing and teasing me because I had ridged indentions from the tree bark on my forehead due to the impact.

Family time was always a lot of fun. We'd go to the Brooklyn Museum, the Botanic Garden, Prospect Park Zoo. We'd have picnics on the meadow in Prospect Park—all these places were a huge part of our childhood. Going to the beach was a big deal—our parents would pack a picnic and we'd all pile into the car, leaving super early so we could get a good spot. We built sandcastles, buried each other in the sand, and played in the water all day.

Of course, as in everyone's childhoods, there were some tough parts as well. When Jean-Michel, I, and Jeanine were eight, four, and one, respectively, our parents split up. They both wanted to ensure that their goals for us stayed on track, and ultimately they determined that we would live with Papa. Jean-Michel was, understandably, very sad and confused about the transition. As the eldest, he became even more protective of us. It was tough for everyone involved, each in our own way. LISANE

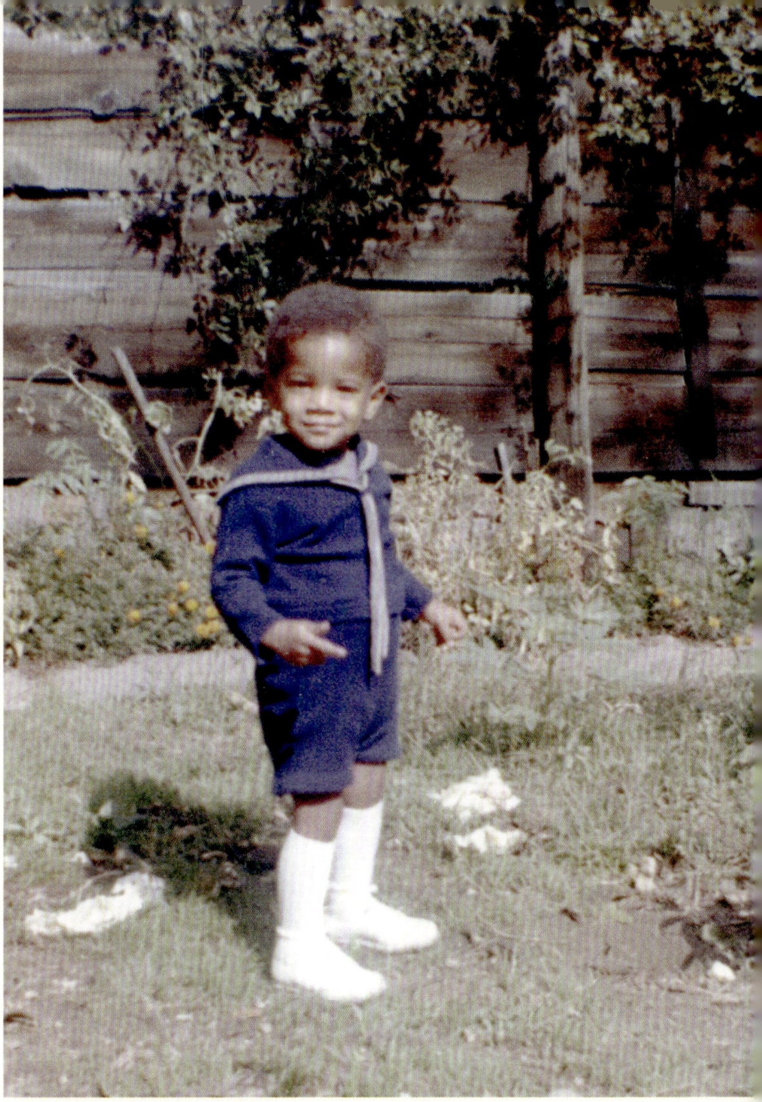

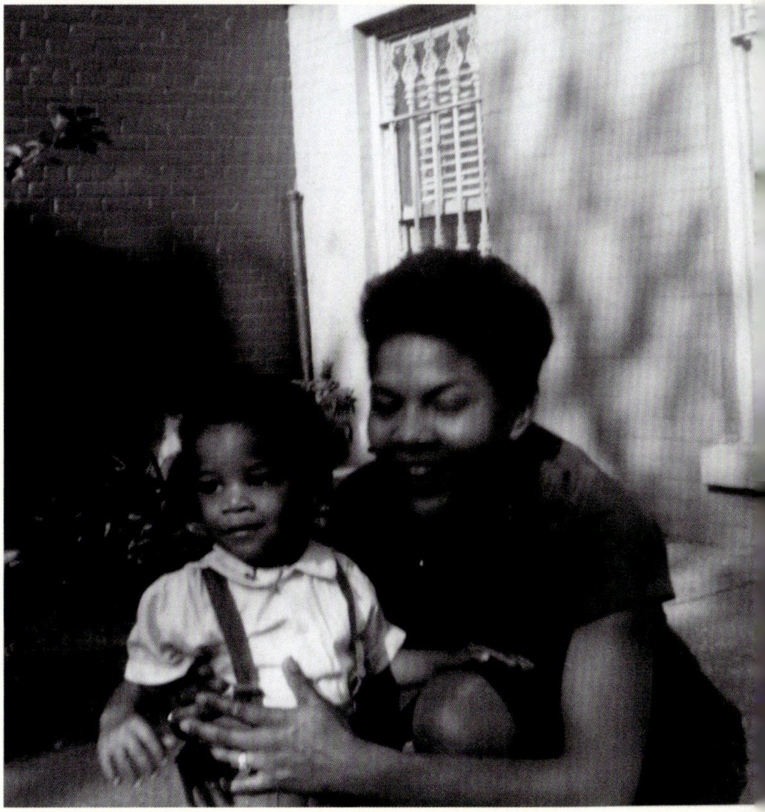

Jean-Michel in Abuelita's garden, Bushwick, Brooklyn, ca. 1962

Jean-Michel and Matilde, Bushwick, Brooklyn, ca. 1962

Jean-Michel at Abuelita's house, Bushwick, Brooklyn, ca. 1963

Gerard with Jean-Michel at the beach, Jacob Riis Park, Queens, ca. 1963

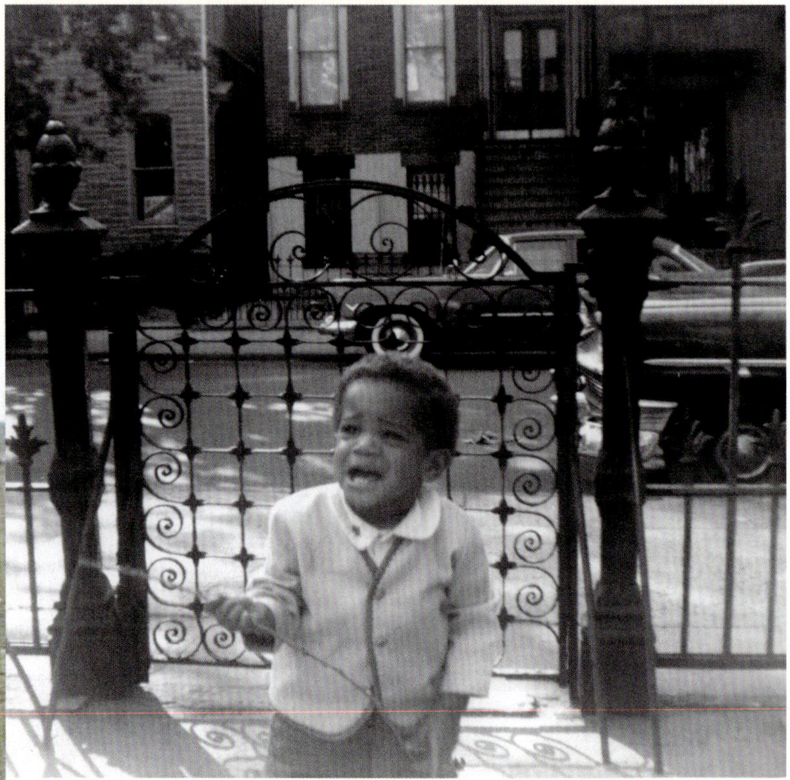

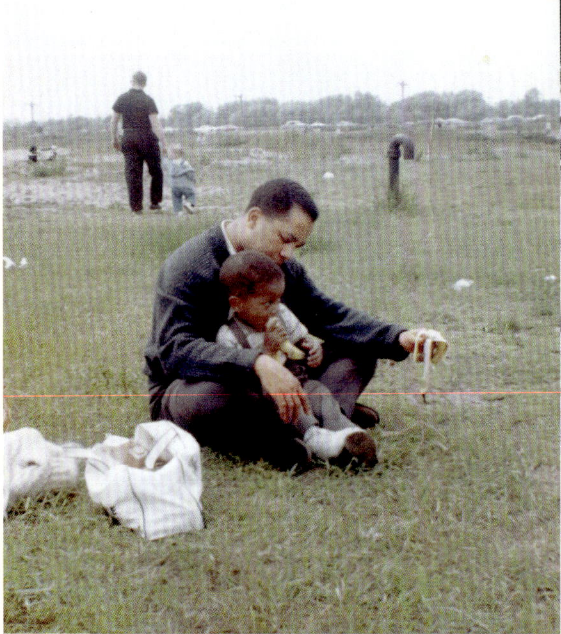

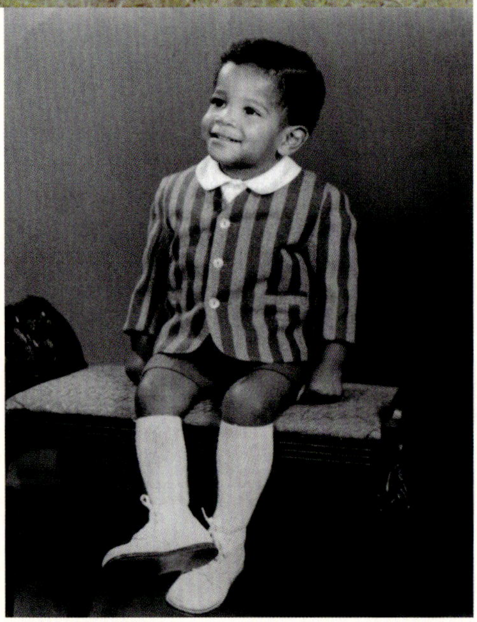

Jean-Michel, 1962.
He was so darned cute dressed in a suit as a little boy. LISANE

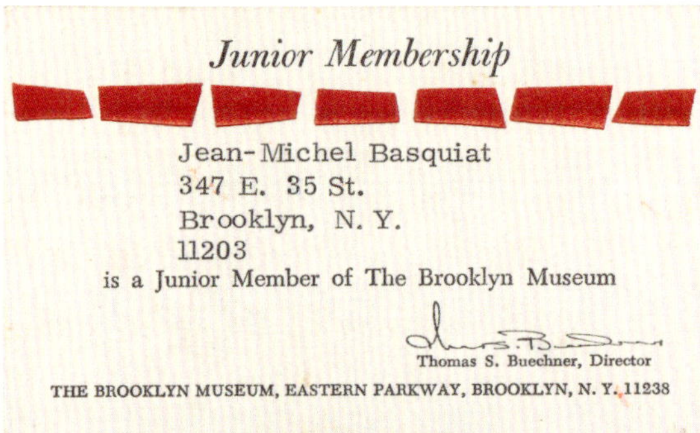

Junior Membership

Jean-Michel Basquiat
347 E. 35 St.
Brooklyn, N. Y.
11203
is a Junior Member of The Brooklyn Museum

Thomas S. Buechner, Director

THE BROOKLYN MUSEUM, EASTERN PARKWAY, BROOKLYN, N. Y. 11238

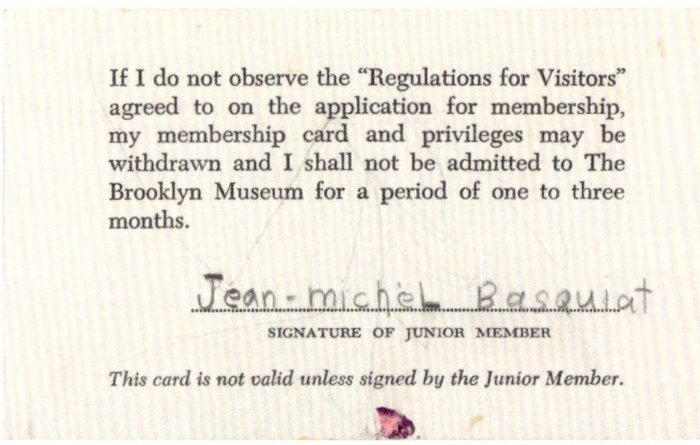

If I do not observe the "Regulations for Visitors" agreed to on the application for membership, my membership card and privileges may be withdrawn and I shall not be admitted to The Brooklyn Museum for a period of one to three months.

Jean-michel Basquiat
SIGNATURE OF JUNIOR MEMBER

This card is not valid unless signed by the Junior Member.

Brooklyn Museum junior membership card with Jean-Michel's name written in his hand on the back, ca. 1966. *As a child, Jean-Michel visited the museum often with his mother Matilde. Jean-Michel once remarked in an interview, "I'd say my mother gave me all the primary things. The art came from her."*

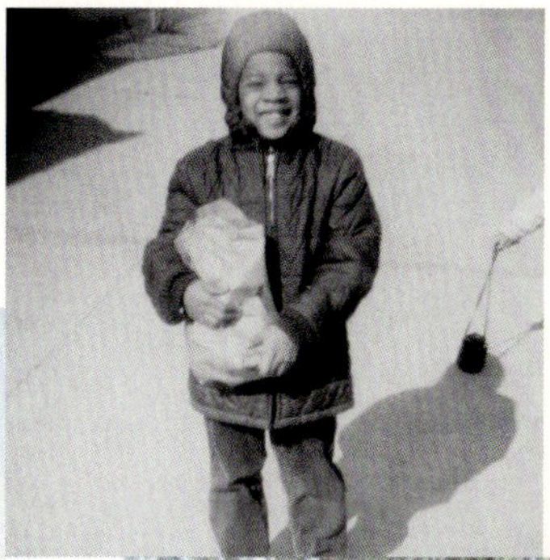

Jean-Michel,
Park Slope, Brooklyn,
February 1967

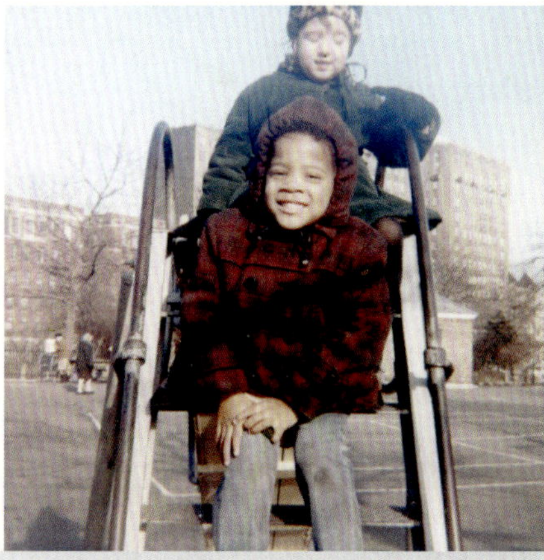

Jean-Michel with unidentified playmate, Prospect Park, Brooklyn, ca. 1967

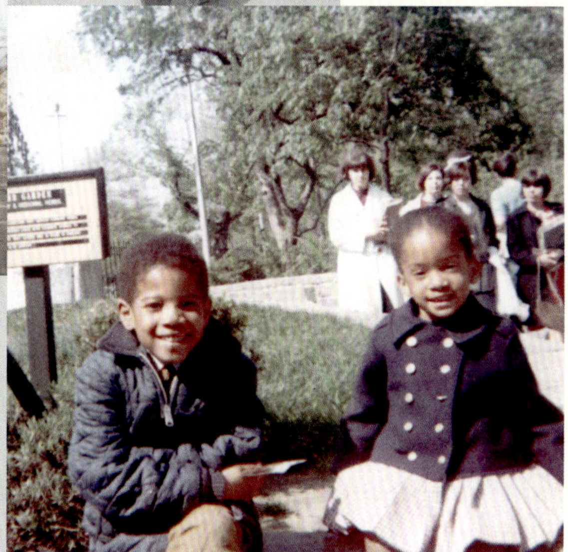

Jean-Michel and Lisane, Prospect Park, Brooklyn, Spring 1967

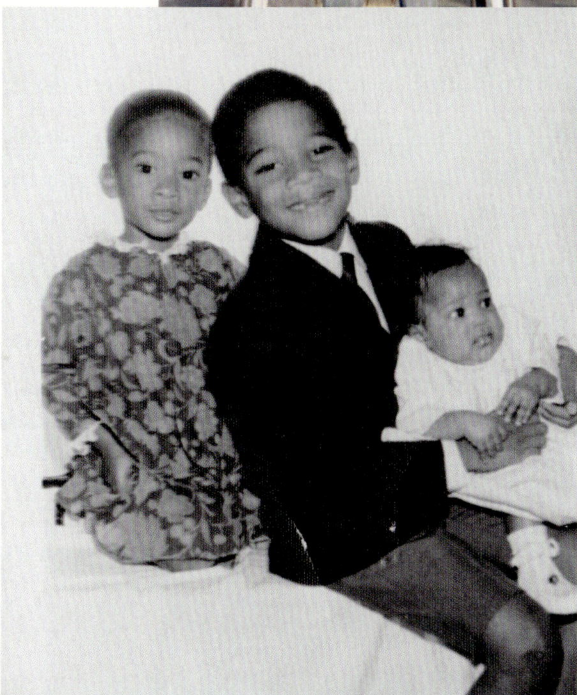

Lisane, Jean-Michel, and Jeanine, 1967

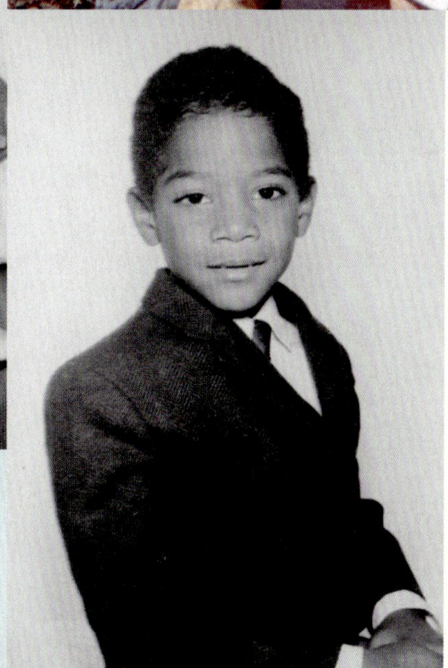

Jean-Michel, 1967

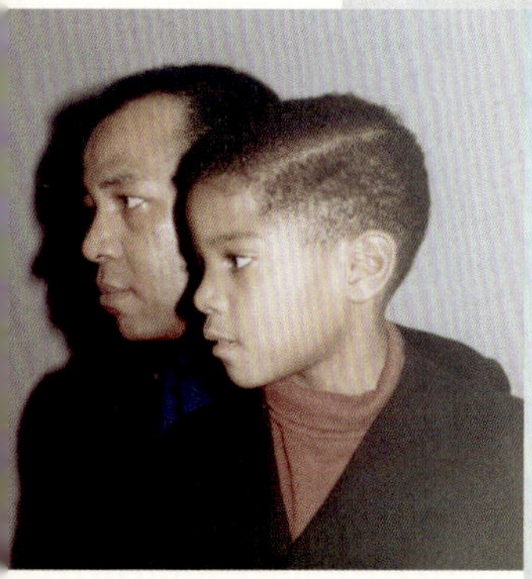

Gerard and Jean-Michel, 1968

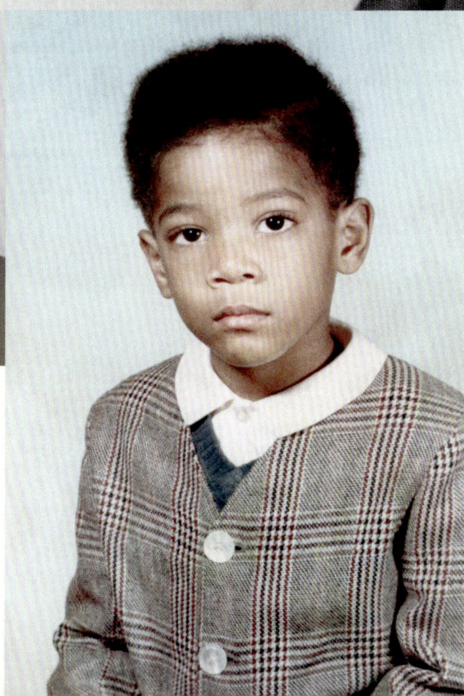

Jean-Michel's elementary school picture, Saint Ann's School, Brooklyn Heights, ca. 1968

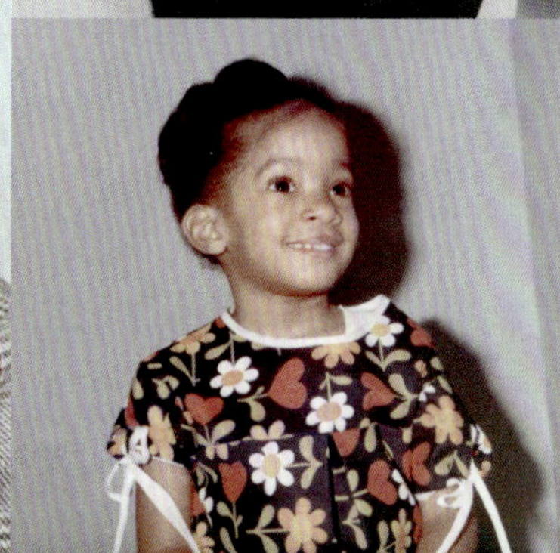

Lisane, 1968

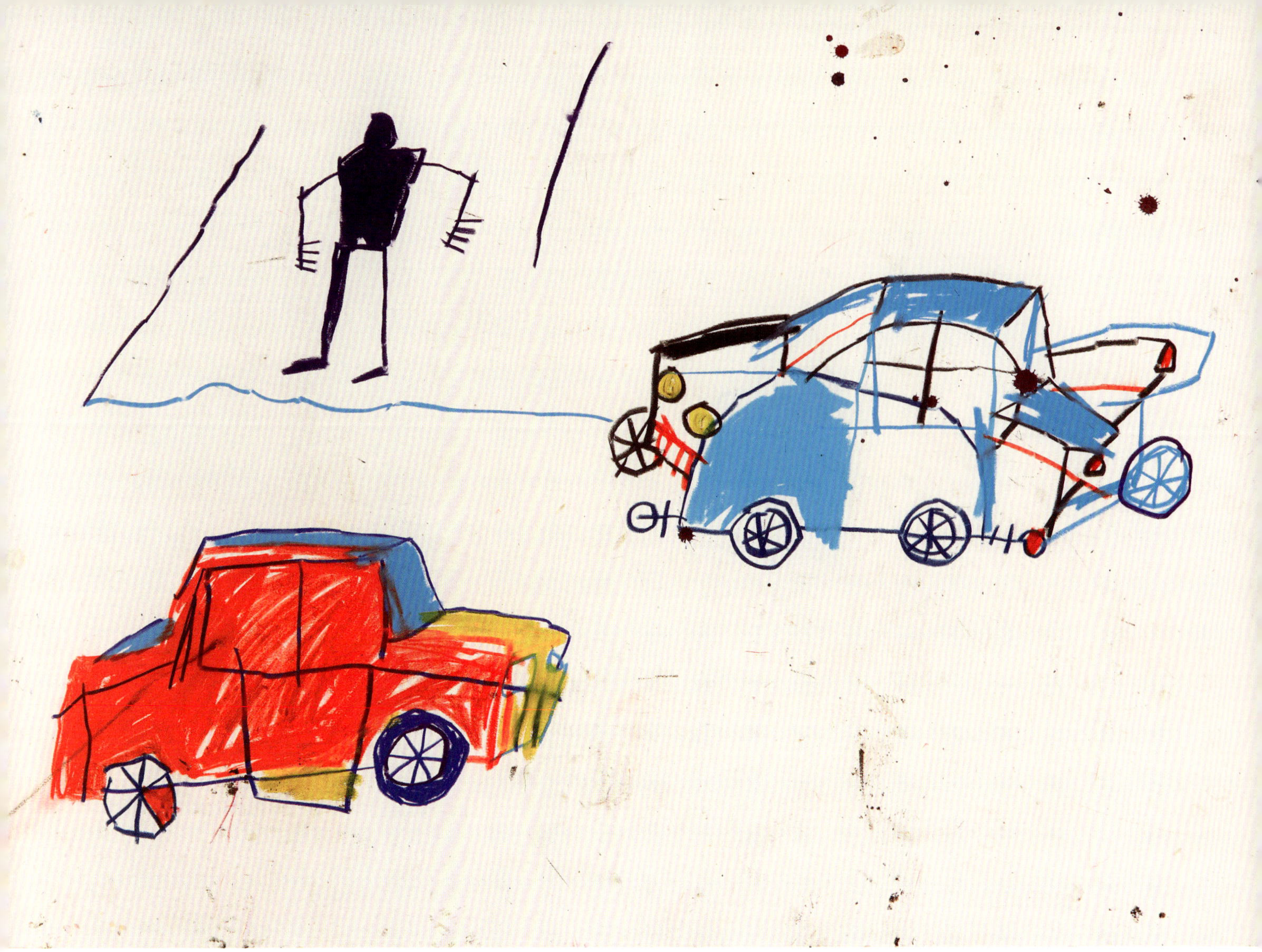

1968: JEAN-MICHEL'S CAR ACCIDENT

My mother was at home cooking dinner. Jean-Michel, who was eight years old at the time, was playing with his friends on the corner stoop, and my mother sent me to get him. I went out and called to him—he was across the street. I remember his face as he ran down the steps and into the street. We were looking at each other, a car hit him, he disappeared, and then it was mayhem. People screaming, going to get my mother, and my mother screaming and crying and running into the street. He was taken to the hospital and had his spleen removed. I remember him being in there for quite some time, but we were not allowed to visit him. LISANE

Untitled, n.d.
Oil stick on paper
22 × 30 in. (55.88 × 76.2 cm)

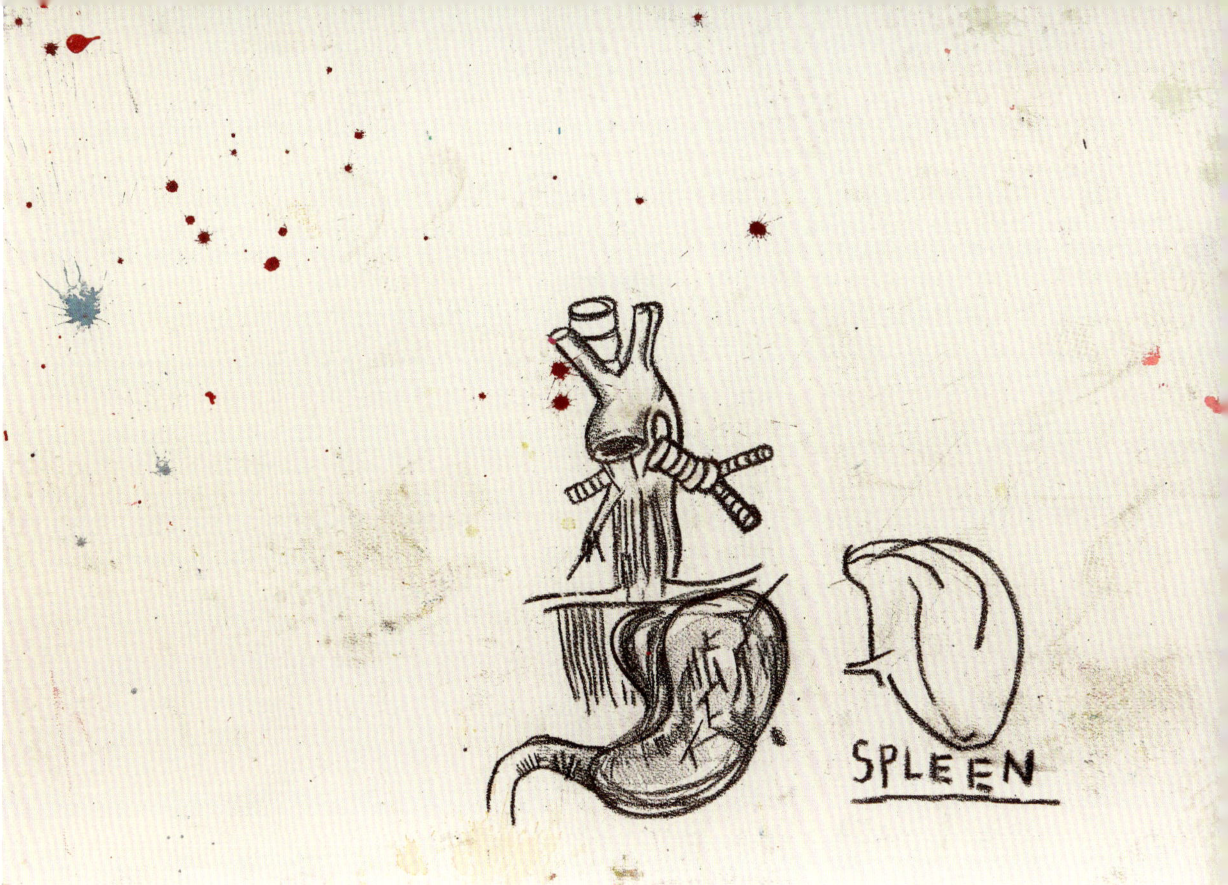

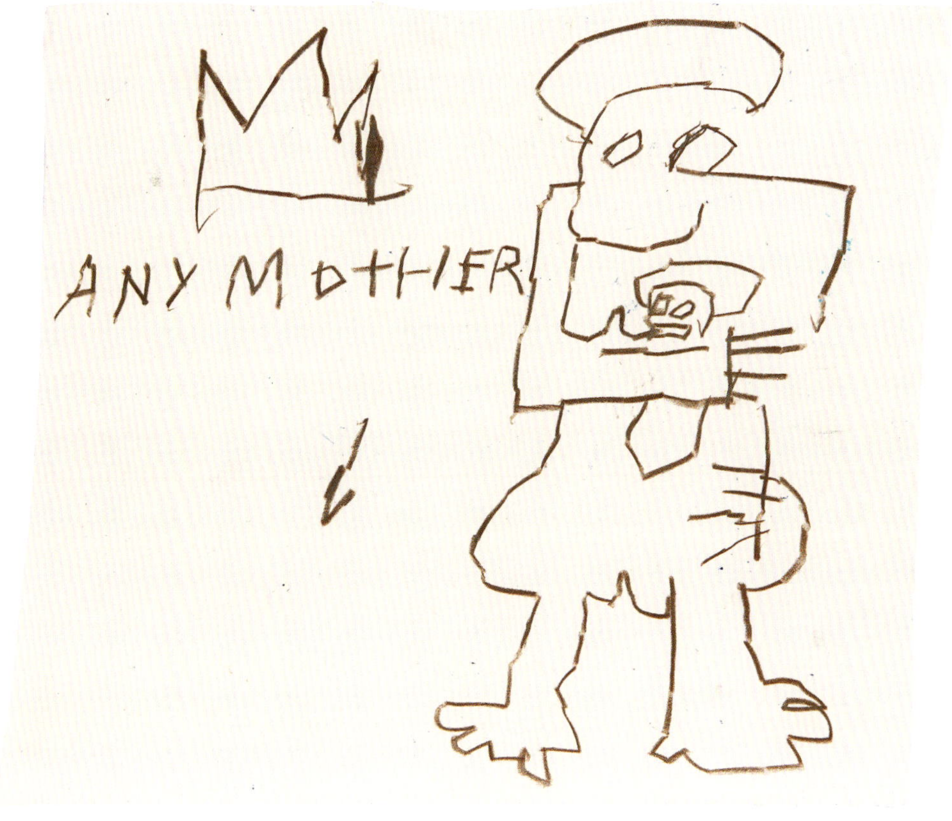

TOP
Untitled (Spleen), n.d.
Crayon on paper
22¼ × 30 in. (56.52 × 762 cm)

LEFT
Untitled, n.d.
Oil stick on paper
13¾ × 15¼ in. (34.93 × 38.74 cm)

LIVING IN PUERTO RICO

Our family relocated to Puerto Rico from Boerum Hill for two years in the mid-1970s. By that time my parents had already separated, and my father was raising Jean-Michel, Lisane, and me as a single dad. Moving from a duplex in a brownstone in a big city to an apartment in the Caribbean took some getting used to. We lived on Calle Estado in the Miramar section of San Juan, in a four-bedroom railroad apartment.

Ice skating was an activity that we enjoyed with our mom and missed while being away from New York. One day Jean-Michel came up with the idea to turn the long hallway in our apartment into our own version of an ice-skating rink while my father was at work. To achieve this, he suggested using soap to emulate skating. We threw soapy water on the floor and "skated" for hours. When my dad came home, he wondered why the floor was so sticky, but of course we didn't let him in on our secret. We simply said that we mopped the floor because we had spilled something. I think he knew something was up after we admitted to mopping the floor three times that week. One of things I most admired about Jean-Michel was his ability to test out and explore all his ideas, no matter how bizarre or if it was going to get him in trouble. His creativity was fueled by his curiosity and sense of adventure.

One of the best things about living in Puerto Rico was living near the beach. We went every weekend with Papa, and during our summer school breaks, we went almost every day with Jean-Michel. There was no shortage of pranks Jean-Michel enlisted us into. I recall a time when he convinced us to dig a large hole in the sand and cover it with a blanket so that our dad and his girlfriend would fall into it when they came back from their walk. JEANINE

Coming from Brooklyn, Puerto Rico was a real adventure. We rode our bikes to the beach every day. There was a house across the street from our apartment building and no one lived in it. Jeanine and I would climb up to the roof and lie there talking, eating tamarind and *quenepa* from the trees. While we lived there, Jean-Michel started taking photos and even created a darkroom in his closet. He learned how to develop film from a man who owned a camera shop. LISANE

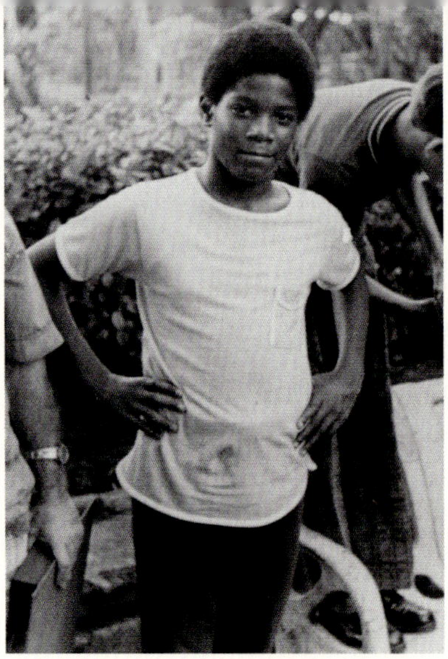

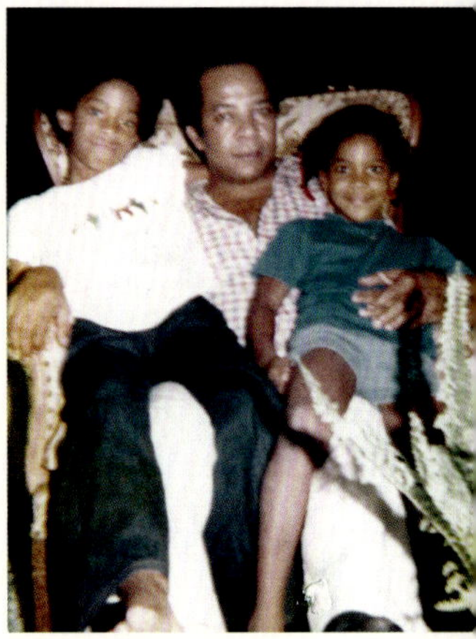

Jean-Michel in Puerto Rico, ca. 1975

Lisane, Gerard, and Jeanine in Puerto Rico, ca. 1975

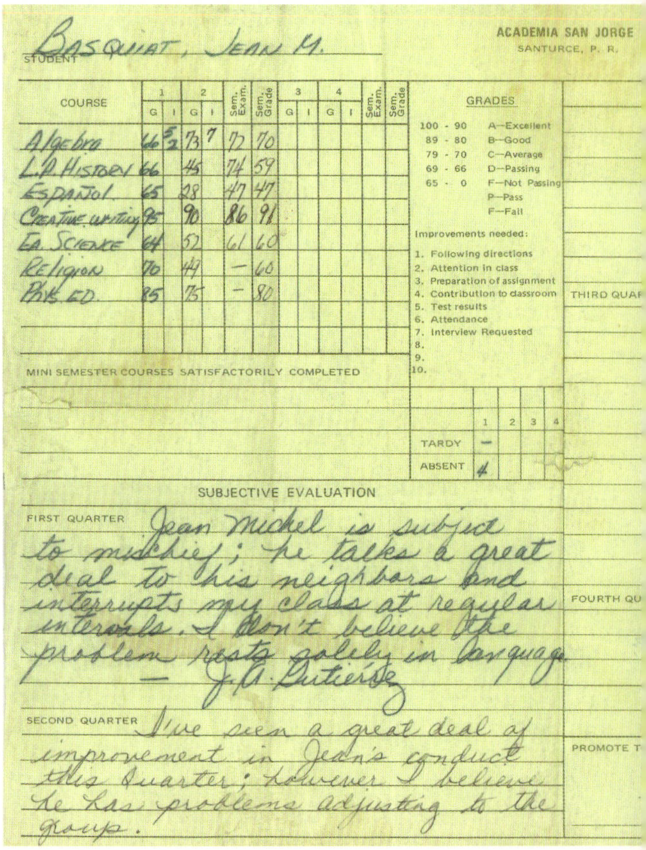

ACADEMIA SAN JORGE
SANTURCE, P. R.

STUDENT: BASQUIAT, JEAN M.

COURSE	1 G	1 I	2 G	2 I	Sem. Exam.	Sem. Grade	3 G	3 I	4 G	4 I	Sem. Exam.	Sem. Grade
Algebra	66	5/2	73	7	72	70						
L.A. History	66		45		74	59						
Español	65		28		47	47						
Creative writing	95		90		86	91						
Ea. Science	64		52		61	60						
Religion	70		49		—	60						
Phys. Ed.	85		75		—	80						

GRADES
100 - 90 A—Excellent
89 - 80 B—Good
79 - 70 C—Average
69 - 66 D—Passing
65 - 0 F—Not Passing
P—Pass
F—Fail

Improvements needed:
1. Following directions
2. Attention in class
3. Preparation of assignment
4. Contribution to classroom
5. Test results
6. Attendance
7. Interview Requested
8.
9.
10.

MINI SEMESTER COURSES SATISFACTORILY COMPLETED

	1	2	3	4
TARDY	—			
ABSENT	4			

SUBJECTIVE EVALUATION

FIRST QUARTER: Jean Michel is subject to mischief; he talks a great deal to his neighbors and interrupts my class at regular intervals. I don't believe the problem rests solely in language. — J. A. Gutierrez

SECOND QUARTER: I've seen a great deal of improvement in Jean's conduct this quarter; however I believe he has problems adjusting to the group.

THIRD QUAR

FOURTH QU

PROMOTE T

Jean-Michel's report card from Academia San Jorge, Santurce, Puerto Rico, 1974–75

BACK TO BROOKLYN: LIVING IN BOERUM HILL

My dad purchased a townhouse in Boerum Hill before moving to Puerto Rico, and we returned to that house when his assignment was complete. Transitioning from Puerto Rico back to Brooklyn wasn't difficult, but it was quite a change from the beach life that we had grown accustomed to. New York's weather was vastly different, but it was so nice to get back to friends, snow, and Christmas trees!

Boerum Hill in the 1970s was not the neighborhood that it is today. The cool hipster cafés, bistros, and boutiques were once dive bars, warehouses, and bodegas all along Atlantic Avenue. Prostitutes hung out on the corners. Our block consisted of only six or seven brownstones that were renovated and occupied. Many of the buildings were abandoned and empty, waiting for someone to see the potential of the neighborhood as my father and neighbors had. They created a block association, developed a tight-knit community, and looked out for each other as the area changed for the better. Neighbors sat on each other's stoops, drank wine, and socialized as their kids played. We had our own version of an impromptu block party every weekend. The Atlantic Antic, a local festival that is over forty-five years old and now brings hundreds of thousands of people to downtown Brooklyn, was created by our next-door neighbors. In the mid-1970s, it was a much smaller affair with only a few hundred people attending.

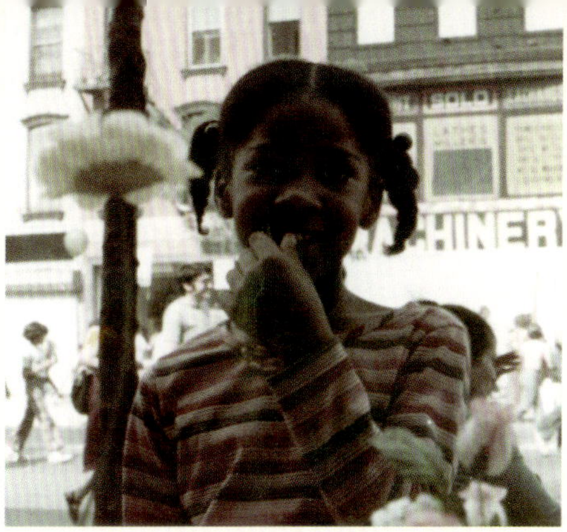

Jeanine at the Atlantic Antic, Brooklyn, ca. 1977

The summer of 1977 in New York City was an eventful one. There was a strike by sanitation department workers. In July there was a twenty-five-hour, citywide blackout. Families came out on their stoops to cool down and pass the time talking. And the notorious serial killer Son of Sam continued his killing spree. Jean-Michel enjoyed telling Lisane and me the Son of Sam story to scare us. It was especially scary during a blackout!

The year 1977 was important to us as a family because Nora Fitzpatrick came into our lives as our father's partner. Nora never tried to replace our mother. She didn't say "you need to call me mom" or try to be our disciplinarian. We respected her. She came in as a friend and was motherly. JEANINE

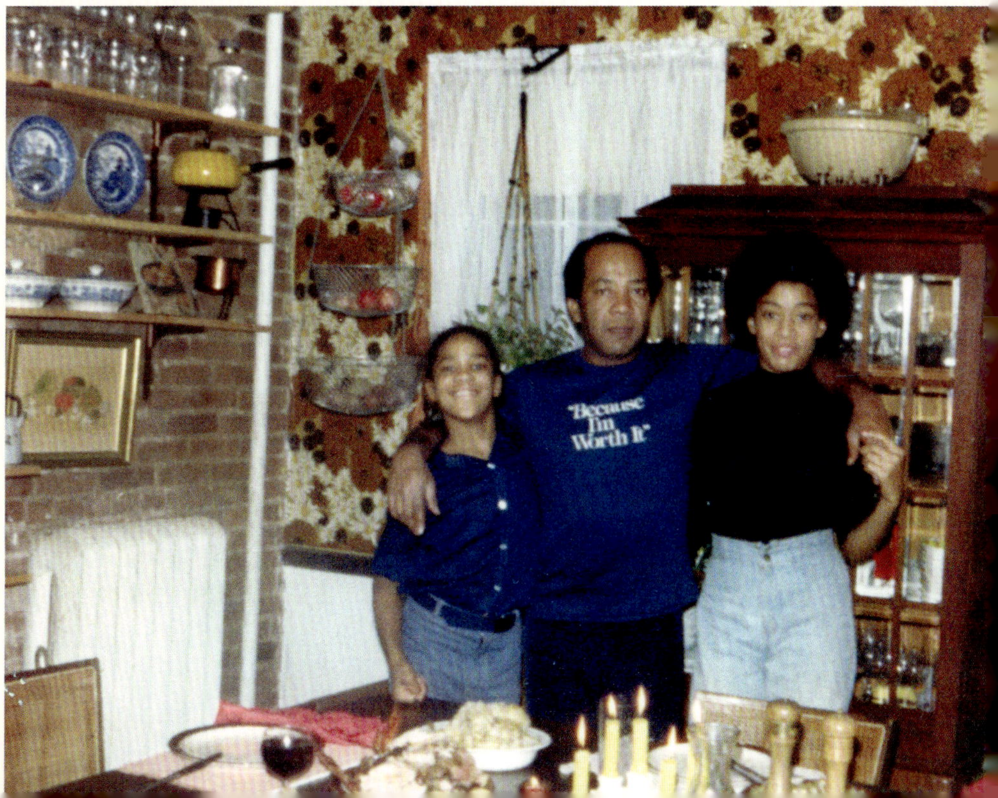

Jeanine, Gerard, and Lisane, Boerum Hill, Brooklyn, ca. 1977. *I still marvel that our family ate dinner at the table together every night, candles and all.* LISANE

THE MUSIC OF JEAN-MICHEL'S CHILDHOOD

"Ain't No Mountain High Enough"
Diana Ross

"And I Love Him"
Shirley Horn

"Big Spender"
Peggy Lee

"Cast Your Fate to the Wind"
Vince Guaraldi Trio

"The Christmas Song"
Nat King Cole

"Feel Like Makin' Love"
Roberta Flack

"If You Leave Me Now"
Chicago

"I'm in the Mood for Love" (aka "Moody's Mood for Love")
King Pleasure

"Imagine"
John Lennon

"Linus and Lucy"
Vince Guaraldi Trio

"Love Hangover"
Diana Ross

"Love Is Here to Stay"
Ella Fitzgerald, Louis Armstrong

"Love to Love You Baby"
Donna Summer

"Lowdown"
Boz Scaggs

"MacArthur Park"
Richard Harris

"Manhã de Carnaval"
Vince Guaraldi Trio

"Mr. Bojangles"
Sammy Davis Jr.

"My Baby Just Cares for Me"
Nina Simone

"My Favorite Things"
John Coltrane

"People"
Barbra Streisand

"Samba de Orpheus"
Vince Guaraldi Trio

"Something"
Shirley Bassey

"Soul Makossa"
The Mighty Tom Cats

"Stormy Weather"
Lena Horne

"A Taste of Honey"
Herb Albert and the Tijuana Brass

"Theme from *Shaft*"
Isaac Hayes

"(They Long to Be) Close to You"
Carpenters

"What a Diff'rence a Day Makes"
Dinah Washington

"What a Wonderful World"
Louis Armstrong

GROWING UP BASQUIAT: MUSIC AND PARTIES

Papa played a huge range of music in our home. He had a stereo with a turntable that was on and playing records most of the time. We grew up listening to jazz, merengue, classical, and disco—from Miles Davis and Ella Fitzgerald to Donna Summer and Tito Puente. JEANINE

Our home was always filled with music, and the three of us had an appreciation for diverse genres. Our father was often listening to his music downstairs while we each had our own playing in our bedrooms upstairs. He played everything, including Aretha Franklin, Jimmy Smith, Chicago, Peggy Lee, Vince Guaraldi, Donna Summer, Diana Ross, and Shirley Bassey. When he got home from work, he would play music while making dinner. And on the weekends, it was the same routine: Nora, our stepmother, and Papa played tennis Saturday and Sunday mornings, and the music would come on as soon as they came home and stayed on while Papa made brunch, either eggs benedict or french toast. Papa spent his afternoons yelling at tennis players on TV, followed by more music while he cooked dinner.

My father and Nora also hosted frequent dinner parties with neighbors and friends. Guests would sit around having drinks and talking, and we were completely underfoot. He didn't subscribe to the idea that "children should be seen and not heard." It was great to be in the middle of all that was going on and privy to the animated conversations the adults were having.

He threw a party once where he actually had me bartend, which seems crazy from our vantage point today since I was barely in high school at the time. I had so much fun doing it! The adults were so impressed that I knew what I was doing, and they kept coming back and getting more and more sloshed. I was already heavy-handed with the alcohol but decided to up the ante by making a game out of it and putting even more liquor in the drinks. By the end of the evening the guests were completely drunk.

Jeanine and I eventually started putting on little productions during these parties using the show tunes, movie soundtracks, and other great music we listened to and loved. Our father would actually tell his friends, "The girls are going to perform for you on Saturday." We would spend all week rehearsing dance routines, songs, and comedy skits.

Inspiration for our party performances was not hard to come by: Jeanine and I would start the day at the matinee at the Duffield Theatre and watch *The Wiz* over and over and over and over again until it was time to go home. We *loved* that movie, and it sparked a whole lot of the singing and dancing we did in our routines; the same was true of *West Side Story* and other productions. We would perform Diana Ross and Barbra Streisand songs. It was the disco era, so Donna Summer's hit "Love to Love You Baby" made it into our repertoire too, as did classics like "Big Spender" by Peggy Lee. The adults would all laugh, and Papa would be beaming. We had such a blast.

It felt good to be brought up in a home where there was so much music and creativity. We could express ourselves through singing, dancing, and playing music as loud as we wanted. My father was very strict about other things, but when it came to this part of our upbringing, we had a lot of freedom. LISANE

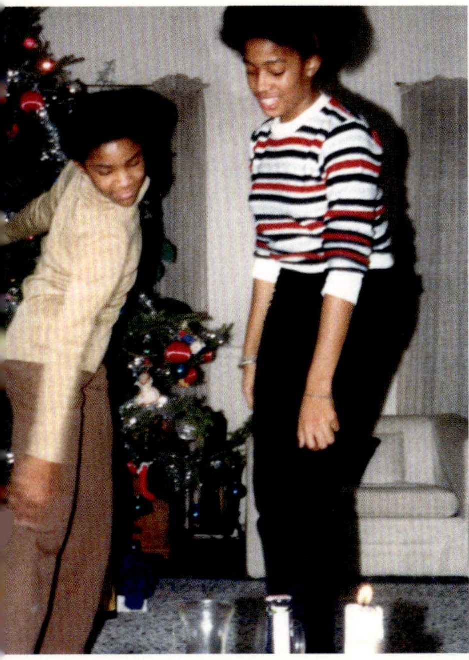

Jeanine and Lisane dancing, Boerum Hill, Brooklyn, Christmas, ca. 1977

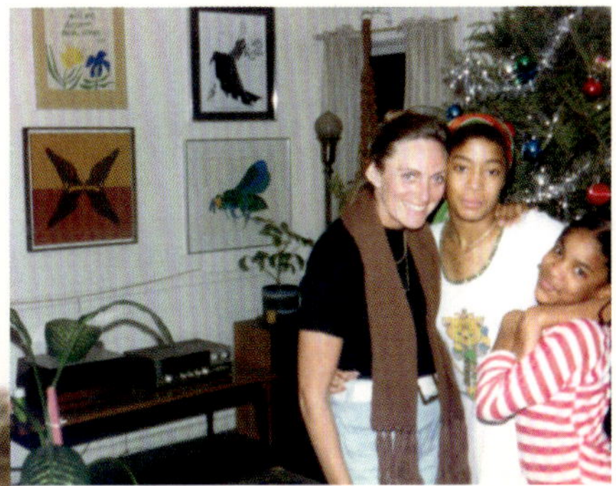

Nora Fitzpatrick, the Basquiat children's stepmother, Lisane, and Jeanine celebrating Christmas, Boerum Hill, Brooklyn, ca. 1977.
In 1977, Nora Fitzpatrick joined the Basquiat family as Gerard's partner.

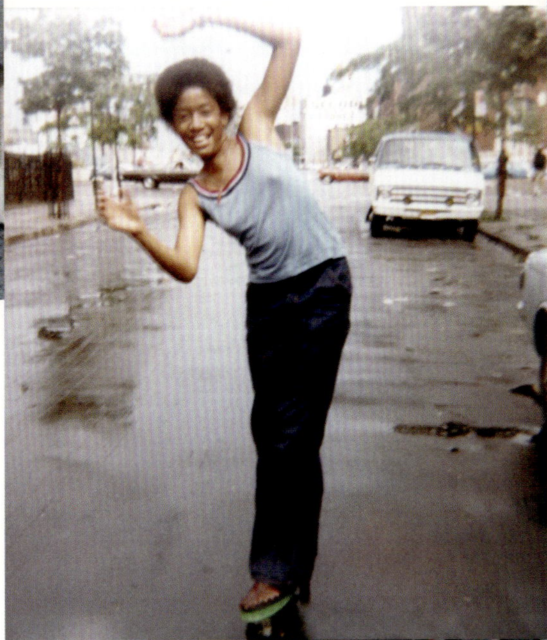

Lisane, Boerum Hill, Brooklyn, ca. 1977

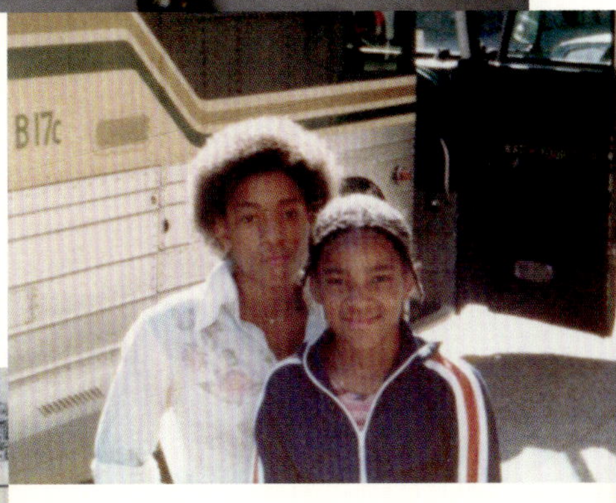

Lisane and Jeanine on their way to sleepaway camp in upstate New York, ca. 1978.
I remember that blouse but have no idea why I looked so serious. LISANE

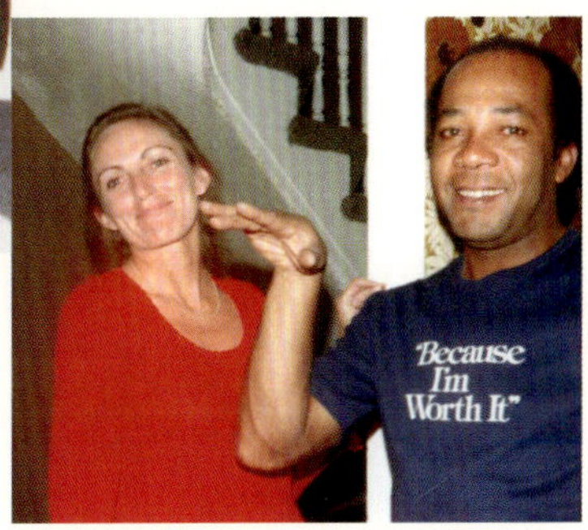

Nora Fitzpatrick and Gerard, Boerum Hill, Brooklyn

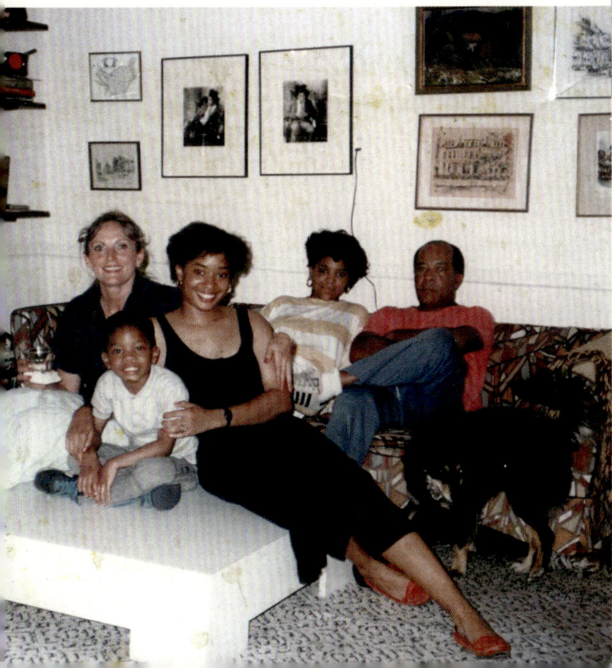

Nora Fitzpatrick, Lisane's son Joseph, Lisane, Jeanine, Gerard, and their dog Ginger, Boerum Hill, Brooklyn, 1986

JEAN-MICHEL'S LOVE OF CARTOONS

In an interview with the curator Henry Geldzahler in 1983 Jean-Michel remarked that he wanted to be a cartoonist when he was young. Cartoon characters can be found throughout Jean-Michel's work, many of which are reminiscent of the ones we watched every Saturday morning as children.

The works on this and the pages following feel so animated and alive. Jean-Michel's characters and penchant for satire bring back memories of the playfulness of our childhood—giggling over cartoons, dancing and wrestling around our home, playing freeze-tag, hide-and-go-seek, and merciless games of punch-car in the back seat of our car during long drives. JEANINE

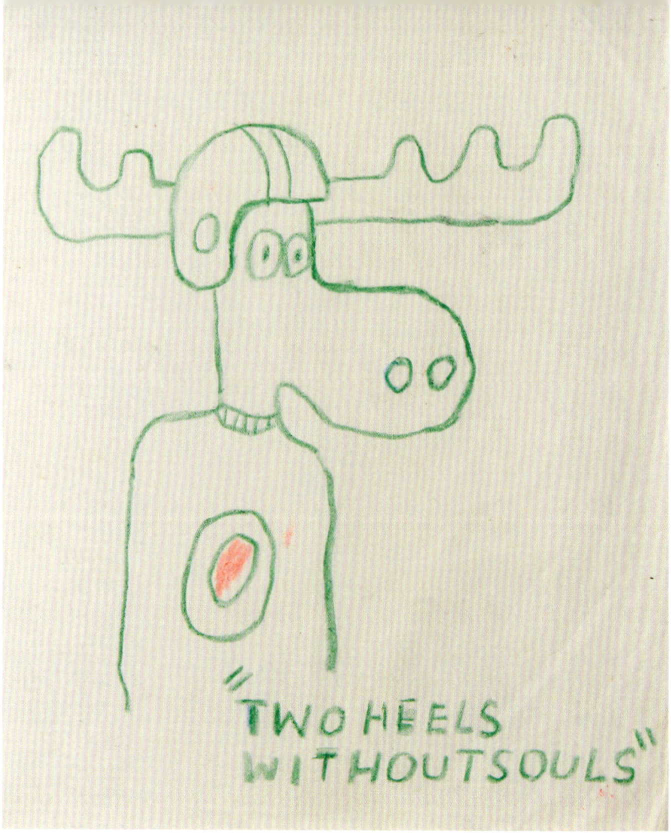

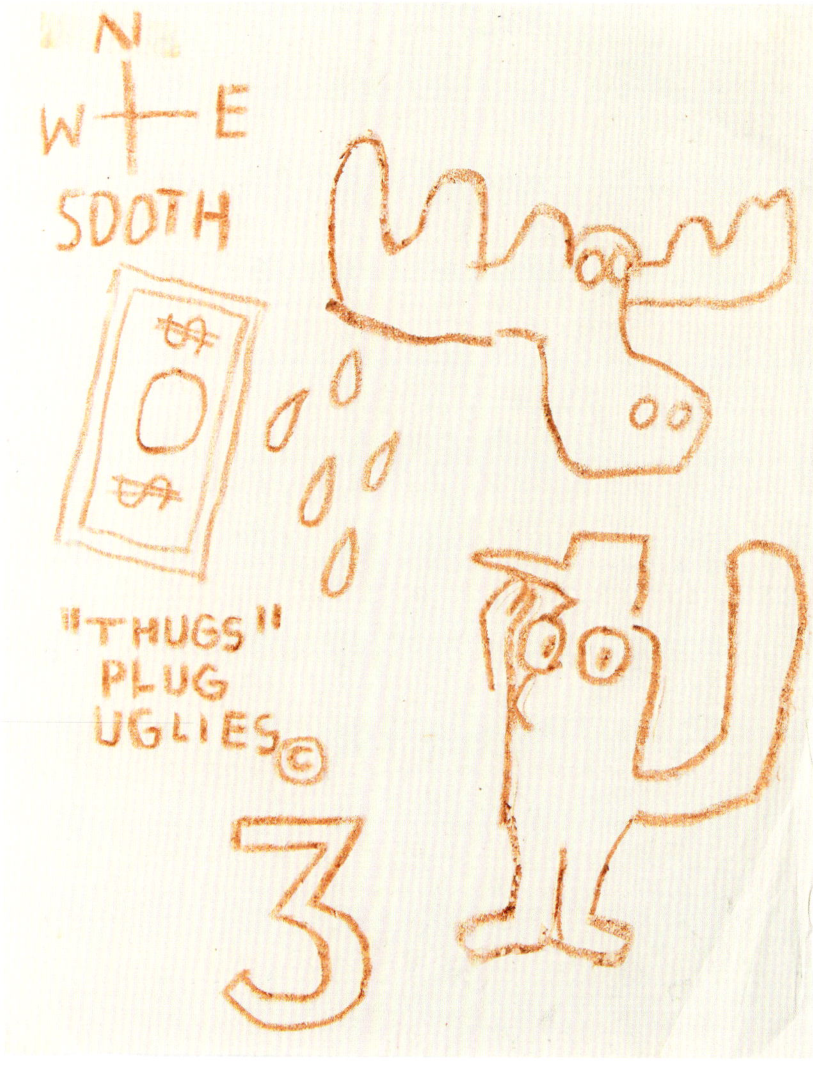

TOP
Untitled (Two Heels Without Souls), n.d.
Crayon on paper
11 × 8½ in. (27.94 × 21.59 cm)

LEFT
Untitled (Thugs), n.d.
Crayon on paper
11 × 8½ in. (27.94 × 21.59 cm)

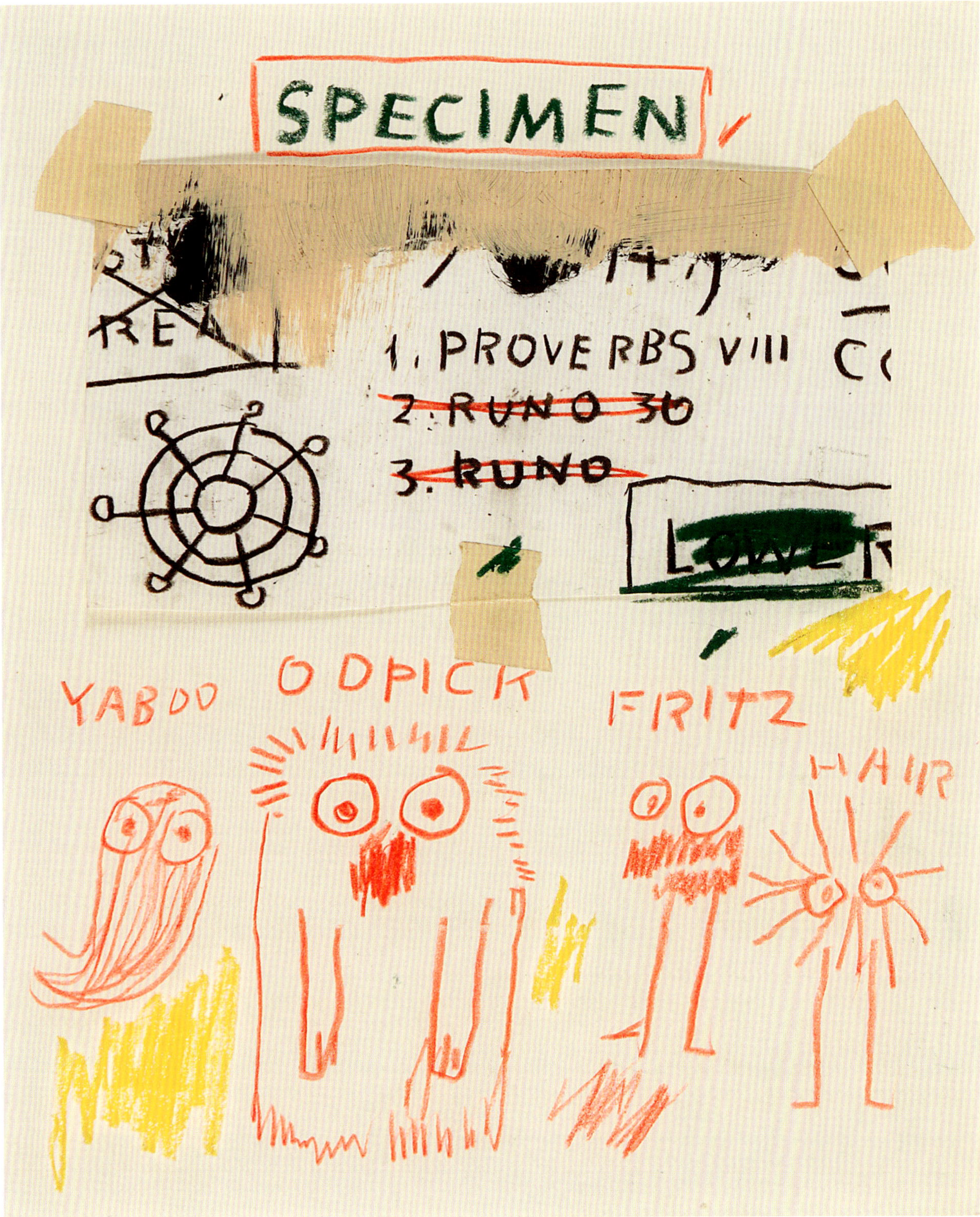

Untitled (Specimen), n.d.
Acrylic, crayon, and masking
tape with collage on paper
10½ × 8½ in. (26.67 × 21.59 cm)

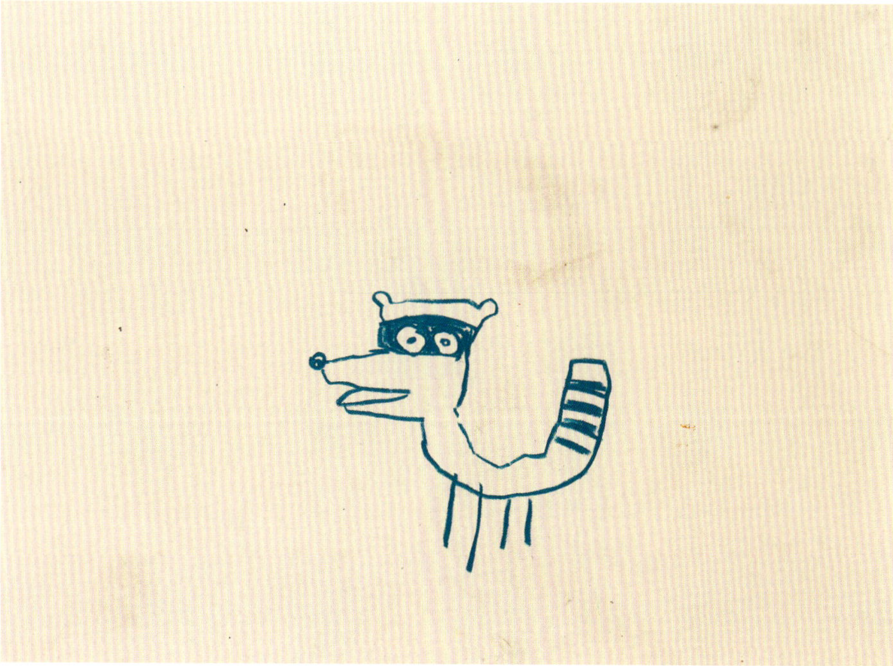

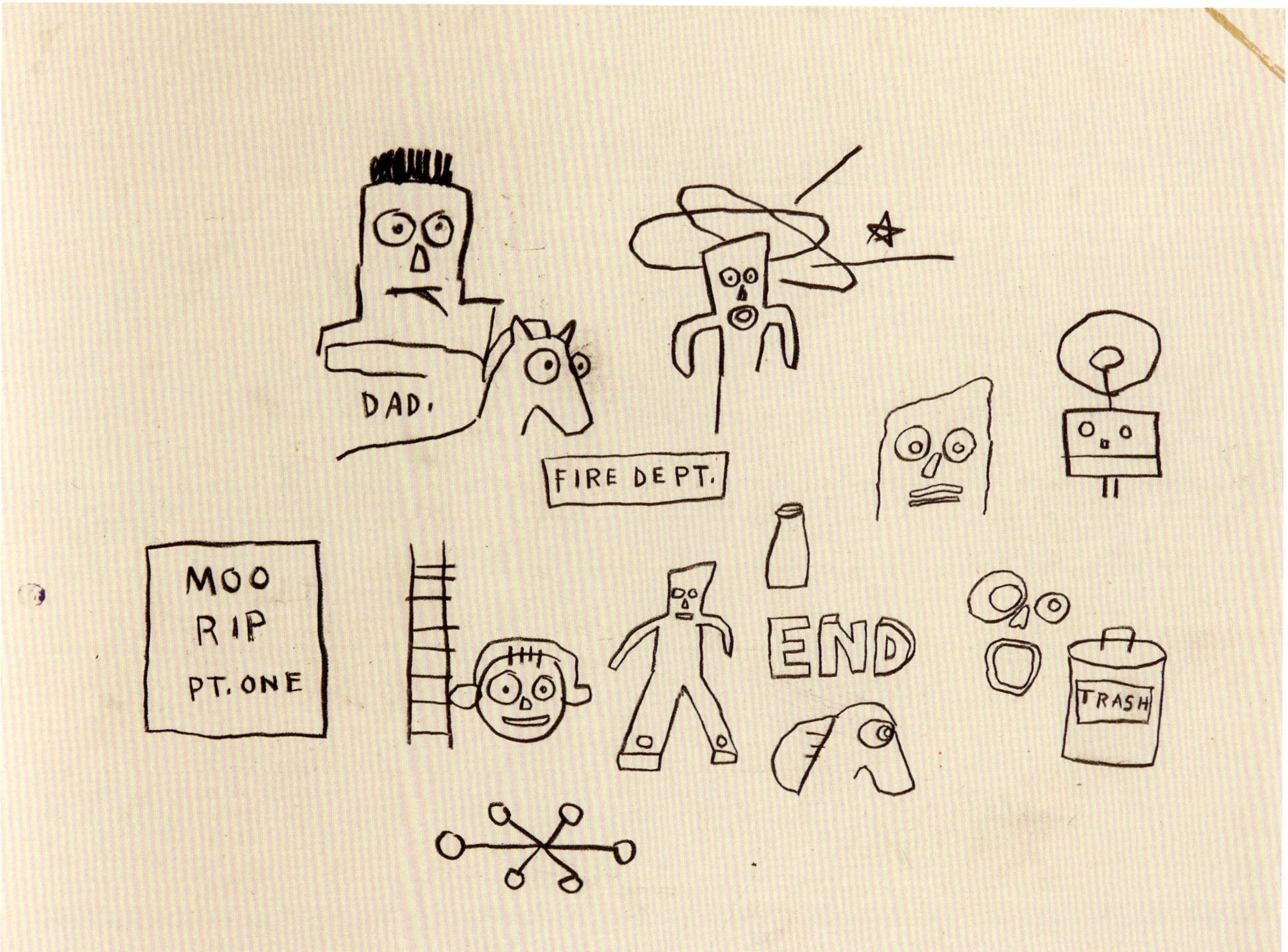

LEFT
Untitled (Rocky Racoon), n.d.
Oil stick on canvas
22¼ × 30 in. (56.52 × 76.2 cm)

BELOW
Untitled (Gumby), n.d.
Oil stick on paper
22¼ × 30 in. (56.52 × 76.2 cm)

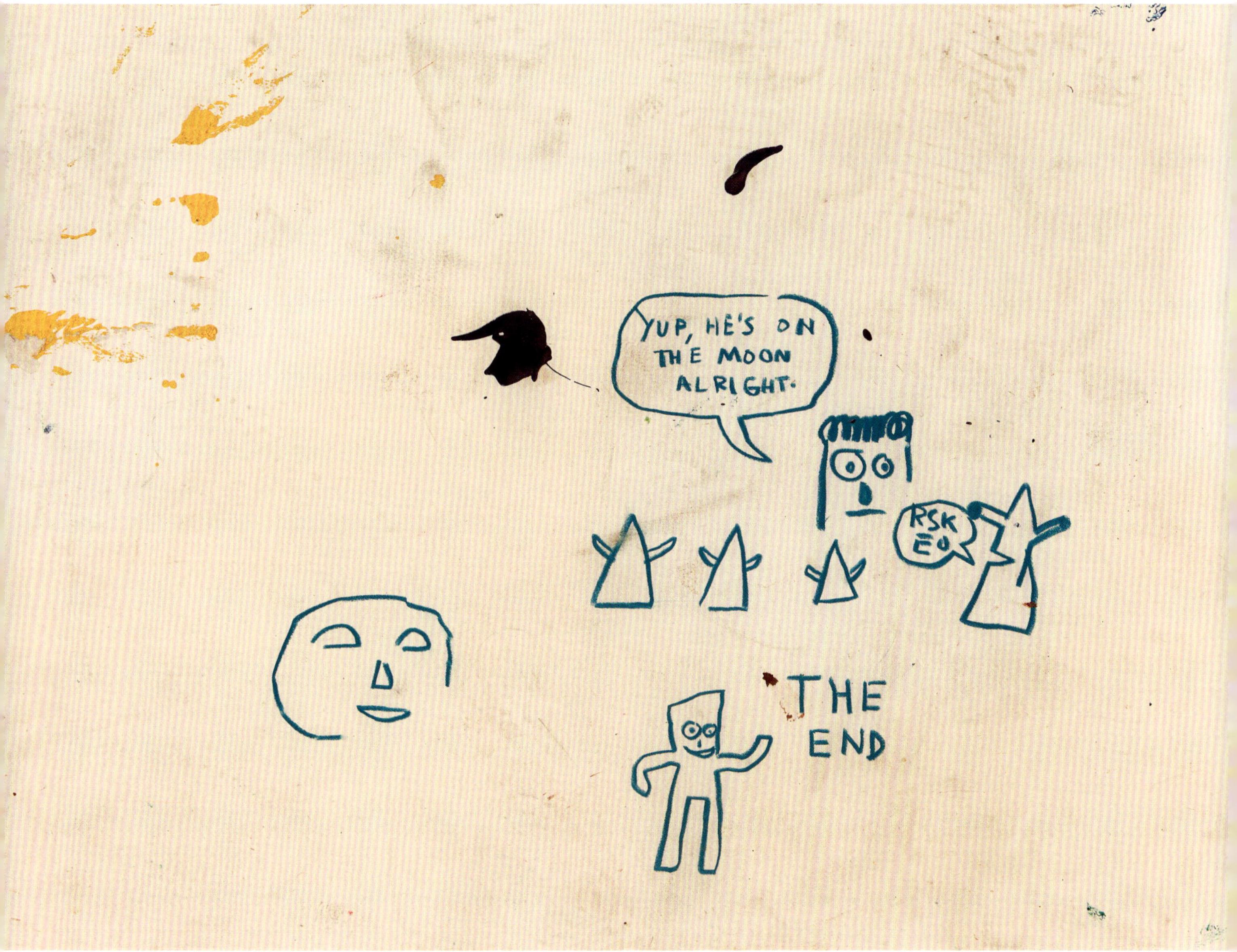

Untitled (Yup, He's on the Moon Alright), n.d.
Acrylic and oil stick on paper
22½ × 30 in. (57.2 × 76.2 cm)

Untitled (Pink Moose), n.d.
Crayon and masking tape
with collage on paper
10½ × 8½ in. (26.67 × 21.59 cm)

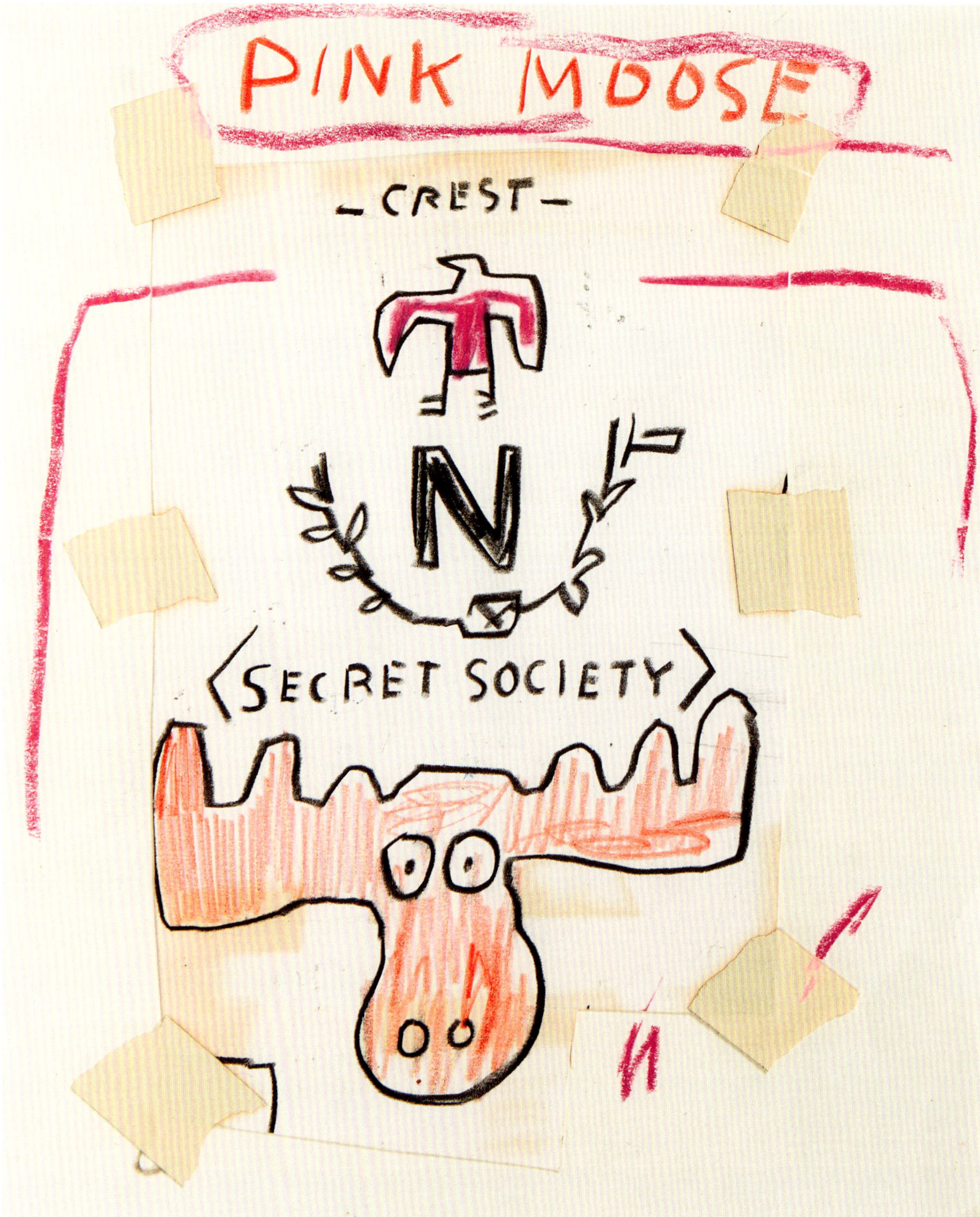

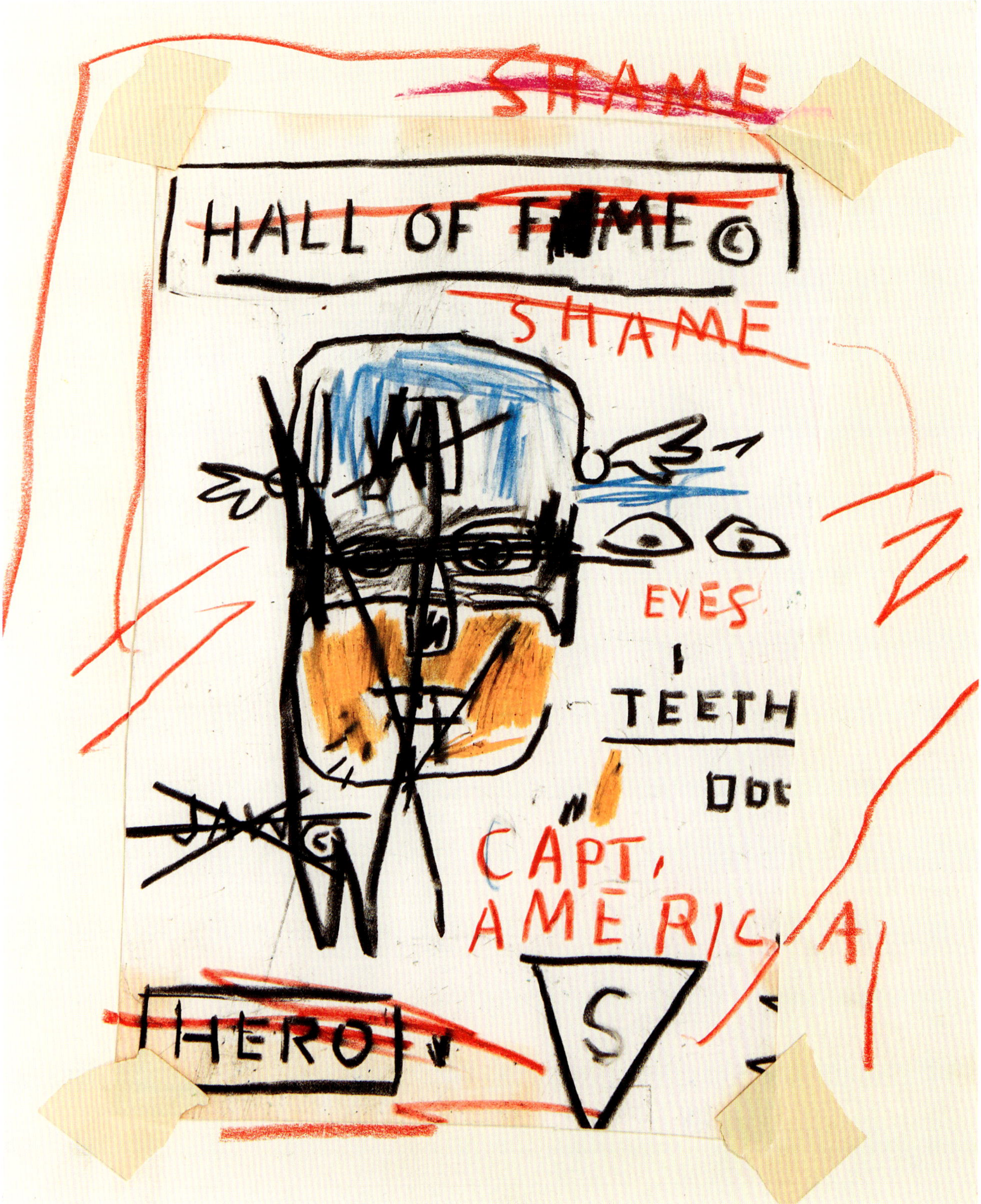

Untitled (Hall of Fame), n.d.
Crayon and masking tape
with collage on paper
10½ × 8½ in. (26.67 × 21.59 cm)

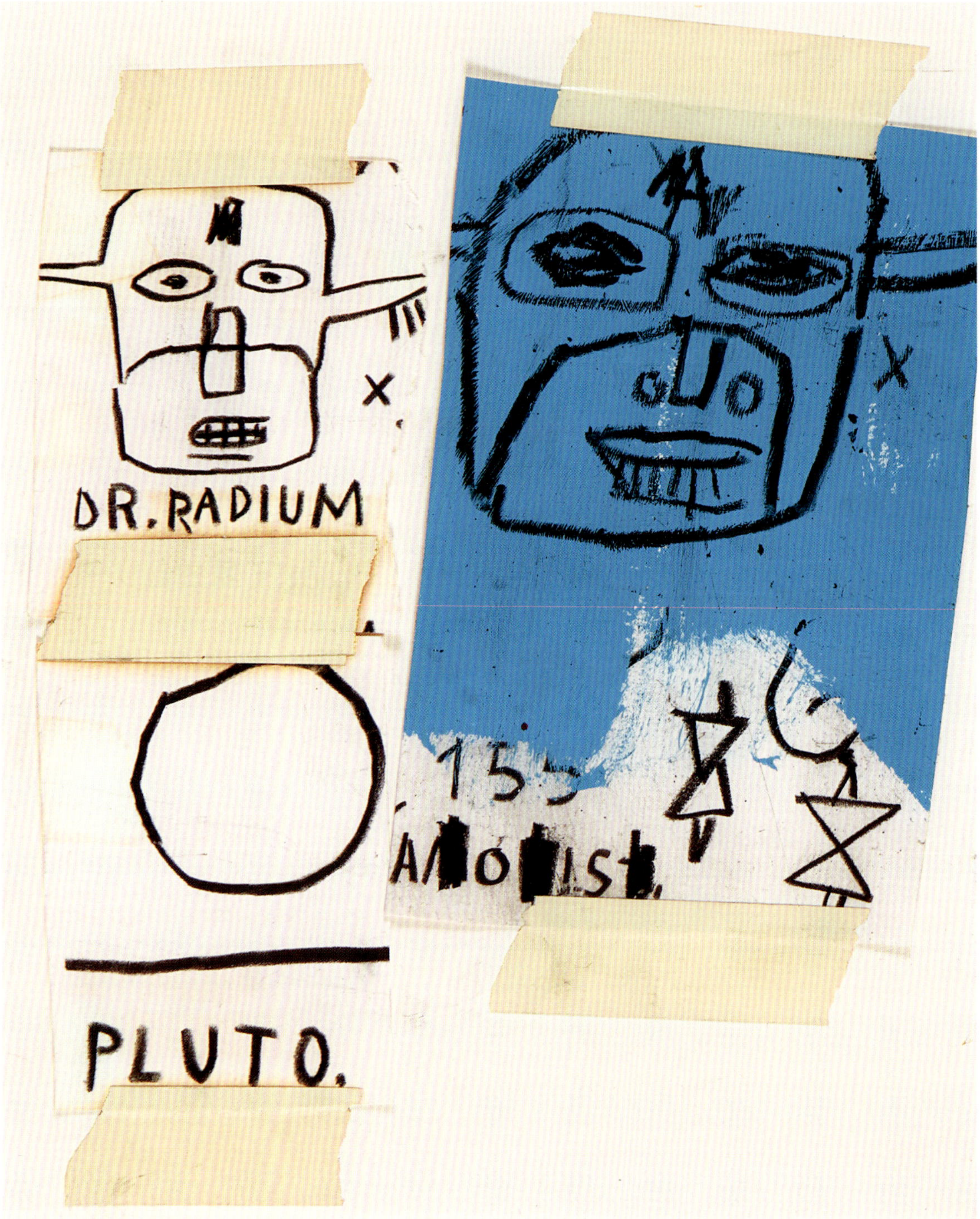

Untitled (Pluto), n.d.
Acrylic, masking tape, and
oil stick with collage on paper
10½ × 8½ in. (26.67 × 21. 59 cm)

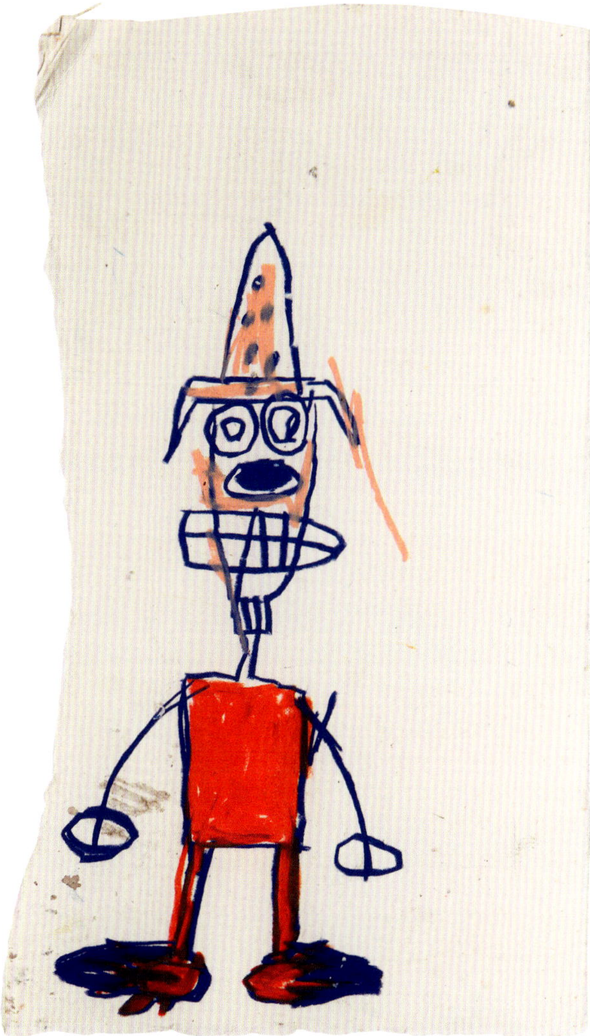

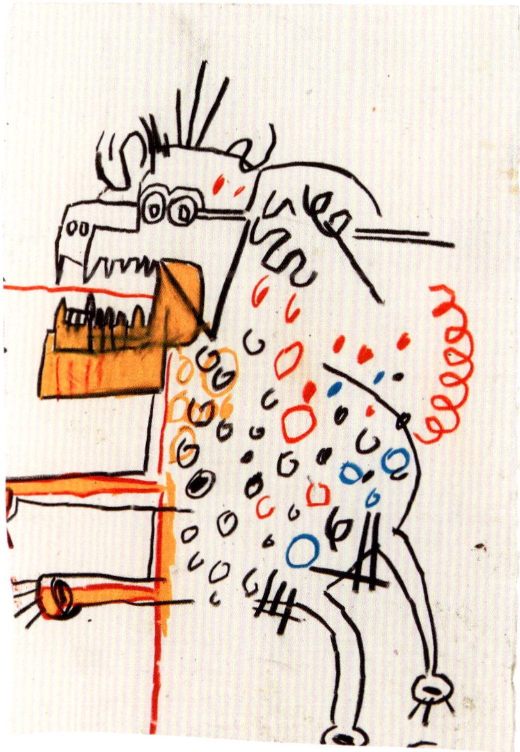

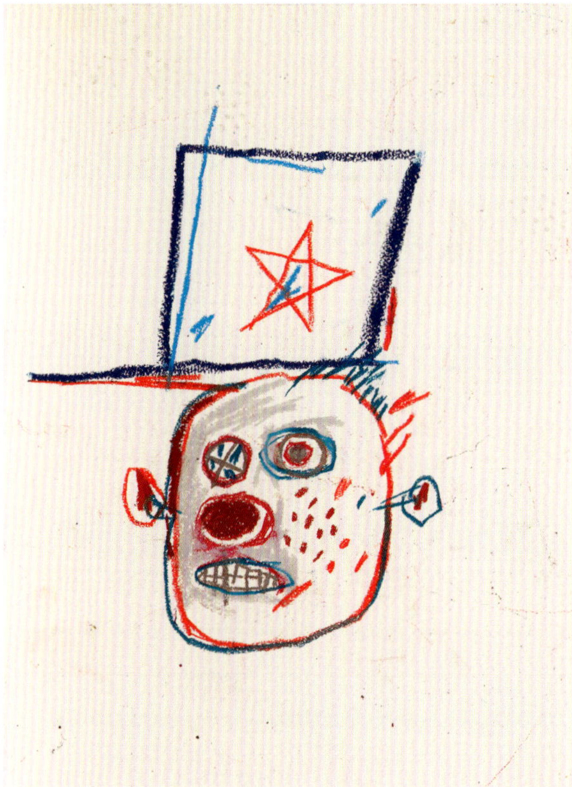

ABOVE
Untitled (Figure), n.d.
Oil stick on paper
14 × 7¼ in. (35.56 × 18.42 cm)

TOP RIGHT
Untitled (Animal), n.d.
Oil stick on paper
16½ × 11¼ in. (41.91 × 28.58 cm)

BOTTOM RIGHT
Untitled, n.d.
Oil stick on paper
30 × 22¼ in. (76.2 × 56.52 cm)

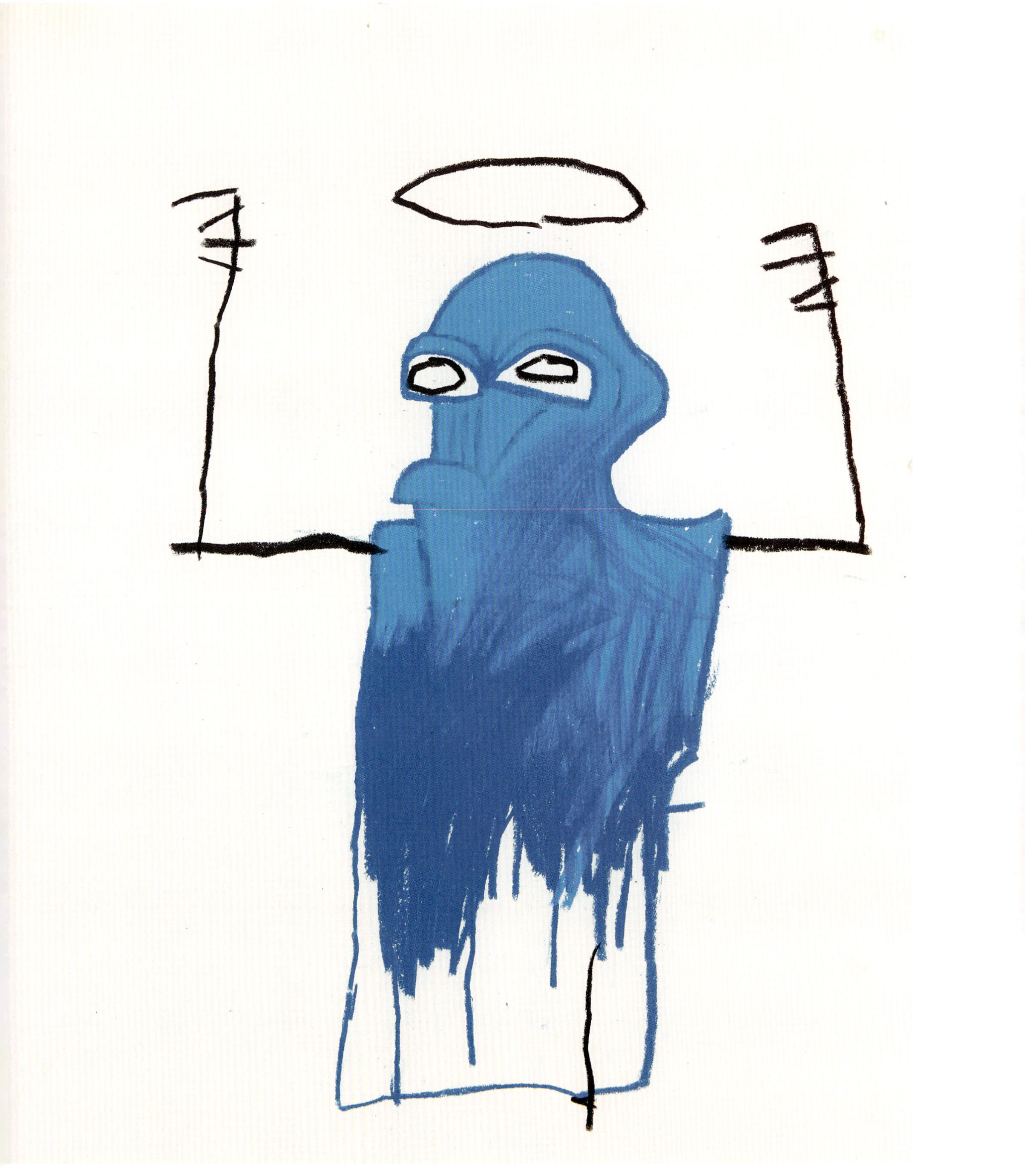

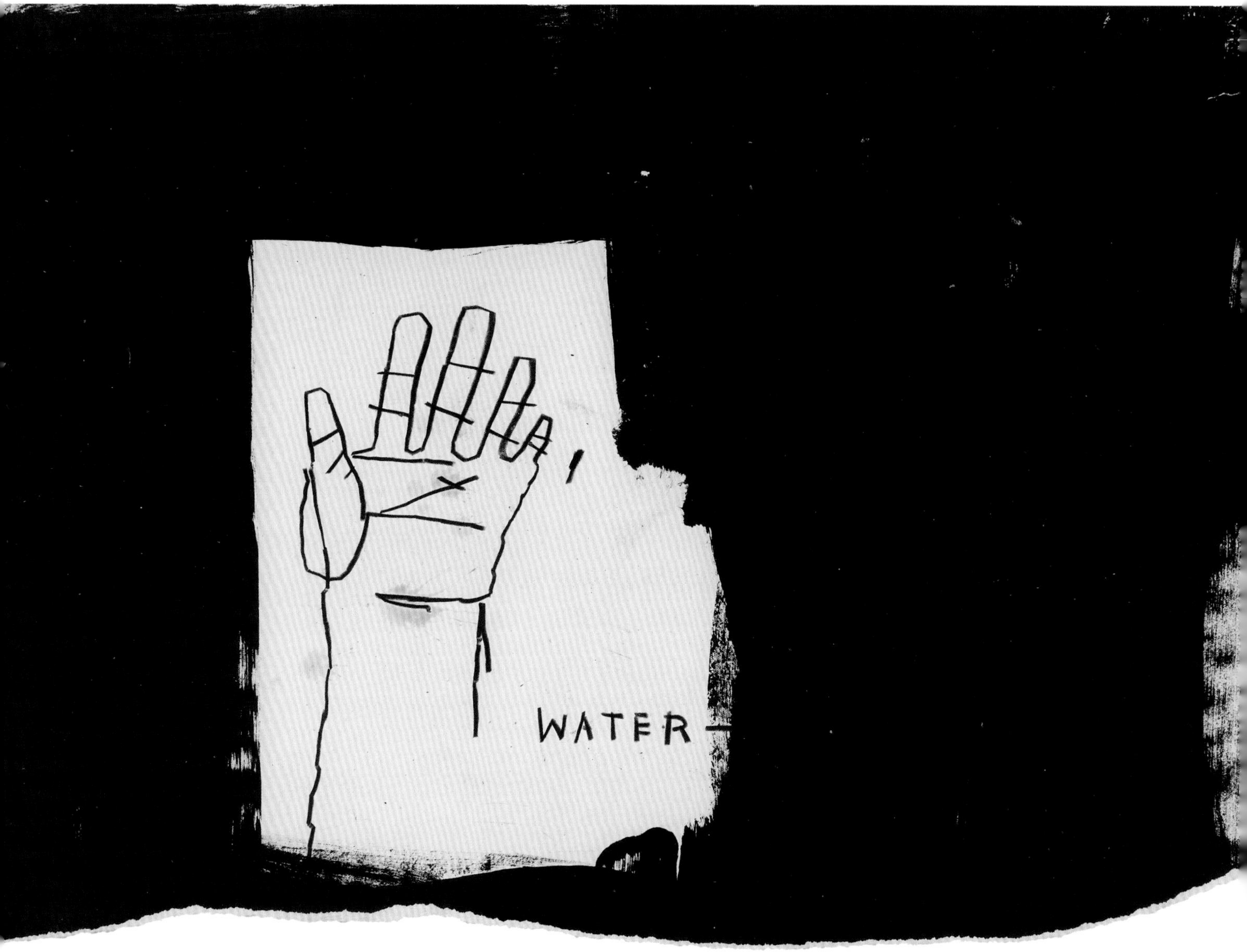

OPPOSITE
Untitled, n.d.
Oil stick on paper
16 × 13¼ in. (40.64 × 33.66 cm)

ABOVE
Untitled (Water), n.d
Acrylic and crayon on paper
16 × 22¼ in. (40.64 × 56.52 cm)

GRADE SCHOOL

Jean-Michel attended Saint Ann's School when we lived in East Flatbush. Papa, Jean-Michel, and I would take the subway to Brooklyn Heights every morning. I would sit on Jean-Michel's lap if we managed to get a seat, and Papa would stand over us and hold on to the rail. We would drop Jean-Michel off at the gate of the school. It's funny: I remember those drop-offs for Jean-Michel well but have no recollection of where my own drop-off was. LISANE

MIDDLE SCHOOL

We all attended the same middle school, I.S. 293, Nathan Hale Junior High School. On my first day—I believe it was in history class—I sat in the first row because we were seated alphabetically. I was a very shy kid. The teacher started taking attendance and when she got to my name, she stopped and said, "Oh my god, there's another one!" She got up, went into the hall, and called the teacher from next door into the room and said, "There's another one." The Basquiat kids definitely left their mark on that school. JEANINE

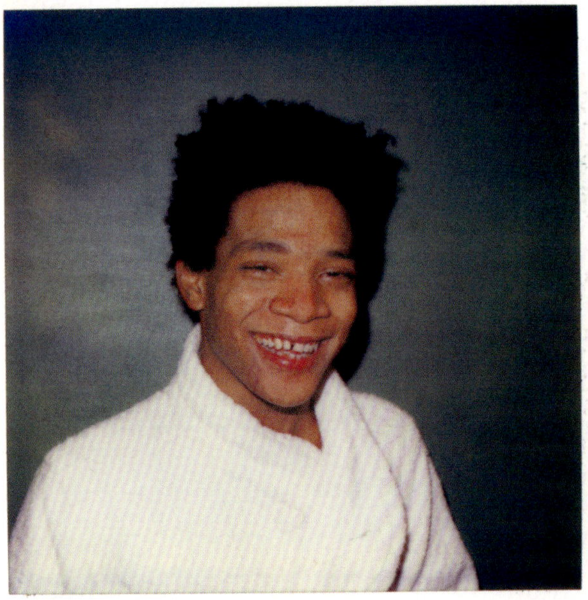

BOTTOM
Jean-Michel, ca. 1978.
It's hard to look at this picture of Jean-Michel because it was taken during a time when he was struggling to make his way. But it also reminds me that in spite of his difficulties he was determined to keep going. LISANE

OPPOSITE TOP
City-as-School newsletter, week of May 9, 1977, issue number 4

OPPOSITE RIGHT AND OPPOSITE BOTTOM
City-As-School newsletter, week of September 26, 1977, issue number 6
13¾ × 8½ in. (34.93 × 21.59 cm).
Jean-Michel was the illustrator for the school newsletter.

HIGH SCHOOL

Jean-Michel struggled a lot in school. It's hard to imagine someone carrying that kind of energy within their soul and not knowing what to do with it, or not having anyone around who really understood it. That was very, very difficult for Jean-Michel. It was also very challenging for my father, who was raised in a culture where being a fully educated, white-collar professional or business person was the only barometer of success. They both had ambitions but saw the path to fulfilling them through two completely different lenses.

After going to several schools, including Edward R. Murrow, Jean-Michel wound up at City-as-School. I think my father had a difficult time seeing this—i.e., Jean-Michel not attending a "traditional" school—not as a failure on his or Jean-Michel's part but simply as an environment better suited for his son. Jean-Michel excelled there, and seeing the work he did on the school's newsletter felt good; it provided an outlet and structure for his creativity as well as an opportunity to express himself.

It was such a stressful and anxious time in our family. I was a young teenager going through puberty, and Jeanine was a few years younger. Our father was raising three adolescents at the same time as a single parent. Jean-Michel was committed to being an artist, and my father's fears for him—not having a life with stability and security—came out as anger and frustration.

Jean-Michel ran away a few times. One day he was there, and then one day he wasn't—there was really no discussion about it. Jean-Michel was never going to conform to the vision my father had for his life. He was out of the house quite a bit, and sometimes he'd stay away longer than others. Eventually, there was more clarity about the fact that Jean-Michel was officially leaving home. I was very sad. I loved my brother—Jeanine and I were very close, and Jean-Michel and I were very close. It was hard not having him home, though I understood—it was just very difficult not having him be part of our lives every day. LISANE

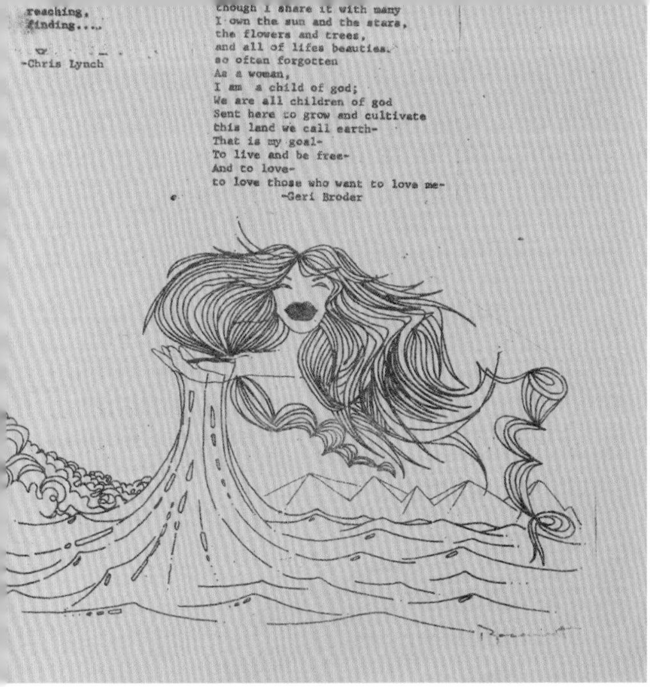

reaching,
finding....

-Chris Lynch

though I share it with many
I own the sun and the stars,
the flowers and trees,
and all of lifes beauties.
so often forgotten
As a woman,
I am a child of god;
We are all children of god
Sent here to grow and cultivate
this land we call earth-
That is my goal-
To live and be free-
And to love-
to love those who want to love me-
-Geri Broder

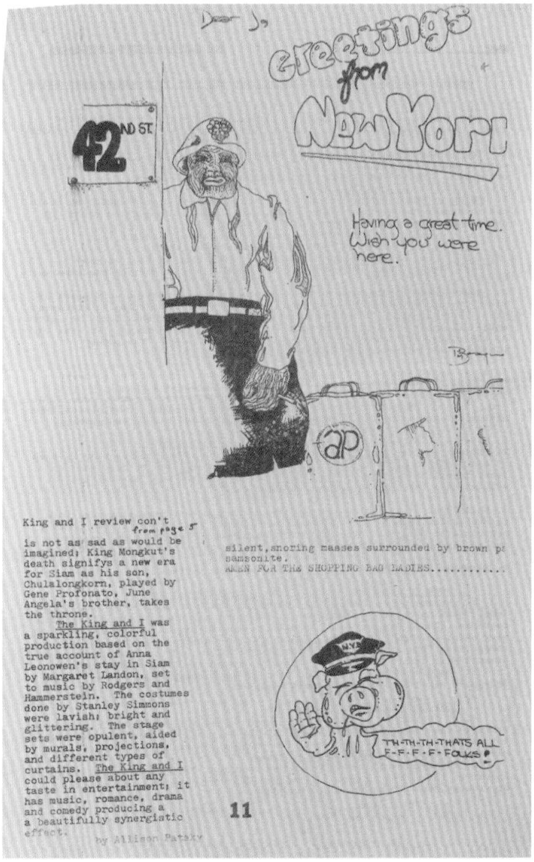

King and I review con't
from page 5
is not as sad as would be imagined; King Mongkut's death signifys a new era for Siam as his son, Chulalongkorn, played by Gene Profonato, June Angela's brother, takes the throne.

The King and I was a sparkling, colorful production based on the true account of Anna Leonowen's stay in Siam by Margaret Landon, set to music by Rodgers and Hammerstein. The costumes done by Stanley Simmons were lavish; bright and glittering. The stage sets were opulent, aided by murals, projections, and different types of curtains. The King and I could please about any taste in entertainment; it has music, romance, drama and comedy producing a a beautifully synergistic effect.

by Allison Pataky

silent, snoring masses surrounded by brown p
samsonite.
AMEN FOR THE SHOPPING BAG LADIES...........

11

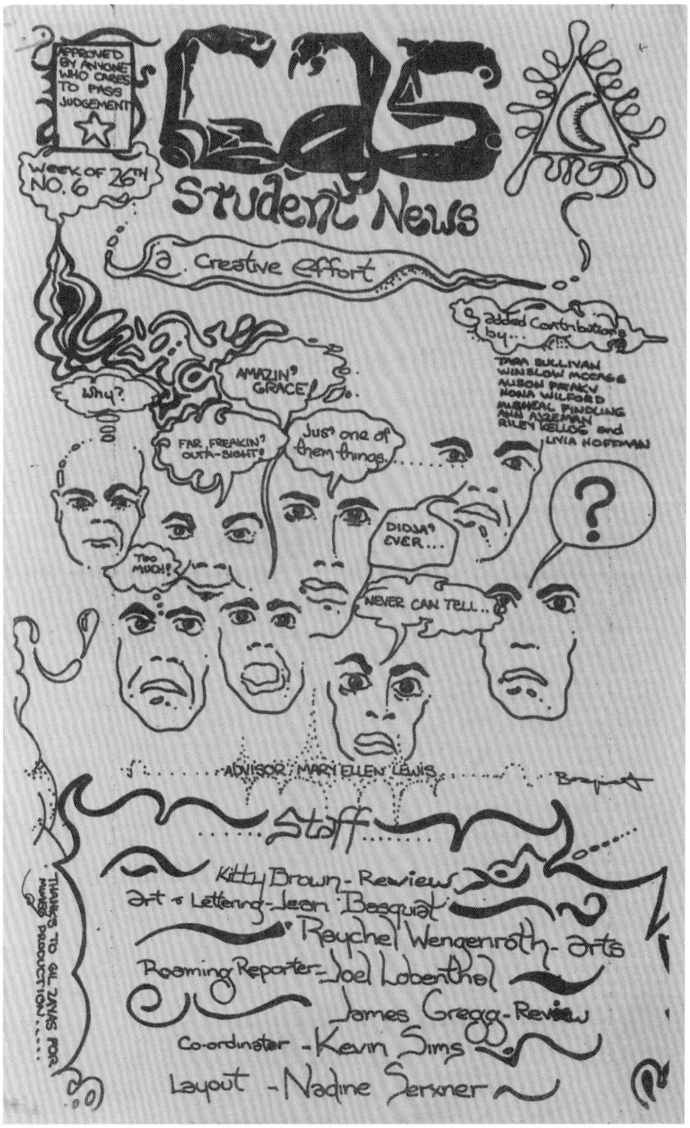

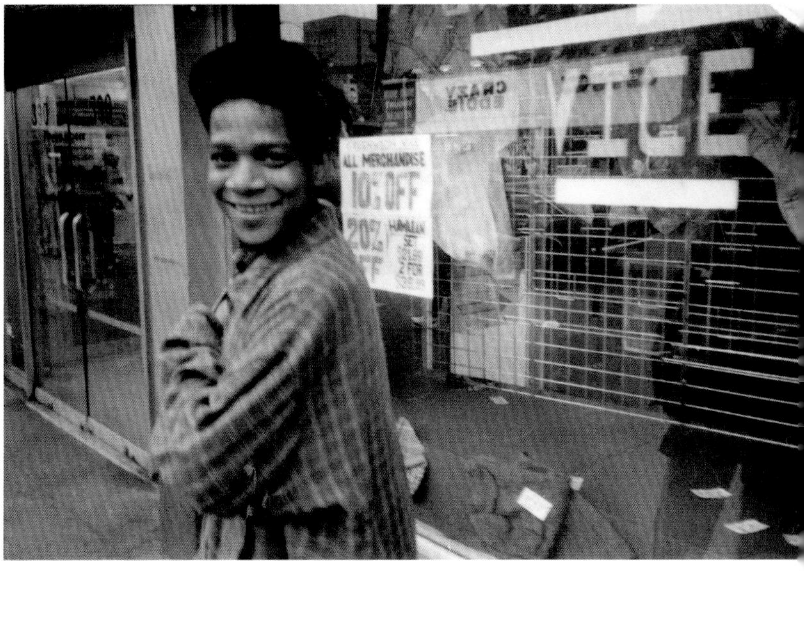

Jean-Michel, ca. 1986

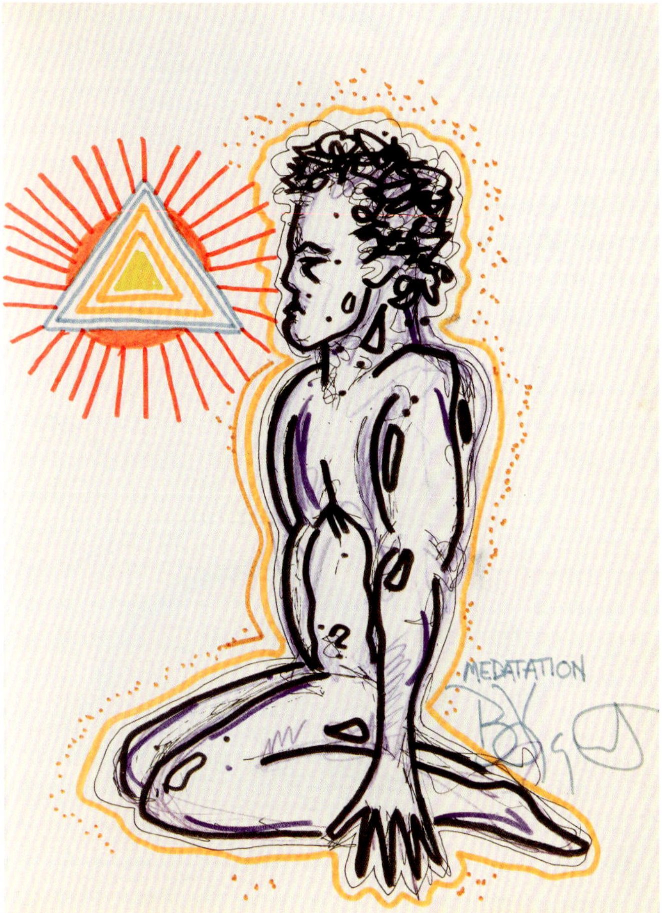

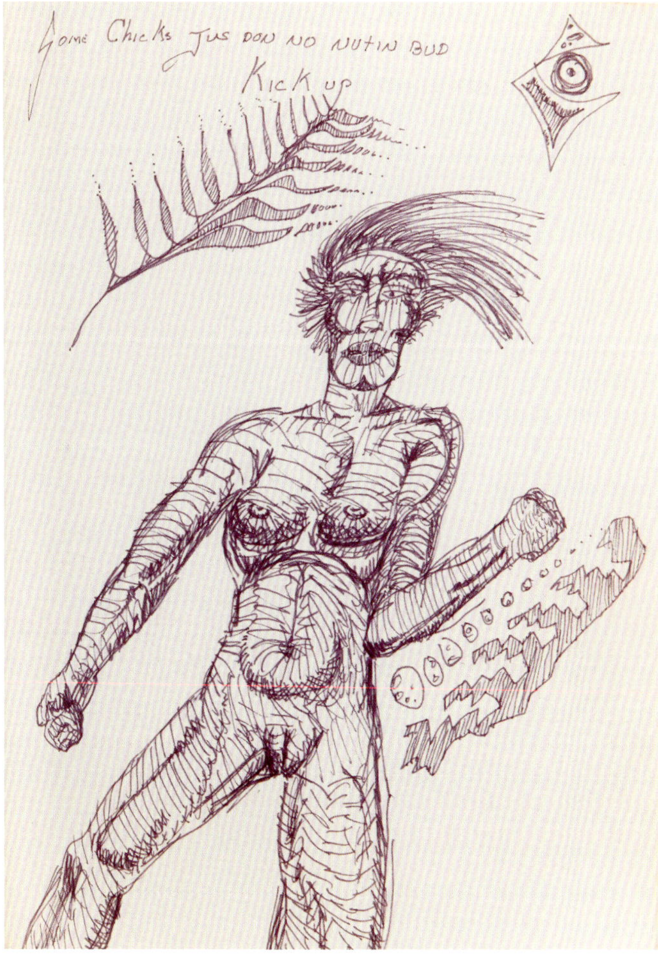

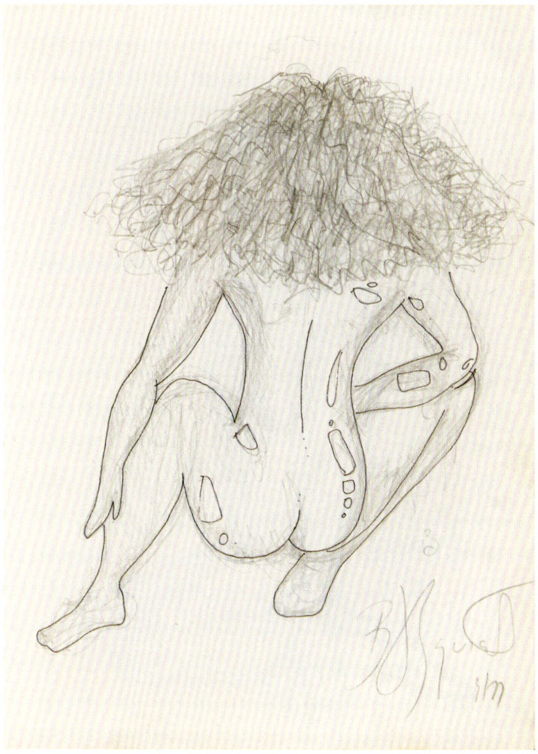

Sketchbook drawings, 1977
Ink on paper.
These are pages from a sketchbook Jean-Michel created as a seventeen-year-old.

JEAN-MICHEL AS A YOUNG ARTIST

My brother was always drawing, scribbling, creating—his mind was always in "create" mode. He could sit down and have a conversation and, before you knew it, he'd come up with some master plan to do something incredible. He was just creative about everything. He even once made moonshine in his room. LISANE

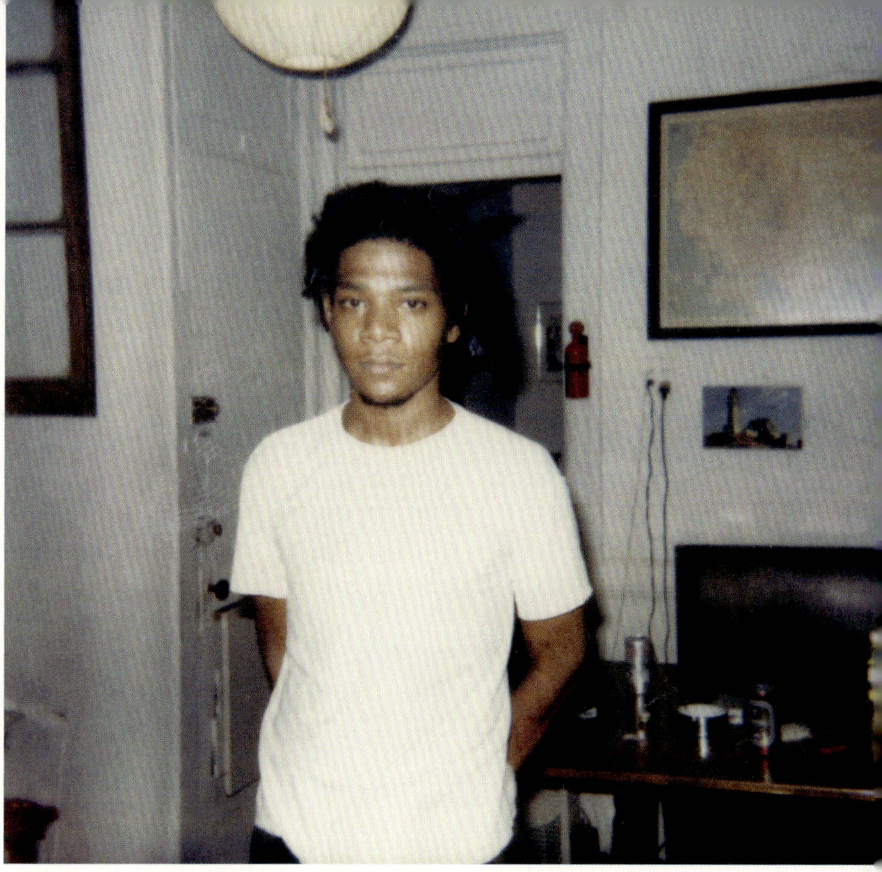

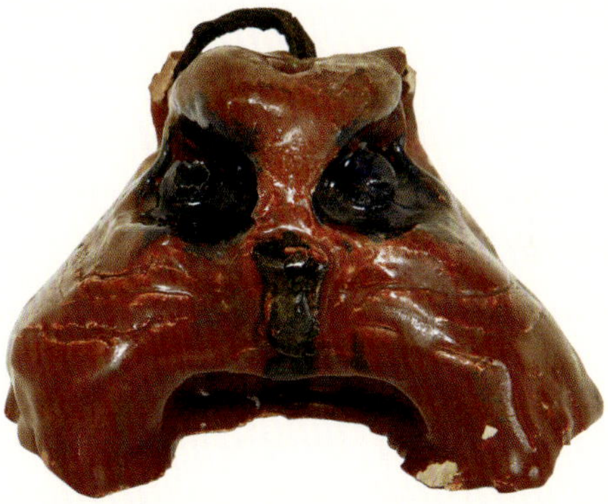

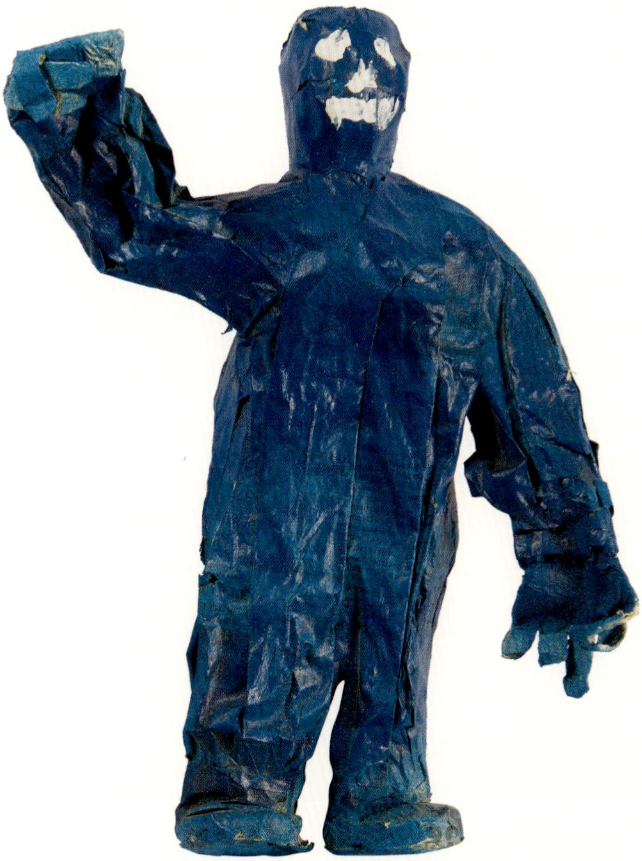

TOP
Jean-Michel, ca. late 1970s

ABOVE
Untitled (Cat), ca. 1971
Clay
3 × 5 × 4 in.
(7.62 × 12.7 × 10.16 cm)

LEFT
Untitled (Standing Man), n.d.
Papier-mâché with spray paint and touches of acrylic
Height: 13 in. (33.2 cm).

Sketches done by:

Name JeaN Basquiat

Address

966-9845

Reorder No. 57-158

Also available in 6 x 4", 8½ x 5½" and 14 x 11" sizes

AmArt® American Pad and Paper Co. Holyoke, Massachusetts 01040

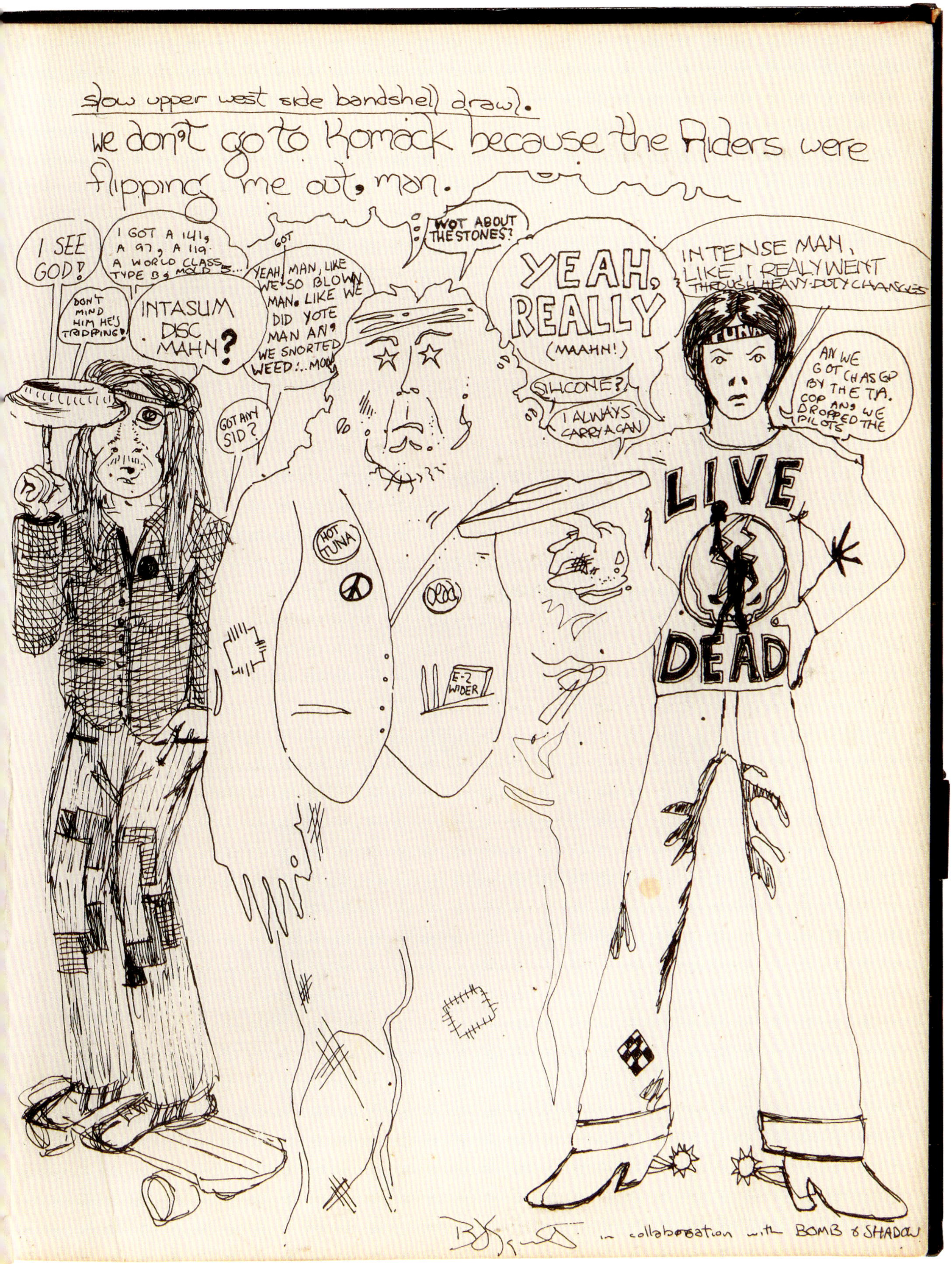
slow upper west side bandshell drawl.
we don't go to Komack because the Riders were flipping me out, man.
I SEE GOD!
I GOT A 141, A 97, A 119. A WORLD CLASS TYPE B, MOLD 5...
DON'T MIND HIM HE'S TRIPPING!
INTASUM DISC MAHN?
YEAH, MAN, LIKE WE SO BLOWN MAN. LIKE WE DID YOTE MAN AN' WE SNORTED WEED!...MON
GOT ANY SID?
WOT ABOUT THE STONES?
YEAH, REALLY (MAAHN!)
SILICONE?
I ALWAYS CARRY A CAN
INTENSE MAN, LIKE, I REALY WENT THROUGH HEAVY-DUTY CHANGES
AN WE GOT CHASED BY THE T.A. COP AN' WE DROPPED THE PILOTS
TUNA
HOT TUNA
Dead
E-Z WIDER
LIVE DEAD
in collaboration with BOMB & SHADOW

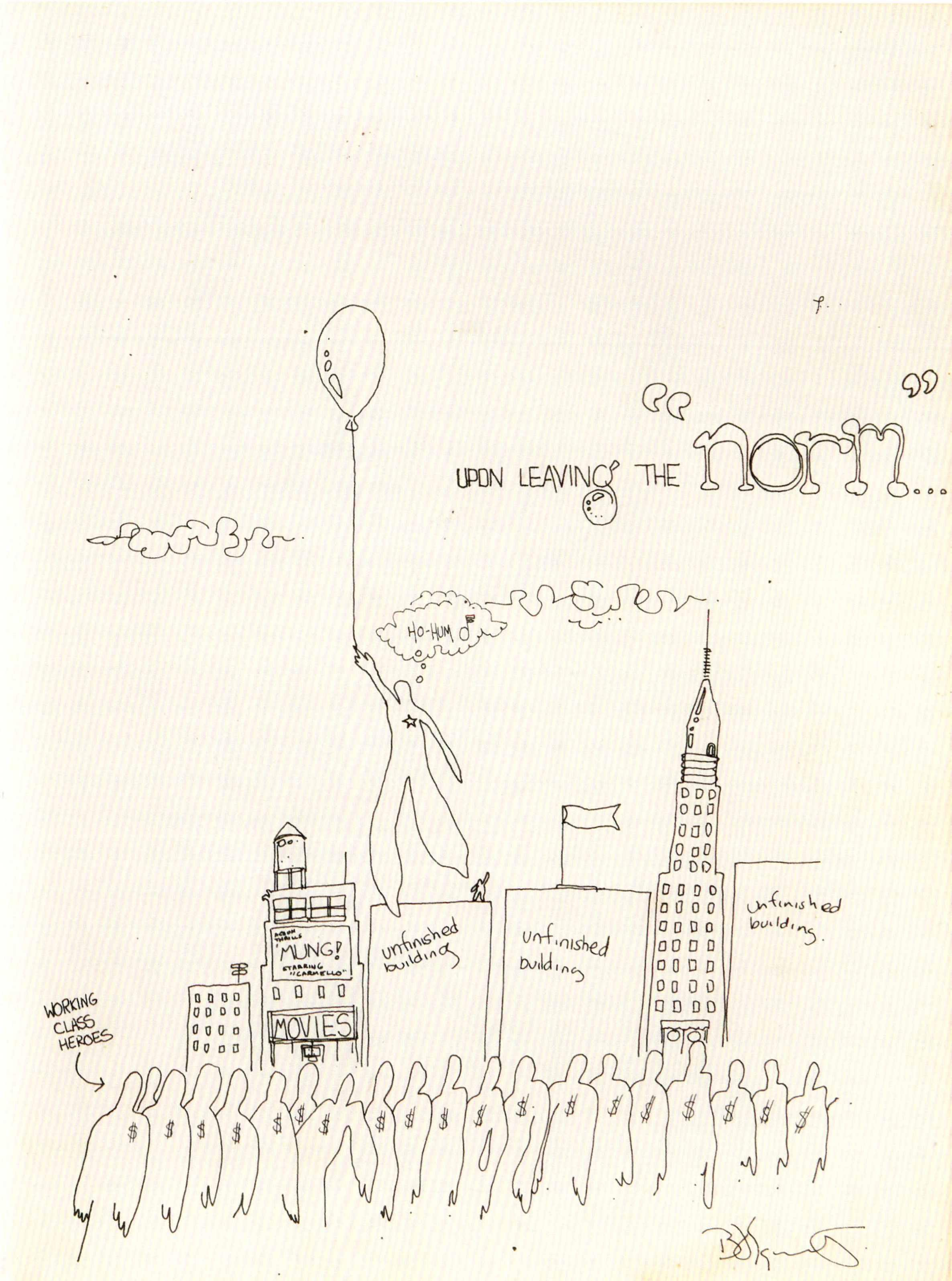

PAGES 40–47
Sketchbook drawings, 1977
Ink on paper.
I can almost see Jean-Michel sitting in a subway car and taking in the scene around him while he made these sketches. LISANE

To whom it may concern:

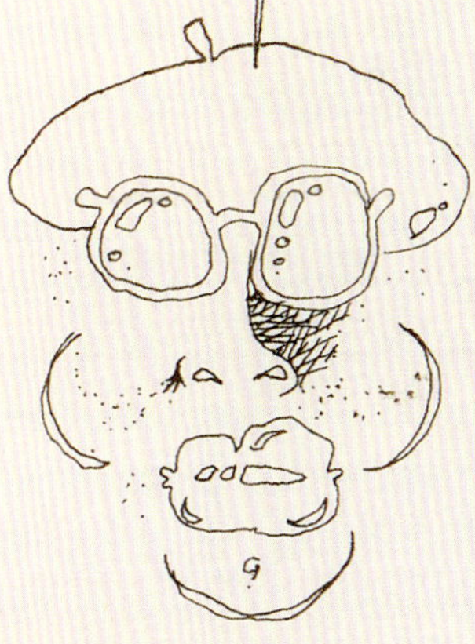

Poem for the Subway

RUMBLE RUMBLE RUMBLE RUMBLE RUMBLE RUMBLE RUMBLE RUMBLE RUMBLE

a liberal-looking lady probably a dancer or a secretary
an old security cop twidling his thumbs and probably dreaming of
Elliot Ness.

Preporation "H" releives hemmoroids.
Doors open, Doors close nobody gets off.
Some 9 to 5 small talk about this one getting married and
that one looking at her across the train. and how fun
mopeds are.
Sleeping derelicts snoring in unison.
RUMBLE RUMBLE RUMBLE RUMBLE RUMBLE RUMBLE RUMBLE
Scrawlings on the wall of live, love, sex & drugs.
The advertisments bombard me and cloud my mind
with visions of Newports, Cream cheese and 6% interest.

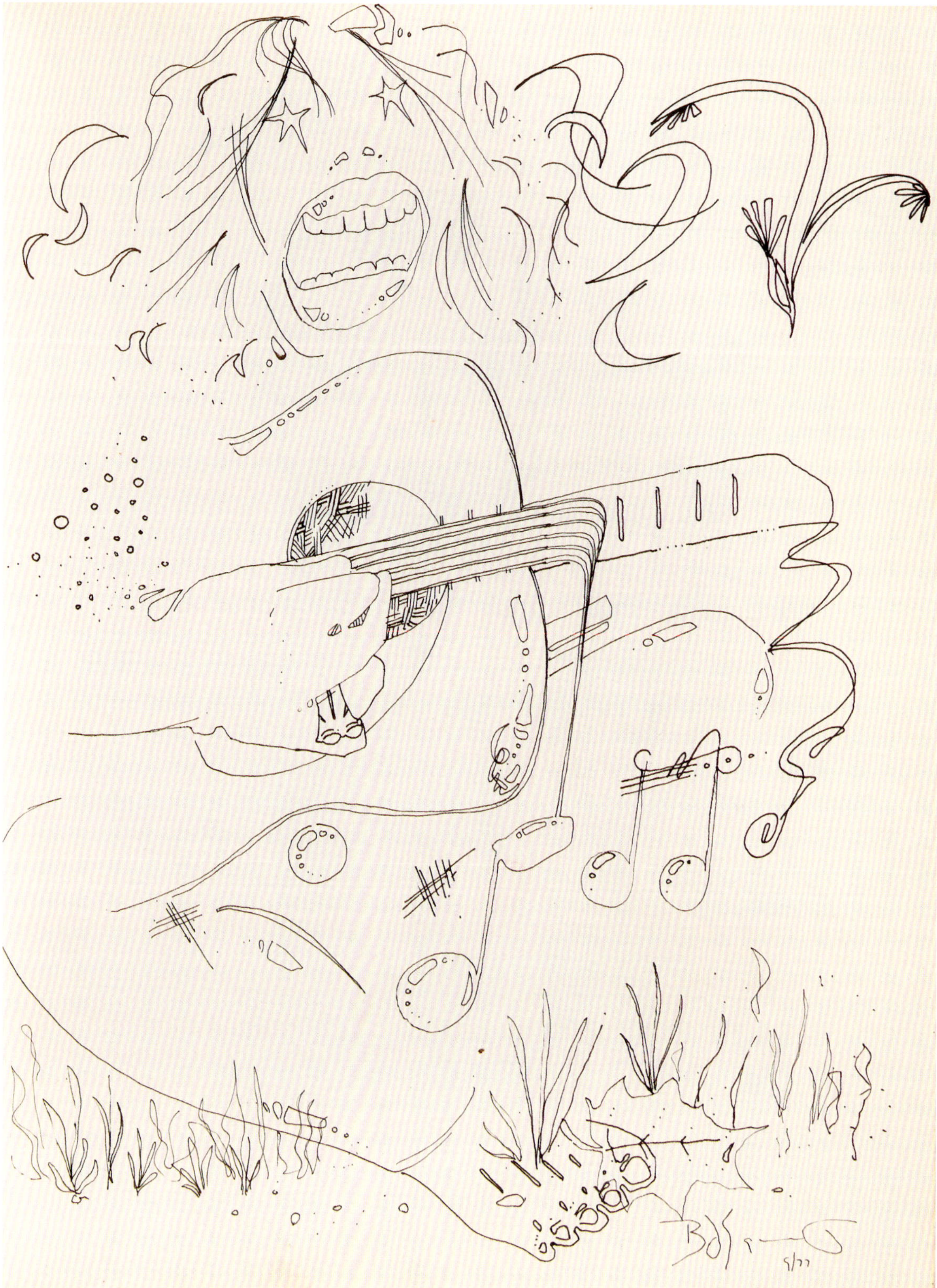

The conveyer bett of life.

This is a little doodah for those not on the mainstream.

Ahem !(Sniffle)..... Uhm....

For those of you who are here on official buisness concerning most pots

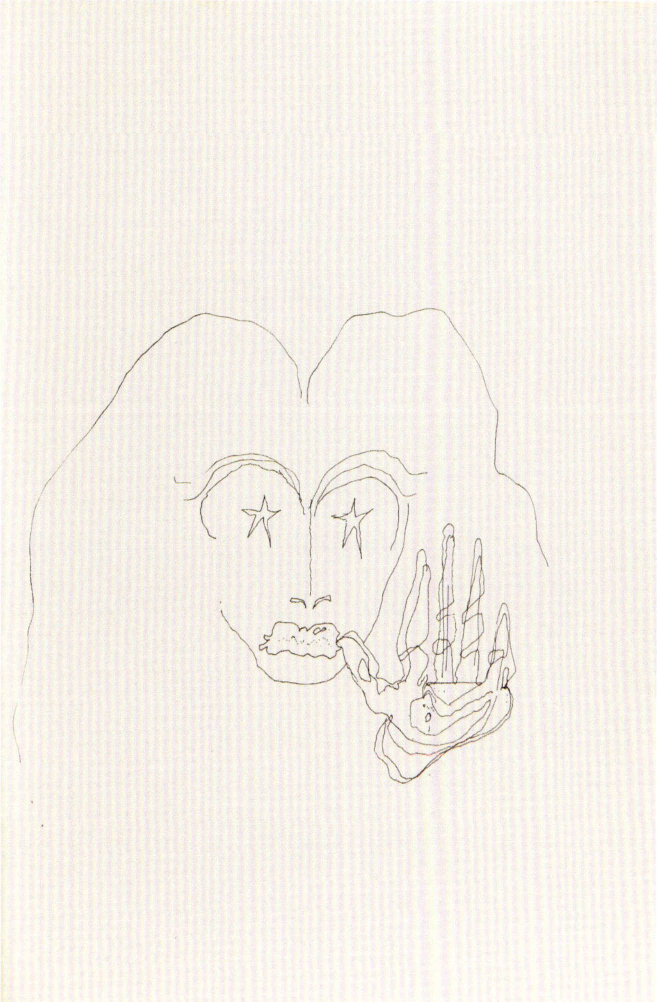

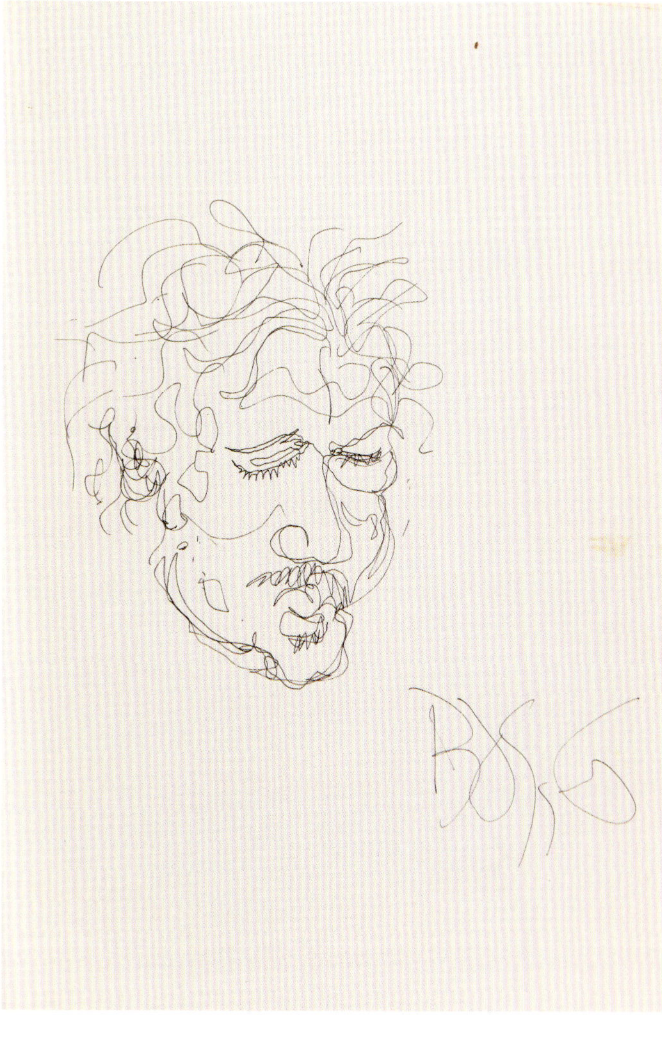

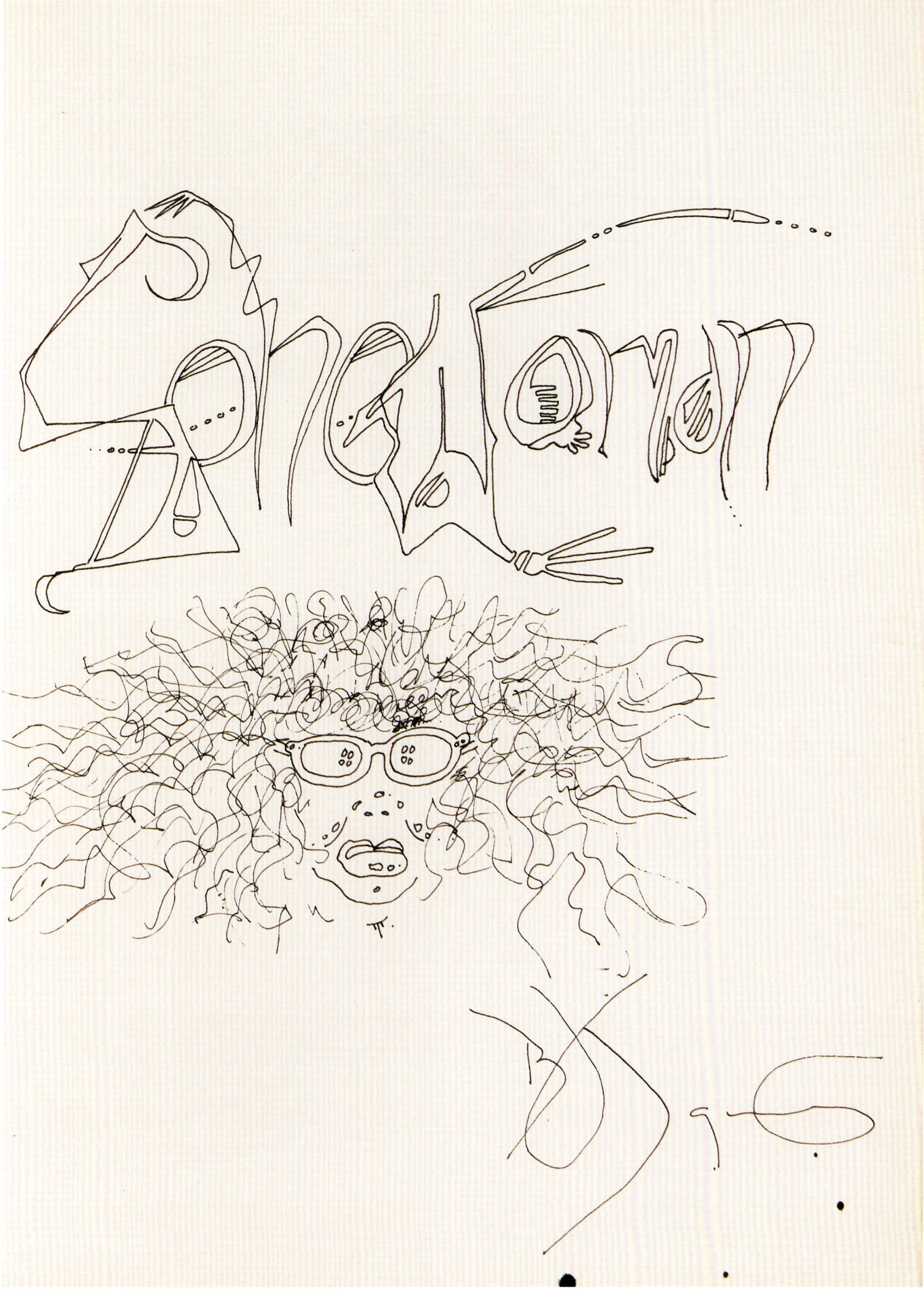

GERARD BASQUIAT

My father could be loving and sweet one moment, and then very harsh the next. He could make you laugh, cry, scream, or see something from a new perspective, all inside of three minutes.

As we were growing up, he was building a career. He was the first Black controller to work for Macmillan Films—and the youngest. He was the primary caregiver for three children, and he was traveling quite a bit for work. Yet, we still had dinner every night at the table as a family unless he was out of town.

He was a great cook and loved good food. We weren't a TV dinner kind of family at all—we had London broil, eggs benedict, boeuf bourguignon, and quiche lorraine. Papa would also make the best beans and rice. His love of good food rubbed off on his kids—I remember Jean-Michel once made us all fondue. We Basquiats were certainly foodies before it became cool. LISANE

When I first met Gerard, Jeanine was nine, Lisane was thirteen, and Jean-Michel was seventeen. It was amazing how bright and independent they all were. Their independence was out of necessity—Gerard had been taking care of them on his own and relying on babysitters when he was at work. In fact, they had several babysitters, and Jean-Michel used to play tricks on them. They never lasted very long! Gerard made sure to spend as much time as he could with his children; there was a family dinner every night. NORA

Our father and mother both took 100 percent responsibility and accountability for their roles as parents, even though it was an unconventional arrangement at the time, with my father as the primary caregiver. In hindsight, he was stretched thin. And his teenage son's desire to pursue a career path where success was completely unheard of was a disruption to the order my father very much wanted to have in our lives and our home. He was anxious about Jean-Michel's desire to be an artist, and it took him a long time to really understand what was going on with Jean-Michel because his own experience was so different. Jean-Michel was a young Black man and my father was terrified for his future. He was completely blindsided by Jean-Michel's gifts and talent. It wasn't until my father started to see that making a living as an artist was actually a possibility for Jean-Michel that his perspective shifted, but it was tough for him and led to a lot of tension between them. LISANE

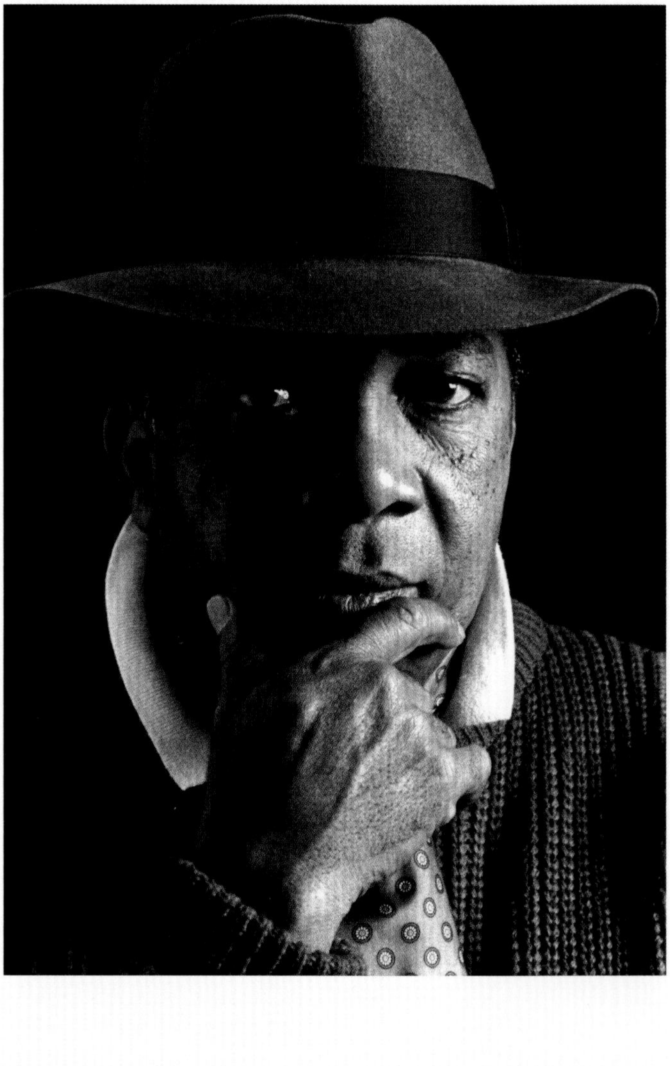

Portrait of Gerard
© GEORGE-DUBOSE.COM

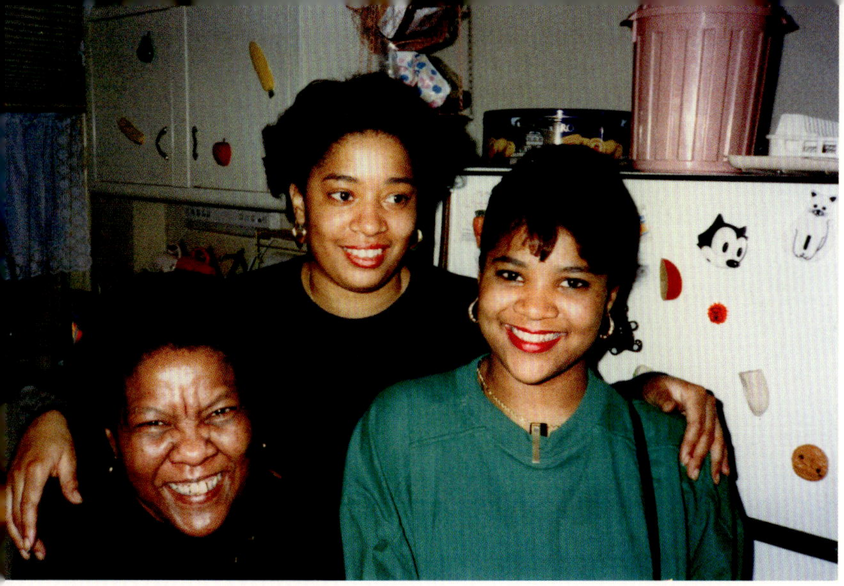

Matilde, Lisane, and Jeanine
at Abuelita's house, Bushwick,
Brooklyn, ca. 1991

MATILDE BASQUIAT

After my parents' separation, Papa always encouraged our relationship with our mother. He would give me $20 and tell me to take her to Junior's, a popular restaurant in Brooklyn, for Mother's Day. We saw her most weekends. She was living with her mother, my Abuelita (the affectionate way to say grandmother, *abuela*, in Spanish), who would make the best fried chicken and *arroz con gandules*, and we would spend the whole day together. She loved taking us to amusement parks, either Great Adventure or Coney Island Astroland. We would ride the Cyclone roller coaster over and over—she never said no. She planned day trips to museums and the planetarium. We went ice and roller skating; we would ride the Staten Island ferry back and forth. And for several years, we never missed the Puerto Rican Day Parade.

Jean-Michel and my mother were close. He spoke fluent Spanish with her and my grandmother. He was very protective of Lisane and me, and very protective of our mom. After he left home, I would go with her to visit Jean-Michel at his apartment, and he would visit her and our grandmother in Brooklyn. JEANINE

Our mother Matilde was beautiful, fashionable, and loved to dance. She was incredibly creative and sewed many of her own clothes. She was an extraordinary woman in so many ways.

Jean-Michel had a very soft spot in his heart for her. When he was in grade school, she received a promotion while working for the telephone company, which meant more time away from home. He would call her, though, and be very upset that she wasn't home. Eventually, she gave up the promotion because she didn't feel he was ready. He was the oldest and our parents' breakup affected him deeply—he always worried about her.

We led a very unconventional life. In hindsight though, my parents were amazing human beings who took their roles as parents very seriously. They got some things wrong and missed a few things, but they really showed up. I have always appreciated that.

After they split, we spent every Saturday with our mother. She would take us to plays, museums, parks, roller-skating rinks, shows, rides on the *Circle Line*, the movies. Jeanine and I once convinced her to take us to see *Richard Pryor: Live in Concert*. We laughed just as hard at the jokes as we did at watching our mother try to maintain her composure.

What I really admire about my mother is that, while she may not have had the ability to show up as a day-to-day mother, she was willing to have any conversation, to answer any question, to clarify any of her decisions, no matter how uncomfortable for her, and no matter how painful. We were incredibly close until she passed away in 2008. LISANE

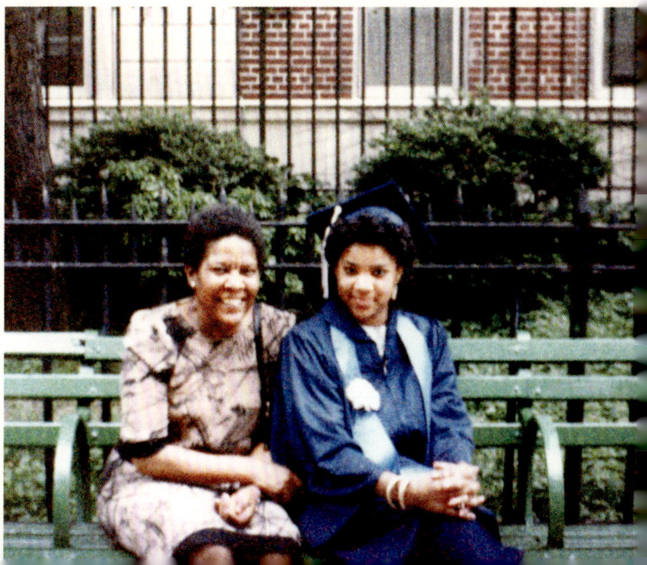

Matilde and Jeanine on
high school graduation day,
Brooklyn, 1985

LATCHKEY KIDS

When you are raised by a single parent who is working and doing their best to provide, you tend to learn responsibility early. I learned to iron at seven, barely reaching the top of the ironing board. I was also cooking at nine, because we usually had to get dinner started before Papa got home from the office, which was in New Jersey. JEANINE

We were latchkey kids, but with lots of structure and routine. We had a system: call Papa as soon as we each got home. He would tell us what to take out of the freezer to defrost for dinner. He'd come home, change his clothes, sit on the couch for a few minutes to unwind, and then he'd make dinner, and we'd sit down to eat. This happened like clockwork every night, unless he was traveling for work. We had housekeepers when we were younger, but when we were older we simply sustained the routine ourselves. LISANE

JEAN-MICHEL: LEADER OF THE MISCHIEF-MAKERS

Jean-Michel was good at convincing you to do things that you might not have agreed to if you knew the outcome. He once convinced me to jump off the top of an armoire with an umbrella to emulate Mary Poppins. Needless to say, it didn't work.

Jean-Michel would come up with spooky ways to scare us during Halloween. Our bedrooms were on the top floor, and he would take Lisane's big Raggedy Ann doll, dress it up in clothes, and put it in a rocking chair. He would then proceed to turn out the lights, make knocking sounds with a broom, and act like the doll was talking.

Jean-Michel actually liked to cook. When he was a teenager, he experimented with cooking. He decided he wanted to roast a London broil like a pot roast. That didn't work out too well. He didn't cook for a while after that one. I think his ego was bruised a little bit. JEANINE

I was the sidekick to Jean-Michel's shenanigans—and there were antics. When you think about the man who created the unbelievably brilliant and unique artwork that he did, you can imagine the creative, crazy-ass genius he was as a kid.

One day, we ordered pizza from a bunch of restaurants, and we ordered all of it to go to one address, but it wasn't our house, of course. We watched from the window while all of these delivery people showed up at the same time scratching their heads.

We had one housekeeper who watched soap operas all day long. We only had one TV and she watched it the entire time she was there. We were always kids with a cause, and in this case it was that our father was paying her to sit around and watch TV. So one day we decided we were going to put an end to it. We wanted to watch something, so Jean-Michel had one of us in front of the TV and situated himself at the outlet. (He didn't want me to electrocute myself.) We got into position—he waited for the most suspenseful moment in the soap opera and then told me to click the TV off. She screamed, and when she ran over to turn it back on, he unplugged it from the wall. She frantically tried to get to the plug from him, and as soon as she plugged it back in, I clicked the TV back off. That was the game; she was completely pissed off and beside herself.

We went through a few housekeepers that summer. One sat on the couch eating potato starch (perhaps she suffered from pica—who knows!), others didn't clean the right way, or something else would be wrong. We took the position that our father was paying someone to work and they weren't doing the work. Finally, our dad said, "You know what, let's do this. You guys stay by yourselves then. We're gonna test this out." And so that's what he did. It worked out well. LISANE

BIG BROTHER

By the time I got to high school, I'd told Jean-Michel that my friends and I had started drinking wine coolers, which were popular at the time. His response was, "Okay, if that's what's happening, come with me. I don't want anyone to ever be able to take advantage of you. So get drunk with me and I'll show you how." And he did—he taught me how to drink and got me super high. And, eventually, the guys in school would try to get me drunk, just like Jean-Michel said they would. They would always wind up drunk and I'd just go home. He taught me how to hold my liquor and how to get stoned so that someone else didn't introduce that to me. LISANE

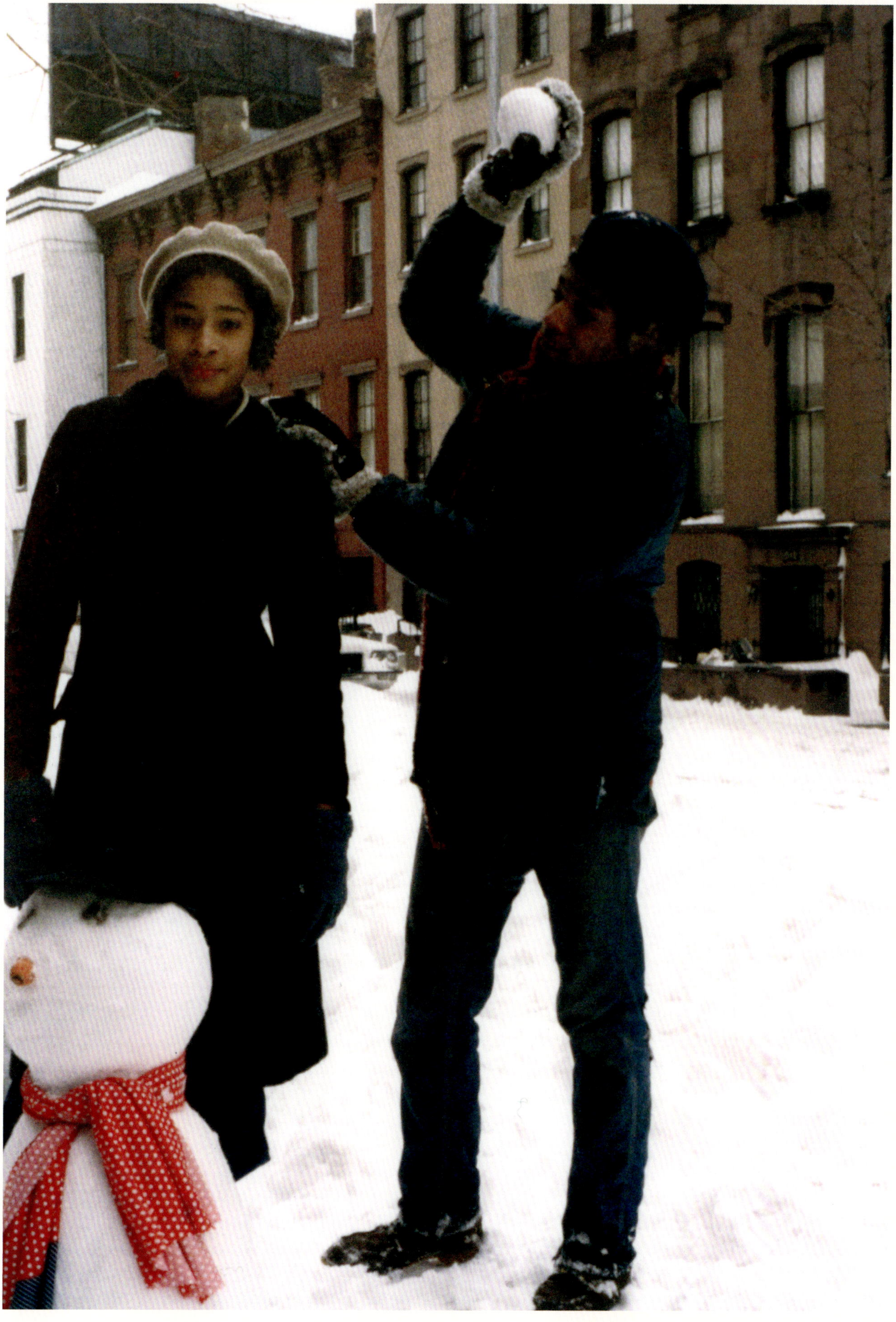

Lisane and Jean-Michel in a snowball fight, Boerum Hill, Brooklyn, ca. 1976

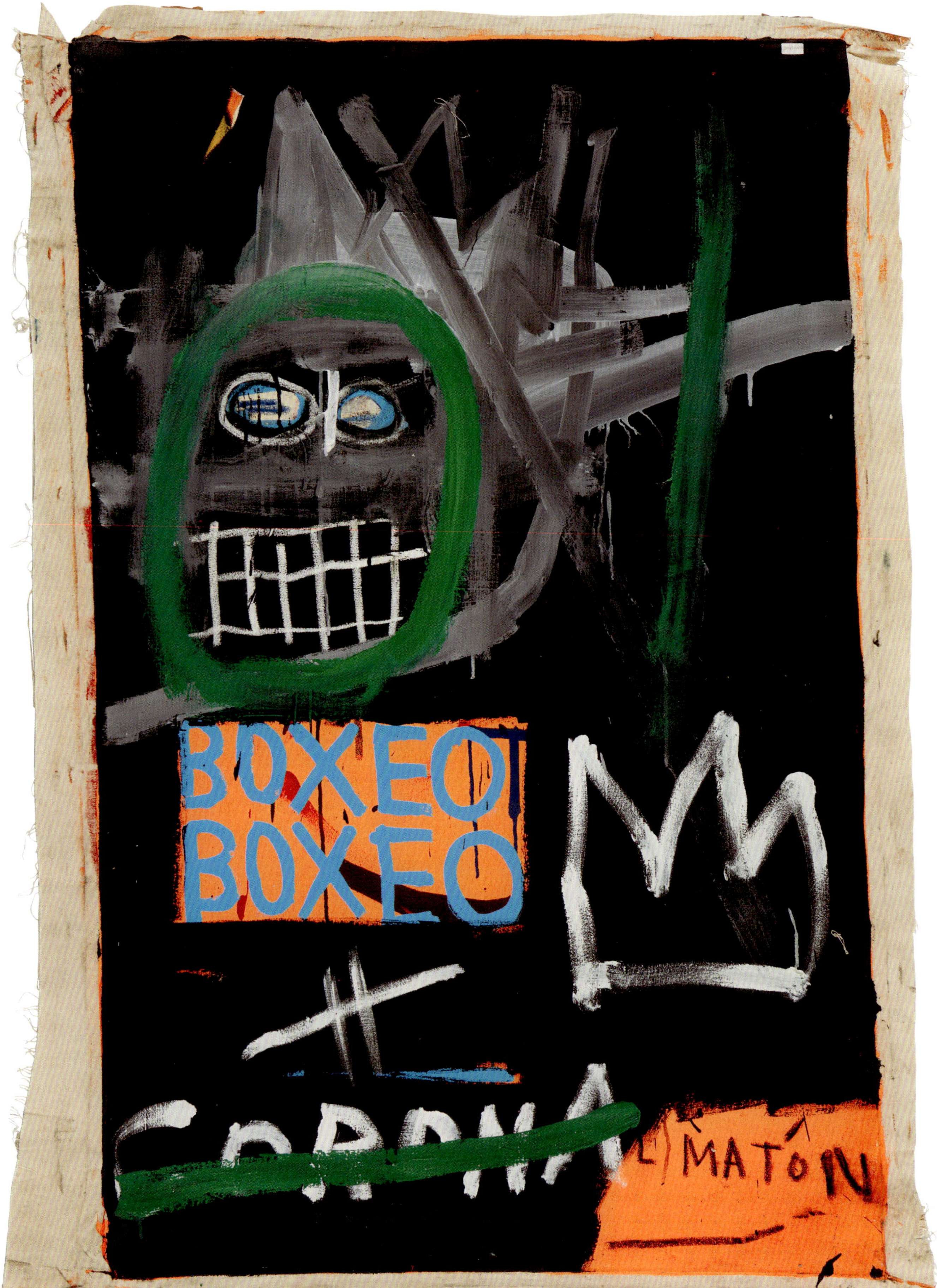
BOXEO
BOXEO
MATÓN

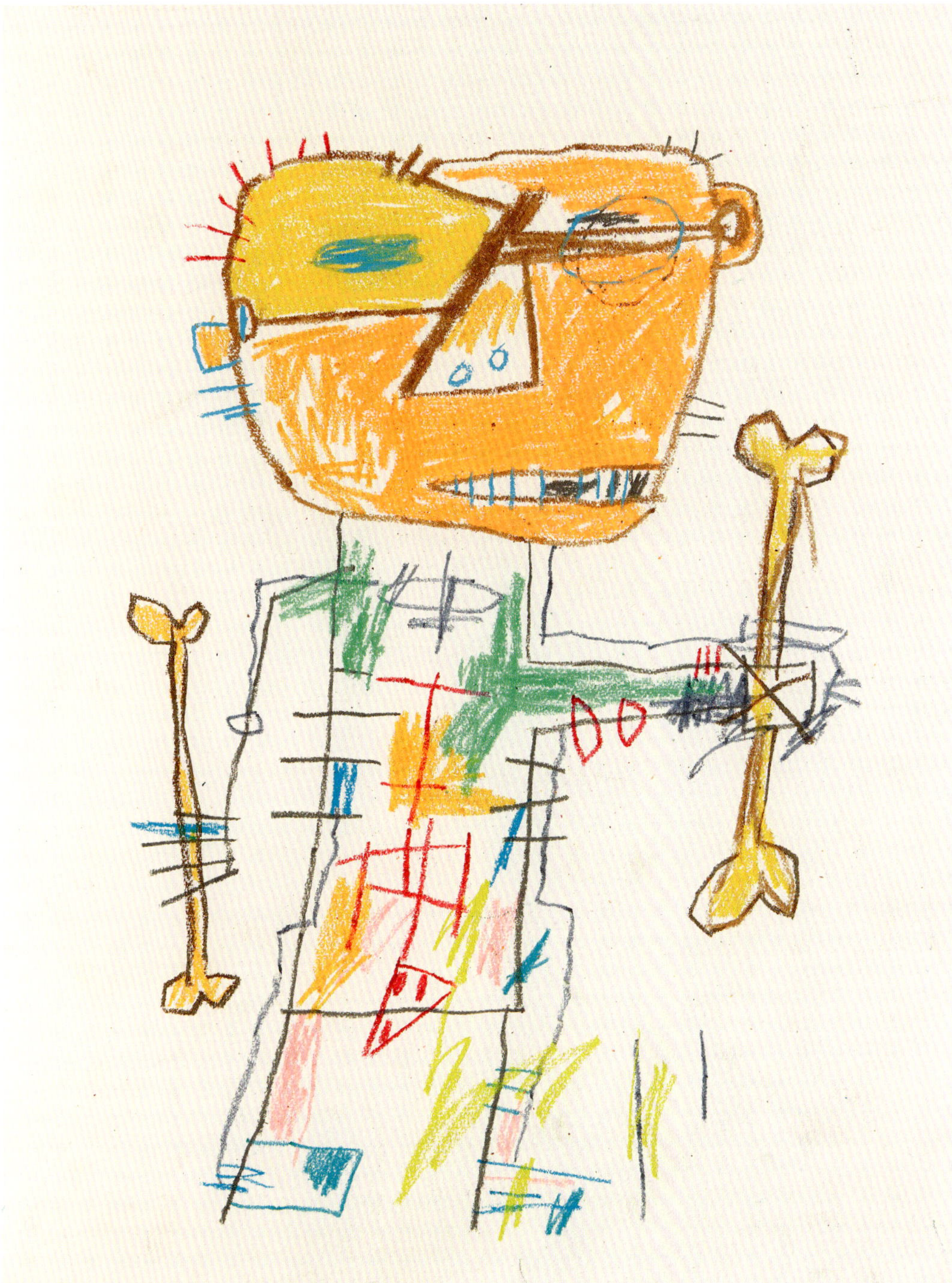

OPPOSITE
Untitled (Boxeo), n.d.
Acrylic and oil stick on paper
59¼ × 40 in. (150.50 × 101.6 cm).
We often watched boxing with our dad on Saturday evenings. "Boxeo" was a program on the Spanish sports channel. JEANINE

He would be so into it. Lots of yelling at the screen. Our father always favored the underdog, unless Muhammad Ali was fighting. He was Ali all the way. LISANE

ABOVE
Untitled, n.d.
Oil stick on paper
24¼ × 18 in. (61.60 × 45.72 cm)

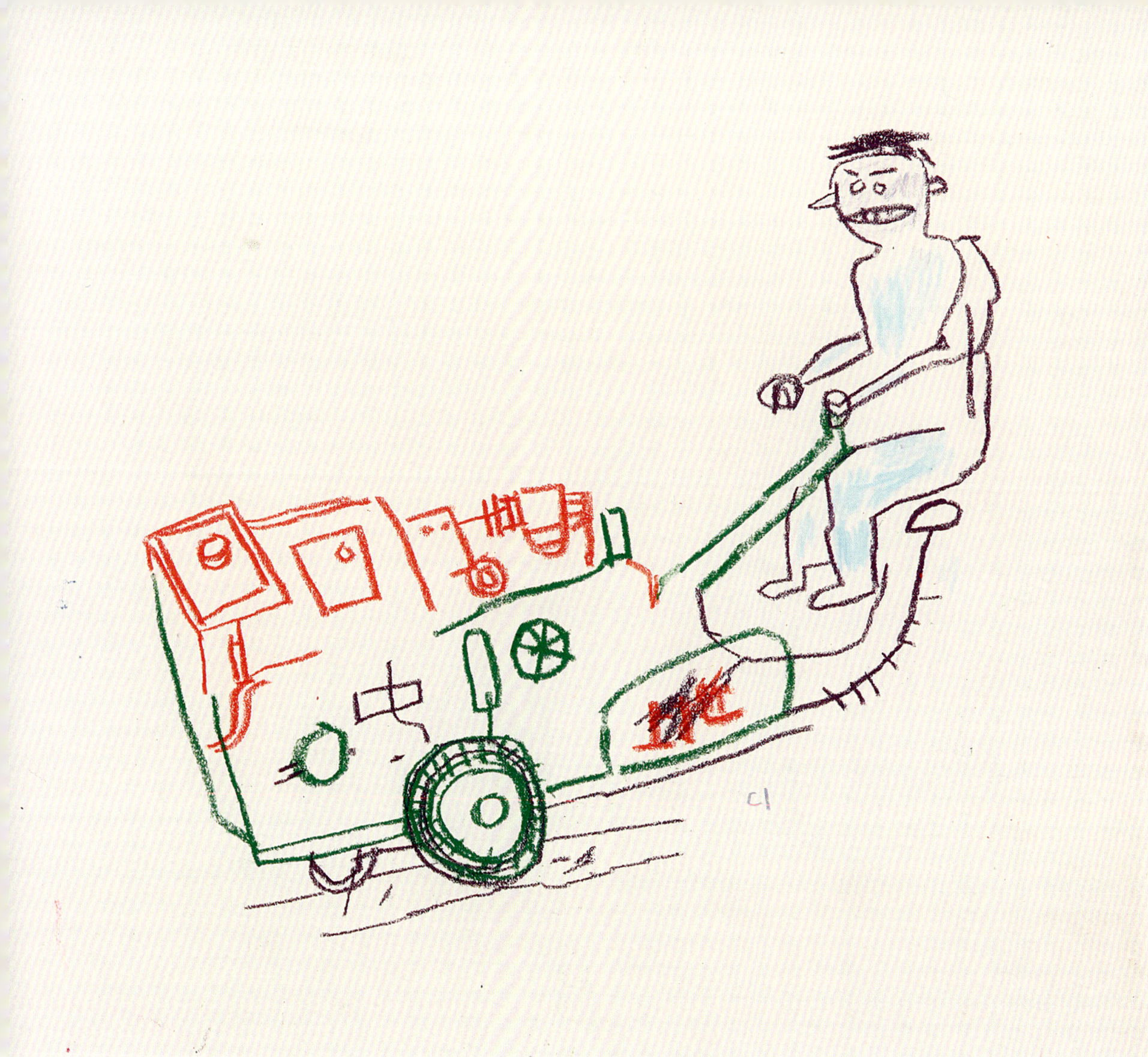

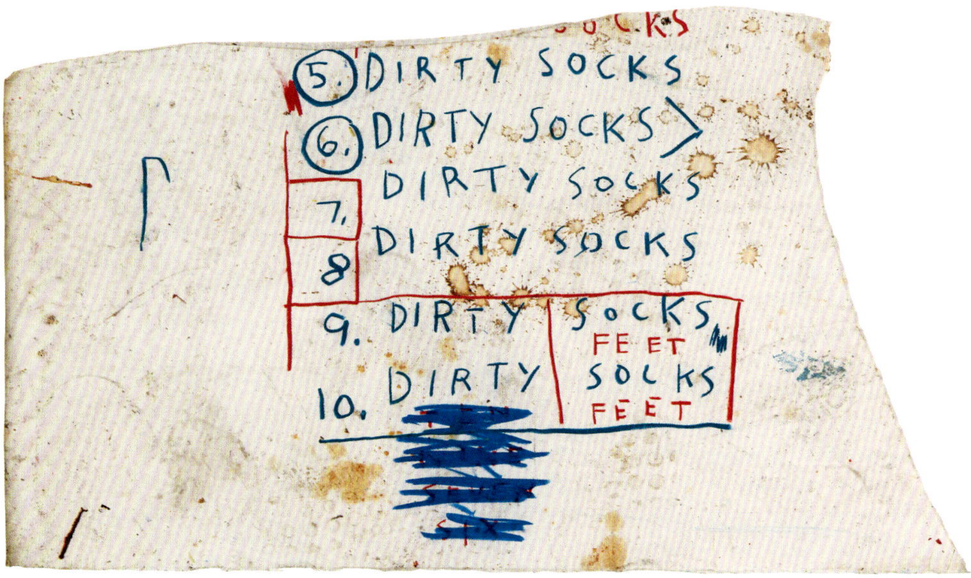

TOP
Untitled, n.d.
Crayon on paper
30 × 22½ in. (76.20 × 57.15 cm).
This drawing is reminiscent of piragua *carts in Puerto Rico and certain Latino sections of New York City.* Piragua *is shaved ice shaped like a cone and covered with fruit-flavored syrup.* JEANINE

RIGHT
Untitled (Dirty Socks), n.d.
Crayon and oil stick on paper
16¼ × 27 in. (41.28 × 68.58 cm)

Untitled, n.d.
Oil stick on paper
24½ × 18 in. (62.23 × 45.72 cm).
Skully is a children's game played on the streets of New York City. The board was sketched using chalk, and the colorful playing pieces were made from bottle caps filled with melted crayons.

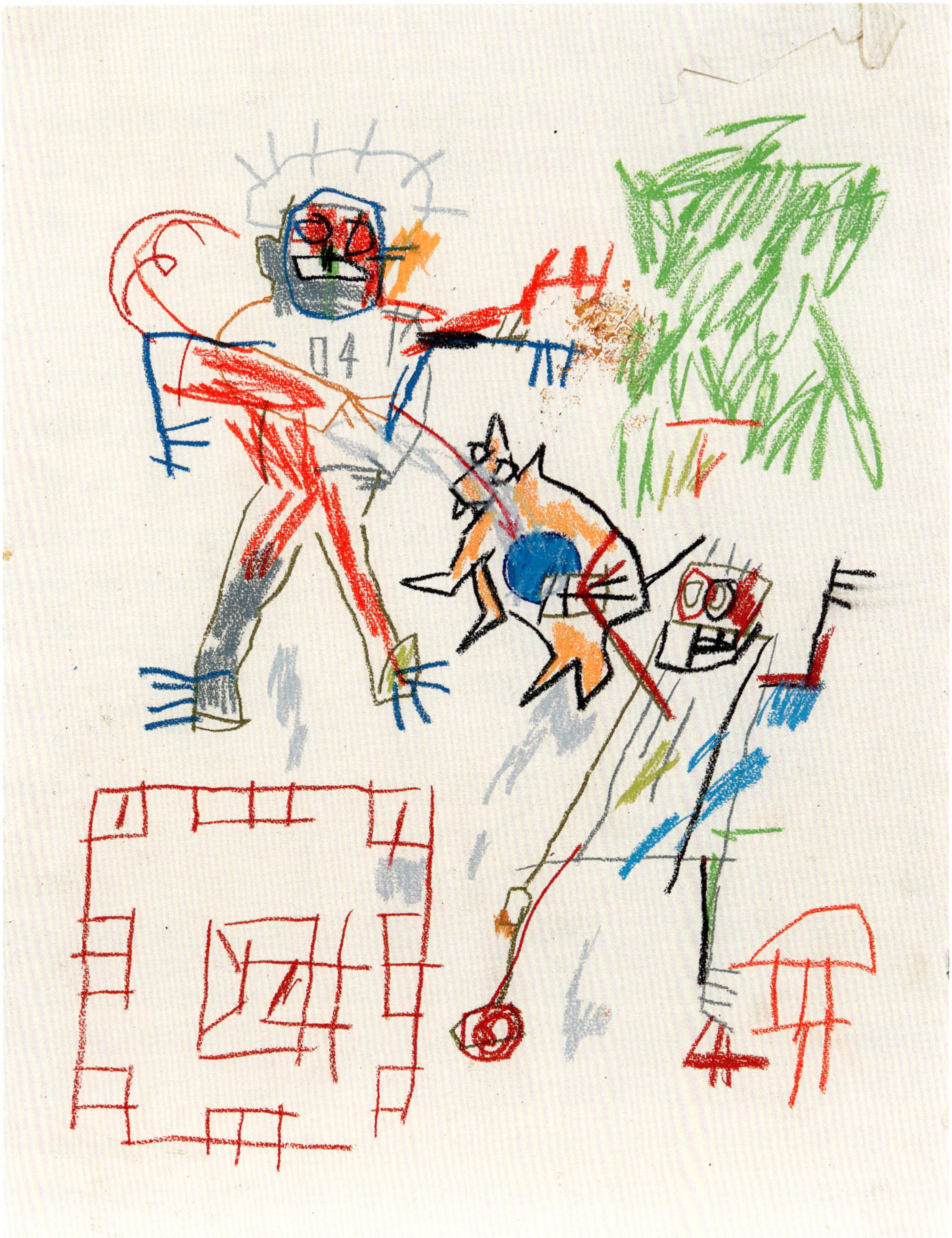

If Jean-Michel were here, I would ask him to share the moment he knew that everything he'd professed about his success and making his mark on the world was, indeed, coming to fruition. From the outside, it seemed that all the obstacles and roadblocks were too tough to surmount, but then, suddenly, it all unfolded for him. The year 1982 was pivotal: solo shows in New York and Los Angeles, as well as being the youngest of 176 artists exhibited at Documenta 7 in Kassel, Germany. And that was just the beginning. It was so excellently done. LISANE

Jean-Michel at Bruno Bischofberger Gallery, Zurich, Switzerland, with Bischofberger in the background, 1982. *Jean-Michel made locks cool long before everyone else.* LISANE

WORLD FAMOUS

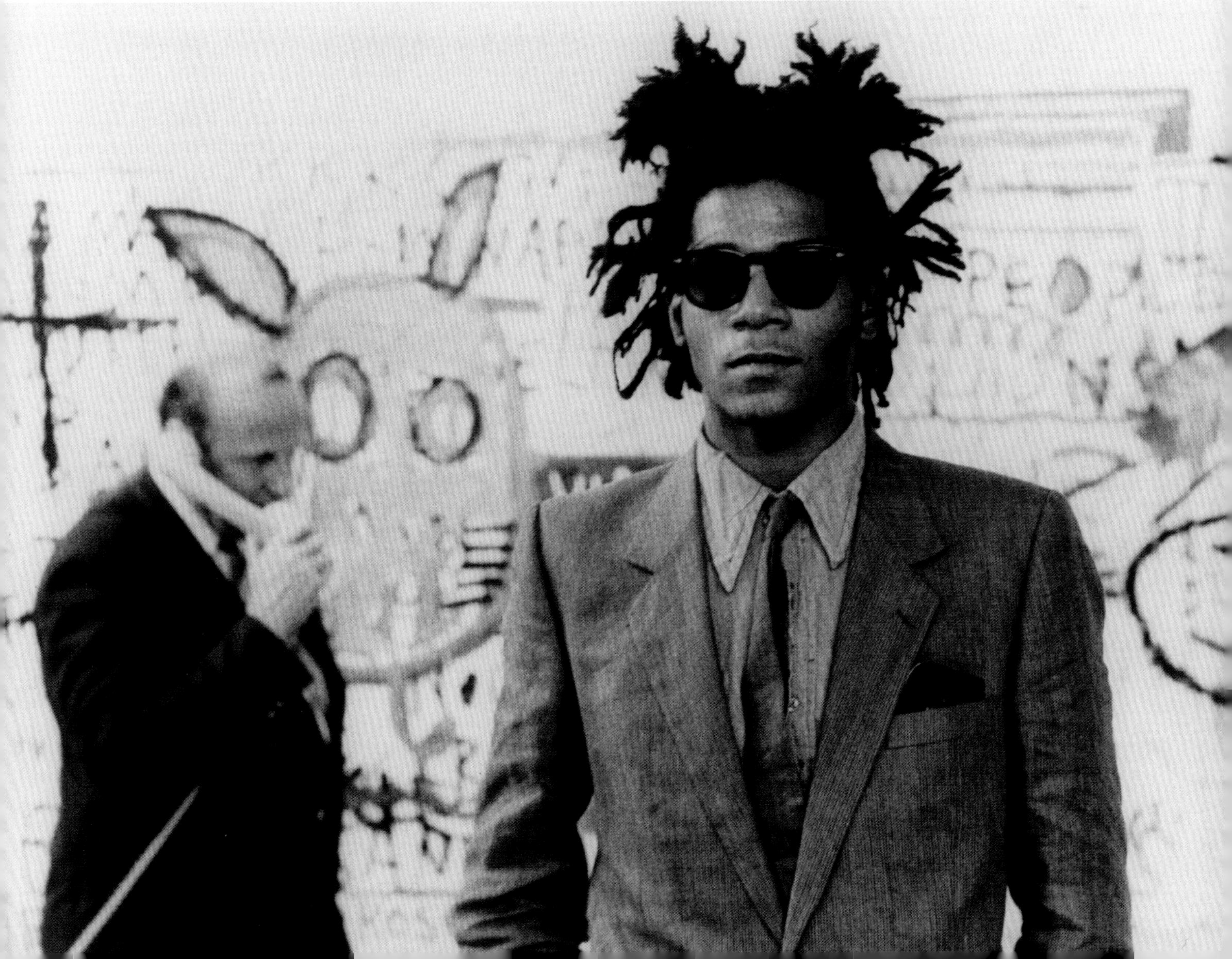

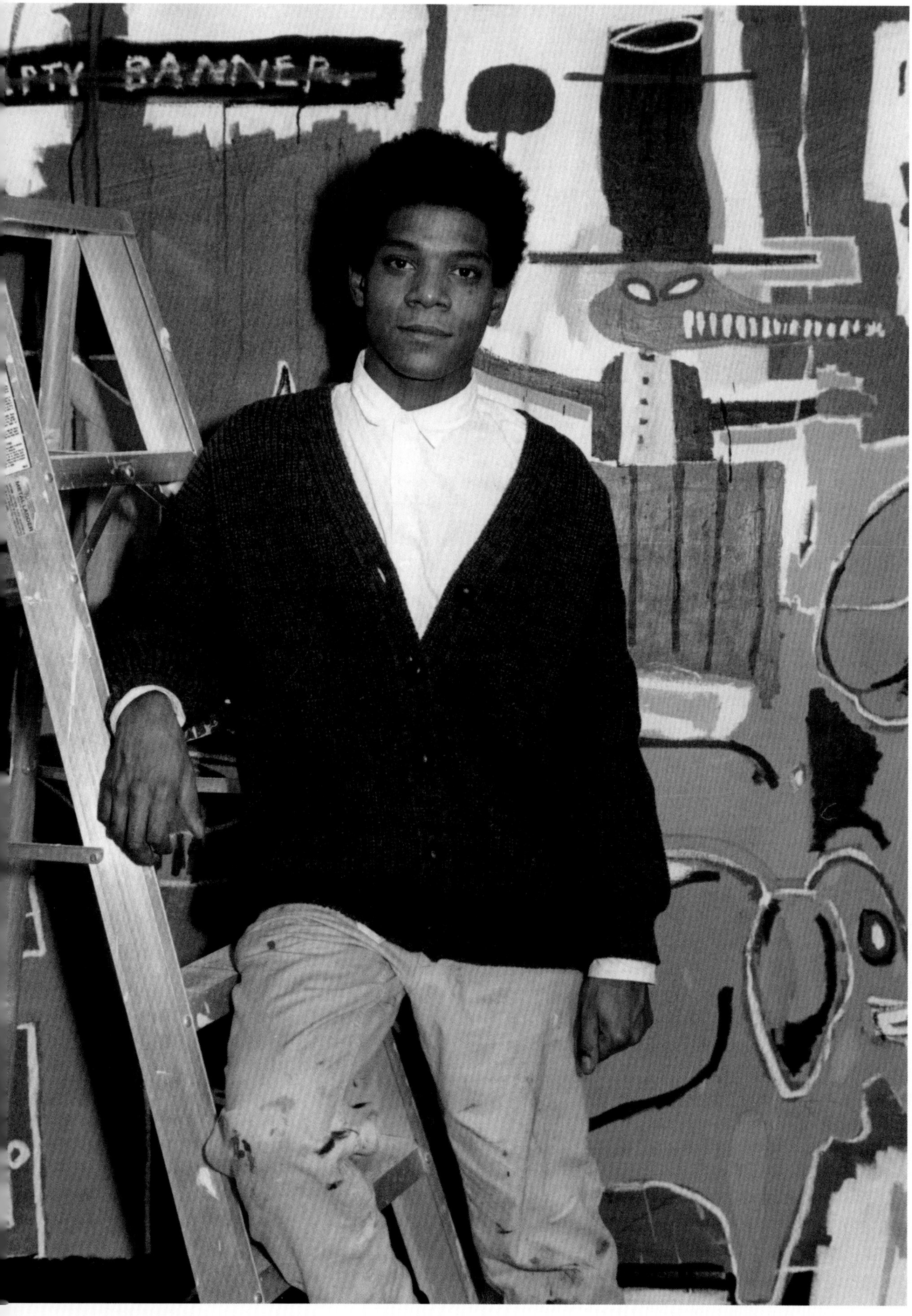

Jean-Michel in BP Photography Studio, New York, 1985 © BETH PHILLIPS

Many Haitians of our father's generation measured success by getting a formal education and pursuing a white-collar profession. Our father saw evidence of that all around him, so he had reasons to believe that his approach to success was *the* way. Going to school, getting a job, having a family, buying a house, etc.—this was the tried and true formula for achieving the American Dream. Yet his son, at least from Papa's perspective, did not appear to value any of that.

They were speaking a completely different language but wanted the very same thing. For Jean-Michel, it was to stand on his own feet and take care of himself: to be respected as a man—a Black man—in this country, to be prosperous, to explore the world, to be relevant, and lead a meaningful life; to work hard and play even harder, to live it up, and enjoy his life. There was no visible evidence that Jean-Michel's master plan to be the greatest painter made any sense at all. Papa saw Jean-Michel's smoking weed, floundering, hanging out, and couch surfing as things that took him away from that path. He simply did not have evidence that Jean-Michel's approach would work. Jean-Michel wanted our dad to believe that he knew what he was doing. Our father was afraid for him and wanted to help. It was terrible for them both, but I believe they were getting to a place of mutual understanding.

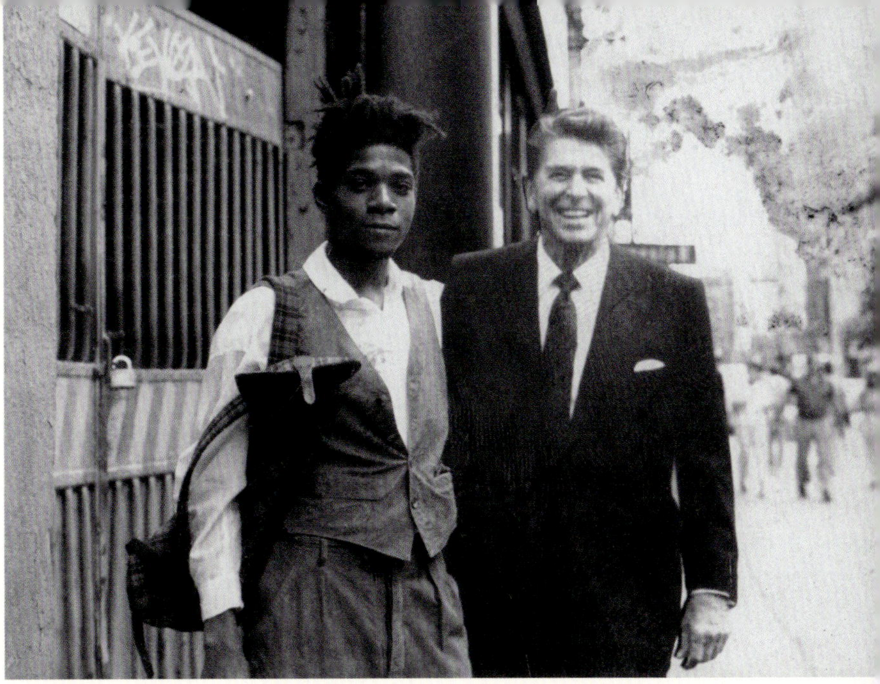

Eventually, of course, my father got to see Jean-Michel realize many of his dreams: he had gallery and museum shows, collectors clamoring for the work, and the critical acclaim that was so important to him.

I remember going to the opening of one of Jean-Michel's shows at the gallery of Annina Nosei, his first art dealer. He'd been working hard and struggling so much before that; it was overwhelming to see him go from painting on anything he could get his hands on because he couldn't afford materials to being celebrated inside the "white cube" of a gallery filled with people who'd come to see what he'd done.

It is one thing to know, intellectually, that your brother has made a mark on contemporary art and culture in the way that Jean-Michel has, but it's quite another to experience how he touched so many people or how far his reach extends beyond the art world. A couple of years after his passing, I made a service call to a utility company, and at one point in the conversation the agent stopped to tell me how much he admired Jean-Michel's work. It still feels very surreal and humbling. Even now I'm still very, very happy for him. LISANE

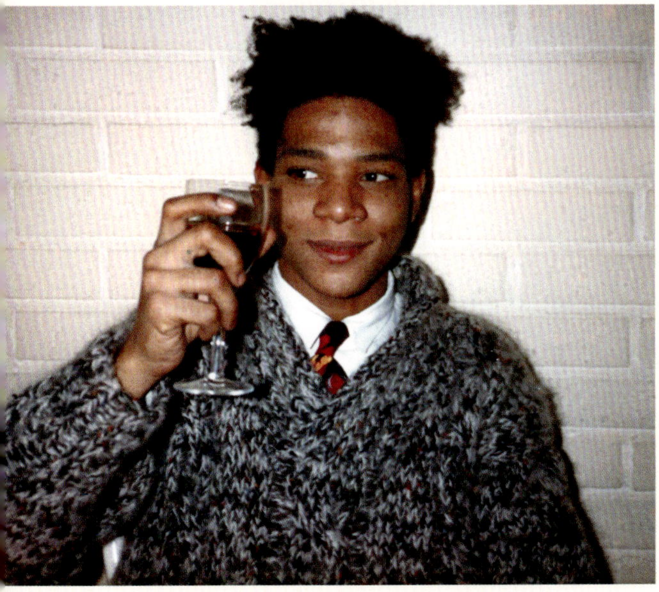

TOP
Jean-Michel with a cutout of Ronald Reagan, New York

LEFT
Jean-Michel at a restaurant in Stockholm, Sweden, 1984
© STELLAN HOLM

BELOW
Untitled, 1984
Acrylic, oil stick, marker, graphite, and Xerox collage on canvas
30 × 24 in. (76.2 × 60.96 cm)

OPPOSITE
Untitled (Self-Portrait), 1984
Acrylic, oil stick, and paper collage on wood
33 × 23 in. (83.82 × 58.42 cm)

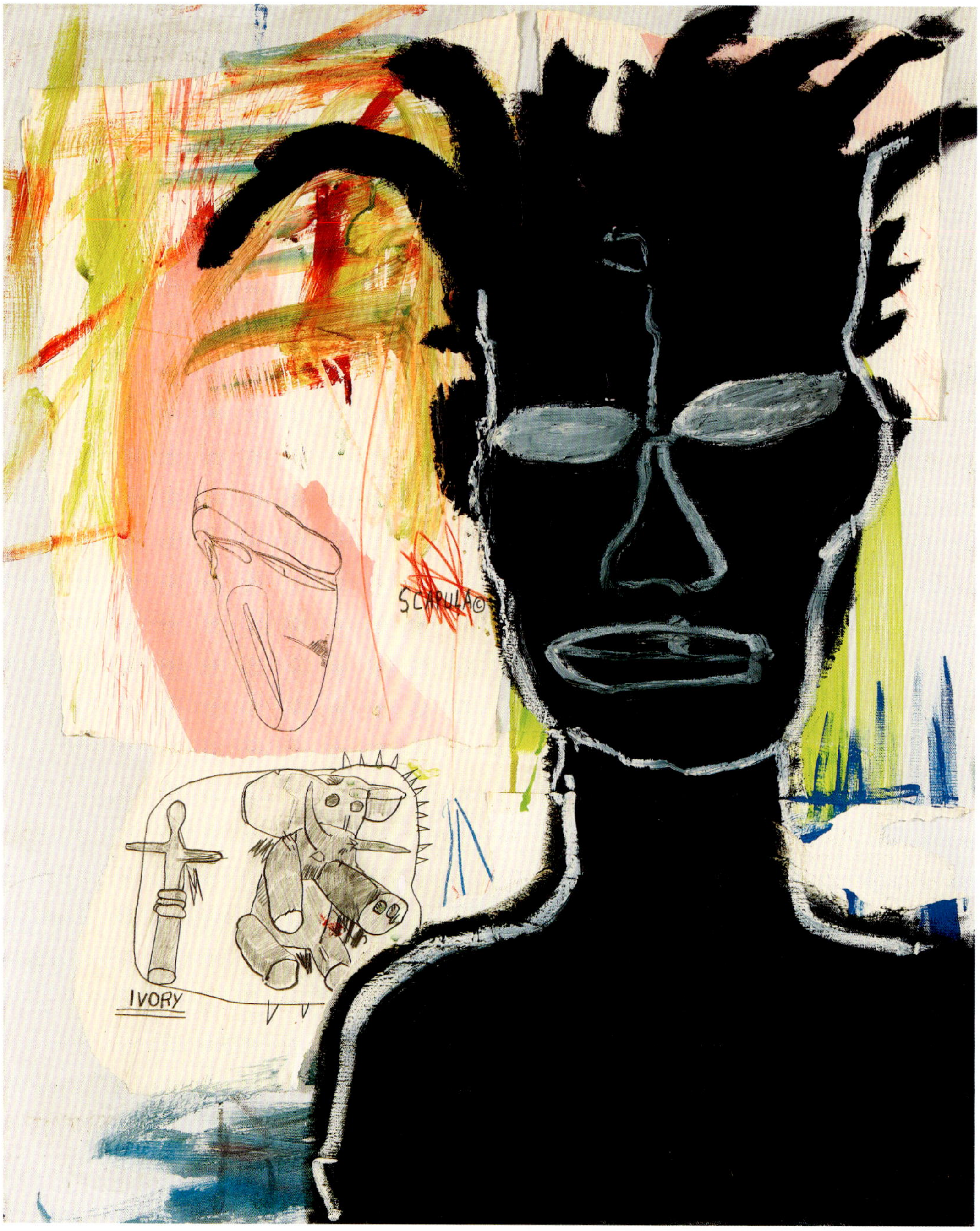

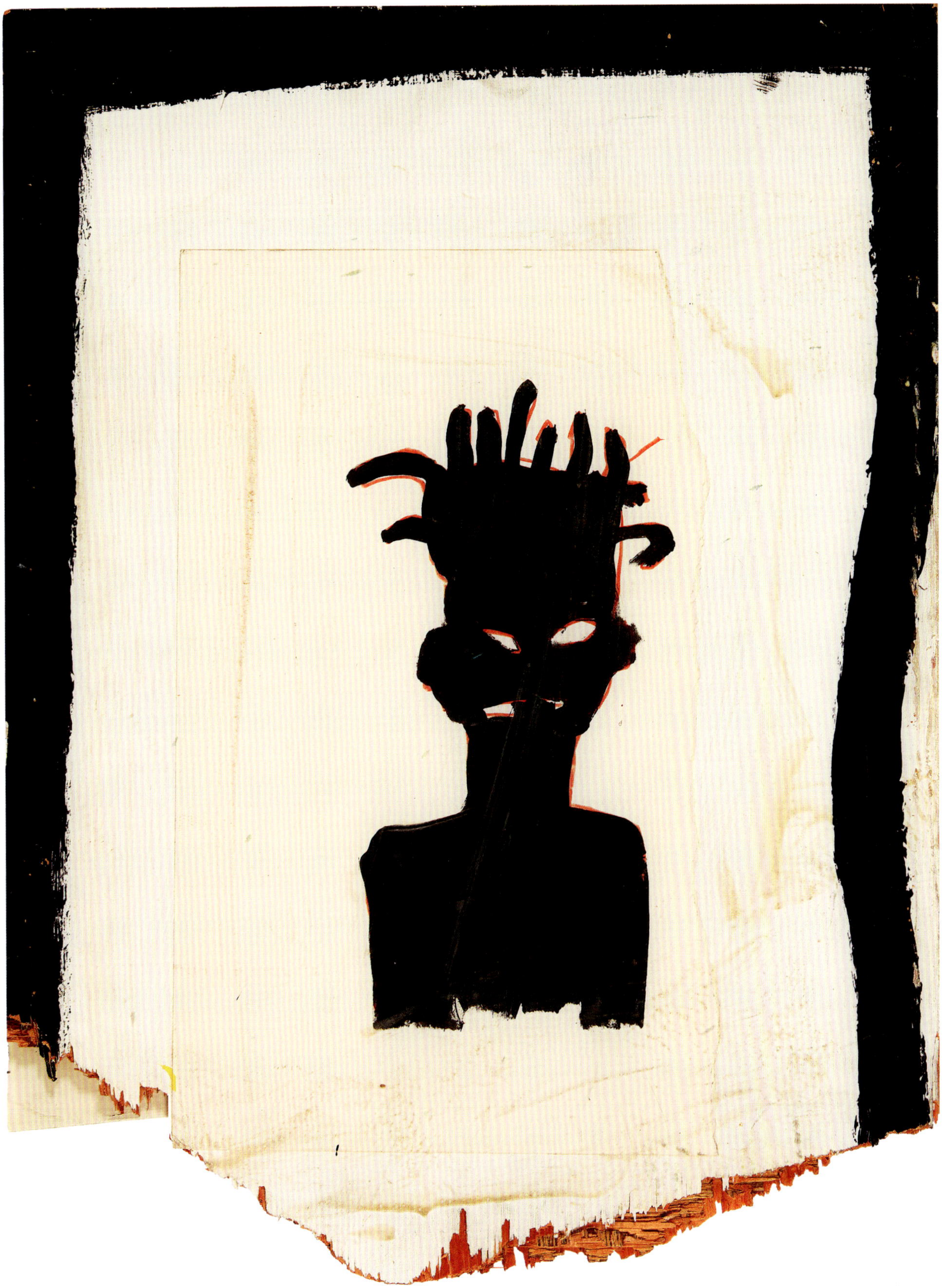

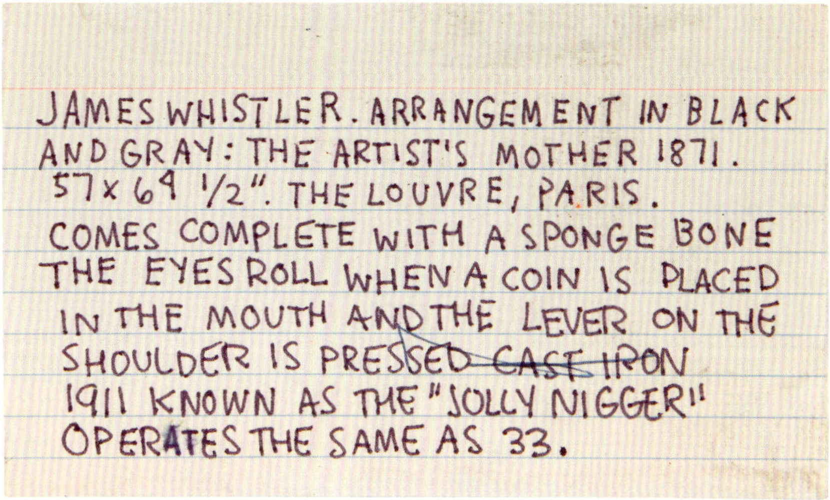

JAMES WHISTLER. ARRANGEMENT IN BLACK AND GRAY: THE ARTIST'S MOTHER 1871. 57 x 64 1/2". THE LOUVRE, PARIS.
COMES COMPLETE WITH A SPONGE BONE THE EYES ROLL WHEN A COIN IS PLACED IN THE MOUTH AND THE LEVER ON THE SHOULDER IS PRESSED ~~CAST IRON~~ 1911 KNOWN AS THE "JOLLY NIGGER" OPERATES THE SAME AS 33.

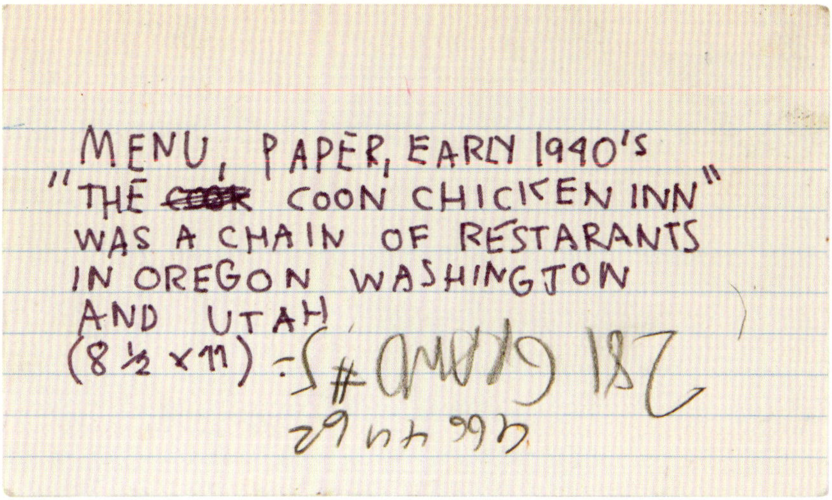

MENU, PAPER, EARLY 1940'S
"THE ~~COOR~~ COON CHICKEN INN"
WAS A CHAIN OF RESTARANTS IN OREGON WASHINGTON AND UTAH
(8 ½ x 11)

281 GRAND #5

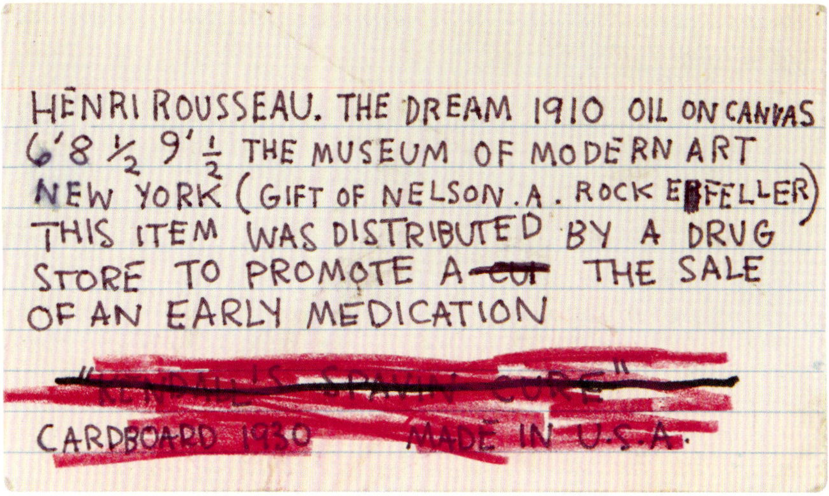

HENRI ROUSSEAU. THE DREAM 1910 OIL ON CANVAS 6'8 ½ 9' ½ THE MUSEUM OF MODERN ART NEW YORK (GIFT OF NELSON. A. ROCKEFELLER)
THIS ITEM WAS DISTRIBUTED BY A DRUG STORE TO PROMOTE A ~~CUT~~ THE SALE OF AN EARLY MEDICATION
~~"KENDALL'S SPAVIN CURE"~~
~~CARDBOARD 1930 MADE IN U.S.A.~~

Index cards found in Jean-Michel's studio, n.d.

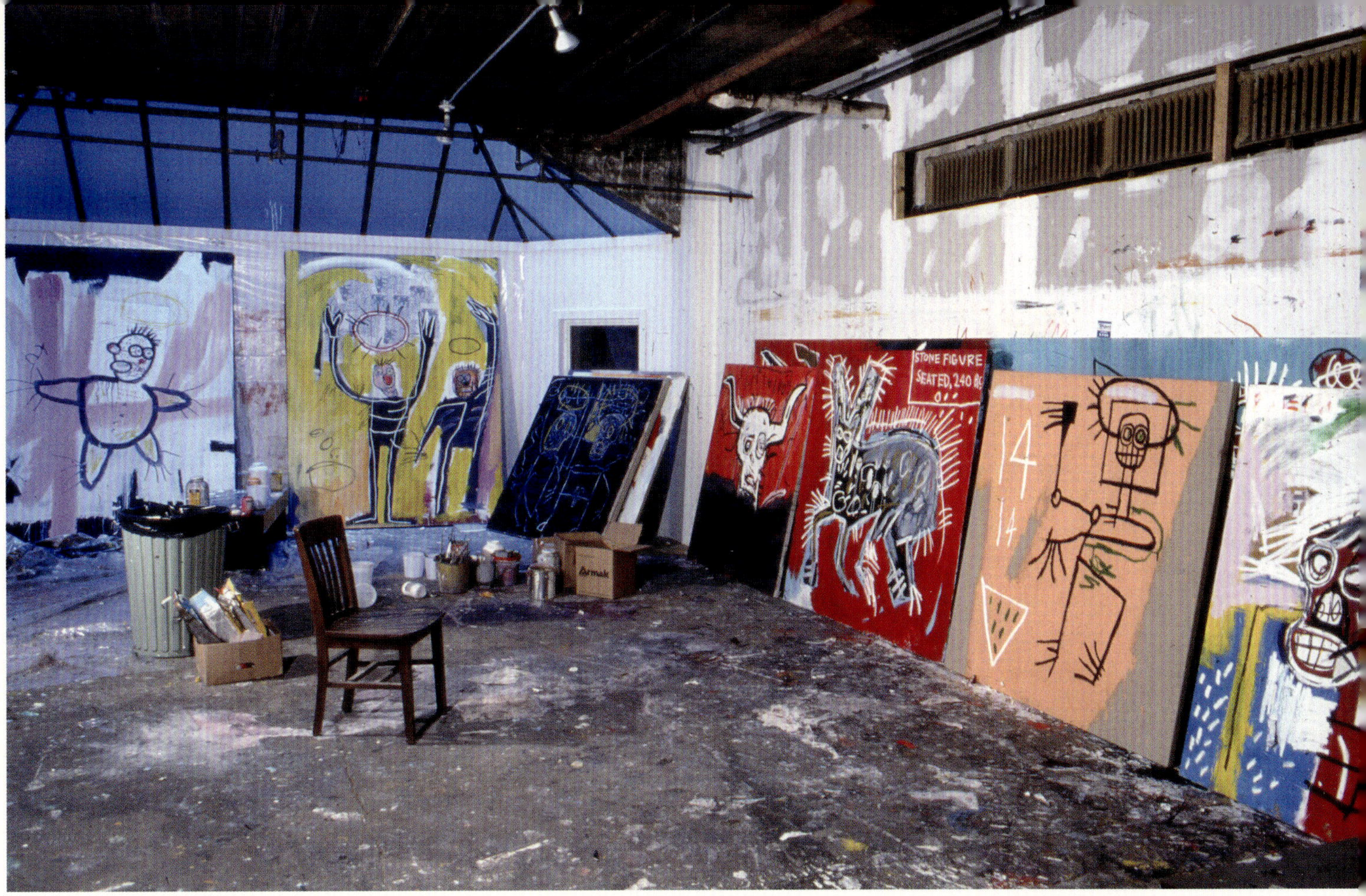

Jean-Michel's studio adjacent to Annina Nosei Gallery, 100 Prince Street, New York, 1982

MEETING JEAN-MICHEL

Annina Nosei, art dealer

In 1980, I opened my gallery in New York at 100 Prince Street. Prior to coming to New York, I lived in Italy, and then France, and eventually made my way to the US to teach at the University of Michigan and the University of California, Los Angeles.

I knew Larry Gagosian, and we worked together on various projects. He was not the famous dealer that he is now; he was just doing small projects. We decided to rent a loft together at 421 West Broadway. He was in California, and I was working out of the apartment, but we made a lot of sales. Both of us procured work to sell—I would find a Jasper Johns and Larry would sell it, or he would find a Cy Twombly and I would sell it.

In 1981, Diego Cortez organized an important show at P.S. 1 in Queens titled *New York / New Wave*. There were about one hundred artists, and I saw two that I liked. One was Roberto Juarez and the other was Jean-Michel Basquiat. I called Diego and asked for Jean-Michel's phone number but he wouldn't give it to me. So, I looked him up in the telephone book and I called his family's number in Brooklyn, but he wasn't there. Somehow he heard that I had called him because he rang me at the gallery, but I missed him. But eventually we met: I didn't go to many openings, but at one of the few that I did attend, a young man, very young, came over and said, "I am Jean-Michel Basquiat. I wanted to meet you."

He asked me come to the East Village and meet him at his friend Suzanne Mallouk's house. It was a small apartment and full of drawings. Fabulous! We left and went to a nearby coffee shop. We talked about everything, particularly how much I liked the work. And he asked, "If you like the work so much, why don't you show me in your gallery?" I told him my program was full. He then asked to put his work in a group show, and I told him the group shows were also full. He asked about my next show, and I told him it was called *Public Address*, but I told him his work didn't fit with that group of artists. "All of your drawings, they are referring to yourself, they are autobiographical somehow." And Jean-Michel replied, "No, you're wrong. I am making work that is addressing the public." He convinced me—he clearly understood everything. He was wise and intelligent well beyond his years.

He asked where he could work, and I offered him a studio space that was connected to the gallery—it had a skylight and two windows. I told him that someone who worked for me could go with him to buy the materials he wanted, such as canvases. He then asked, "What kind of materials should I get?"

When I went to the P.S. 1 show, I liked Roberto Juarez's work because the paintings reminded me of Wifredo Lam—they were reminiscent of Tropicália. At that time, I was particularly interested in the Caribbean, in the music and the culture. When I looked at Jean-Michel's paintings, I saw that they were completely different from anybody else's. They were really new and unique. There were elements of the work that made me think of some of the signs and symbols of Haitian Vodou. It turned out he was Haitian, which I didn't know when I first saw the work. His work also reminded me of concrete poetry, and the poetry one would find written on the streets in France—graffiti. Jean-Michel had actually done graffiti himself, which I was also unaware of when I first met him. The words he used in his paintings were very meaningful.

I was so excited about the works, and people bought them. I wasn't thinking about the future though, unfortunately, because I should have kept some of them. But I was so happy to be selling them. I told Larry Gagosian to do a show in Los Angeles, which he did. And that's when he opened his own gallery. ANNINA NOSEI

JEAN-MICHEL'S PERSONALITY

At the University of Rome, I studied the work of Marcel Duchamp with a very famous professor, and let me tell you something about Jean-Michel: He knew everything about art history. One of the first presents that Jean-Michel gave me for my birthday was a little booklet on Duchamp.

He was not always a happy person. Matilde, his mother, was sick and this was difficult for him. But he tried! He liked music very much. He thought about other people a lot and was very generous.

When Andy Warhol died, I went to visit Jean-Michel at his studio on Great Jones Street, and he was very sad. He said—nearly crying—"Annina, how am I going to talk with anybody? There is nobody that I really like that I can talk to." ANNINA NOSEI

THE ESTATE

I was part of the authentication committee for Jean-Michel's work that was founded by Gerard Basquiat in 1994. It was very interesting and important work. It was nice to meet all together in the estate's office with Gerard, Nora Fitzpatrick, and Fred Hoffman, the curator and dealer, and on occasion other people joined us as well. Eventually the committee was dissolved—our work was done. ANNINA NOSEI

OPPOSITE
Jean-Michel in Stockholm, Sweden, 1984.
According to gallerist Stellan Holm, Jean-Michel was in Stockholm for just one week to prepare for an exhibition. The artist Knut Swane, a friend of Holm's, let Basquiat borrow his studio for one night where Jean-Michel was able to produce eighteen paintings. Holm assisted him during the evening and took a few photos while Jean-Michel was working.

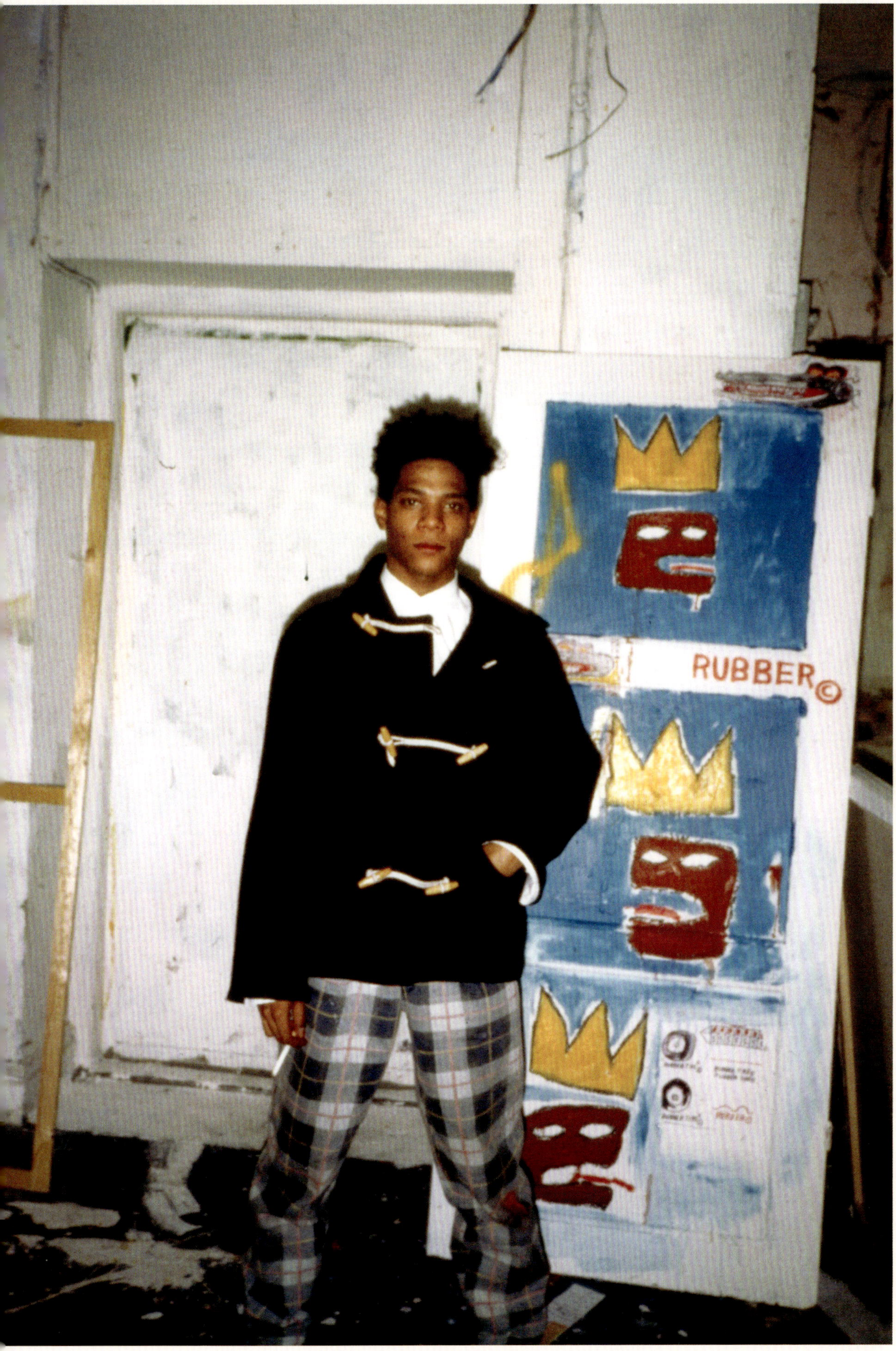
RUBBER©

ON FAME

Jean-Michel always wanted to be famous for his art. He wanted to be recognized along with all the "greats" that he read about and admired. His childhood museum trips certainly had an influence on his work.

Painting seemed to be something that Jean-Michel needed in his life—he needed it in the way others need air to breathe. His work was an open diary to the world; it was how he communicated his thoughts, fears, and anger. The body of work that he left on this earth shows how much he needed to express. It's beautiful in a way. The fact that he was able to earn a good living as an artist while he was alive is incredible. Ultimately, I am happy he was able to accomplish what he wanted. I respect the drive, commitment, and unwavering determination—by any means necessary. Not many are willing to do that.

Fame is a funny thing. I think everyone wants a degree of fame. We all want to be recognized and acknowledged for our achievements. But often fame comes with negative feedback, which can be debilitating for some. For Jean-Michel, the criticism of his work was difficult to hear, and not being exhibited in some art institutions hurt him. I admire those who can let things roll off their backs, but it's difficult for most. We are all human, after all.

In the 1980s, Jean-Michel was recognized mostly by the art world. Prior to becoming more well-known and mainstream, journalists and critics didn't really get him or even want to try to understand him. There were many contentious interviews in which they questioned his intellect, challenged his creative process, and belittled his work. Jean-Michel just wanted to be seen.

I never discussed celebrity with Jean-Michel—it wasn't something that ever really came up in conversation. He always showed up as just my brother. For me, he was the older brother that I laughed and hung out with, so I see him through a completely different lens. It's both surreal and humbling to hear his fans speak of him in a manner that is so different from my perspective. But I am incredibly proud to hear others talk about how he has inspired them.

If he were alive today, my guess is that he would have ventured into other creative outlets and would be mentoring aspiring young artists. JEANINE

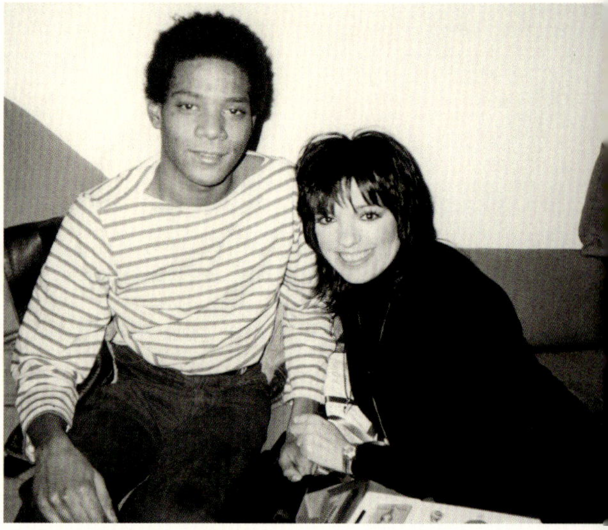

Jean-Michel with Liza Minnelli at a Christmas party, New York, ca. 1983

Jean-Michel's success was a double-edged sword. He felt quite a bit of pressure. He was so ahead of his time, and he was also very young. There was money involved, and so much recognition—things many people aspire to. He had surpassed many of the folks that he started the journey with, in terms of his success. They were still friends, but his life and what he was dealing with was different from their reality. In spite of that success, though, he was still seen as "the other" by the art world establishment; he didn't fit in anywhere, really. Being put into a position of having to constantly correct how people saw him deeply annoyed Jean-Michel. He wanted to be seen as an artist, first and foremost, and to have *that* conversation. It frustrated him to defend himself against people's prejudices, stereotypes, and assumptions.

Jean-Michel was on a journey to figure out where he belonged and what he was going to do with his particular set of circumstances, while continuing to grow and develop his work. I would have loved to see what else he would have done with all of this. I would have loved to sit down with him and talk about life. LISANE

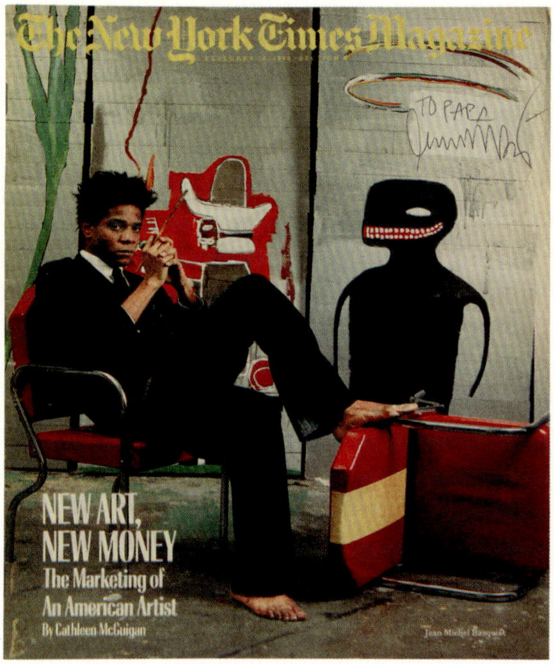

New York Times Magazine,
February 10, 1985
Inscribed by Jean-Michel:
"To Papa"

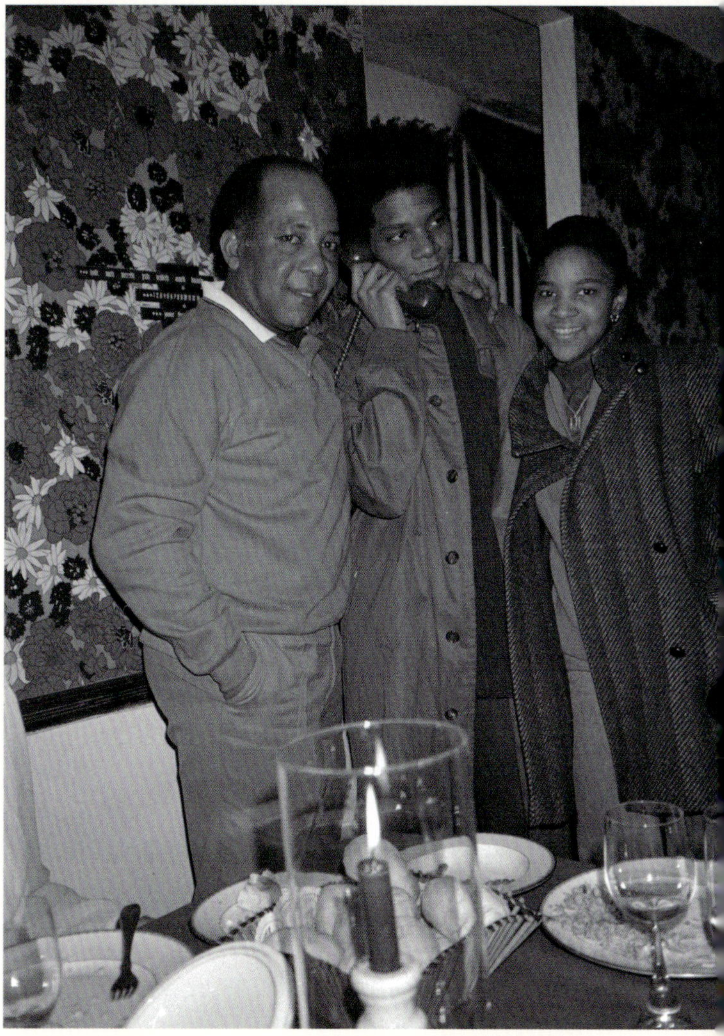

Gerard, Jean-Michel, and Jeanine, Boerum Hill, Brooklyn, ca. 1985.
When he was on the cover of the Sunday New York Times Magazine, *Jean-Michel brought Andy Warhol to our house to meet us, have dinner, and celebrate.* JEANINE

This was taken the night Andy Warhol came to visit our family home in Brooklyn. I was so annoyed I wasn't home for this! LISANE

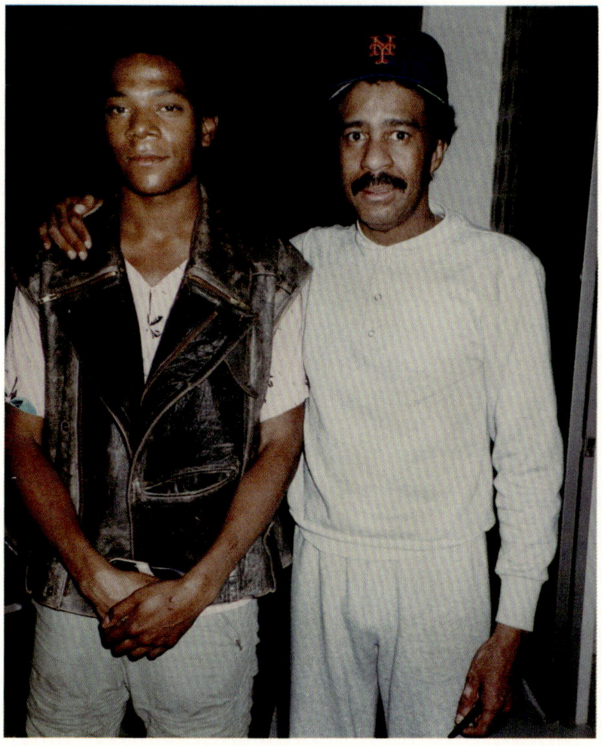

Jean-Michel and Richard Pryor, Los Angeles, California, ca. 1982
PHOTO: MARGARET GOLDSMITH, COURTESY OF FRED HOFFMAN FINE ART

I remember hearing that Jean-Michel and Madonna were dating. It was very matter-of-fact. After that, I would party extra hard to "Everybody," LOL. LISANE

It was Thanksgiving in the early 1980s. Jean-Michel was on the phone with Gerard, inviting us for dinner. Several calls later he found a restaurant and made a reservation at One Fifth Avenue. Gerard, Jeanine, and I went to the restaurant, and Jean-Michel was already there with Madonna and some friends. (We didn't know who Madonna was at the time.) He knew that I liked vodka gimlets, so everybody was drinking vodka gimlets. He was so very thoughtful and charming. We had a lovely dinner, after which there was the usual fight between Jean-Michel and Gerard about who would pay the bill. After dinner we went to his apartment on Crosby Street to hang out. It was a lovely occasion that I will always remember. NORA

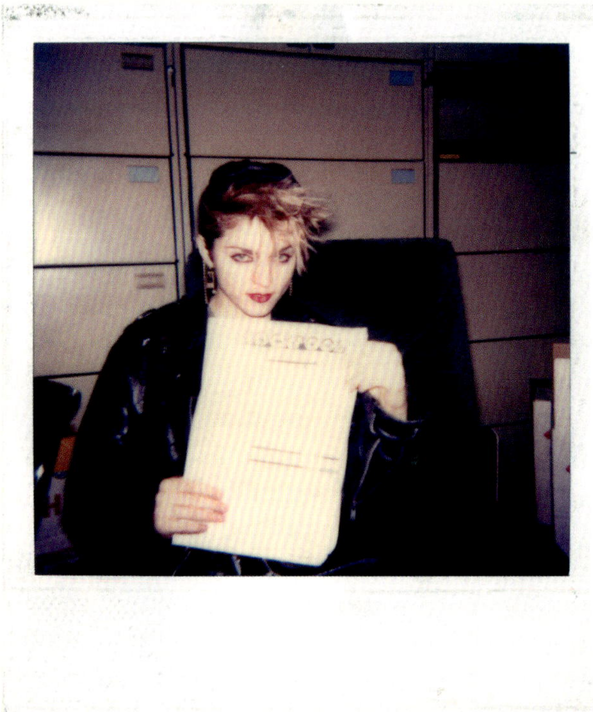

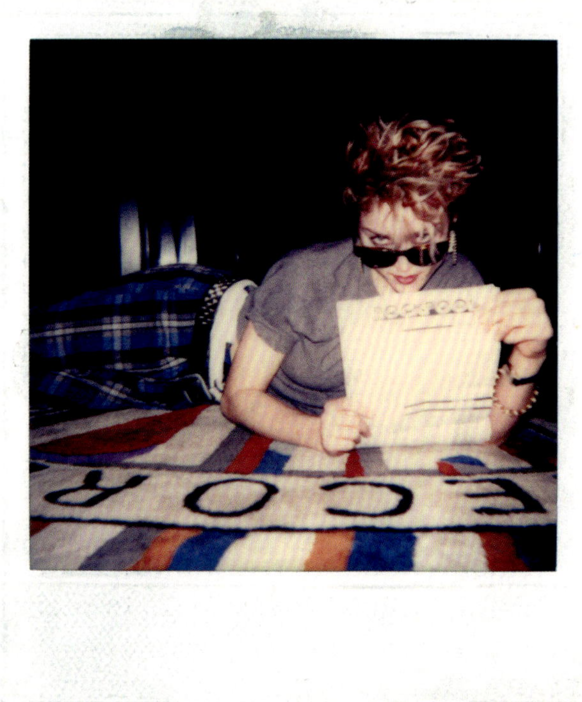

I remember the night that we (Papa, Nora, and I) met Madonna. It was the only time I saw her. We went to dinner at the restaurant One Fifth Avenue. Jean-Michel introduced his girlfriend: "This is Madonna. And she has a song out right now." I had no idea who she was at the time, but he showed us her first single "Everybody." After dinner we went to his loft on Crosby Street. While we were there, Madonna asked if I knew how to do a popular dance at the time, because I was a teenager. I did—I showed her how to do "the Webo." JEANINE

Madonna, ca. 1982

RIGHT
Jean-Michel and the artist Dominque Philbert, aka ERO

BOTTOM
Jean-Michel outside Akira Ikeda Gallery, Tokyo, Japan, November 9, 1985.
Jean-Michel traveled to Japan with then-girlfriend Jennifer Goode on the occasion of his one-person show at Akira Ikeda Gallery.

PHOTO: YOSHITAKA UCHIDA, © IKEDA GALLERY, JAPAN

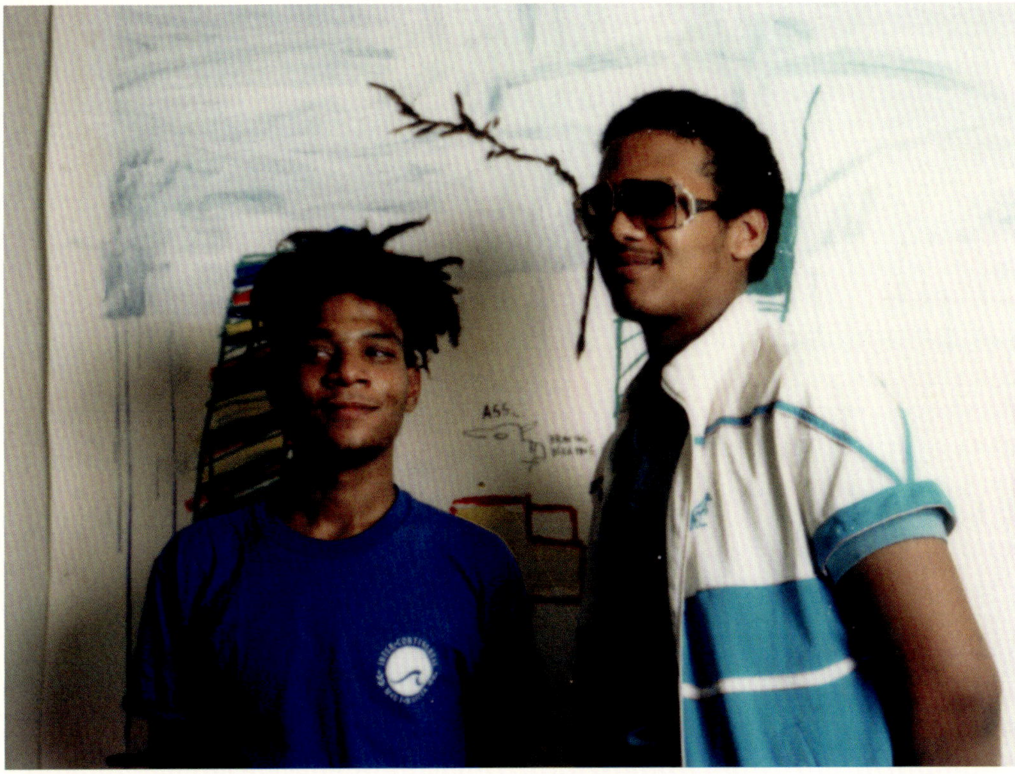

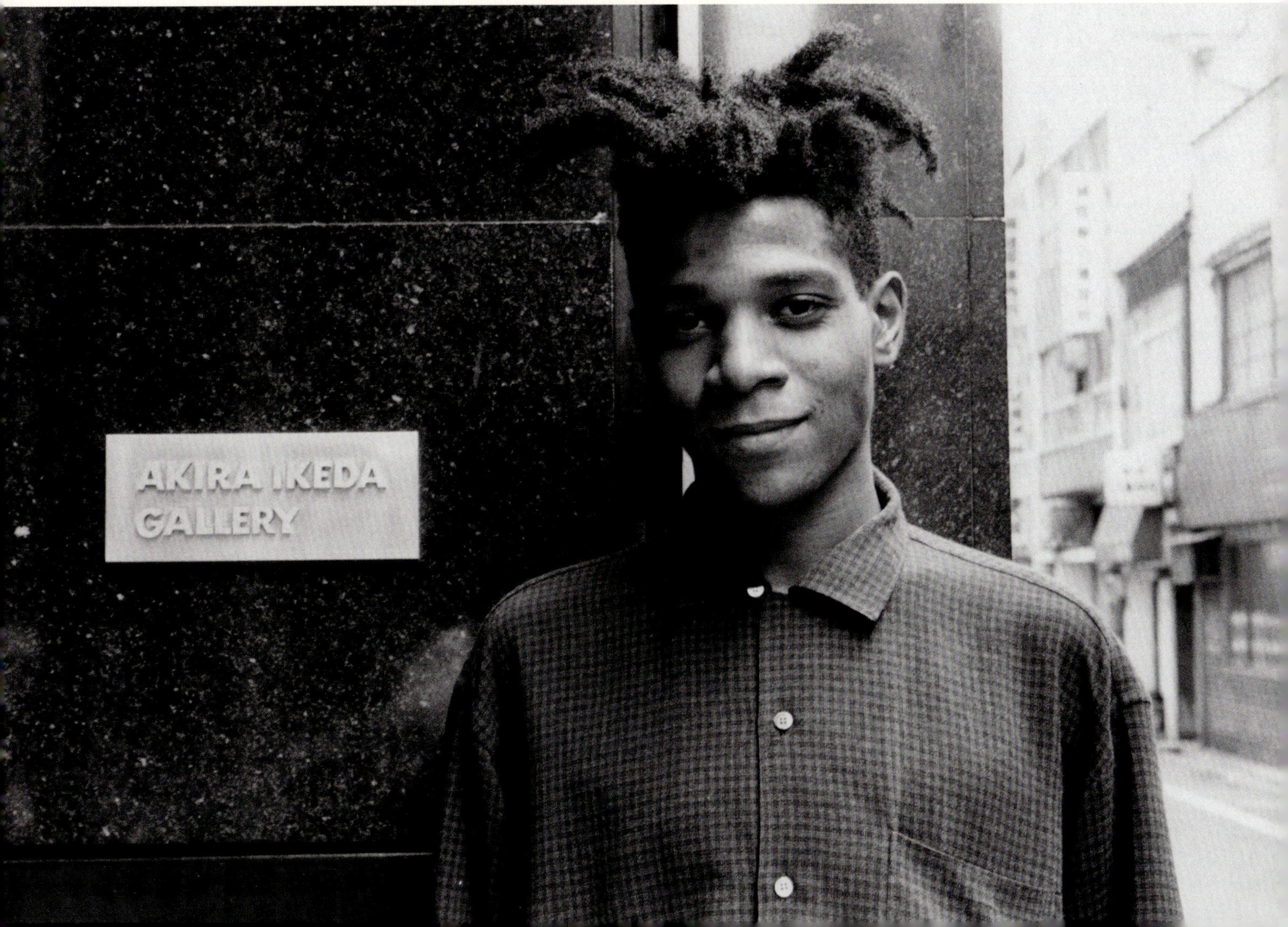

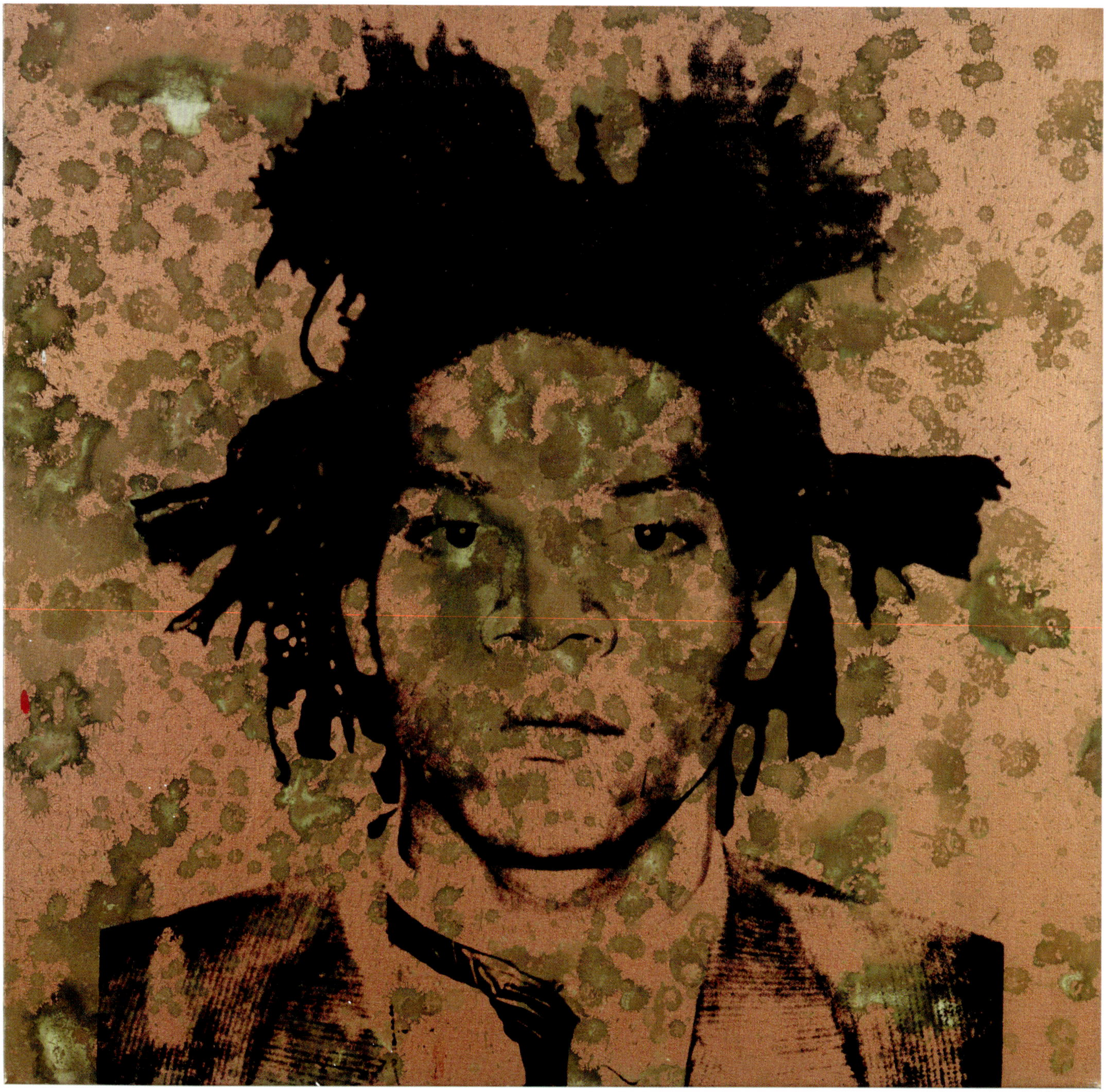

Andy Warhol
Jean-Michel Basquiat, 1982
Oxidized silkscreen on canvas
40 × 40 in. (101.6 × 101.6 cm)

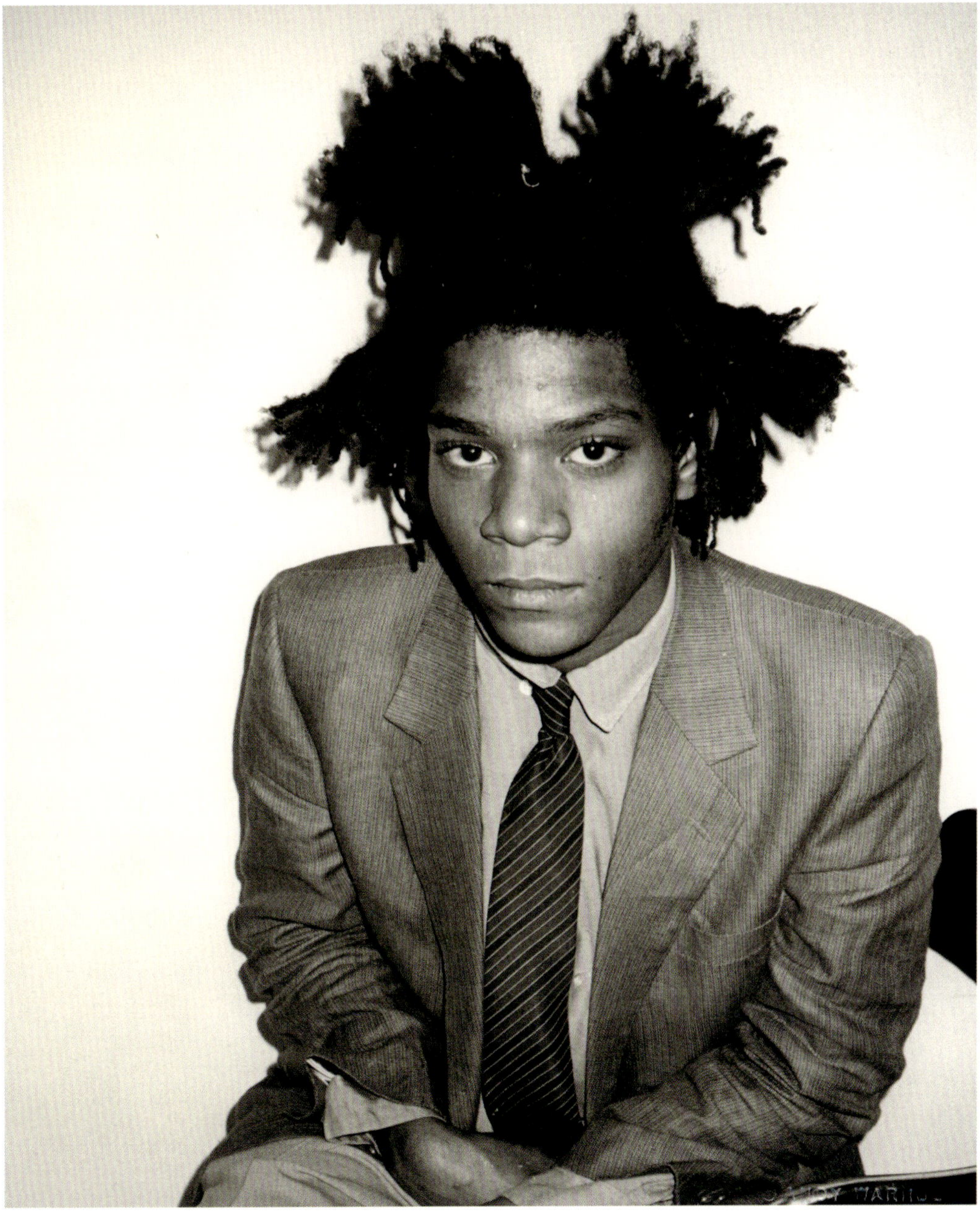

Photograph of Jean-Michel for a painting by Andy Warhol, 1982

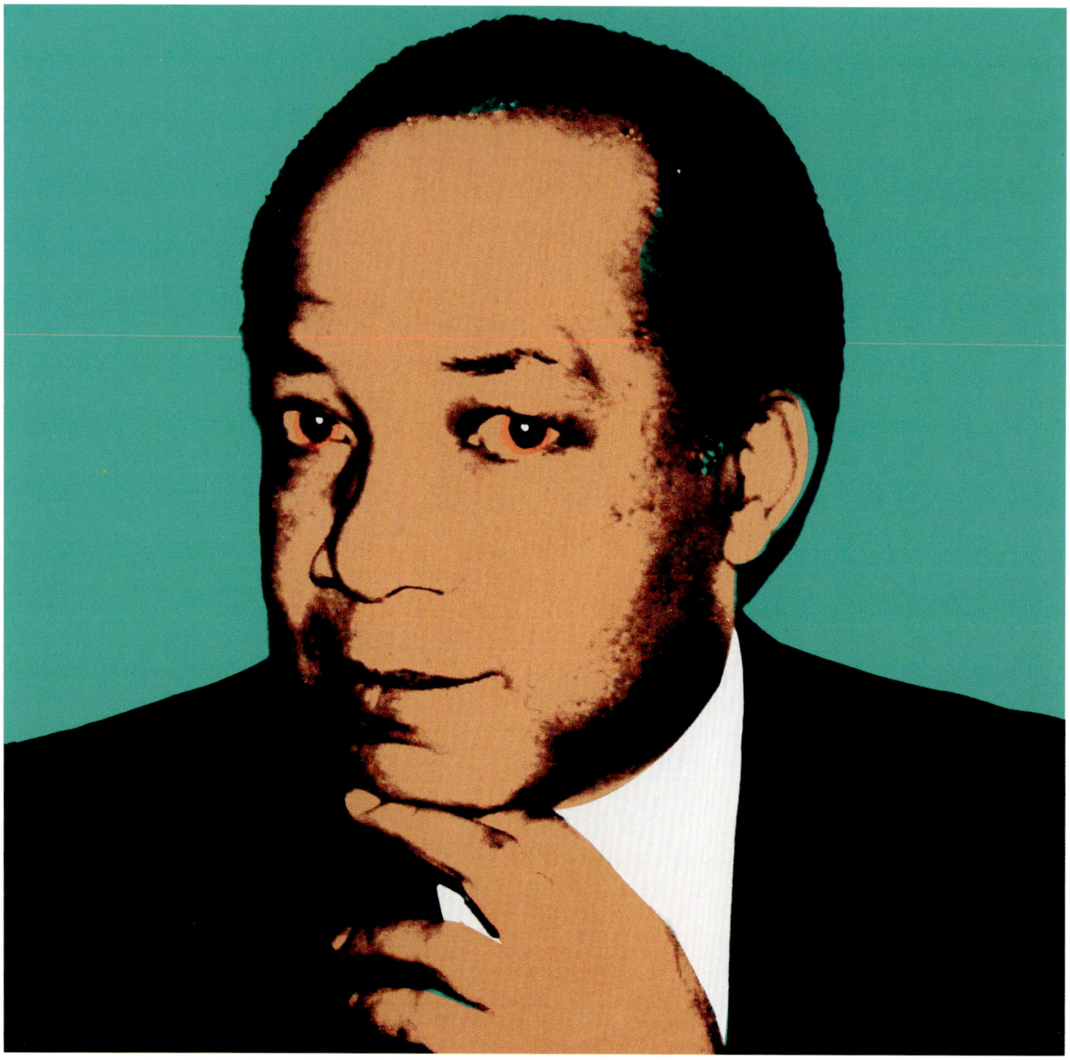

Andy Warhol
Gerard Basquiat, 1986
Acrylic and silkscreen on canvas
40 × 40 in. (101.6 × 101.6 cm)

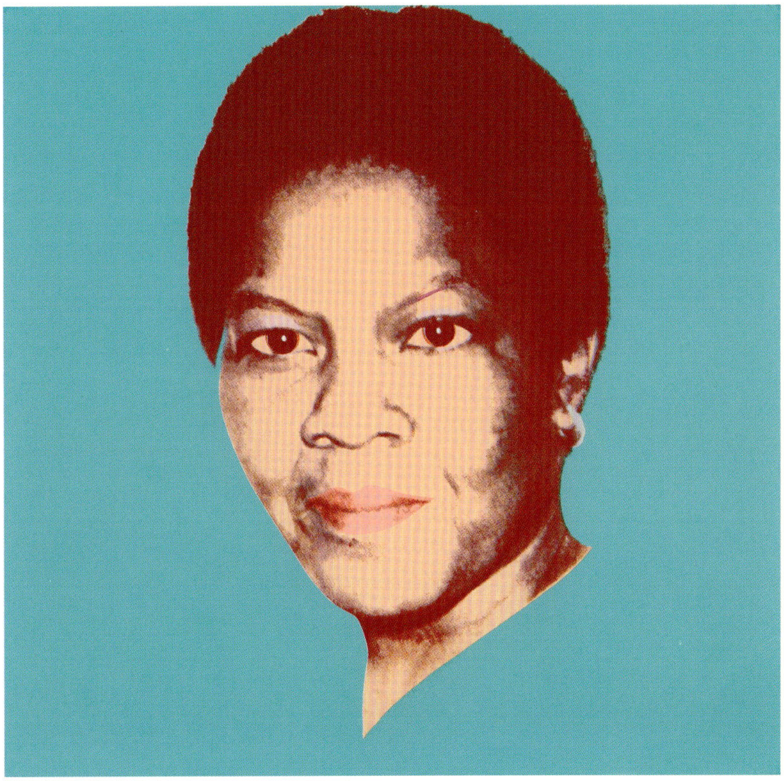

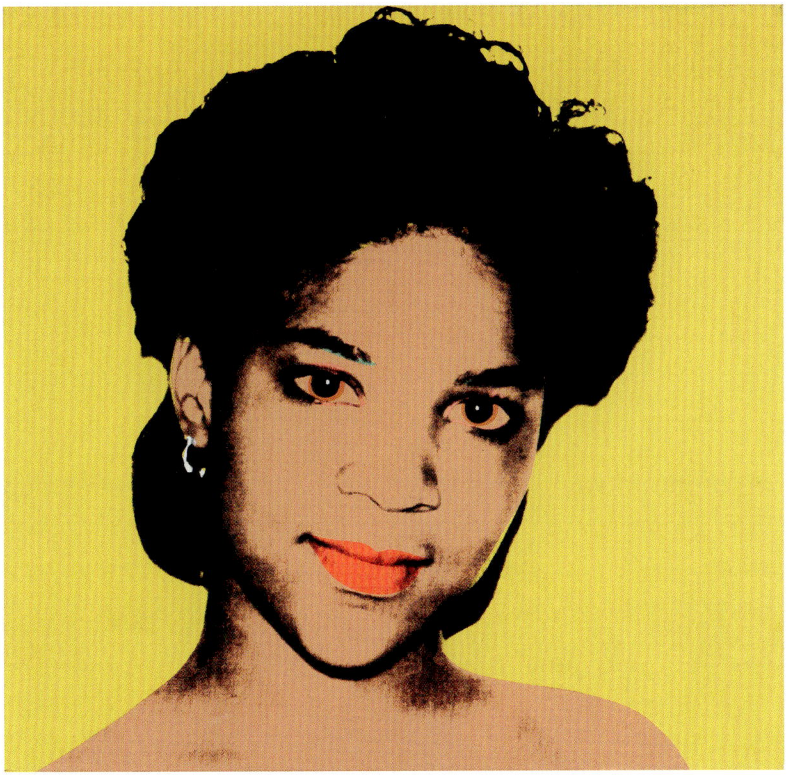

TOP
Andy Warhol
Matilde Basquiat, 1986
Acrylic and silkscreen on canvas
40 × 40 in. (101.6 × 101.6 cm)

LEFT
Andy Warhol
Jeanine Basquiat, 1986
Acrylic and silkscreen on canvas
40 × 40 in. (101.6 × 101.6 cm).
It was fun to sit down for a portrait with Andy. It really didn't take that long. He took a photo with his Polaroid camera and created a silkscreen of the image. JEANINE

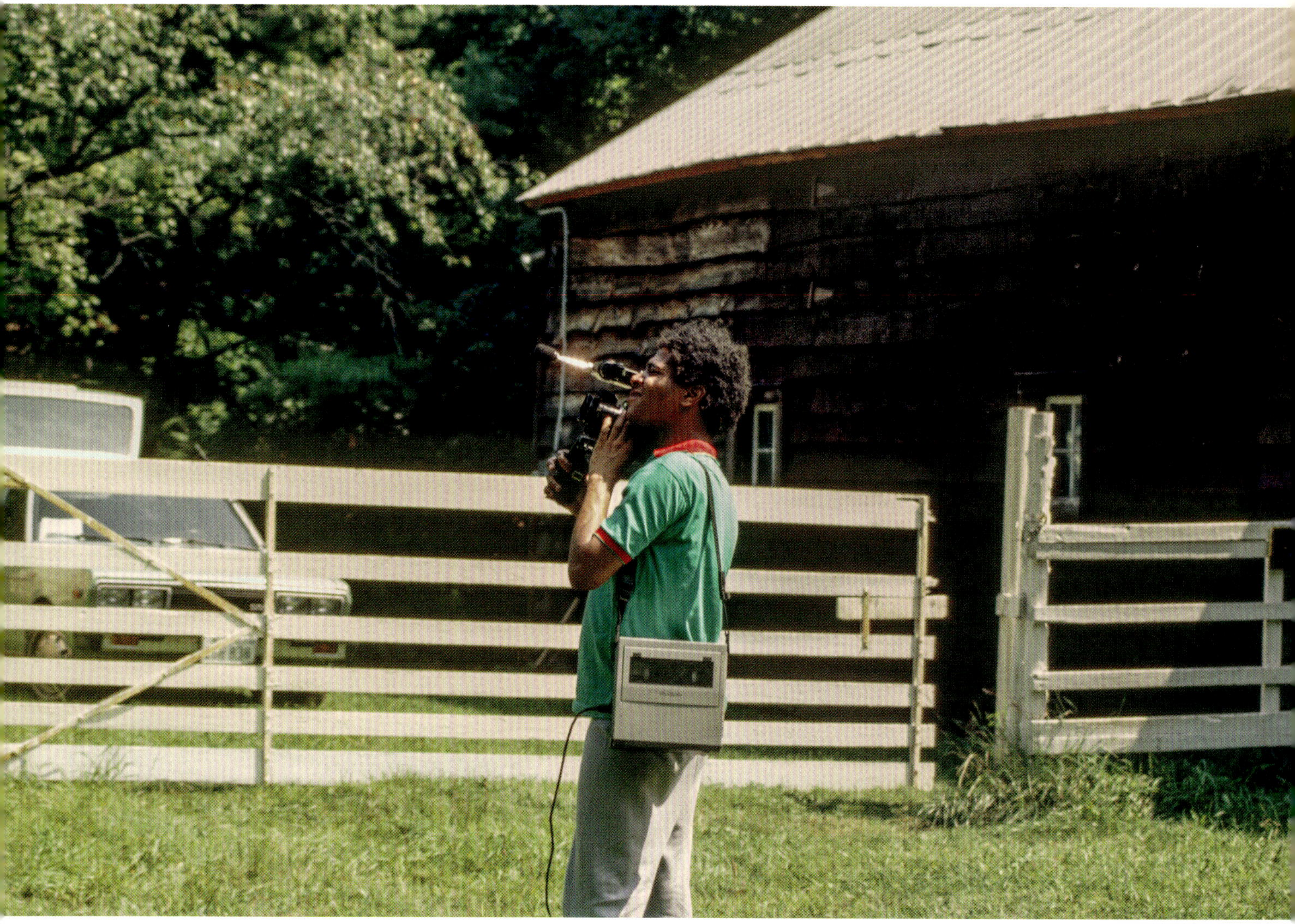

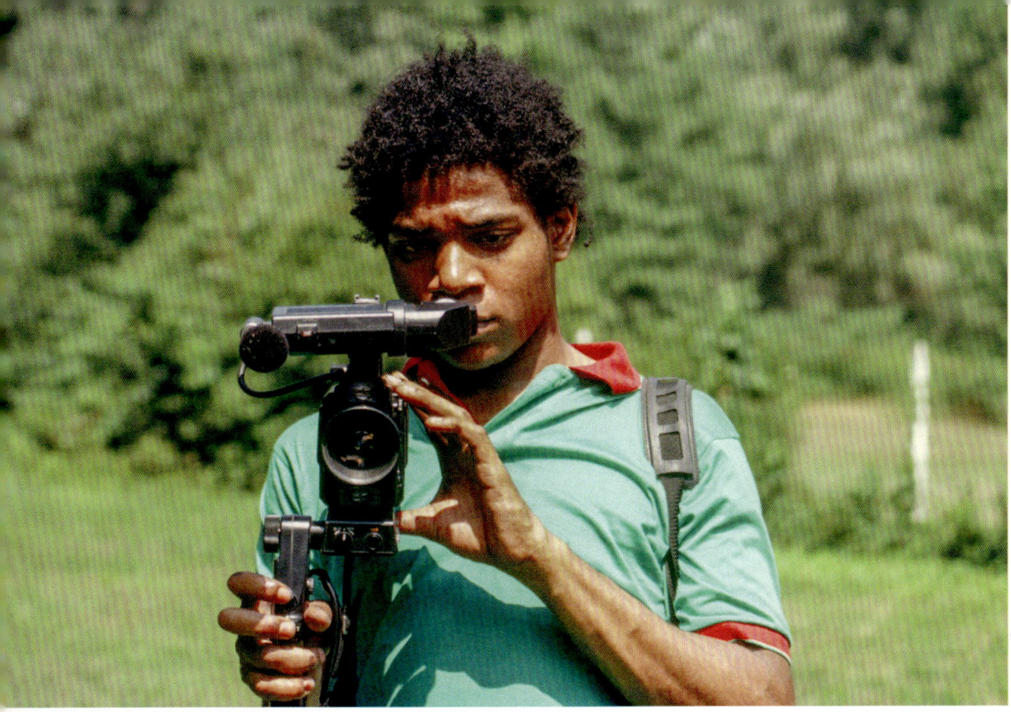

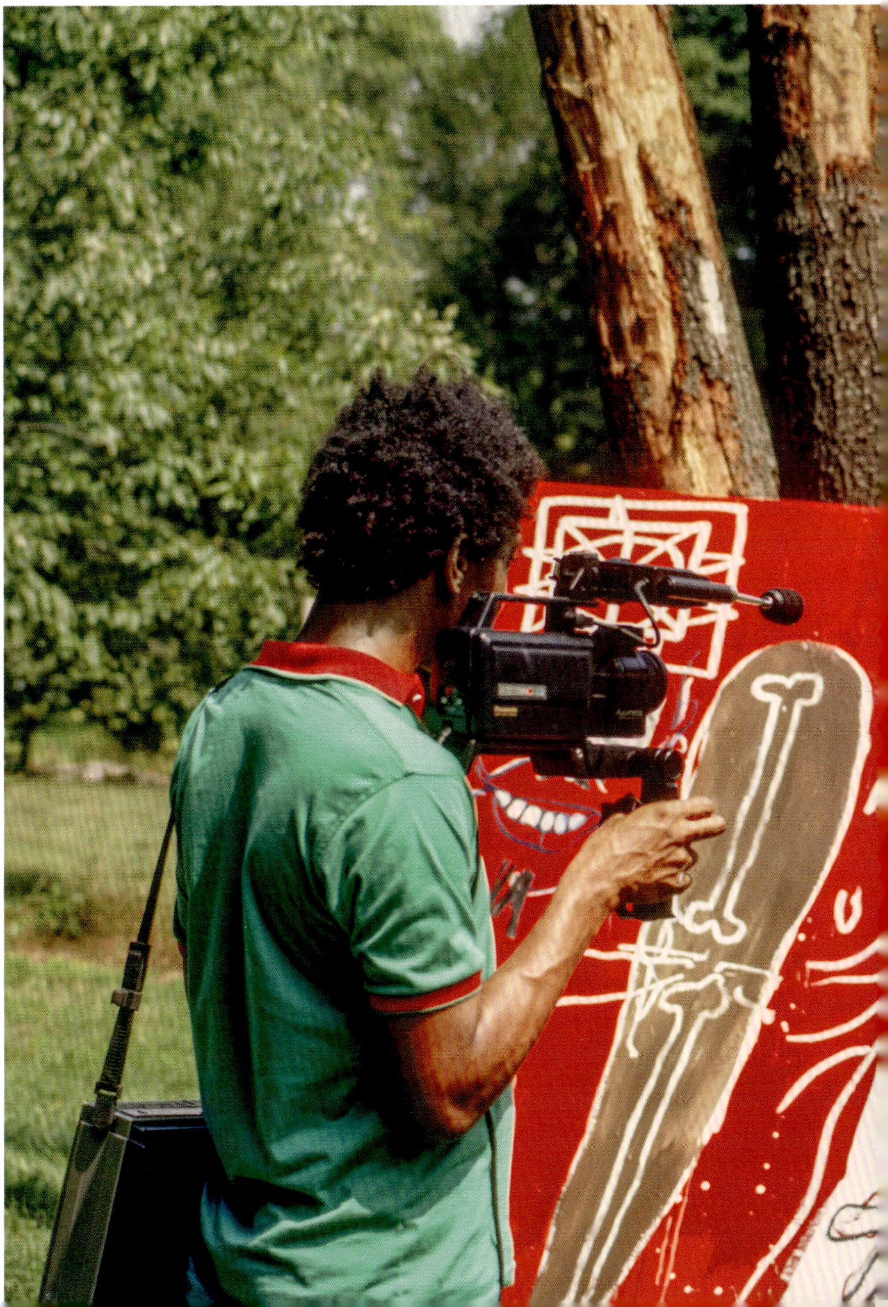

THIS SPREAD
Jean-Michel at Lee Jaffe's studio, Carmel, New York, 1983

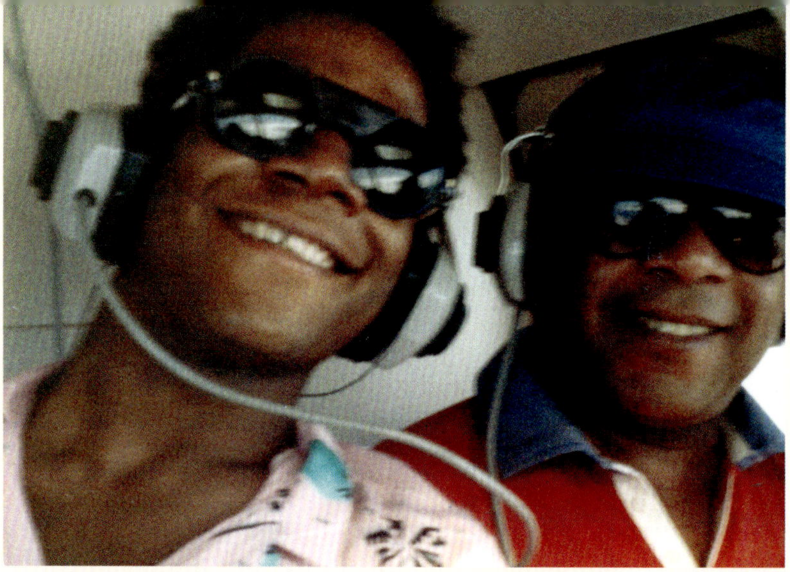

Jean-Michel and Gerard on a helicopter ride in Hawaii, 1984
PHOTO COURTESY OF NORA FITZPATRICK

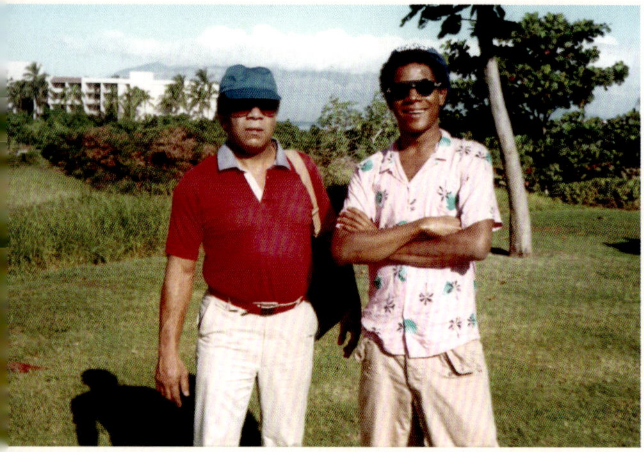

Gerard and Jean-Michel in Hana, Maui, Hawaii, 1984
PHOTO COURTESY OF NORA FITZPATRICK

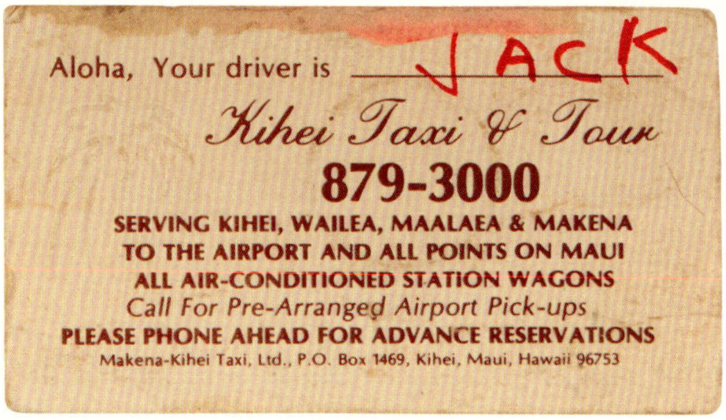

Taxi driver's business card from Jean-Michel's trip to Hawaii, 1984

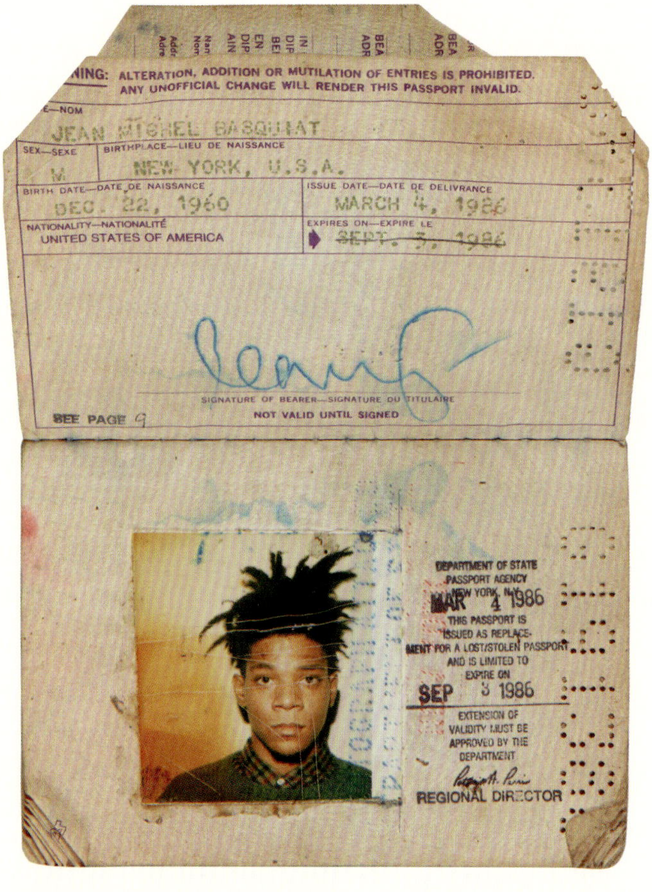

Jean-Michel's passport, 1986

TRAVEL

Travel was an integral part of Jean-Michel's life. Besides needing to travel for his exhibitions around the world, he also had a love for different cuisines and cultures. The two places that I know were life-changing for him were Hawaii and Abidjan, capital of the Ivory Coast in Africa.

He loved Hawaii—Maui in particular. He felt at peace and free there, and the tranquility allowed him the opportunity to reset. From my recollection, he would always stay at a particular property with two cottages. When our family visited, we stayed at that property. I experienced my first helicopter ride on that trip. It was incredible, and I still remember it vividly. The beaches had black sand from the volcanos. We played tennis and rode horses, and Jean-Michel was really serene. It was time spent with him that I will never forget. JEANINE

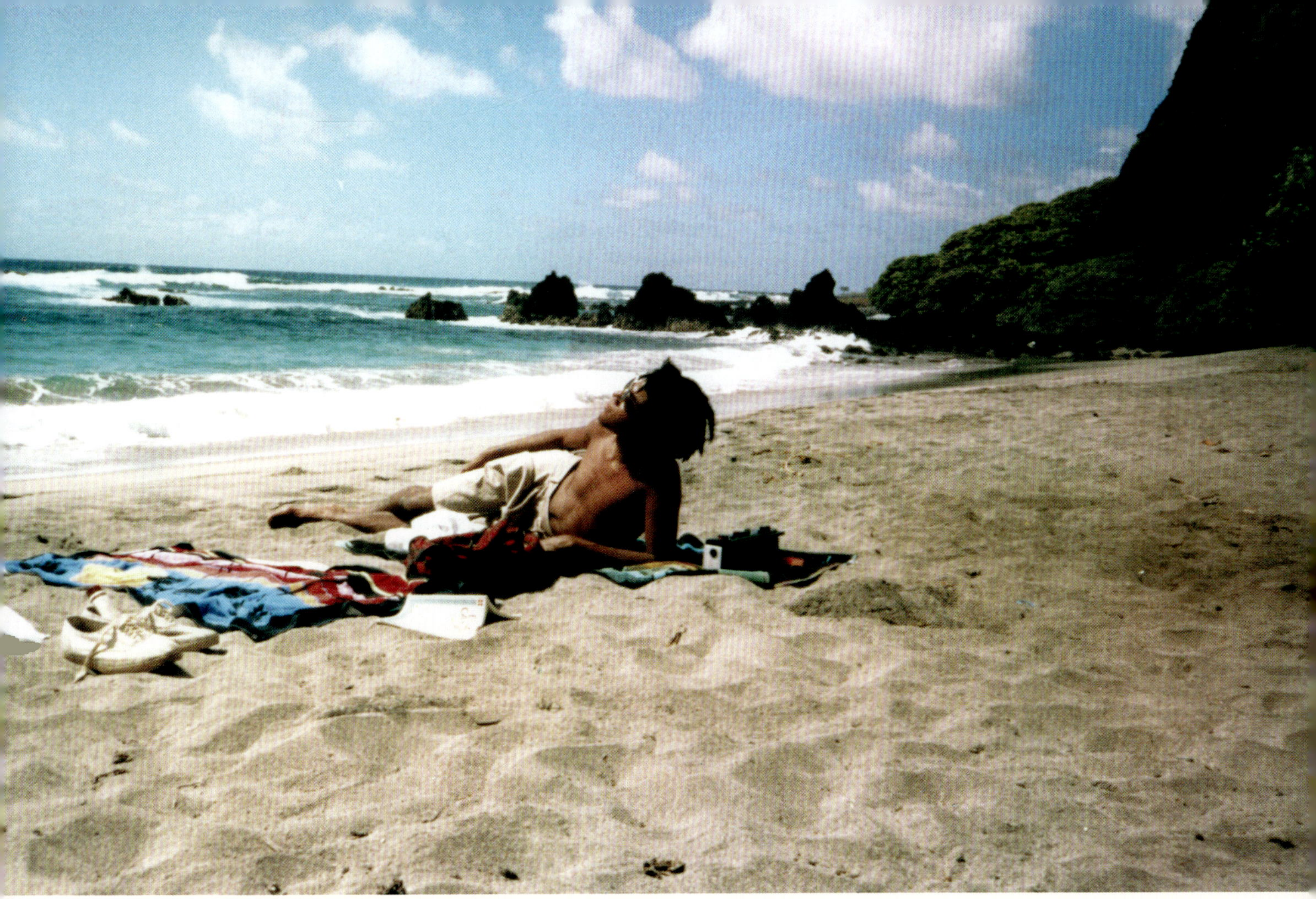

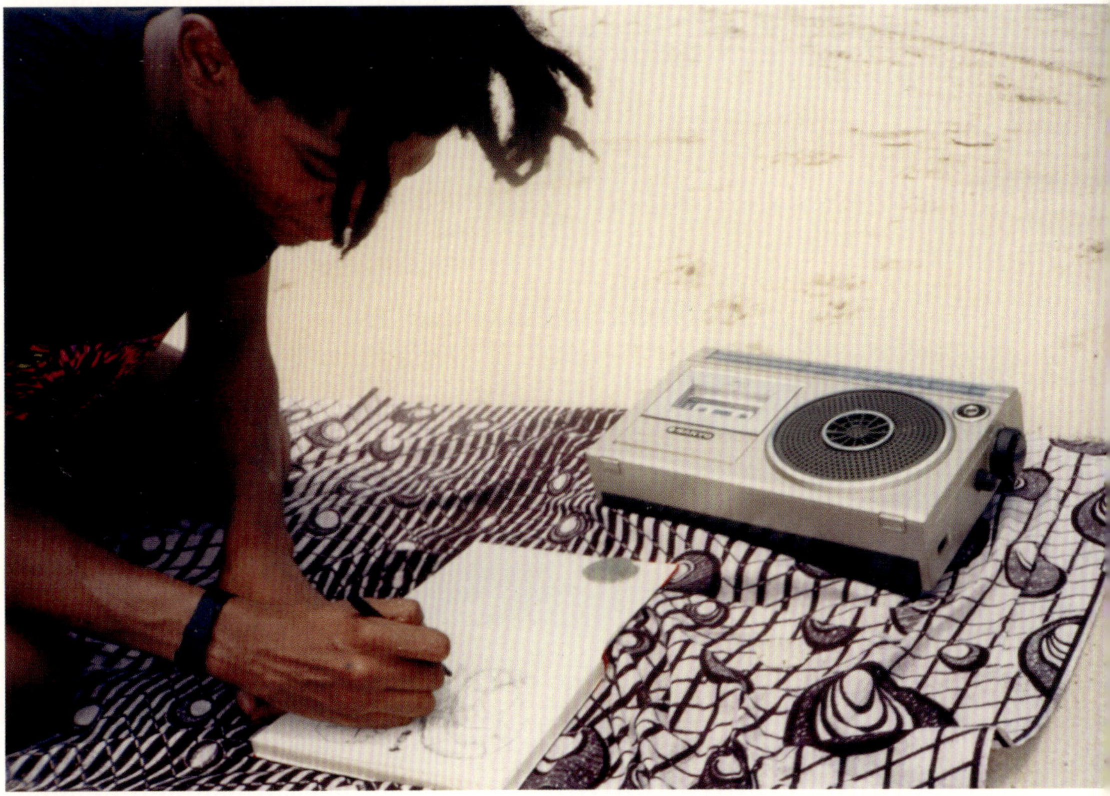

Jean-Michel on the beach in Africa, November 1986
PHOTOS: JENNIFER GOODE

JEAN-MICHEL'S TRIP TO THE IVORY COAST

Jean-Michel and I were dating at the time of his trip to the Ivory Coast, and I joined him there. We arrived in Abidjan on Sunday afternoon October 12, 1986. Jean-Michel's exhibition at the Centre Culturel Français opened on Friday, October 10. I cannot remember why we arrived after the opening. A missed flight? Who knows. Georges Courrèges—a photographer who showed us around during our trip—picked us up from the airport and drove us to the CCF.

JENNIFER GOODE

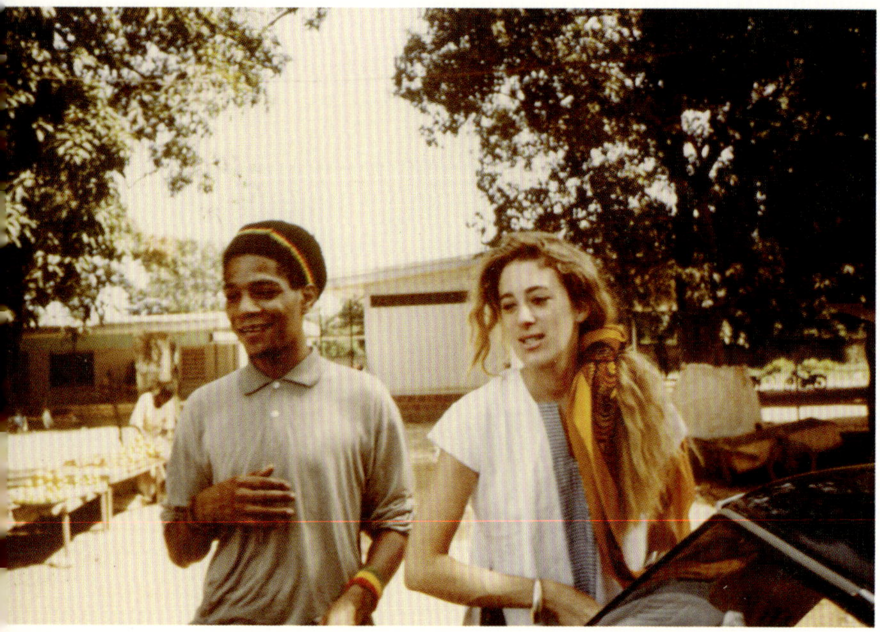

LEFT
Jean-Michel and Jennifer Goode, Ivory Coast, Africa, 1986
PHOTO: CHRISTINA BISCHOFBERGER

BOTTOM
Unknown man, Philippe Briet, Jean-Michel, and Jennifer Goode in Tiagba, Ivory Coast, Africa, October 1986
PHOTO: GEORGES COURRÈGES

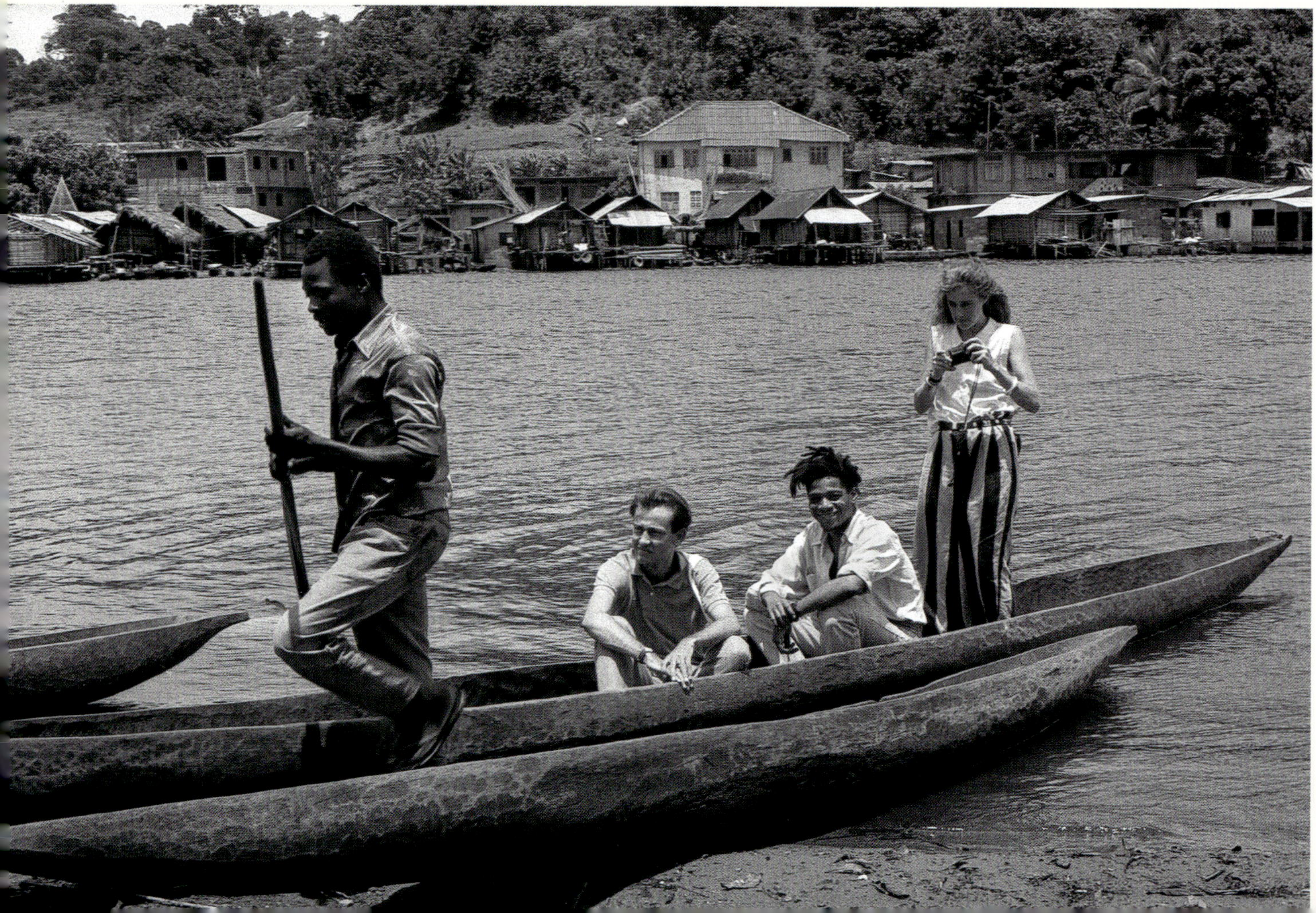

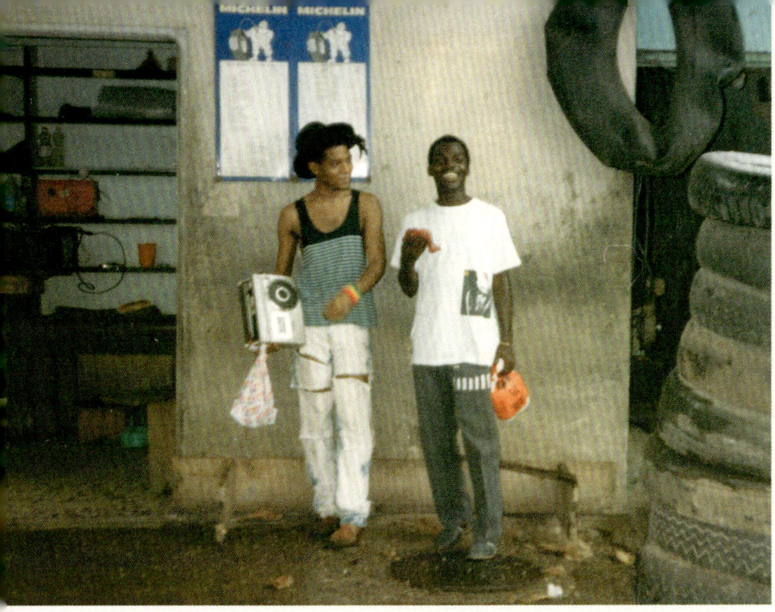

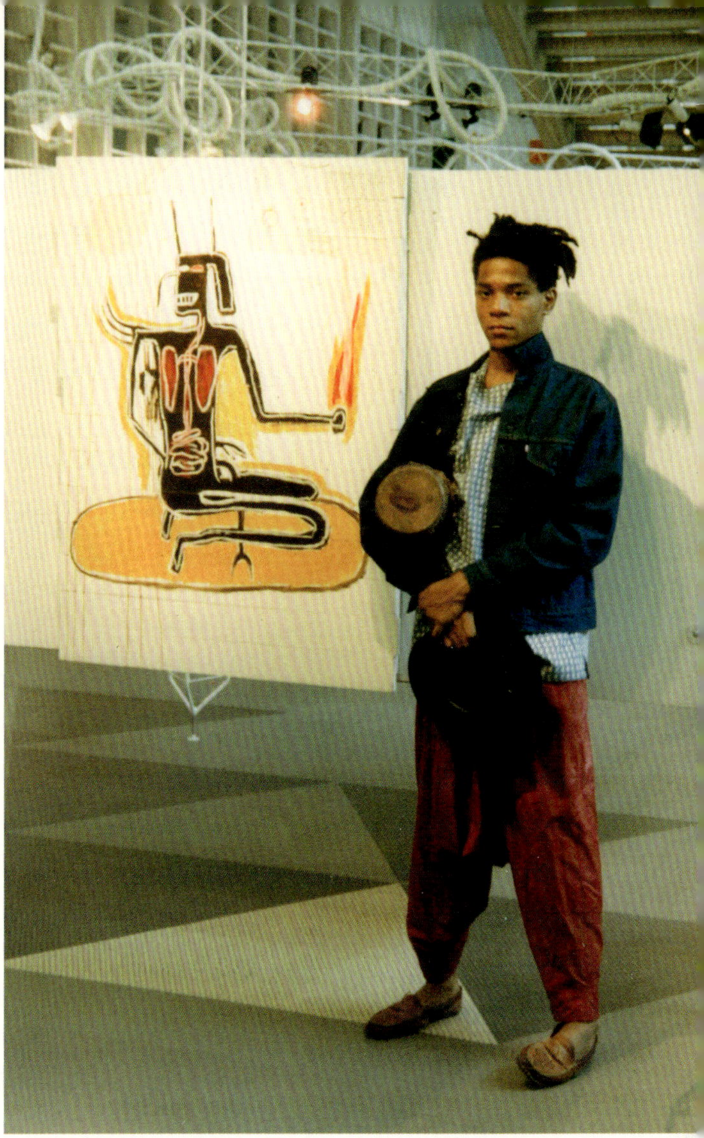

TOP LEFT AND BOTTOM
Jean-Michel, Ivory Coast, Africa, November 1986
PHOTOS: JENNIFER GOODE

TOP RIGHT
Jean-Michel in front of his painting at his exhibition at the Centre Culturel Français, Abidjan, Ivory Coast, 1986, arranged by gallerist Bruno Bischofberger.
PHOTO: CHRISTINA BISCHOFBERGER

As always, there were many people for the opening for Jean-Michel's show at the Centre Culturel Français: Ivorian artists, diplomats from different embassies, journalists, press from national TV, professors of fine arts, etc.

During their time in Abidjan, I took Jennifer and Jean-Michel to the "hot" district of Treichville to have dinner in a "maquis" (a small African restaurant) which was run by a friend. We had dinner sitting on the floor on cushions. Jean-Michel was delighted and Jennifer was too—both were amazed by this incredible place.

A few days later Jean-Michel met the Ivorian artists of the Vohou Vohou group—N'Guessan Kra, Théodore Koudougnon, and Youssouf Bath—that I had exhibited at the same time but in another venue. Jean-Michel was interested in the recycled materials such as *tapa* (a tree bark) on which the Ivorian artists worked as well as the colors, much of which was not paint but created with the juice of herbs, fruits, earth, and sand.

I wanted Jean-Michel to discover parts of the Ivory Coast beyond Abidjan so I went with him, Jennifer, and Philippe Briet to the island of Tiagba. We took a pirogue and went to a small fishermen's village on stilts. While there, I brought them to a friend's house who had a small plane and he flew them over the Azagny National Reserve and the Bandama River where one could see elephants bathing in the river.

GEORGES COURRÈGES

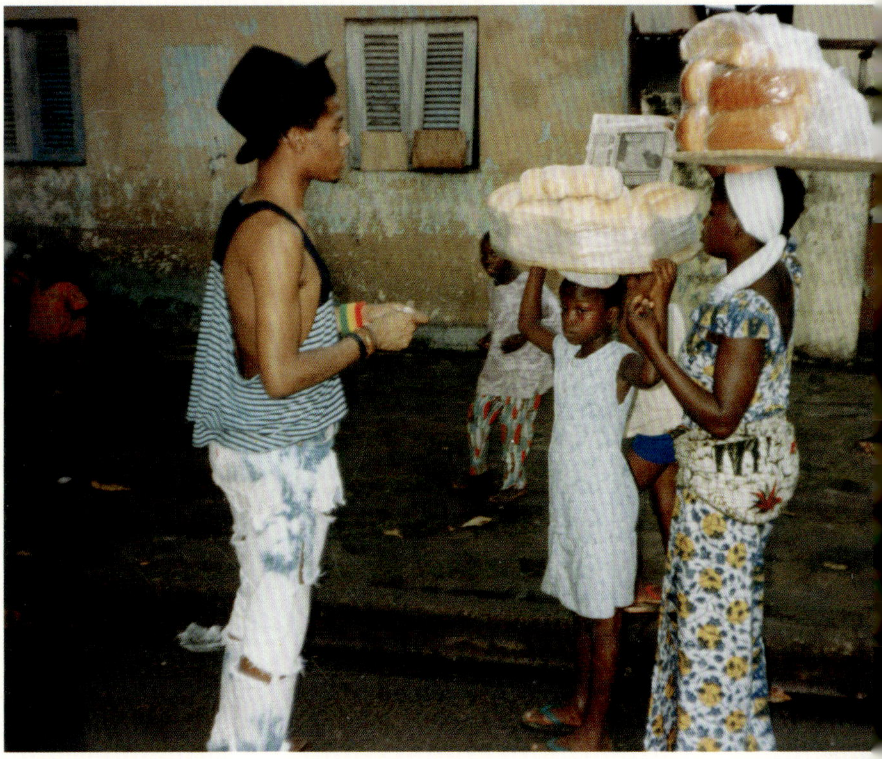

COMME DES GARÇONS

I started my career in fashion in 1982 at Comme des Garçons, where I served as the US general manager for seventeen years. I met Jean-Michel in 1984. Mary Boone had escorted him into the flagship store in SoHo and asked that he be dressed for his first opening at her gallery. She had a blank check and said she needed a wardrobe for him. From the moment he walked into the store, I was struck by his natural sense of style. He had a beautiful physique. He wore clothes beautifully and, being thin and tall, he could wear very relaxed silhouettes. The men's collection suited him because it was sort of a juxtaposition of fine tailoring and a relaxed kind of ease. From that point on, Jean-Michel was a regular customer.

Comme des Garçons had the practice of casting interesting men that were not models for its runway shows in Paris. In the summer of 1986, Jean-Michel was invited to walk the runway for the Spring/Summer 1987 collection. We traveled together to Paris, as I was the buyer for the brand. I was also entrusted with keeping an eye on him and making sure that he was at the fittings, the dress rehearsal, and, of course, the final show. He enjoyed himself and took to the runway effortlessly. He seemed to be truly amused and interested. He was curious and had a good sense of humor.

When we finished our work in Paris, Jean-Michel and I returned to New York. We were on the same Air France flight but, because he was the model, he was in business class and I was in coach. He saw me board the plane and asked the flight attendant if I could join him as he had an empty seat next to him, but she said it was impossible.

He came down the aisle from business to find me in coach. I was struck by just how fabulous he looked in the suit that Comme des Garçons had given him for modeling in the show. He had personalized the suit with a fantastic collection of necklaces. The flight had originated in Tel Aviv, and the passenger sitting on the aisle in my row was a rabbi with all his sacred books on his lap. Jean-Michel gestured to him that he wanted to sit next to me. The rabbi realized that he'd have to either stand up with all of his books or stay seated. Jean-Michel didn't wait for him to react—he jumped over him and plopped himself down in the middle seat. And we took off. JOHANNE SHEPLEY SIFF

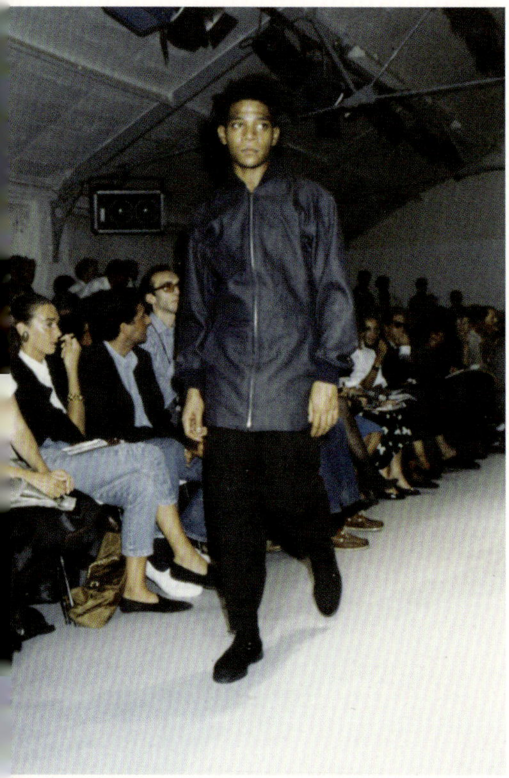

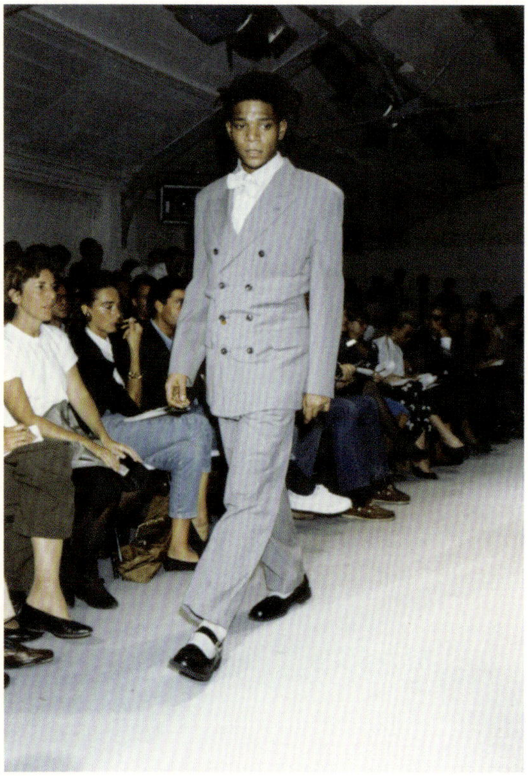

Jean-Michel walking the runway for the Comme des Garçons Homme Plus Spring/Summer 1987 fashion show, Paris, 1986

PHOTOS COURTESY OF COMME DES GARÇONS

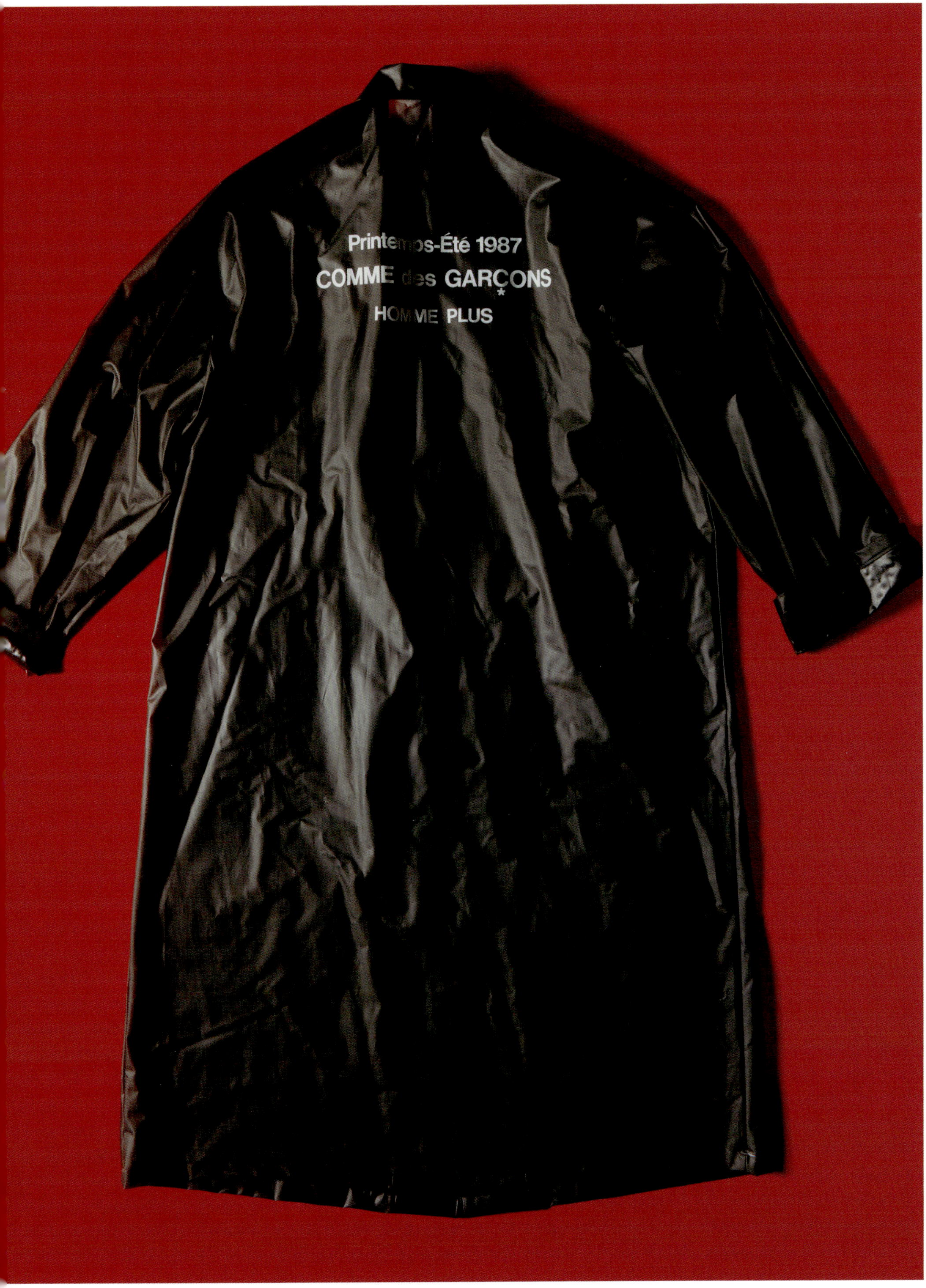

Jean-Michel's Comme des Garçons raincoat

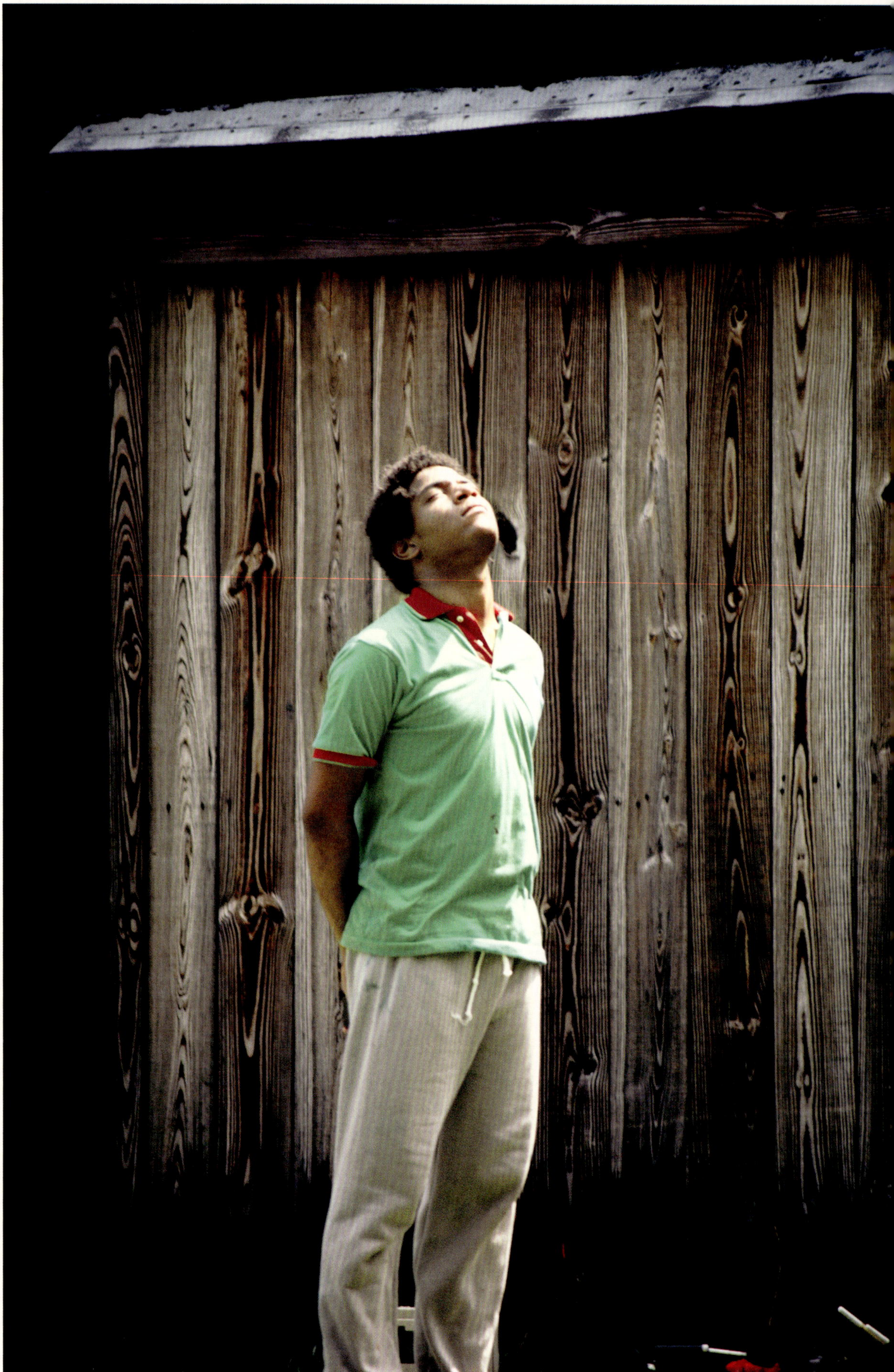

Jean-Michel in Carmel, New York, 1983 © LEE JAFFE

GENERROSITY

Jean-Michel was the human embodiment of an act of generosity in every area of his life. LISANE

Jean-Michel was always incredibly generous. Whatever he enjoyed, he shared freely with others. Whether vacationing in Hawaii or dining at The Odeon or Mr Chow, Jean-Michel took care of those who were with him. He wanted to share his success and experiences with others. It was not uncommon for Jean-Michel to arrive at the house completely by surprise with gifts. He showed up once in a cab with big screen TVs and VCRs.

One weekend when I was visiting him, he took me to the Comme des Garçons store close to his apartment to do some shopping. At that time, kids my age wore Pumas, Levi's, and Lacoste polo shirts—there was no appreciation for designers who were avant-garde and conceptual. I'm embarrassed to say that at the time I only wore a few pieces, but I do still have a large caftan shirt that is very sentimental to me.

Jean-Michel often reflected on his early struggles before making a living from his work. He was known to walk through the Bowery just to hand out money to the homeless on the street, usually one-hundred-dollar bills. And he didn't just hand out money, he would stop, sit, talk, and listen to their stories. Since he had also spent time not knowing where he would rest his head at night, he was curious to know how others had come to their circumstances. JEANINE

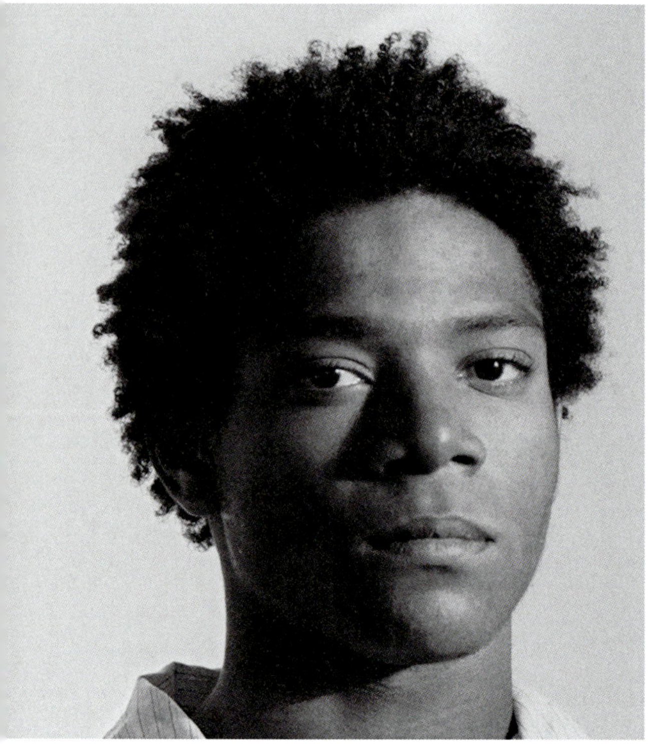

LEFT
Jean-Michel at Mary Boone Gallery, New York, 1984

BOTTOM
Untitled (Portrait), n.d.
Oil stick on paper
24 × 18 in. (60.96 × 45.72 cm)

OPPOSITE
Untitled (1960), 1983
Acrylic and oil stick on paper mounted on wood
36 × 24 in. (91.44 × 60.96).
Jean-Michel was born in 1960.

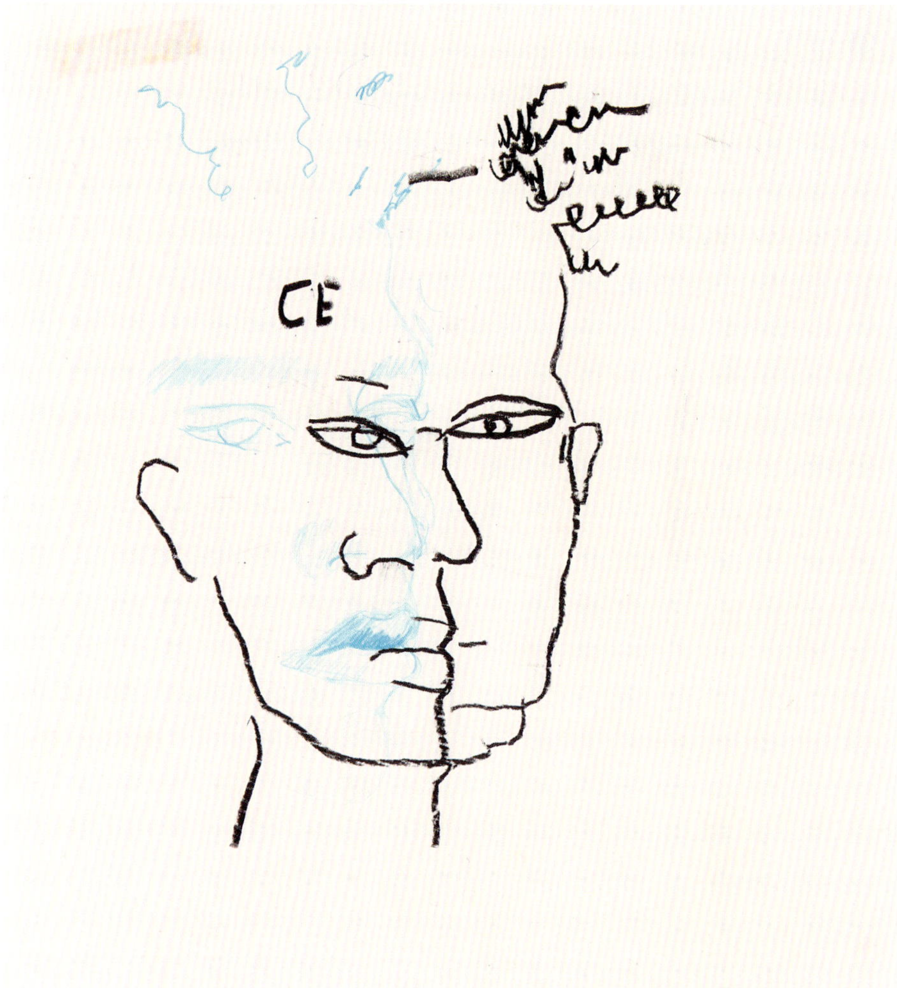

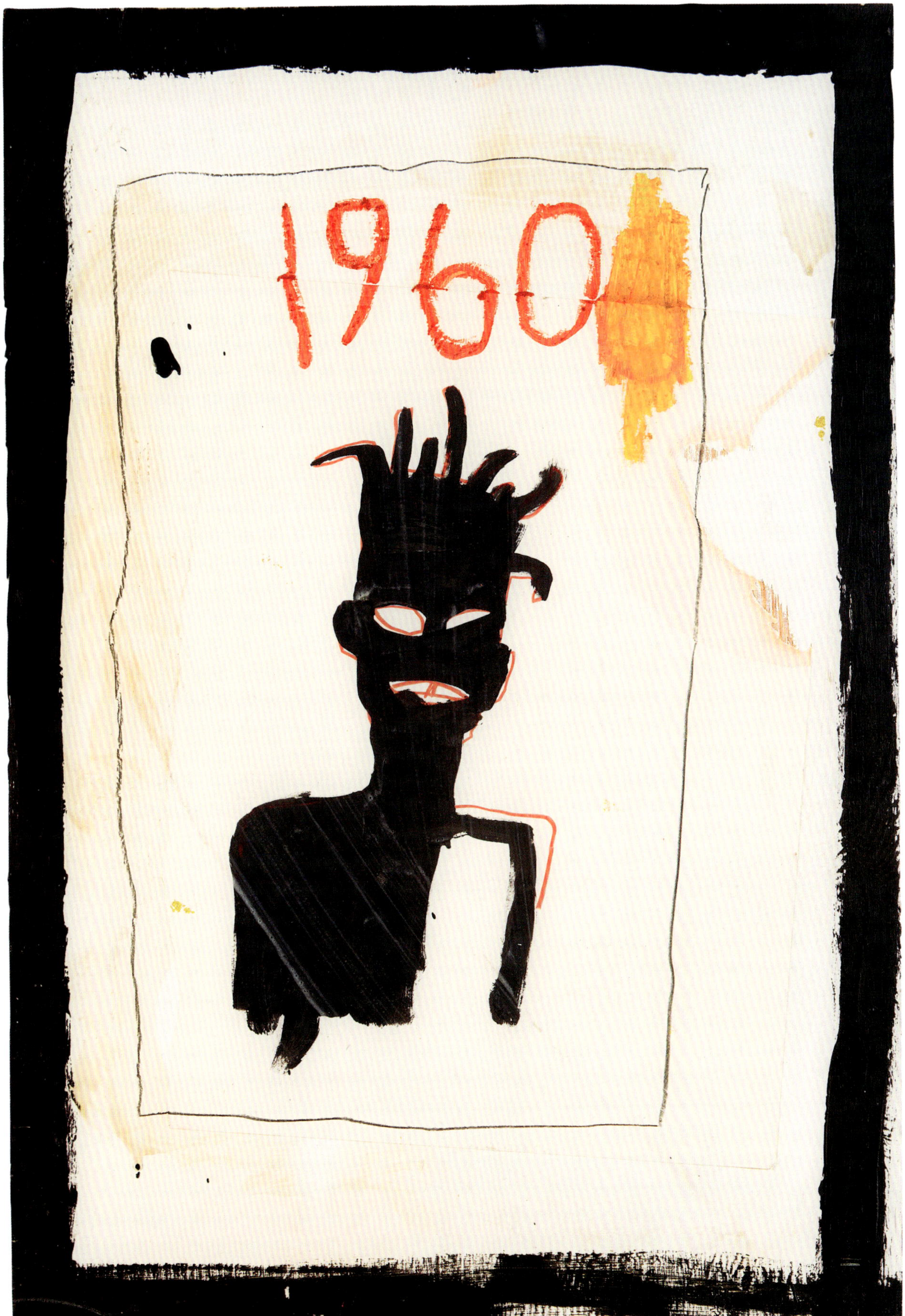
1960

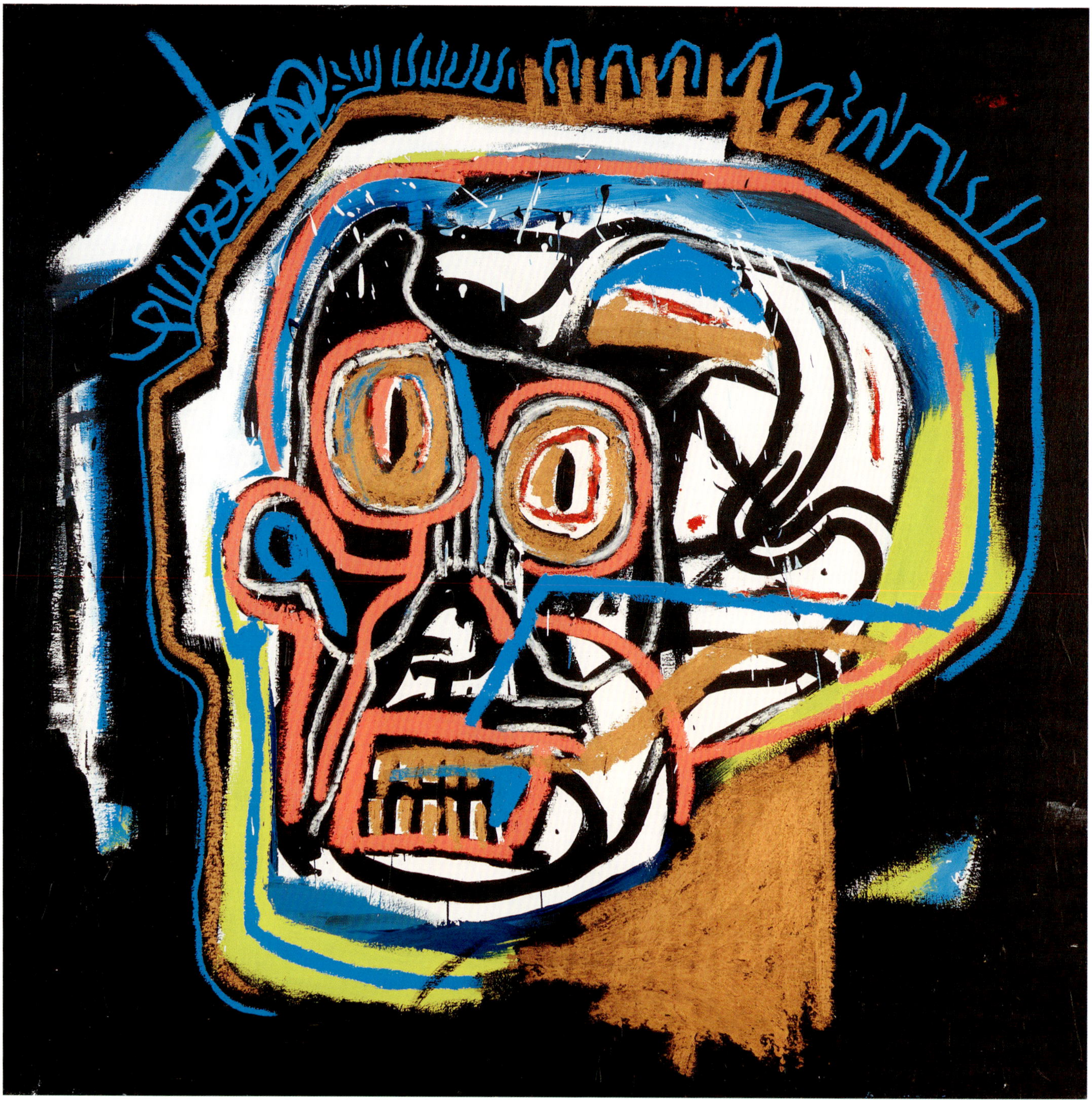

Untitled, 1983
Acrylic and oil stick on wood
48 × 48 in. (121.92 × 121.92 cm)

Untitled (Dry Goods©), 1982
Oil stick on Plexiglas and wood
46 × 39 × 2 in.
(116.84 × 99.06 × 5.08 cm)

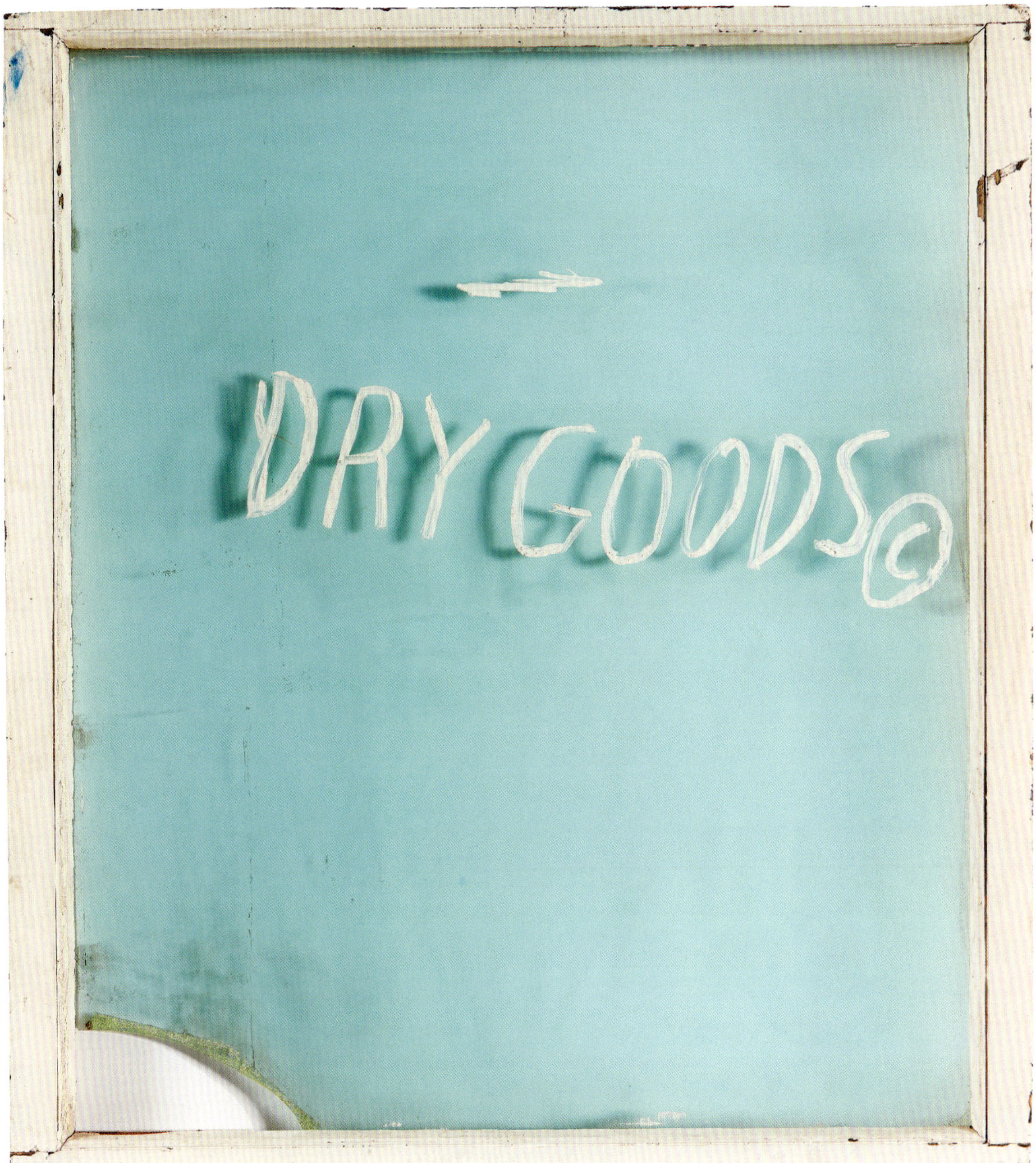

Untitled (Crowned Head), n.d.
Oil stick on paper
24 × 18 in. (60.96 × 45.72 cm)

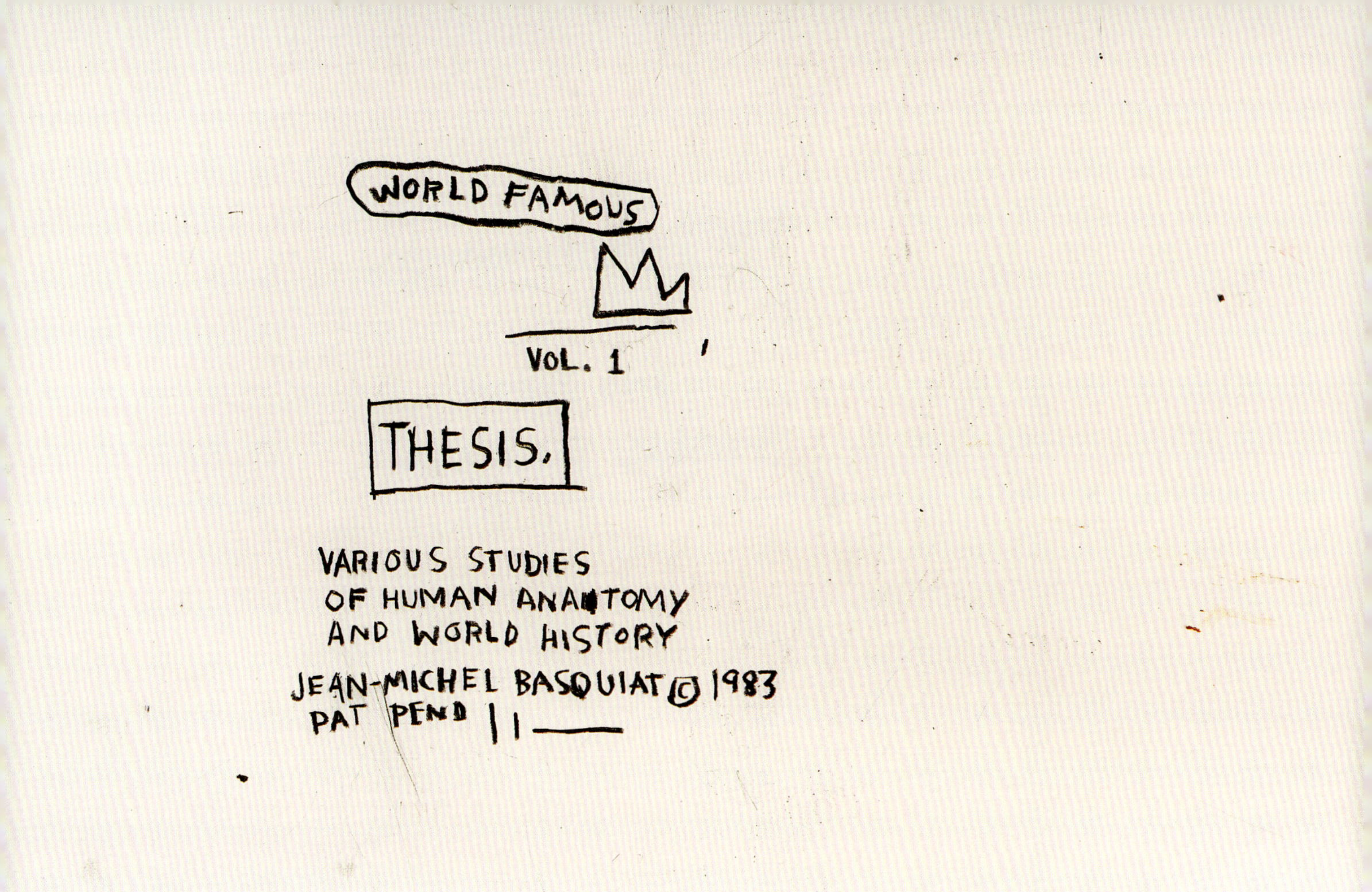

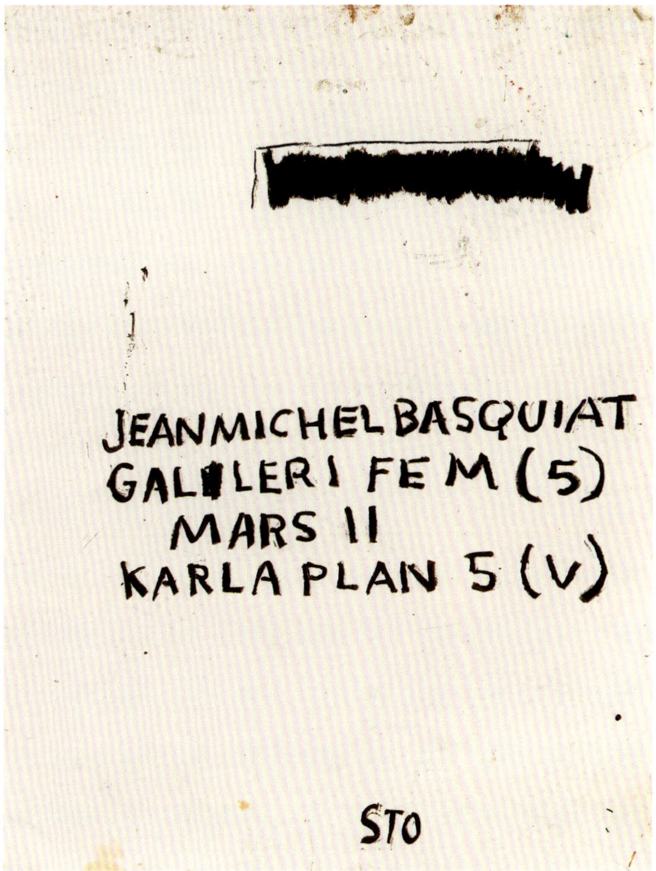

TOP
Untitled (World Famous Vol. 1 Thesis), n.d.
Crayon on paper
22½ × 30 in. (57.15 × 76.2 cm)

RIGHT
Untitled (JeanMichel Basquiat), n.d.
Oil stick on paper
30 × 22¼ in. (76.2 × 56.52 cm)

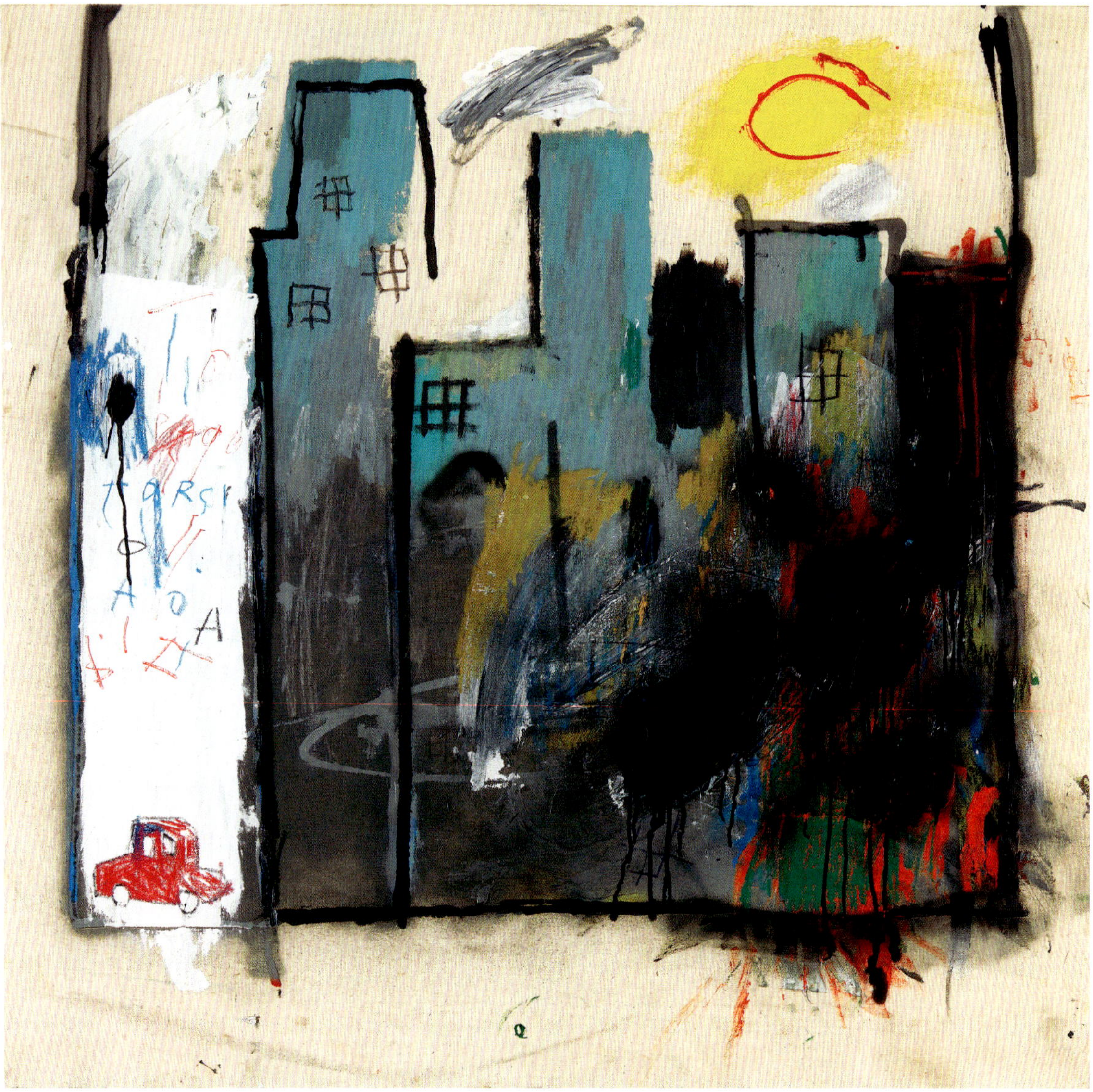

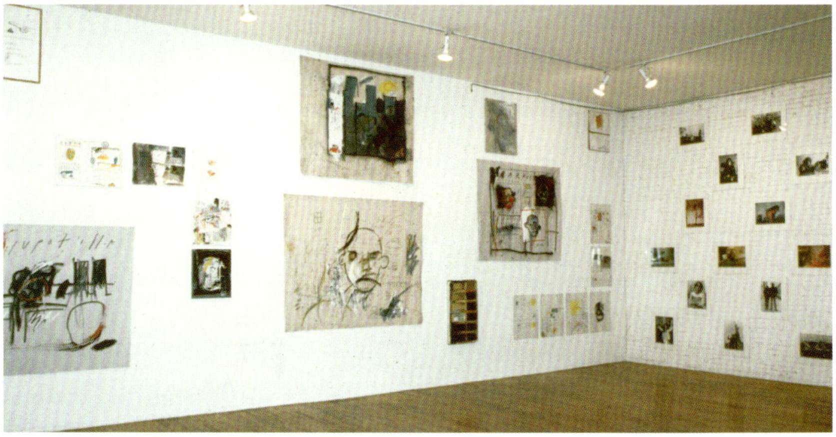

TOP
Untitled, ca. 1980–81
Acrylic, spray paint, and
oil stick on canvas
40 × 41 in. (101.6 × 104.14 cm).
This work was included in the New York / New Wave *exhibition organized by Diego Cortez at P.S. 1, Institute for Art and Urban Resources, Long Island City, New York.*

RIGHT
Installation view, *New York / New Wave* exhibition with works by Jean-Michel and Bob Gruen, at P.S. 1 Institute for Art and Urban Resources, Long Island City, New York, February 15–April 5, 1981. (MoMA P.S. 1 Archives, II.A.298, The Museum of Modern Art Archives.)

Untitled, 1983–84
Acrylic, oil stick and
photocopy on canvas
66 × 60 in. (167.64 × 152.4 cm)

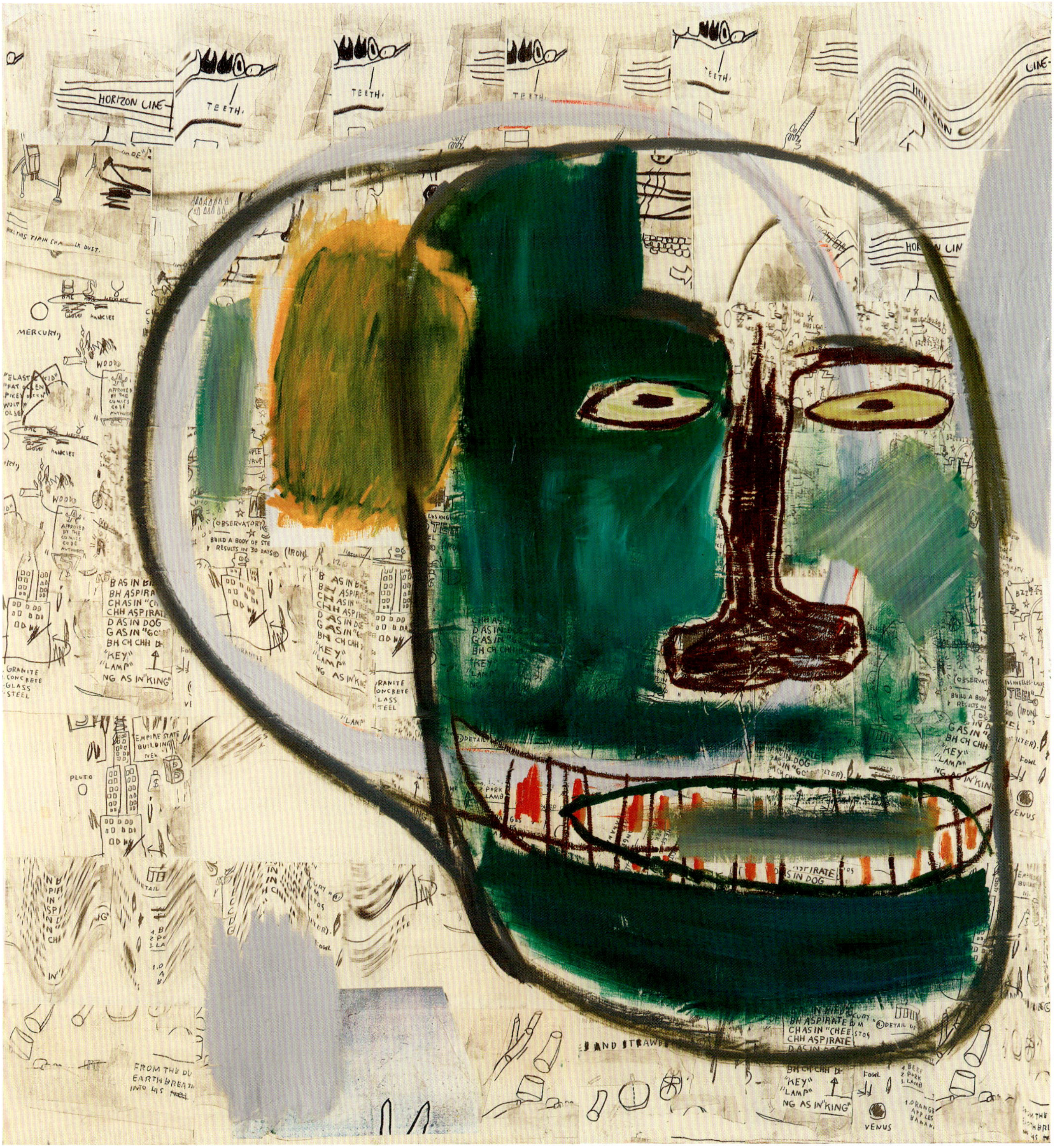

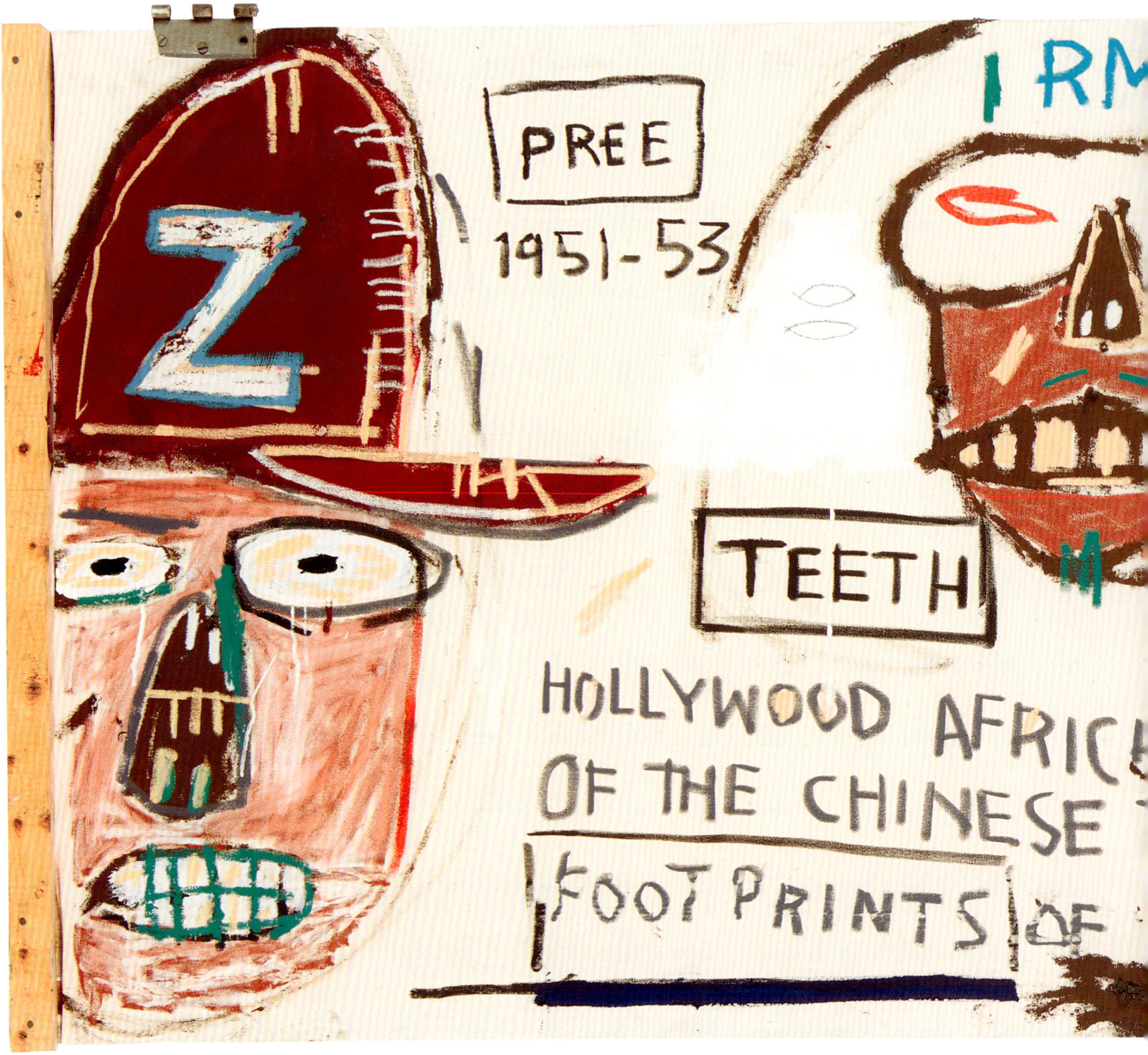
PREE
1951-53
TEETH
HOLLYWOOD AFRIC
OF THE CHINESE
FOOT PRINTS
Z

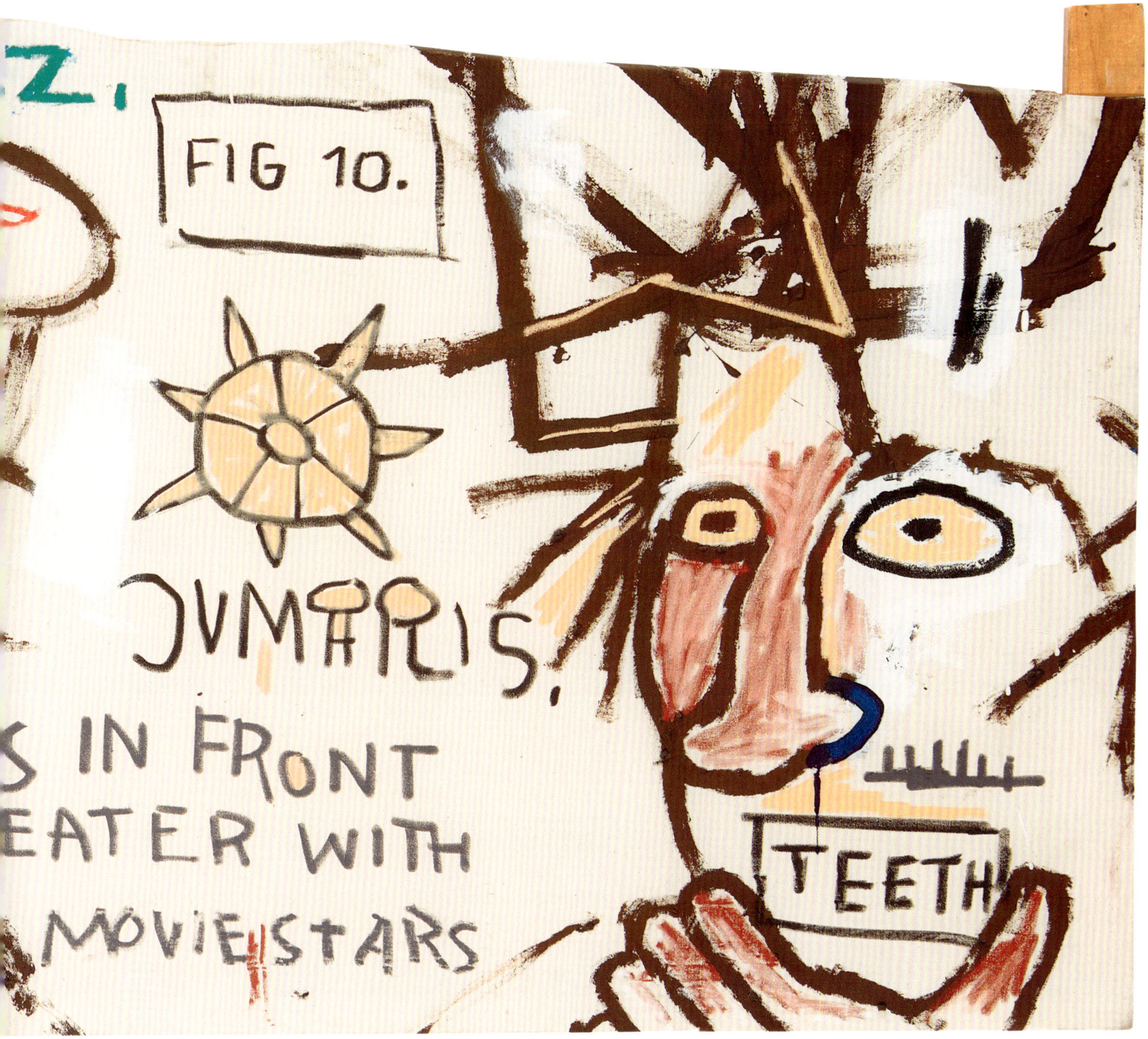

Hollywood Africans in Front of the Chinese Theater with Footprints of Movie Stars, 1983
Acrylic and oil stick on canvas mounted on wood supports
31½ × 81½ in.
(80.01 × 207.01 cm).
Jean-Michel created this painting after a trip to Los Angeles with Rammellzee and Toxic.

BLUE RIBBON

Named after Jean-Michel's *Blue Ribbon* series of paintings, this chapter highlights some of the more important works in the estate's collection, works that are extraordinary for their depth of meaning, their scale, or because of their significance to our family. According to many observers, Jean-Michel produced his best works in 1982, and some attribute this to him painting in a proper studio space for the first time. Five of the works featured—*Untitled (Ernok)* (opposite), *Untitled (Venus)* (page 102), *Untitled (Ajax)* (page 103), *Cabeza* (page 108), and *Untitled (Rinso)* (page 116)—were painted in 1982 and all were created with wood supports.

Several works featured are from 1984, including two untitled paintings (pages 98–101), works Jean-Michel made from wood fencing taken from behind the studio he rented in Venice Beach, California. In his book *The Art of Jean-Michel Basquiat* (2017), gallerist and curator Fred Hoffman recalls that the back door of Jean-Michel's studio, which was a block from the beach, opened onto a small courtyard that was enclosed by a wood fence. One evening Jean-Michel walked out into the courtyard and was startled by a homeless man who had managed to enter through a hole in the fence. He decided to have the wood fence removed and brought into his studio, ultimately using it as his "canvas" for several paintings.

Dry Cell (page 111), also featured here, was painted in 1988 and was one of the last paintings created by Jean-Michel. He gave it to our father as a gift. JEANINE

Untitled (Ernok), 1982
Acrylic and oil stick on canvas mounted on tied wood supports
83½ × 60 in. (210.09 × 152.4 cm)

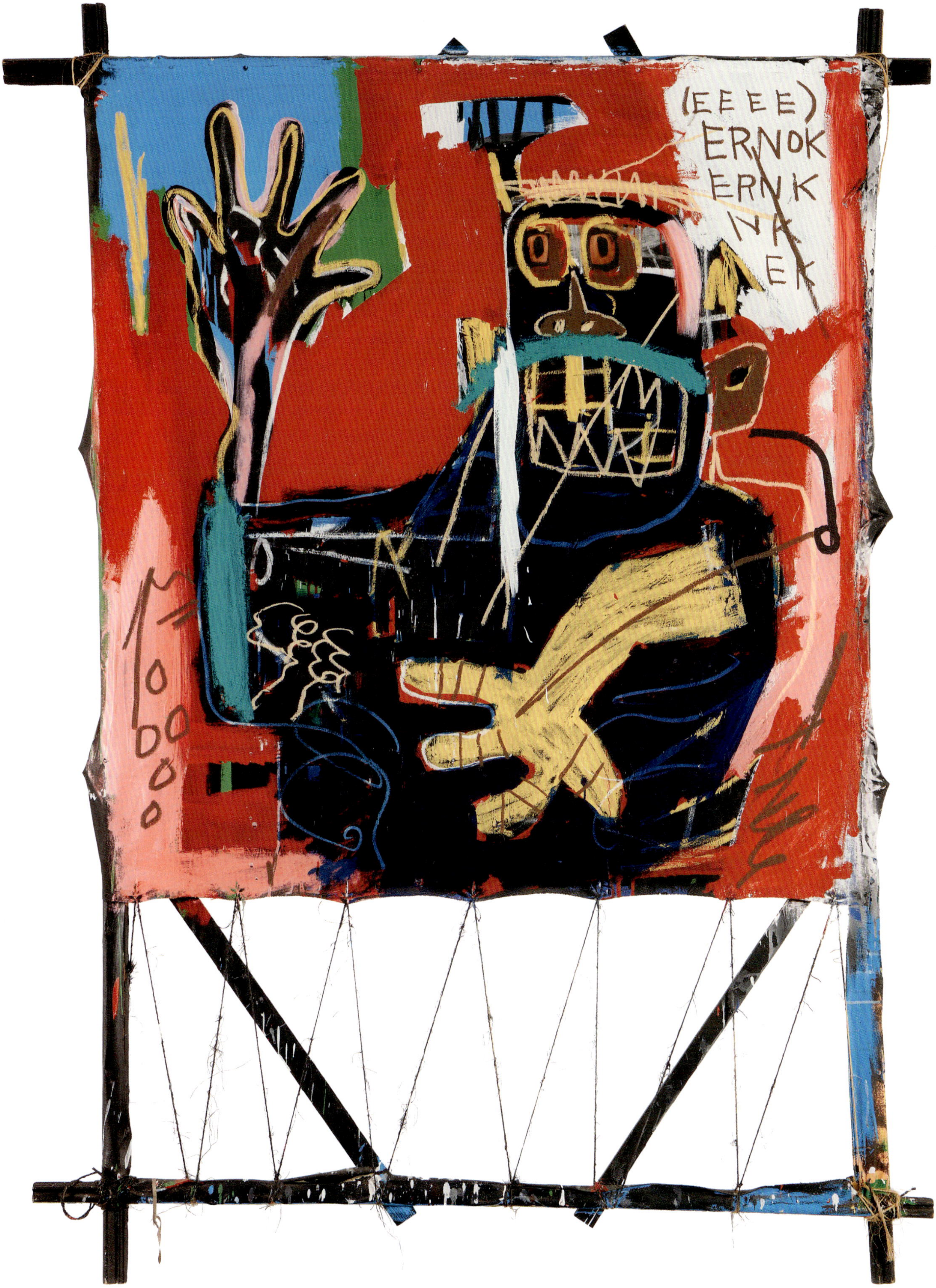
(EEEE)
ERNOK
ERNK
NA
EK

THE WORK: JEAN-MICHEL'S PAINTINGS AND DRAWINGS

I love Jean-Michel's palette and the vibrancy of the colors he painted with. Color was key in expressing mood and emotion for Jean-Michel. The words and phrases that feature so prominently in much of his work were also essential in conveying meaning. His method of crossing out words is wholly unique—it's genius. With words and phrases either partially covered up or almost completely obscured, the gesture invites the viewer to ask, "Why?" To draw more attention to the words underneath? To negate them entirely? Jean-Michel's paintings are not about leading viewers to appreciate their beauty—they are about prompting the viewer to ask questions, pushing them to learn more.

As for my favorite works, there are so many but here are a few: I love *Cabeza* (page 108). I love the colors, and the figure is so striking. *Hollywood Africans in Front of the Chinese Theater with Footprints of Movie Stars* (pages 92–93) has been on quite a journey recently—it's been borrowed by numerous museums. The painting memorializes a trip Jean-Michel made to Los Angeles with friends—three young Black men hanging out and having their LA experience. It is probably the best way he could have recorded the experience. I love that one.

The drawings are even more personal. Some speak of us as a family, with thoughts that were going through his mind at the time. *Untitled (World Famous Vol. 1 Thesis)* (page 89) is such a simple drawing but important in that it's about Jean-Michel's aspirations. In another drawing, *Untitled (Out Getting Ribs JM)* (page 206), I imagine that he left that as a note on his door for someone who was coming to meet him and it wound up inspiring a drawing. It's so him. I love it.

When I was a teenager—which was at the height of Jean-Michel's career—I wasn't able to fully appreciate his work, its rich, layered content, and the complex network of associations and meanings. As I've matured, certain works strike me differently—I see and understand so much more now. Standing in front of them, you see texture and other nuanced aspects of the materials he worked with. You see the evidence of his hand, too. None of these things can be properly conveyed in print, unfortunately. I'm blown away, really, by how powerful, how significant, how grand the scale. I recall someone saying to me once that the paintings are filled with so much rage, and I didn't process that until later. In preparation for making selections of the work to be featured in the exhibition and this book, we've spent a lot of time with his paintings and drawings at the warehouse where they've been stored. I have been able to sit with the work, to really see it, to take it all in privately, outside of a museum or gallery. This time has been invaluable, and it allowed me to see parts I didn't before. JEANINE

Choosing the works to be included in this exhibition and book was overwhelming but also a lot of fun. It took us a long time to narrow down the list of works featured. Throughout the process, we thought about Jean-Michel: his love of cartoons and the characters that populated them, his wry, comedic slant on things, his observations, his pain. We learned so much as we researched the subjects he painted about. His works with words really resonate with me—I hear his voice and the way that he spoke quickly when he felt passionately about something. It was like there were more thoughts in his head than he could ever get out of his mouth. So he wrote them down, at his own pace. A work like *Untitled (World Famous Vol. 1 Thesis)*—which I love—kind of sums it all up.

The meaning of the crown that appears in so many of his works is obvious, and he had the courage to make sure the world knew that he was recognizing the kings and queens that defined *his* world history. It also signals to us that he knew he was himself a King.

We were raised to have incredible pride and confidence in who we are, what we can do, and where we came from. Our family would say, "You're a Basquiat, and this is the family that you come from. This is who we are." We were each clear about our identity through the many stories we were told about the roads that led us to where we are, and we—Jean-Michel, Jeanine, and I—feel, and felt, very confident in who we are individually and in who we are as Basquiats. Jean-Michel went into the world with that. LISANE

Pink Amos or Andy, 1983
Acrylic, oil stick, and Xerox collage on canvas
48 × 35⅝ in. (121.92 × 90.5 cm)

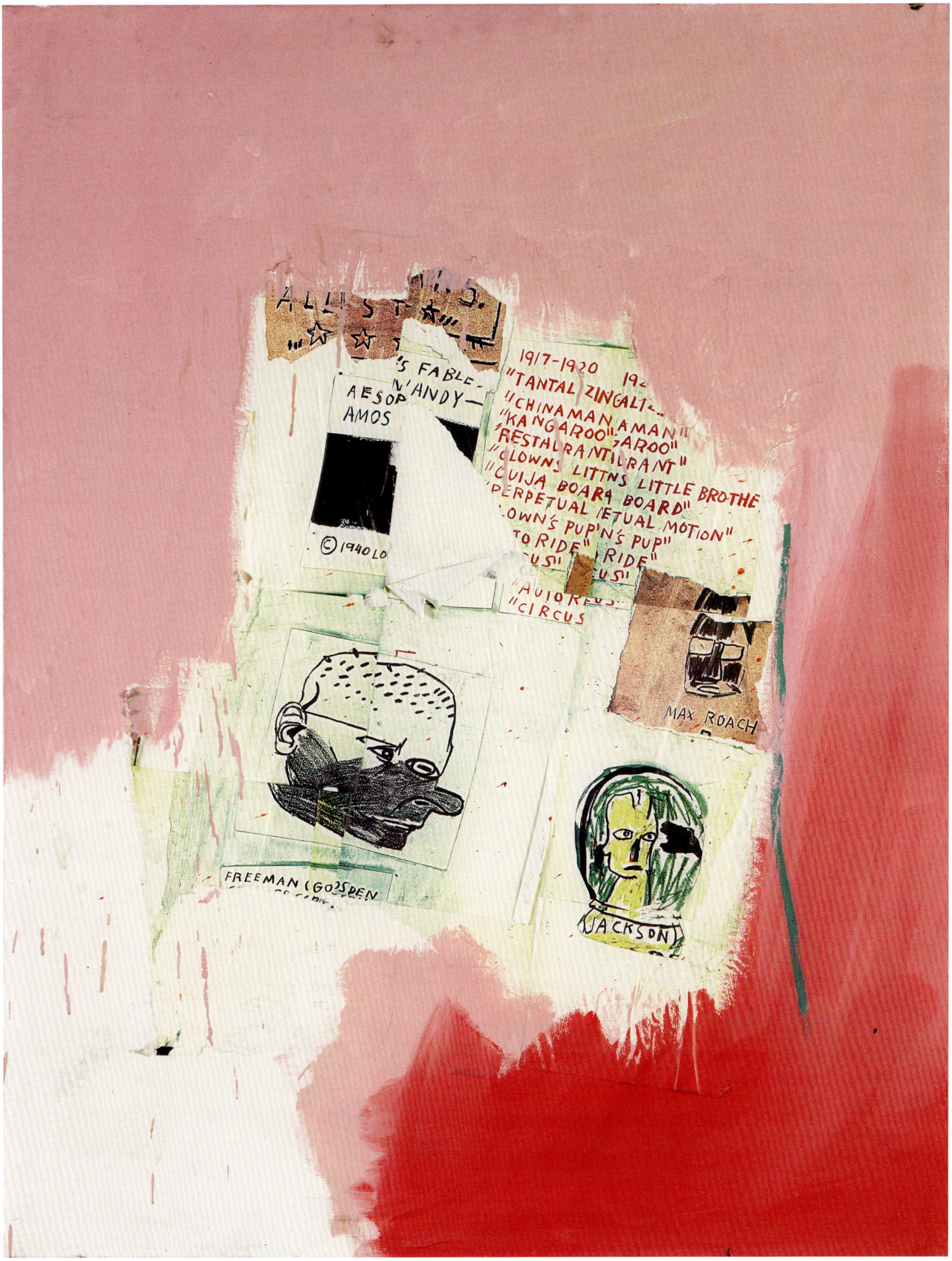
AESOP
AMOS
©1940
1917-1920
"CHINAMAN
"KANGAROO"
"CLOWNS
LITTLE BROTHE
"PERPETUAL
MOTION"
"CIRCUS
MAX ROACH
FREEMAN (GOSDEN
JACKSON

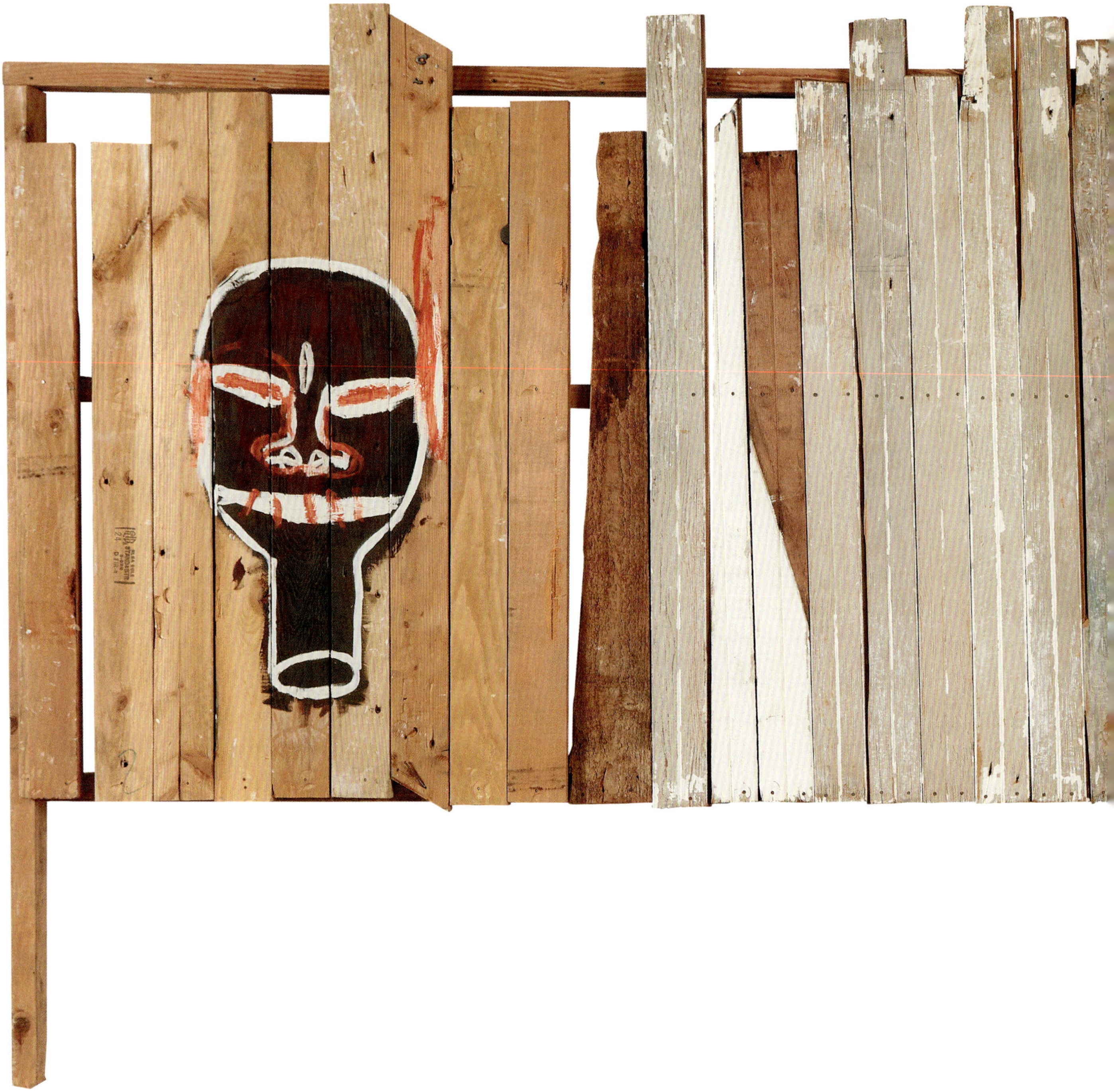

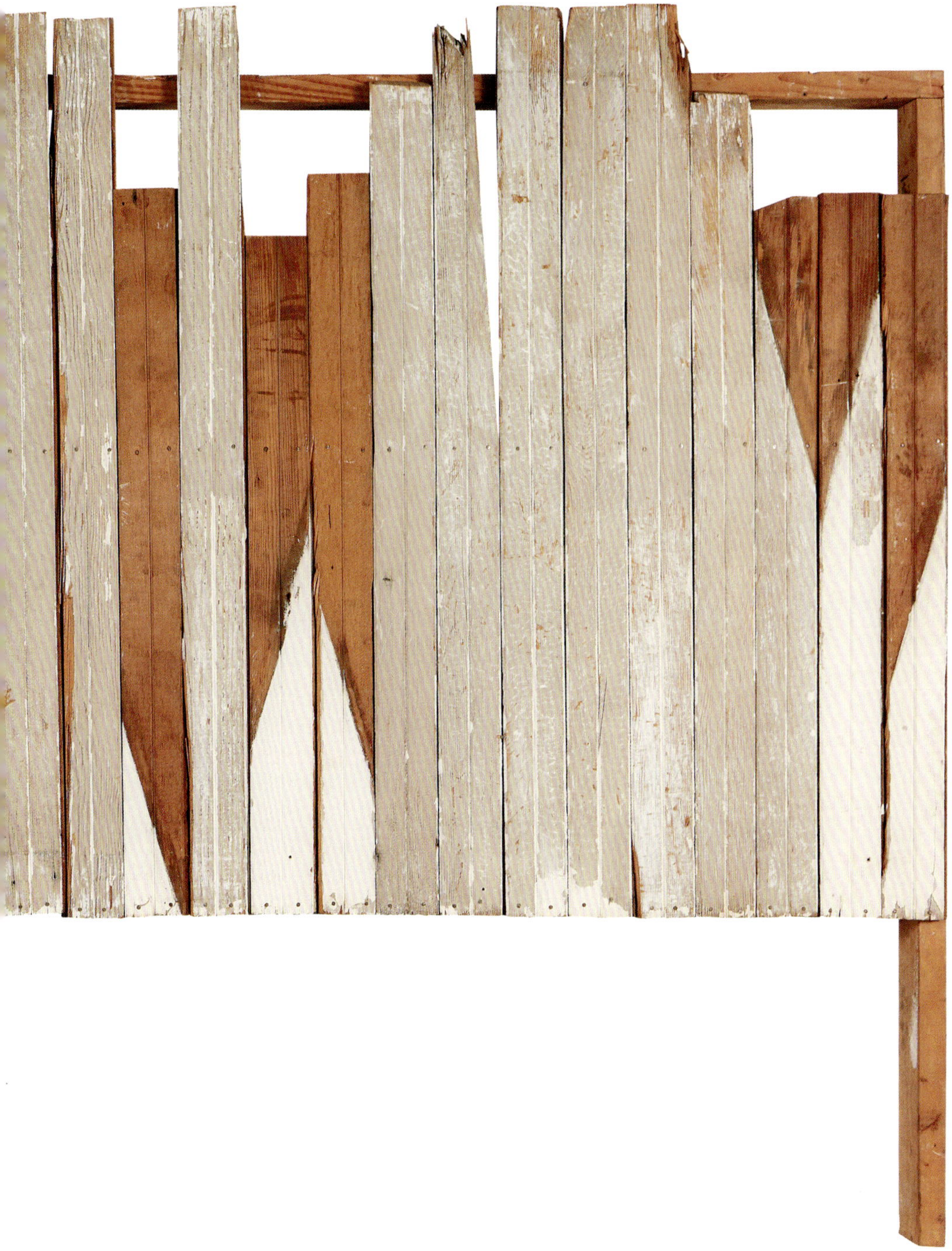

Untitled, 1984
Acrylic and oil stick on wood
67 × 120 × 4 in.
(170.18 × 304.8 × 10.16 cm)

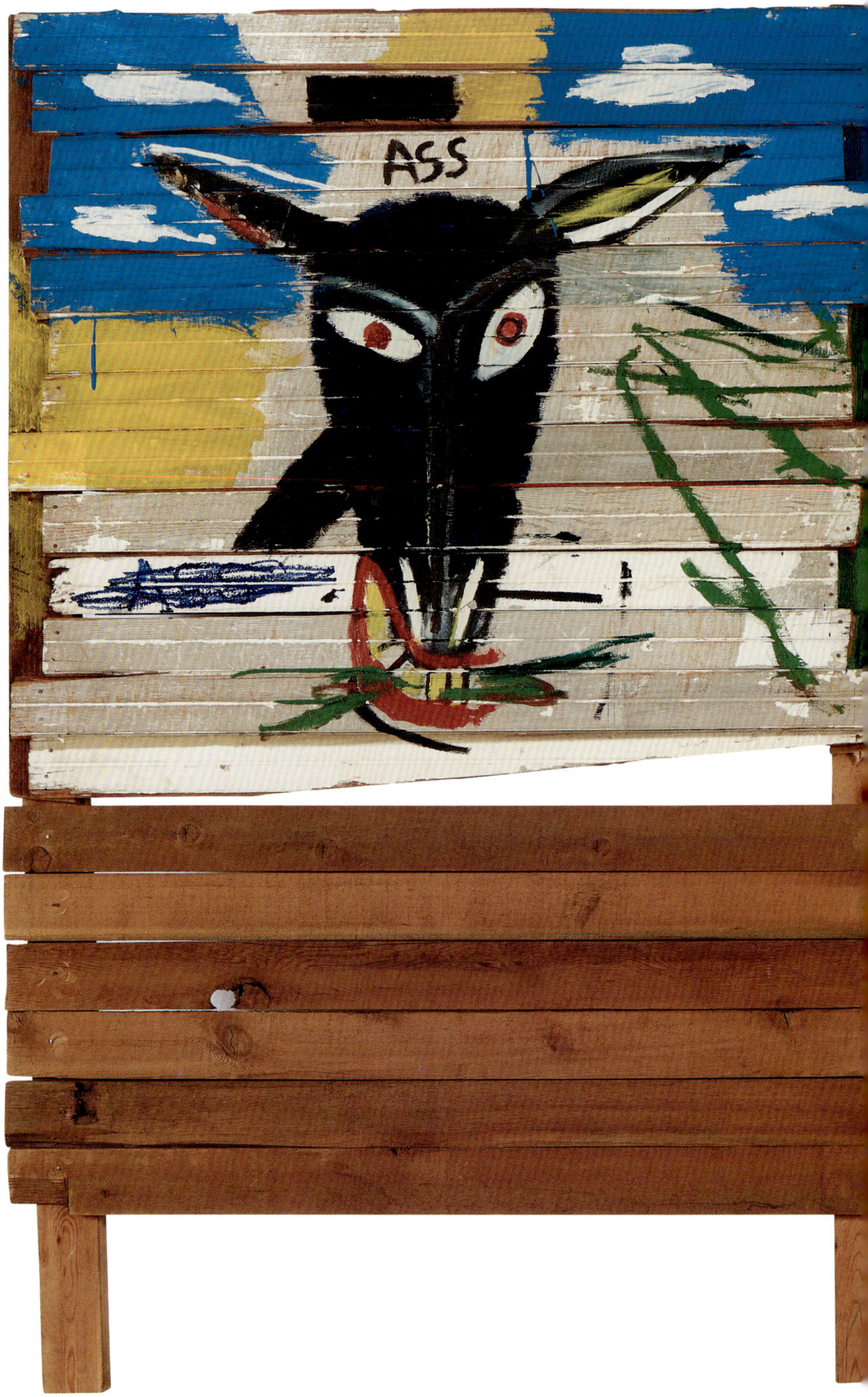
ASS

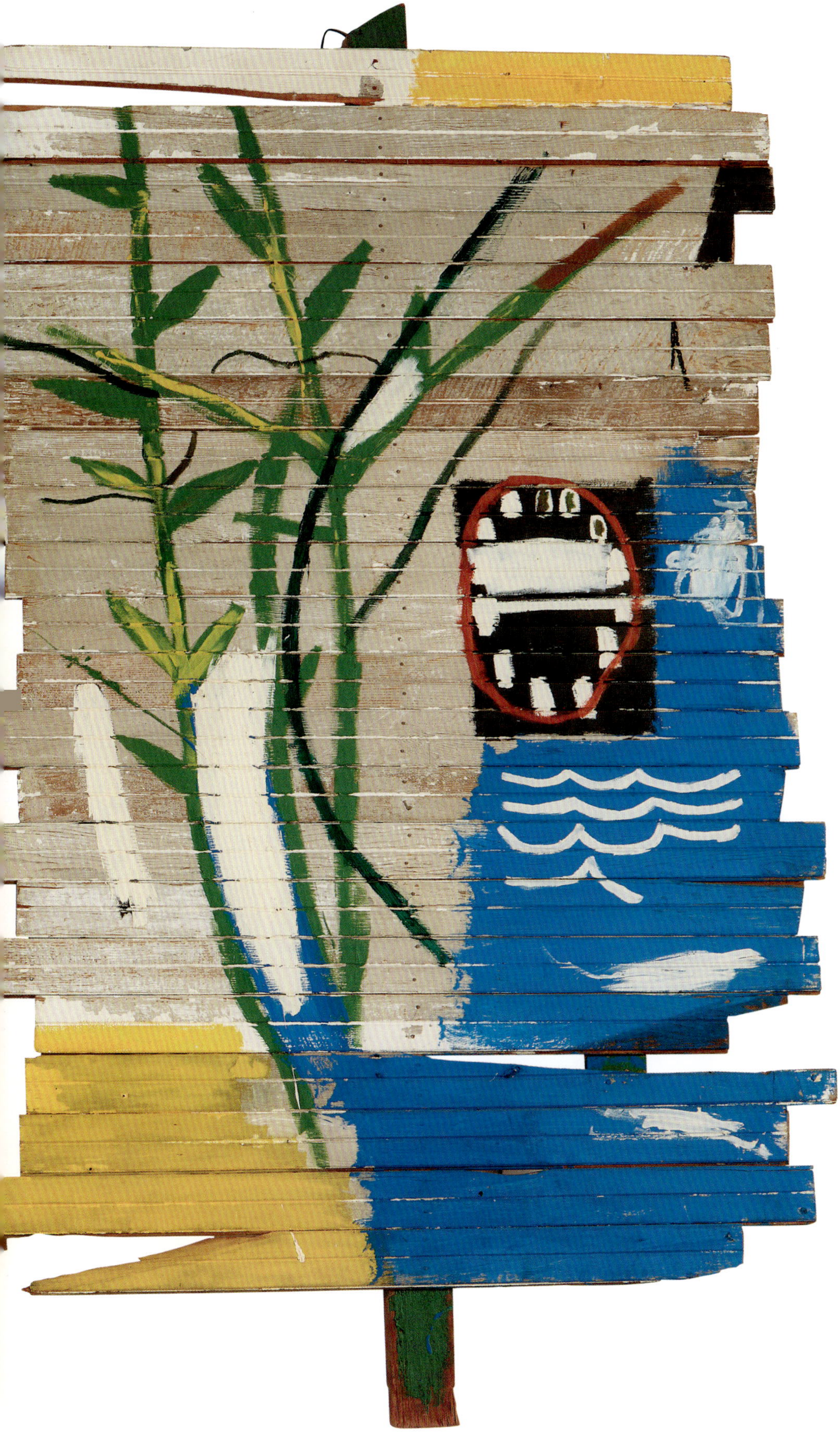

Untitled, 1984
Acrylic and oil stick on wood
84 × 99 × 10 in.
(213.36 × 251.46 × 25.4 cm)

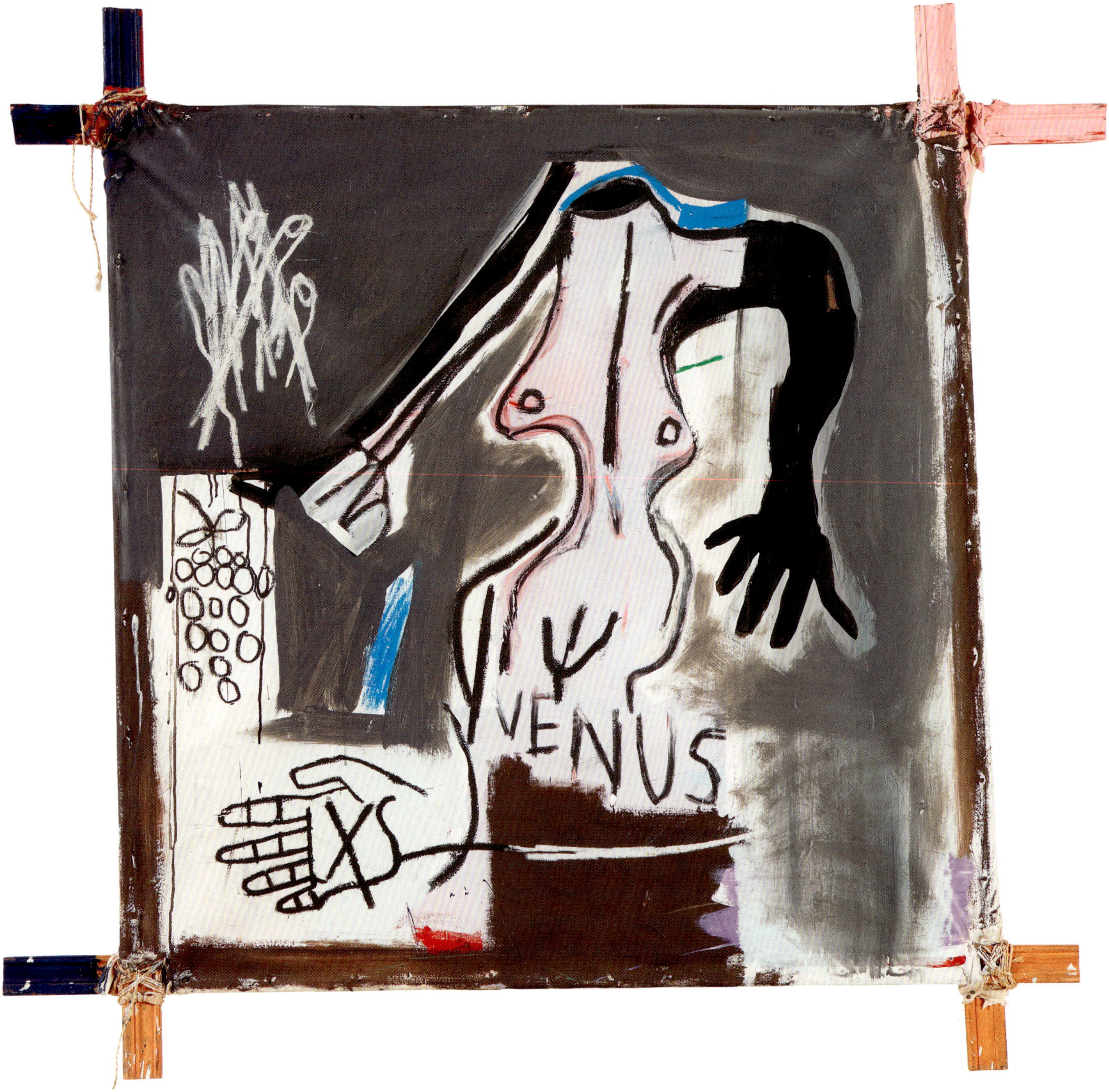

Untitled (Venus), 1982
Mixed media on canvas
with wood supports
61 × 61 in. (154.94 × 154.94 cm)

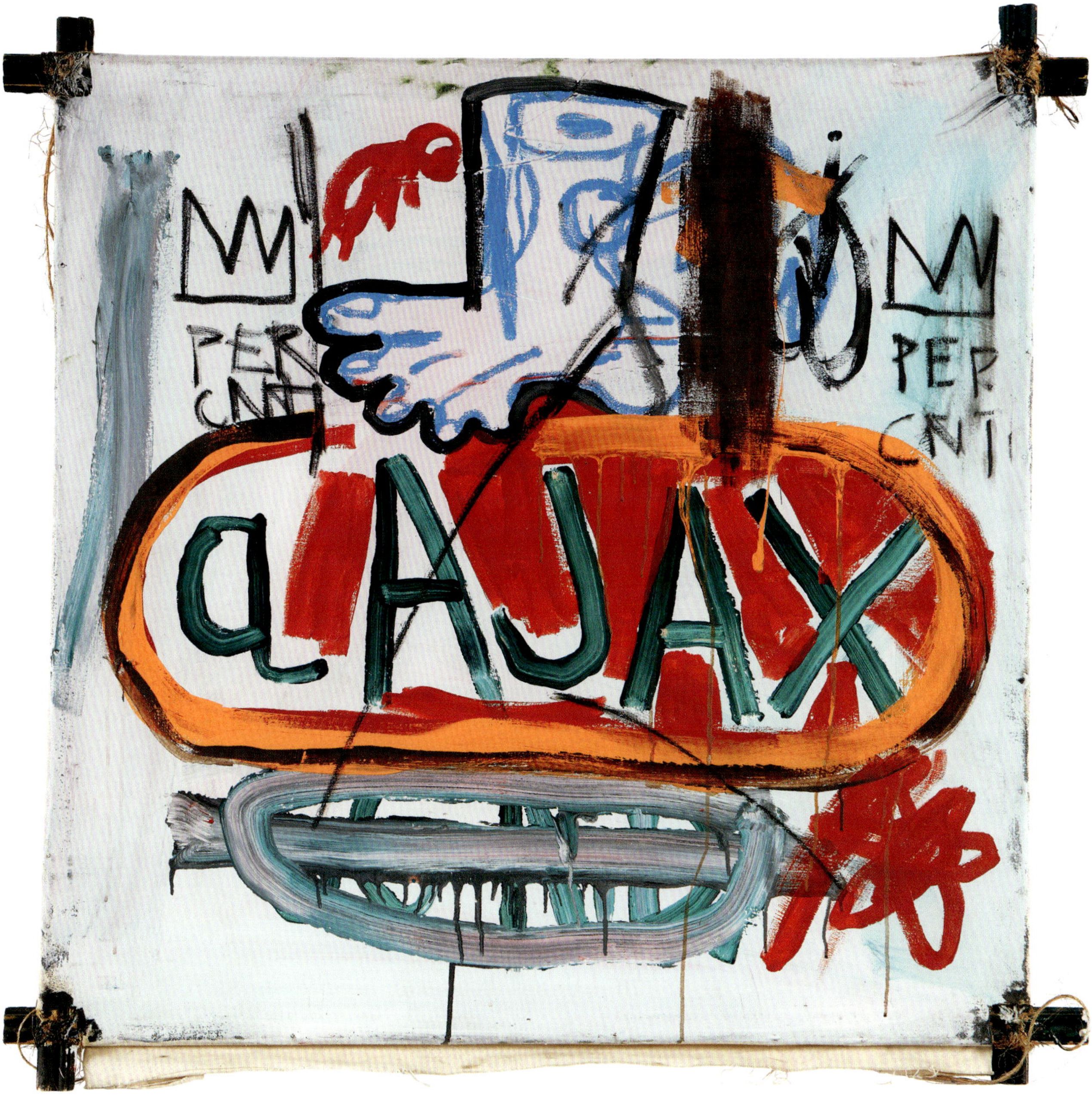

Untitled (Ajax), 1982
Acrylic and oil stick on
canvas with wood supports
48 × 48 in. (121.92 × 121.92 cm)

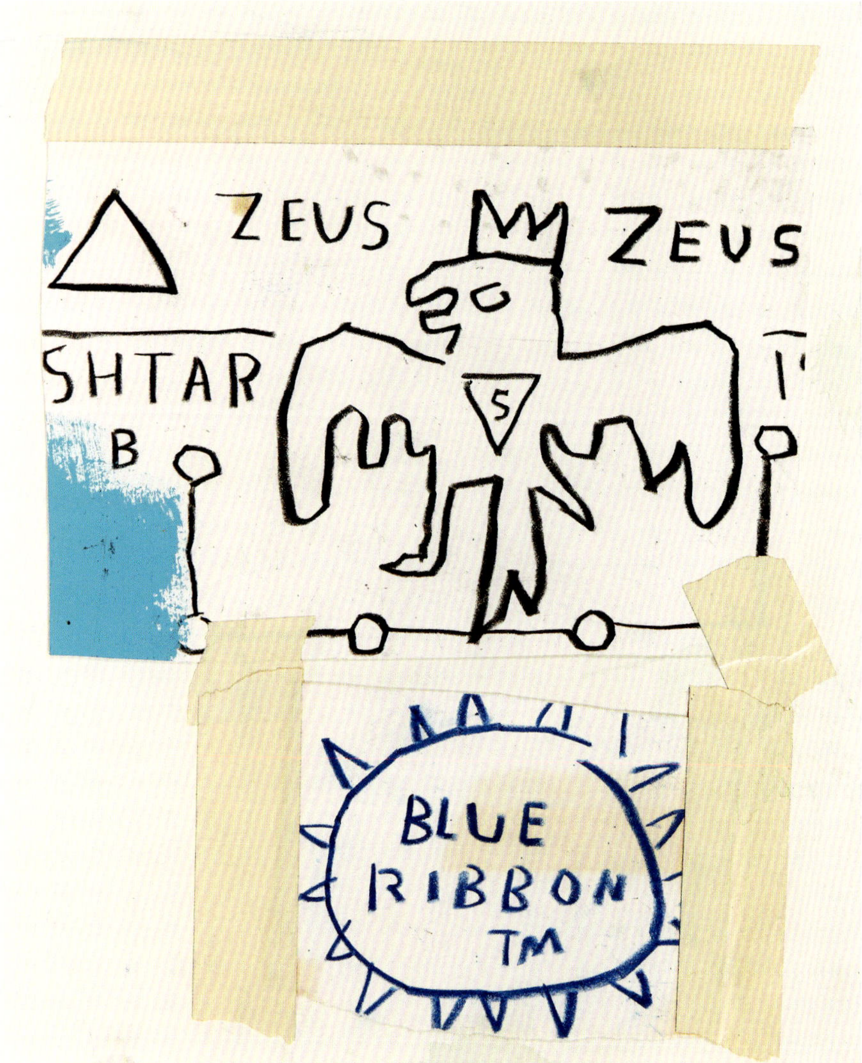

LEFT
Untitled (Zeus), n.d.
Acrylic, crayon, and masking tape with collage on paper
10½ × 8½ in. (26.67 × 21.59 cm)

BOTTOM
Untitled (Zoomorphic), n.d.
Acrylic and oil stick on paper
5¾ × 5 in. (14.6 × 12.7 cm)

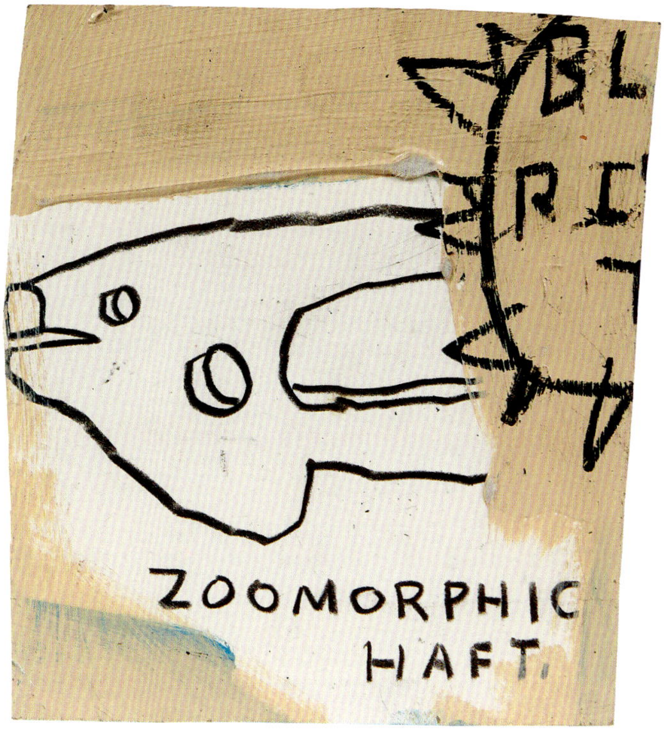

Untitled (Blue Ribbon), n.d.
Acrylic, masking tape, and
oil stick with collage on paper
10½ × 8½ in. (26.67 × 21.59 cm)

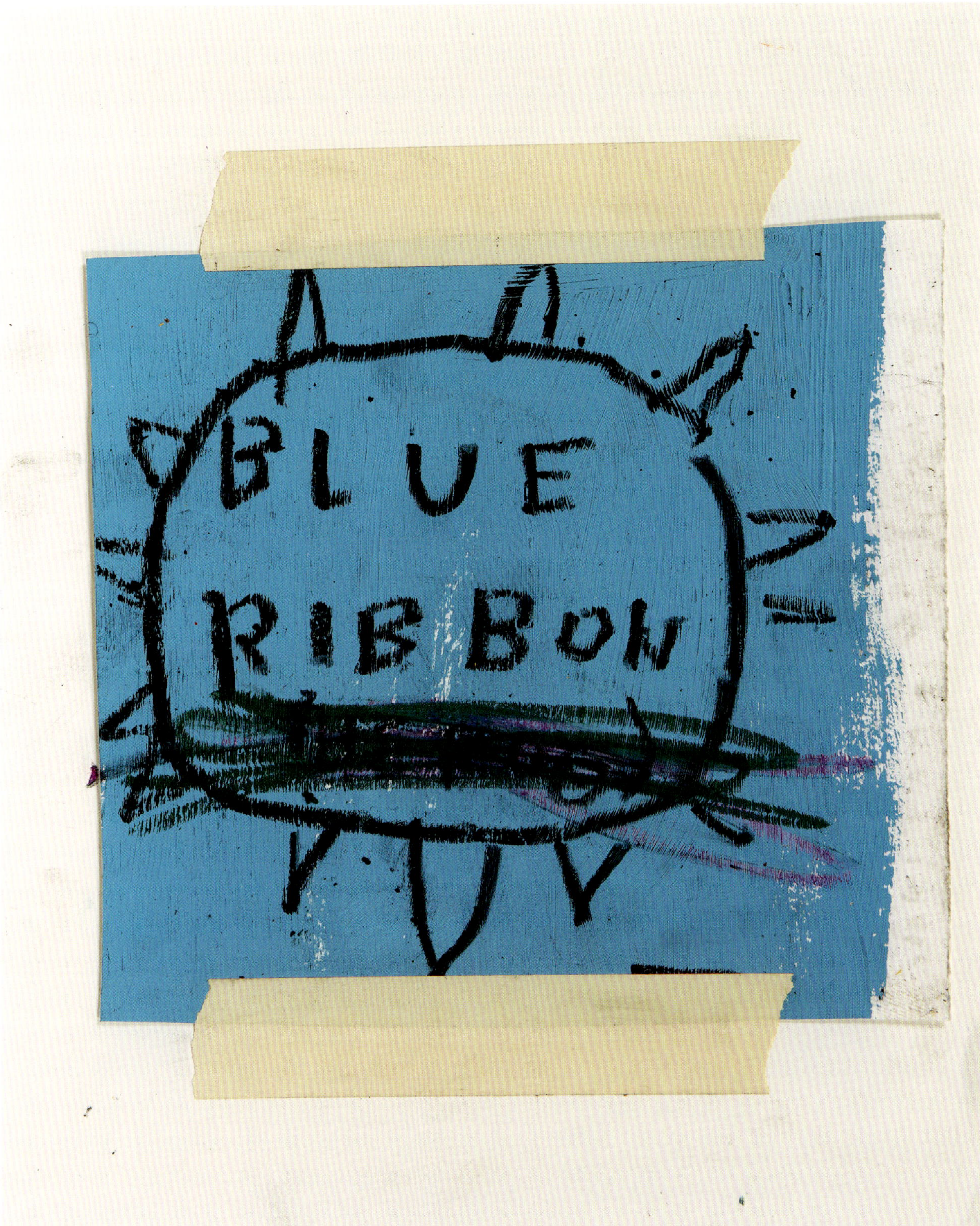

Untitled, 1985
Acrylic and silkscreen on canvas
66 × 60½ in. (167.64 × 153.67 cm)

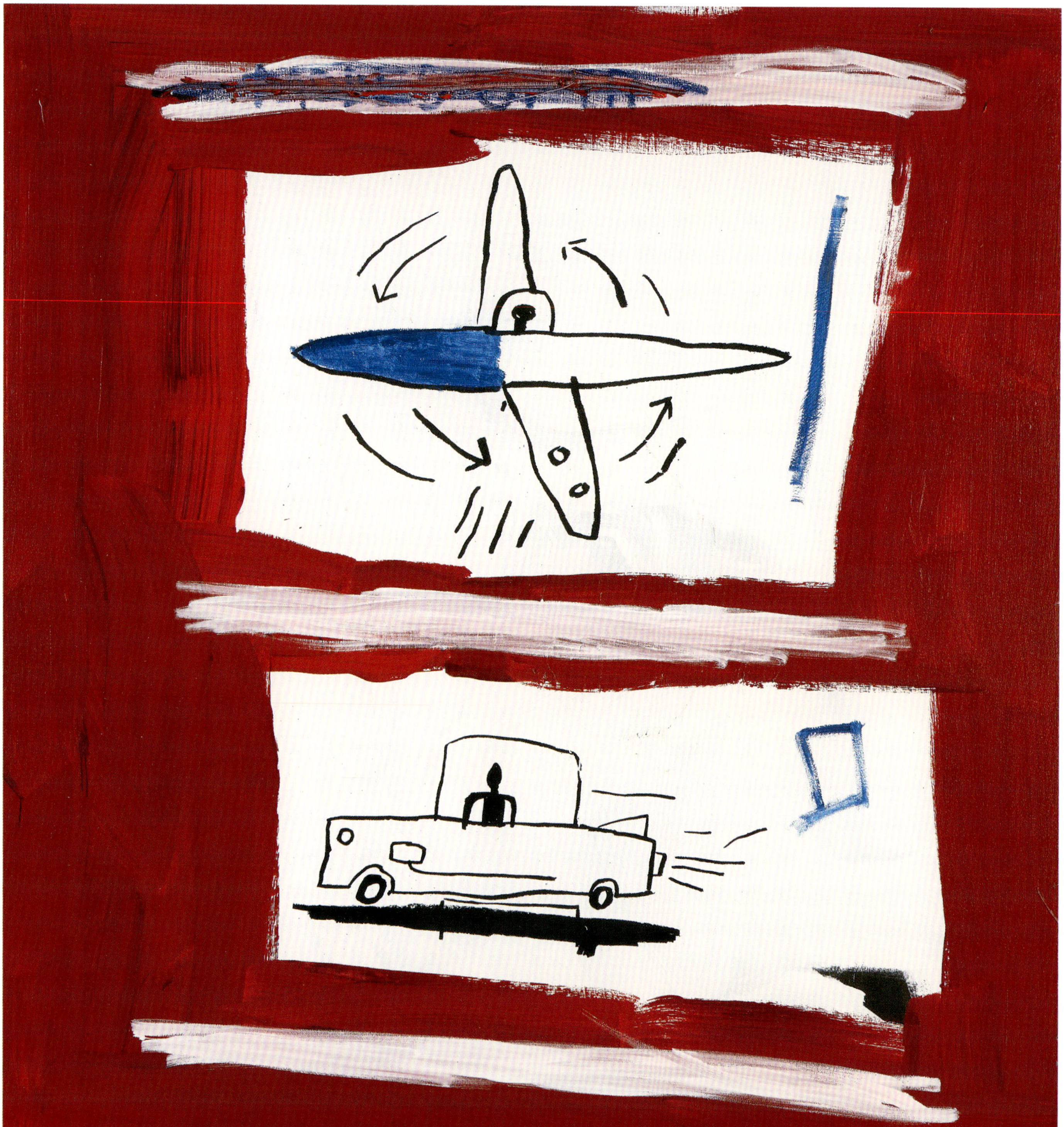

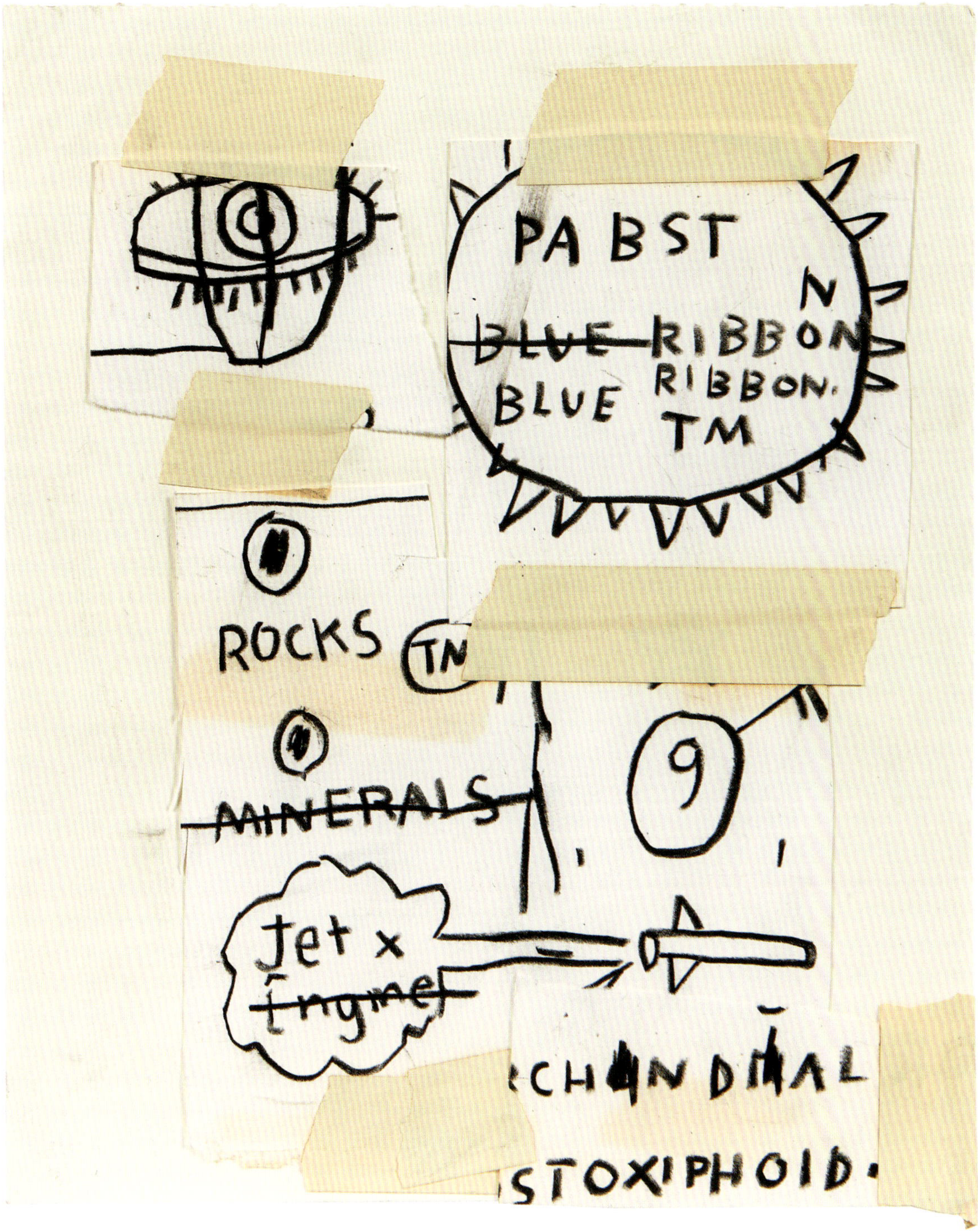

Untitled (Pabst), n.d.
Graphite and masking tape
with collage on paper
10½ × 8⅜ in. (26.67 × 20.42 cm)

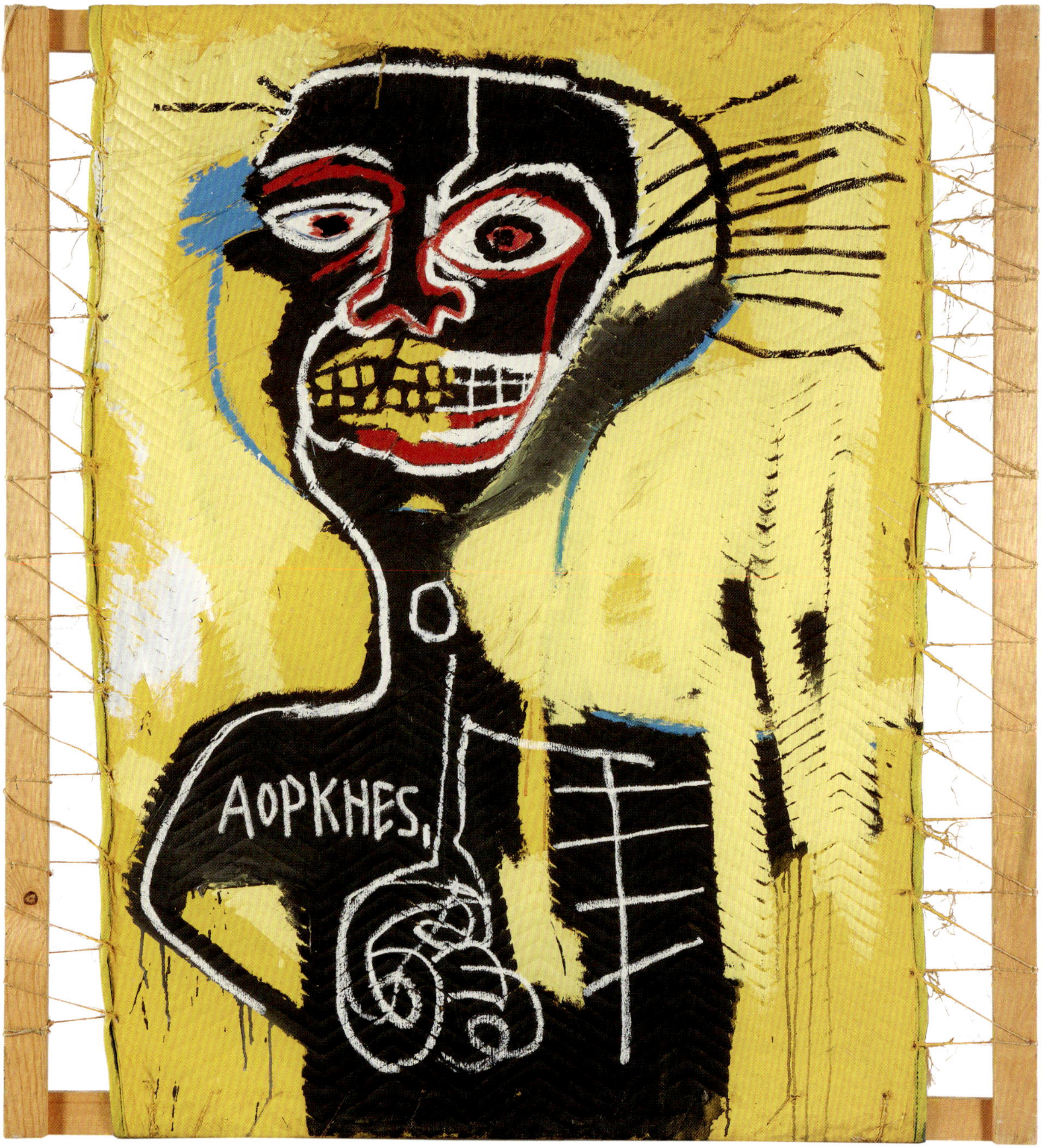

Cabeza, 1982
Acrylic and oil stick on blanket mounted on tied wood supports
66¾ × 60 in. (169.55 × 15.4 cm)

Untitled (Sin Hueso), n.d.
Acrylic, crayon, and oil stick
on paper
20¼ × 14½ in. (51.44 × 36.83 cm)

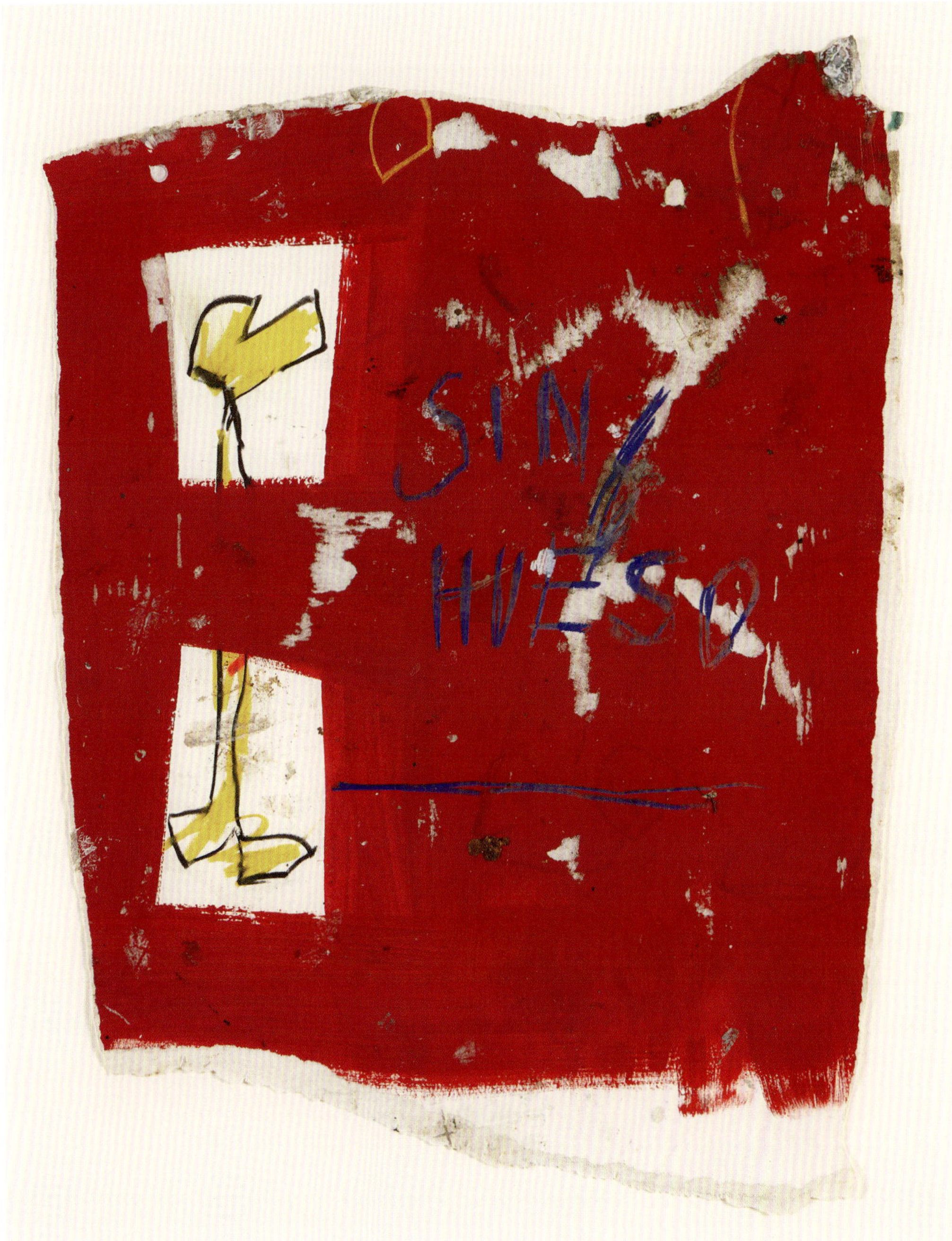

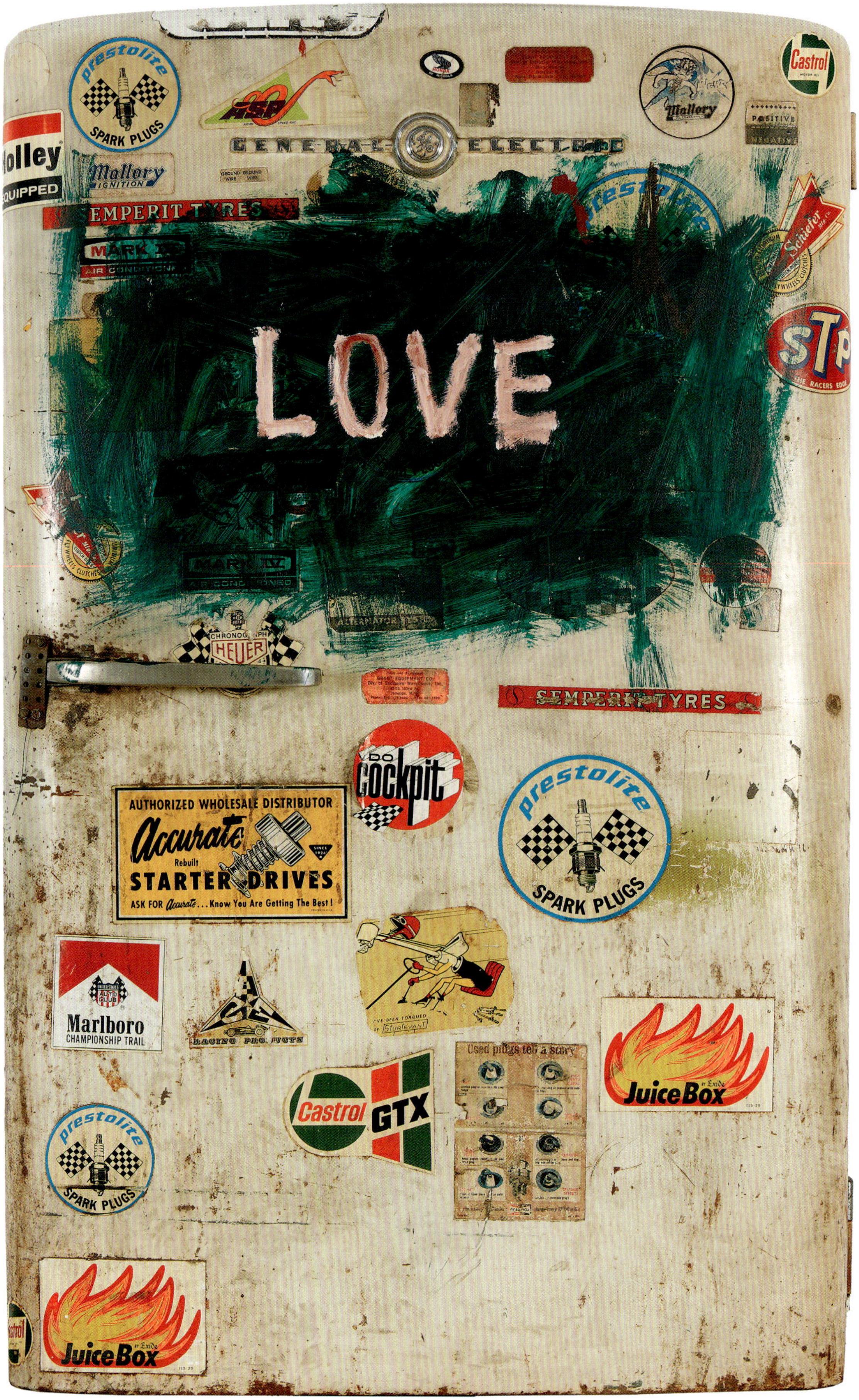
prestolite
SPARK PLUGS
Castrol
Mallory
Holley
EQUIPPED
Mallory
IGNITION
SEMPERIT TYRES
LOVE
STP
THE RACERS EDGE
CHRONOGRAPH
HEUER
SEMPERIT TYRES
cockpit
AUTHORIZED WHOLESALE DISTRIBUTOR
Accurate
Rebuilt
STARTER DRIVES
ASK FOR Accurate... Know You Are Getting The Best!
prestolite
SPARK PLUGS
Marlboro
CHAMPIONSHIP TRAIL
RACING PRODUCTS
Castrol GTX
Used plugs tell a story
Juice Box
by Exide
prestolite
SPARK PLUGS
Juice Box
by Exide

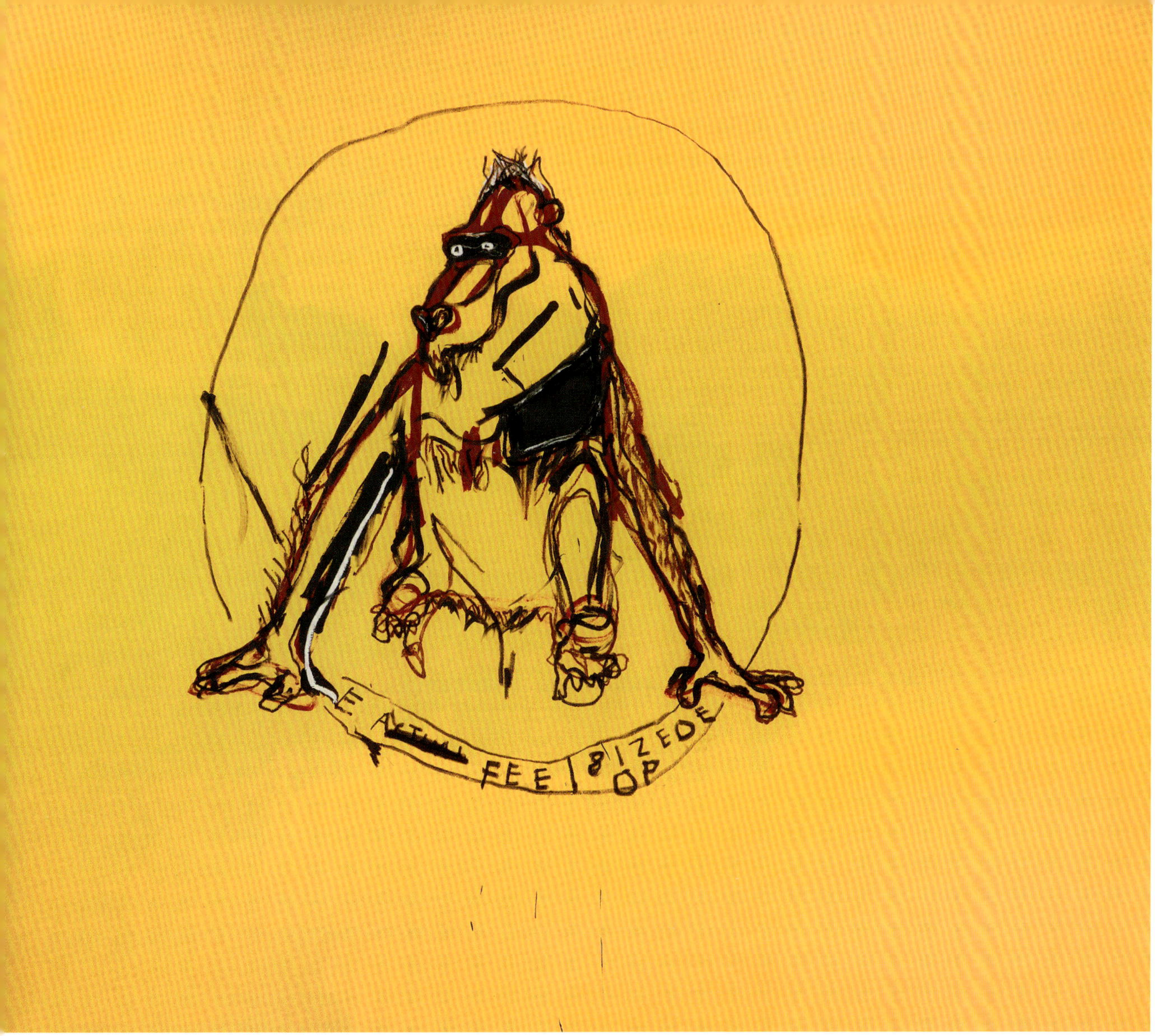

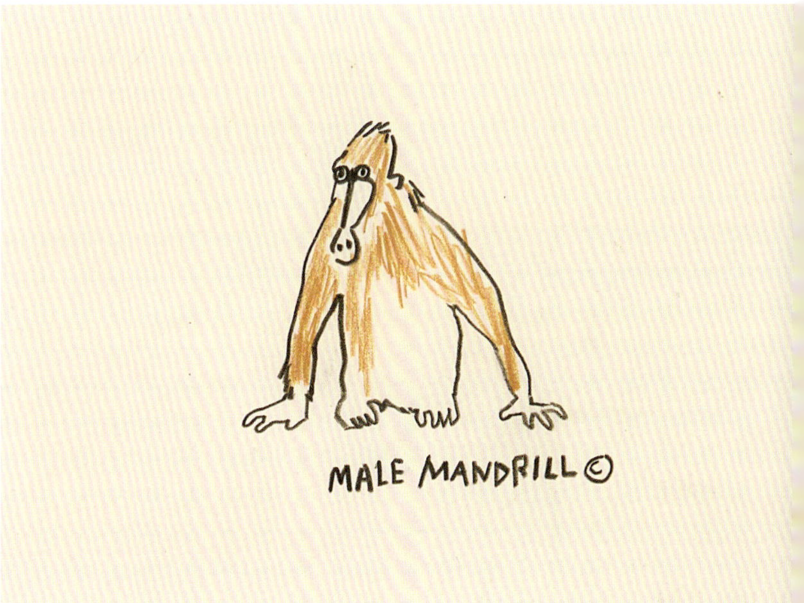

OPPOSITE
Untitled (Love), 1984
Acrylic, oil stick, and paper collage on refrigerator door
49¼ × 30 × 5 in.
(125.10 × 76.2 × 12.7 cm)

TOP
Dry Cell, 1988
Acrylic on canvas
120 × 120 in. (304.8 × 304.8 cm)
COLLECTION OF NORA FITZPATRICK

RIGHT
Untitled (Male Mandrill), n.d.
Colored pencil and graphite on paper
22¼ × 30 in. (56.52 × 76.2 cm)

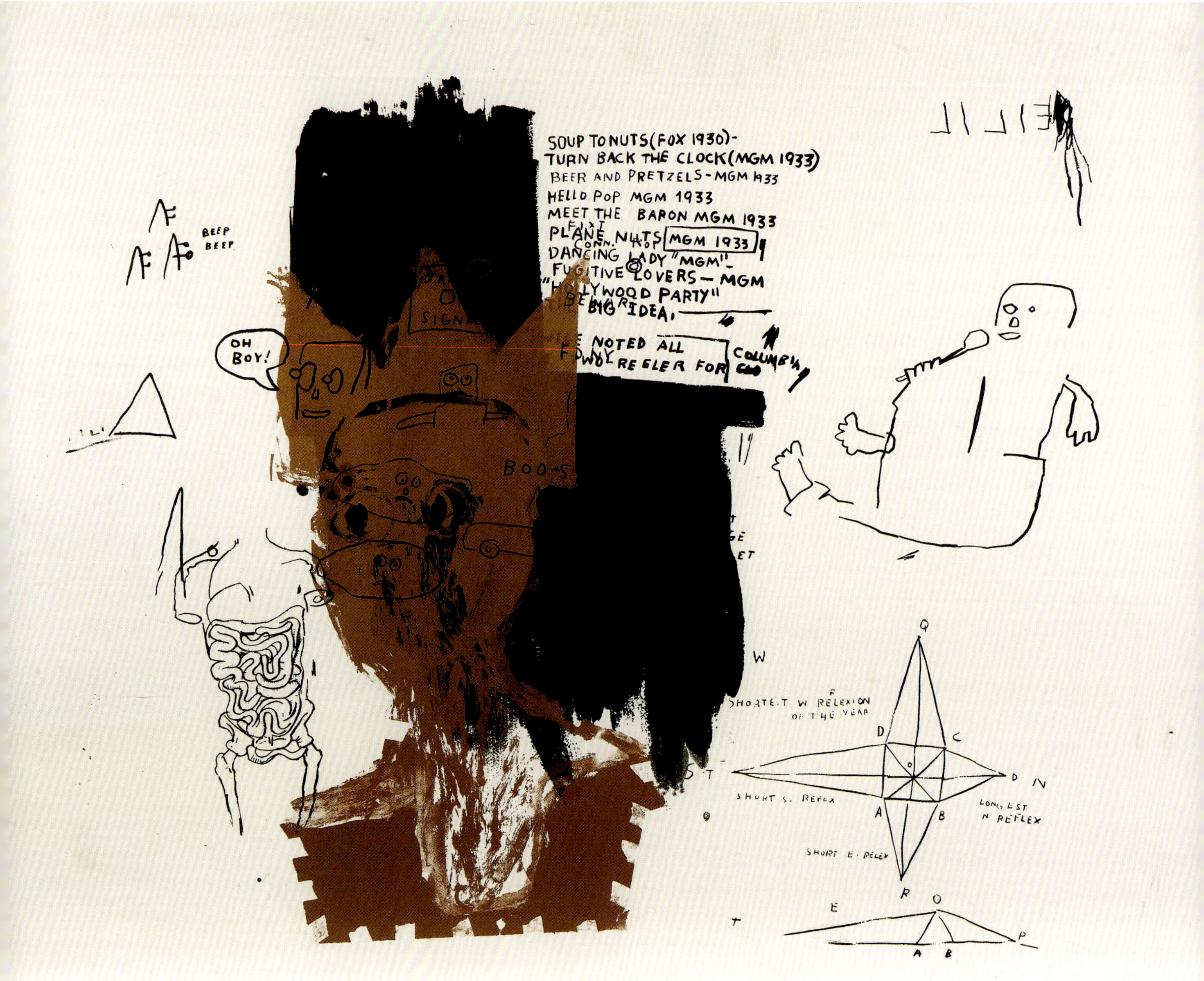

ABOVE
Untitled (Soup to Nuts), n.d.
Color monotype on paper
36 × 60 in. (91.44 × 152.4 cm)

OPPOSITE
Untitled, 1982
Acrylic and oil stick on canvas
48 × 29⅝ in. (121.92 × 75.62 cm)

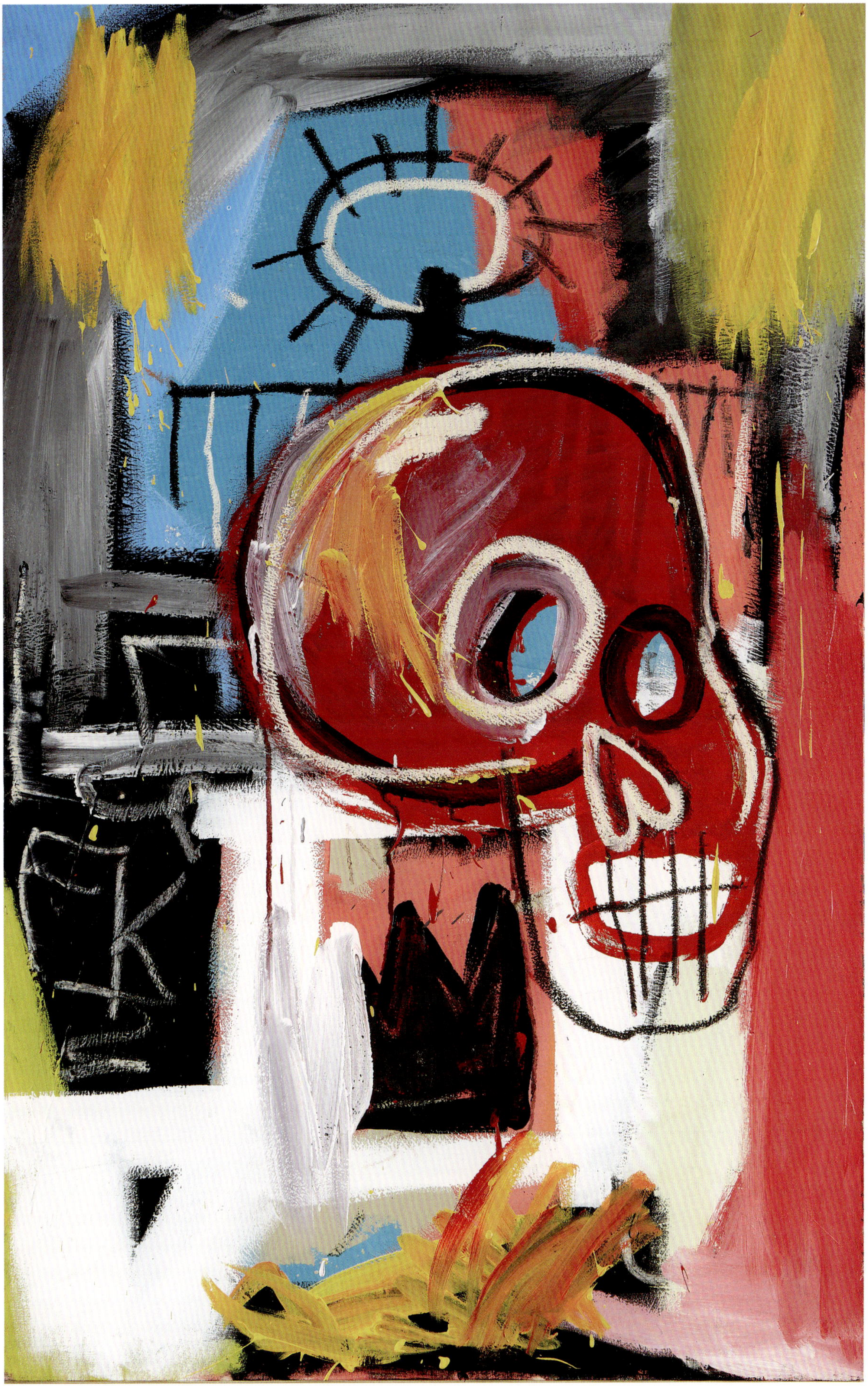

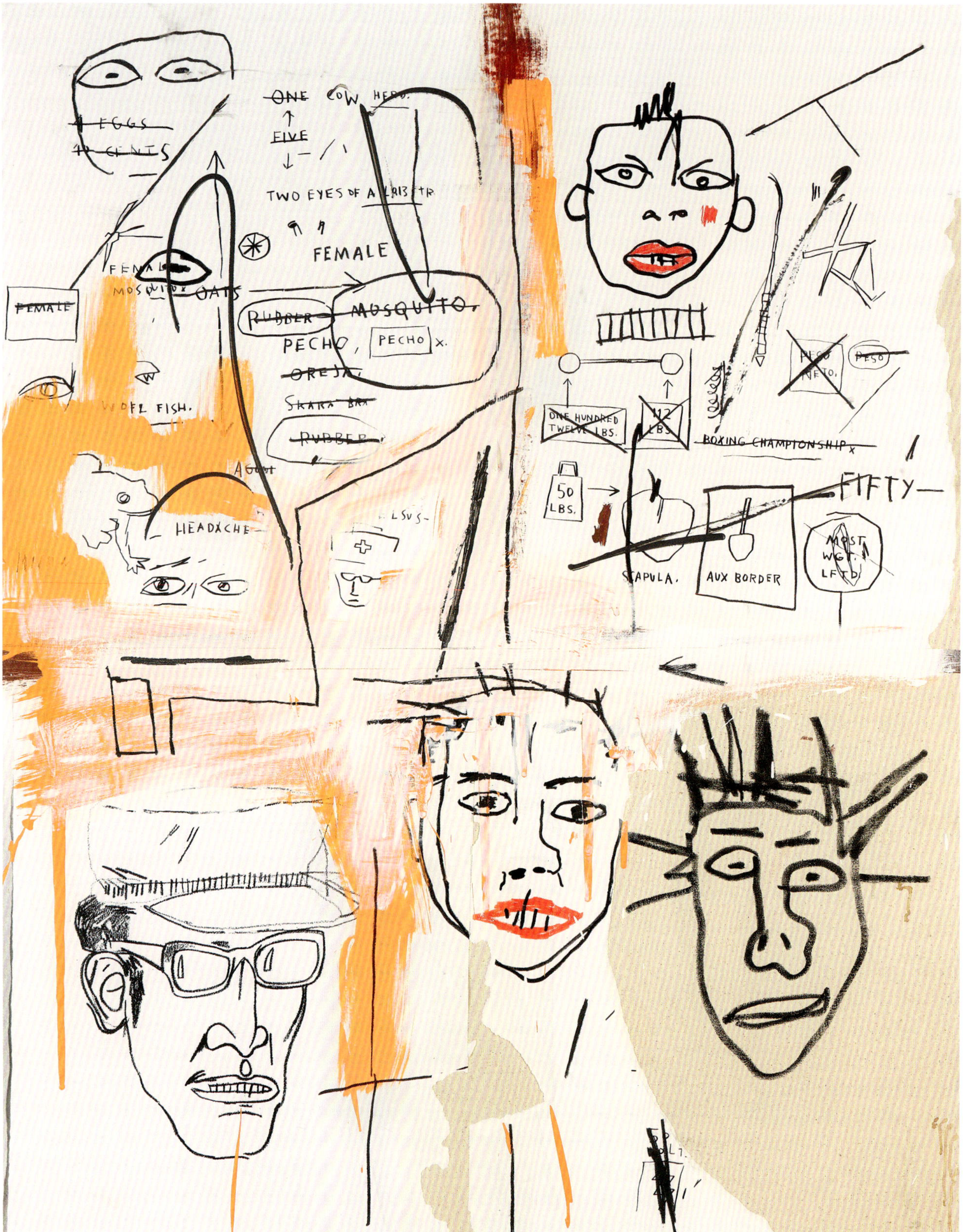
ONE COW HERD.
FIVE
EGGS
CENTS
TWO EYES OF A
FEMALE
OATS
FEMALE
RUBBER
MOSQUITO.
PECHO,
PECHO x.
OREJA
WOLF FISH.
RUBBER
HEADACHE
ONE HUNDRED TWELVE LBS.
112 LBS.
PESO
BOXING CHAMPIONSHIP x
50 LBS.
FIFTY
SCAPULA.
AUX BORDER
MOST WGT. LFTD.
TREE

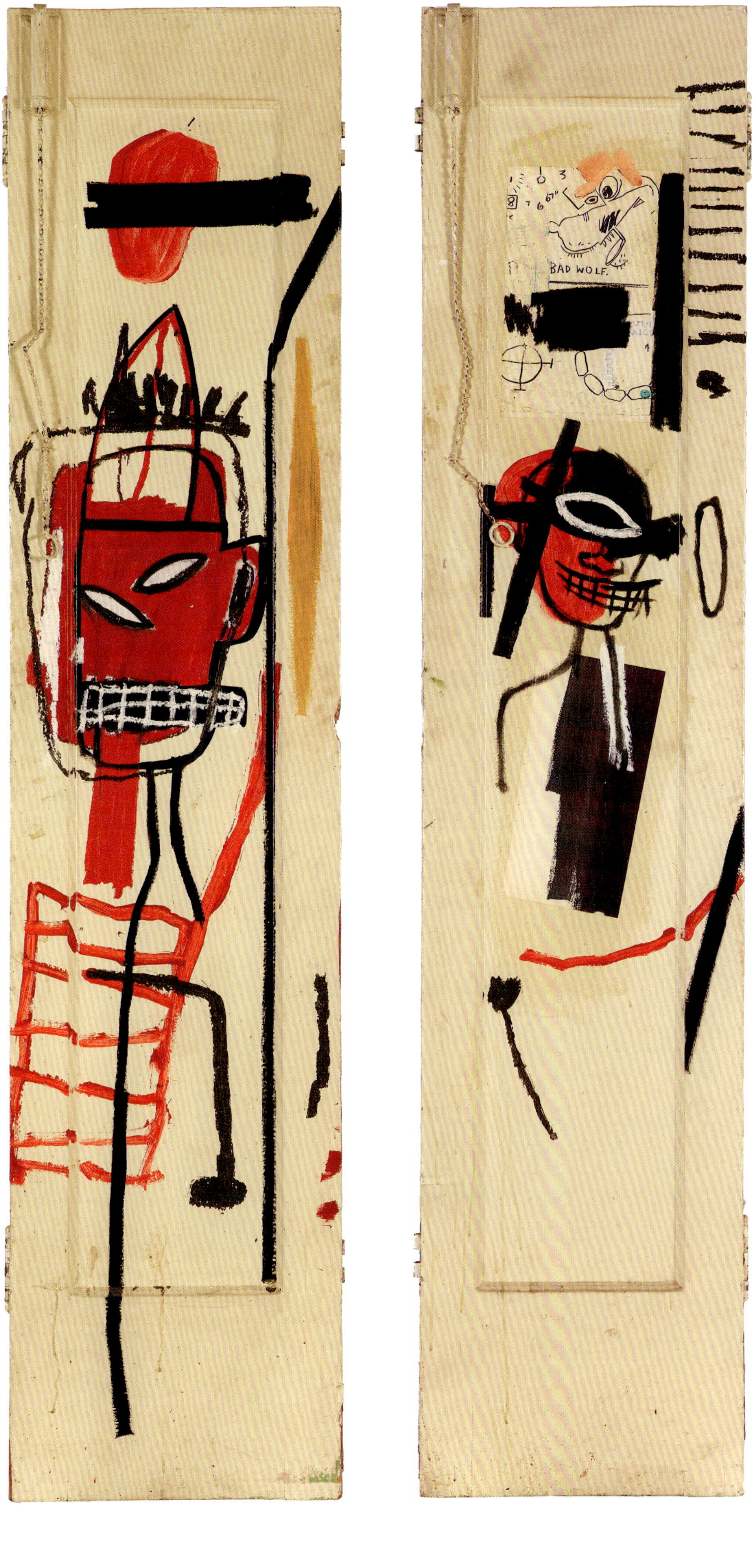

OPPOSITE
Untitled, n.d.
Acrylic, oil stick, and photocopy on canvas
84 × 60 in. (213.36 × 152.4 cm)

RIGHT
Untitled, n.d.
Acrylic, oil stick, and color photocopy on wood hinged door (double-sided)
82 × 18 in. (208.28 × 45.72 cm)

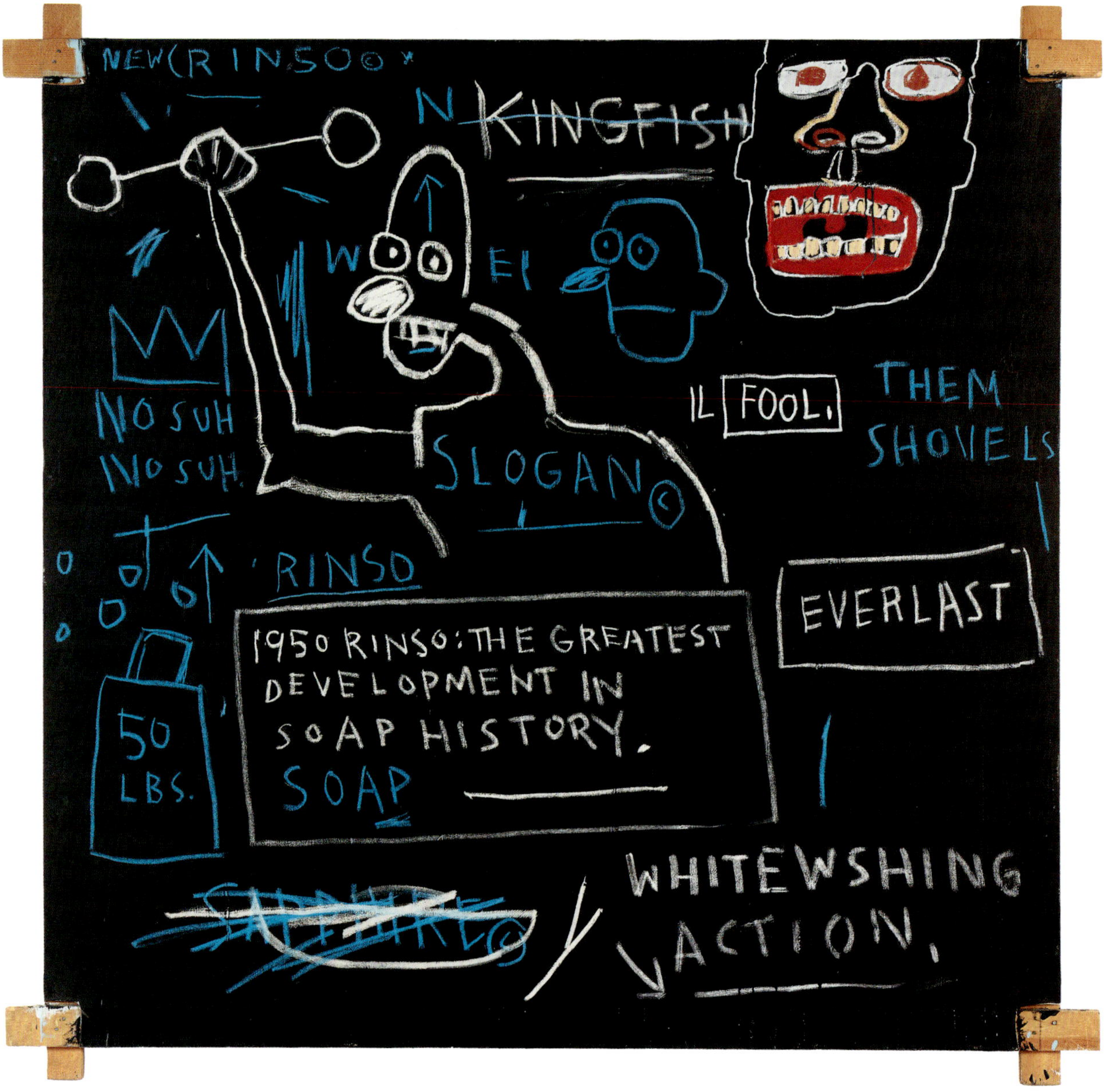

Untitled (Rinso), 1982
Acrylic and oil stick on canvas
with wood supports
72 × 72 in. (182.88 × 182.88 cm)

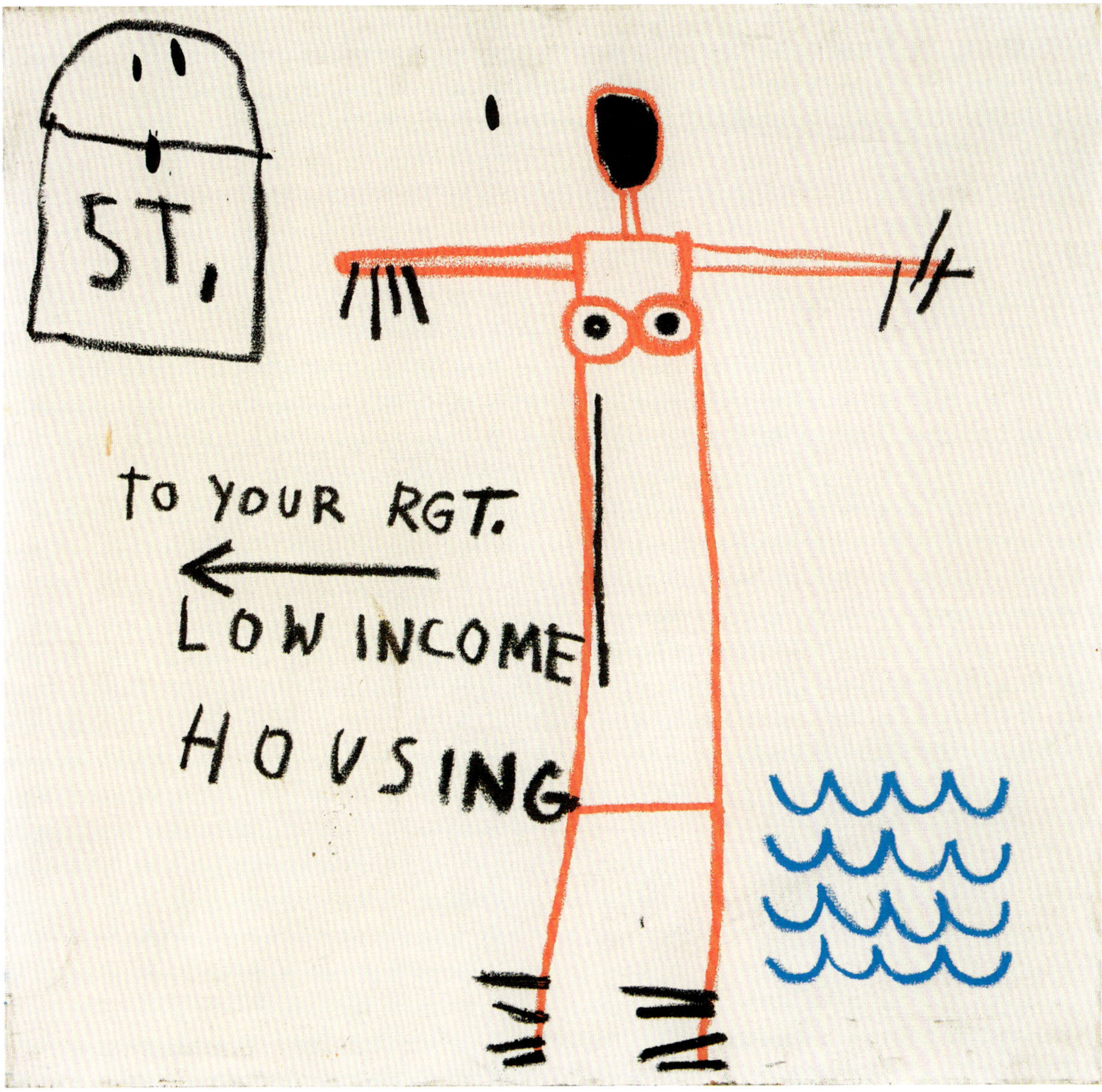

Untitled (Low Income Housing), n.d.
Acrylic and oil stick on canvas
36 × 36 in. (91.44 × 91.44 cm)

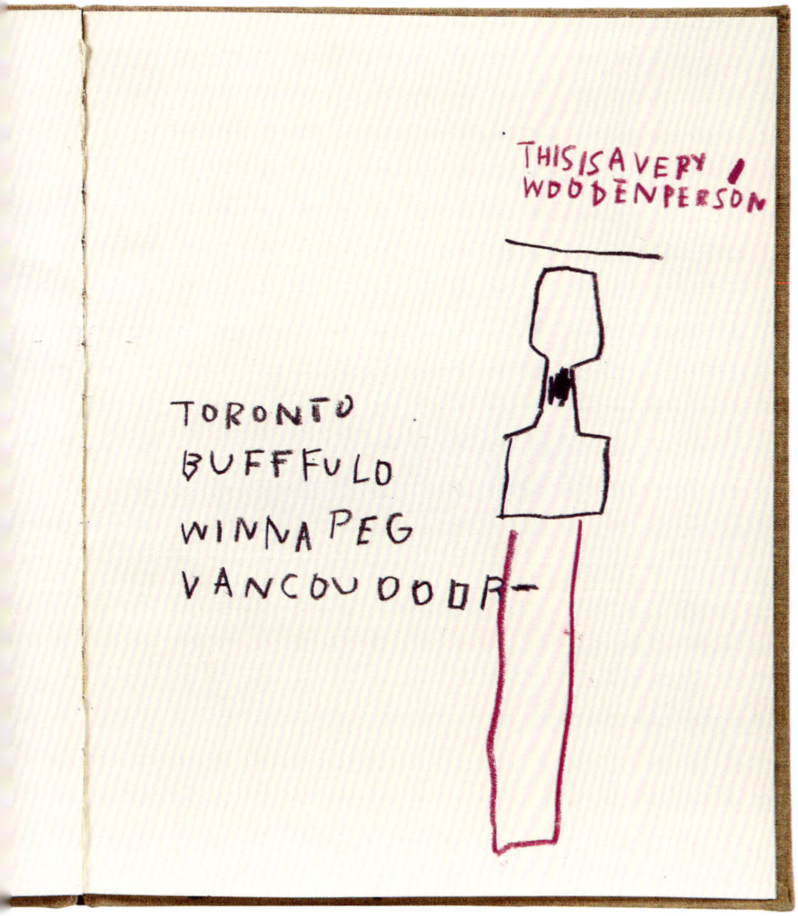
THISISAVERY
WOODENPERSON
TORONTO
BUFFFULO
WINNAPEG
VANCOUOOOR-

GRACE JONES
15,000$
JEAN MICHEL BASQ.
57 GREAT JONES ST.
N.Y.C.

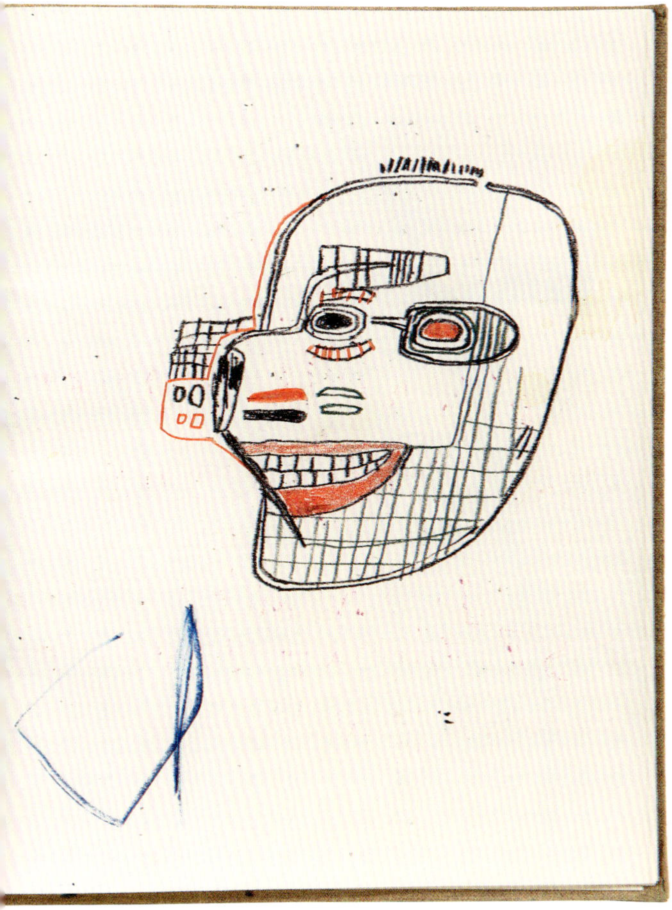

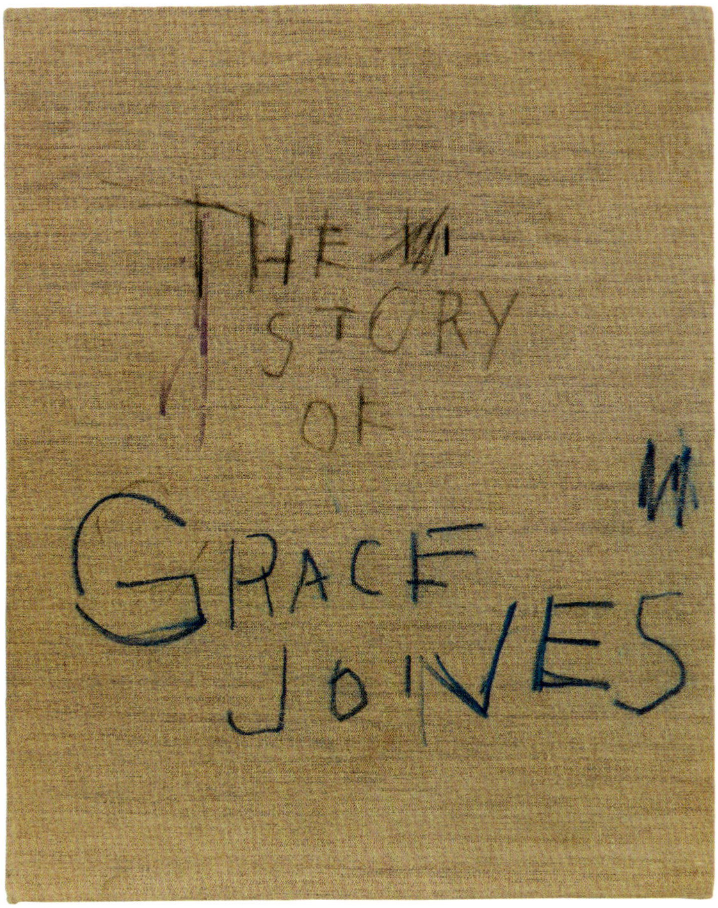

OPPOSITE AND ABOVE
The Story of Grace Jones notebook, interior pages, n.d.
Graphite, colored pencil, ink, and oil stick on paper
28 × 48 in (71.12 × 121.92 cm)

ABOVE RIGHT
The Story of Grace Jones notebook, n.d.
Colored pencil and oil stick on cloth covered cardboard
18 × 24 in. (45.72 × 35.56 cm)

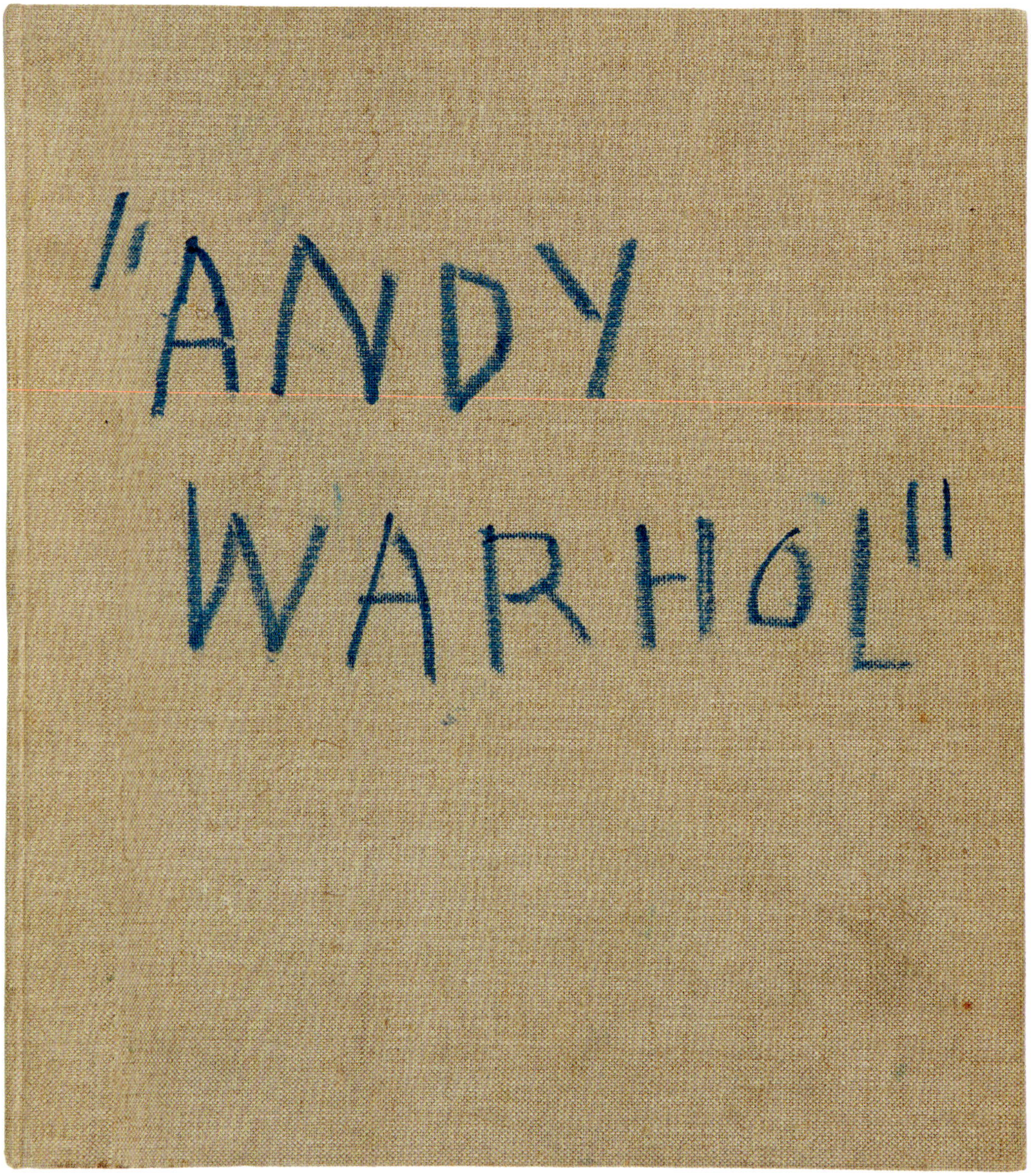

"Andy Warhol" notebook, n.d.
Graphite, colored pencil, ink, and oil stick on paper; cloth cover, 25 pages of handwritten text and drawings
14¾ × 12¾ in. (37.47 × 32.39 cm)

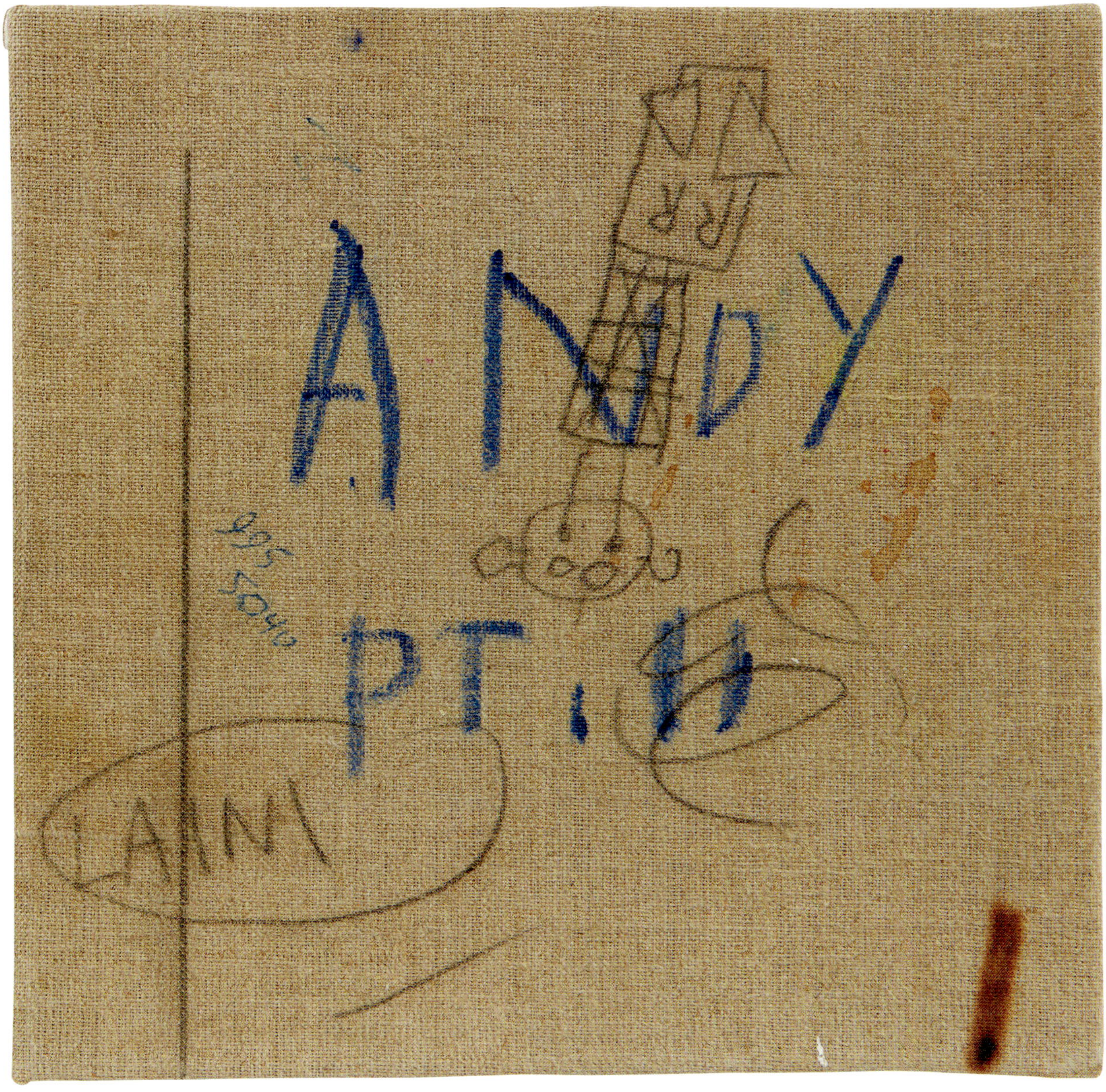

Andy PT. II notebook, n.d.
Colored pencil, graphite, and crayon on paper; cloth cover, 13 pages of handwritten text and drawings
10 × 10 in. (25.4 × 25.4 cm)

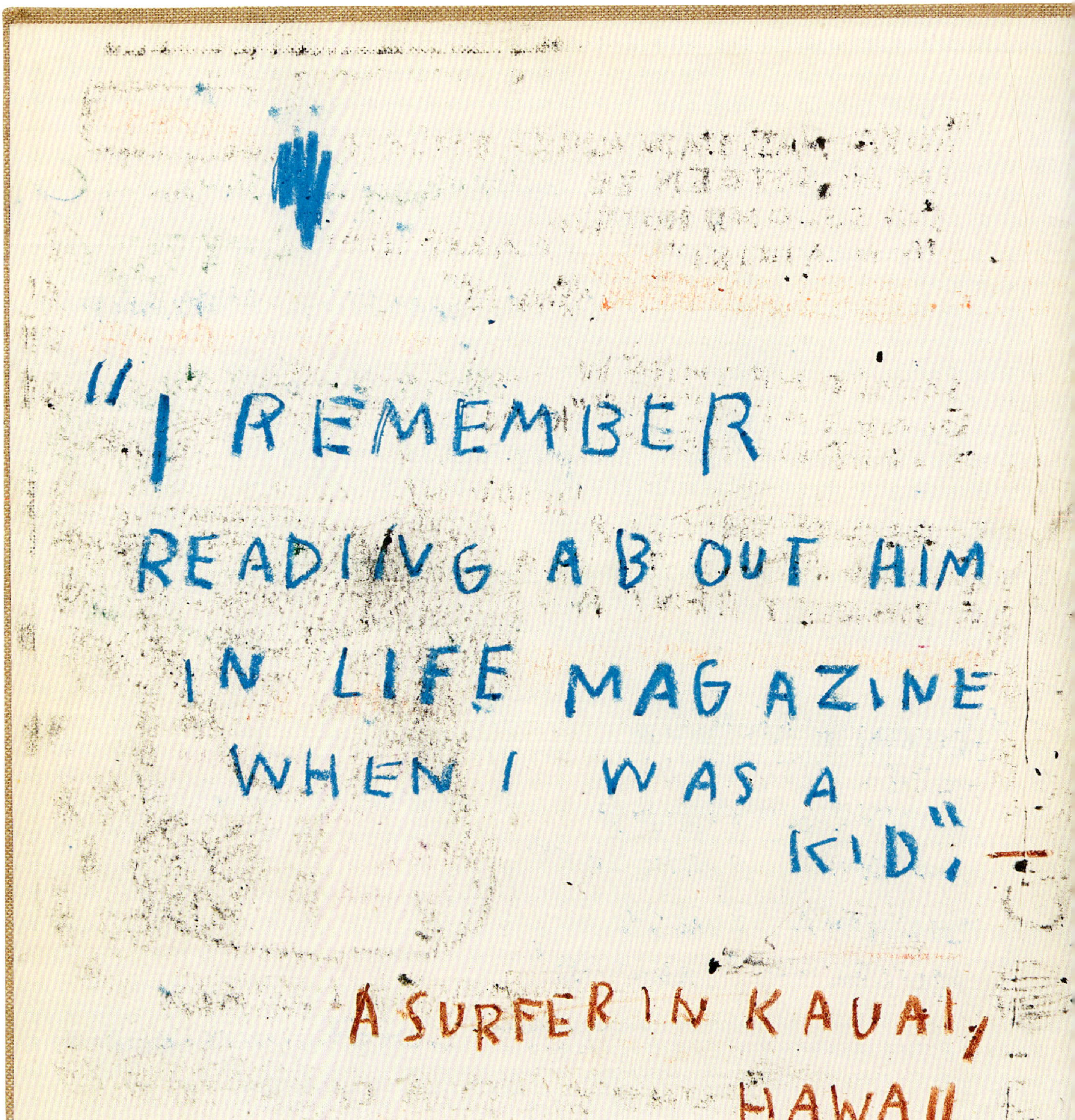
"I REMEMBER
READING ABOUT HIM
IN LIFE MAGAZINE
WHEN I WAS A
KID".
A SURFER IN KAUAI,
HAWAII
NOV, 12 · 1983

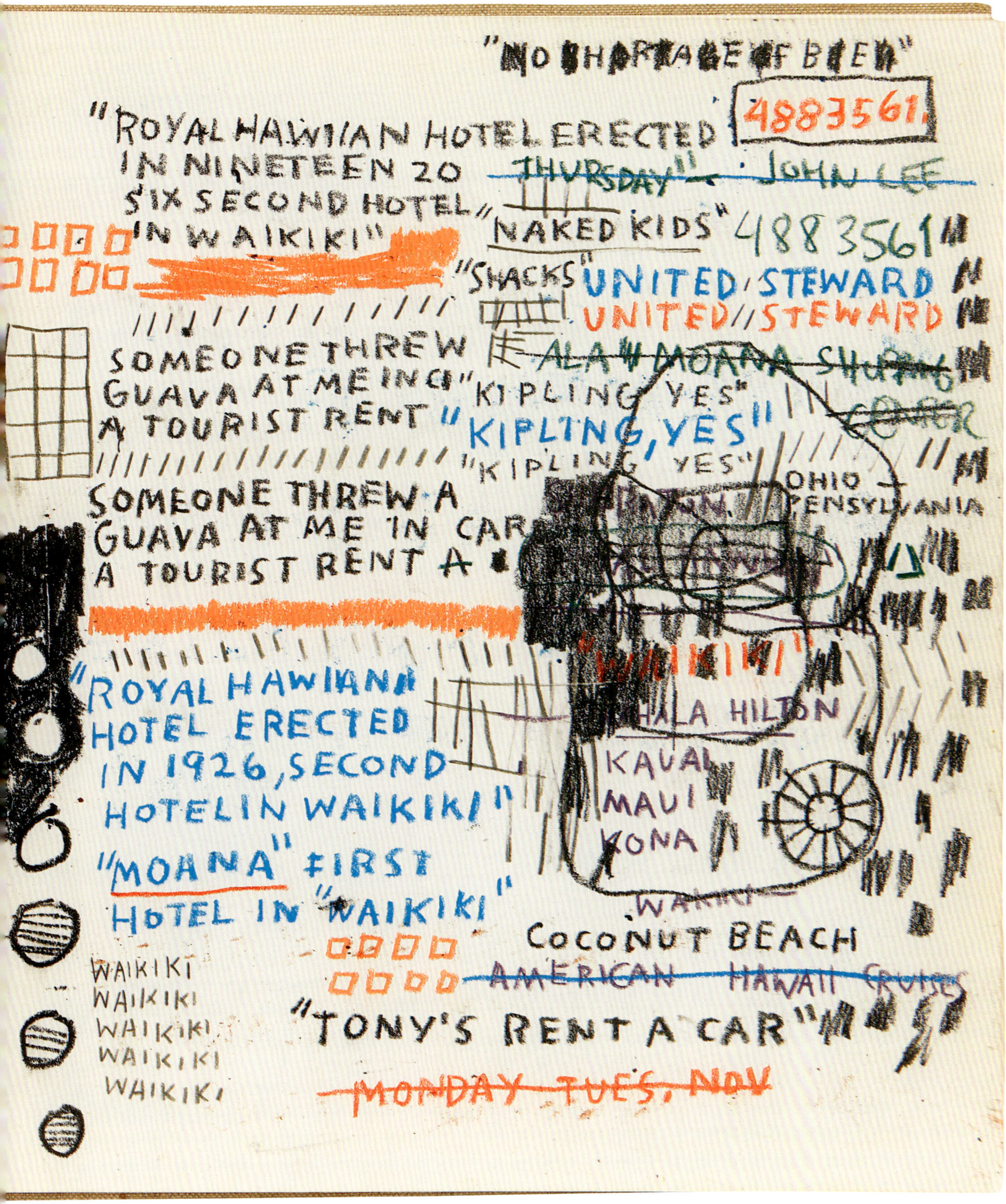
"NO SHORTAGE OF BEER"
4883561.
"ROYAL HAWAIIAN HOTEL ERECTED
IN NINETEEN 20
SIX SECOND HOTEL
IN WAIKIKI"
THURSDAY" · JOHN LEE
"NAKED KIDS" 4883561
"SHACKS" UNITED STEWARD
UNITED STEWARD
ALA MOANA SHOPPING
CENTER
SOMEONE THREW
GUAVA AT ME IN C"
A TOURIST RENT
"KIPLING YES"
"KIPLING, YES"
"KIPLING YES"
OHIO
PENSYLVANIA
SOMEONE THREW A
GUAVA AT ME IN CAR
A TOURIST RENT A
"WAIKIKI"
KAHALA HILTON
KAUAI
MAUI
KONA
"ROYAL HAWIIAN
HOTEL ERECTED
IN 1926, SECOND
HOTEL IN WAIKIKI"
"MOANA" FIRST
HOTEL IN "WAIKIKI"
COCONUT BEACH
AMERICAN HAWAII CRUISES
WAIKIKI
WAIKIKI
WAIKIKI
WAIKIKI
WAIKIKI
"TONY'S RENT A CAR"
MONDAY TUES, NOV

PAGES 122–23

"Andy Warhol" notebook, interior cover spread, n.d.
Graphite, colored pencil, ink, and oil stick on paper
30¼ × 25¼ in. (74.94 × 64.78 cm)

Andy Warhol PT. II notebook, n.d.
Colored pencil, graphite, and crayon on paper; 13 pages of handwritten text and drawings
20 × 20 in. (50.8 × 50.8 cm)

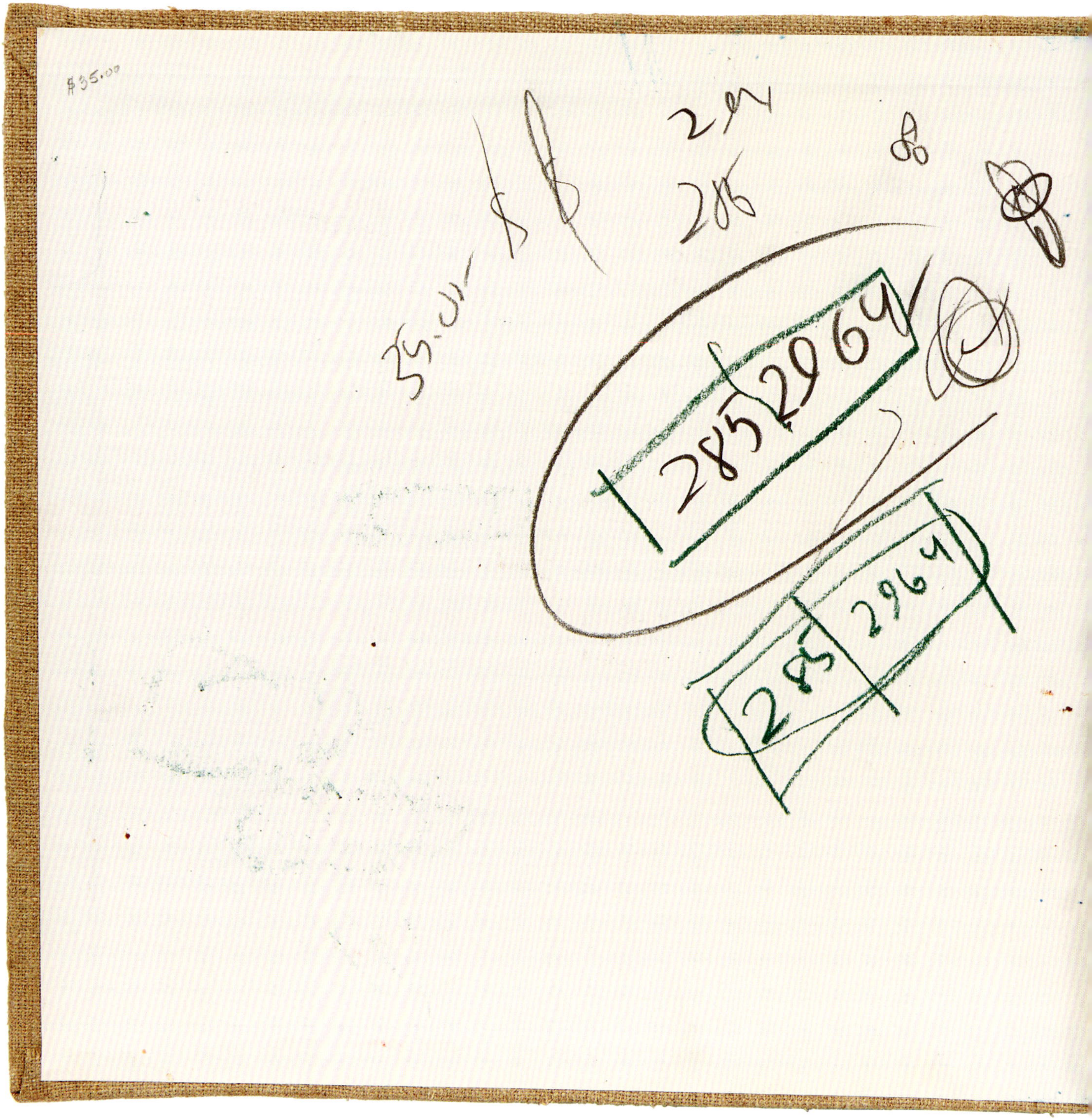

SEND A GIRL A POSTCARD
LEAVE A SISTER HANGING

~~ROA~~

ROYAL HAWAIIAN

~~BANKOK~~
WAIKIKI
~~WAIKK~~
~~WAK~~
~~BANGKOK~~
MONTEGO BAY
~~ZURICH~~

IN WAIKIKI THEY HAVE THESE PEDICABS SOMETHING LIKE
THE THREE-WHEELED MOTO-RICKSHAWS OF BANGKOK—
ONLY NOISELESS

TEN HOURS ON AN AIRPLANE —

I APPROACHED TWO OF THE PEDICAB DRIVERS BOTH
CLEANCUT LOOKING SURF JOCK TYPES
I ASKED FOR A "~~TOURIST RIDE~~"
ONE WAS EATING A HAMBURGER SO THE SECOND
WAS ELECTED
AFTER HE ACCUSED ME OF BEING A COP HE
SOLD ME SOME ~~PAKOLO~~
PAKALOLO

AND THEN TOLD ME ABOUT ~~GIGACARET~~ CIGARETTE
CURRENCY IN JAIL OR IN "THE CAN" —
AND THAT HE WAS NOT IN WORDS, ~~DEFENSIVELY~~
A THREE TIME LOSER
HIS —

OVER A PANCAKE AND EGG HIS
SPECIAL —
FIVE KINDS OF SYRUP

HE TOLD ME HE "SHOT A FOOL'S HEAD OFF"

LAS VEGAS —

COCONUT
MAPLE
ORANGE
PASSION FRUIT

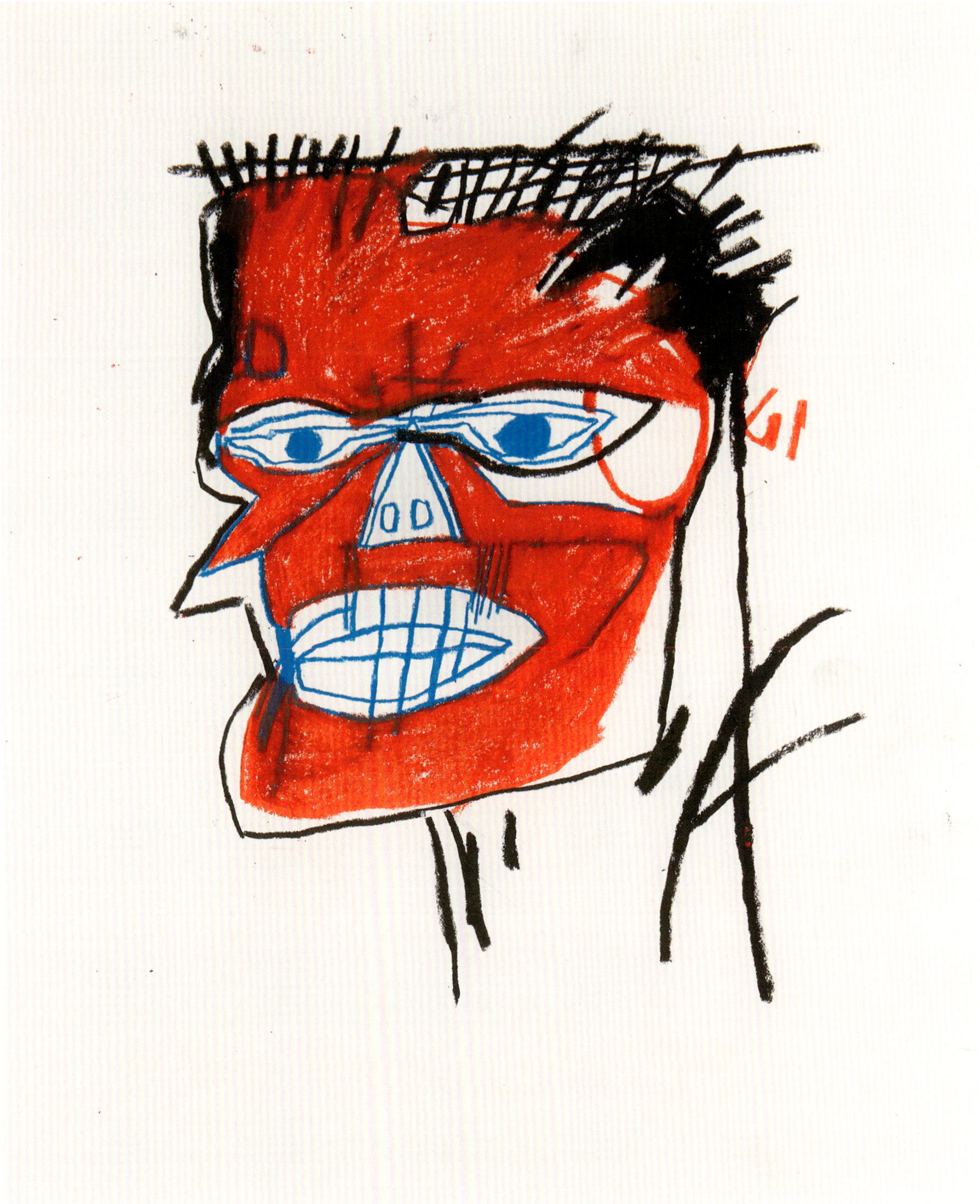

Untitled, n.d.
Oil stick on paper
16 × 13¼ in. (40.64 × 33.66 cm)

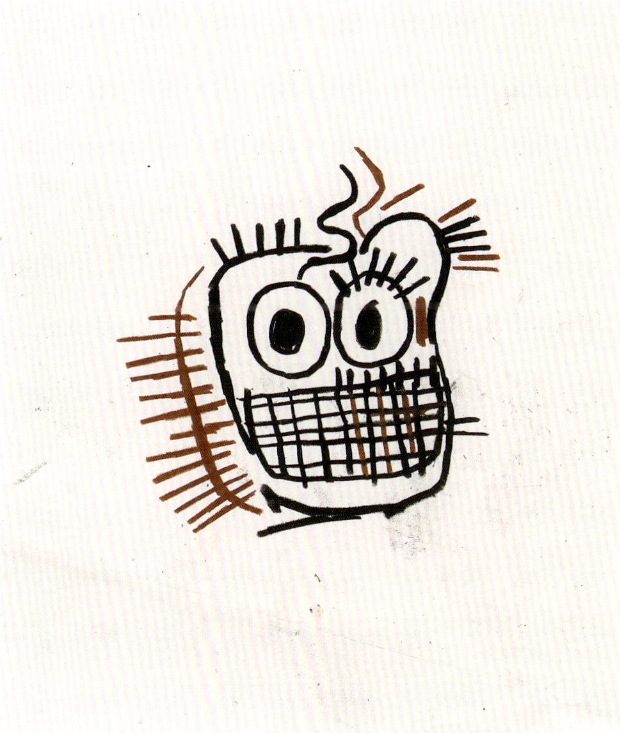

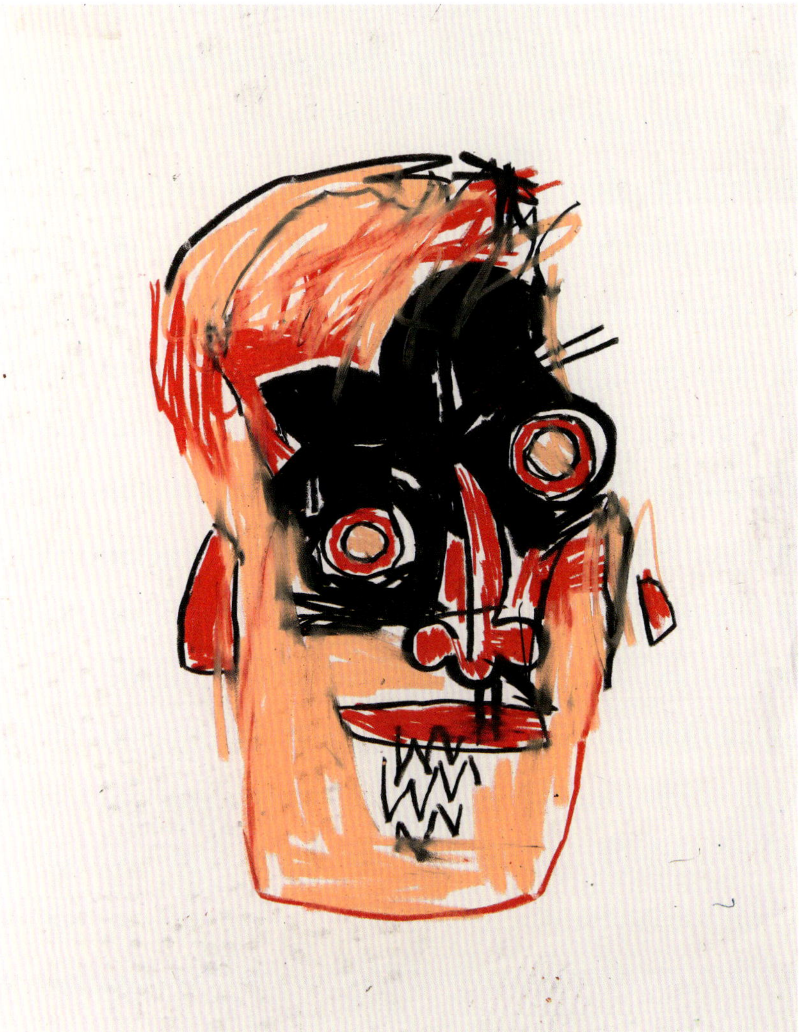

TOP
Untitled, n.d.
Oil stick on paper
24 × 19 in. (60.96 × 48.26 cm)

LEFT
Untitled, n.d.
Oil stick on paper
15½ × 11¾ in. (39.37 × 29.85 cm)

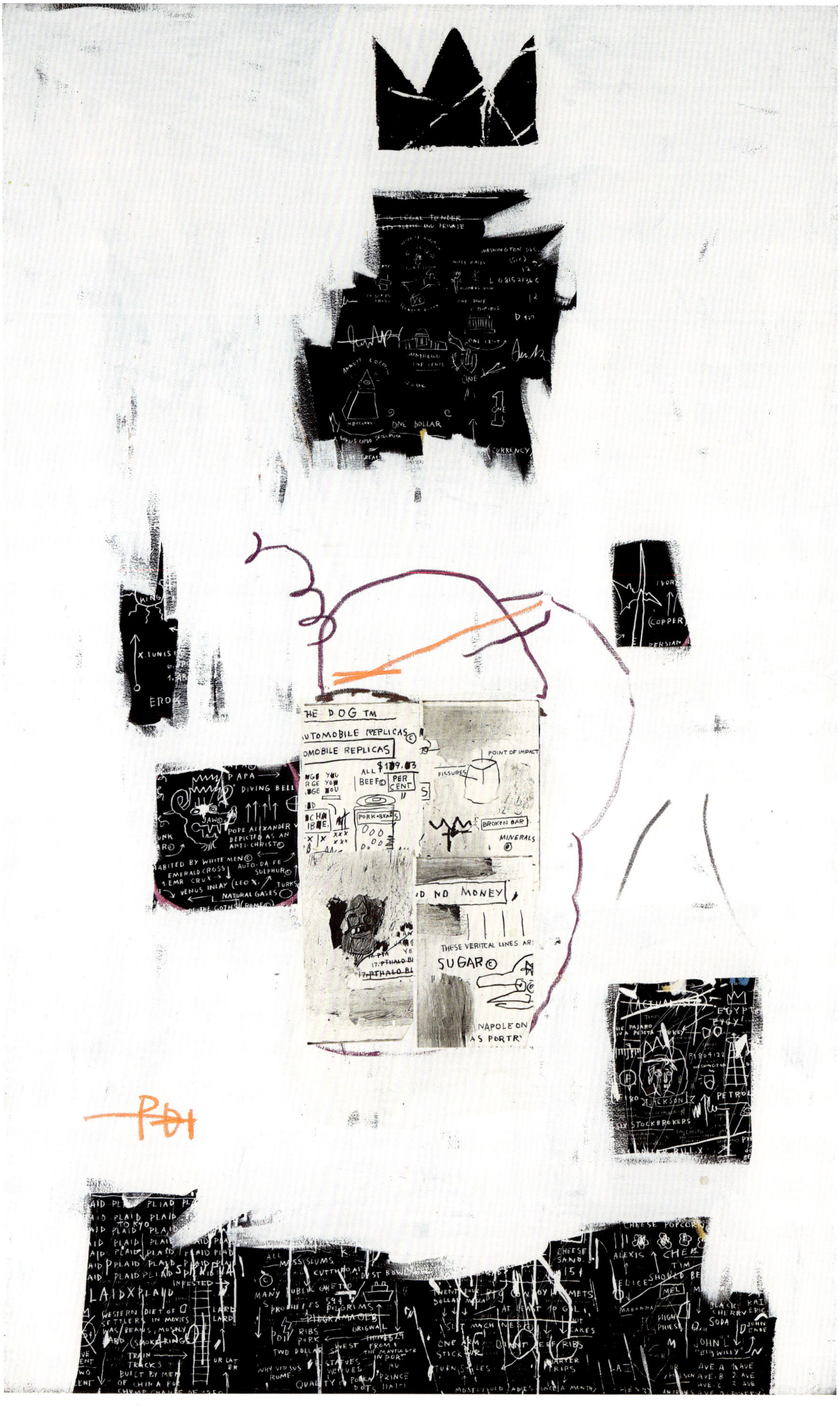
ONE DOLLAR
CURRENCY
COPPER
PERSIAN
PAPA
DIVING BELL
POPE ALEXANDER
DEPICTED AS AN
ANTI-CHRIST©
EMERALD CROSS
SULPHUR©
NATURAL GASES
AUTOMOBILE REPLICAS
ALL
BEEF©
PER CENT
PORK+BEANS
POINT OF IMPACT
FISSURES
BROKEN BAR
MINERALS
THESE VERITCAL LINES AR
SUGAR©
STOCKBROKERS
EGYPT
PETROL
JACKSON
SLUMS
PILGRIMS
CHEESE POPCORN
ALEXIS
SODA
HIGH PRIEST

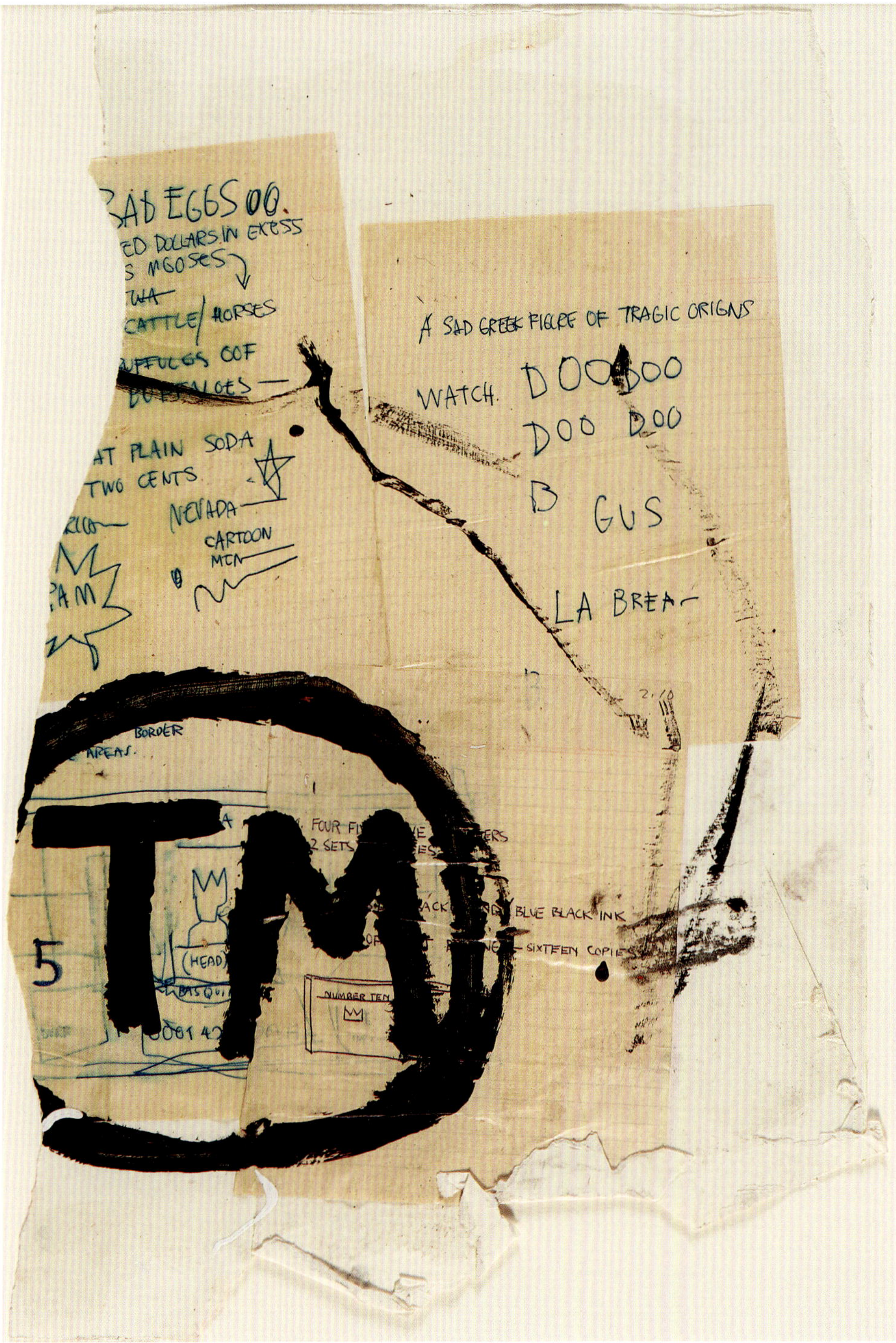

OPPOSITE
Tuxedo, n.d.
Acrylic, oil stick, photocopy, and ink on canvas
101½ × 50½ in.
(257.81 × 128.27 cm)

ABOVE
Untitled (TM), n.d.
Collage of paper with ink and acrylic on paper
20 × 12¾ in. (50.8 × 32.29 cm)

This chapter takes its title from the painting of the same name created by Jean-Michel in 1988. It is a simple but striking work and, like everything Jean-Michel created, filled with meaning. That work is featured here, along with others from earlier in his career.

In 1983, five years before Jean-Michel painted *Ideal*, he moved to his Great Jones Street studio, where he lived and worked for the rest of his life. Much of what he surrounded himself with there has been preserved: handwritten notes, clothing, records, books, movies, and objects, from African art to toys he collected. Bringing them together here affords the reader a glimpse into how he lived and the things he kept close. JEANINE

Jean-Michel outside his Great Jones Street studio, ca. 1985

IDEAL

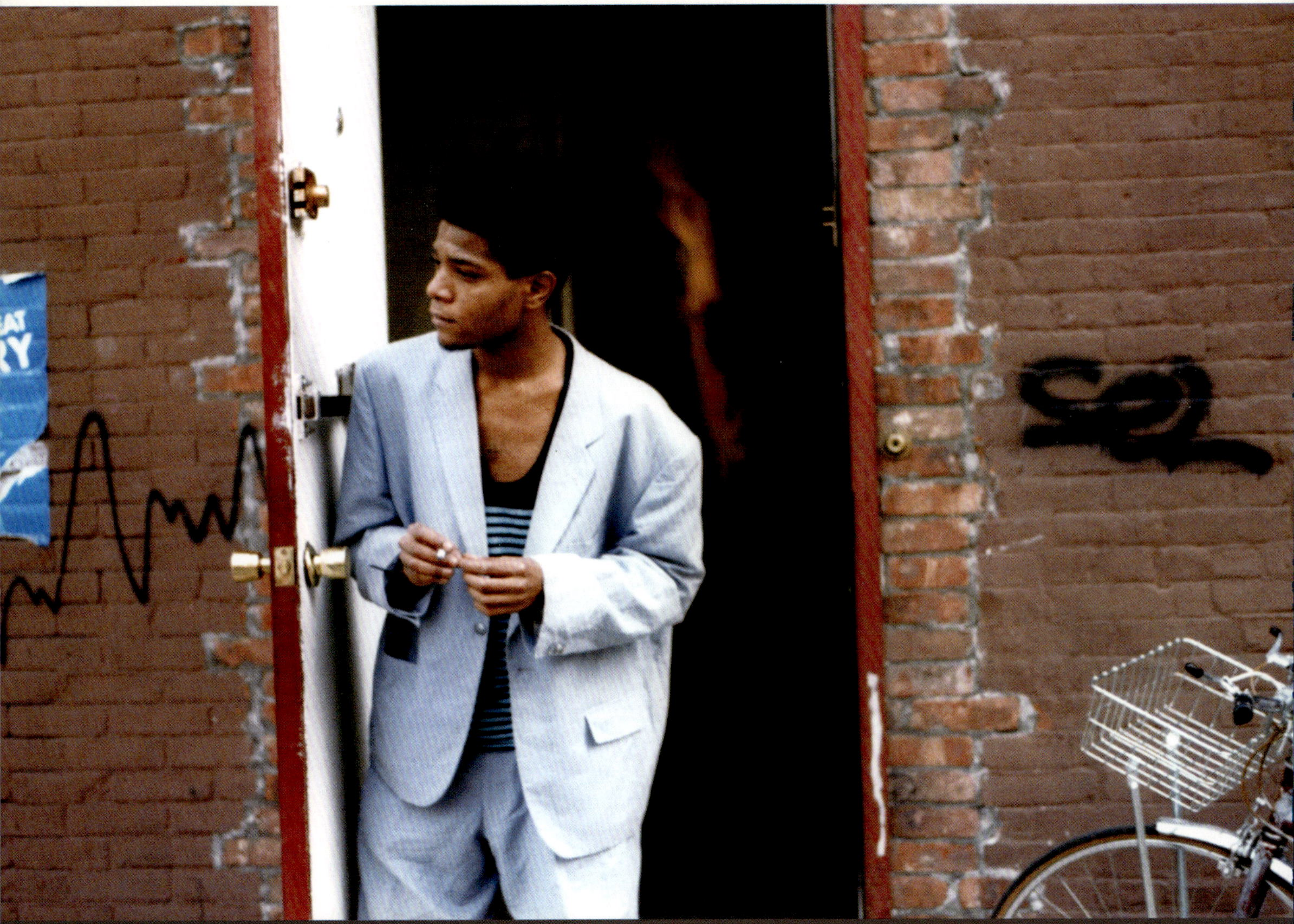

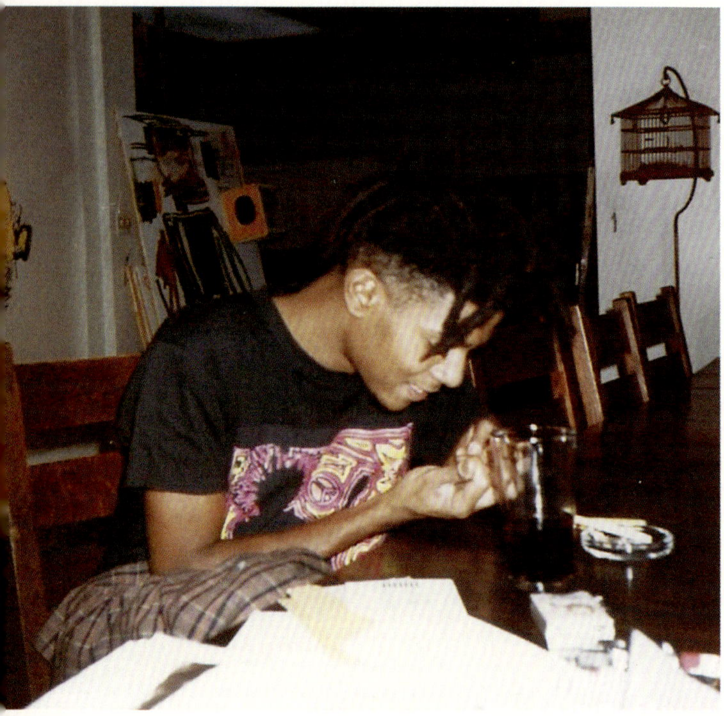

LEFT
Jean-Michel in his Great Jones Street studio, June 1986

BOTTOM
Jean-Michel in his Great Jones Street studio, 1987

TSENG KWONG CHI © MUNA TSENG DANCE PROJECTS, INC.

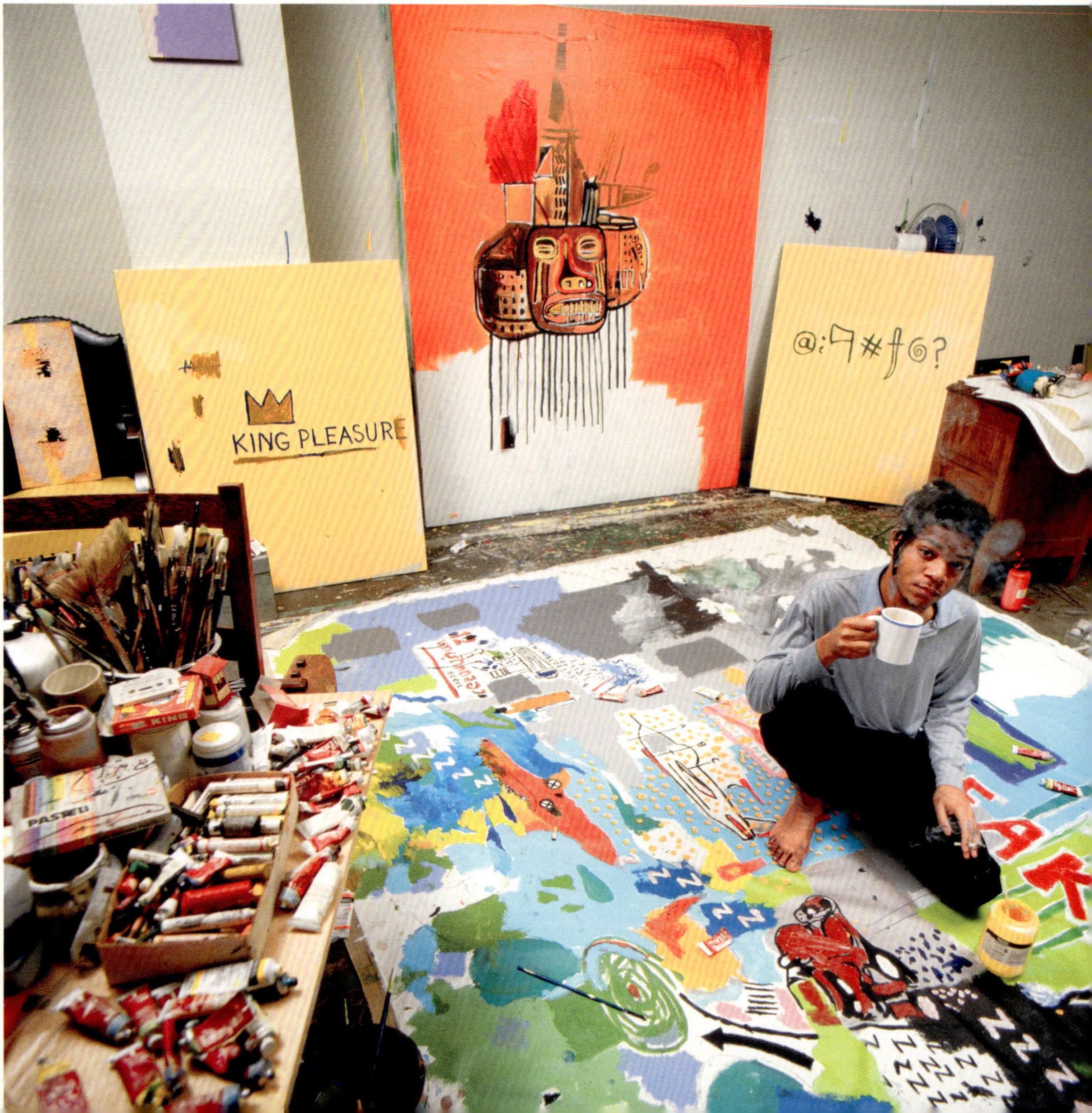

57 GREAT JONES STREET

Upon entering Jean-Michel's studio, the first thing you noticed to the right was an incredibly long dining table that easily sat ten to twelve people. Jean-Michel loved entertaining and great food. Dean & DeLuca was a gourmet market that he frequented, and when visiting him, food from the local shop would usually be laid out on the table. We would sit around that table and talk, but the painting never stopped. Mid-conversation, he would hop up, paint something, come back and sit down. JEANINE

I loved that space for him. The building was so unassuming from the outside, and then you walked in and *wow*—you found yourself in the center of Jean-Michel's world. While it was such a seemingly busy place, there was a grounded stability to it. It felt like his home; it felt good in there. It was a beautiful, open space, so well put together, with a huge farmhouselike table as the centerpiece.

It was a foodie's paradise. Jean-Michel had a very discerning palate. Gourmet food, exotic libations, a water cooler (which wasn't common at the time)—the best of everything. I visited once right after his trip to Japan, and he excitedly turned me on to sake. In typical Jean-Michel fashion, he didn't just turn me on to it, he schooled me on how it was made, how delicate it was, and how to drink it.

His studio was behind the living room/ kitchen area. I was initially taken aback at the size of the space and the sheer energy that seemed to bounce off the walls—music playing, TV on, huge canvases all over the place, him walking across things on the floor, and a medley of works in progress everywhere, waiting for him to get to them.

My brother knew how to party, and people wanted to be around him. Folks were constantly calling and stopping by. He would be at the center of all the activity while also popping in and out. Jean-Michel would literally walk away from a person as they were talking, walk over to a work and, with extreme focus, he'd paint something, write something, scribble something. It was magic!

It was beautiful to see how he created a space for himself where everything supported the flow of his creativity. He had his home, studio, music he was inspired by, food, TV, things he collected during his travels, and he was working on establishing a team to help him. So many parts of his life were coming together all of which were in service to him being able to do his thing. LISANE

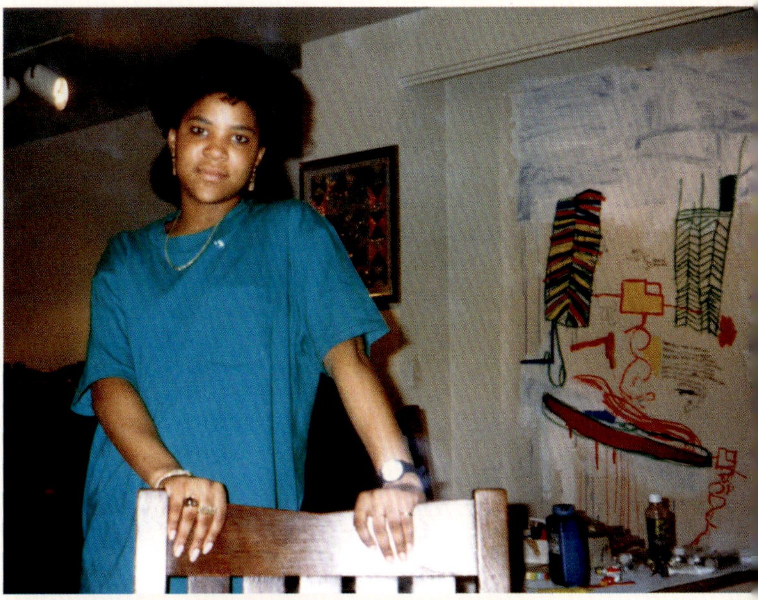

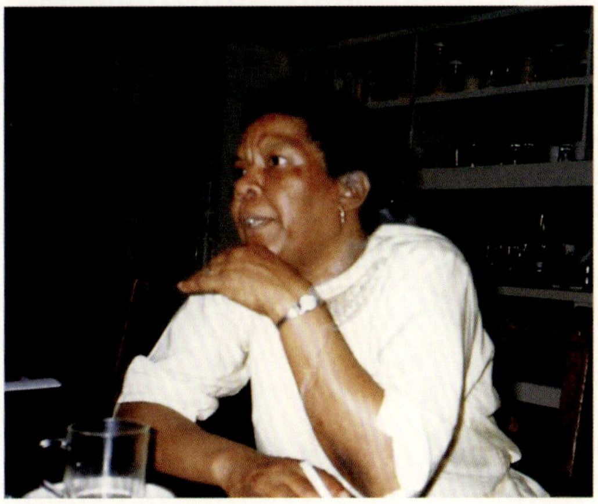

TOP
Jeanine in the Great Jones Street studio, 1986

BOTTOM
Matilde in the Great Jones Street studio, June 1986

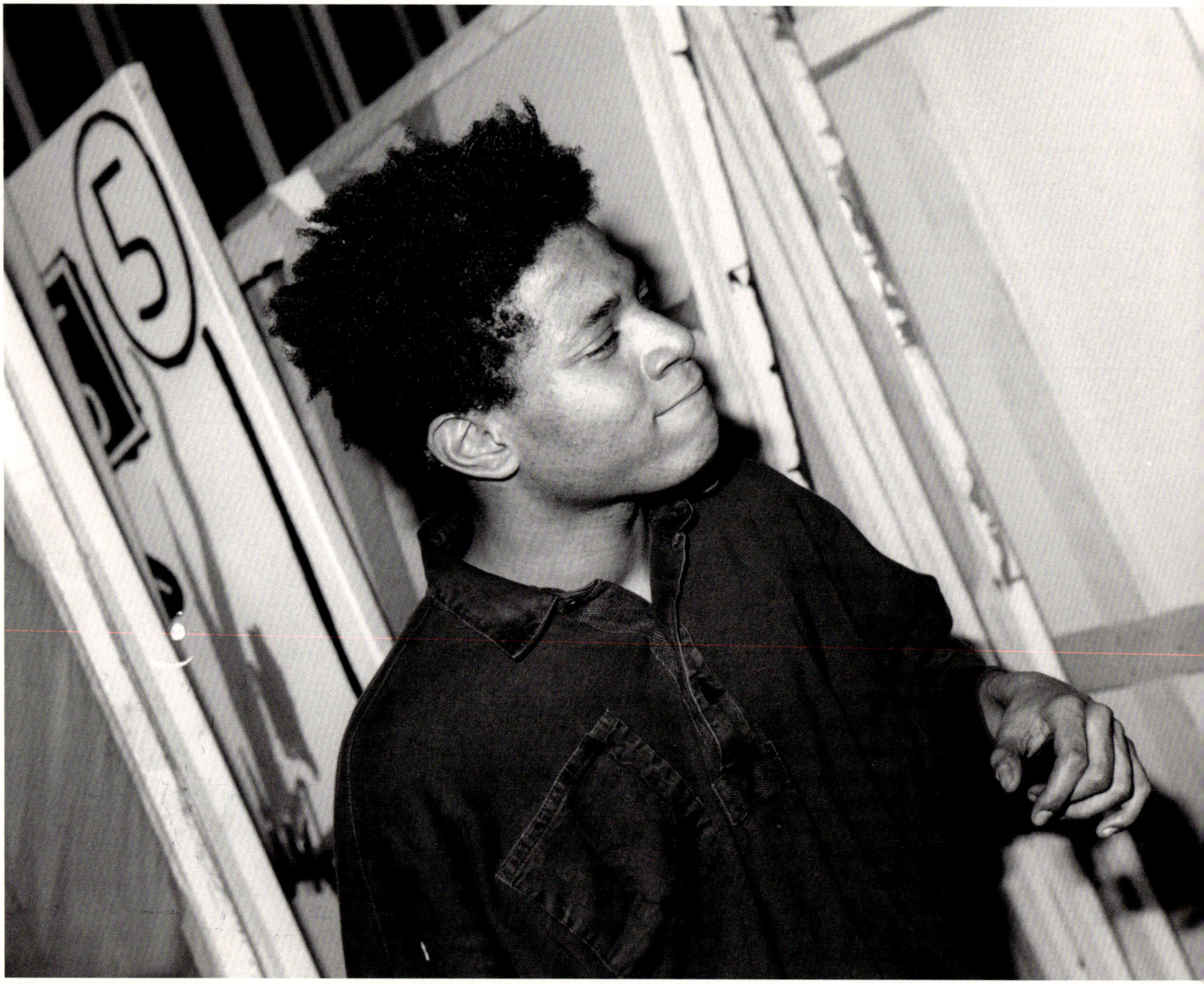

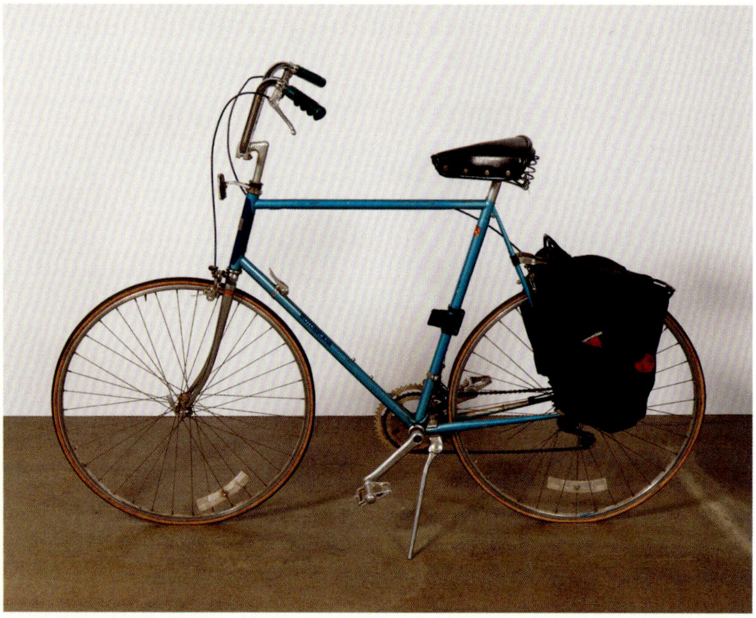

Jean-Michel in his Great Jones Street studio, 1984. *This photo was taken on Jean-Michel's 24th birthday, according to the photographer.*
© BETH PHILLIPS

Jean-Michel's bicycle. *Jean-Michel often rode his bicycle around New York City because taxi drivers frequently refused to pick him up.*

In addition to good food, Jean-Michel loved music, movies, and reading, which was evident by his expansive book, record, and movie collections. I recall frequent visits to nearby bookstores and Tower Records on the corner of 4th Street and Broadway. We would walk out with dozens of records at a time. Looking at his paintings, it was clear they were used as source material. Jean-Michel's thirst for knowledge wasn't the by-product of spending time in a traditional classroom—it was an innate part of who he was. Whatever he read he soaked up like a sponge, and when he traveled he completely immersed himself in the culture.

So many different types of music could be heard playing in Jean-Michel's studio. We bonded over the latest rap record or dances that were popular at the time—Grandmaster Flash, The Fearless Four, T La Rock, and Jazzy Jay. I remember at one of his parties we were discussing and admiring "Super Rhymes" by Jimmy Spicer. JEANINE

JEAN-MICHEL'S STUDIO PLAYLIST

"Another Brick in the Wall"
Pink Floyd

"Bennie and the Jets"
Elton John

"Billie's Bounce"
Charlie Parker

"Black Man"
Stevie Wonder

"Blue in Green"
Miles Davis, John Coltrane

"Bohemian Rhapsody"
Queen

"Careless Whisper"
George Michael

"Come On"
Jimi Hendrix

"Freddie Freeloader"
Miles Davis, John Coltrane

"In the Air Tonight"
Phil Collins

"Is This Love"
Bob Marley and the Wailers

"Klaunstance"
Charlie Parker

"Lucy in the Sky with Diamonds"
Elton John

"Now's the Time"
Charlie Parker

"Ornithology"
Charlie Parker

"Pinball Wizard"
Elton John

"Pinball Wizard"
The Who

"Purple Haze"
Jimi Hendrix

"Red Red Wine"
UB40

"'Round Midnight"
Miles Davis, John Coltrane

"Salt Peanuts"
Charlie Parker, Dizzy Gillespie

"Star Spangled Banner"
Jimi Hendrix

"Voodoo Chile"
Jimi Hendrix

"We Will Rock You"
Queen

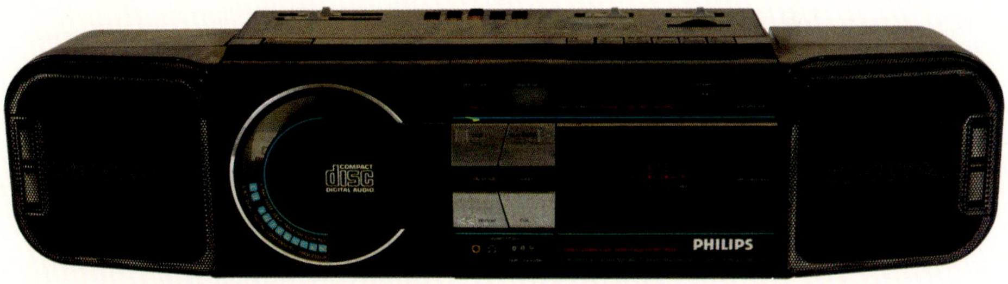

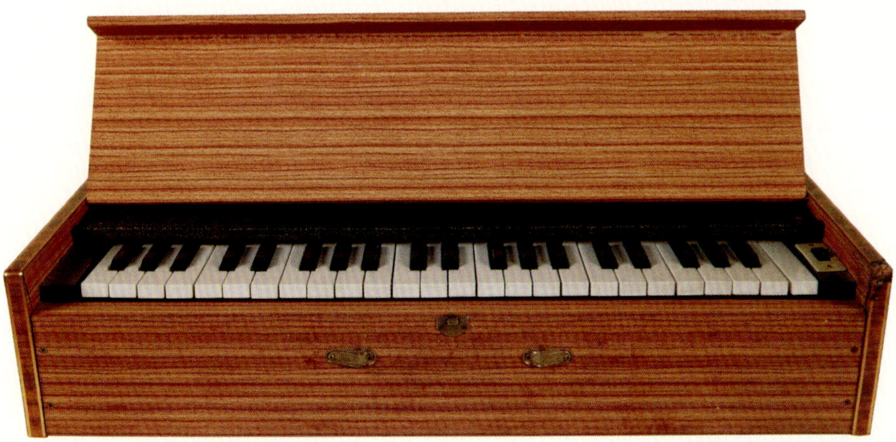

Jean-Michel's boombox and portable piano

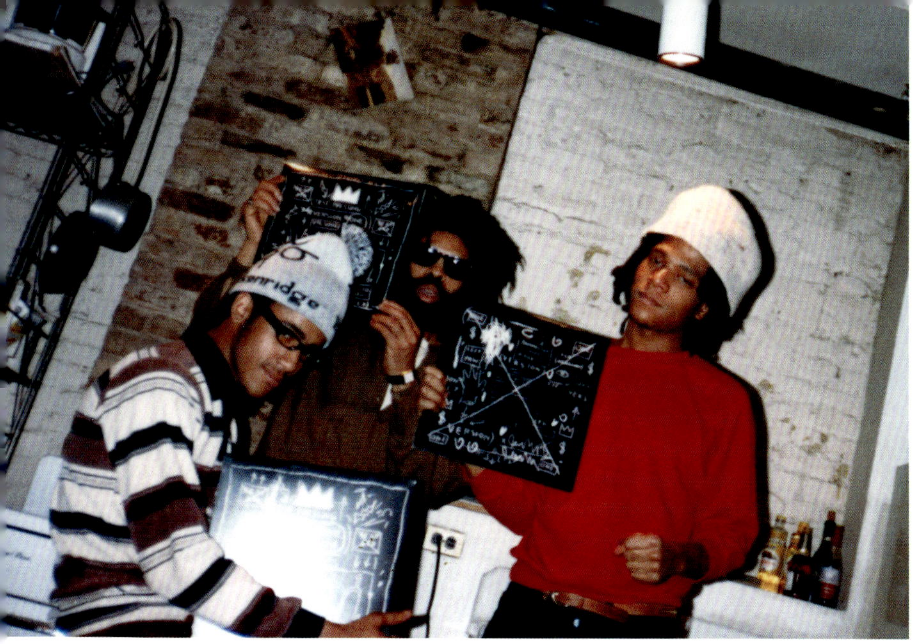

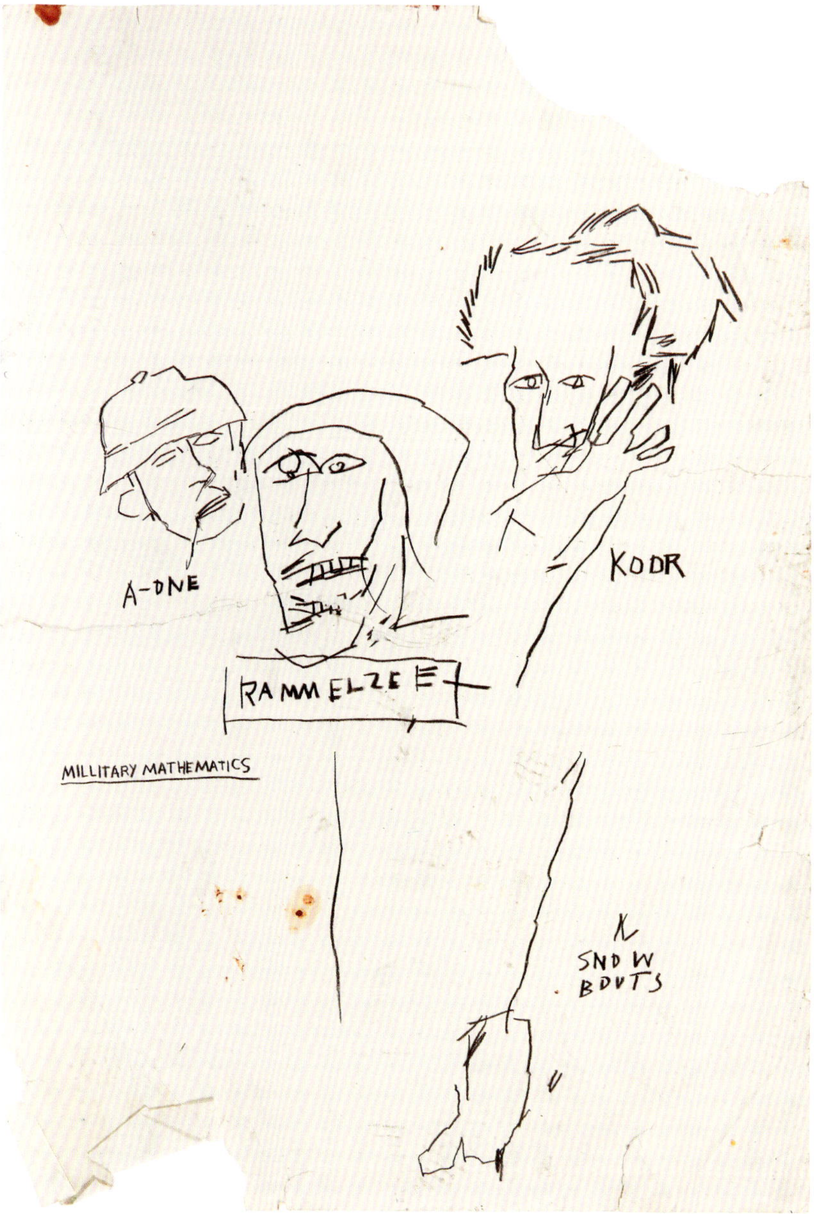

TOP
Toxic, Shenge Ka Pharaoh, and Jean-Michel (left to right) with the *Beat Bop* single, 1983

RIGHT
Untitled (Rammelzee), n.d.
Oil stick on canvas
38 × 25 in. (96.52 × 63.5 cm)

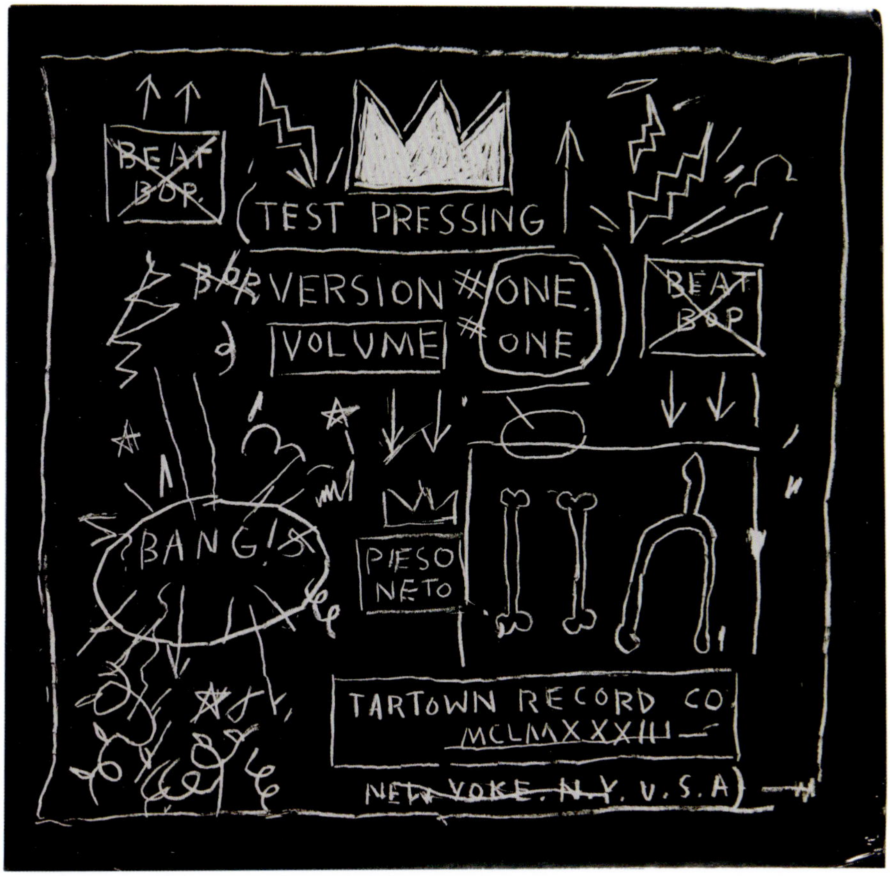

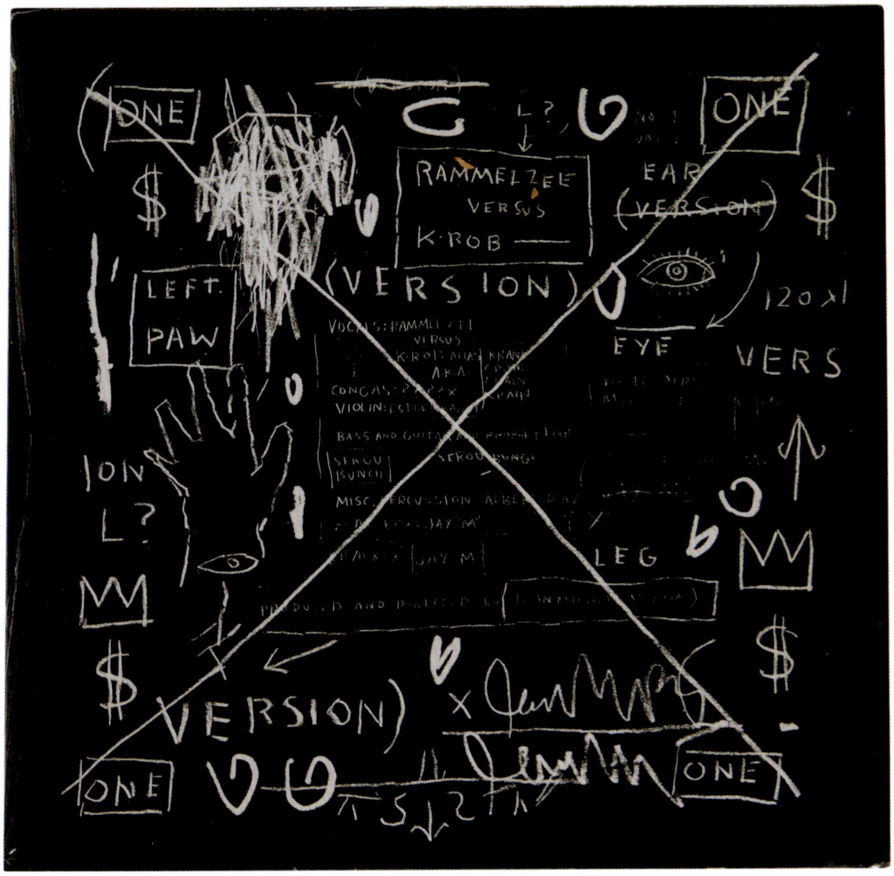

Beat Bop (front and back), 1983
Music: K-Rob, Rammellzee
Cover artwork: Jean-Michel Basquiat

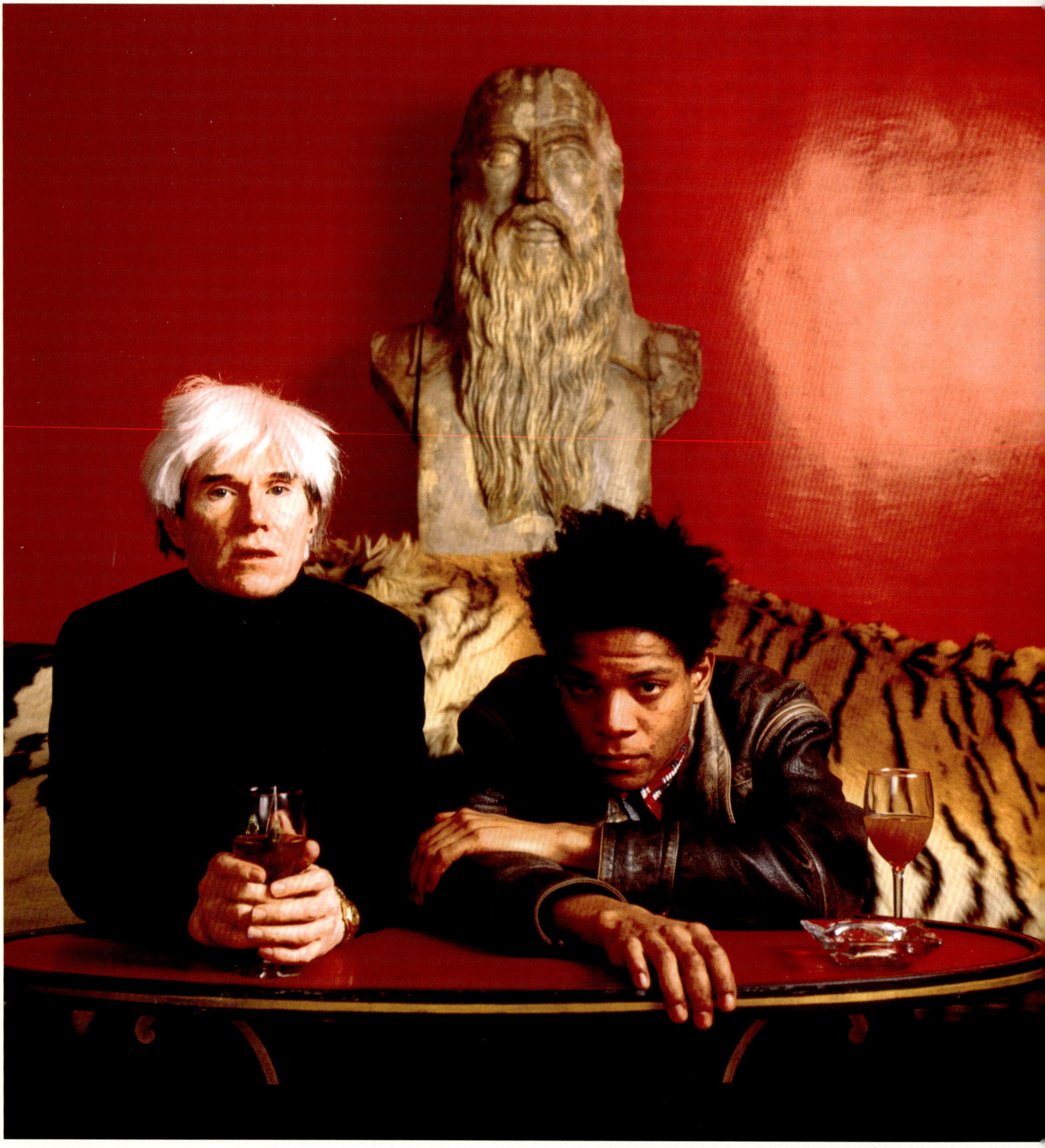

Andy Warhol and Jean-Michel,
New York, 1985

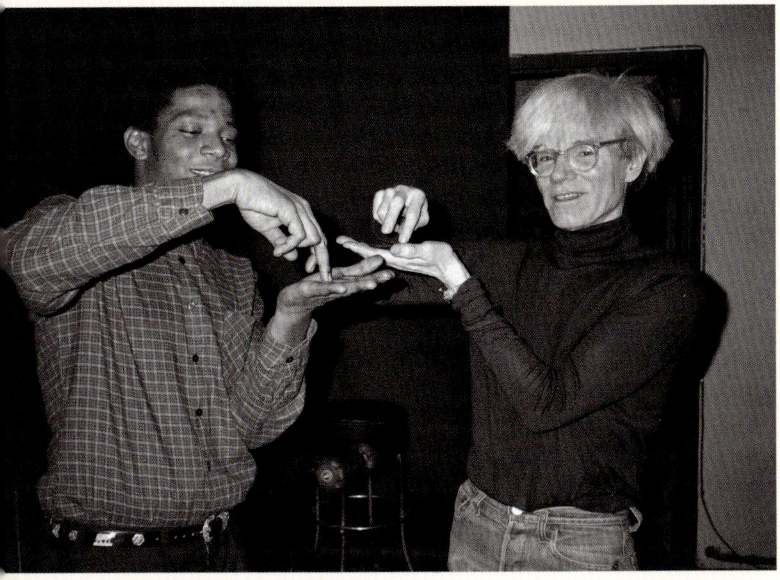

Jean-Michel and Andy Warhol at 860 Broadway, October 26, 1983

ANDY WARHOL

As a teen, Jean-Michel admired Andy Warhol and made it a point to meet and sell postcards to him, which he did in their first encounter. Not long after, the two artists were properly introduced and eventually Andy became a mentor to Jean-Michel and they shared a deep friendship. When Jean-Michel was on the cover of the Sunday *New York Times Magazine*, he brought Andy to our house to have dinner and celebrate.

My brother sought Andy's advice on navigating the art world and Jean-Michel, in turn, encouraged Andy to start painting again. As artists, they understood each other. Both Jean-Michel and Andy were often misunderstood, and certainly the art world wasn't always kind to my brother. When Andy passed away, Jean-Michel was devastated. It didn't help that they weren't on the best of terms at the time. When I called him to express my condolences, he could barely stay on the phone. JEANINE

The first time they met was in SoHo in 1978. Warhol was with well-known curator Henry Geldzahler at the restaurant W.P.A., and Jean-Michel approached them to try to sell some of his art.

When they became friends a little while later, Andy helped him a lot. He was the one who told Jean-Michel that he should save some of his artwork instead of selling it all. He truly needed the money when he was first starting out, but Andy was very clear about that—it was very good advice. Jean-Michel was very upset when he passed. NORA

He'd always wanted to meet Andy and, of course, he made it happen. People have said that Andy was a father figure to Jean-Michel. I suppose that is a convenient assumption, given the difference in their age, but Jean-Michel had a father. I don't think he was looking for one. Jean-Michel and Andy developed a mutual admiration, respect, and friendship for one another. People can do that at any age. They seemed to inspire and encourage each other.

They were friends who entered each other's lives at a time when Jean-Michel probably needed mentorship and friendship with someone who wasn't going to want anything from him and in whom he could trust. He needed people around him who understood the place he was in and the significance of the trajectory he was on. Andy was one of very few who truly understood, firsthand, the enormity of what Jean-Michel was facing in his career. When Andy passed, Jean-Michel was deeply hurt. LISANE

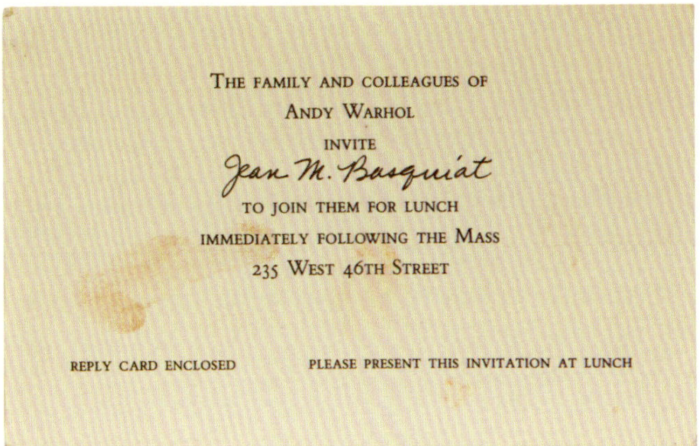

THE FAMILY AND COLLEAGUES OF
ANDY WARHOL
INVITE
Jean M. Basquiat
TO JOIN THEM FOR LUNCH
IMMEDIATELY FOLLOWING THE MASS
235 WEST 46TH STREET

REPLY CARD ENCLOSED

PLEASE PRESENT THIS INVITATION AT LUNCH

Lunch invitation following Andy Warhol's funeral service, New York, 1987

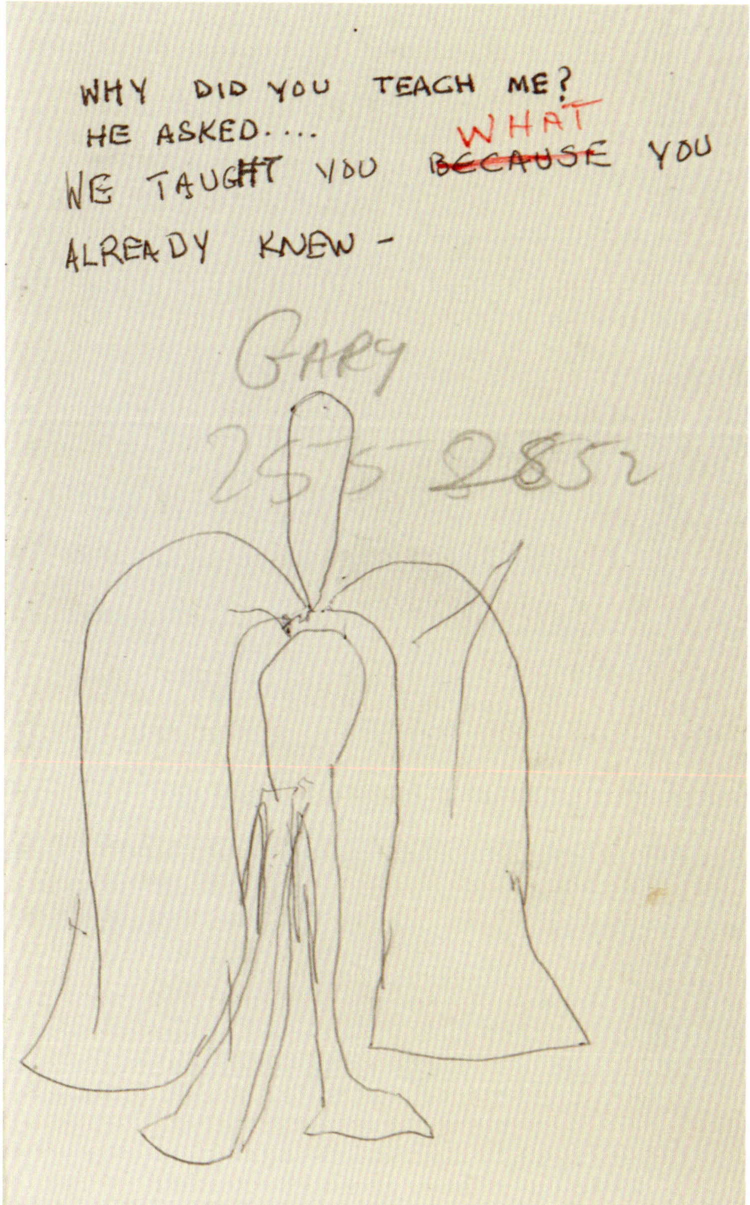

RIGHT
Notebook, inside cover, n.d.

BELOW AND BOTTOM
Notes found in Jean-Michel's studio, n.d.

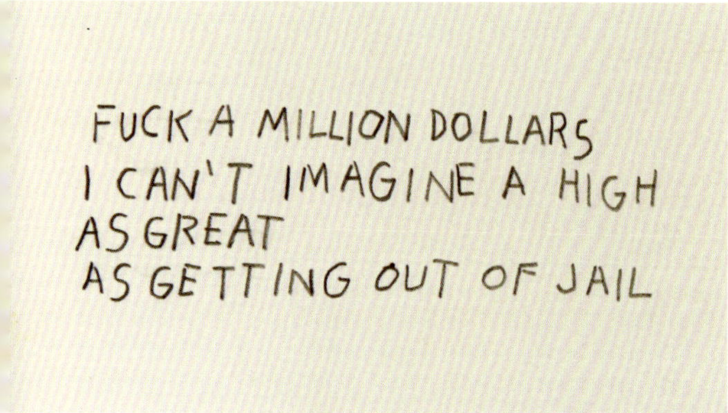
FUCK A MILLION DOLLARS
I CAN'T IMAGINE A HIGH
AS GREAT
AS GETTING OUT OF JAIL

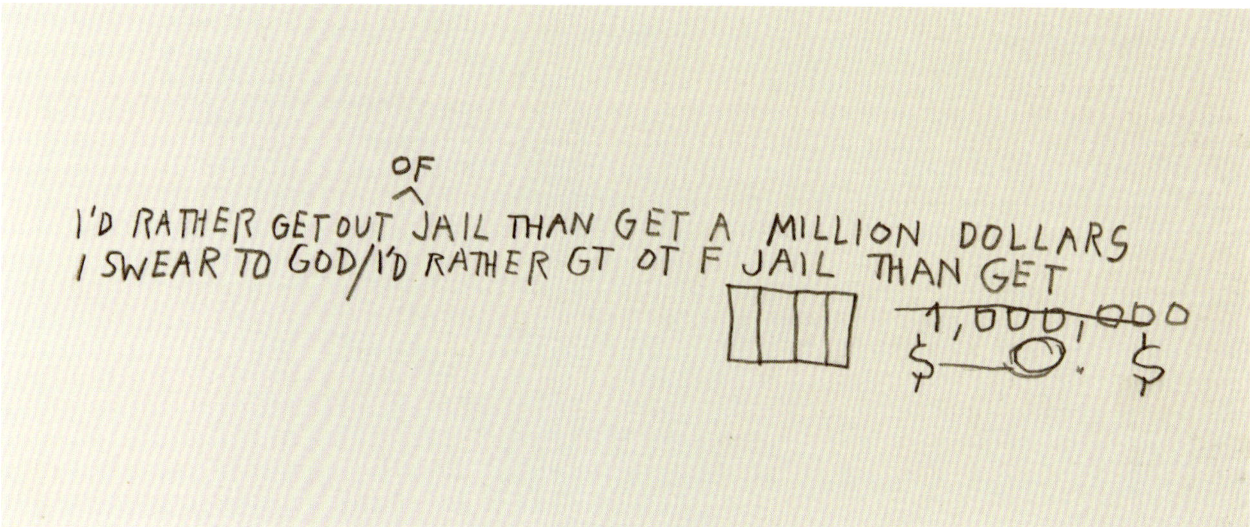
I'D RATHER GET OUT OF JAIL THAN GET A MILLION DOLLARS
I SWEAR TO GOD/I'D RATHER GT OT F JAIL THAN GET
~~1,000,000~~
$ 0. $

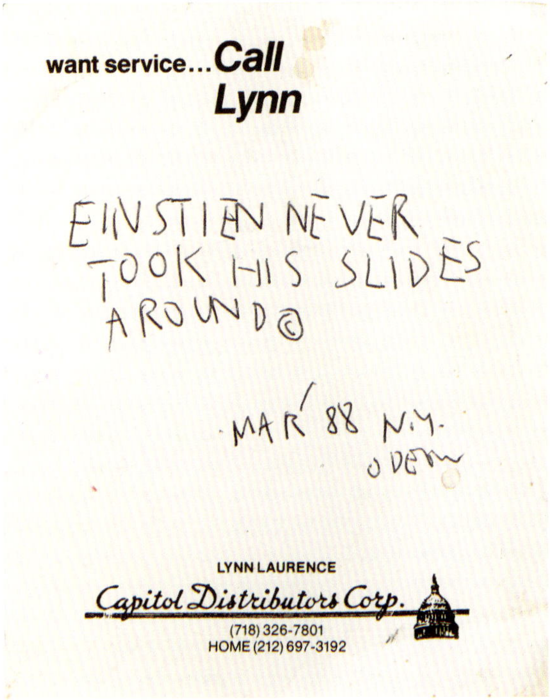

want service... **Call Lynn**

EINSTIEN NEVER TOOK HIS SLIDES AROUND ©

MAR '88 N.Y.
ODEM

LYNN LAURENCE
Capitol Distributors Corp.
(718) 326-7801
HOME (212) 697-3192

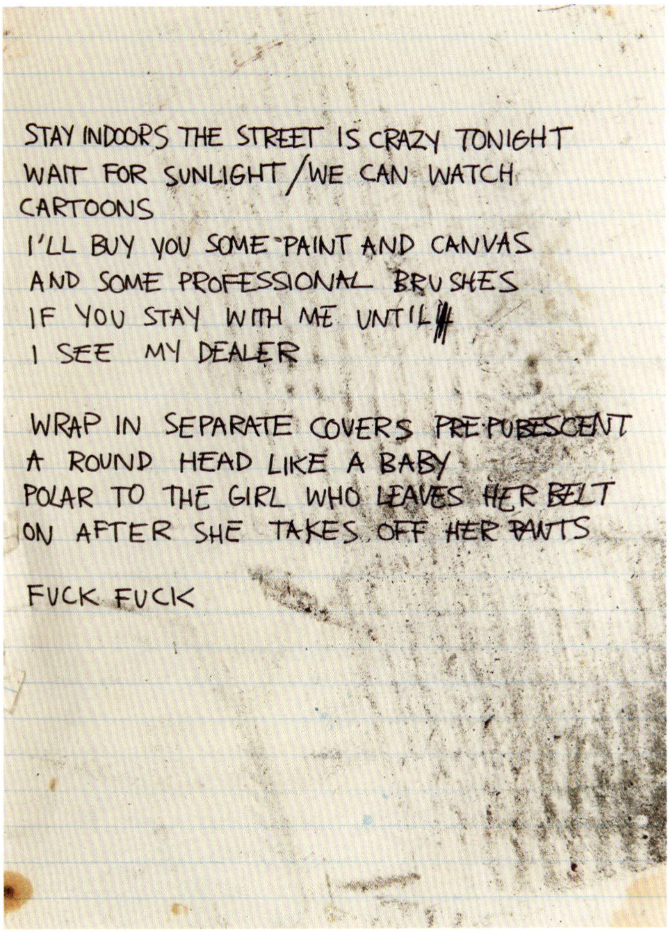

STAY INDOORS THE STREET IS CRAZY TONIGHT
WAIT FOR SUNLIGHT / WE CAN WATCH
CARTOONS
I'LL BUY YOU SOME PAINT AND CANVAS
AND SOME PROFESSIONAL BRUSHES
IF YOU STAY WITH ME UNTIL
I SEE MY DEALER

WRAP IN SEPARATE COVERS PRE-PUBESCENT
A ROUND HEAD LIKE A BABY
POLAR TO THE GIRL WHO LEAVES HER BELT
ON AFTER SHE TAKES OFF HER PANTS

FUCK FUCK

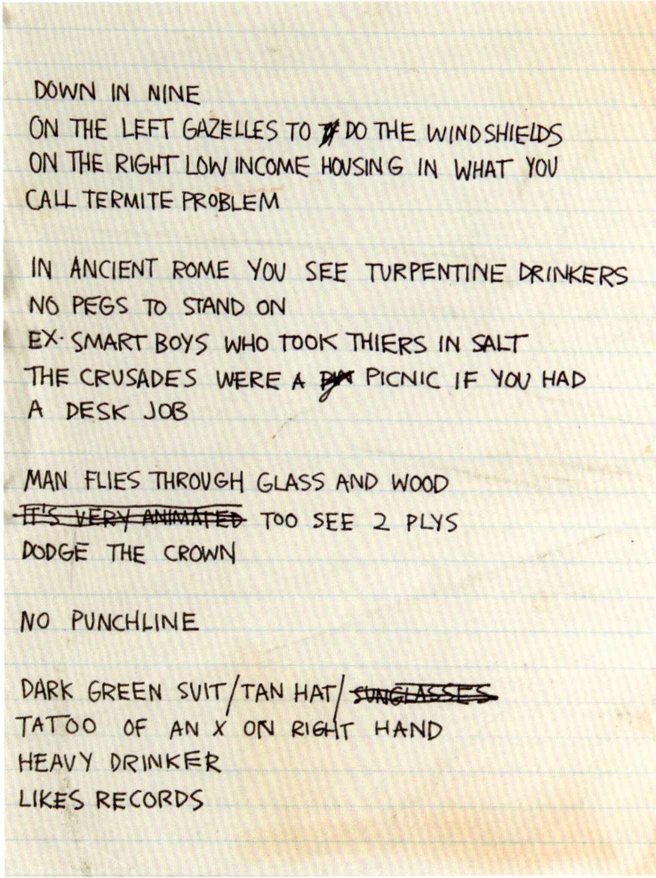

DOWN IN NINE
ON THE LEFT GAZELLES TO DO THE WINDSHIELDS
ON THE RIGHT LOW INCOME HOUSING IN WHAT YOU
CALL TERMITE PROBLEM

IN ANCIENT ROME YOU SEE TURPENTINE DRINKERS
NO PEGS TO STAND ON
EX-SMART BOYS WHO TOOK THIERS IN SALT
THE CRUSADES WERE A PICNIC IF YOU HAD
A DESK JOB

MAN FLIES THROUGH GLASS AND WOOD
~~IT'S VERY ANIMATED~~ TOO SEE 2 PLYS
DODGE THE CROWN

NO PUNCHLINE

DARK GREEN SUIT / TAN HAT / ~~SUNGLASSES~~
TATOO OF AN X ON RIGHT HAND
HEAVY DRINKER
LIKES RECORDS

Notes found in Jean-Michel's studio, n.d.

Notes found in Jean-Michel's studio, n.d.

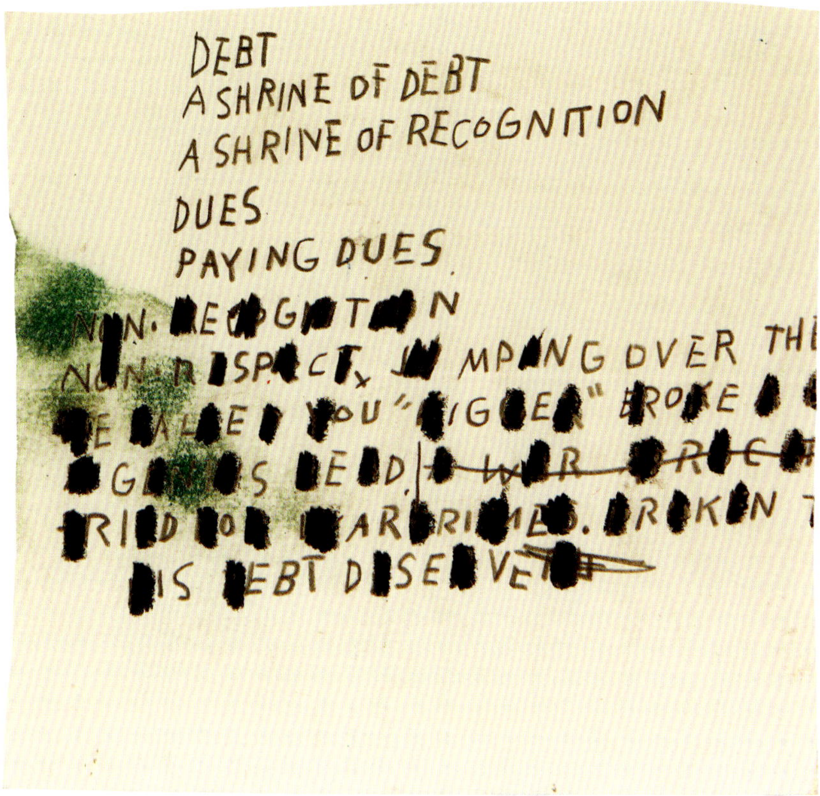

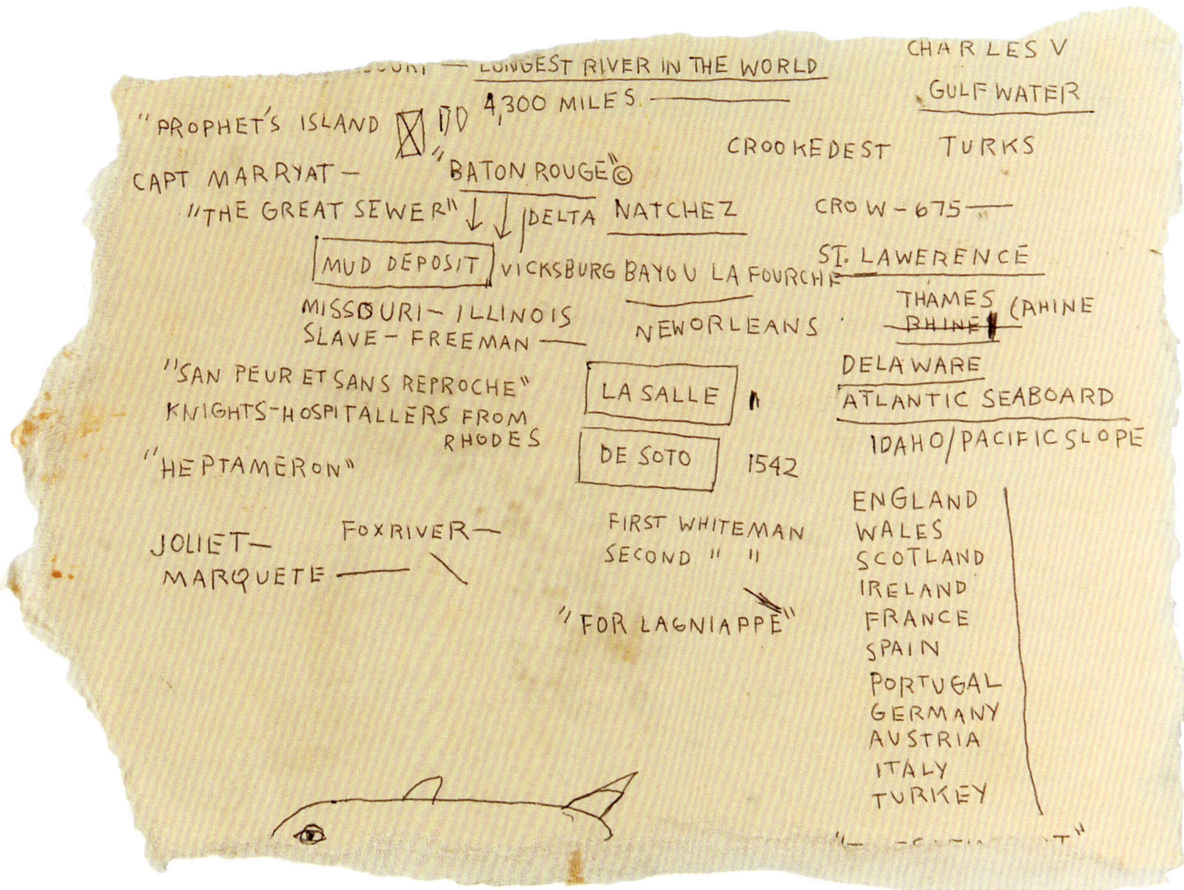

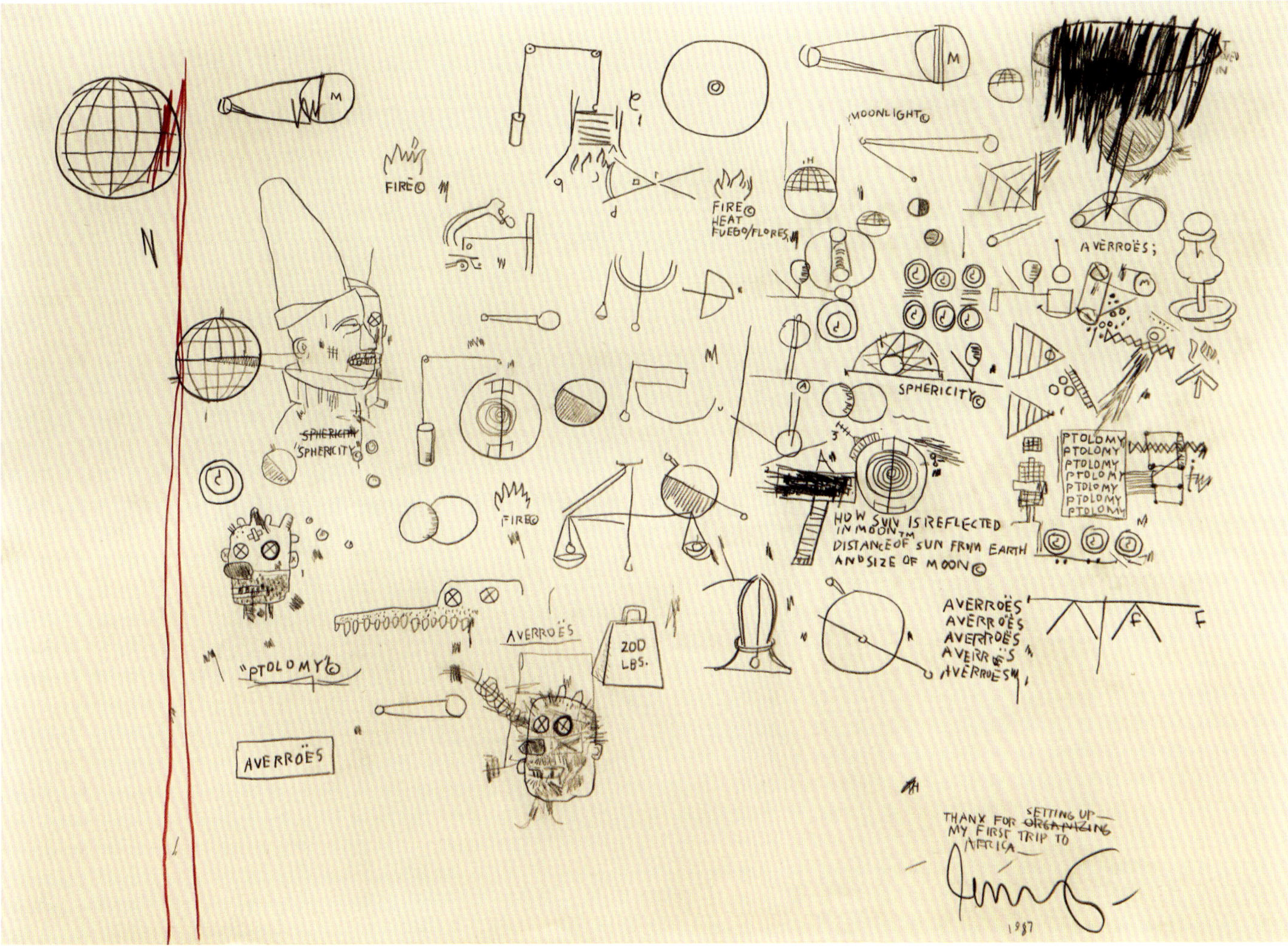

Untitled, 1986
Pencil and crayon on paper
22¼ × 30 in. (56.5 × 76 cm)

Jean-Michel in his Great Jones Street studio, 1987

TSENG KWONG CHI © MUNA TSENG DANCE PROJECTS, INC.

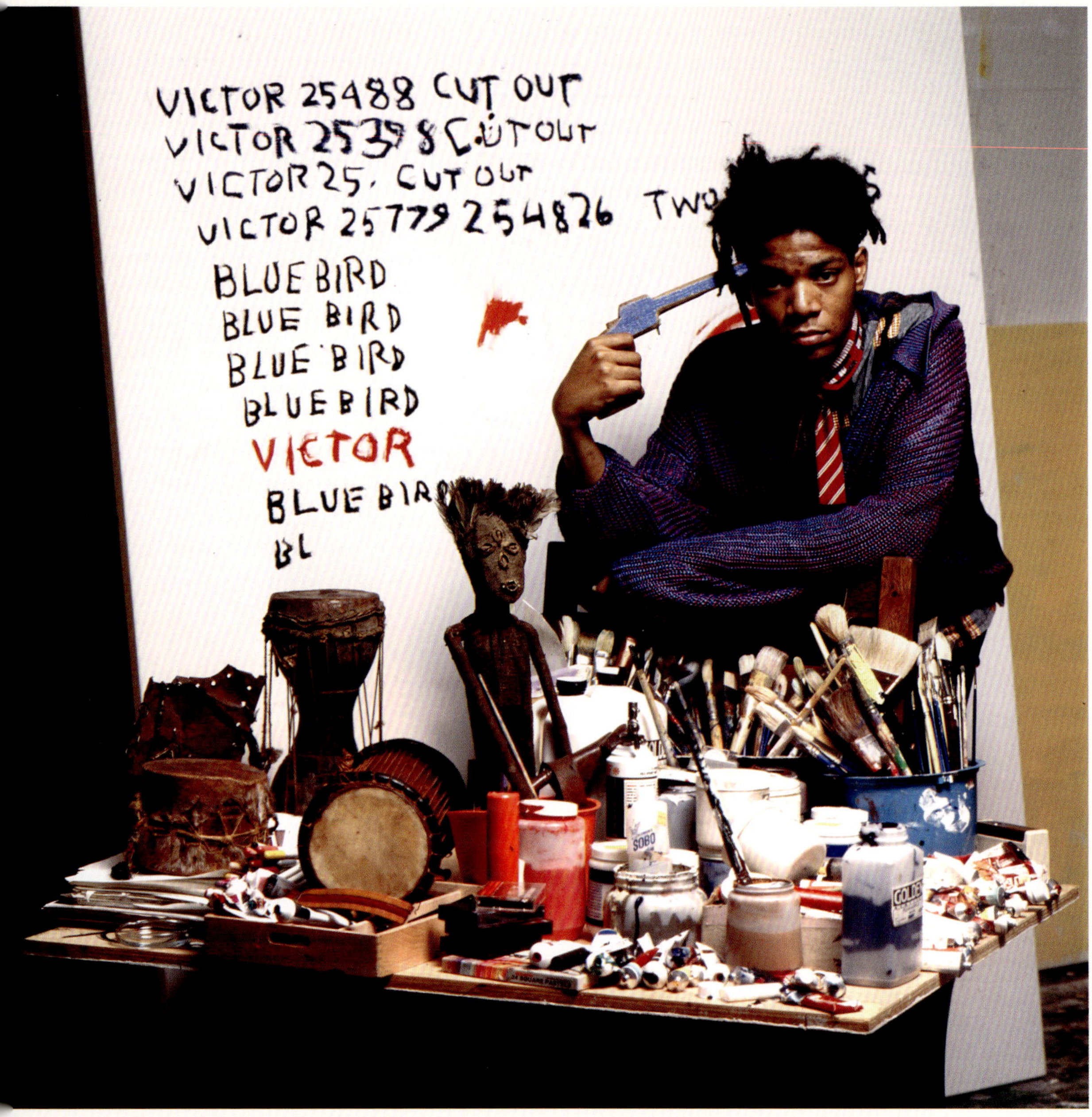

Cloth doll from
Jean-Michel's studio

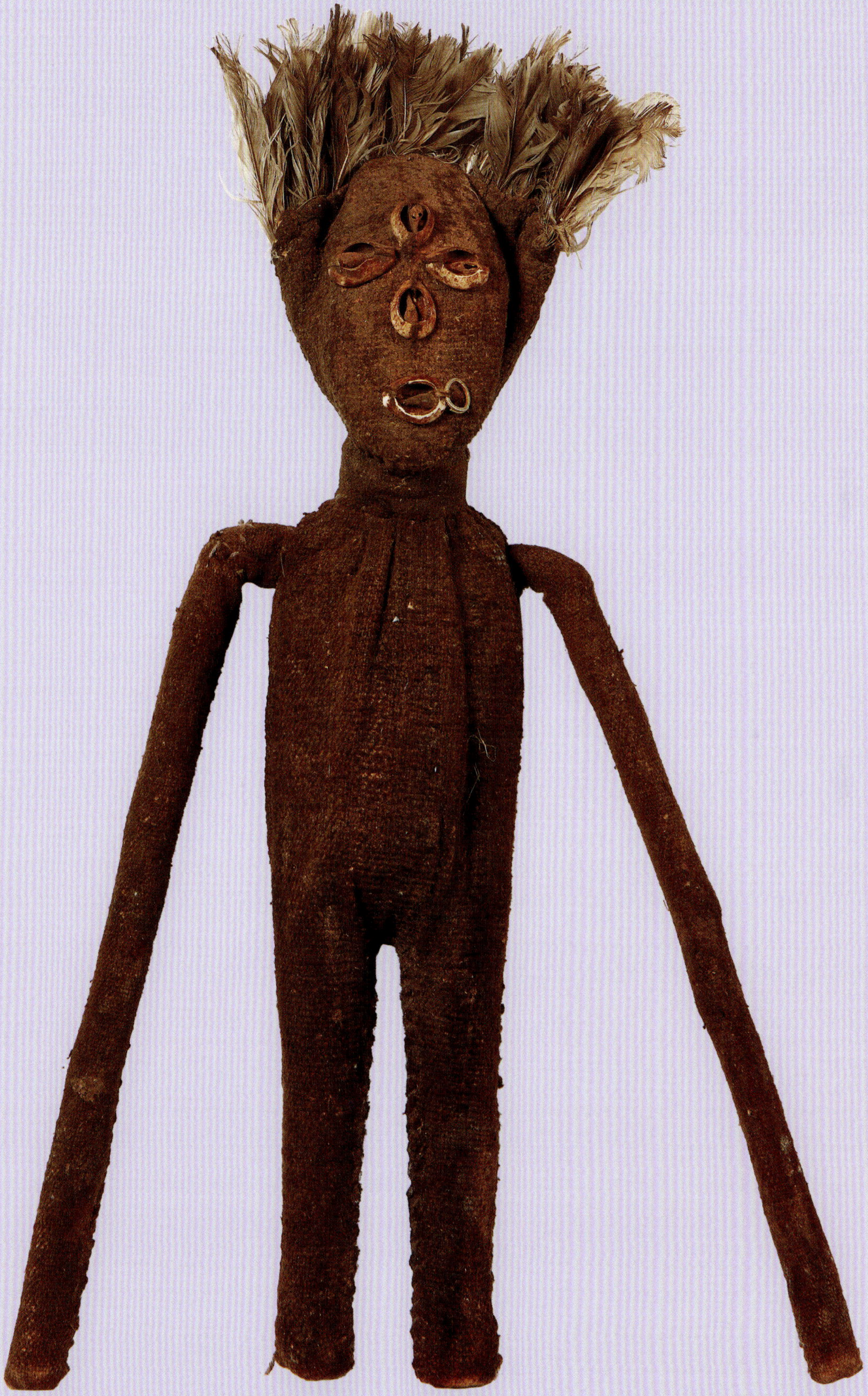

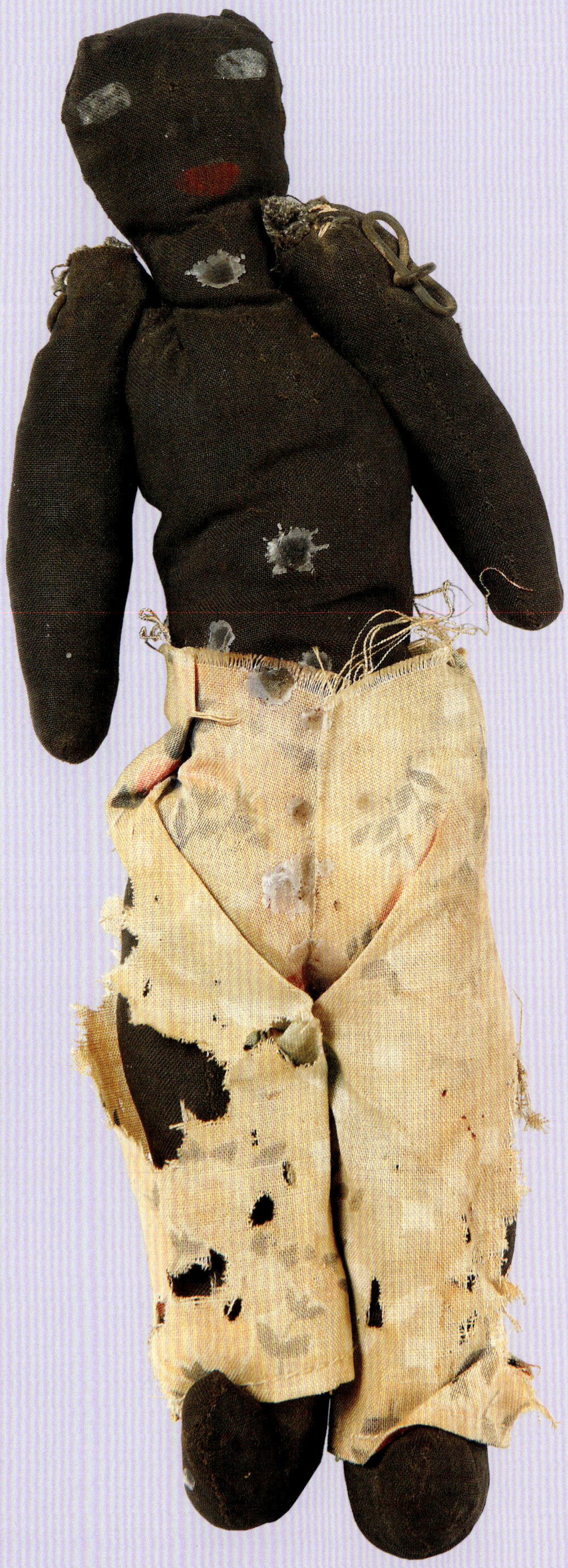

Cloth doll from
Jean-Michel's studio

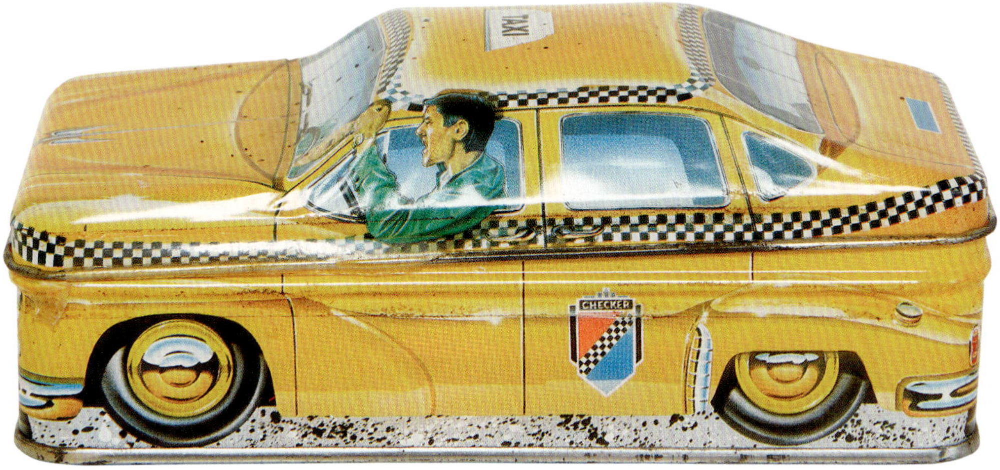

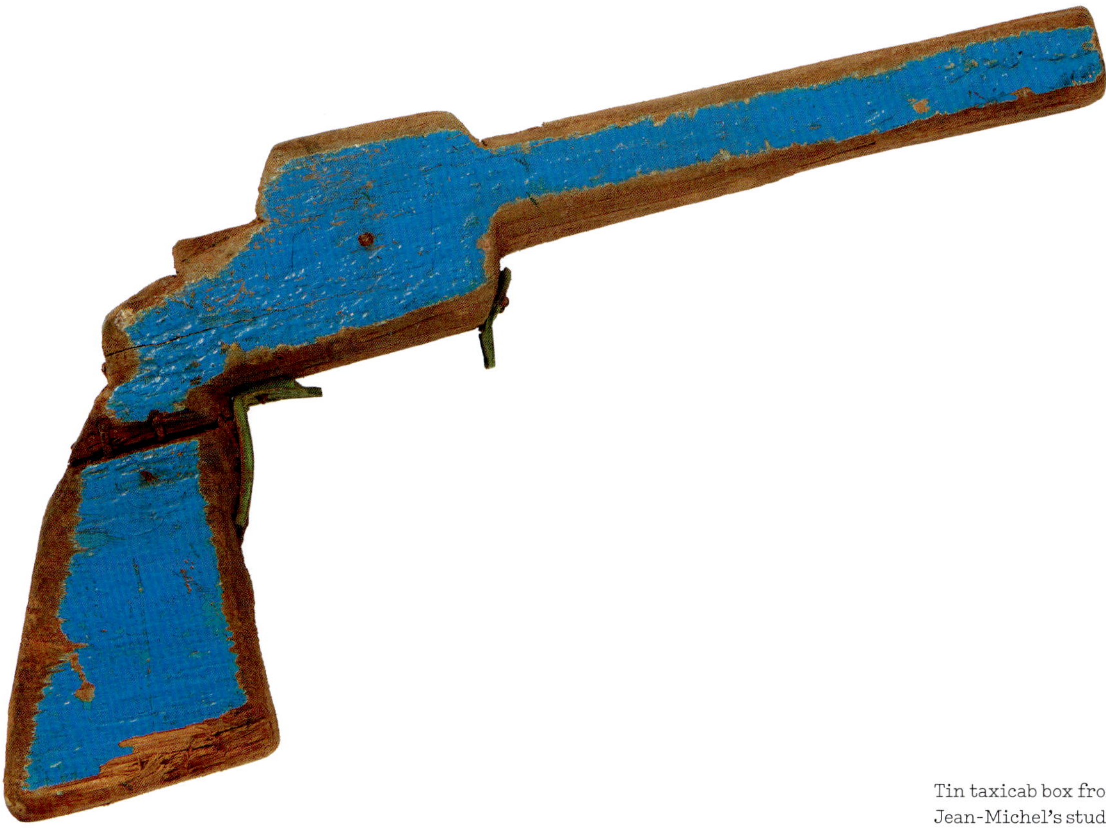

Tin taxicab box from
Jean-Michel's studio

Wood toy gun from
Jean-Michel's studio

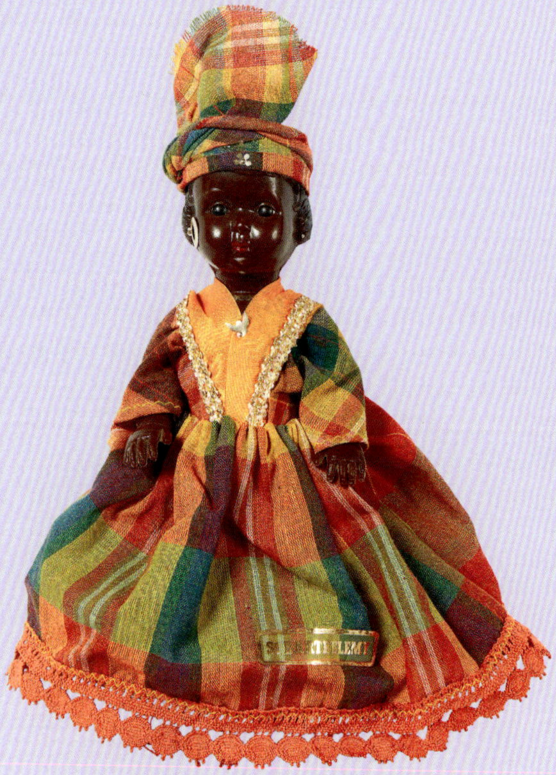

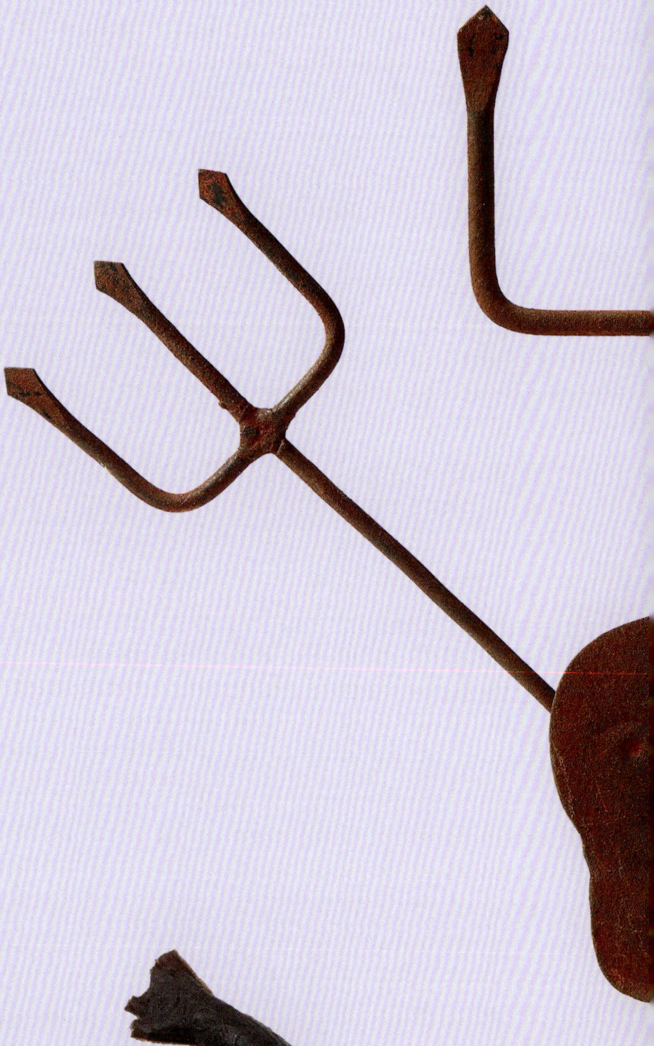

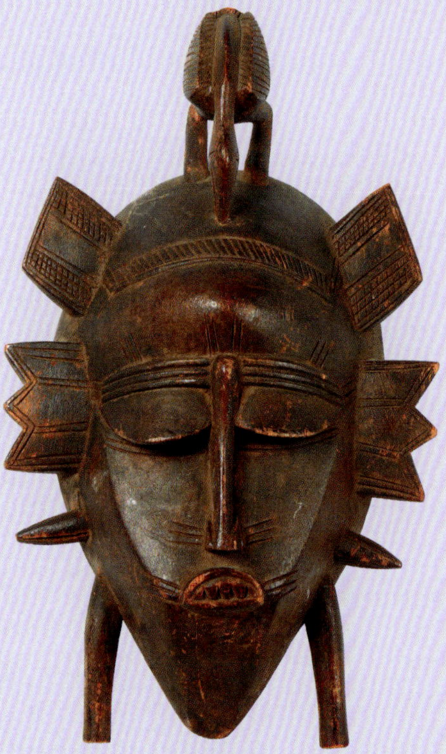

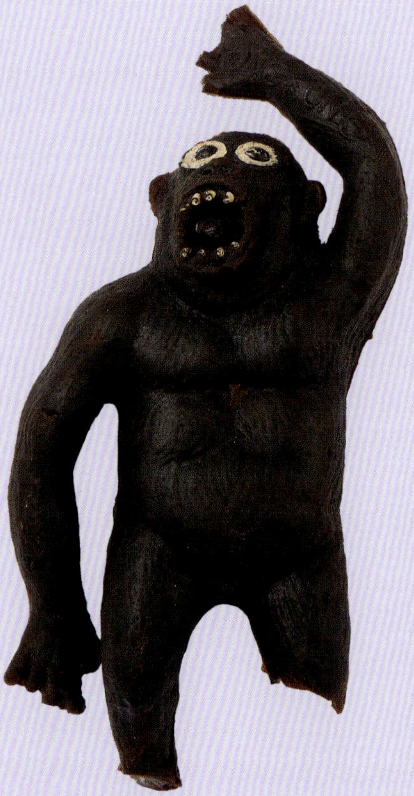

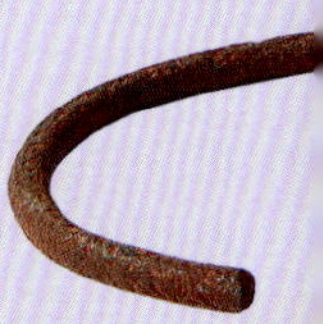

Objects from Jean-Michel's studio (top to bottom, left to right): St. Barthelemy doll, carved wood mask, rubber ape, metal skull sculpture, monkey sculpture, wood mask, and wood animal sculpture purchased by Jean-Michel on his trip to the Ivory Coast

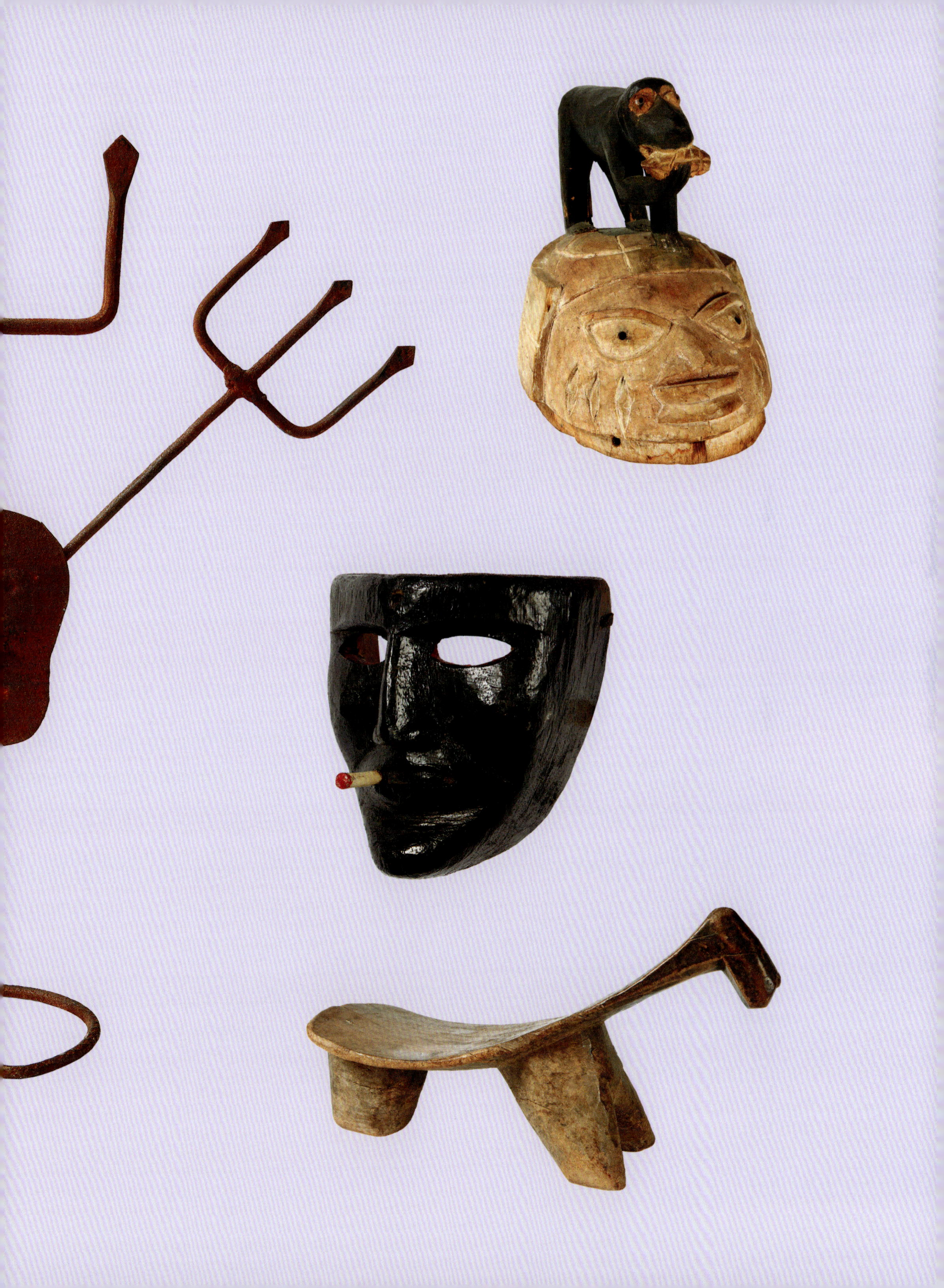

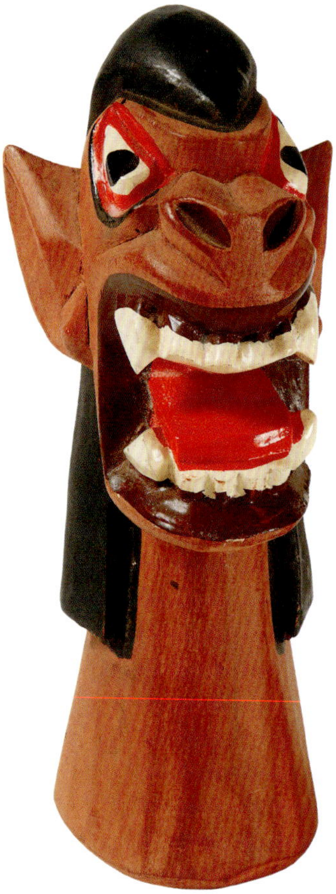

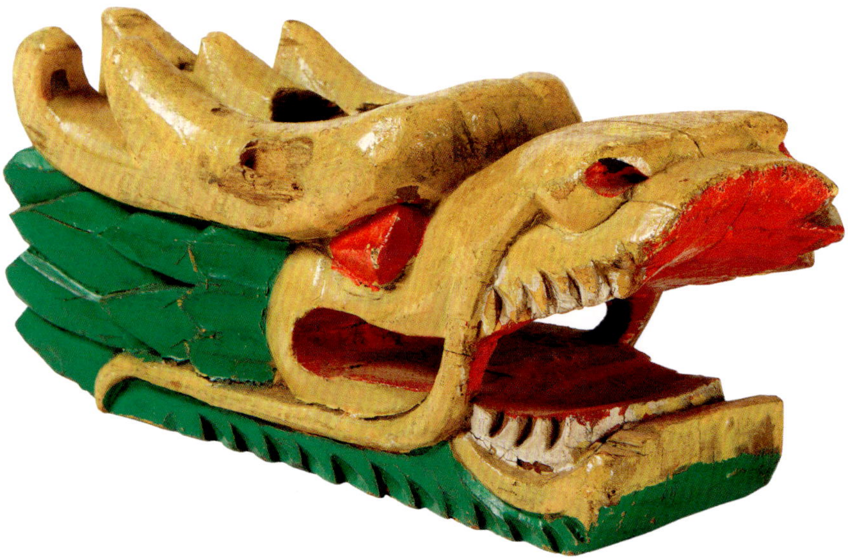

TOP
Wood sculpture from Jean-Michel's studio

BOTTOM
Wood sculpture used as source material for Jean-Michel's *Untitled (Palladium)* painting

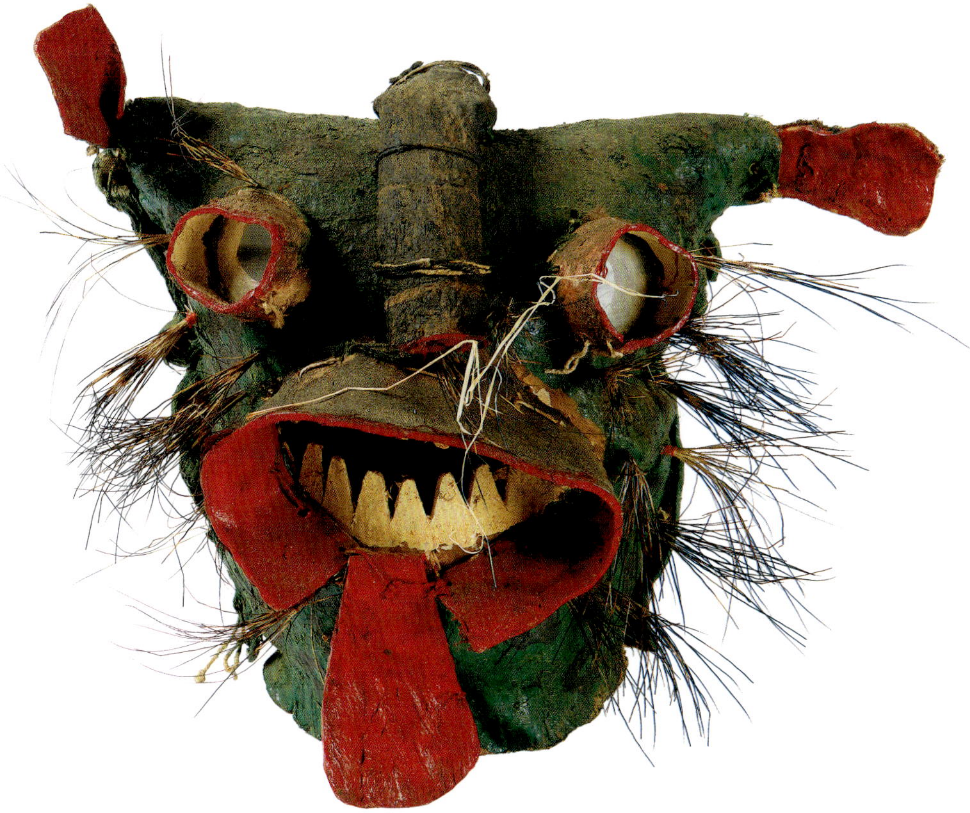

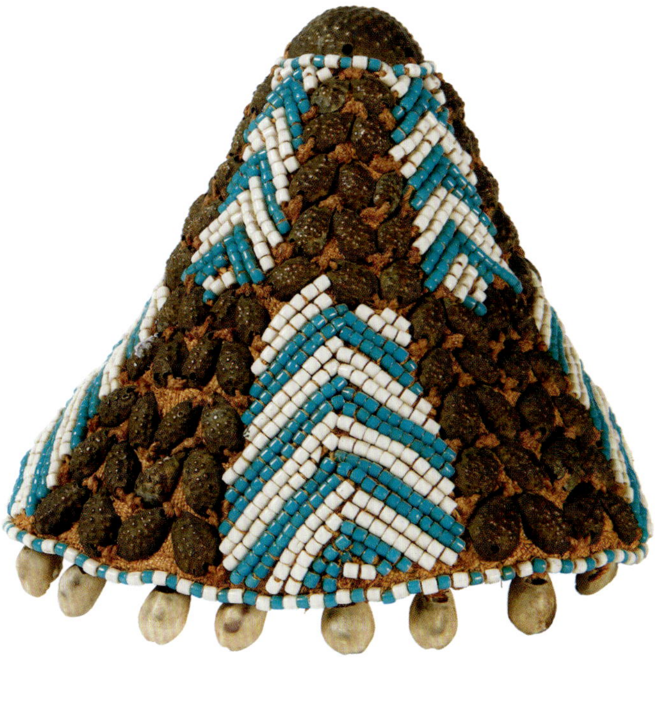

TOP
African mask purchased by Jean-Michel on his trip to the Ivory Coast

BOTTOM
Beaded sculpture from Jean-Michel's studio

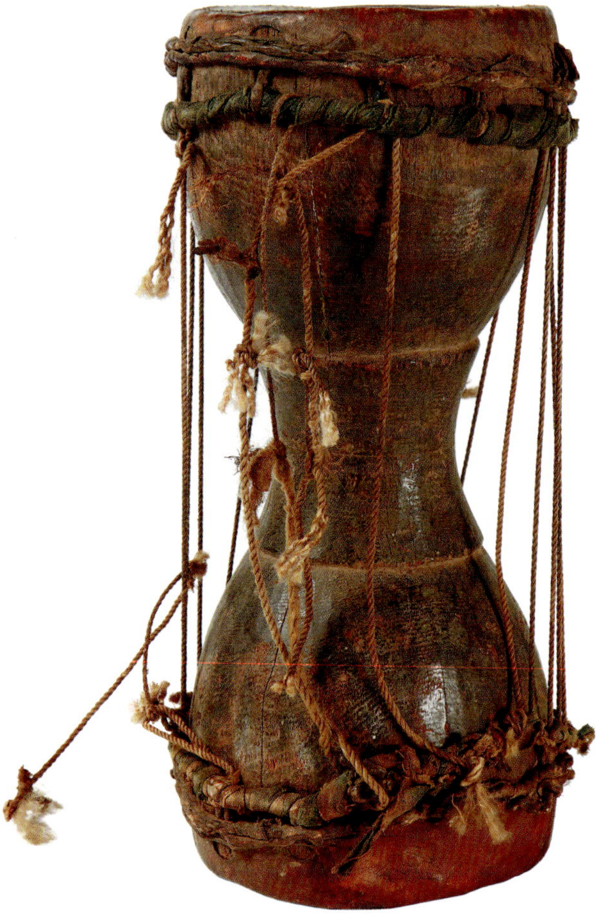

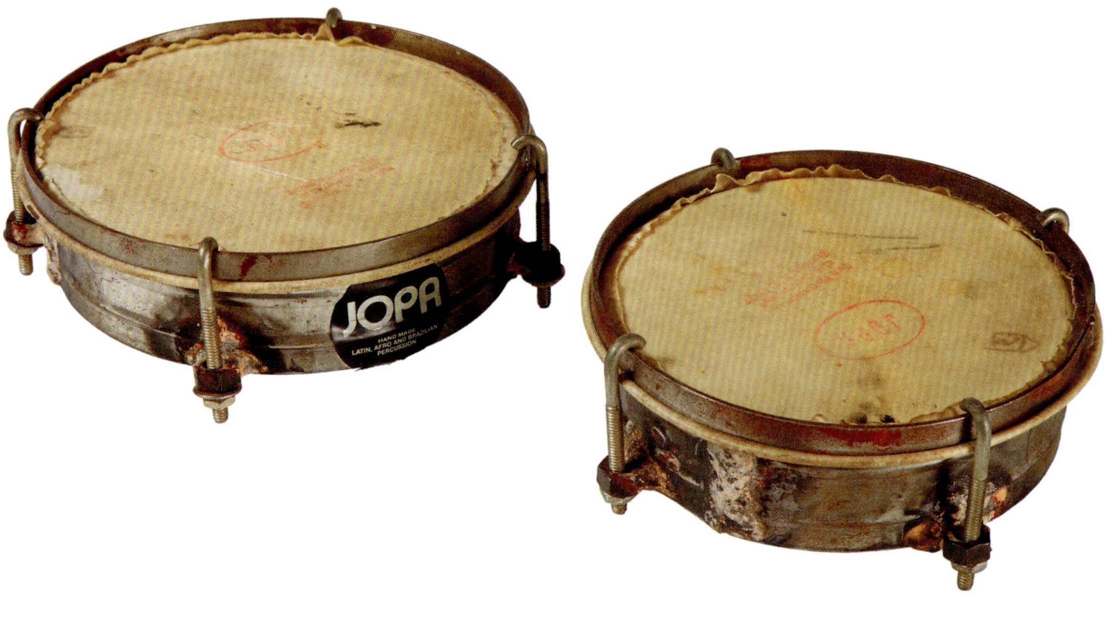

Drums from
Jean-Michel's studio

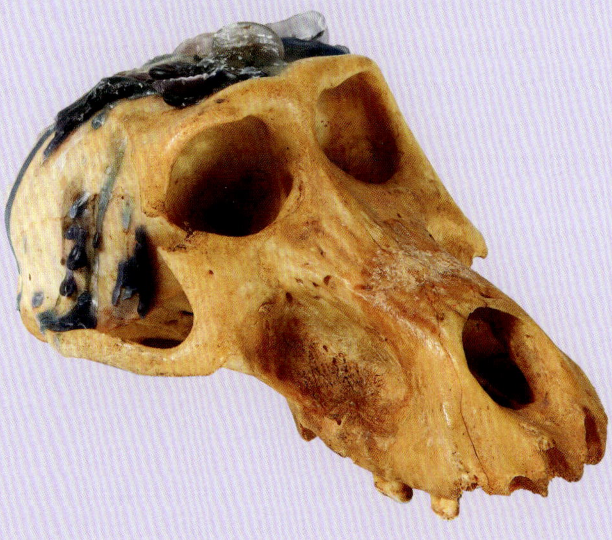
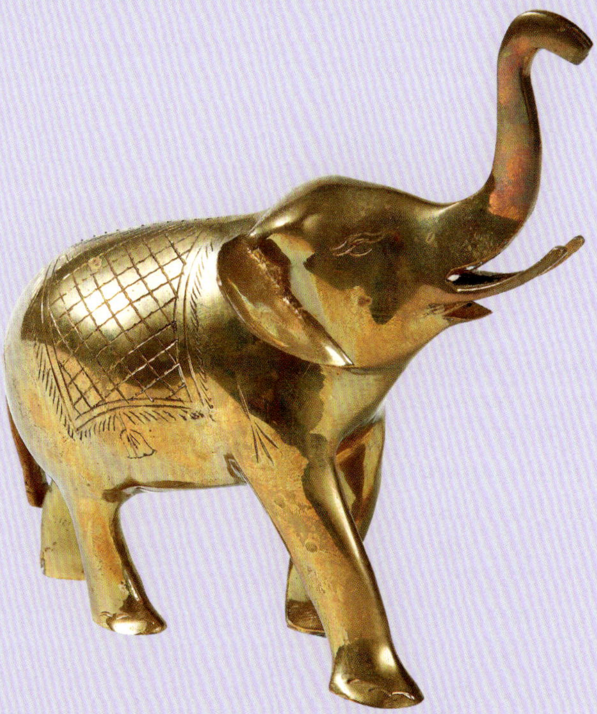
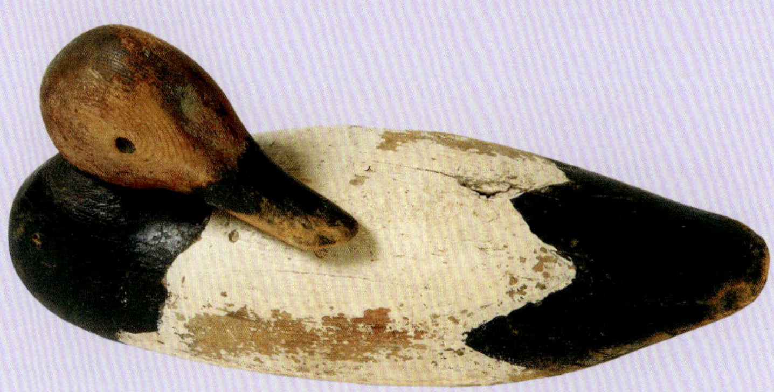
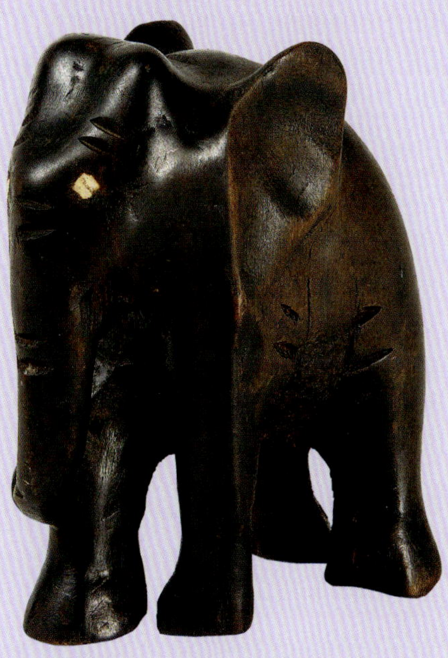
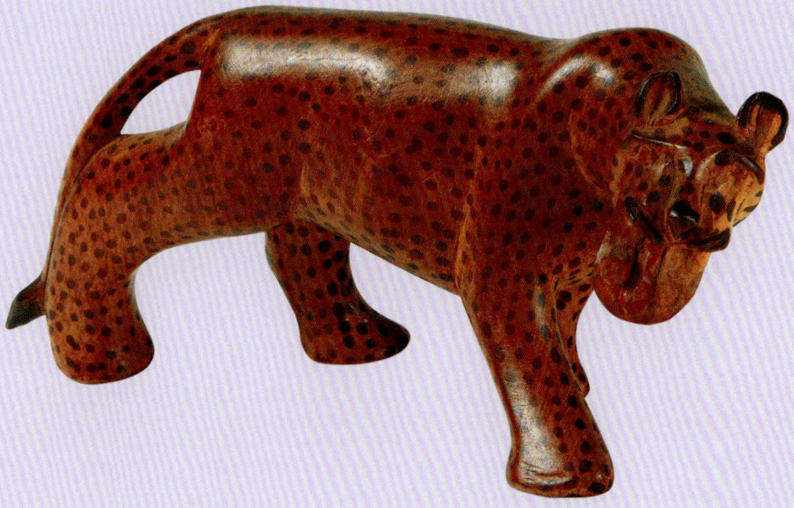

Objects from Jean-Michel's studio (clockwise from top left): Monkey skull, metal elephant sculpture, wood duck decoy, wood leopard sculpture, and wood elephant sculpture

Objects from Jean-Michel's studio (top to bottom): Decorated globe, box camera, bronze candle holder, and metal steamboat sculpture

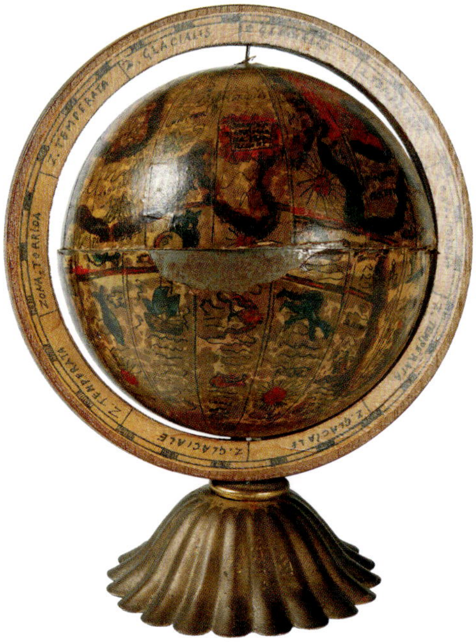

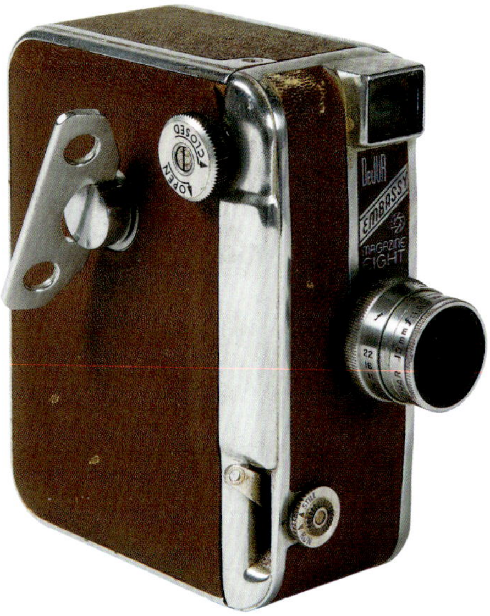

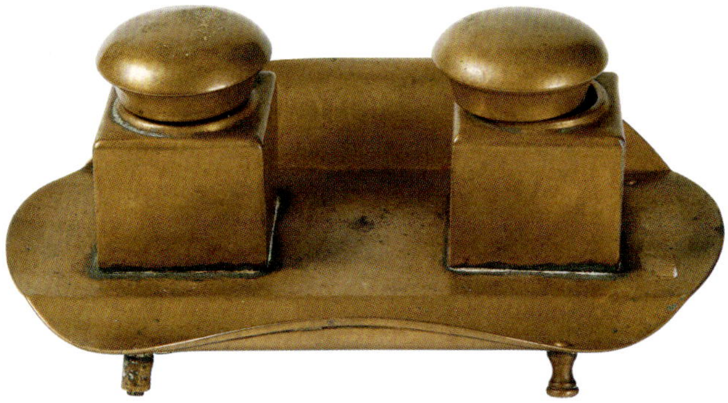

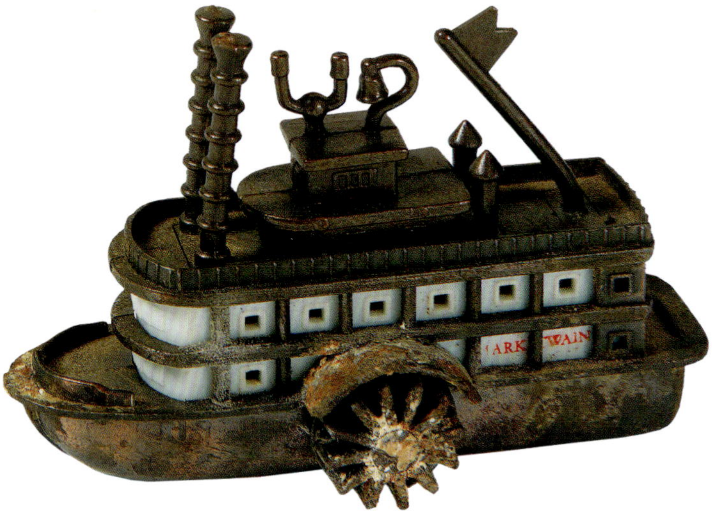

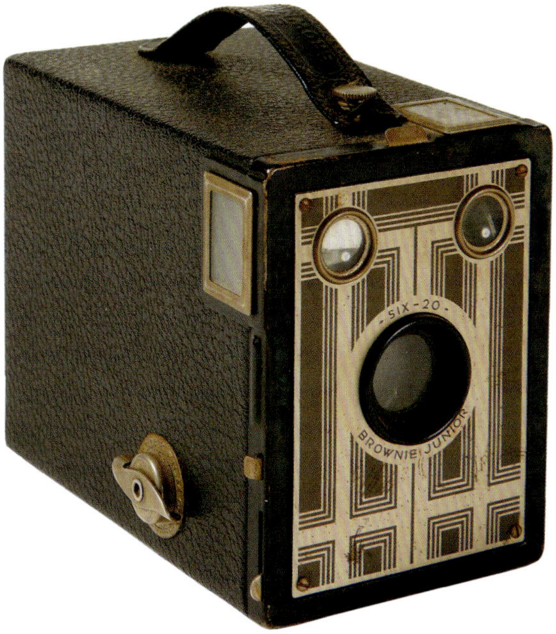

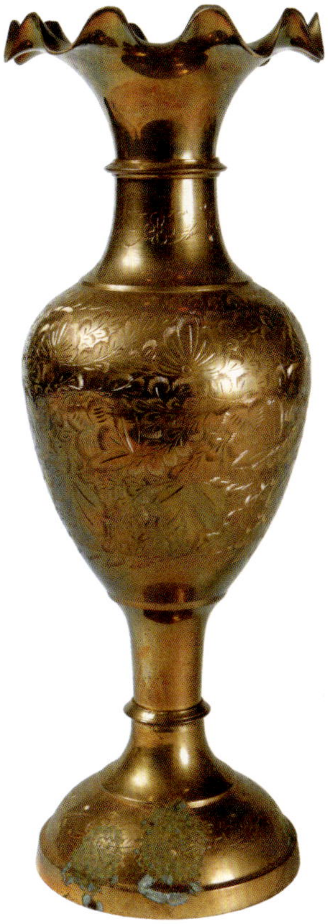

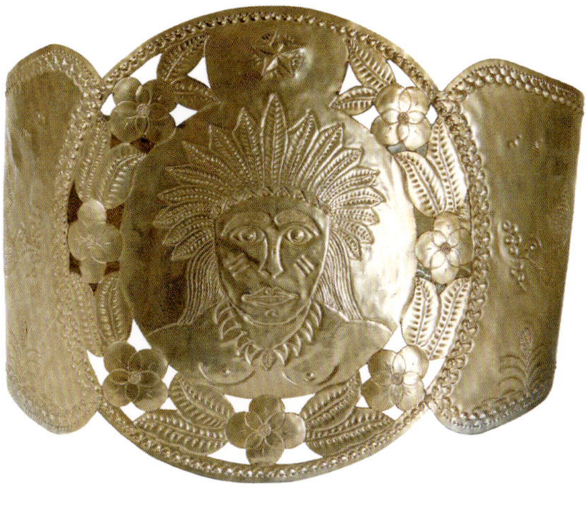

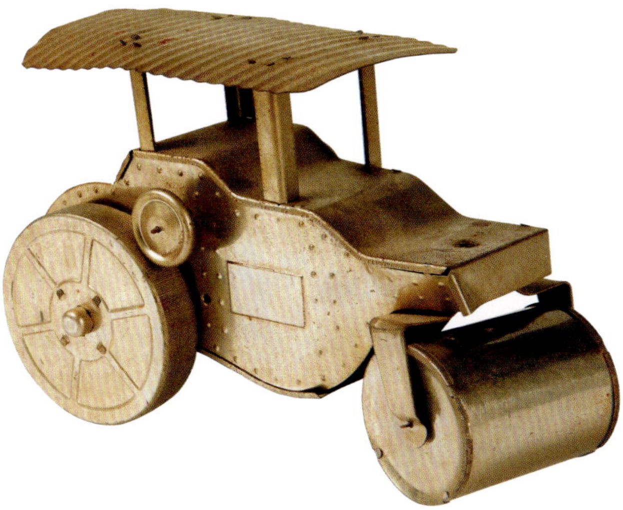

Objects from Jean-Michel's studio (top to bottom): Box camera, decorative metal vase, metal belt purchased by Jean-Michel on his trip to the Ivory Coast, and tin car

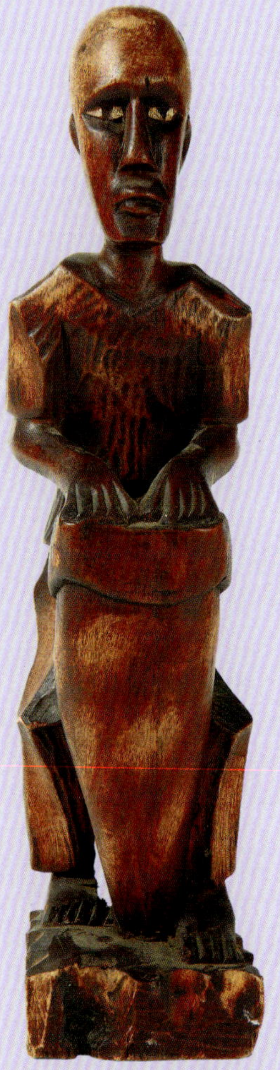

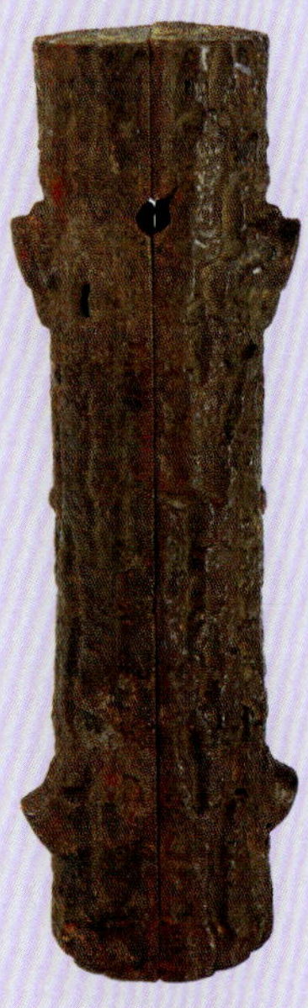

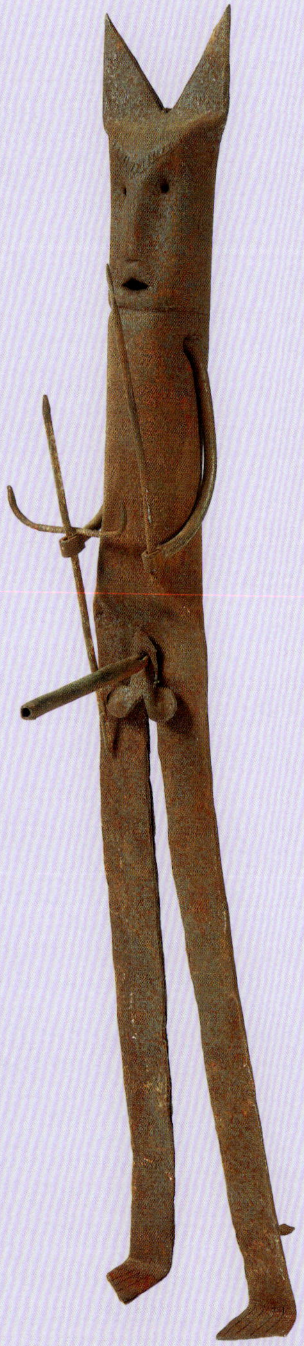

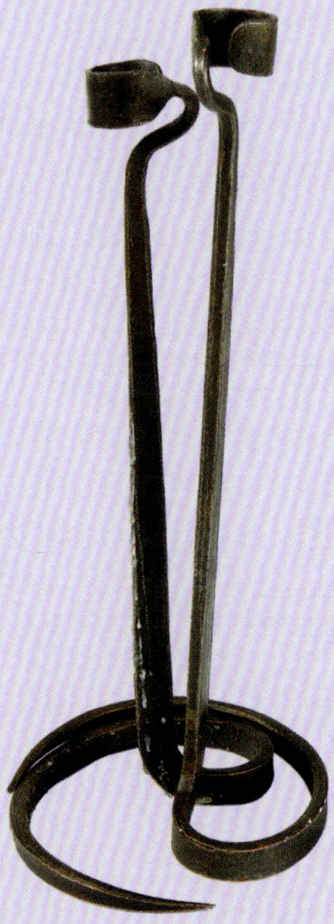

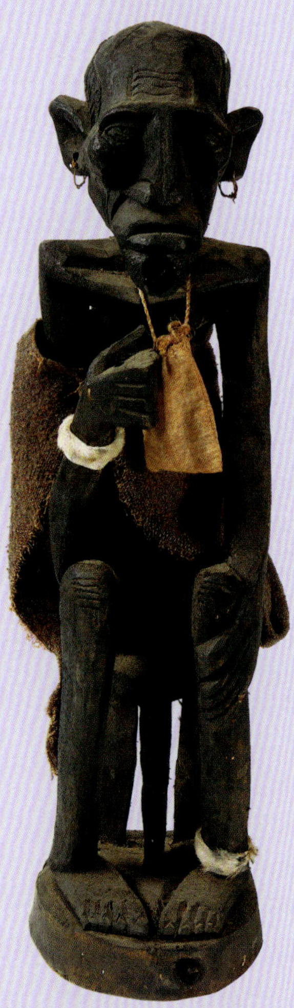

Objects from Jean-Michel's studio (clockwise from top left): Wood statue, wood tree trunk sculpture, metal sculpture, wood sculpture purchased by Jean-Michel on his trip to the Ivory Coast, and pair of iron candle holders

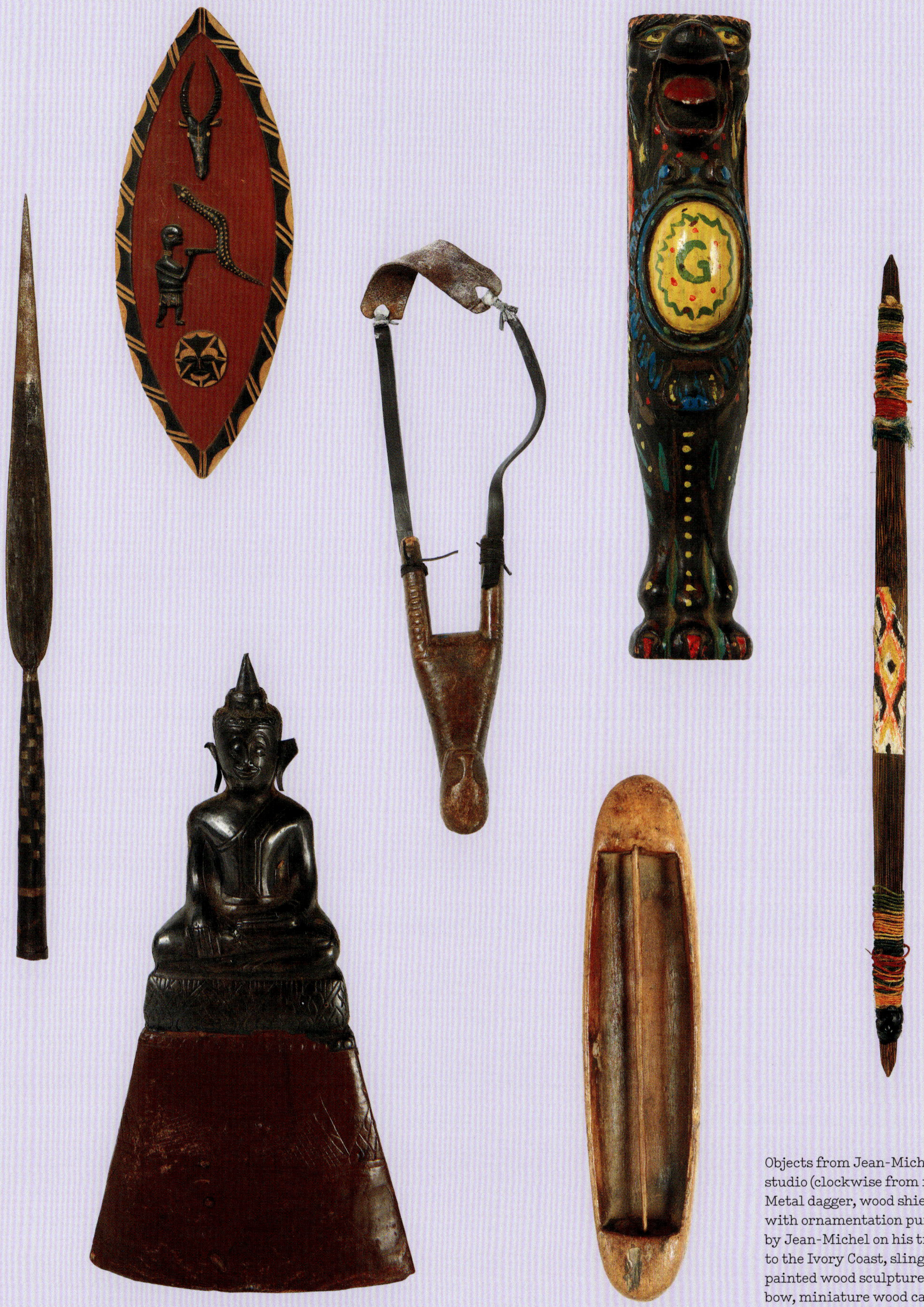

Objects from Jean-Michel's studio (clockwise from far left): Metal dagger, wood shield with ornamentation purchased by Jean-Michel on his trip to the Ivory Coast, sling shot, painted wood sculpture, wood bow, miniature wood canoe, and metal and wood Buddhist sculpture

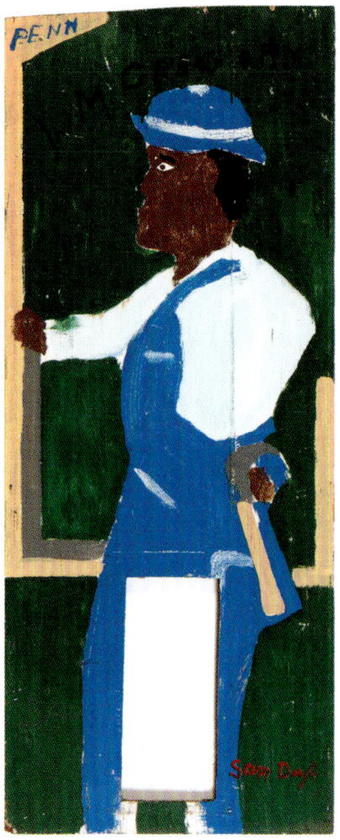
PENN

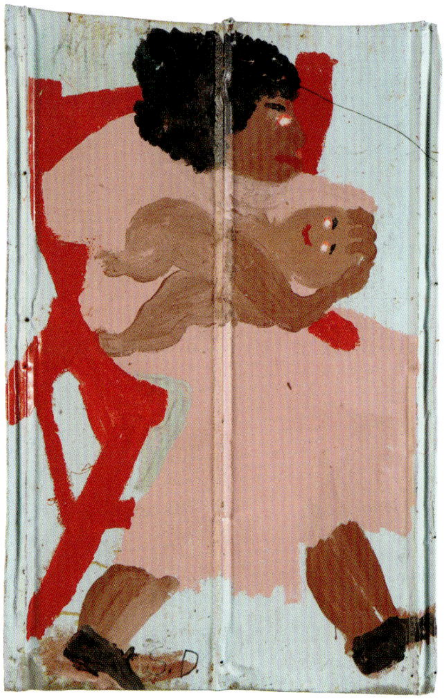

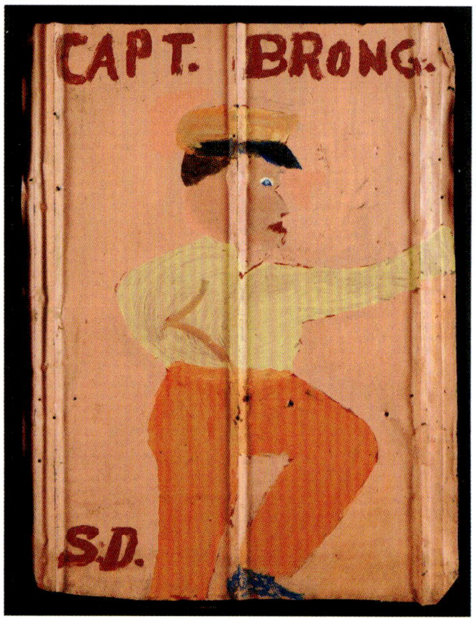
CAPT. BRONG.
S.D.

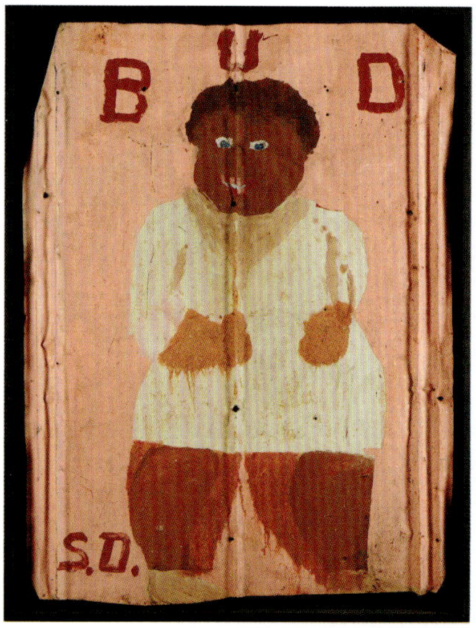
B U D
S.D.

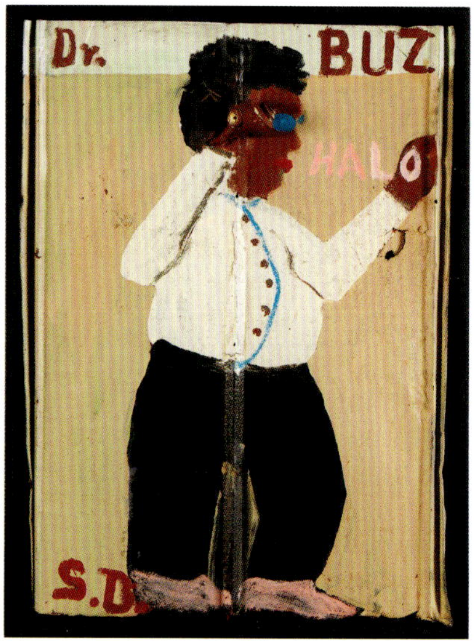
Dr. BUZ
HALO
S.D

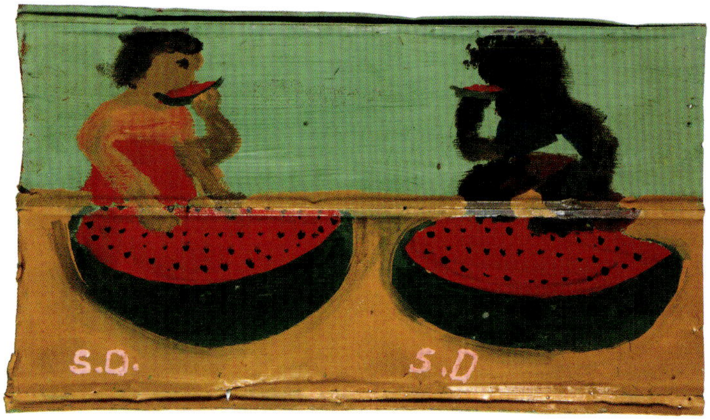
S.D.
S.D

JEAN-MICHEL AS COLLECTOR

Jean-Michel collected many things as he went through life, and he often bought the work of fellow artists, including friends. He owned several works by Sam Doyle, a Black artist from South Carolina who painted on wood and sheet metal depicting the people of his St. Helena Gullah community. He also collected works by Alison Saar, who painted Black figures and athletes on metal and mat board. JEANINE

Jean-Michel purchased ten Sam Doyle paintings from my gallery in 1985 while he was in Atlanta for an exhibition of his drawings. He gave away four of the paintings as gifts and kept the others. When I went to New York to select the drawings for his show, I played with his beautiful, large white cat who seemed to like me. Back in New York after his show, he called to ask if he could send me the cat since he was traveling a lot. He bought a crate and flew to Atlanta. I renamed it Basquiat, and it lived to be seventeen years old. FAY GOLD, FAY GOLD GALLERY

OPPOSITE
All works are by Sam Doyle and were acquired from Fay Gold Gallery, Atlanta, Georgia.

OPPOSITE TOP, LEFT TO RIGHT
Portrait of William Gregory, n.d.
House paint on wood
50¼ × 20 in. (127.64 × 50.8 cm)

Sam's Grandmother, n.d.
Oil on metal
41 × 25½ in. (104.14 × 64.77 cm)

OPPOSITE MIDDLE, LEFT TO RIGHT
Untitled (Capt. Brong), n.d.
Oil on metal
36½ × 27 in. (9271 × 58 cm)

Bud, n.d.
Oil on metal
37 × 27 in. (9398 × 68.58 cm)

Untitled (Dr. Buz), n.d.
Oil on metal with conch shell and bottle cap
36 × 25½ in. (91.44 × 64.77 cm)

OPPOSITE BOTTOM
Two Figures with Watermelon, n.d.
House paint on metal
25 × 42½ in (63.5 × 107.95 cm)

All works are by Alison Saar.

TOP, LEFT TO RIGHT
K.O., 1984
Watercolor and acrylic with collage on mat board
12 × 8½ in. (30.48 × 21.59 cm)

Easy Money, 1984
Painted metal and mat board
20 × 12½ in. (50.8 × 31.75 cm)

BOTTOM, LEFT TO RIGHT
Mr Easy Money, 1984
Watercolor and acrylic on mat board
12 × 10½ in. (30.48 × 26.67 cm)

Slugger Study, 1984
Watercolor and acrylic with collage on mat board
10 × 8 in. (25.4 × 20.32 cm)

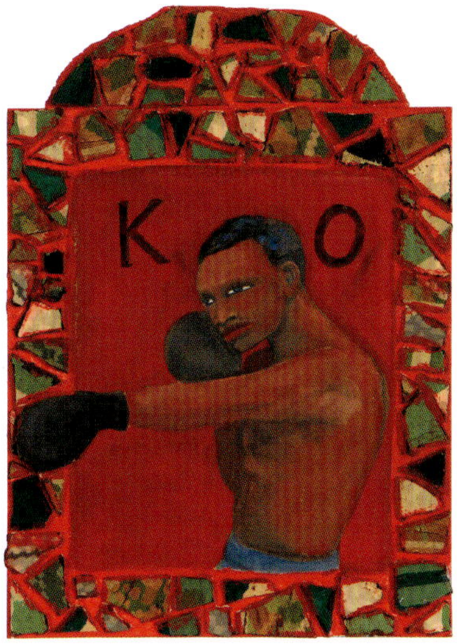

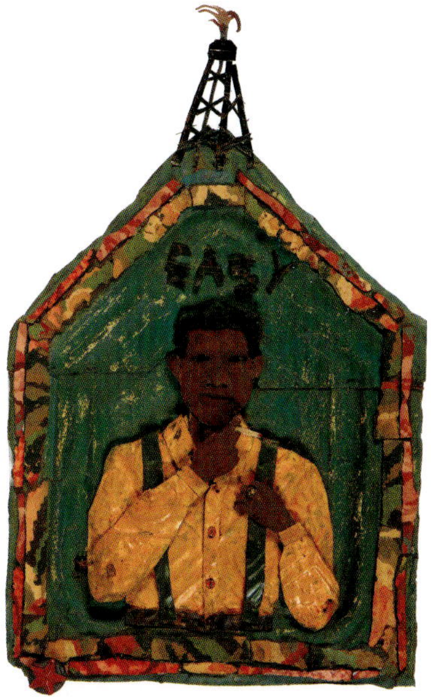

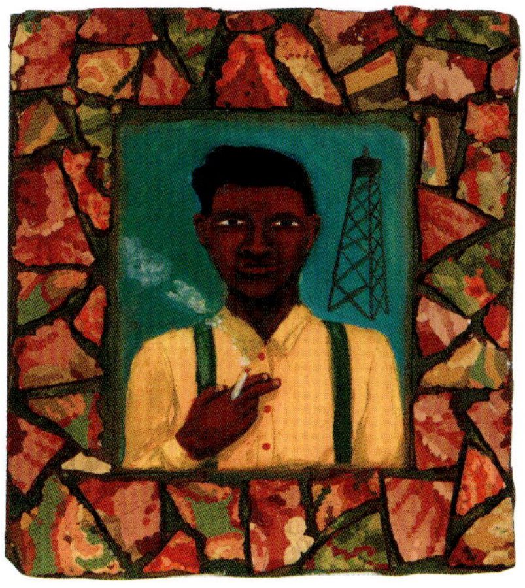

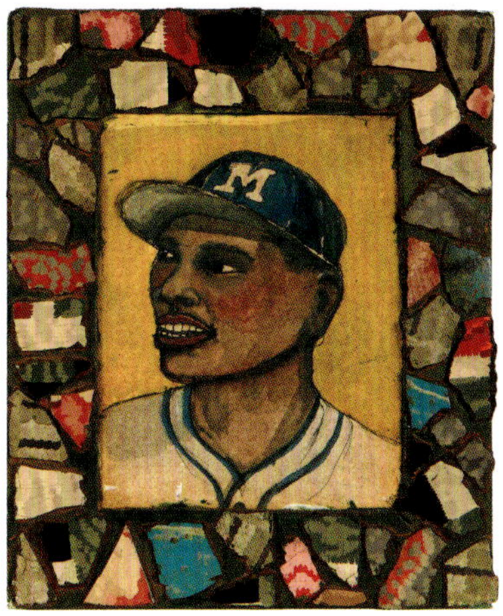

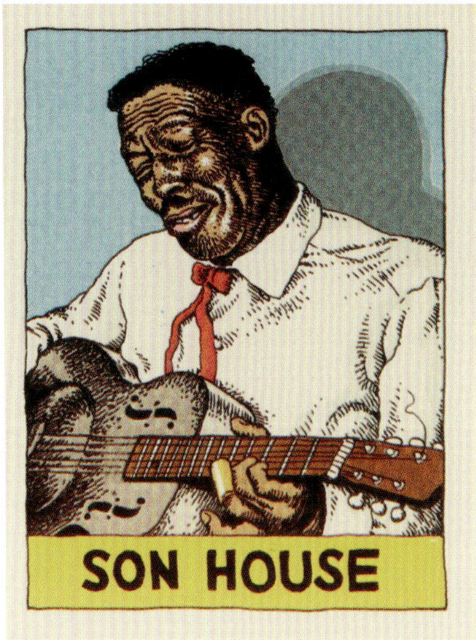

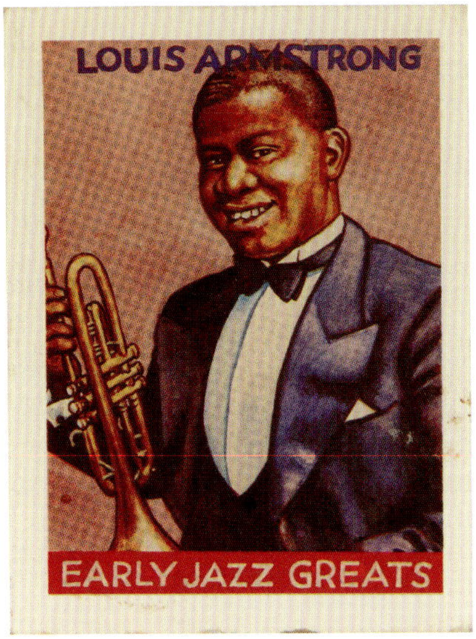

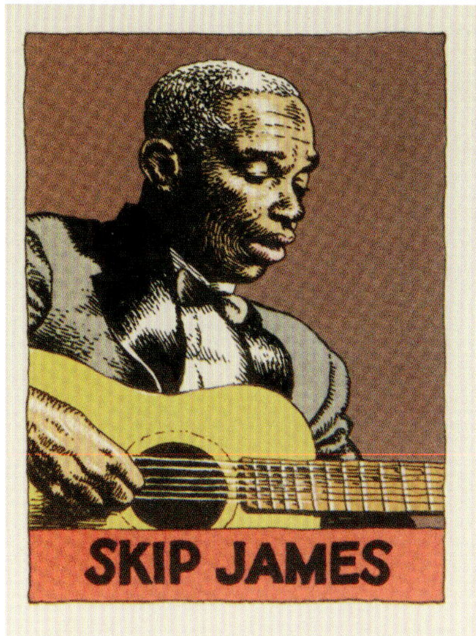

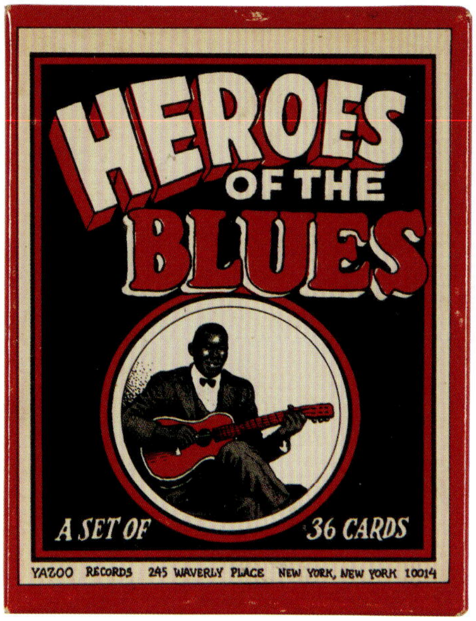

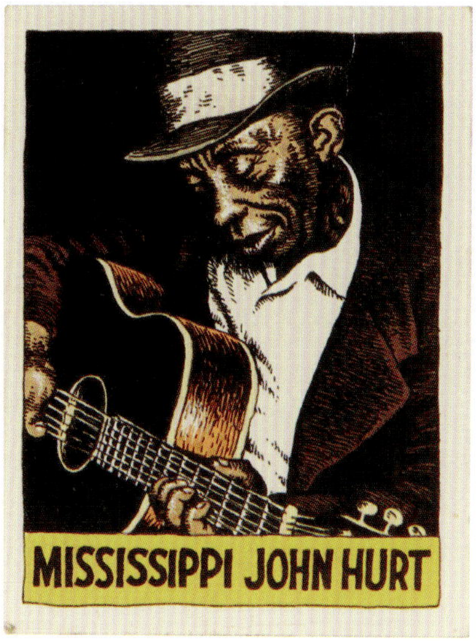

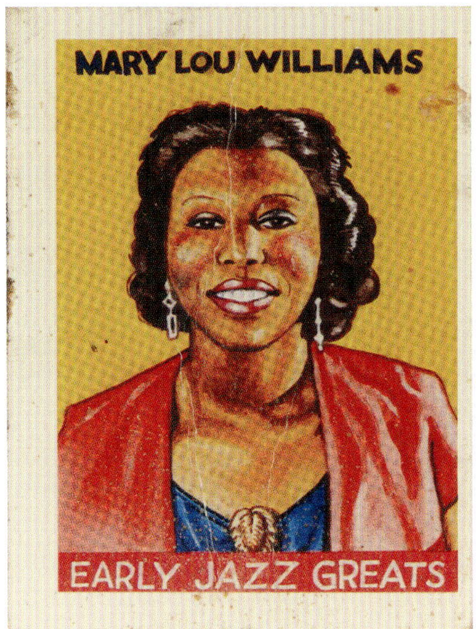

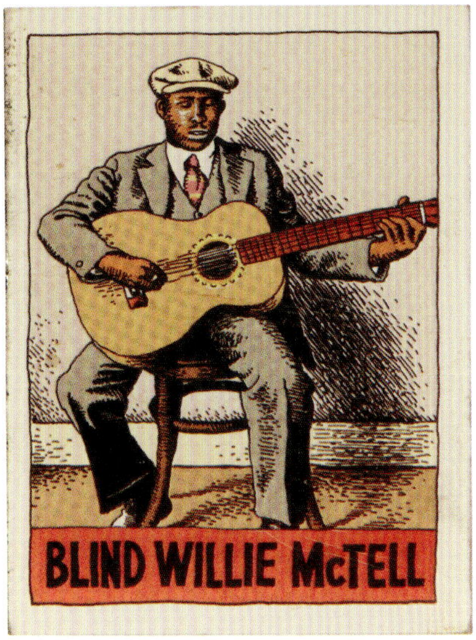

Heroes of the Blues cards. *Jean-Michel was a collector of various trading cards that included Black singers and musicians, superheroes, and ball players.*

OPPOSITE
Marvel superhero cards

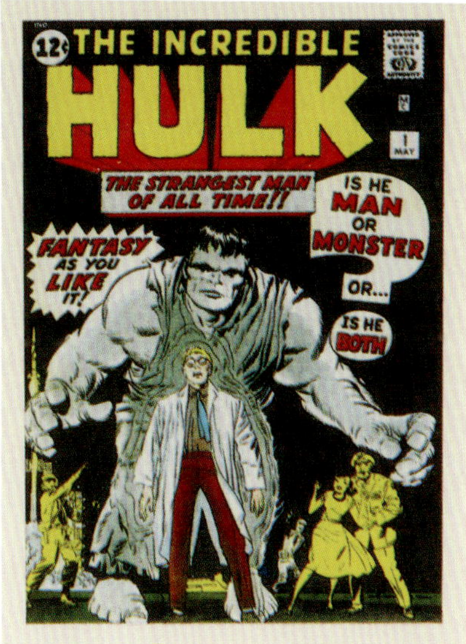
12¢
THE INCREDIBLE
HULK
1 MAY
THE STRANGEST MAN OF ALL TIME!!
IS HE MAN OR MONSTER OR... IS HE BOTH
FANTASY AS YOU LIKE IT!

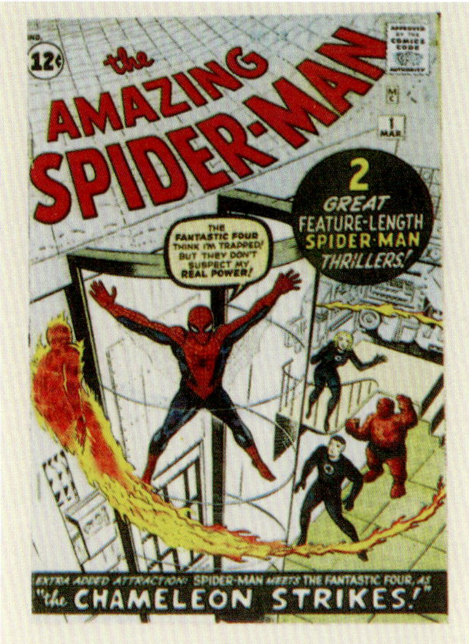
12¢
the AMAZING SPIDER-MAN
1 MAR.
2 GREAT FEATURE-LENGTH SPIDER-MAN THRILLERS!
THE FANTASTIC FOUR THINK I'M TRAPPED! BUT THEY DON'T SUSPECT MY REAL POWER!
EXTRA ADDED ATTRACTION: SPIDER-MAN MEETS THE FANTASTIC FOUR, AS
"the CHAMELEON STRIKES!"

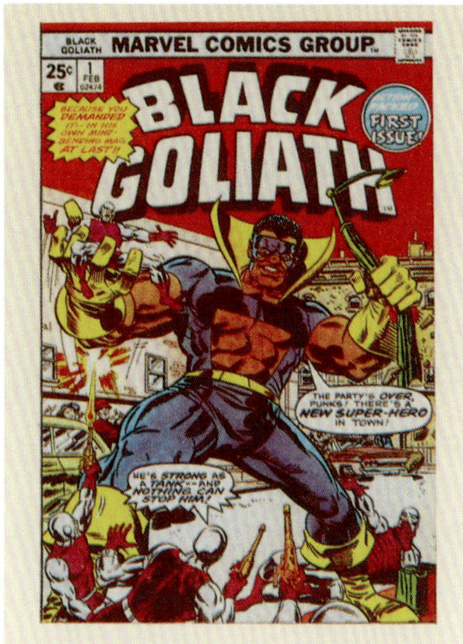
BLACK GOLIATH
MARVEL COMICS GROUP
25¢
1 FEB
BLACK GOLIATH
FIRST ISSUE!
THE PARTY'S OVER, PUNKS! THERE'S A NEW SUPER-HERO IN TOWN!

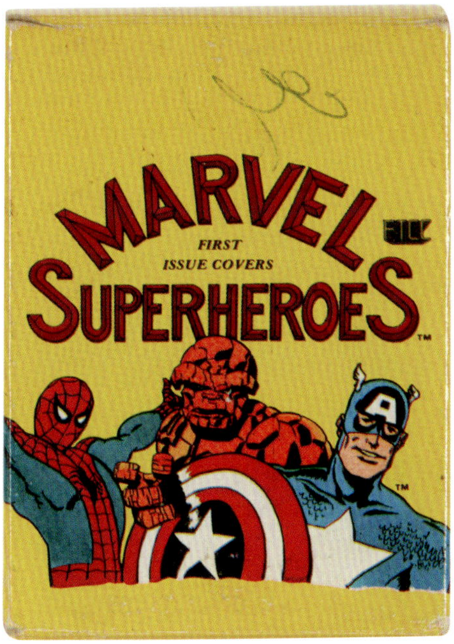
MARVEL
FIRST
ISSUE COVERS
SUPERHEROES
TM

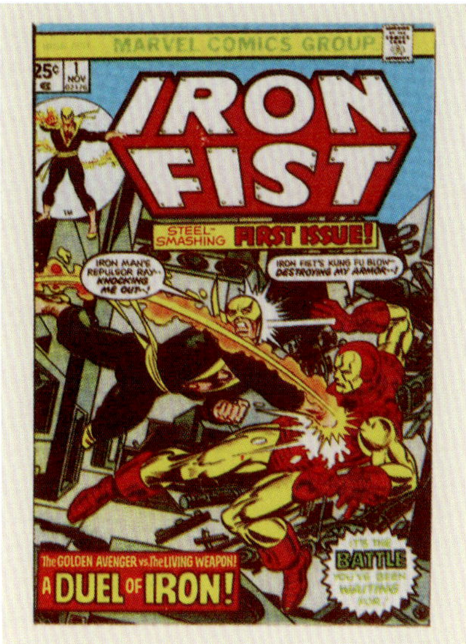
MARVEL COMICS GROUP
25¢
1 NOV
IRON FIST
STEEL-SMASHING FIRST ISSUE!
The GOLDEN AVENGER vs. The LIVING WEAPON!
A DUEL OF IRON!

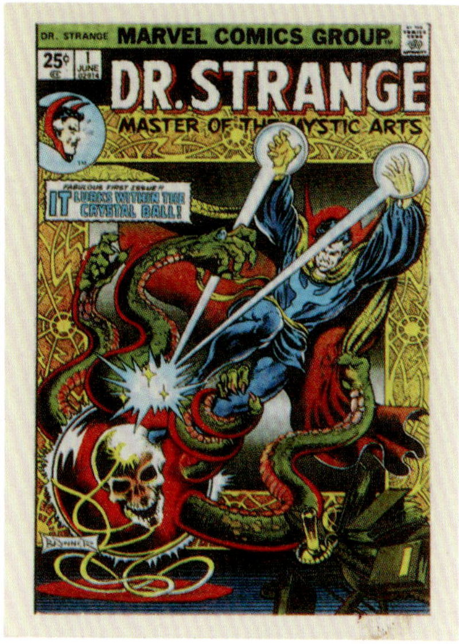
DR. STRANGE
MARVEL COMICS GROUP
25¢
1 JUNE
DR. STRANGE
MASTER OF THE MYSTIC ARTS

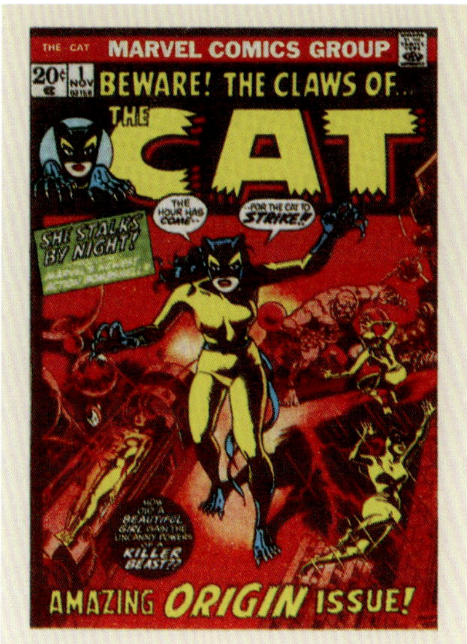
THE CAT
MARVEL COMICS GROUP
20¢
1 NOV
BEWARE! THE CLAWS OF...
THE CAT
AMAZING ORIGIN ISSUE!

JEAN-MICHEL'S COLLECTION OF BOOKS AND MAGAZINES

ART, ARCHITECTURE, AND ANATOMY

African Art: An Introduction. Frank Willett. New York: Oxford University Press, 1971.
Anatomy: A Complete Guide for Artists. Joseph Sheppard. New York: Watson-Guptill Publications, 1975.
Anatomy for the Artist. Improve Your Painting and Drawing Series, No. 9. J. M. Parramón. Hemel Hempstead, UK: Fountain Press, 1973.
Aphrodisiac Erotic Drawings by John Boyce for Selected Passages from the Works of Anaïs Nin. New York: Crown, 1976.
Art about Art. Jean Lipman and Richard Marshall. New York: E. P. Dutton in association with the Whitney Museum of American Art, 1978.
The Art of Cameroon. Tamara Northern. Washington, DC: Smithsonian Institution Traveling Exhibition Service, 1984.
Art USA Now. 2 vols. Allen S. Weller. New York: Viking, 1963.
ARTnews Annual (1955).
Arts Magazine, March 1985.
The Best of "Life." New York: Avon, 1975.
Comix: A History of Comic Books in America. Les Daniels. New York: Bonanza, 1971.
Content: A Contemporary Focus 1974–1984. Hirshhorn Museum and Sculpture Garden. Washington, DC: Smithsonian Institution Press, 1984 (including press clippings, exhibition reviews, press releases, gallery handouts, etc.).
The Cut-outs of Henri Matisse. John Elderfield. New York: George Braziller, 1978.
Draw 50 Famous Faces. Lee J. Ames. Garden City, NY: Doubleday, 1978.
Drawing the Human Form: Methods, Sources, Concepts. William A. Berry. New York: Van Nostrand Reinhold, 1977.
Egyptian Painting. Arpag Mekhitarian. London: Macmillan, 1978.
Gaudi. Ignasi de Solà-Morales. New York: Rizzoli, 1983.
The Human Figure: An Anatomy for Artists. David K. Rubins. Harmondsworth, UK: Penguin, 1977.

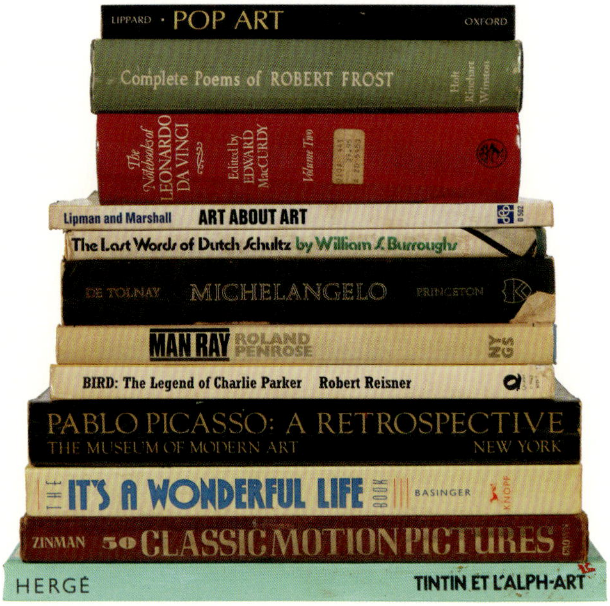

Images of the Mind: Selections from the Edward L. Elliott Family and John B. Elliott Collections of Chinese Calligraphy and Painting at the Art Museum, Princeton University. Wen C. Fong. Princeton, NJ: Art Museum, Princeton, in association with Princeton University Press, 1984.
Italian Primitives: Panel Painting of the Twelfth and Thirteenth Centuries. Enzo Carli. New York: Harry N. Abrams, 1965.
Joseph Beuys, Robert Rauschenberg, Cy Twombly, Andy Warhol: Sammlung Marx. Berlin: Arkadien, 1983.
Krazy Kat: The Comic Art of George Herriman. New York: Harry N. Abrams, 1986.
Little Arena: Drawings and Sculptures from the Collection [of] Adri, Martin, and Geertjan Visser. Toos van Kooten. Otterlo, Neth.: Rijksmuseum Kröller-Müller, 1984.
Man Ray. Roland Penrose. New York: Thames and Hudson, 1975.
Michelangelo. Charles de Tolnay. Princeton, NJ: Princeton University Press, 1975.
Michelangelo: Drawings. Pavel Preiss. Minneapolis: Control Data Arts, 1982.
Mimmo Paladino: Arbeiten auf Papier, 1973–1987. Salzburg: Editions Galerie Thaddaeus Ropac, 1987.
The Natural Way to Draw: A Working Plan for Art Study. Kimon Nicolaides. Boston: Houghton Mifflin, 1941.
The Notebooks of Leonardo da Vinci. 2 vols. Edward MacCurdy, comp., trans. 2nd ed. London: Jonathan Cape, 1977.
Pablo Picasso: A Retrospective. William Rubin, ed. New York: Museum of Modern Art, 1980 (inscribed "For Jean-Michel with my warmest wishes, Annina, Nov. 1981").
Picasso, in Collaboration with Edward Quinn. Pierre Descargues. New York: Felicie, 1974.
Pop Art. Lucy R. Lippard. New York: Oxford University Press, 1966.
The Pop Sixties: A Personal and Irreverent Guide. Andrew J. Edelstein. New York: World Almanac, 1985.
Primitive Art: Its Traditions and Styles. Paul S. Wingert. New York: New American Library, 1962.
"Primitivism" in 20th Century Art: Affinity of the Tribal and the Modern. 2 vols. William Rubin, ed. New York: Museum of Modern Art, 1984.
The Sculpture of Picasso. Roland Penrose. New York: Museum of Modern Art, 1967.
The Story of Painting: From Cave Painting to Modern Times. H. W. Janson and Dora Jane Janson. New York: Harry N. Abrams, 1977.
The Success and Failure of Picasso. John Berger. New York: Pantheon, 1965.
Tintin et L'alph-art. Hergé, Paris: Casterman, 1986.
Van Gogh. Paris: Skira, 1948.
Westkunst zeitgenössische Kunst seit 1939. Laszlo Glozer. Cologne: DuMont, 1981.

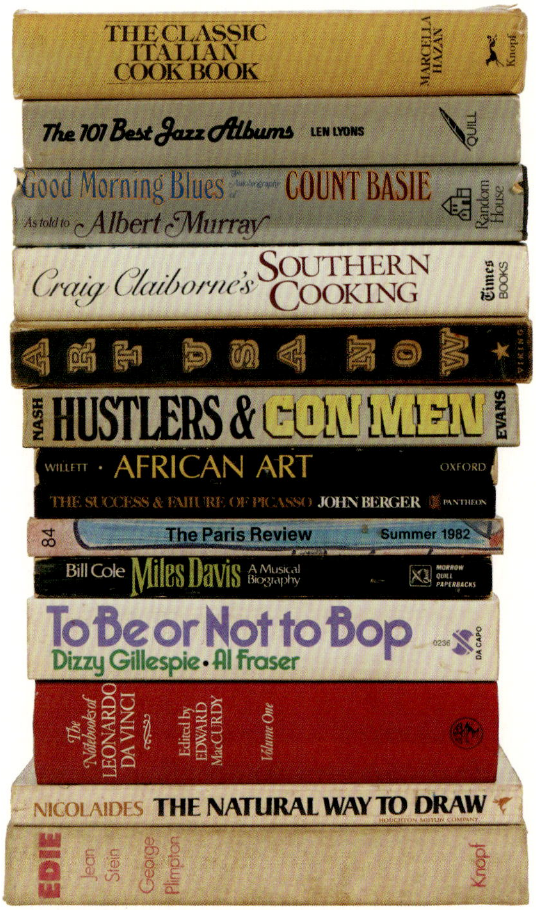

COOKING

Aunt Sammy's Radio Recipes: The Great Depression Cookbook. Ruth Van Deman and Fanny Walker Yeatman. New York: Universe Books, 1975.

Chef Paul Prudhomme's Louisiana Kitchen. Paul Prudhomme. New York: William Morrow, 1984.

The Chez Panisse Menu Cookbook. Alice Waters. New York: Random House, 1982.

The Classic Italian Cookbook. Marcella Hazan. New York: Alfred A. Knopf, 1983.

Craig Claiborne's Southern Cooking. Craig Claiborne. New York: Times Books, 1987.

Mastering the Art of French Cooking. Julia Child, Louisette Bertholle, and Simone Beck. Vol. 1. New York: Alfred A. Knopf, 1983.

Uta Hagen's Love for Cooking. Uta Hagen. New York: Macmillan, 1976.

White Trash Cooking. Ernest Matthew Mickler. Winston-Salem, NC: Jargon Society; Berkeley, CA: Ten Speed Press, 1986.

HISTORY AND ATLASES

Cultural Atlas of Africa. Jocelyn Murray, ed. New York: Facts on File, 1981.

The Earth and Man: A Rand McNally World Atlas. New York: Rand McNally, 1972.

"Life's" Picture History of Western Man. Joseph J. Thorndike Jr. and Joseph Kastner, eds. New York: Time, 1951.

The Times Atlas of the World. 7th comprehensive ed. London: Times Books, 1987.

The White House and Its Thirty-Three Families. New enlarged ed. Amy La Follette Jensen. New York: McGraw-Hill, 1962.

LITERATURE

Complete Poems of Robert Frost. Robert Frost. New York: Holt, Rinehart and Winston, 1963.

Edie. Jean Stein. New York: Alfred A. Knopf, 1982.

Fernando & Marta: A Boy and Girl of Spain. G. Warren Schloat and Anson Wilson Schloat. New York: Alfred A. Knopf, 1970.

Howl. Allen Ginsberg. Barry Miles, ed. New York: Harper and Row, 1984 (inscribed: "For Jean-Michel Basquiat at dinner with W.S. Burroughs December 20, 1986")

Humans at Work. Mike Dowdall, Dennis Welch, and Pat Welch. New York: Simon and Schuster, 1986.

Hustlers and Con Men. Jay Robert Nash. New York: M. Evans, 1976.

The Last Words of Dutch Schultz: A Fiction in the Form of a Film Script. William S. Burroughs. New York: Viking, 1975.

Mussolini. Denis Mack Smith. Milan: Rizzoli, 1983.

Our Literary Heritage: A Pictorial History of the Writer in America. Van Wyck Brooks and Otto L. Bettmann. New York: E. P. Dutton, 1956.

Paris Review, no. 84 (Summer 1982).

MOVIES AND TELEVISION

The Art of Alfred Hitchcock: Fifty Years of His Motion Pictures. Donald Spoto. Garden City, NY: Doubleday, 1976.

Black Hollywood: The Negro in Motion Pictures. Gary Null. Secaucus, NJ: Citadel, 1980.

50 Classic Motion Pictures: The Stuff That Dreams Are Made Of. David Zinman. New York: Crown, 1971.

Flesh and Fantasy. Penny Stallings, with Howard Mandelbaum. New York: Bell, 1978.

Getting into Film. Mel London. New York: Ballantine, 1977.

Hitchcock: Tutti I Film. Riccardo Rosetti. Rome: Savelli, 1980.

Hollywood Babylon II. Kenneth Anger. New York: E. P. Dutton, 1984.

I Need More: The Stooges and Other Stories. Iggy Pop, with Anne Wehrer. New York: Karz-Cohl, 1982.

Incredibly Strange Films. Jim Morton. San Francisco: Re/Search, 1986.

The "It's a Wonderful Life" Book. Jeanine Basinger. New York: Alfred A. Knopf, 1986.

Ladies and Gentlemen, Lenny Bruce!! Albert Goldman, from the journalism of Lawrence Schiller. New York: Random House, 1971.

"Life" Goes to the Movies. New York: Time-Life Books, 1975.

Movie Greats. Paul Michael, ed. New York: Garland, 1969.

A Pictorial History of Horror Movies. Denis Gifford. London: Hamlyn, 1973.

Tallulah. Brendan Gill. New York: Holt, Rinehart and Winston, 1972.

The Universal Story. Clive Hirschhorn. New York: Crown, 1983.

The Warner Bros. Story. Clive Hirschhorn. New York: Crown, 1979.

MUSIC

Bird: The Legend of Charlie Parker. Robert George Reisner. London: Quartet, 1974.

Bird Lives! Ross Russell. London: Quartet, 1980.

Charlie Parker: A Discography. 4 vols. Piet Koster and Dick M. Bakker. Alphen aan den Rijn, Neth.: Micrography, 1974–76.

Good Morning Blues: The Autobiography of Count Basie as told to Albert Murray. New York: Random House, 1985.

Jazz. William Claxton. Santa Fe, NM: Twelvetrees Press, 1987.

Miles Davis: A Musical Biography. Bill Cole. New York: William Morrow, 1974.

The 101 Best Jazz Albums: A History of Jazz on Records. Len Lyons. William Morrow, 1980.

To Be, or Not . . . to Bop. Dizzy Gillespie, with Al Fraser. New York: Da Capo, 1979.

To Bird with Love. Chan Parker. Poitiers, France: Wizlov, 1981.

MISCELLANEOUS

Collecting Toys: A Collector's Identification and Value Guide. Richard O'Brien. 3rd ed. Florence, AL: Books Americana, 1982.

Eastvillage 86: A Guide. A Documentary. New York: Egret, 1986.

Gerry Frank's Where to Find it, Buy it, Eat it, in New York. Gerry Frank. 5th ed. Salem, OR: Gerry's Frankly Speaking, 1987.

Les Aventures de Tintin, Reporter du Petit "Vingtième" au Congo. Hergé. Brussels: Casterman, 1982.

Luna Luna. André Heller. Hamburg: Heyne/Peter Schmidt Studios, 1987.

L'Uomo Vogue, October 1984 (Jean-Michel is profiled on page 388).

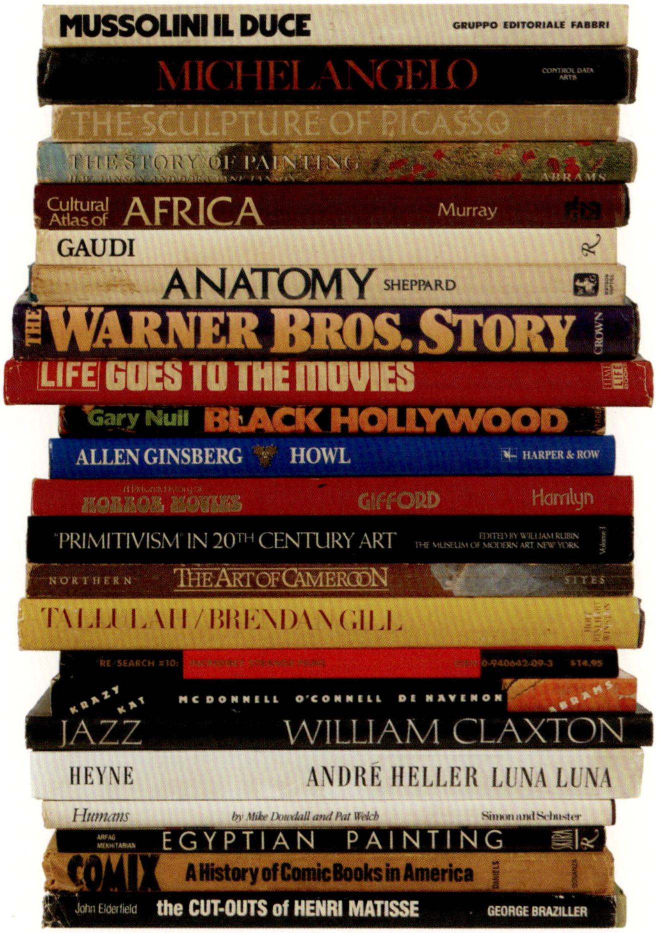

Books from Jean-Michel's Great Jones Street studio

JEAN-MICHEL'S COLLECTION OF MOVIES ON VIDEOTAPE

We always felt that Jean-Michel was a genius from a very young age. As we went through his extensive book and movie collection, I was reminded of Howard Gardner's theory of multiple intelligences—everyone learns differently and those subjects should be taught in various ways. It's clear that Jean-Michel was a visual learner. JEANINE

1910s

The Birth of a Nation, D. W. Griffith, 1915
The Count and *The Adventurer*, Charlie Chaplin, 1916, 1917
Intolerance, D. W. Griffith, 1916
The Original Keystone Comedies, Mack Sennett, 1915 (2 vols.)
Tarzan of the Apes, Scott Sidney, 1918

1920s

Blackmail, Alfred Hitchcock, 1929
Bulldog Drummond, F. Richard Jones, 1929
The Cabinet of Dr. Caligari, Robert Wiene, 1920
The Circus / A Day's Pleasure, Charlie Chaplin, 1928
The Iron Mask, Allan Dwan, 1929
The Lodger, Alfred Hitchcock, 1926
The Lost World, Harry O. Hoyt, 1925
Metropolis, Fritz Lang, 1927
Napoleon, Abel Gance, 1927
Nosferatu, F. W. Murnau, 1922
Spies, Fritz Lang, 1928
Ten Days That Shook the World (originally titled *October*), Sergei Eisenstein, 1927
Wild Orchids, Sidney Franklin, 1929

1930s

Abraham Lincoln, D. W. Griffith, 1930
The Adventures of Robin Hood, Michael Curtiz and William Keighley, 1938
After the Thin Man, W. S. Van Dyke, 1936
Algiers, John Cromwell, 1938
Angels with Dirty Faces, Michael Curtiz, 1938
Animal Crackers, Victor Heerman, 1930
Anna Christie, Clarence Brown, 1930
Anthony Adverse, Mervyn LeRoy, 1936
At the Circus (Marx Bros.), Edward Buzzell, 1939
Beachcomber, Erich Pommer, 1938
Black Fury, Michael Curtiz, 1935
The Blue Angel, Josef von Sternberg, 1930
The Bride of Frankenstein, James Whale, 1935
Call It Murder (originally titled *Midnight*), Chester Erskin[e], 1934
Captain Blood, Michael Curtiz, 1935
Captains Courageous, Victor Fleming, 1937
The Criminal Code, Howard Hawks, 1931
Dames, Ray Enright, 1934
Dark Victory, Edmund Goulding, 1939
David Copperfield, George Cukor, 1935
Dead End, William Wyler, 1937
Dinner at Eight, George Cukor, 1933
Dodge City, Michael Curtiz, 1939
Dodsworth, William Wyler, 1936
Duck Soup, Leo McCarey, 1933
A Farewell to Arms, Frank Borzage, 1932
The Flying Deuces (Laurel & Hardy), A. Edward Sutherland, 1939
Footlight Parade, Lloyd Bacon, 1933
42nd Street, Lloyd Bacon, 1933
Frankenstein, James Whale, 1931
Gold Diggers of 1933, Mervyn LeRoy, 1933
Golden Boy, Rouben Mamoulian, 1939
Gone with the Wind, Victor Fleming, George Cukor, 1939
The Good Earth, Sidney Franklin, 1937
Gunga Din, George Stevens, 1939
Hal Roach Comedy Classics, vol. 3, 1936
Hell's House, Howard Higgin, 1934
The Hurricane, John Ford, 1937
I Am a Fugitive from a Chain Gang, Mervyn LeRoy, 1932
I Cover the Waterfront, James Cruze, 1933
It Happened One Night, Frank Capra, 1934
Juarez, William Dieterle, 1939
King of Jazz, John Murray Anderson, 1930
The Lady Vanishes, Alfred Hitchcock, 1938
M, Fritz Lang, 1931
A Midsummer Night's Dream, Max Reinhardt, 1935
Min and Bill, George Hill, 1930
Modern Times, Charlie Chaplin, 1936
Monkey Business (Marx Bros.), Norman Z. McLeod, 1931

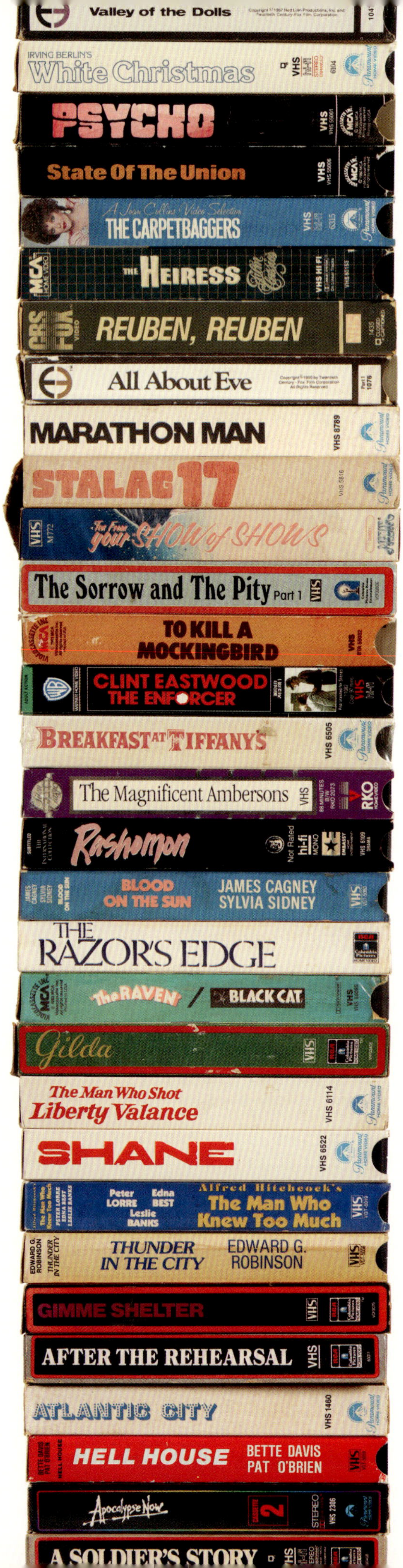

Videotapes from Jean-Michel's Great Jones Street studio

Mr. Moto's Last Warning, Norman Foster, 1939, double feature with *Meeting at Midnight* (originally titled *Black Magic*) (Charlie Chan), Phil Rosen, 1944
Mr. Smith Goes to Washington, Frank Capra, 1939
Murder by Television, Clifford Sanforth, 1935
My Man Godfrey, Gregory La Cava, 1936
A Night at the Opera, Sam Wood, 1935
Ninotchka, Ernst Lubitsch, 1939
Nothing Sacred, William A. Wellman, 1937
Number Seventeen, Alfred Hitchcock, 1932
Our Daily Bread, King Vidor, 1934
Palooka, Benjamin Stoloff, 1934
The Petrified Forest, Archie Mayo, 1936
Possessed, Clarence Brown, 1931
The Private Lives of Elizabeth and Essex, Michael Curtiz, 1939
Public Enemy, William A. Wellman, 1931
Rain, Lewis Milestone, 1932
The Raven, Louis Friedlander, 1935, double feature with *The Black Cat*, Edgar G. Ulmer, 1934
The Roaring Twenties, Raoul Walsh, 1939
Sabotage, Alfred Hitchcock, 1936
San Francisco, W. S. Van Dyke, 1936
Scarface, Howard Hawks, 1932
Secret Agent, Alfred Hitchcock, 1936
The Shadow Strikes, Lynn Shores, 1937
Something to Sing About, Victor Schertzinger, 1937
Stage Door, Gregory La Cava, 1937
Stagecoach, John Ford, 1939
A Star Is Born, William A. Wellman, 1937
Svengali, Archie Mayo, 1931
Tarzan the Ape Man, W. S. Van Dyke, 1932
They Made Me a Criminal, Busby Berkeley, 1939
The Thin Man, W. S. Van Dyke, 1934
The 39 Steps, Alfred Hitchcock, 1935
Thunder in the City, Marion Gering, 1937
Treasure Island, Victor Fleming, 1934
The Triumph of the Will, Leni Riefenstahl, 1935
Way Out West (Laurel & Hardy), James W. Horne, 1937
The Wizard of Oz, Victor Fleming (credited), George Cukor, Mervyn LeRoy, Norman Taurog, Richard Thorpe, and King Vidor, 1939
The Women, George Cukor, 1939
Wuthering Heights, William Wyler, 1939
Zero for Conduct, Jean Vigo, 1933

1940s

Adventures of Don Juan, Vincent Sherman, 1948
Along Came Jones, Stuart Heisler, 1945
The Ape Man, William Beaudine, 1943
Arsenic and Old Lace, Frank Capra, 1944
The Best Years of Our Lives, William Wyler, 1946
The Big Sleep, Howard Hawks, 1946
The Bishop's Wife, Henry Koster, 1947
Black Narcissus, Michael Powell and Emeric Pressburger, 1947
Blood on the Sun, Frank Lloyd, 1945
Body and Soul, Robert Rossen, 1947
Brewster's Millions, Allan Dwan, 1945
Cabin in the Sky, Vincente Minnelli, 1943
Captain Kidd, Rowland V. Lee, 1945
Casablanca, Michael Curtiz, 1942
Christmas in July, Preston Sturges, 1940
A Chump at Oxford (Laurel & Hardy), Alfred J. Goulding, 1940
Citizen Kane, Orson Welles, 1941
Danny Boy, Terry Morse, 1945
Dark Passage, Delmer Daves, 1947
Detour, Edgar C. Ulmer, 1945
Dr. Jekyll and Mr. Hyde, Victor Fleming, 1941
Foreign Correspondent, Alfred Hitchcock, 1940
The Fountainhead, King Vidor, 1949
Gaslight, George Cukor, 1944
Gilda, Charles Vidor, 1946
Go West, Edward Buzzell, 1940
The Gold Rush (reedited silent film with added narration), Charlie Chaplin, 1942
The Great Dictator, Charlie Chaplin, 1940
The Heiress, William Wyler, 1949
Here Comes Mr. Jordan, Alexander Hall, 1941
High Sierra, Raoul Walsh, 1941
His Girl Friday, Howard Hawks, 1940
The Human Comedy, Clarence Brown, 1943
The Inspector General, Henry Koster, 1949
It's a Wonderful Life, Frank Capra, 1946
It's in the Bag!, Richard Wallace, 1945
Ivan the Terrible, Part I, Sergei Eisenstein, 1944
Key Largo, John Huston, 1948
Kitty Foyle, Sam Wood, 1940
The Lady from Shanghai, Orson Welles, 1948
Laura, Otto Preminger, 1944
The Letter, William Wyler, 1940
Lifeboat, Alfred Hitchcock, 1944
Madame Bovary, Vincente Minnelli, 1949
The Magnificent Ambersons, Orson Welles, 1942
The Maltese Falcon, John Huston, 1941
Meet John Doe, Frank Capra, 1941
Mighty Joe Young, Ernest B. Schoedsack, 1949
Mr. Lucky, H. C. Potter, 1943
My Favorite Brunette, Elliott Nugent, 1947
Northern Pursuit, Raoul Wash, 1943
Notorious, Alfred Hitchcock, 1946
Our Town, Sam Wood, 1940
Passage to Marseille, Michael Curtiz, 1944
Penny Serenade, George Stevens, 1941
The Perils of Pauline, George Marshall, 1947
The Philadelphia Story, George Cukor, 1940
The Picture of Dorian Gray, Albert Lewin, 1945
Prelude to War, Frank Capra, 1942
The Pride of the Yankees, Sam Wood, 1942
The Razor's Edge, Edmund Goulding, 1946
Rebecca, Alfred Hitchcock, 1940
Red River, Howard Hawks, 1948
Rome, Open City, Roberto Rossellini, 1946
Rope, Alfred Hitchcock, 1948
Scarlet Street, Fritz Lang, 1945
The Sea Hawk, Michael Curtiz, 1940
The Senator Was Indiscreet, George S. Kaufman, 1947
The Set-Up, Robert Wise, 1949
The Seventh Victim, Mark Robson, 1943
Spellbound, Alfred Hitchcock, 1945
State of the Union, Frank Capra, 1948
Suspicion, Alfred Hitchcock, 1941
Terror by Night, Roy William Neill, 1946
They Died with Their Boots On, Raoul Walsh, 1941
They Drive by Night, Raoul Walsh, 1940
They Live by Night, Nicholas Ray, 1948
The Third Man, Carol Reed, 1949
This Gun for Hire, Frank Tuttle, 1942
To Be or Not to Be, Ernst Lubitsch, 1942
To Have and Have Not, Howard Hawks, 1944
Topper Returns, Roy Del Ruth, 1941
The Treasure of the Sierra Madre, John Huston, 1948
Under Capricorn, Alfred Hitchcock, 1949
Unfaithfully Yours, Preston Sturges, 1948
A Walk in the Sun, Lewis Milestone, 1945
Watch on the Rhine, Herman Shumlin, 1943
White Heat, Raoul Walsh, 1949
Yankee Doodle Dandy, Michael Curtiz, 1942

1950s

The African Queen, John Huston, 1951
All About Eve, Joseph L. Mankiewicz, 1950
The Amos 'n' Andy Show (TV series), ca. 1951
The Asphalt Jungle, John Huston, 1950
Autumn Leaves, Robert Aldrich, 1956
Baby Doll, Elia Kazan, 1956
Beat the Devil, John Huston, 1954
Ben-Hur, William Wyler, 1959
The Big Heat, Fritz Lang, 1953
Black Orpheus, Marcel Camus, 1959
Born Yesterday, George Cukor, 1950
The Bridge on the River Kwai, David Lean, 1957
The Caine Mutiny, Edward Dmytryk, 1954
Chained for Life, Harry Fraser, 1952
Champagne for Caesar, Richard Whorf, 1950
Daughter of Dr. Jekyll, Edgar G. Ulmer, 1957
The Day the Earth Stood Still, Robert Wise, 1951
Diabolique, Henri-Georges Clouzot, 1955
Dial M for Murder, Alfred Hitchcock, 1954
East of Eden, Elia Kazan, 1955
A Farewell to Arms, Charles Vidor, 1957
Giant, George Stevens, 1956
Glen or Glenda, Edward D. Wood Jr., 1953
Guys and Dolls, Joseph L. Mankiewicz, 1955
Hiroshima Mon Amour, Alain Resnais, 1959
The Honeymooners Hidden Episodes, vol. 1, 1953
I Confess, Alfred Hitchcock, 1953
I Vitelloni, Federico Fellini, 1953
Imitation of Life, Douglas Sirk, 1959
Ivanhoe, Richard Thorpe, 1952
Jail Bait, Edward D. Wood Jr., 1954
Jailhouse Rock, Richard Thorpe, 1957
Journey to the Center of the Earth, Henry Levin, 1959

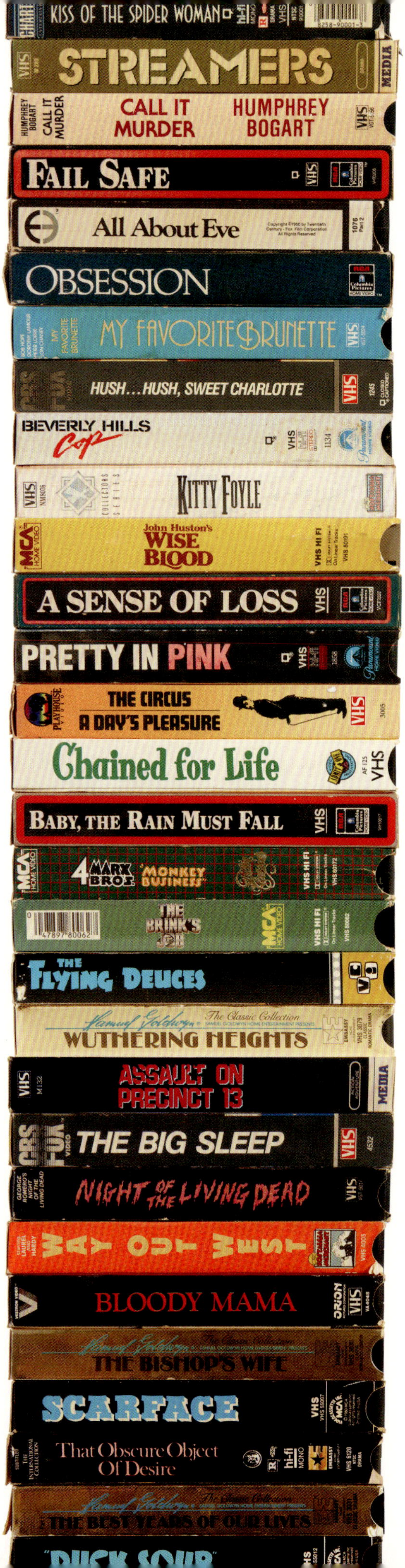

The King and I, Walter Lang, 1956
A King in New York, Charlie Chaplin, 1957
The Left Hand of God, Edward Dmytryk, 1955
Los Olvidados, Luis Buñuel, 1950
Love in the Afternoon, Billy Wilder, 1957
Love in the City, Federico Fellini, 1953
Macao, Josef von Sternberg, 1952
The Man in the White Suit, Alexander Mackendrick, 1951
The Man Who Knew Too Much, Alfred Hitchcock, 1956
Moby Dick, John Huston, 1956
No Time for Sergeants, Mervyn LeRoy, 1958
North by Northwest, Alfred Hitchcock, 1959
On the Waterfront, Elia Kazan, 1954
The Paris Express, Harold French, 1952
A Place in the Sun, George Stevens, 1951
Rashomon, Akira Kurosawa, 1950
Rear Window, Alfred Hitchcock, 1954
Rebel Without a Cause, Nicholas Ray, 1955
The Red Balloon, Albert Lamorisse, 1956
Rififi, Jules Dassin, 1955
Rio Bravo, Howard Hawks, 1959
Sawdust and Tinsel, Ingmar Bergman, 1953
The Searchers, John Ford, 1956
The Seven Samurai, Akira Kurosawa, 1954
The Seven Year Itch, Billy Wilder, 1955
The Seventh Seal, Ingmar Bergman, 1957
Shack Out on 101, Edward Dein, 1955
Shane, George Stevens, 1953
Stalag 17, Billy Wilder, 1953
A Star Is Born, George Cukor, 1954
Strangers on a Train, Alfred Hitchcock, 1951
Sunset Boulevard, Billy Wilder, 1950
The Ten Commandments, Cecil B. DeMille, 1956
Them!, Gordon Douglas, 1954
The Thing from Another World (also known as *The Thing*), Christian Nyby, 1951
To Catch a Thief, Alfred Hitchcock, 1955
Tom Thumb, George Pal, 1958
The Trouble with Harry, Alfred Hitchcock, 1955
12 Angry Men, Sidney Lumet, 1957
Ulysses, Mario Camerini, 1954
Utopia (Laurel & Hardy), Léo Joannon, 1950
Vera Cruz, Robert Aldrich, 1954
Viva Zapata Elia Kazan, 1952
The Wages of Fear, Henri-Georges Clouzot, 1953
While the City Sleeps, Fritz Lang, 1956
White Christmas, Michael Curtiz, 1954
Witness for the Prosecution, Billy Wilder, 1957
The Wrong Man, Alfred Hitchcock, 1956
The Young Philadelphians, Vincent Sherman, 1959

1960s

After the Fox, Vittorio De Sica, 1966
Alfie, Lewis Gilbert, 1966
Alice's Restaurant, Arthur Penn, 1969
The Arrangement, Elia Kazan, 1969
Baby the Rain Must Fall, Robert Mulligan, 1965
Band of Outsiders (originally titled *Bande a Part*), Jean-Luc Godard, 1964
Beach Party, William Asher, 1963
Becket, Peter Glenville, 1964
Blow-Up, Michelangelo Antonioni, 1966
Bonnie and Clyde, Arthur Penn, 1967
Breakfast at Tiffany's, Blake Edwards, 1961
Bullitt, Peter Yates, 1968
Butch Cassidy and the Sundance Kid, George Roy Hill, 1969
The Carpetbaggers, Edward Dmytryk, 1964
Casino Royale, John Huston, Ken Hughes, Val Guest, Robert Parrish, Joseph McGrath, 1967
Charade, Stanley Donen, 1963
Closely Watched Trains, Jirí Menzel, 1966
Contempt, Jean-Luc Godard, 1963
Days of Wine and Roses, Blake Edwards, 1962
Dementia 13, Francis Ford Coppola, 1963
The Dirty Dozen, Robert Aldrich, 1967
Doctor Zhivago, David Lean, 1965
Dr. No, Terence Young, 1962
Dr. Strangelove, Stanley Kubrick, 1964
Fail Safe, Sidney Lumet, 1964
For a Few Dollars More, Sergio Leone, 1965
From Russia with Love, Terence Young, 1963
Goldfinger, Guy Hamilton, 1964
The Graduate, Mike Nichols, 1967
The Greatest Story Ever Told, George Stevens, 1965
A Hard Day's Night, Richard Lester, 1964
Hollywood without Make-up (Ken Murray home movies), 1963
Hombre, Martin Ritt, 1967
Hush . . . Hush, Sweet Charlotte, Robert Aldrich, 1964
In the Heat of the Night, Norman Jewison, 1967

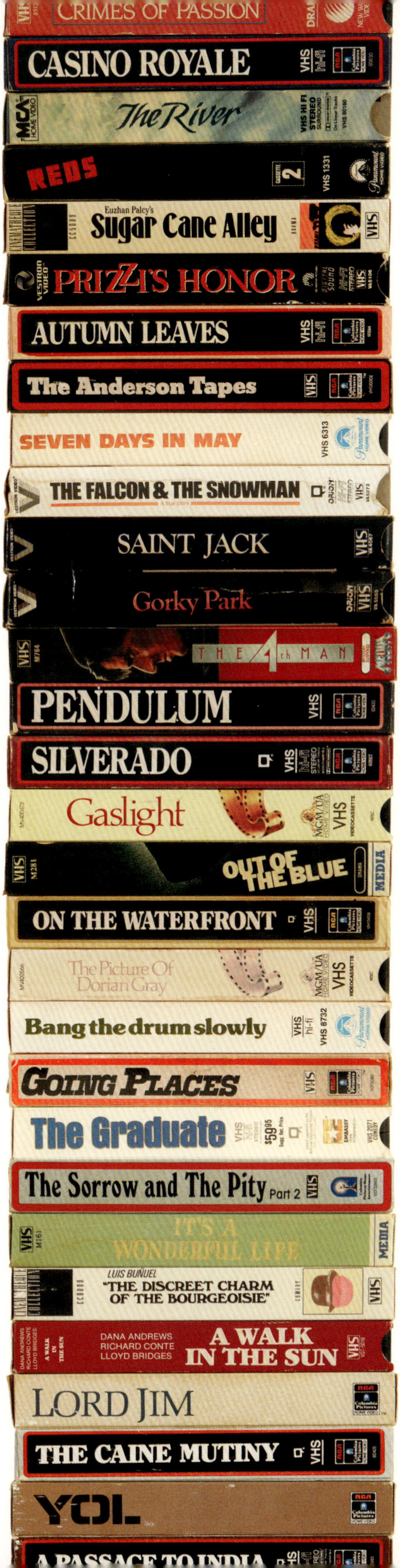

In the Year of the Pig (documentary on Vietnam), Emile de Antonio, 1968
Inherit the Wind, Stanley Kramer, 1960
Invitation to a Gunfighter, Richard Wilson, 1964
Irma la Douce, Billy Wilder, 1963
It's a Mad, Mad, Mad, Mad World, Stanley Kramer, 1963
The Jerry Lewis Show (TV series), September 1968
Judgment at Nuremberg, Stanley Kramer, 1961
La Dolce Vita, Federico Fellini, 1960
The Lion in Winter, Anthony Harvey, 1968
The Little Shop of Horrors, Roger Corman, 1960
Lord Jim, Richard Brooks, 1965
Lost in Space (TV series), Irwin Allen, pilot, September 15, 1965
Madame X, David Lowell Rich, 1966
Magical Mystery Tour (Beatles), 1967
The Magnificent Seven, John Sturges, 1960
A Man for All Seasons, Fred Zinnemann, 1966
The Man Who Shot Liberty Valance, John Ford, 1962
Marnie, Alfred Hitchcock, 1964
Master of the World, William Witney, 1961
Medium Cool, Haskell Wexler, 1969
Midnight Cowboy, John Schlesinger, 1969
The Misfits, John Huston, 1961
Morgan!, Karel Reisz, 1966
Mutiny on the Bounty, Lewis Milestone, 1962
The Night of the Iguana, John Huston, 1964
Night of the Living Dead, George Romero, 1968
Once Upon a Time in the West, Sergio Leone, 1968
One-Eyed Jacks, Marlon Brando, 1961
The Oscar, Russell Rouse, 1966
Paris Blues, Martin Ritt, 1961
The Pawnbroker, Sidney Lumet, 1965
Pendulum, George Schaefer, 1969
Planet of the Apes, Franklin J. Schaffner, 1968
The Prisoner (TV series), 1967
The Producers, Mel Brooks, 1968
The Professionals, Richard Brooks, 1966
Psycho, Alfred Hitchcock, 1960
Putney Swope, Robert Downey [Sr.], 1969
The Rain People, Francis Ford Coppola, 1969
Reflections in a Golden Eye, John Huston, 1967
Requiem for a Heavyweight, Ralph Nelson, 1962
Ride the High Country, Sam Peckinpah, 1962
The Rise and Fall of the Third Reich, Jack Kaufman, 1968
The Servant, Joseph Losey, 1963
Seven Days in May, John Frankenheimer, 1964
7 Faces of Dr. Lao, George Pal, 1963
Ship of Fools, Stanley Kramer, 1965
Simon of the Desert, Luis Buñuel, 1969
The Sorrow and the Pity, Marcel Ophüls, 1969
Spartacus, Stanley Kubrick, 1960
Stagecoach, John Ford, 1967
Star Trek, *"The Alternative Factor"* (TV series episode), Gerd Oswald, 1967
Studs Lonigan, Irving Lerner, 1960
Targets, Peter Bogdanovich, 1968
The Terror, Roger Corman, 1963
This Property Is Condemned, Sydney Pollack, 1966
A Thousand Clowns, Fred Coe, 1965
Thunderball, Terence Young, 1965
To Kill a Mockingbird, Robert Mulligan, 1962
Topaz, Alfred Hitchcock, 1969
Torn Curtain, Alfred Hitchcock, 1966
2001: A Space Odyssey, Stanley Kubrick, 1968
Valley of the Dolls, Mark Robson, 1967
Viridiana, Luis Buñuel, 1961
Viva Las Vegas, George Sidney, 1964
Waltz of the Toreadors, John Guillermin, 1962
What Ever Happened to Baby Jane?, Robert Aldrich, 1962
The Wild Bunch, Sam Peckinpah, 1969
The World of Henry Orient, George Roy Hill, 1964
You Only Live Twice, Lewis Gilbert, 1967
Z, Costa-Gavras, 1969

1970s

Aguirre, the Wrath of God, Werner Herzog, 1972
All the President's Men, Alan J. Pakula, 1976
Allegro Non Troppo, Bruno Bozzetto, 1976
Amarcord, Federico Fellini, 1973
The American Friend, Wim Wenders, 1977
American Graffiti, George Lucas, 1973
The Anderson Tapes, Sidney Lumet, 1971
Apocalypse Now, Francis Ford Coppola, 1979
Assault on Precinct 13, John Carpenter, 1976

Badlands, Terrence Malick, 1973
Bang the Drum Slowly, John D. Hancock, 1973
Barry Lyndon, Stanley Kubrick, 1975
Being There, Hal Ashby, 1979
The Bingo Long Traveling All-Stars & Motor Kings, John Badham, 1976
Bloody Mama, Roger Corman, 1970
Blue Collar, Paul Schrader, 1978
The Blues According to Lightnin' Hopkins, Les Blank with Skip Gerson, 1970
Brewster McCloud, Robert Altman, 1970
The Brink's Job, William Friedkin, 1978
Buck and the Preacher, Sidney Poitier, 1972
Buffalo Bill and the Indians, or Sitting Bull's History Lesson, Robert Altman, 1976
Cabaret, Bob Fosse, 1972
Caligula, (Tinto Brass), 1979
Carnal Knowledge, Mike Nichols, 1971
Catch-22, Mike Nichols, 1970
Chinatown, Roman Polanski, 1974
A Clockwork Orange, Stanley Kubrick, 1971
The Conformist, Bernardo Bertolucci, 1970
The Day of the Jackal, Fred Zinnemann, 1973
The Day of the Locust, John Schlesinger, 1975
Days of Heaven, Terrence Malick, 1978
The Discreet Charm of the Bourgeoisie, Luis Buñuel, 1972
$ (Dollars), Richard Brooks, 1971
11 Harrowhouse, Aram Avakian, 1974
The Enforcer, James Fargo, 1976
Enter the Dragon, Robert Clouse, 1973
Exorcist II: The Heretic, John Boorman, 1977
Family Plot, Alfred Hitchcock, 1976
Farewell, My Lovely, Dick Richards, 1975
Fingers, James Toback, 1978
The Four Feathers, Don Sharp, 1978
Frenzy, Alfred Hitchcock, 1972
The Garden of the Finzi-Continis, Vittorio De Sica, 1970
The Getaway, Sam Peckinpah, 1972
Gimme Shelter, David Maysles, Albert Maysles, Charlotte Zwerin, 1970
The Godfather, Francis Ford Coppola, 1972
Going Places, Bertrand Blier, 1974
Greaser's Palace, Robert Downey [Sr.], 1972
The Great Santini, Lewis John Carlino, 1979
Harry and Tonto, Paul Mazursky, 1974
The Hospital, Arthur Hiller, 1971
Invasion of the Body Snatchers, Phillip Kaufman, 1978
Jaws, Steven Spielberg, 1975
Jimi Hendrix, Joe Boyd, John Head, Gary Weis, 1973
Kelly's Heroes, Brian G. Hutton, 1970
Lenny, Bob Fosse, 1974
The Life and Times of Judge Roy Bean, John Huston, 1972
Little Big Man, Arthur Penn, 1970
Magnum Force, Ted Post, 1973
A Man Called Horse, Elliot Silverstein, 1970
The Man Who Fell to Earth, Nicolas Roeg, 1976
Marathon Man, John Schlesinger, 1976
McCabe & Mrs. Miller, Robert Altman, 1971
Mean Streets, Martin Scorsese, 1973
The Men Who Made the Movies: Alfred Hitchcock (later retitled *Inside Hitchcock*), Richard Schickel, 1973
Midnight Express, Alan Parker, 1978
Nashville, Robert Altman, 1975
Network, Sidney Lumet, 1976
New York, New York, Martin Scorsese, 1977
O Lucky Man!, Lindsay Anderson, 1973
Obsession, Brian De Palma, 1976
One Flew Over the Cuckoo's Nest, Miloš Forman, 1975
The Onion Field, Harold Becker, 1979
Papillon, Franklin J. Schaffner, 1973
The Parallax View, Alan J. Pakula, 1974
Performance, Donald Cammell and Nicolas Roeg, 1970
Phantom of the Paradise, Brian De Palma, 1974
The Plumber, Peter Weir, 1979
Robert et Robert, Claude Lelouch, 1978
The Ruling Class, Peter Medak, 1972
Saint Jack, Peter Bogdanovich, 1979
Scarecrow, Jerry Schatzberg, 1973
A Sense of Loss, Marcel Ophüls, 1972
Shaft, Gordon Parks, 1971
Shampoo, Hal Ashby, 1975
Short Eyes, Robert M. Young, 1977
The Shout, Jerzy Skolimowski, 1978
Silver Streak, Arthur Hiller, 1976
Slaughterhouse-Five, George Roy Hill, 1972
Soldier of Orange, Paul Verhoeven, 1977
Soylent Green, Richard Fleischer, 1973
State of Siege, Costa-Gavras, 1972
The Sting, George Roy Hill, 1973

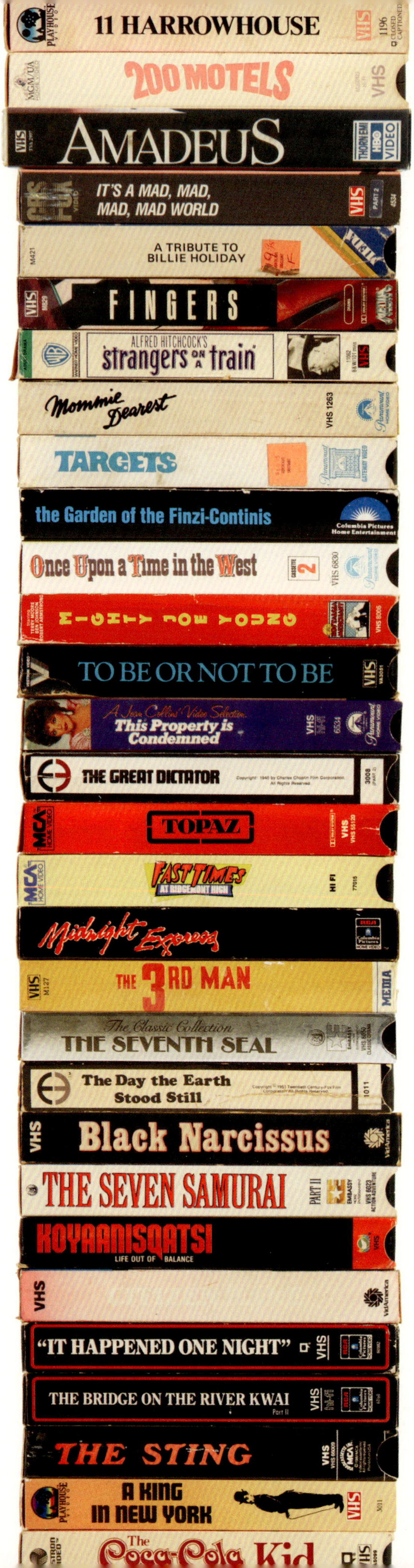

Sunday Bloody Sunday, John Schlesinger, 1971
Super Fly, Gordon Parks Jr., 1972
The Taking of Pelham One Two Three, Joseph Sargent, 1974
That Obscure Object of Desire, Luis Buñuel, 1977
They Call Me Mister Tibbs!, Gordon Douglas, 1970
Three Days of the Condor, Sydney Pollack, 1975
Time After Time, Nicholas Meyer, 1979
The Tin Drum, Volker Schlöndorff, 1979
200 Motels, Tony Palmer and Frank Zappa, 1971
Underground, Emile de Antonio, Mary Lampson, and Haskell Wexler, 1976
Wise Blood, John Huston, 1979
Zabriskie Point, Michelangelo Antonioni, 1970

1980s

After the Rehearsal, Ingmar Bergman, 1984
Against All Odds, Taylor Hackford, 1984
All of Me, Carl Reiner, 1984
Amadeus, Milos Forman, 1984
The Amateur, Charles Jarrott, 1981
American Gigolo, Paul Schrader, 1980
And the Ship Sails On, Federico Fellini, 1983
Another Country, Marek Kanievska, 1984
Antarctica, Koreyoshi Kurahara, 1983
Atlantic City, Louis Malle, 1980
The Awakening, Mike Newell, 1980
The Ballad of Gregorio Cortez, Robert M. Young, 1982
Berlin Alexanderplatz, Rainer Werner Fassbinder, 1980
Beverly Hills Cop, Martin Brest, 1984
Beyond the Walls, Uri Barbash, 1984
Birdy, Alan Parker, 1984
Blade Runner, Ridley Scott, 1982
Blood Simple, Joel and Ethan Coen, 1985
Bob Marley Legend, 1984
Body Heat, Lawrence Kasdan, 1981
The Border, Tony Richardson, 1982
The Bounty, Roger Donaldson, 1984
The Breakfast Club, John Hughes, 1985
Breathless, Jim McBride, 1983
The Brother from Another Planet, John Sayles, 1984
Burden of Dreams, Les Blank, 1982
Careful, He Might Hear You, Carl Schultz, 1983
Carmen, Francesco Rosi, 1984
Christiane F., Uli Edel, 1981
The Coca-Cola Kid, Dusan Makavejev, 1985
Commando, Mark L. Lester, 1985
The Compleat Beatles, Patrick Montgomery, 1982
Countryman, Dickie Jobson, 1982
Coup de Torchon (*Clean Slate*), Bertrand Tavernier, 1981
Crimes of Passion, Ken Russell, 1984
Crossover Dreams, Leon Ichaso, 1985
Cutter's Way, Ivan Passer, 1981
Dance with a Stranger, Mike Newell, 1985
Das Boot (*The Boat*), Wolfgang Petersen, 1981
The Dead Zone, David Cronenberg, 1983
Desperately Seeking Susan, Susan Seidelman, 1985
Diner, Barry Levinson, 1982
Dressed to Kill, Brian De Palma, 1980
The Dresser, Peter Yates, 1983
The Elephant Man, David Lynch, 1980
Elvis: One Night with You, Steve Binder, 1985
Erendira, Ruy Guerra, 1983
Eureka, Nicolas Roeg, 1983
Excalibur, John Boorman, 1981
Experience Preferred... but Not Essential, Peter Duffell, 1982
Eye of the Needle, Richard Marquand, 1981
The Falcon and the Snowman, John Schlesinger, 1985
Fast Times at Ridgemont High, Amy Heckerling, 1982
The First Deadly Sin, Brian G. Hutton, 1980
A Flash of Green, Victor Nunez, 1986
The 4th Man, Paul Verhoeven, 1983
Frank Sinatra: Portrait of an Album (with Quincy Jones), Emil G. Davidson, 1985
F/X, Robert Mandel, 1986
Gabriela, Bruno Barreto, 1983
Gandhi, Richard Attenborough, 1982
Girl Groups: The Story of a Sound, Steve Alpert, 1983
Godfather Epic (parts I and II together, reedited chronologically), Francis Ford Coppola, 1981
Gorky Park, Michael Apted, 1983
Greystoke: The Legend of Tarzan, Lord of the Apes, Hugh Hudson, 1984
Guyana Tragedy: The Story of Jim Jones, William A. Graham, 1980
Heat of Desire, Luc Béraud, 1981
Heaven's Gate, Michael Cimino, 1980
Henry Moore, Thierry Filliard and Alain Vernis, 1983
Indiana Jones and the Temple of Doom, Steven Spielberg, 1984
Jagged Edge, Richard Marquand, 1985
Kamikaze 89, Wolf Gremm, 1982
Kerouac, the Movie, John Antonelli, 1984
The King of Comedy, Martin Scorsese, 1983
Kiss of the Spider Woman, Hector Babenco, 1985
Koyaanisqatsi: Life out of Balance, Godfrey Reggio, 1983
La Traviata, Franco Zeffirelli, 1982
Last Night at the Alamo, Eagle Pennell, 1983
A Love in Germany, Andrzej Wajda, 1983
Love Streams, John Cassavetes, 1984
Manhunter, Michael Mann, 1986
Mephisto, István Szabó, 1981
Missing, Costa-Gavras, 1982
Mommie Dearest, Frank Perry, 1981
The Natural, Barry Levinson, 1984
Never Cry Wolf, Carroll Ballard, 1983
The Night of the Shooting Stars, Paolo and Vittorio Taviani, 1982
A Night with Lou Reed, Clark Santee, 1983
Of Mice and Men, Reza Badiyi, 1981
Once upon a Time in America, Sergio Leone, 1984
Out of the Blue, Dennis Hopper, 1981
Paris, Texas, Wim Wenders, 1984
A Passage to India, David Lean, 1984
Pennies from Heaven, Herbert Ross, 1981
Places in the Heart, Robert Benton, 1984
Polyester, John Waters, 1981
The Pope of Greenwich Village, Stuart Rosenberg, 1984
The Postman Always Rings Twice, Bob Rafelson, 1981
Pretty in Pink, Howard Deutch, 1986
Prince of the City, Sidney Lumet, 1981
A Private Function, Malcolm Mowbray, 1984
Prizzi's Honor, John Huston, 1985
The Purple Rose of Cairo, Woody Allen, 1985
Racing with the Moon, Richard Benjamin, 1984
Raging Bull, Martin Scorsese, 1980
Raiders of the Lost Ark, Steven Spielberg, 1981
The Razor's Edge, John Byrum, 1984
Reds, Warren Beatty, 1981
Reuben, Reuben, Robert Ellis Miller, 1983
The Right Stuff, Philip Kaufman, 1983
The River, Mark Rydell, 1984
Running Scared, Peter Hyams, 1986
Scarface, Brian De Palma, 1983
Silkwood, Mike Nichols, 1983
Silverado, Lawrence Kasdan, 1985
Smithereens, Susan Seidelman, 1982
A Soldier's Story, Norman Jewison, 1984
St. Elmo's Fire, Joel Schumacher, 1985
Star 80, Bob Fosse, 1983
State of Siege, Costa-Gavras, 1972
Stir Crazy, Sidney Poitier, 1980
Streamers, Robert Altman, 1983
Suburbia, Penelope Spheeris, 1984
Sugar Cane Alley, Euzhan Palcy, 1983
Tales of Ordinary Madness, Marco Ferreri, 1981
Tender Mercies, Bruce Beresford, 1983
That Was Rock: The T.A.M.I. Show [1964] and *The Big T.N.T. Show* [1966] (compilation from two 1960s rock concert films), 1984
That's Dancing!, Jack Haley Jr., 1985
Thief, Michael Mann, 1981
This Is Elvis, Andrew Solt, Malcolm Leo, 1981
True Confessions, Ulu Grosbard, 1981
Under the Volcano, John Huston, 1984
Witness, Peter Weir, 1985
The Year of Living Dangerously, Peter Weir, 1982
Year of the Dragon, Michael Cimino, 1985
Young Sherlock Holmes, Barry Levinson, 1985
Zelig, Woody Allen, 1983

Untitled, 1986
Acrylic and oil stick on wood
11 × 9⅛ × 9⅛ in.
(27.94 × 23.18 × 23.18 cm)

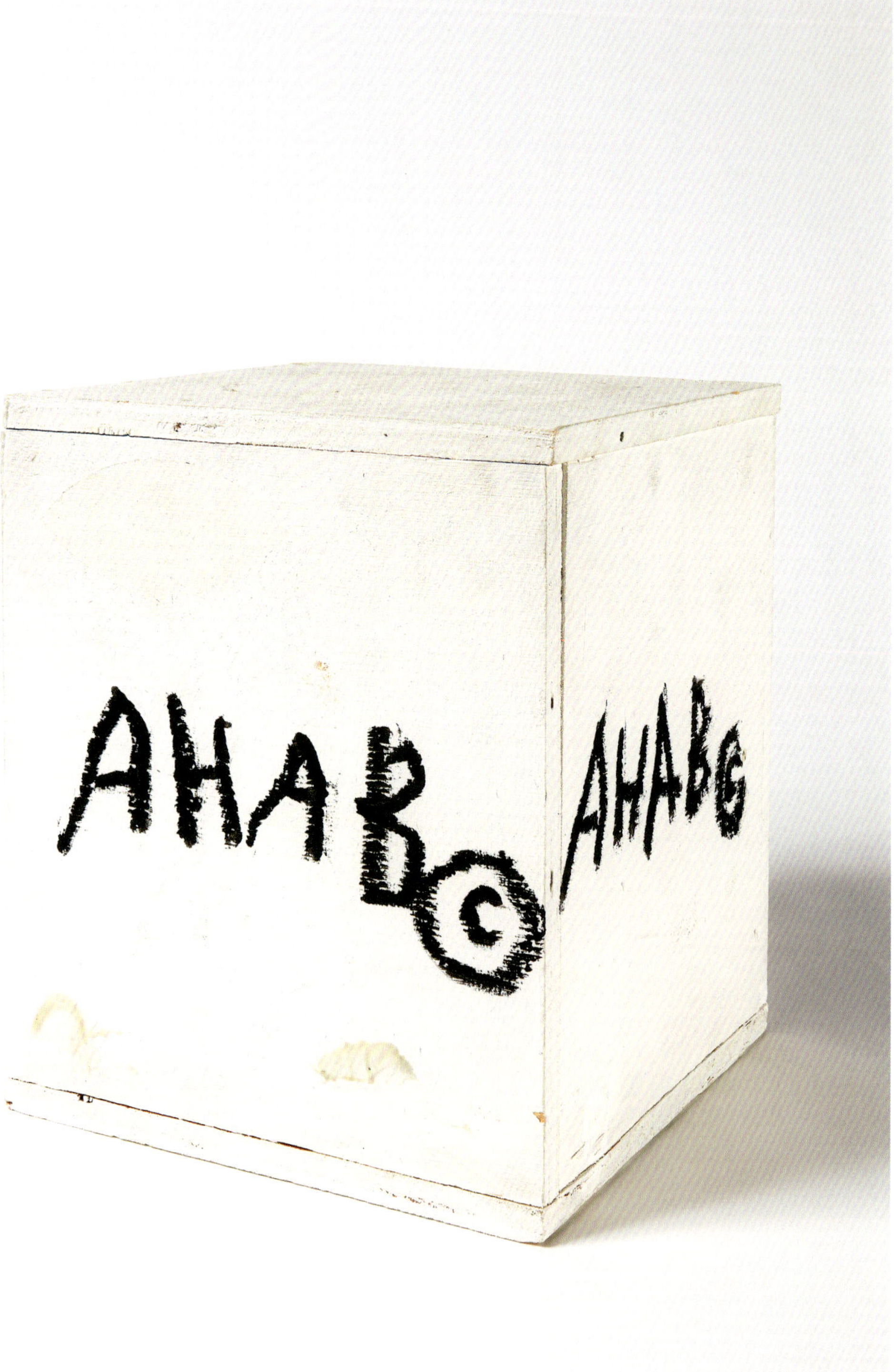

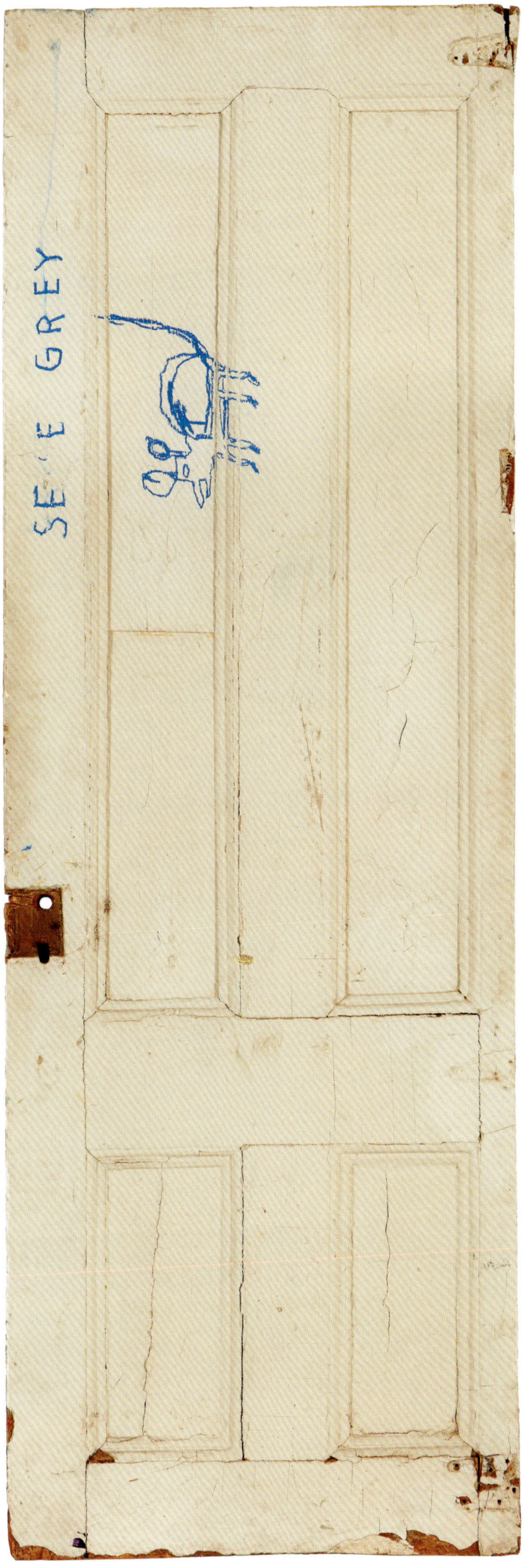

Untitled, n.d.
Oil stick on wood door
27½ × 85 in. (69.85 × 215.9 cm)

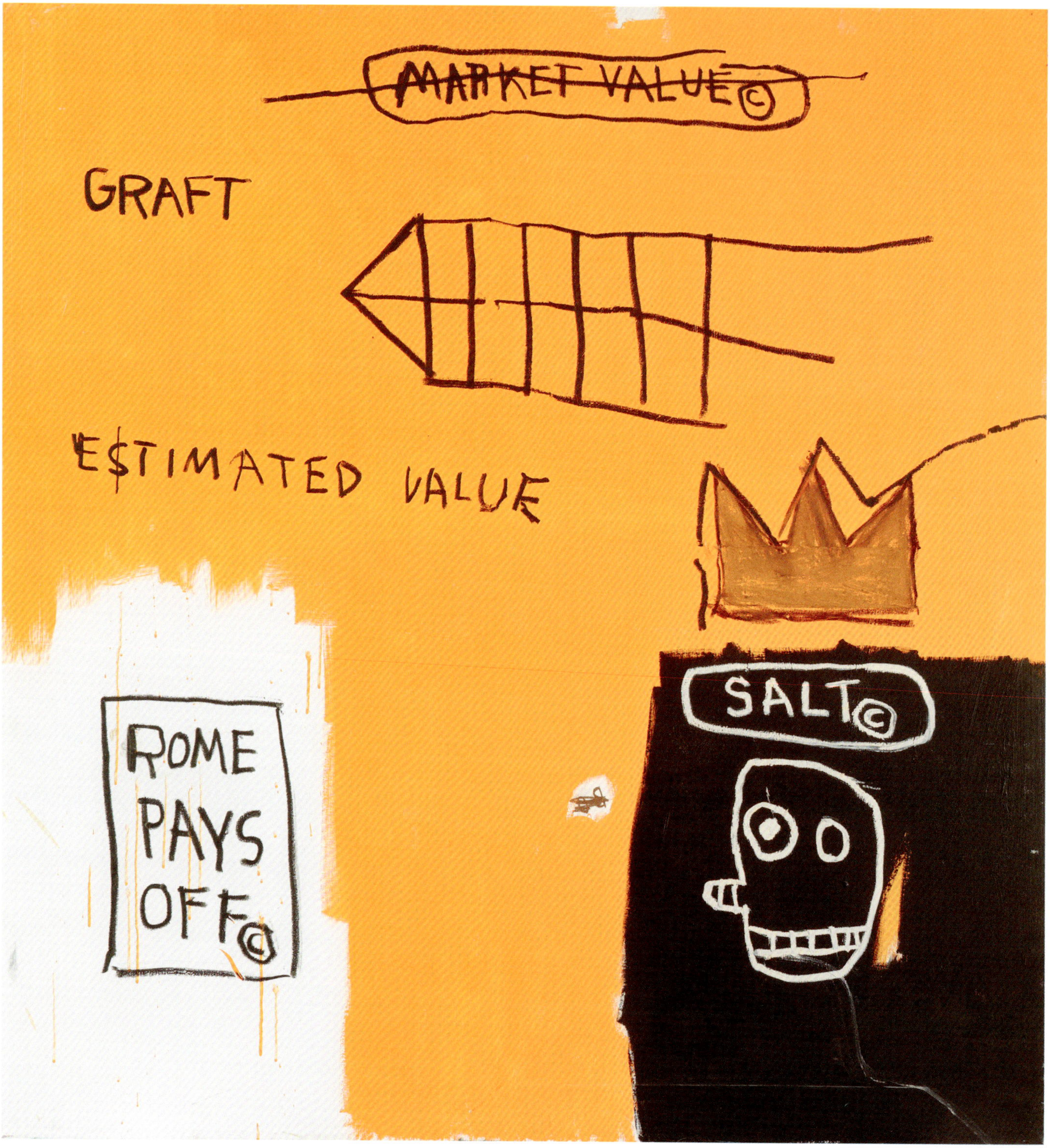
MARKET VALUE©
GRAFT
E$TIMATED VALUE
SALT©
ROME PAYS OFF©

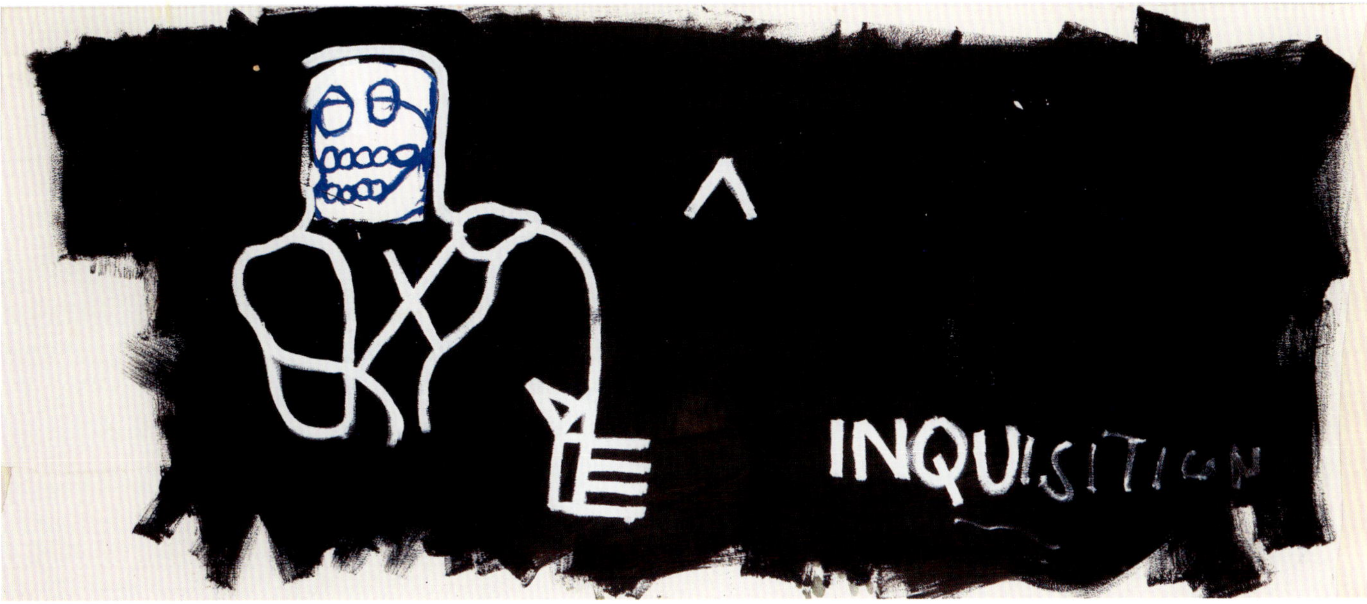

OPPOSITE
Untitled (Rome Pays Off), 1984
Acrylic and oil stick on canvas
66 × 60 in. (167.64 × 152.4 cm)

ABOVE
Untitled (Inquisition), n.d.
Acrylic on paper mounted
on canvas
45 × 101 in. (114.3 × 256.54 cm)

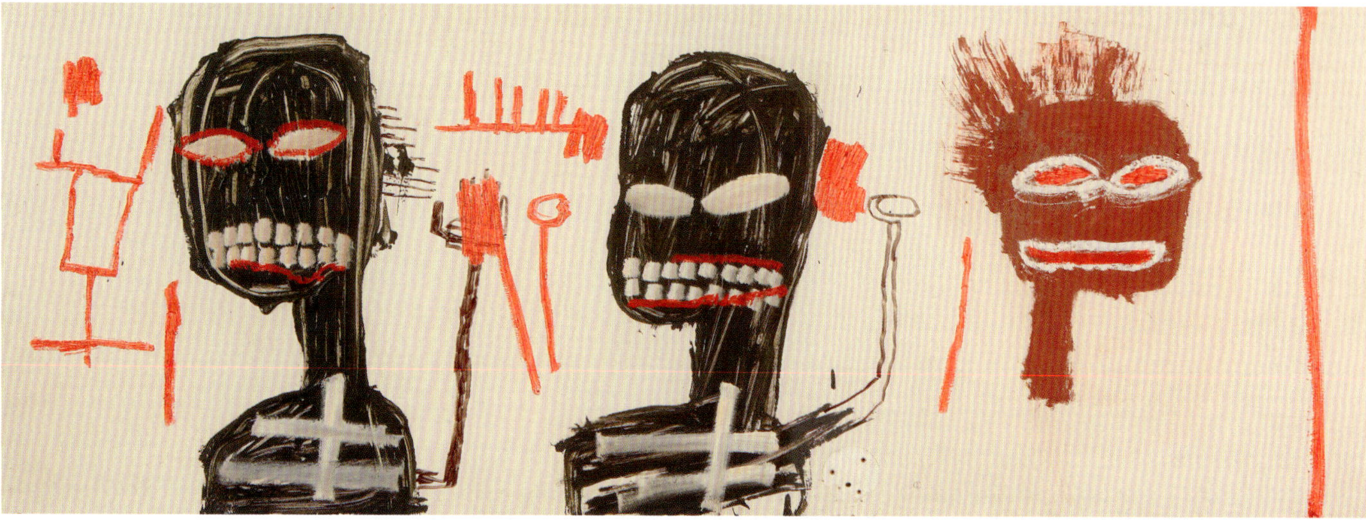

ABOVE
Untitled, n.d.
Acrylic and oil stick on wood door
23½ × 63 in. (59.69 × 160.02 cm)

OPPOSITE
Untitled, 1982
Acrylic and oil stick on canvas
48 × 29¾ in. (121.92 × 75.57 cm)

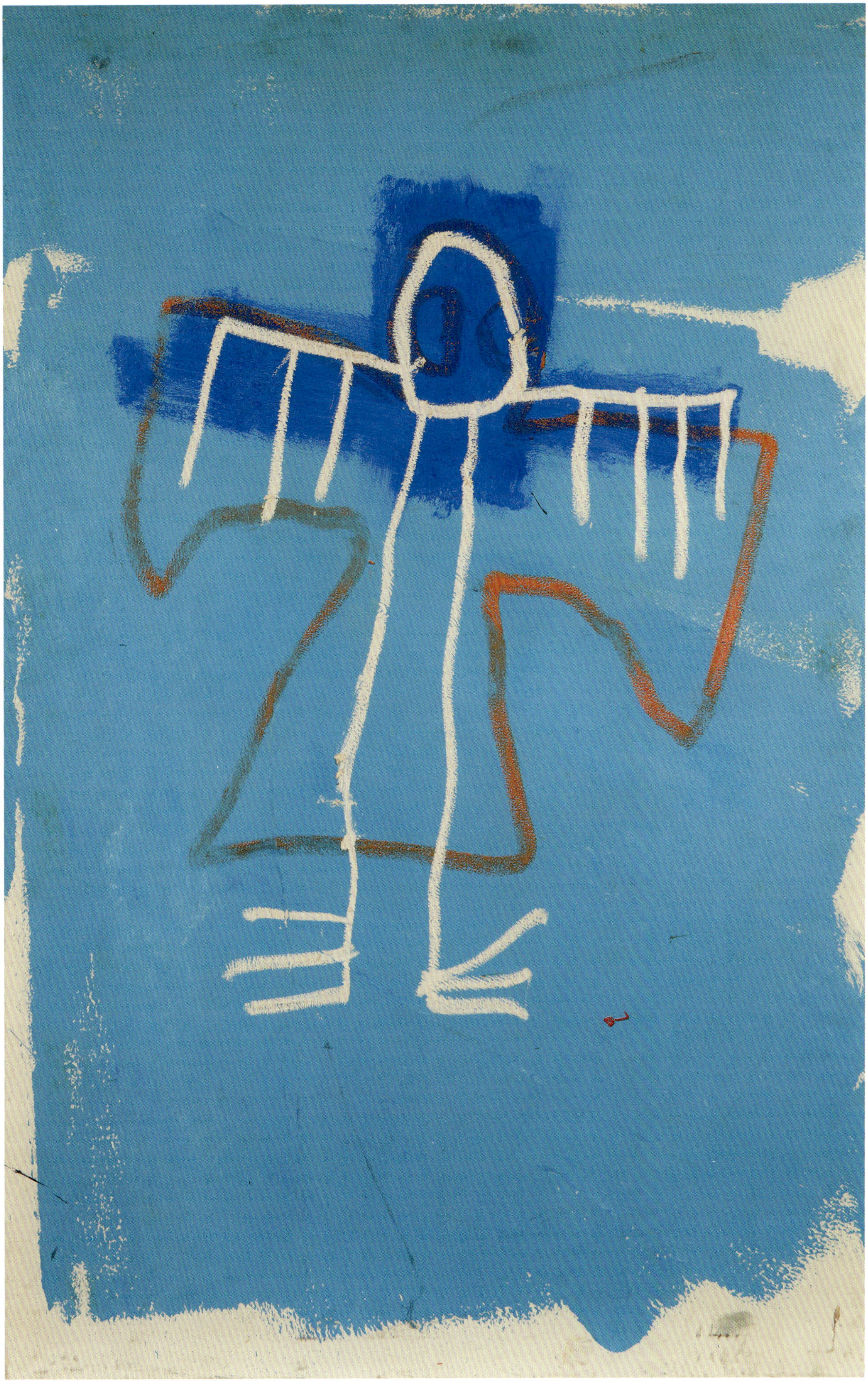

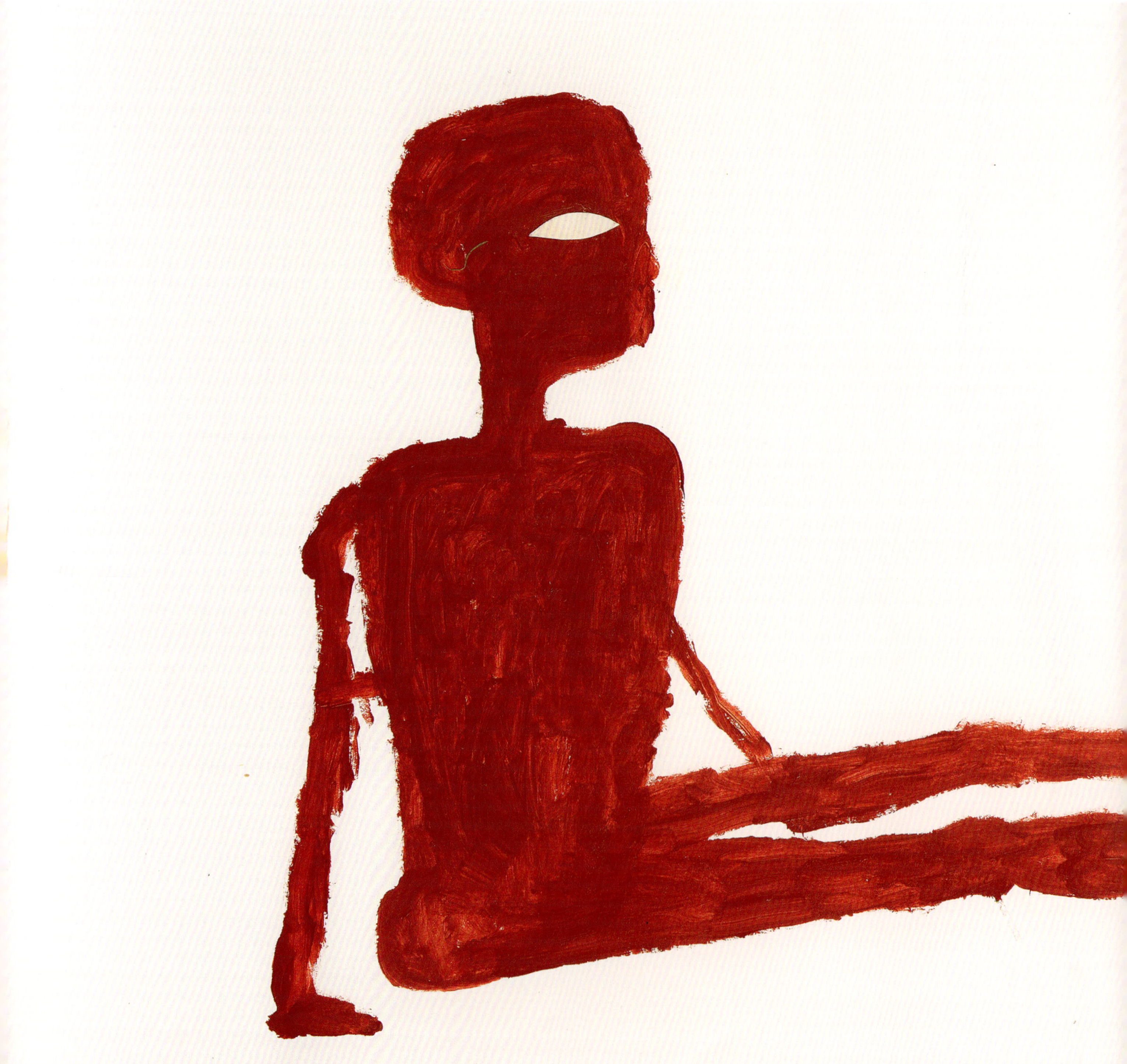

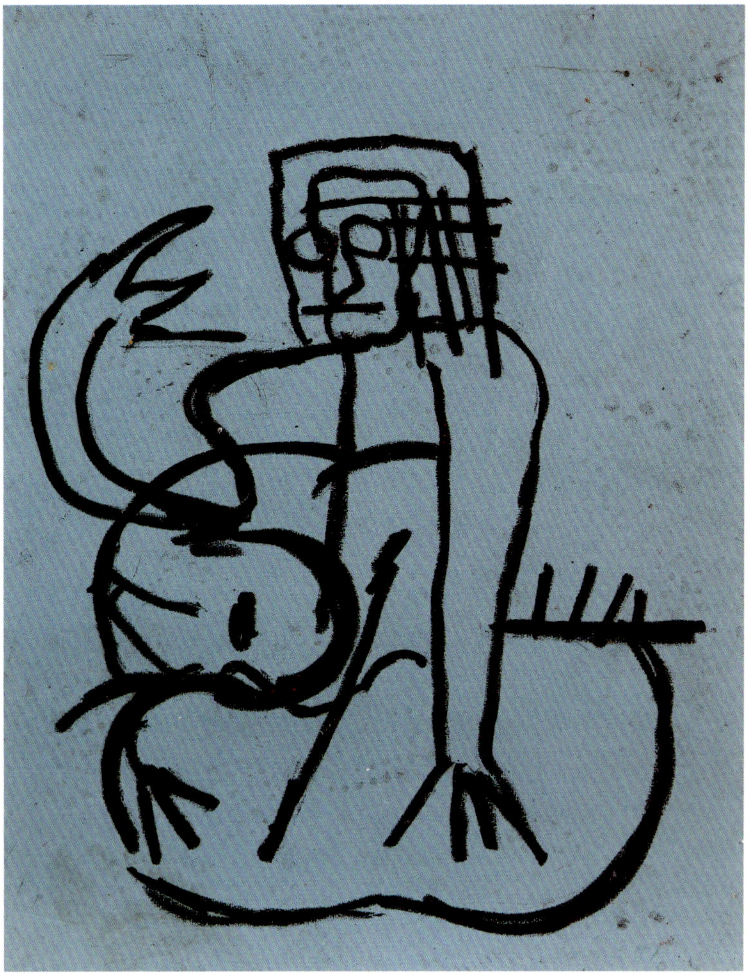

LEFT
Untitled, n.d.
Acrylic with collage on paper
22½ × 30 in. (57.15 × 76.2 cm)

ABOVE
Untitled, n.d.
Oil stick on paper
23¾ × 18 in. (60.33 × 45.72 cm)

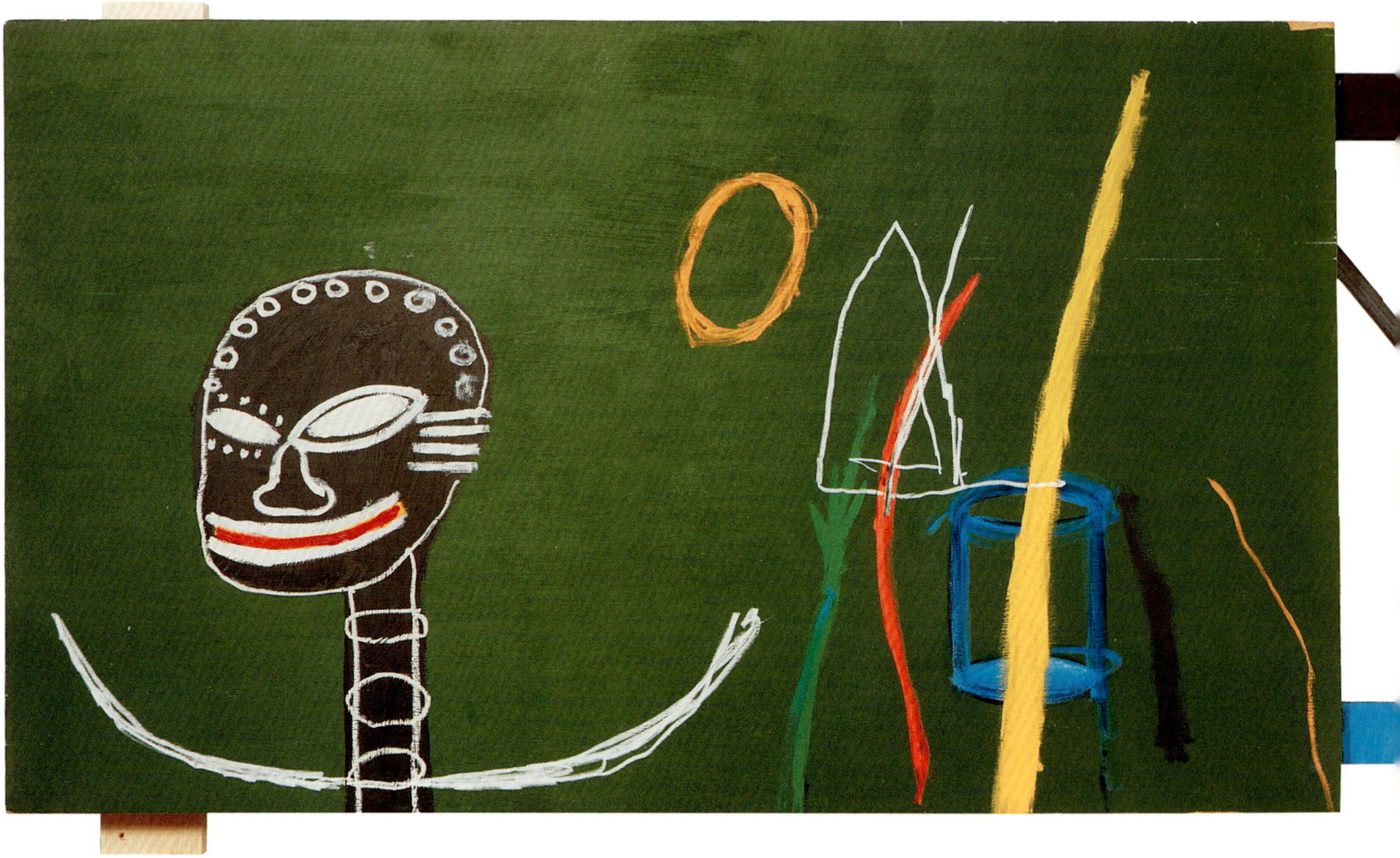

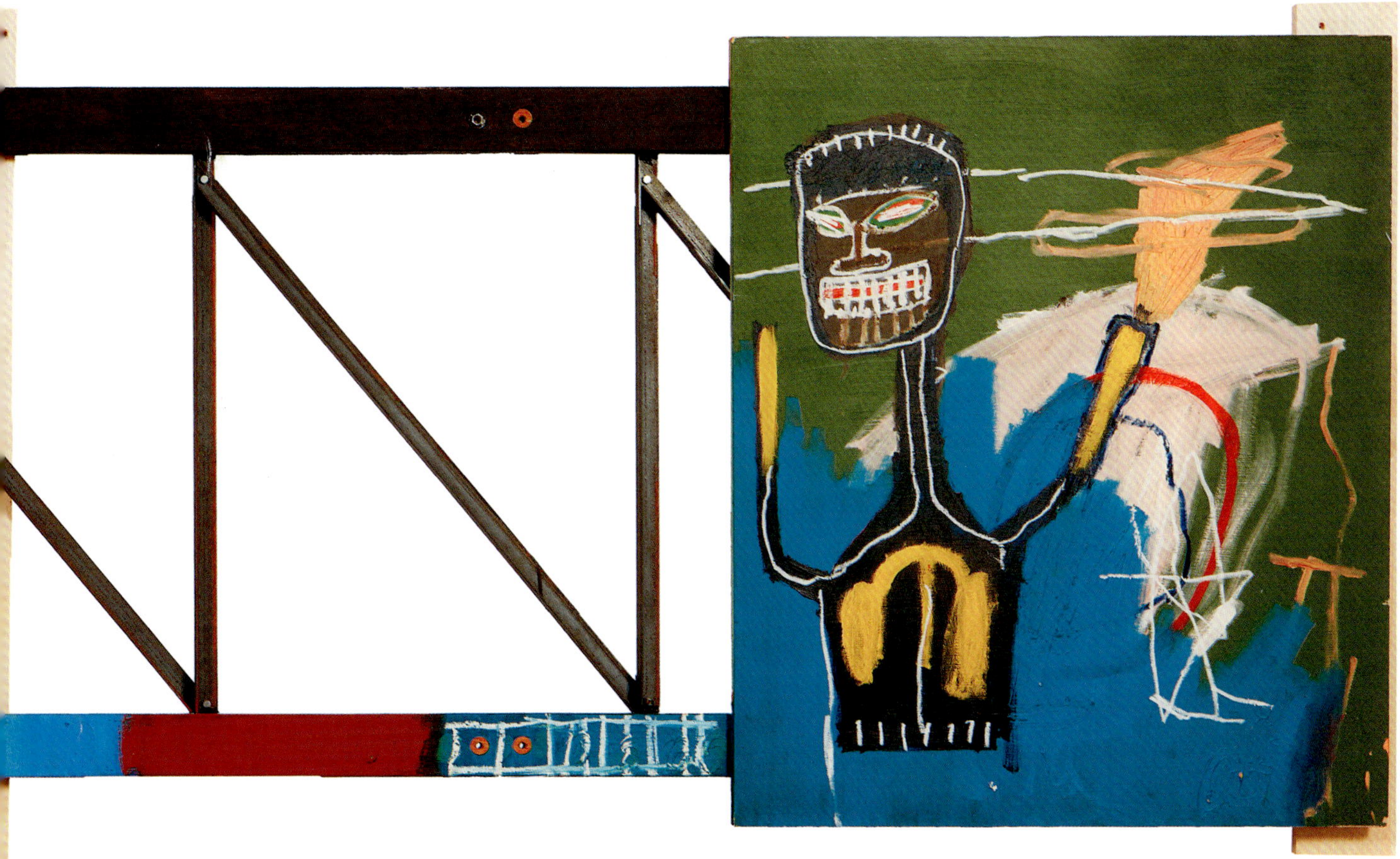

Untitled, 1984
Acrylic paint on metal and
wood supports
42 × 156 in. (106.68 × 396.24 cm)

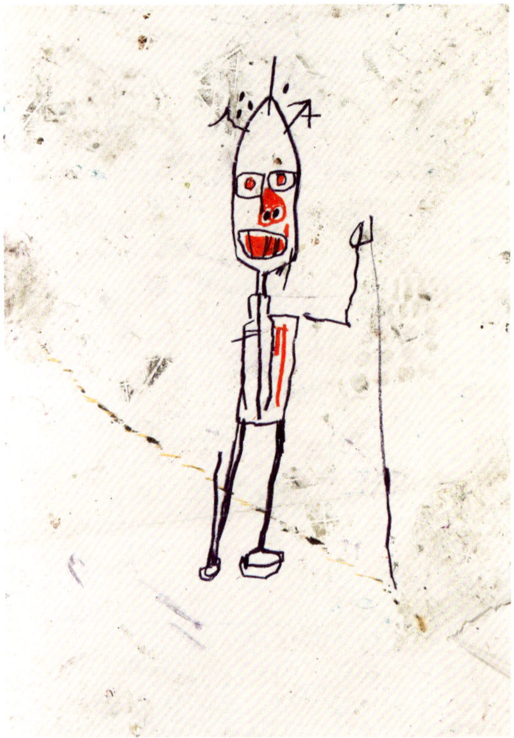

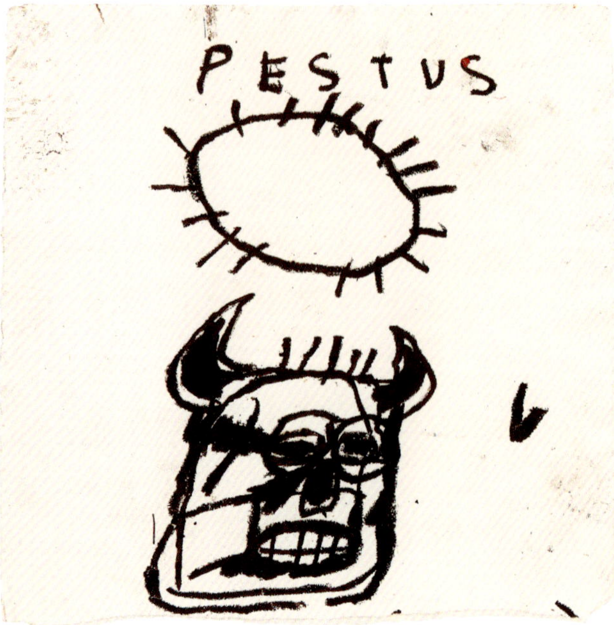

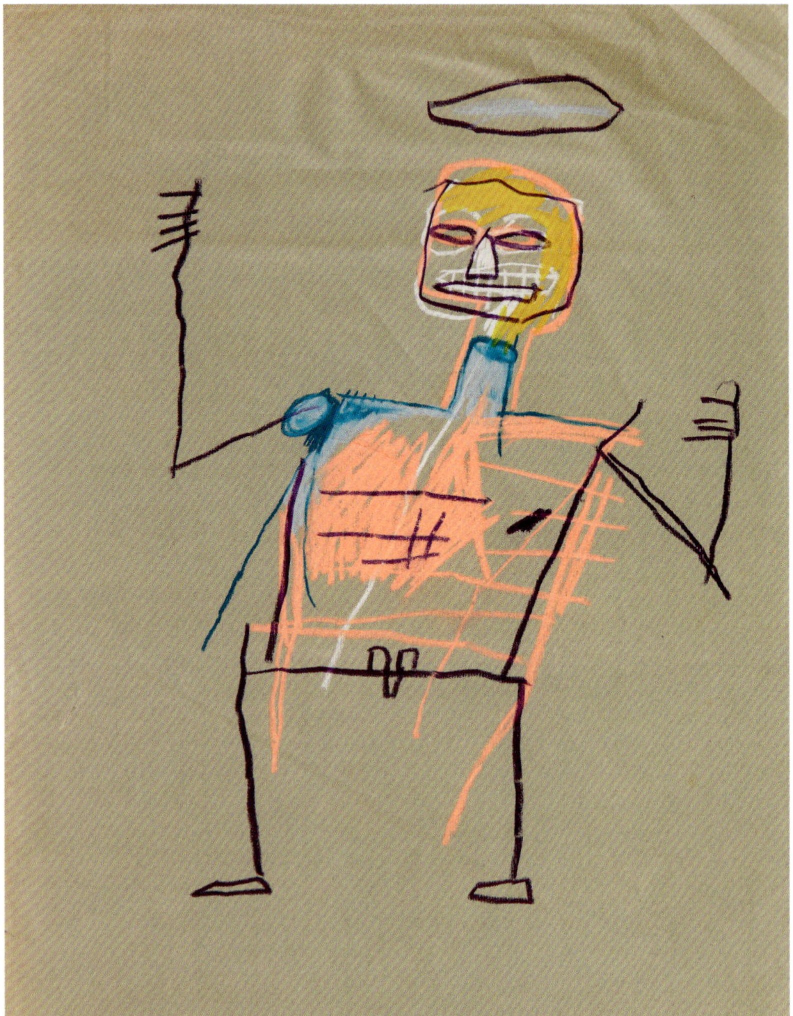

TOP LEFT
Untitled, n.d.
Oil stick on paper
22 × 14½ in. (55.88 × 36.83 cm)

TOP RIGHT
Untitled (Pestus), n.d.
Oil stick on paper
20 × 20 in. (50.8 × 50.8 cm)

RIGHT
Untitled (Haloed Figure), n.d.
Oil stick on paper
23¾ × 18 in. (60.33 × 45.72 cm)

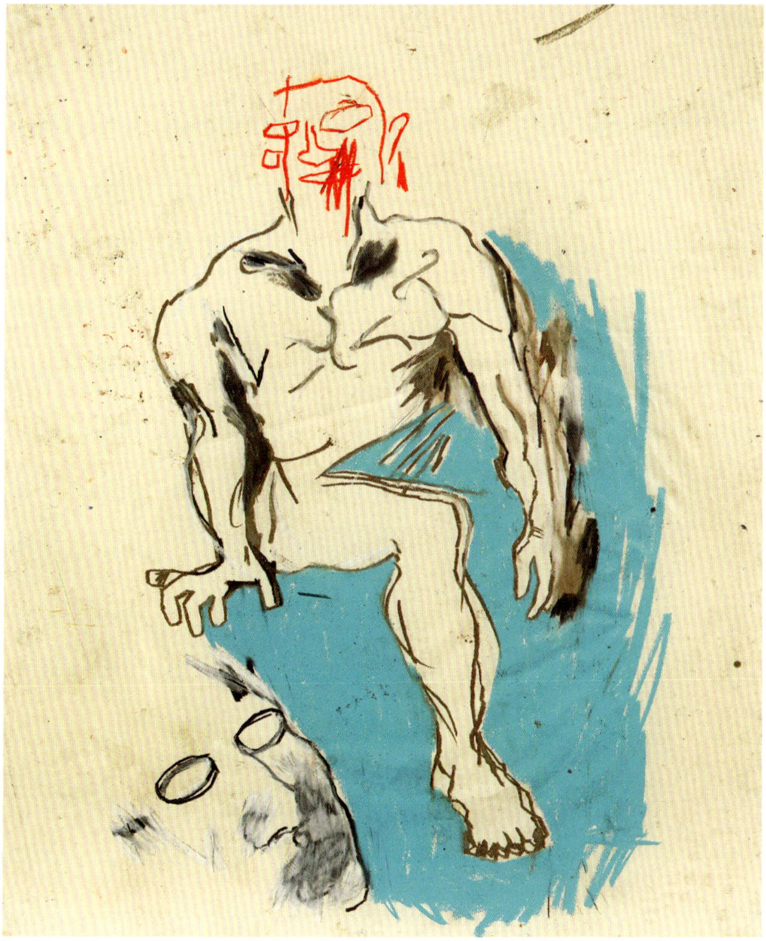

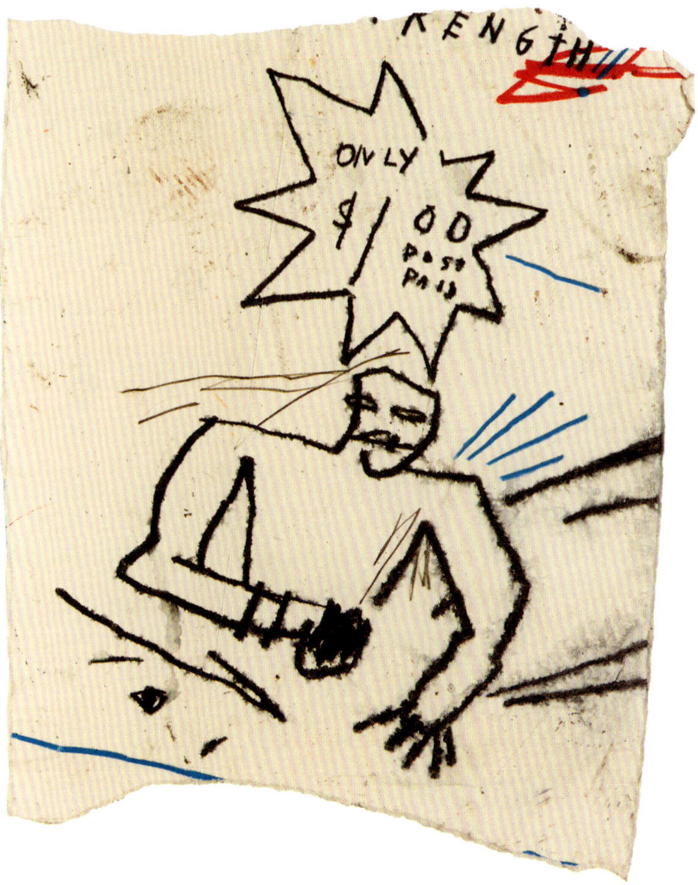

TOP
Untitled, n.d.
Oil stick on paper
29 × 33 in. (73.66 × 88.42 cm)

RIGHT
Untitled (Only $1.00), n.d.
Graphite and oil stick on paper
20 × 15 in. (50.8 × 38.1 cm)

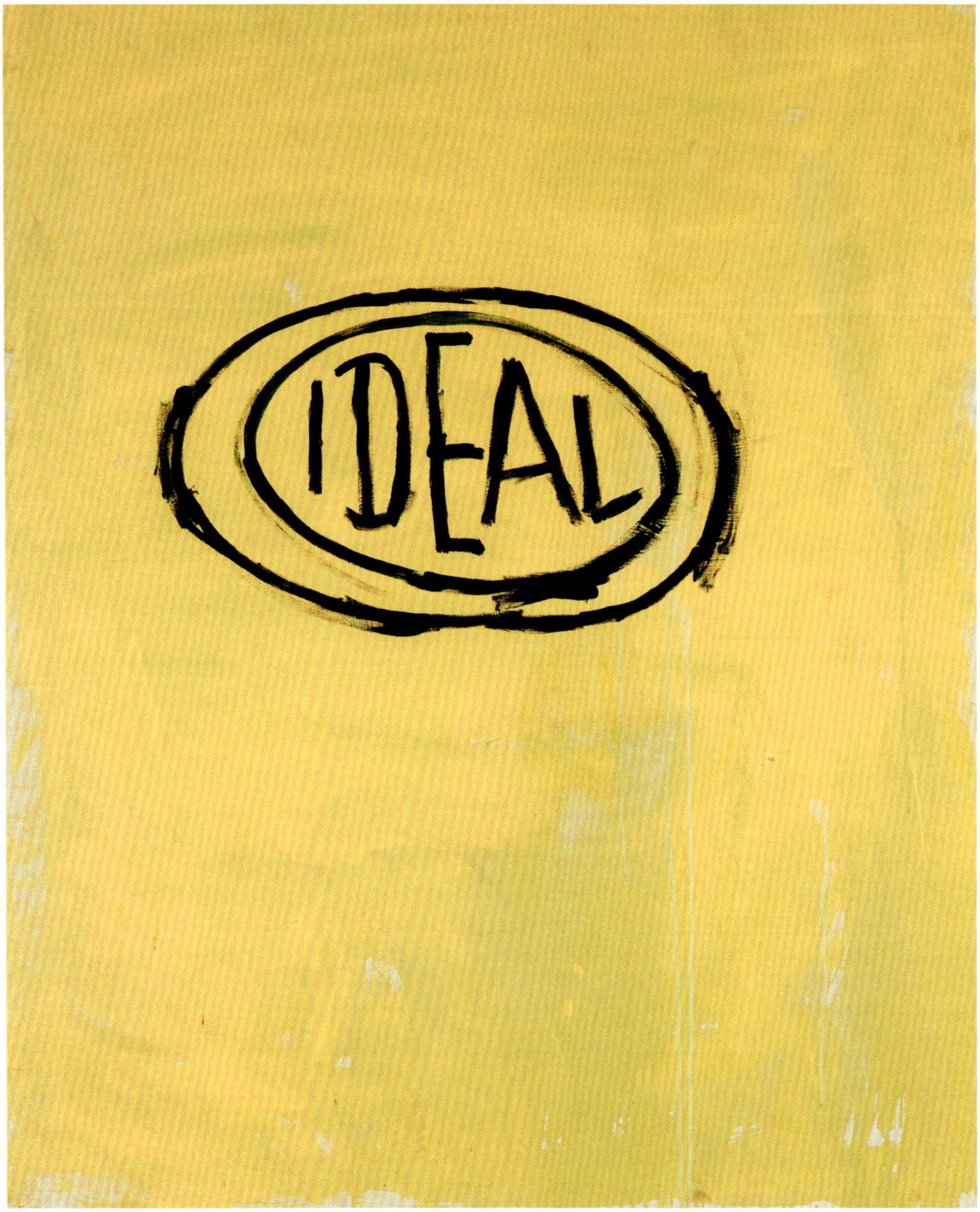

ABOVE
Untitled (Ideal), 1988
Acrylic and oil stick on canvas
49½ × 39½ in.
(125.73 × 100.33 cm)

OPPOSITE
Untitled, 1984
Acrylic and oil stick on canvas
86 × 68 in. (218.44 × 172.72 cm)

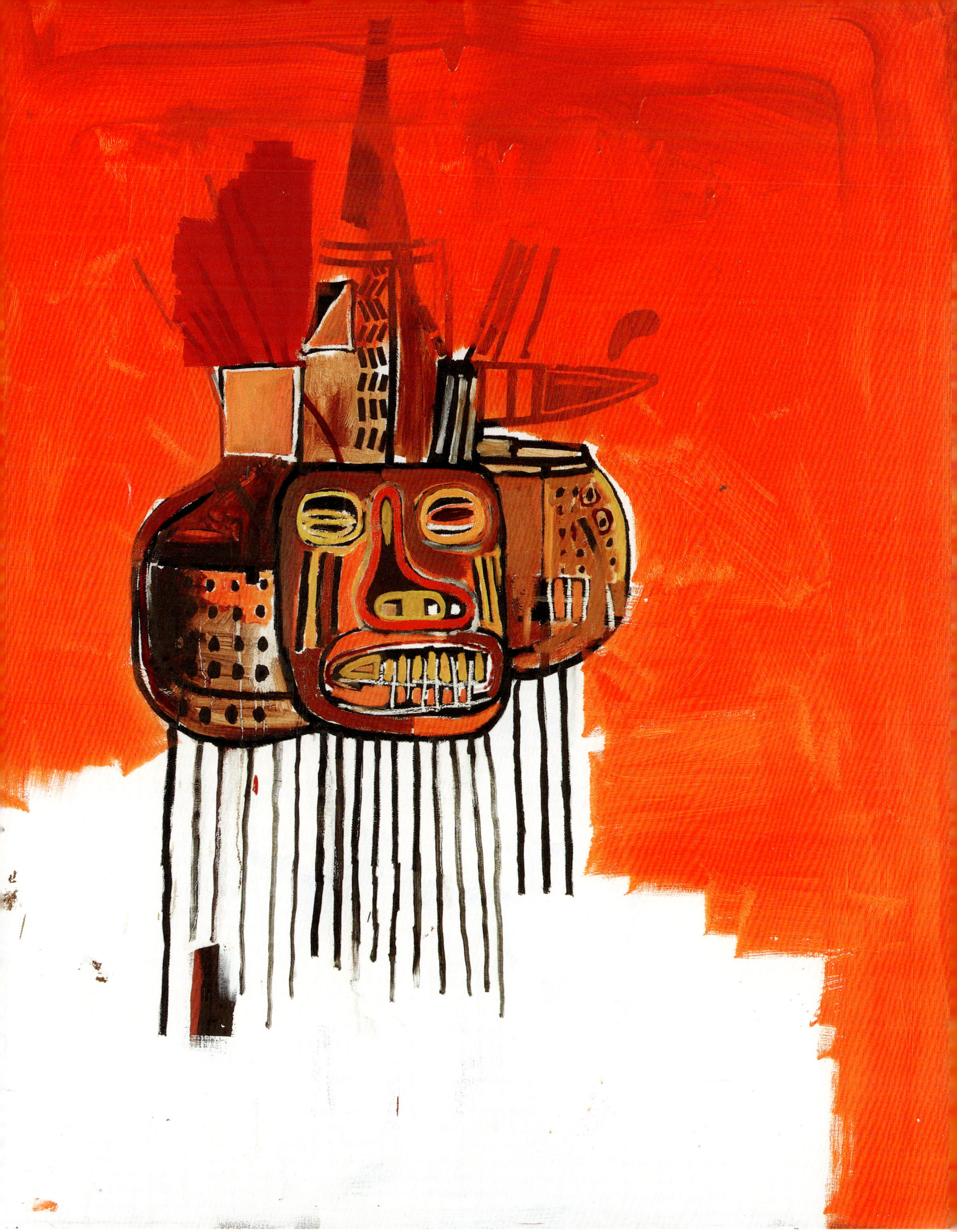

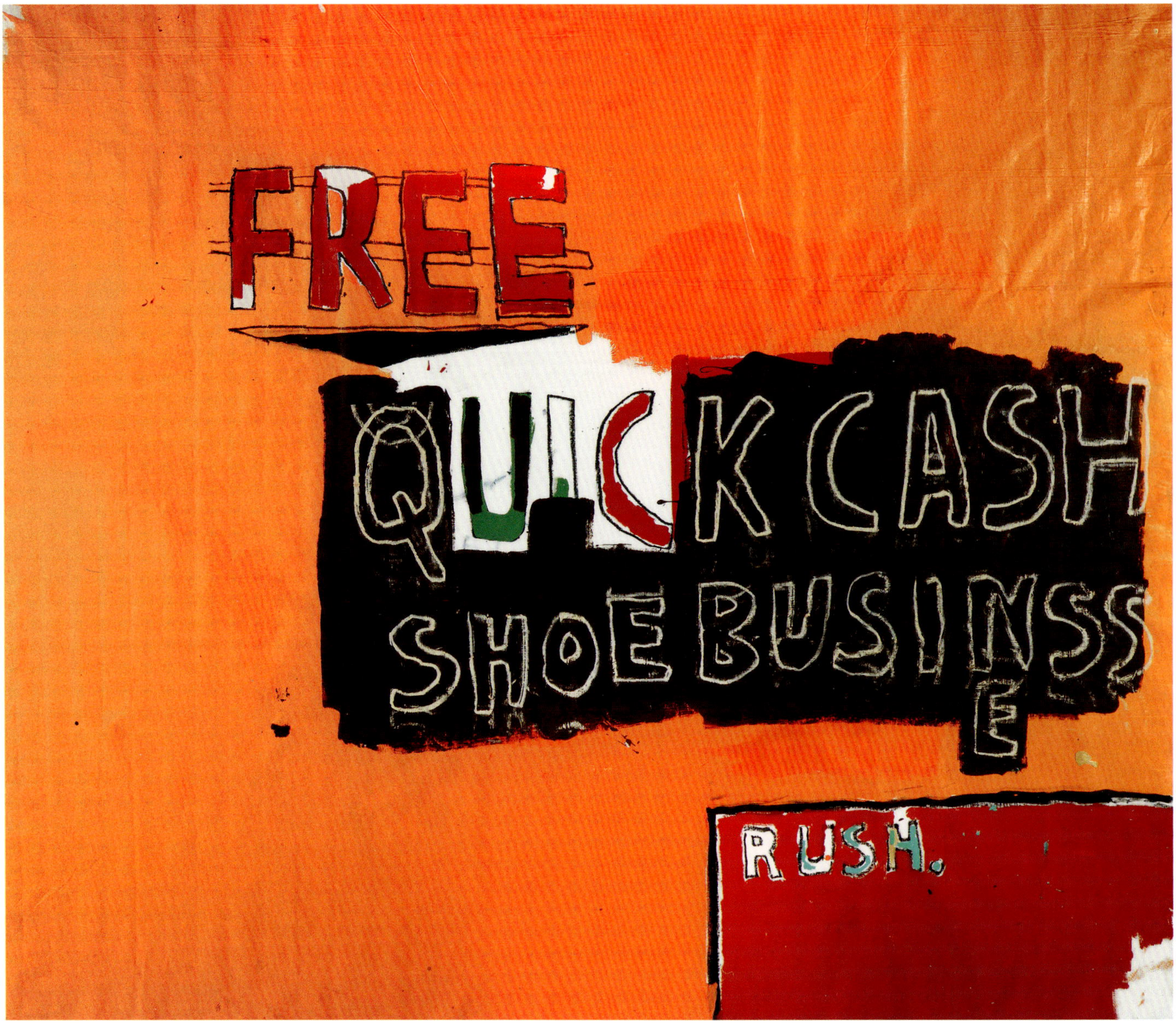

Untitled (Quick Cash Shoe Business), n.d.
Acrylic and oil stick on canvas
113 × 118 in. (287.02 × 299.72 cm)

RIGHT
Untitled (Water Movement), 1988
Acrylic and oil stick on canvas
49½ × 29½ in.
(125.73 × 74.93 cm)

BOTTOM
Untitled, n.d.
Oil stick on paper
24 × 18 in. (60.96 × 45.72 cm)

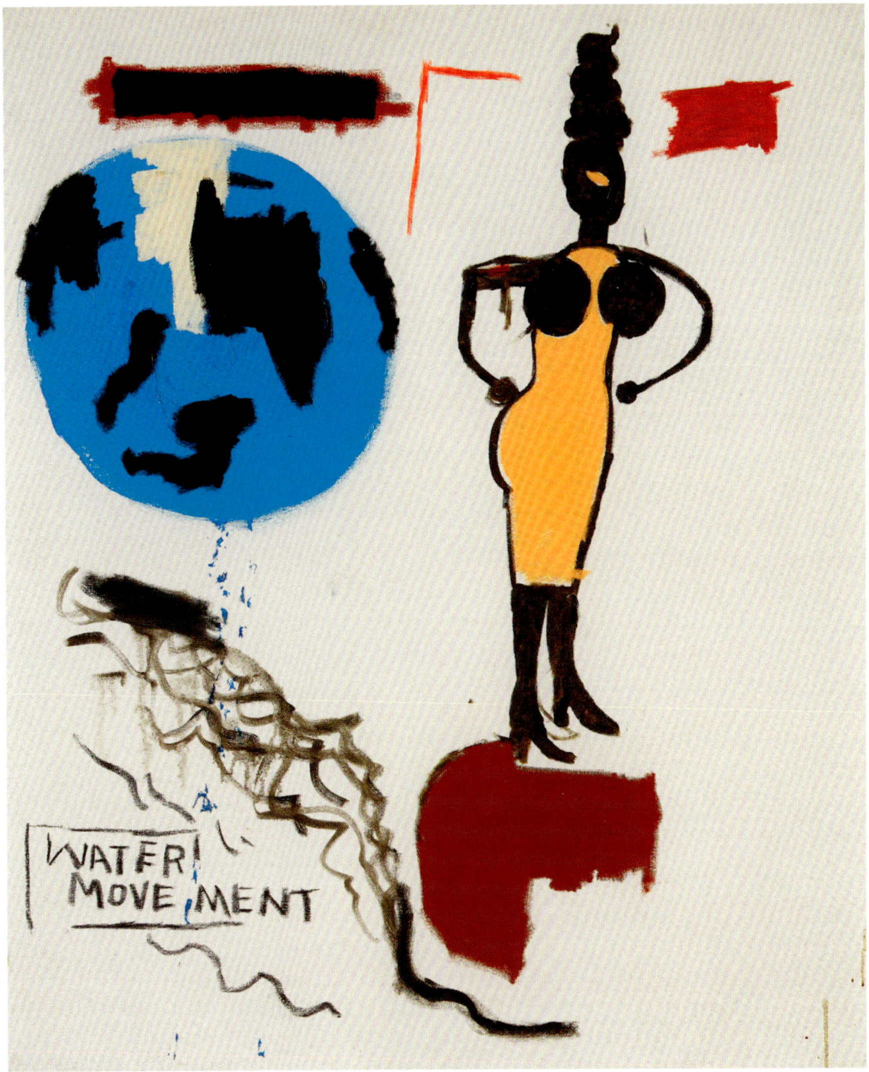

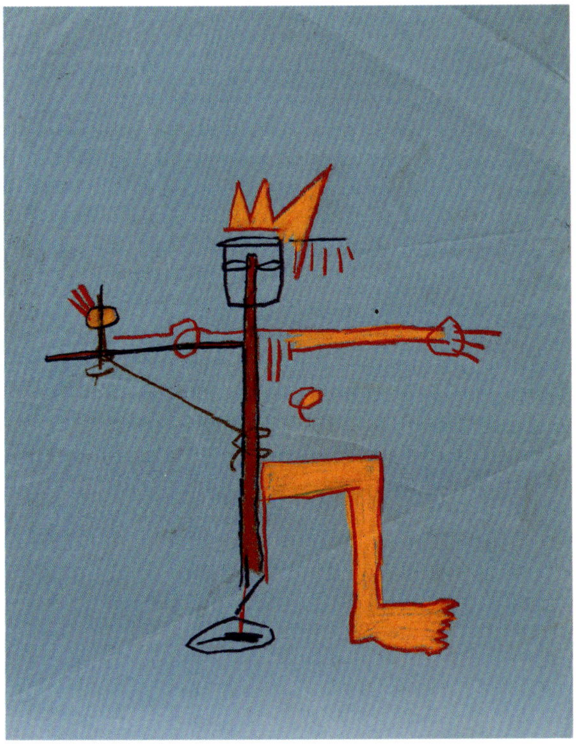

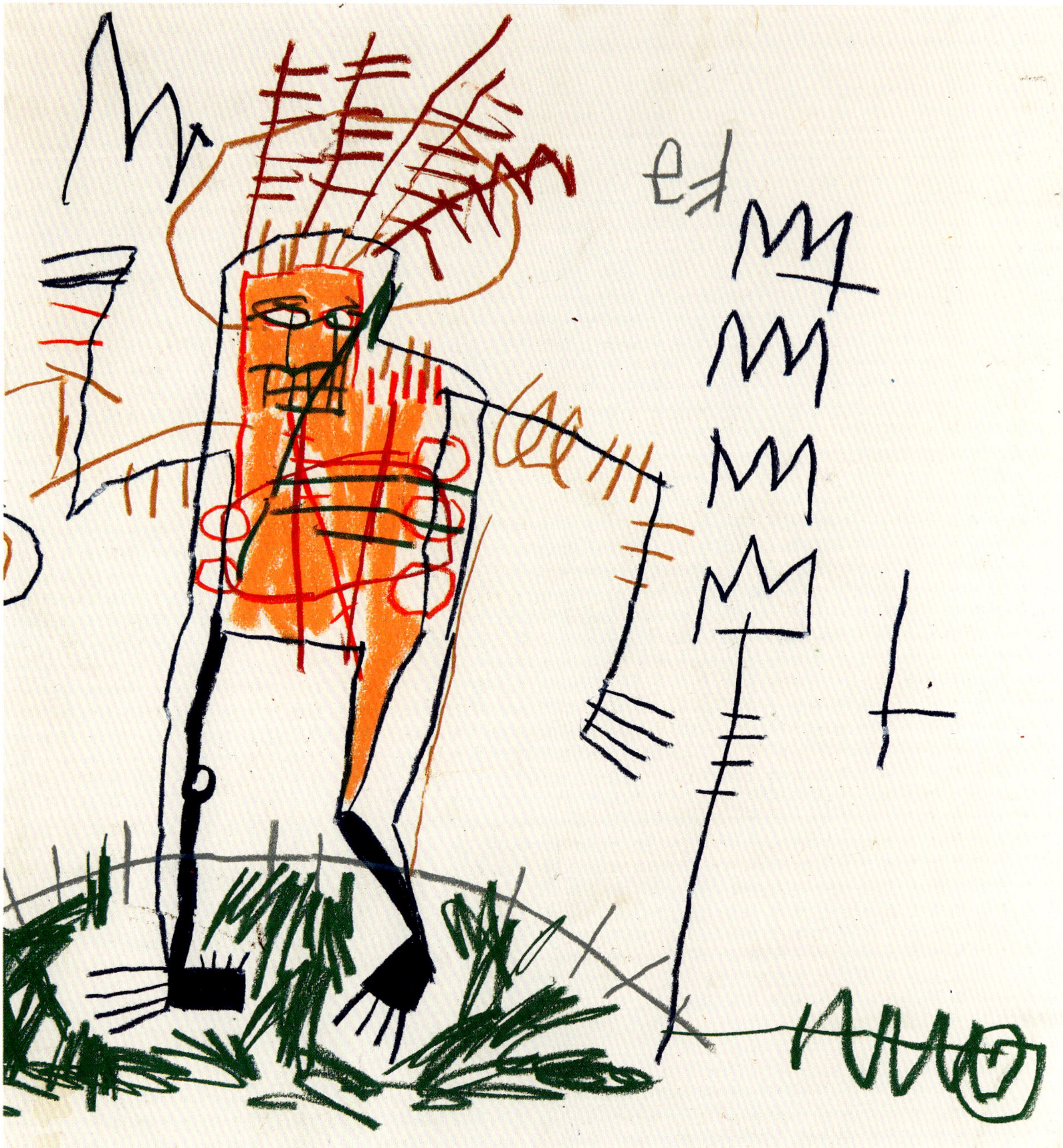

Untitled (Figure), n.d.
Oil stick on paper
18 × 16½ in. (45.72 × 41.91 cm)

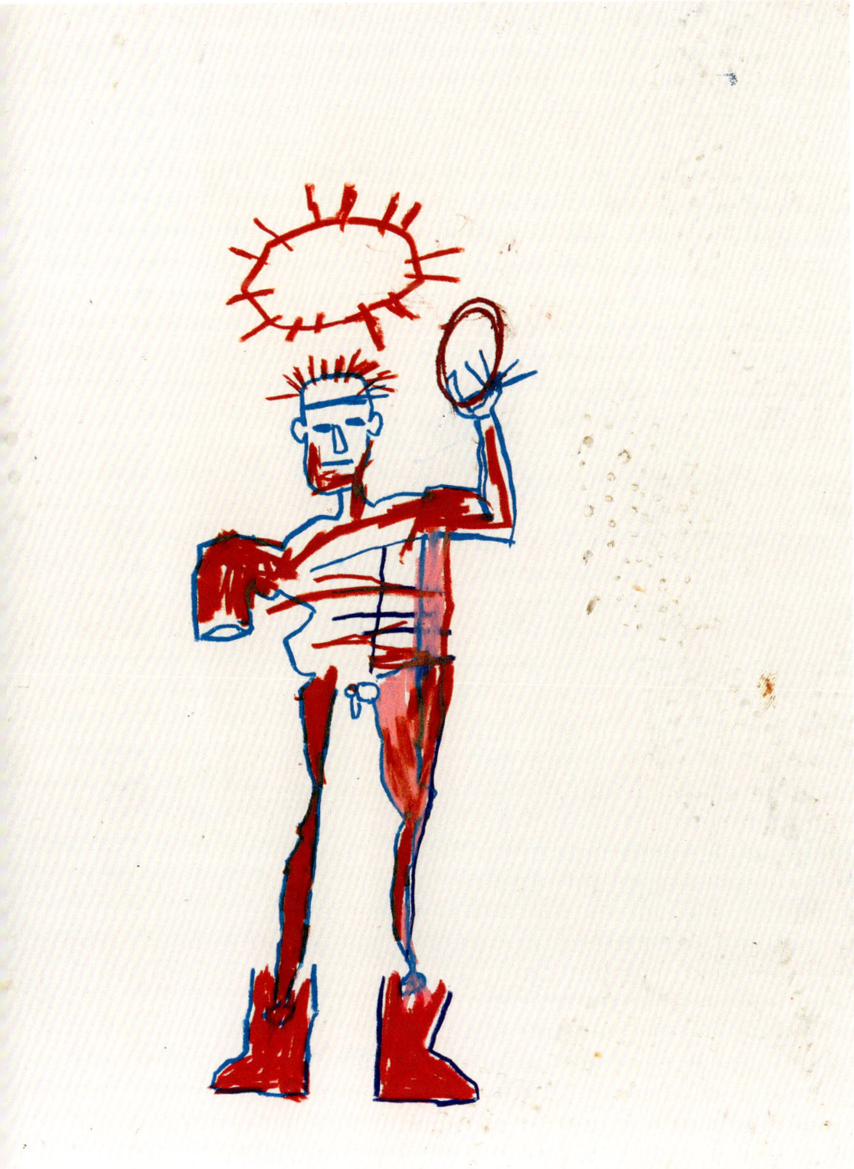

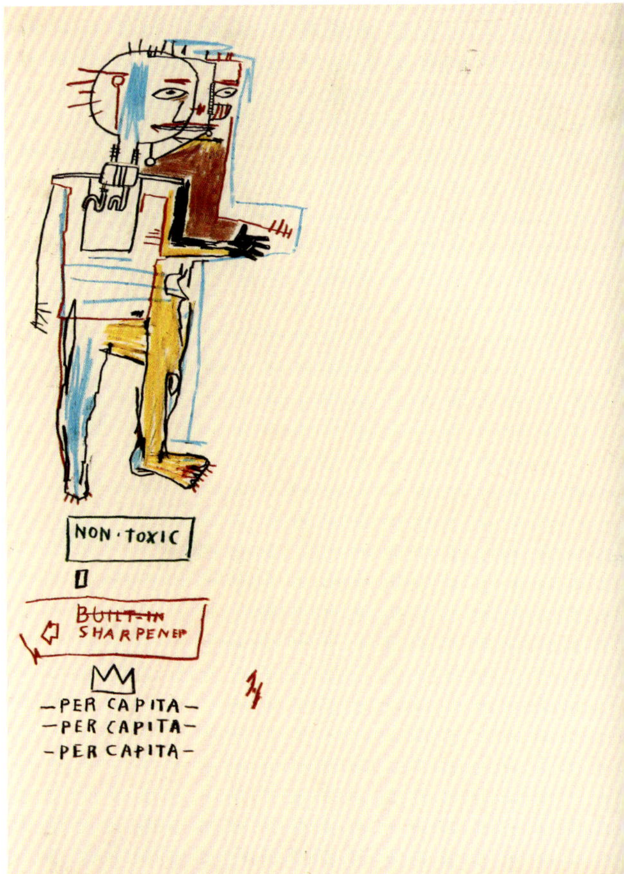

TOP
Untitled, n.d.
Oil stick on paper
22¼ × 17¼ in. (57.15 × 43.82 cm)

RIGHT
Untitled, n.d.
Crayon on paper
30 × 22½ in. (76.2 × 57.15 cm)

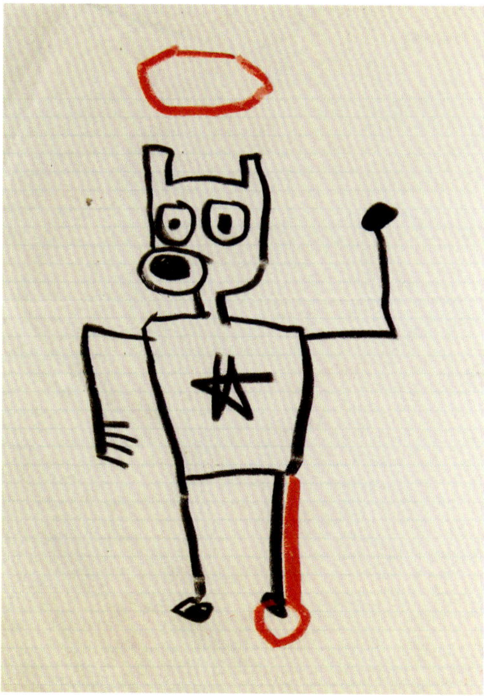

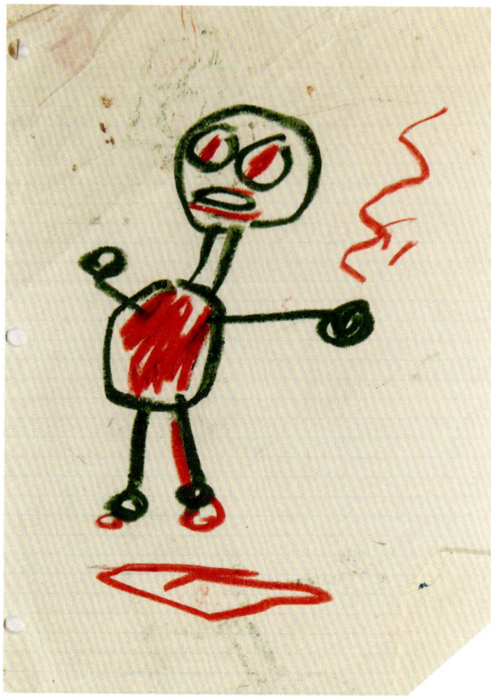

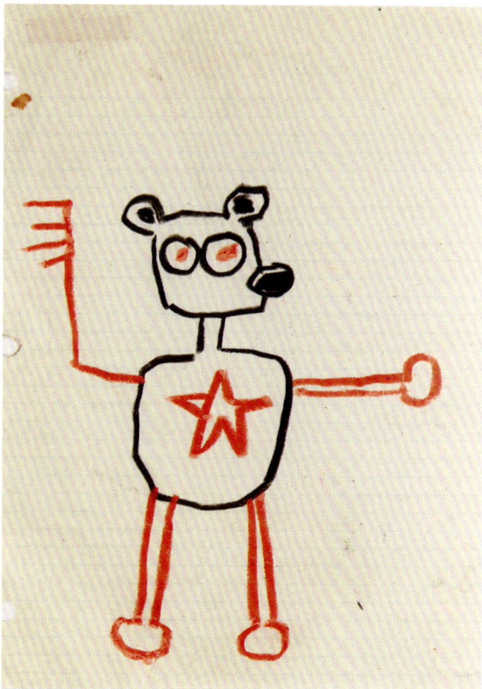

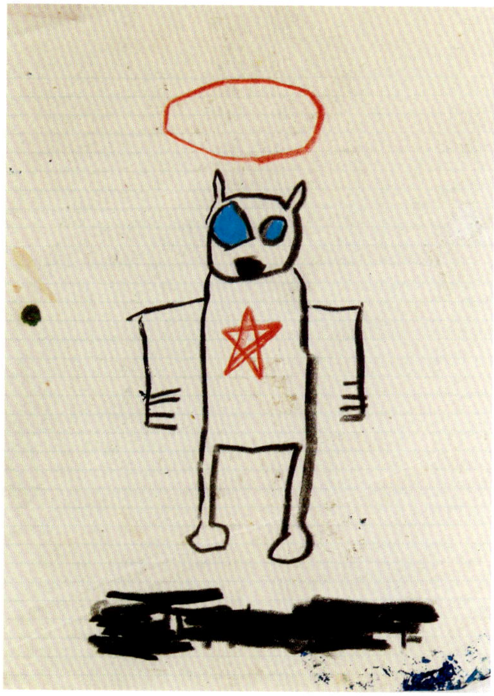

TOP, LEFT TO RIGHT
Untitled, n.d.
Crayon on paper
11 × 8½ in. (27.94 × 21.59 cm)

Untitled, n.d.
Oil stick on paper
11 × 8¼ in. (27.94 × 20.96 cm)

BOTTOM, LEFT TO RIGHT
Untitled, n.d.
Crayon and oil stick on paper
11 × 8¼ in. (27.94 × 20.96 cm)

Untitled, n.d.
Crayon and oil stick on paper
11 × 8¼ in. (27.95 × 20.96 cm)

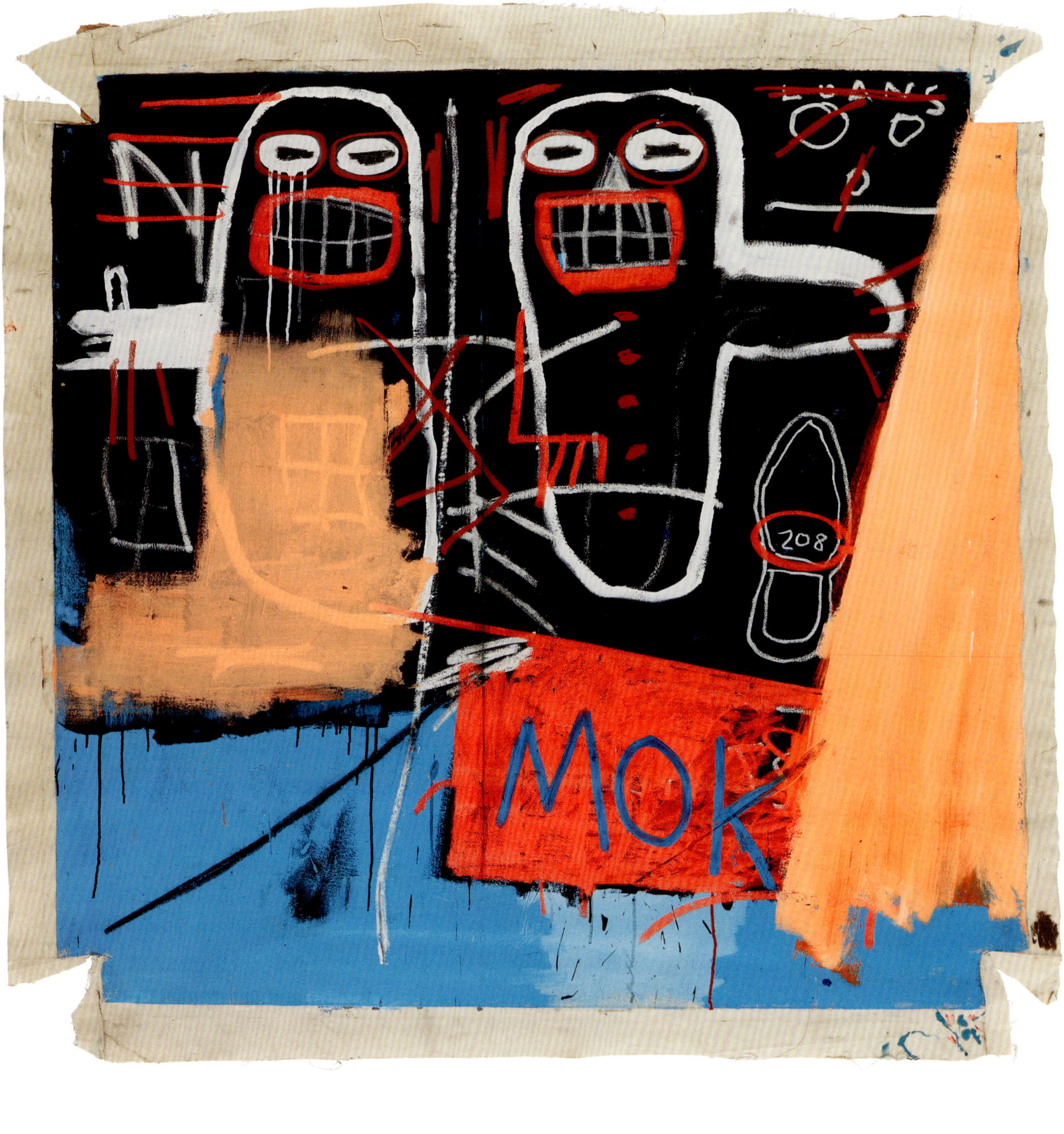

Untitled (Mok), n.d.
Acrylic and oil stick on canvas
61½ × 59 in. (156.21 × 149.86 cm)

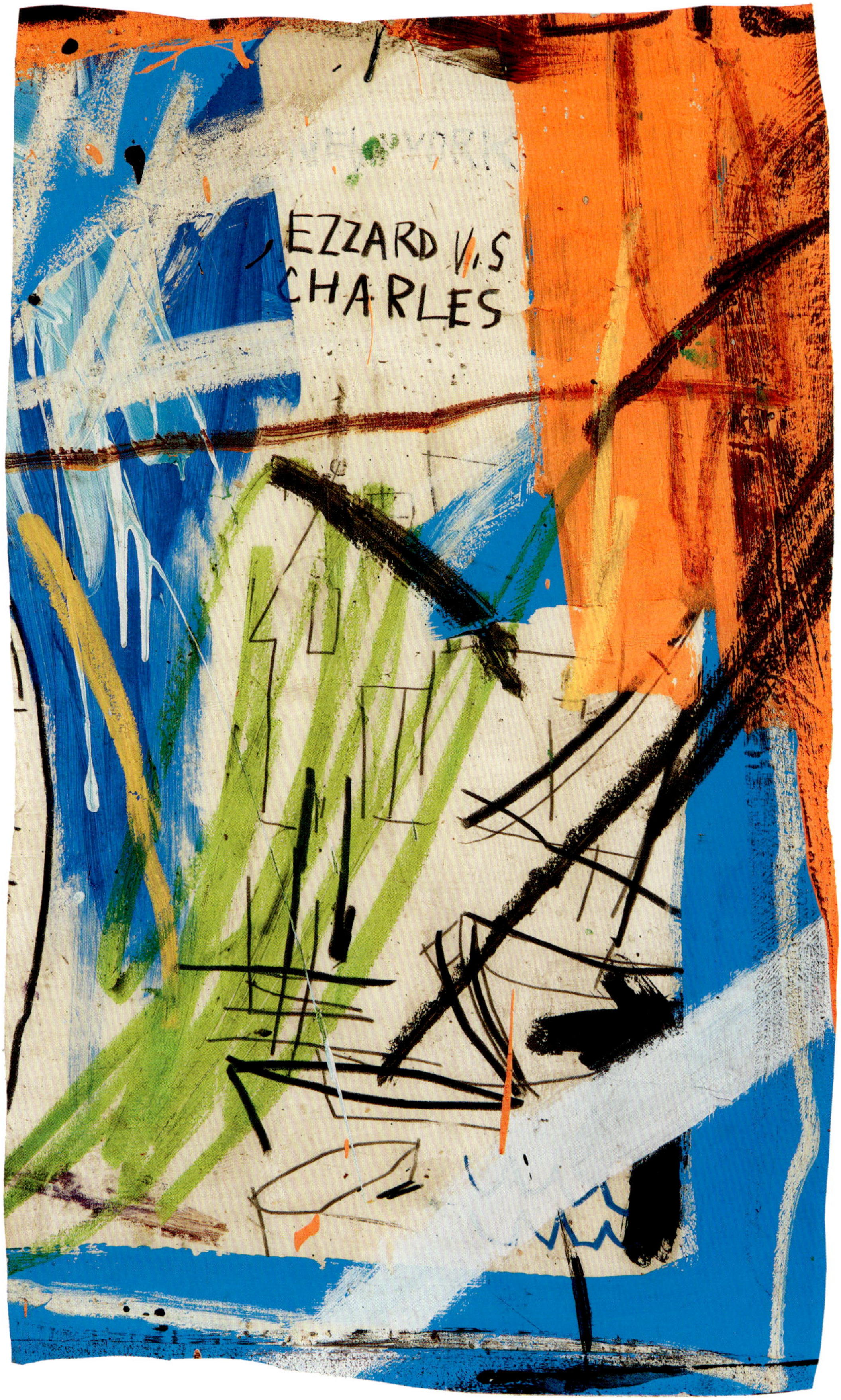
EZZARD V.S
CHARLES

OPPOSITE
Untitled (Painting Fragment), n.d.
Acrylic, oil stick, and crayon on vinyl laid down on canvas
33 × 19½ in. (83.82 × 49.53 cm)

BELOW
Untitled (Portrait), n.d.
Crayon and oil stick on paper
14 × 9¾ in. (35.56 × 24.77 cm)

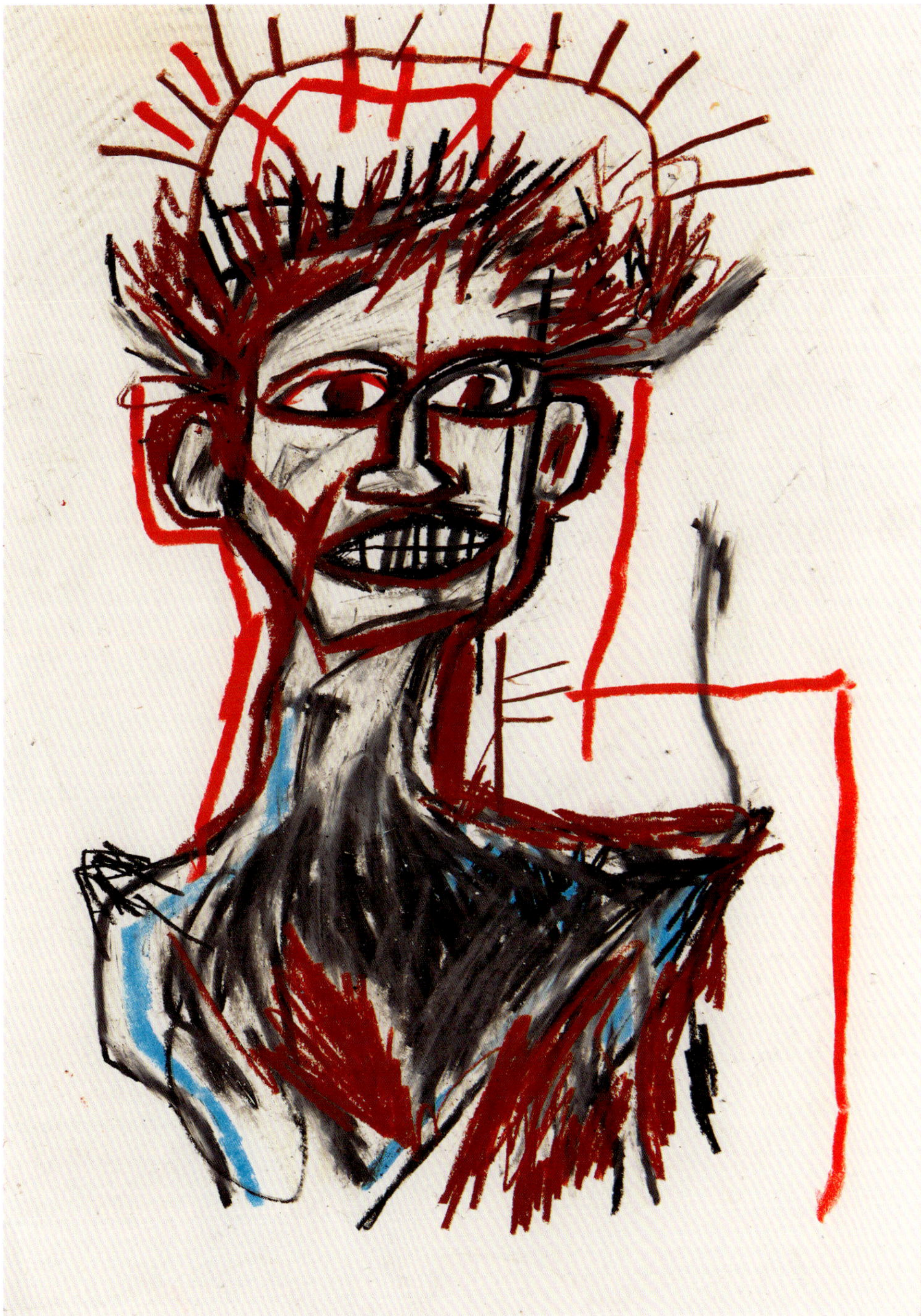

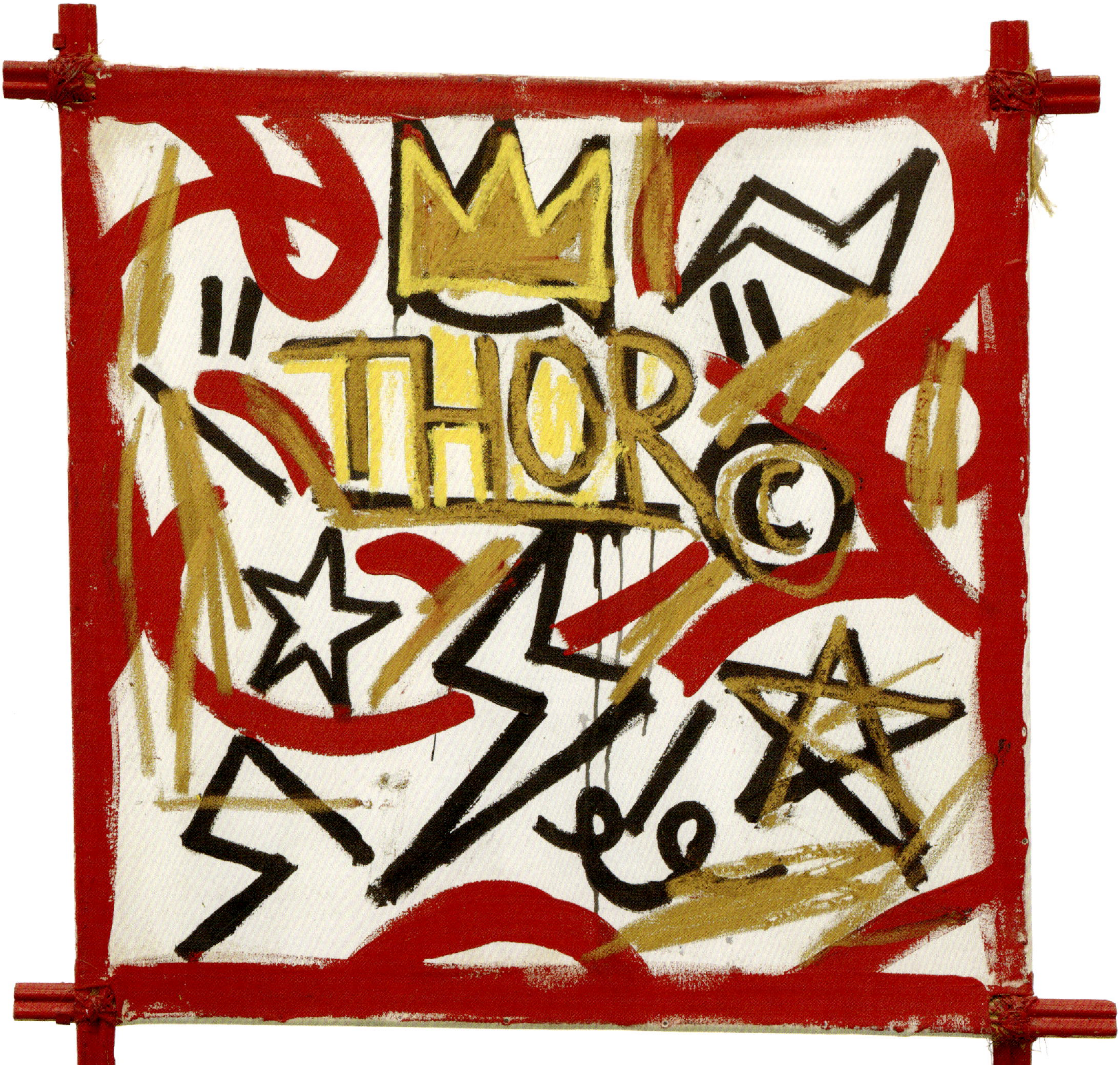

Untitled (Thor), 1982
Acrylic and oil stick on canvas
mounted on tied wood supports
48 × 48 in. (121.92 × 121.92 cm)

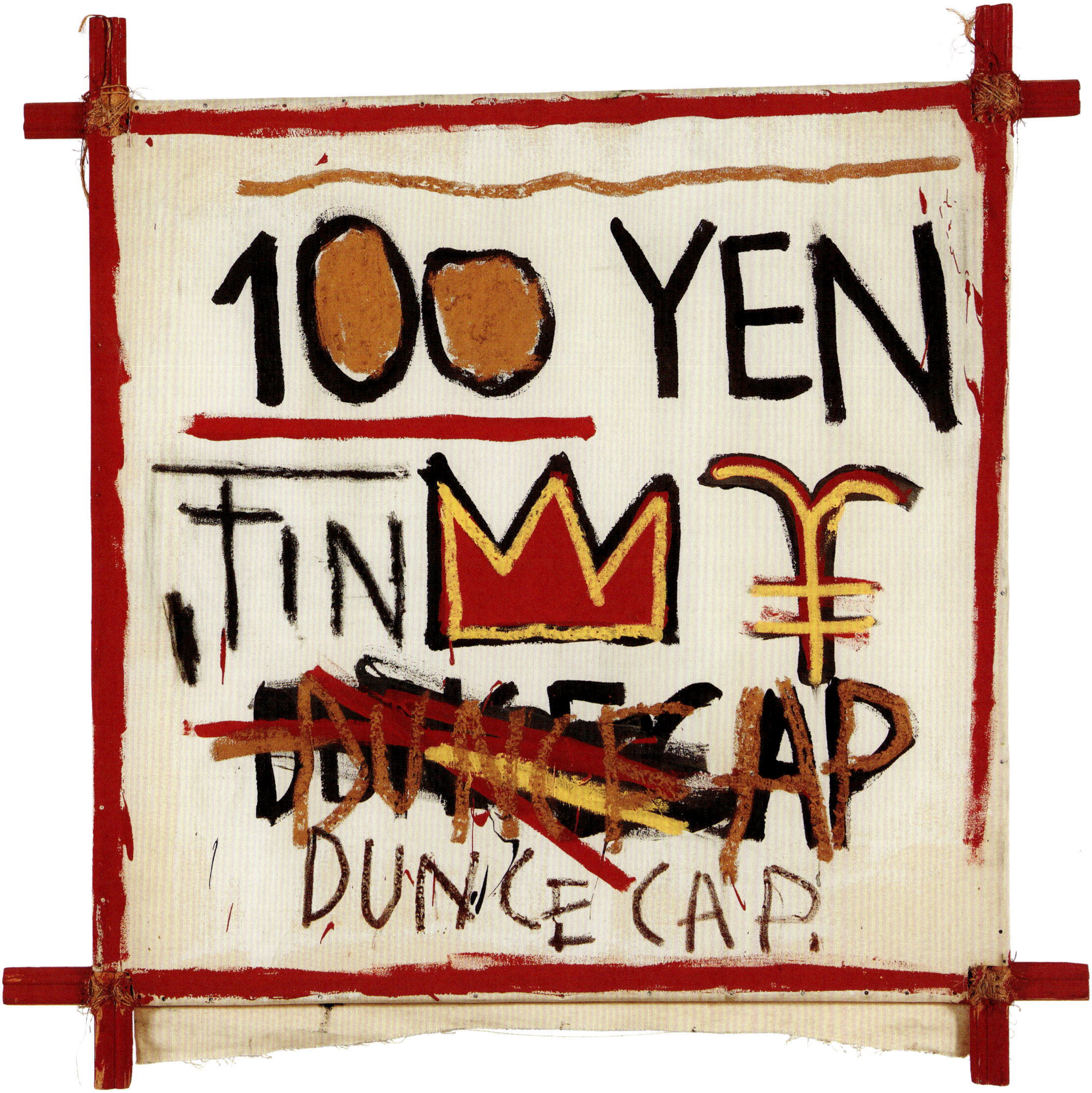

Untitled (100 Yen), 1982
Acrylic and oil stick on canvas
mounted on tied wood supports
48½ × 48 in. (123.19 × 121.92 cm)

Untitled (They Little Know), n.d.
Acrylic, crayon, and masking
tape with collage on paper
10½ × 8½ in. (26.67 × 21.59 cm)

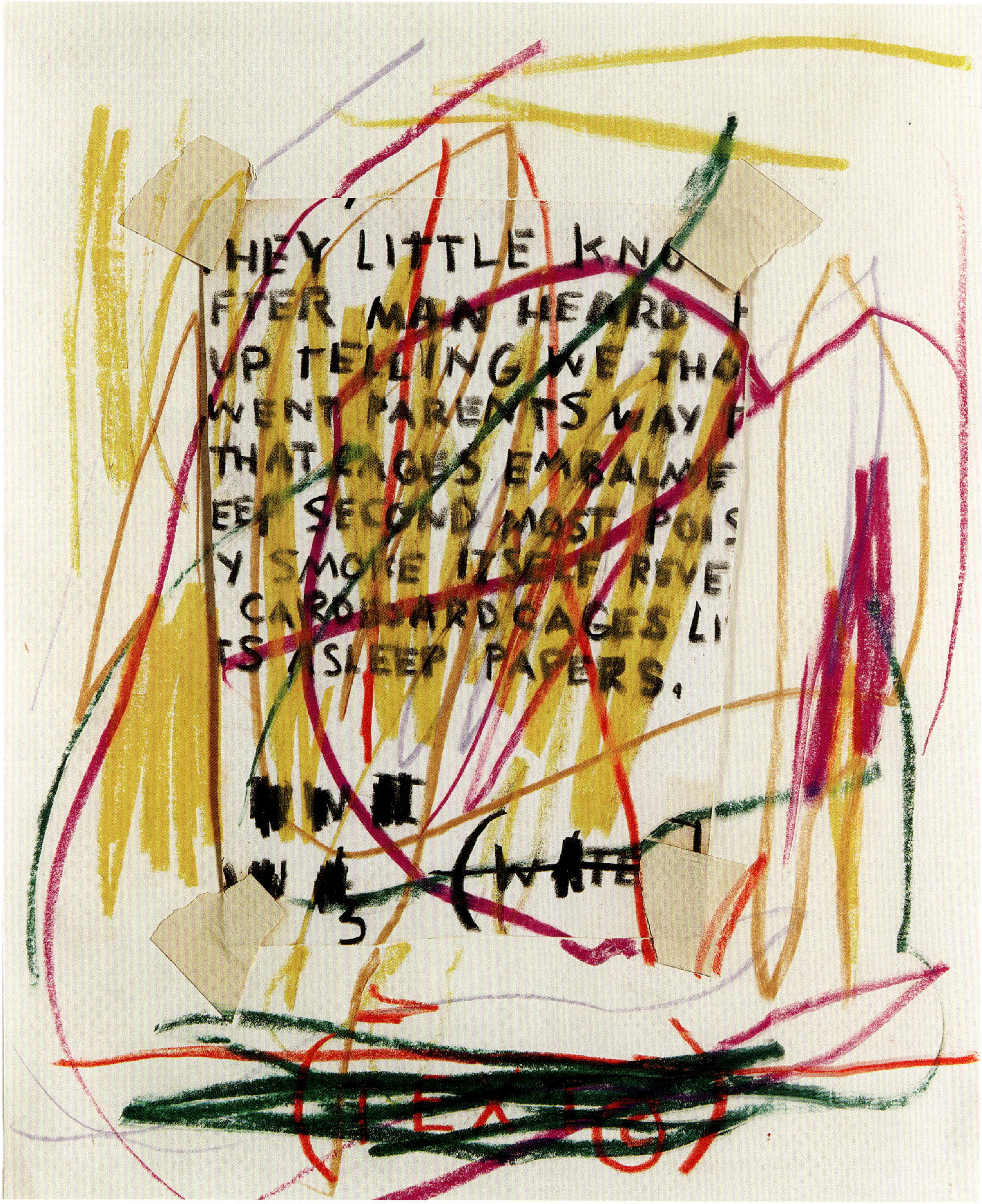

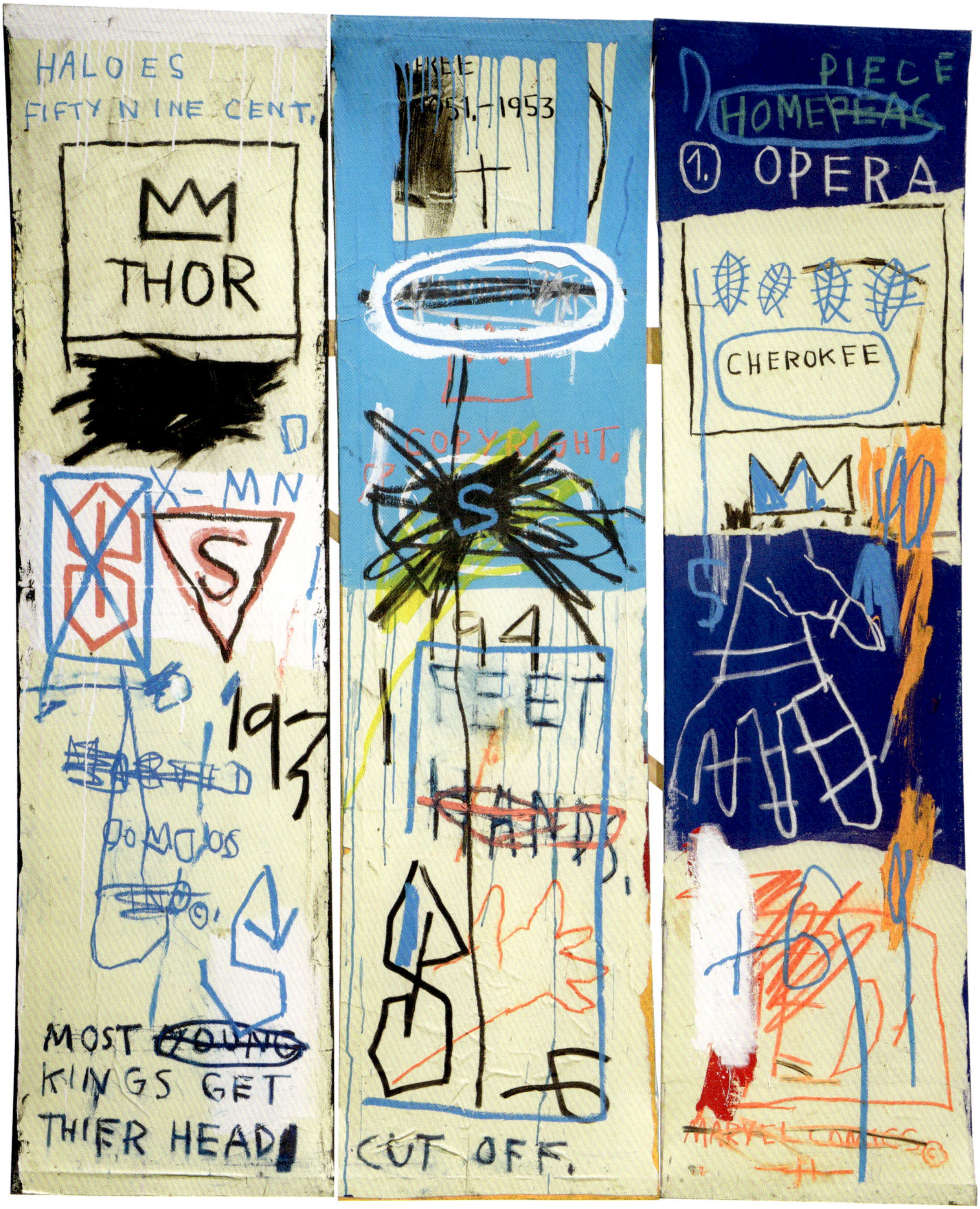

Charles the First, 1982
Acrylic, oil stick, and paper
on canvas
Triptych, 78 × 62 in. overall
(198.12 × 157.48 cm)

BELOW
Untitled (Tar), n.d.
Acrylic on wood in
painted frame
40 × 28 in. (101.6 × 71.12 cm)

OPPOSITE
Untitled (Tar), 1981
Acrylic on wood panel
36 × 21 in. (91.44 × 53.34 cm)

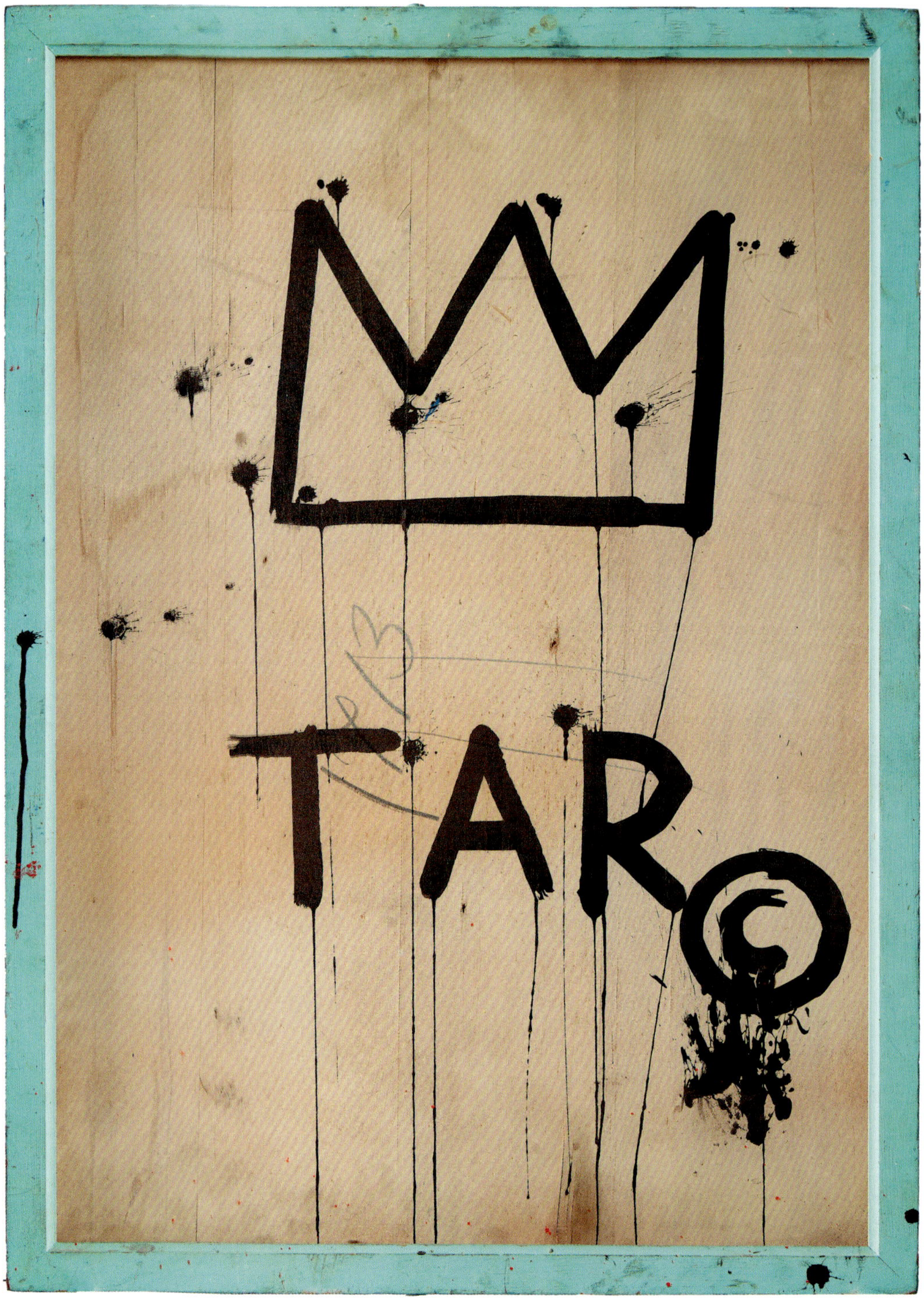

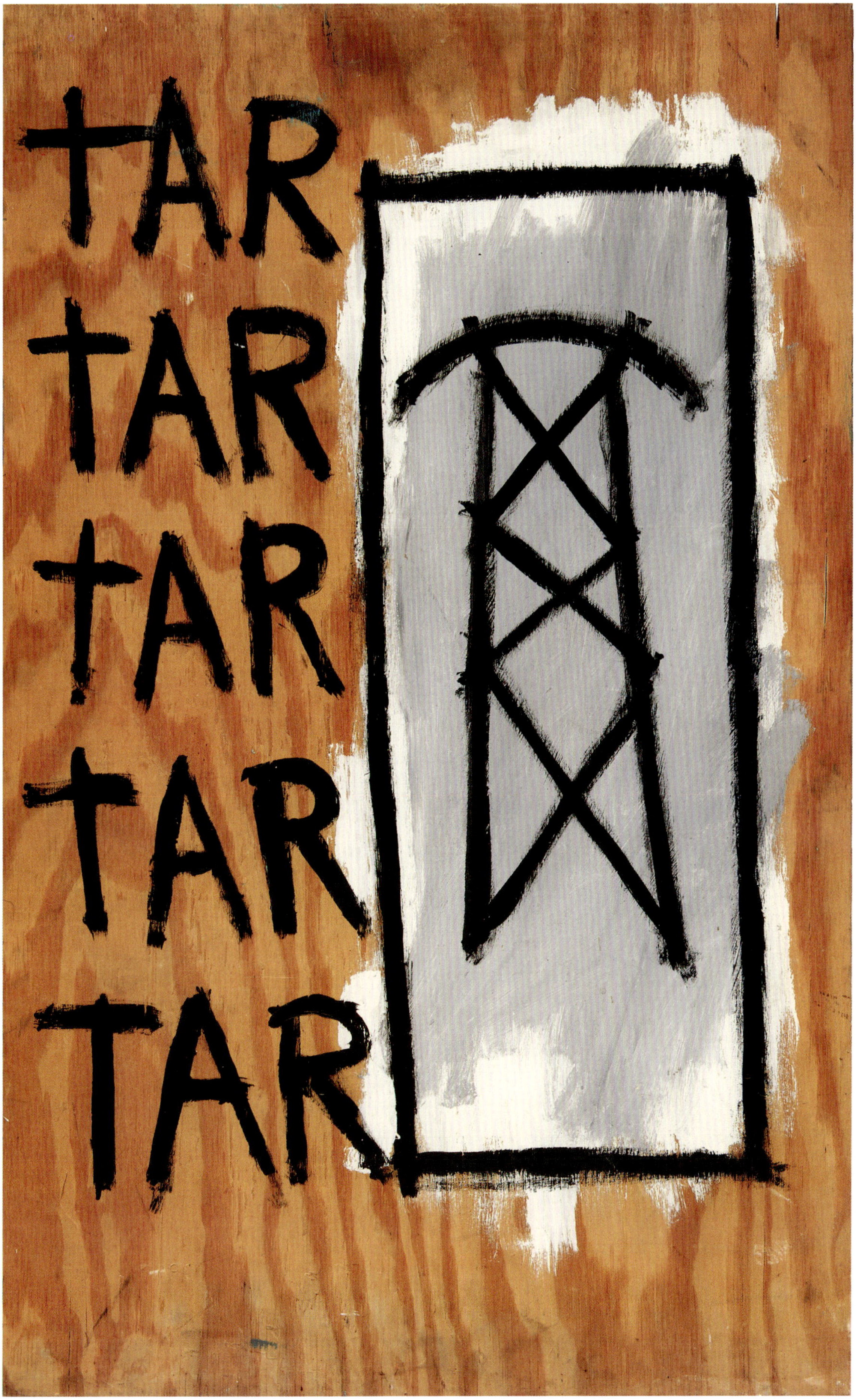
TAR
TAR
TAR
TAR
TAR

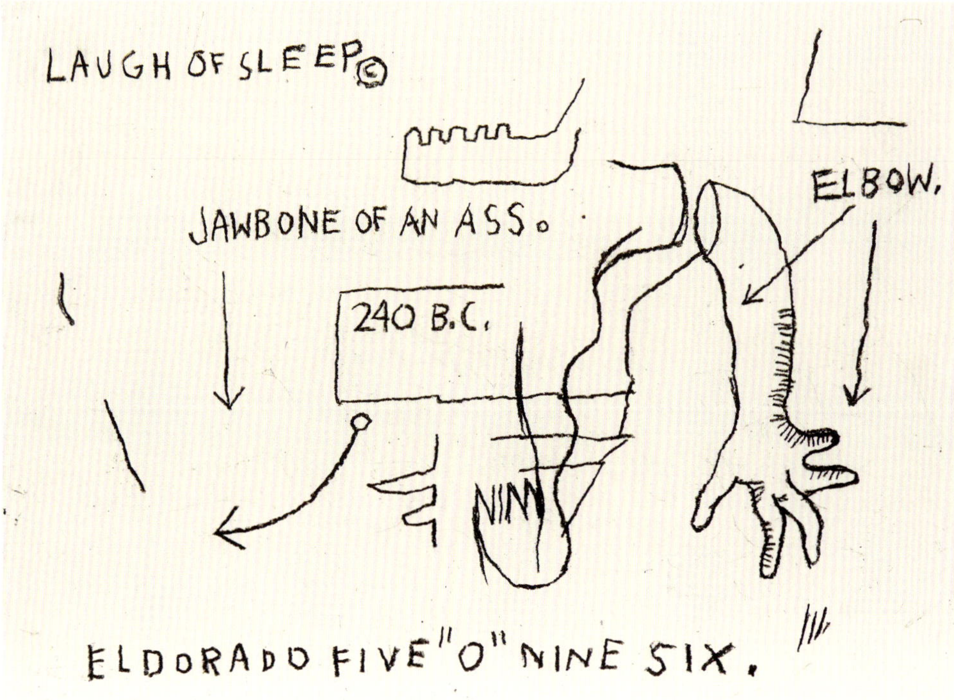

LEFT
Untitled (Laugh of Sleep), n.d.
Oil stick on paper
15 × 20 in. (38.1 × 50.8 cm)

BOTTOM
Untitled, n.d.
Printed paper collage mounted on plywood with spray acrylic
9 × 7 in. (22.86 × 17.78 cm)

OPPOSITE
Untitled (Spine), n.d
Charcoal, oil stick, and paper mounted on wood
36 × 24 in. (91.44 × 60.96 cm)

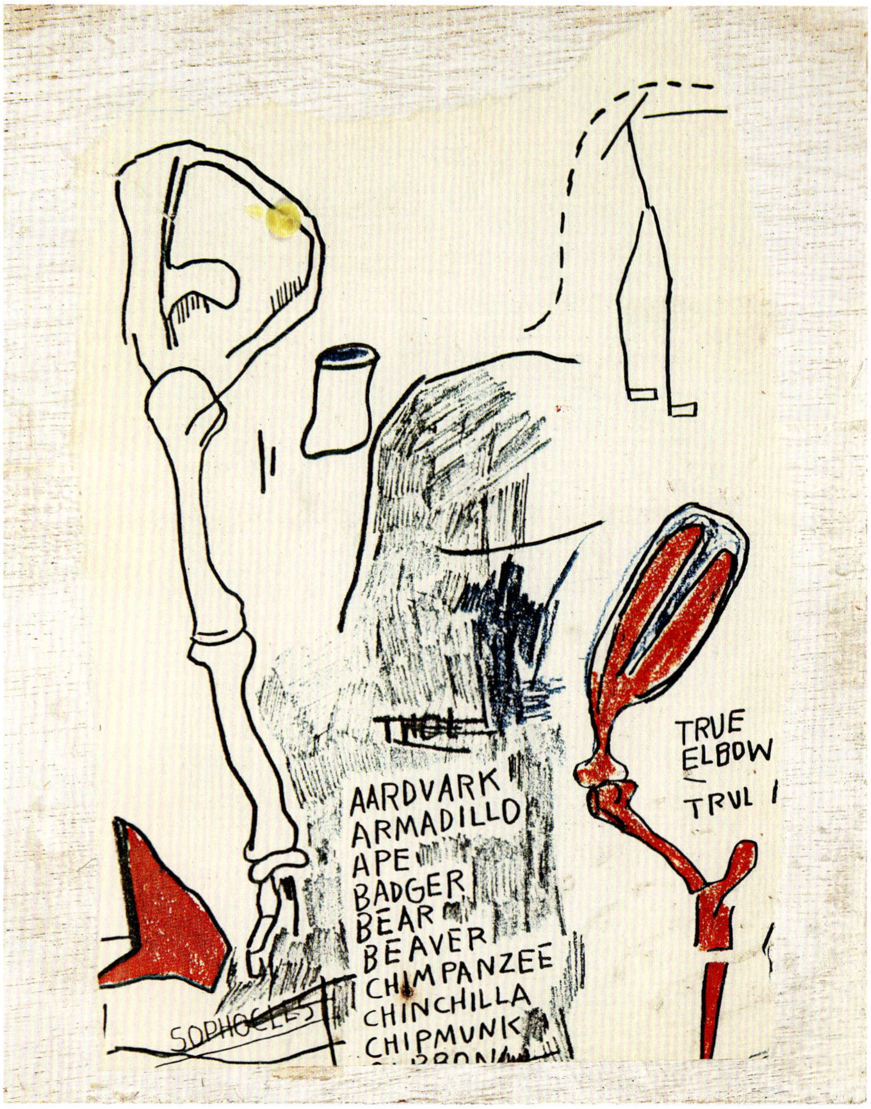

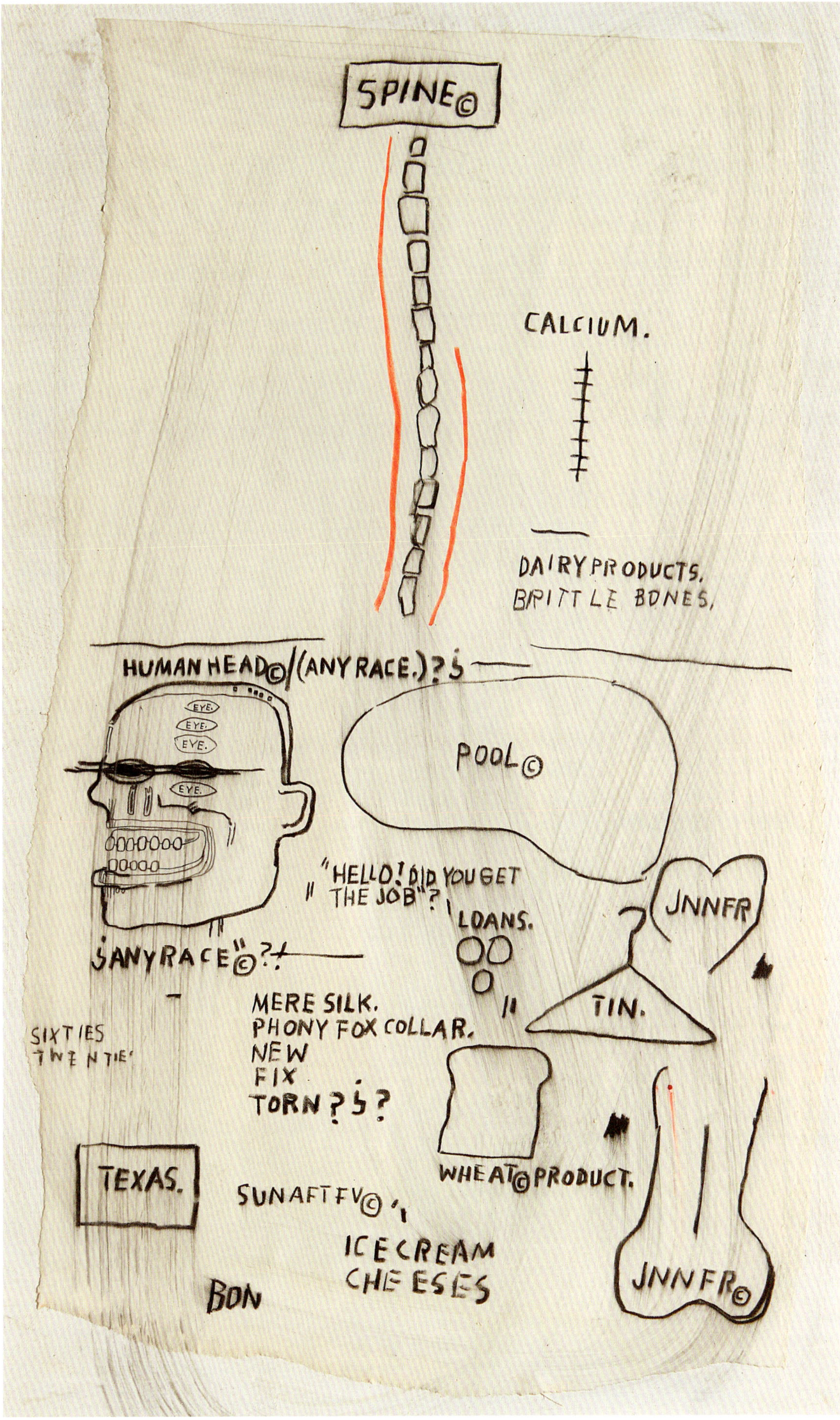
SPINE©
CALCIUM.
DAIRY PRODUCTS.
BRITTLE BONES.
HUMAN HEAD©/(ANY RACE.)?¿
EYE.
EYE.
EYE.
EYE.
POOL©
"HELLO! DID YOU GET THE JOB"?
LOANS.
JNNFR
¿ANY RACE"©?!
MERE SILK.
PHONY FOX COLLAR.
NEW
FIX
TORN?¿?
TIN.
SIXTIES
TWENTIES
TEXAS.
WHEAT© PRODUCT.
SUNAFTFV©
ICE CREAM
CHEESES
BON
JNNFR©

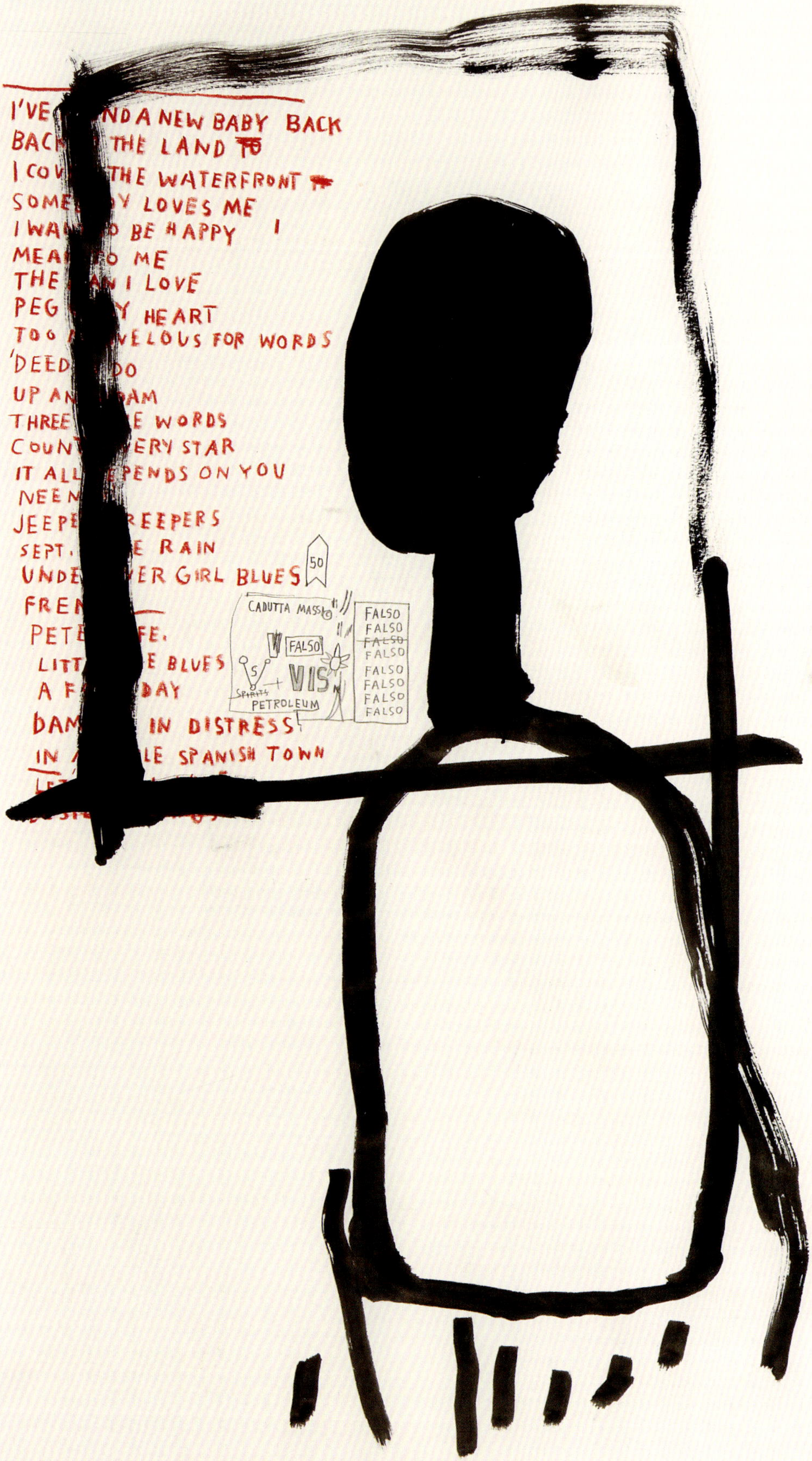
I'VE
ND A NEW BABY BACK
BACK
THE LAND TO
I COV
THE WATERFRONT
SOME
Y LOVES ME
I WA
BE HAPPY I
MEA
O ME
THE
AN I LOVE
PEG
Y HEART
TOO
VELOUS FOR WORDS
'DEED
DO
UP AN
DAM
THREE
E WORDS
COUN
ERY STAR
IT ALL
PENDS ON YOU
NEEN
JEEPE
REEPERS
SEPT.
E RAIN
UNDE
VER GIRL BLUES
50
FREN
PETE
FE.
LITT
E BLUES
A F
DAY
DAM
IN DISTRESS
IN A
LE SPANISH TOWN
CADUTTA MASSI
FALSO
FALSO
FALSO
FALSO
FALSO
FALSO
FALSO
FALSO
FALSO
VIS
PETROLEUM

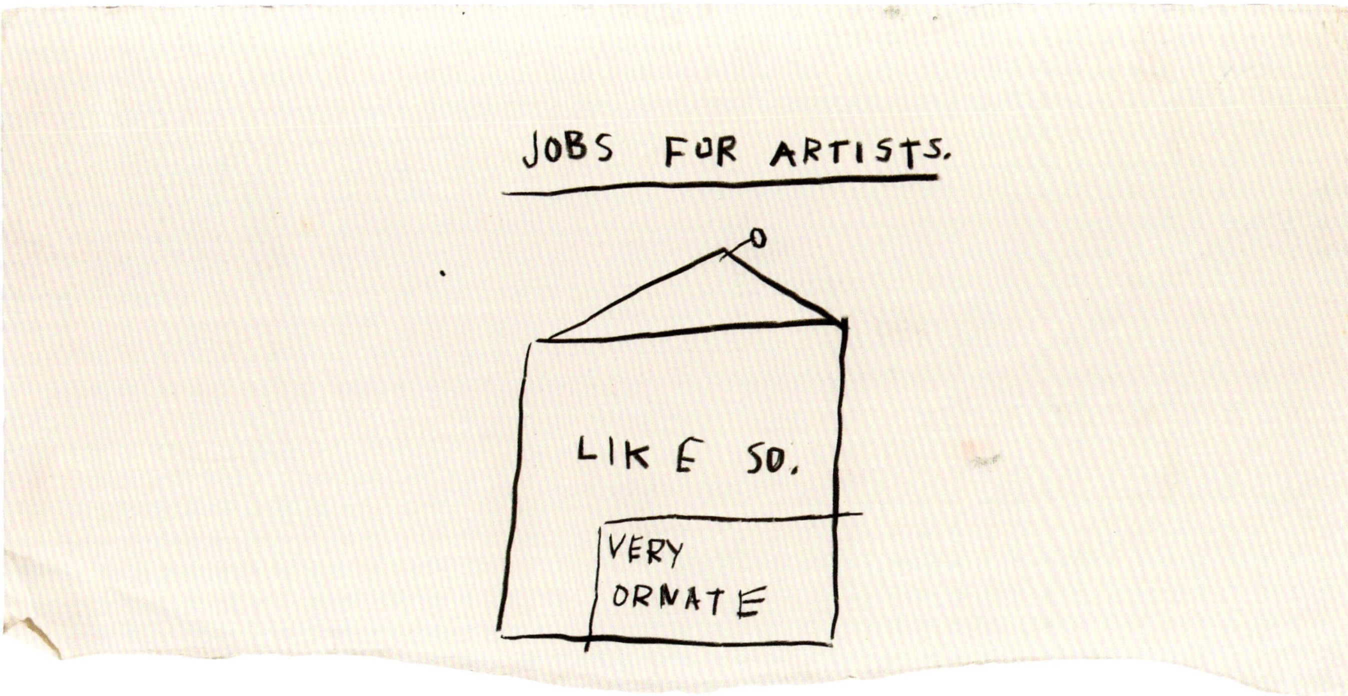

OPPOSITE
Untitled (Falso), n.d.
Crayon, graphite, and ink
on paper
42 × 29½ in. (106.68 × 74.93 cm)

ABOVE
Untitled (Jobs for Artists), n.d.
Oil stick on paper
15 × 30 in. (38.1 × 76.2 cm)

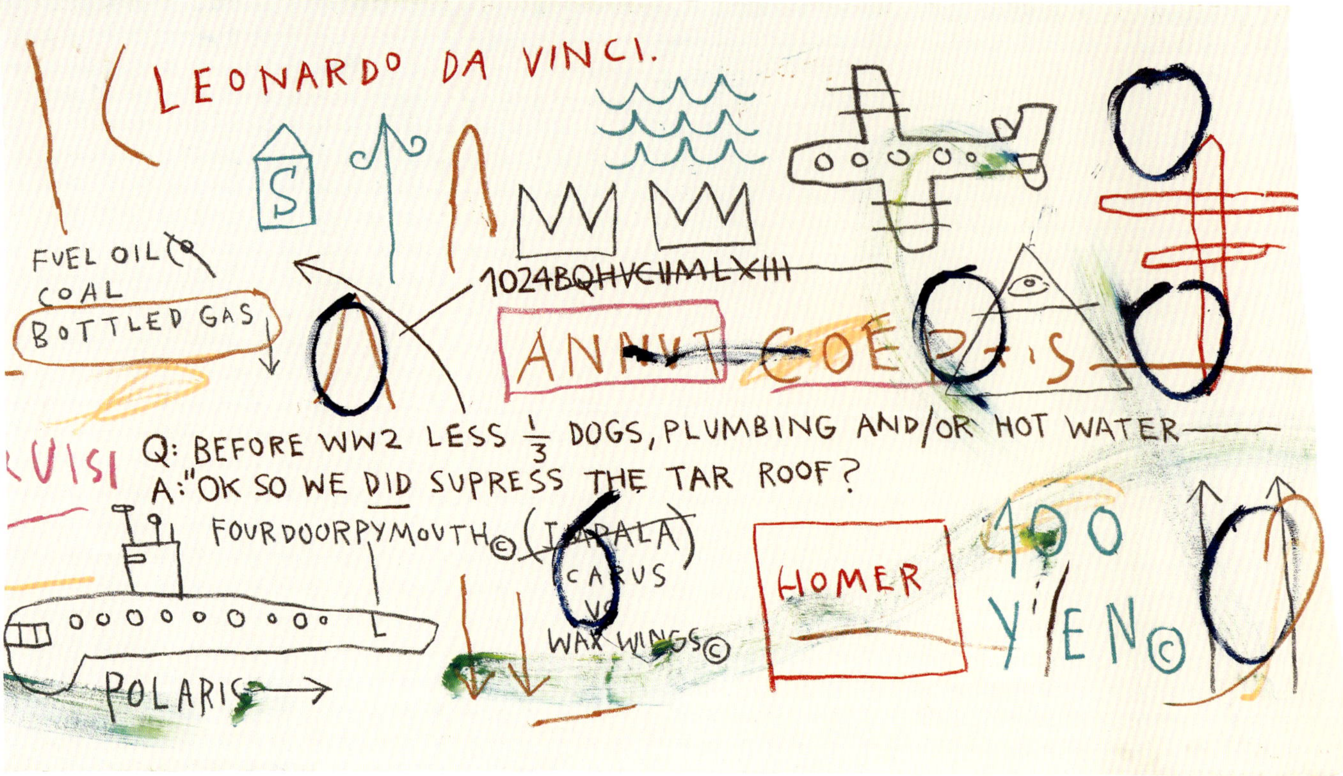

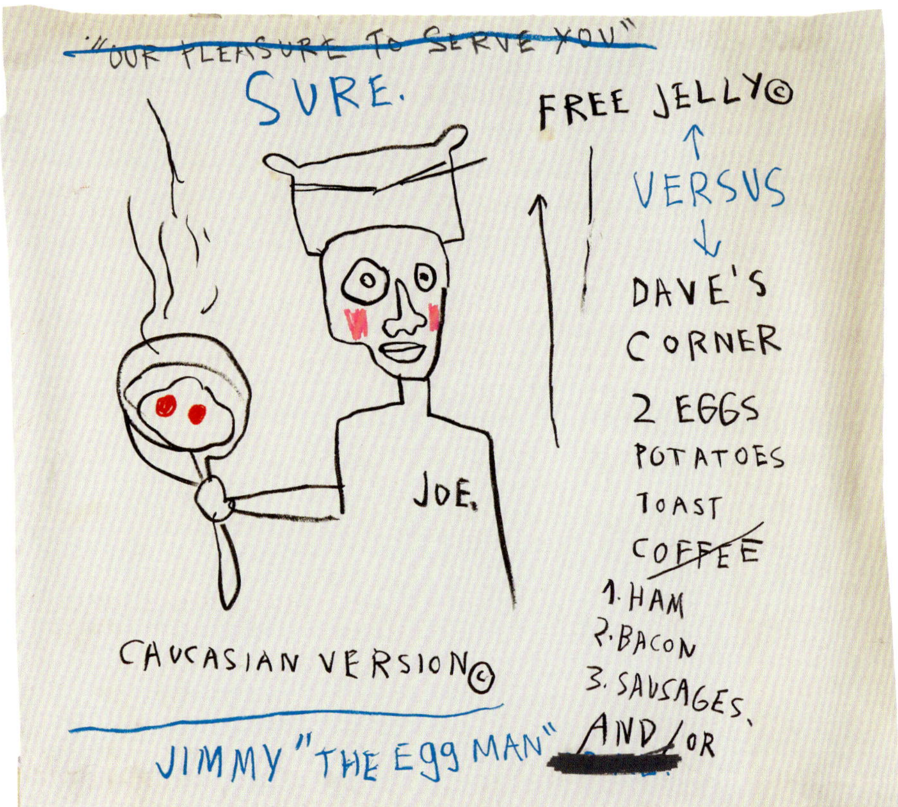

TOP
Untitled (Leonardo da Vinci), n.d.
Acrylic and oil stick on paper
45 × 77 in. (114.3 × 195.58 cm)

LEFT
Untitled (Jimmy the Eggman), n.d.
Oil stick on paper
50¼ × 53½ in.
(127.64 × 135.89 cm)

OPPOSITE
Untitled (Member), n.d.
Crayon on paper
30 × 22¼ in. (76.2 × 56.52 cm).
We watched the television show "Batman" as kids. JEANINE

OVERLEAF
Untitled (Entrance to Descending Passage), n.d.
Color monotype on paper
36 × 60 in. (91.44 × 152.4 cm)

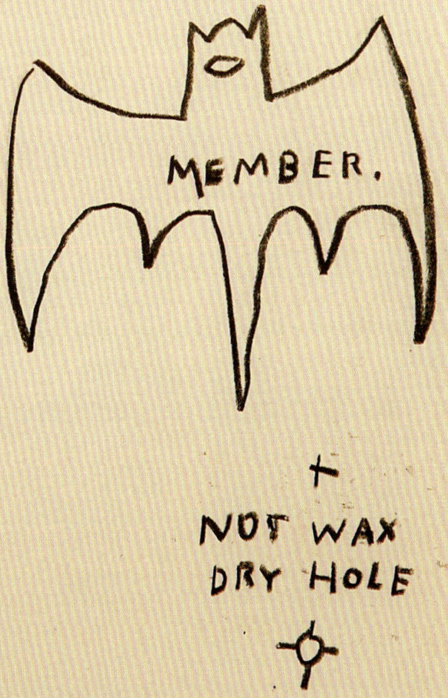
MEMBER.
+
NOT WAX
DRY HOLE

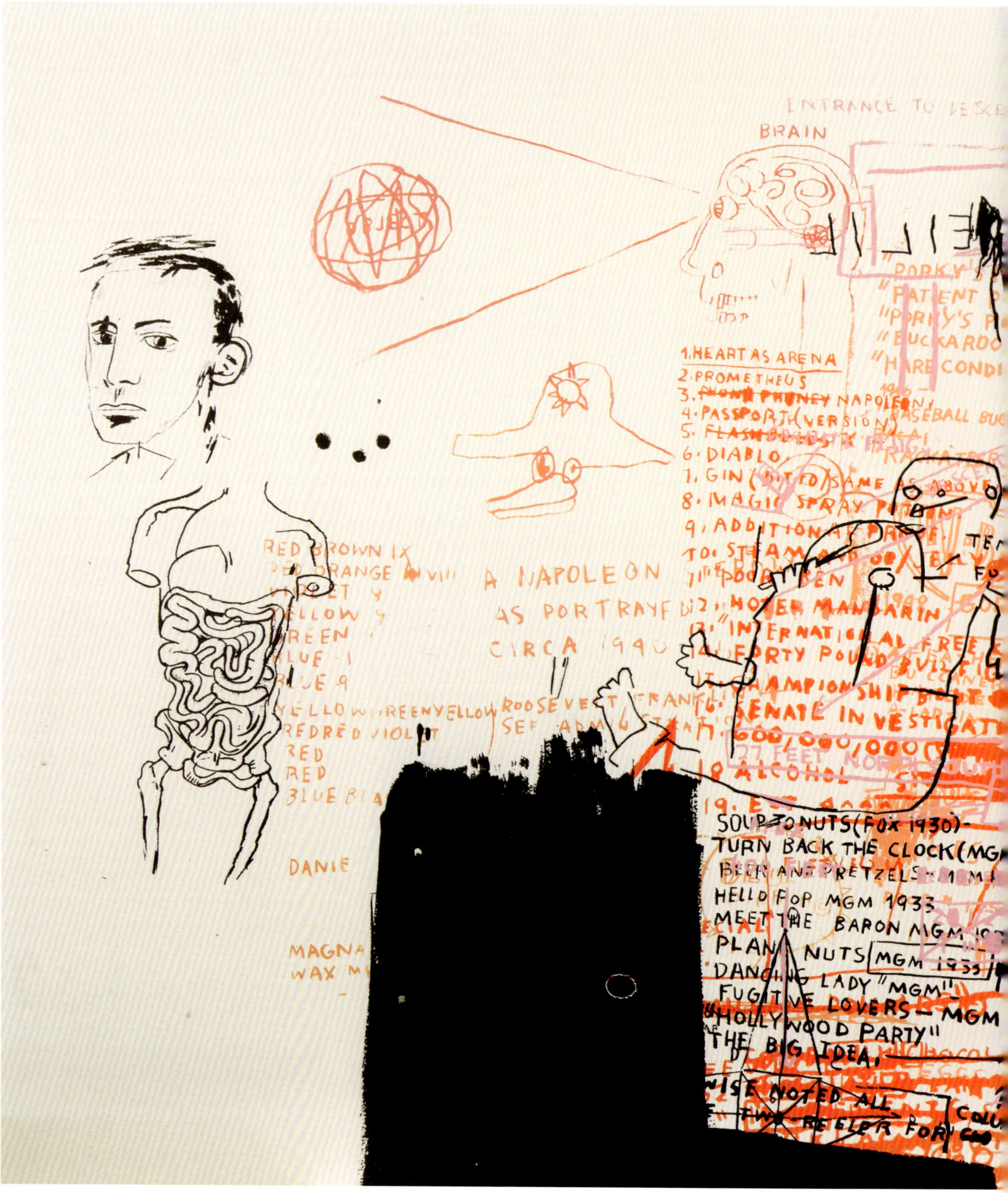

BRAIN
1. HEART AS ARENA
2. PROMETHEUS
4. PASSPORT
6. DIABLO
A NAPOLEON
RED BROWN IX
RED
RED
DANIE
MAGNA
WAX M
SENATE INVESTIGAT
ALCOHOL
SOUP TO NUTS (FOX 1930)-
TURN BACK THE CLOCK (MG
HELLO POP MGM 1933
MEET THE BARON MGM
DANCING LADY "MGM"
FUGITIVE LOVERS — MGM
"HOLLYWOOD PARTY"
THE BIG IDEA

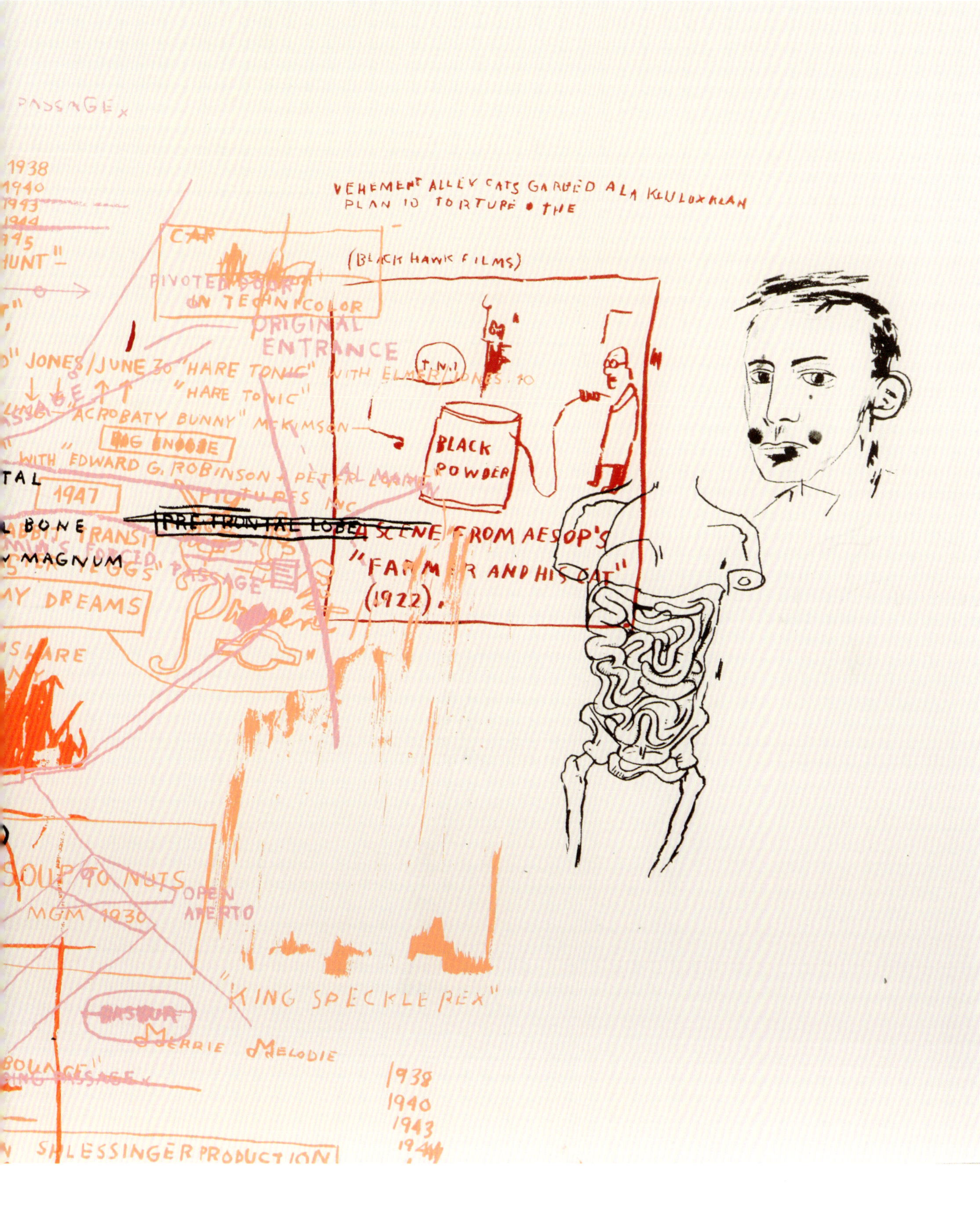
(BLACK HAWK FILMS)
ORIGINAL
ENTRANCE
"HARE TONIC"
"ACROBATY BUNNY" MCKIMSON
WITH EDWARD G. ROBINSON
1947
PRE FRONTAL LOBE
BLACK POWDER
SCENE FROM AESOP'S
"FARMER AND HIS CAT"
(1922).
SOUP TO NUTS
MGM 1930
OPEN
APERTO
"KING SPECKLE REX"
MERRIE MELODIE
1938
1940
1943

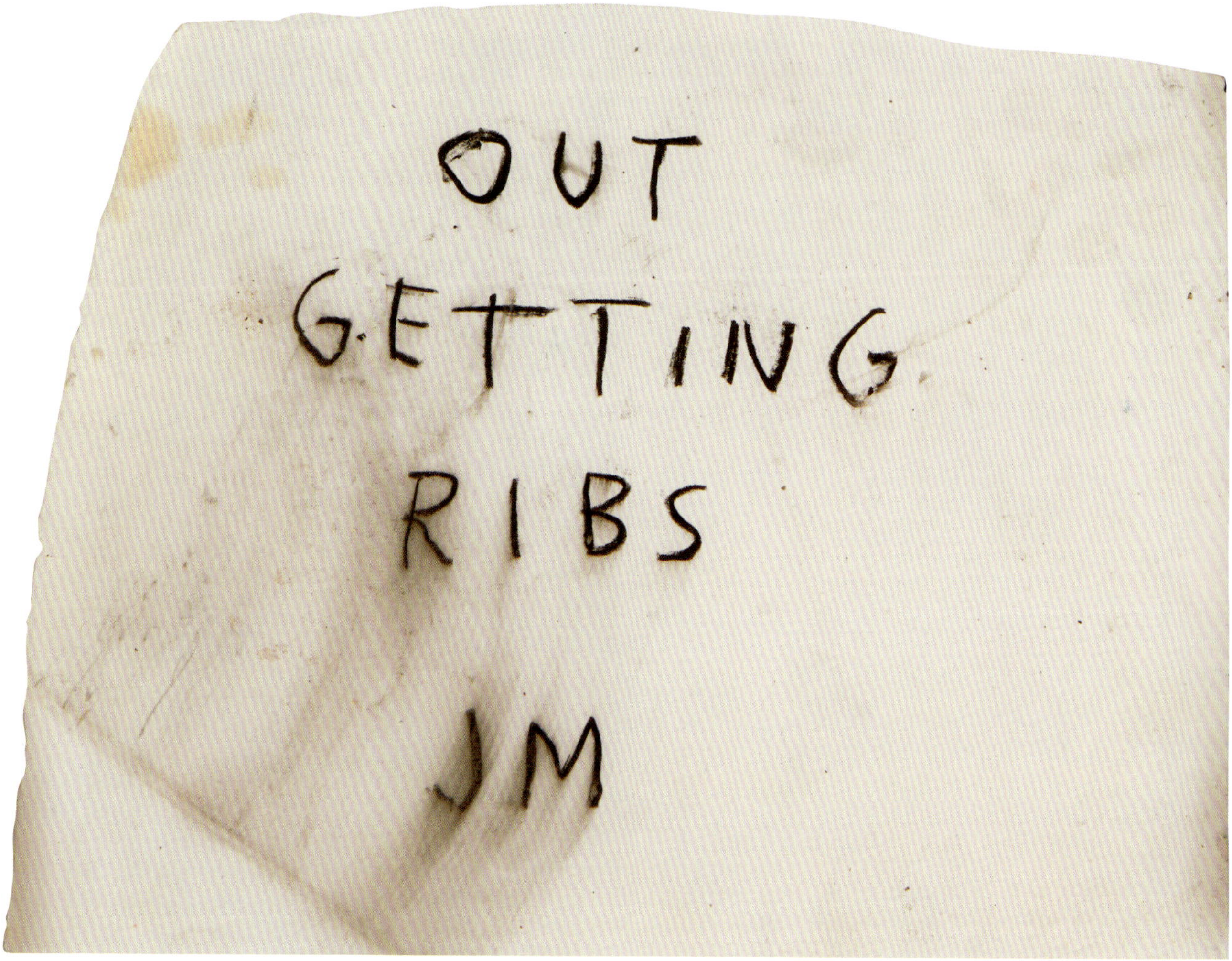

Untitled (Out Getting Ribs JM), n.d.
Crayon on paper
8 × 9¼ in. (20.32 × 24.77 cm)

Untitled (Crown), n.d.
Oil stick on paper
7 × 10 in. (17.78 × 25.4 cm)

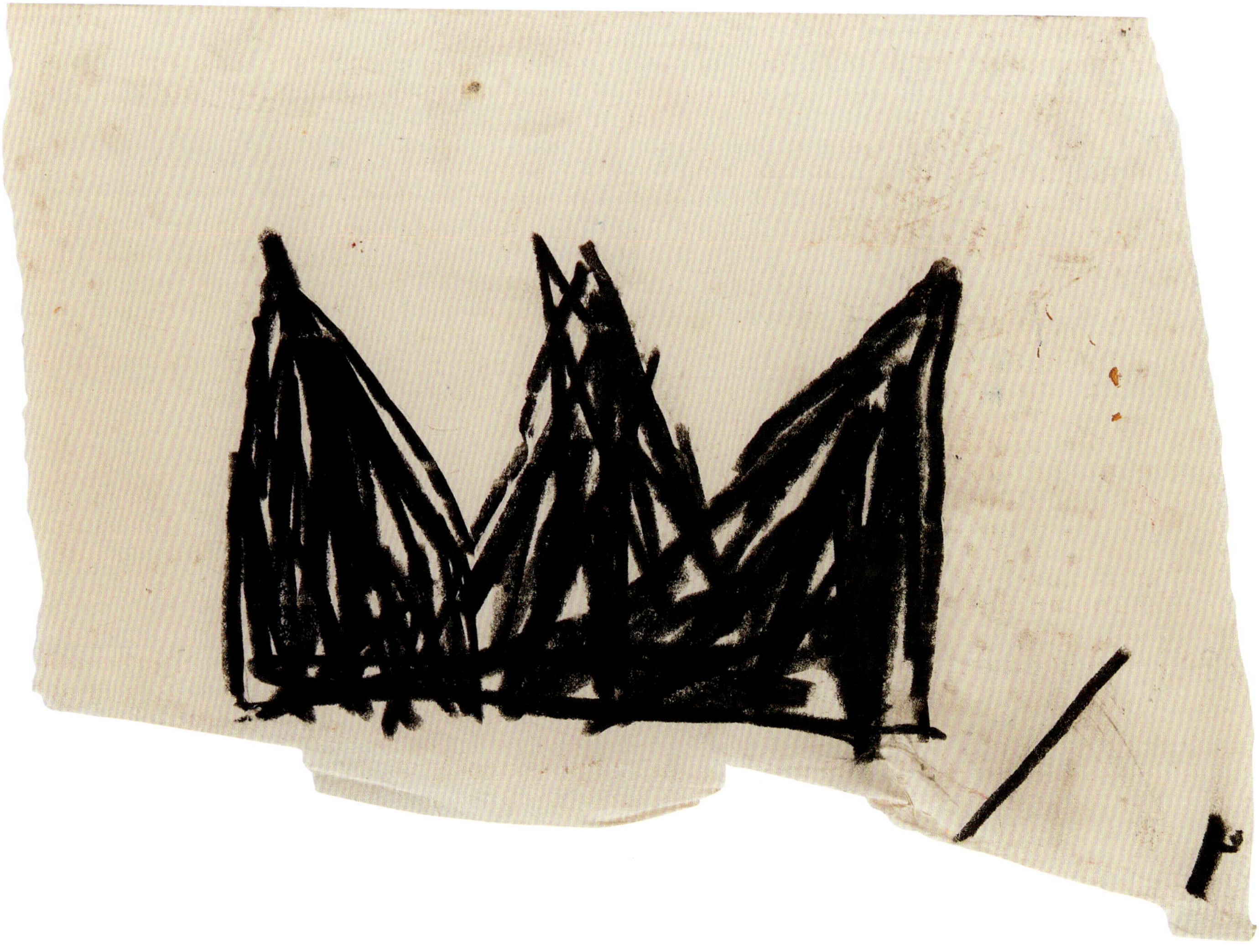

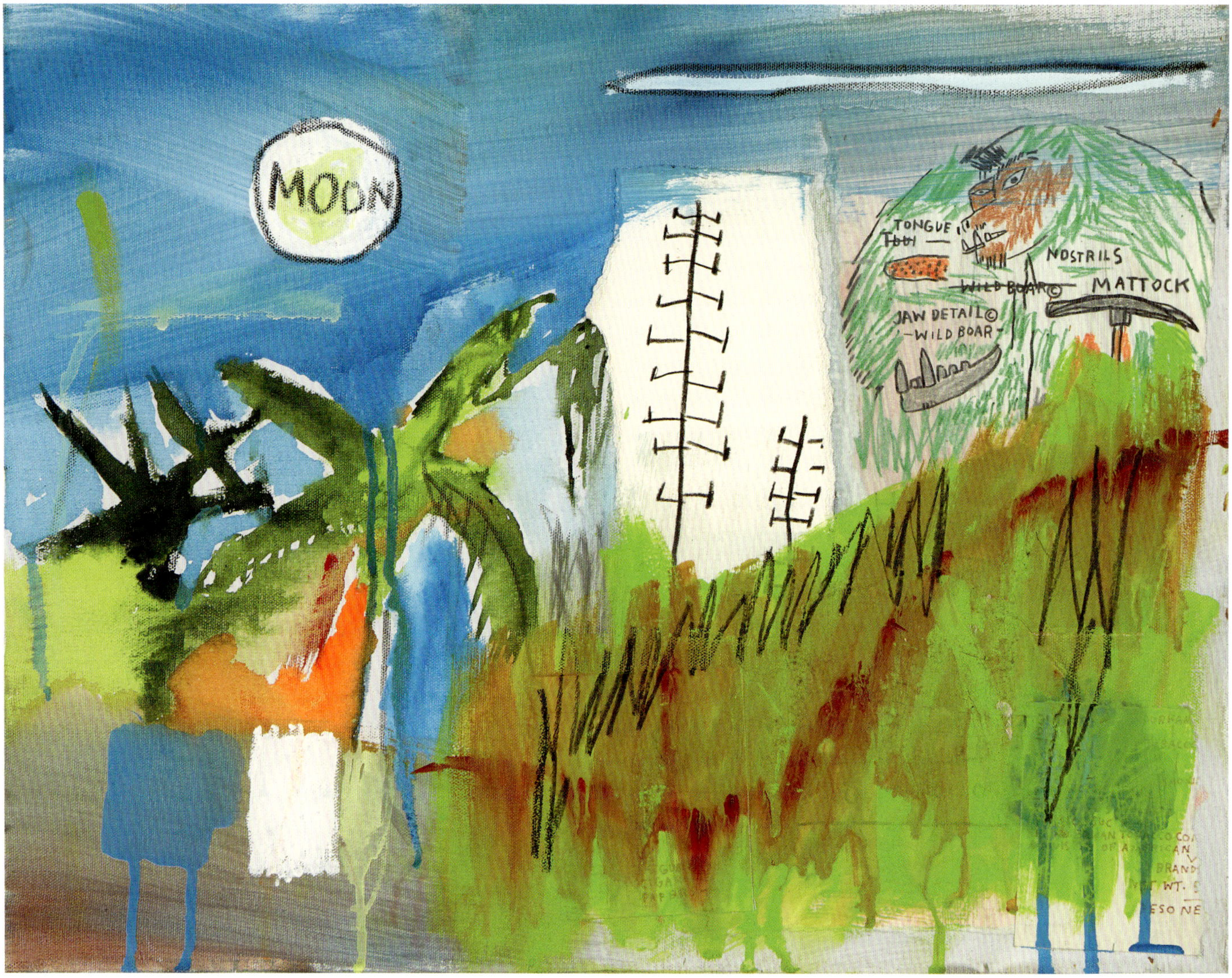

Untitled (Moon), n.d.
Acrylic, oil stick, graphite,
and color copy on canvas
16 × 20 in. (40.64 × 50.8 cm)

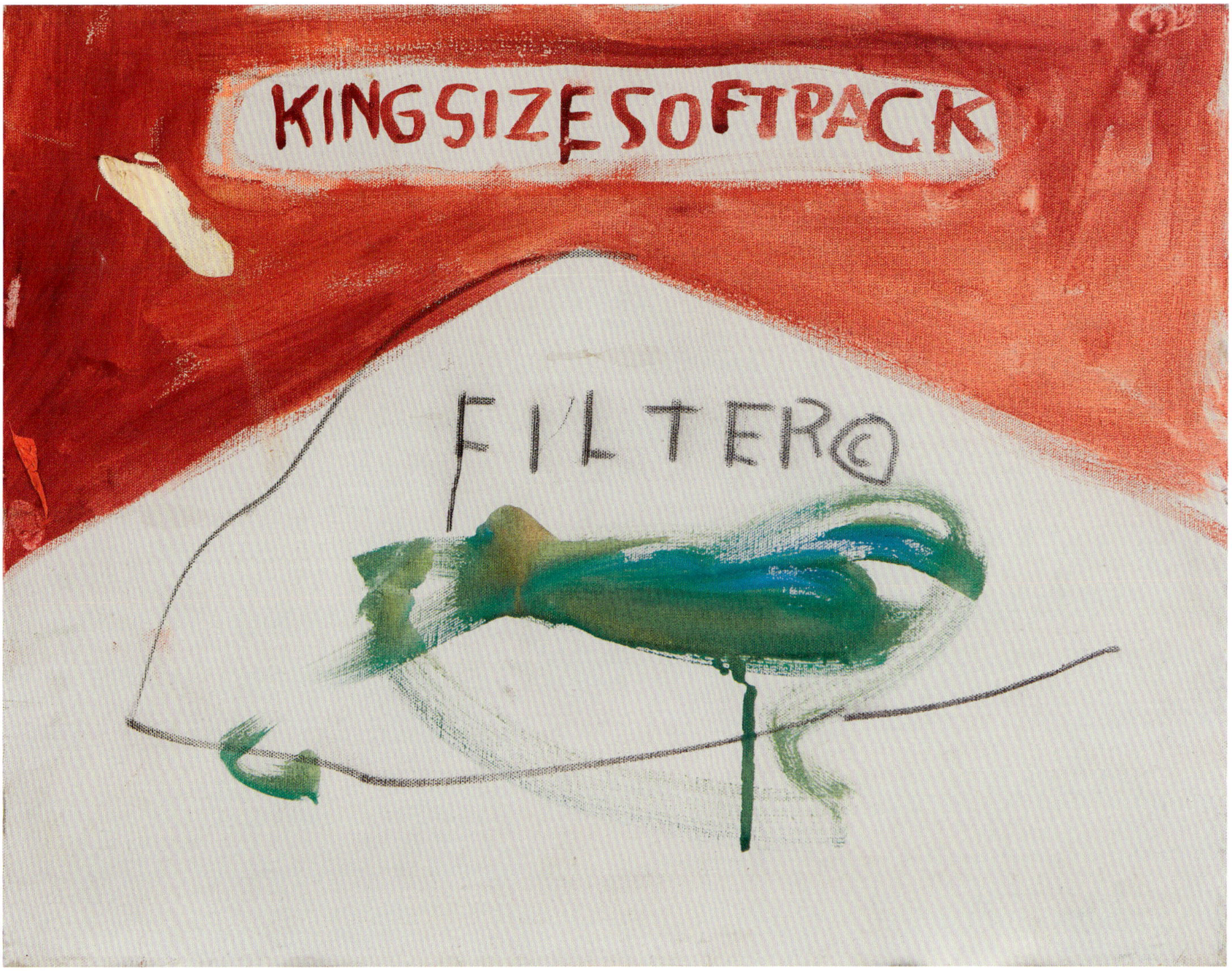

Untitled (King Size Soft Pack), n.d.
Acrylic and crayon on canvas
16 × 20 in. (40.64 × 50.8 cm)

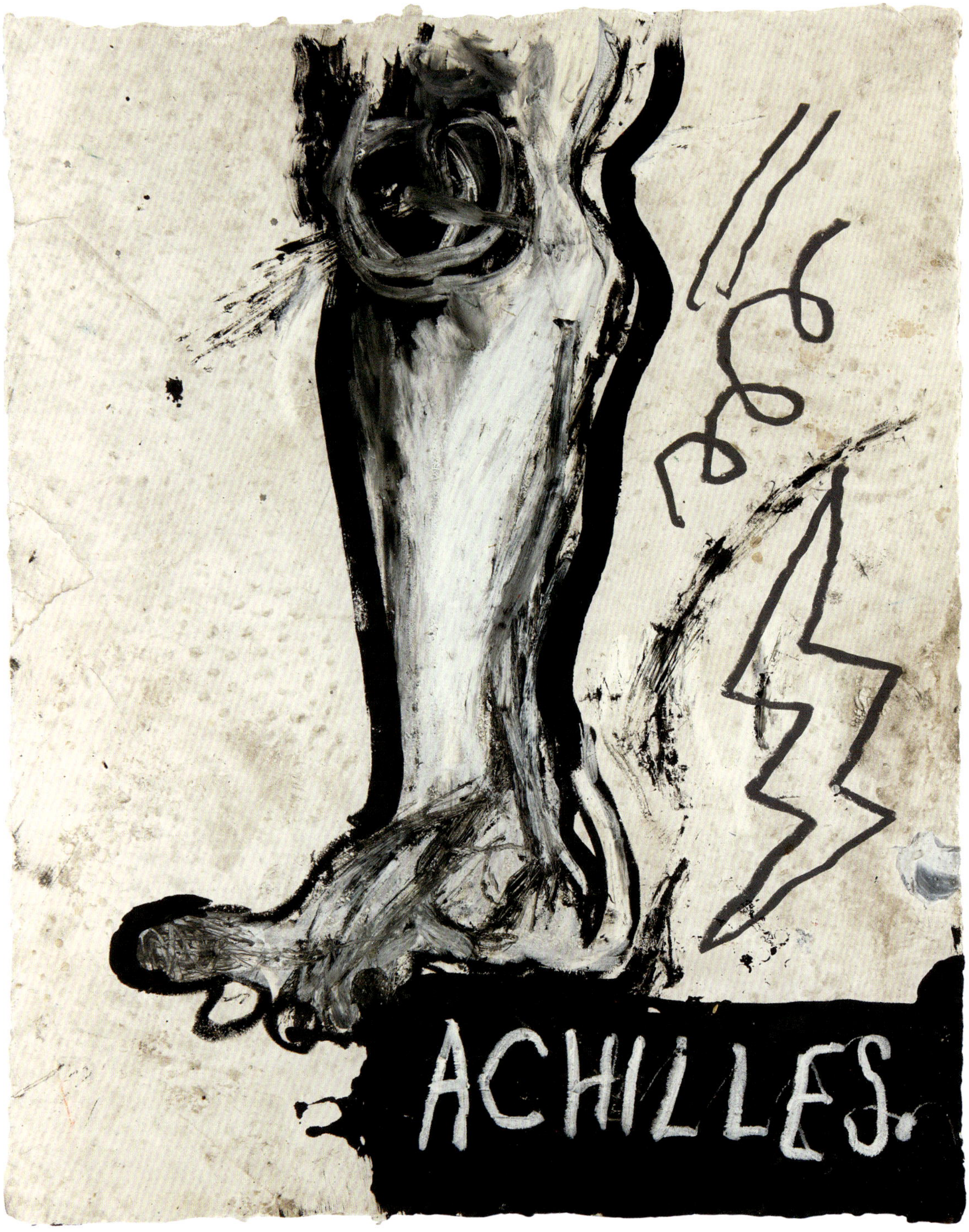

Untitled (Achilles Heel), n.d.
Acrylic and oil stick on paper
19¼ × 15¼ in. (48.90 × 38.74 cm)

Untitled (You Get What You Pay For), n.d.
Acrylic and oil stick on Mylar
68 × 71 in. (172.72 × 180.34 cm)

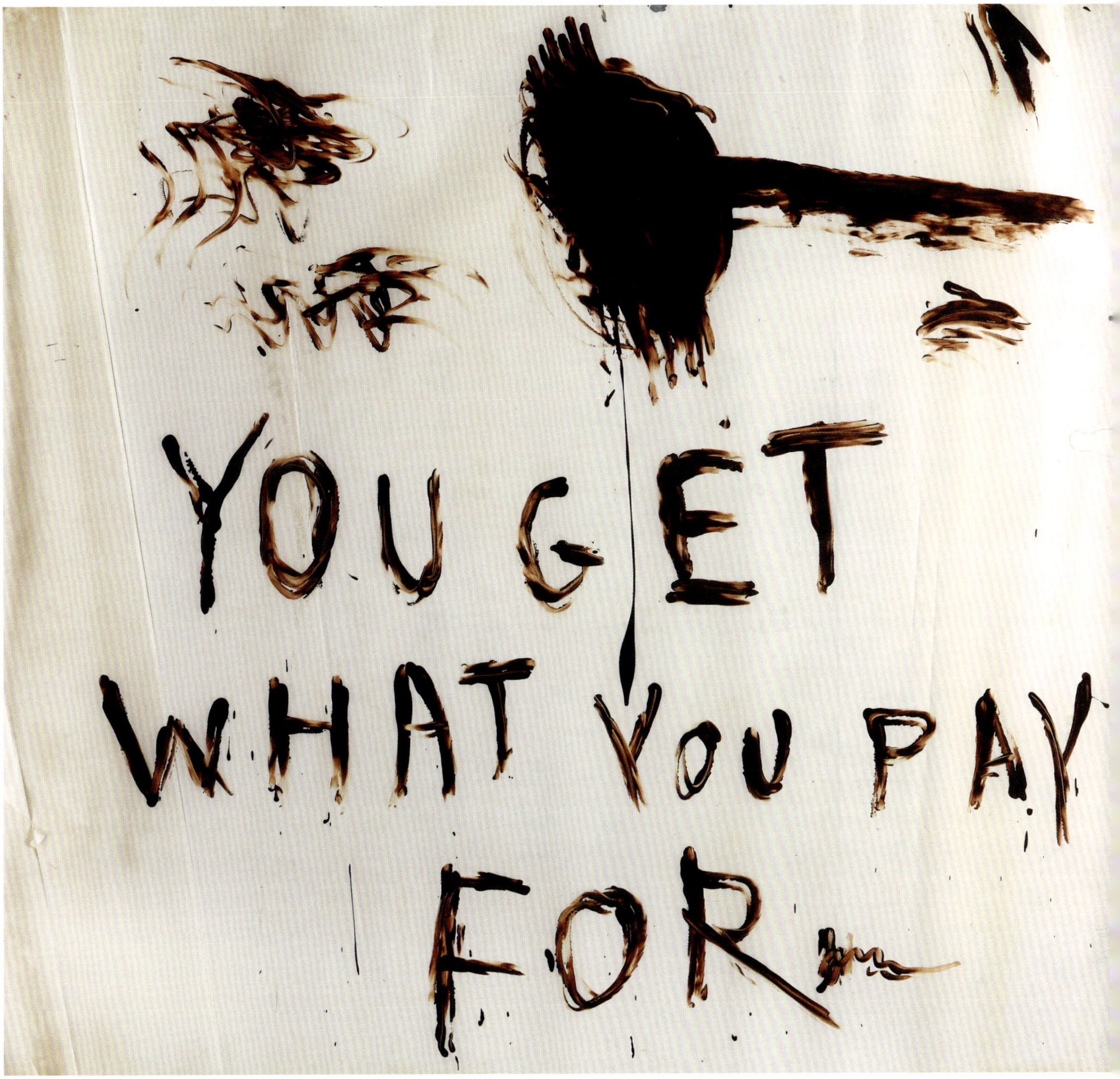

Untitled (600 Dollars in Dimes), n.d.
Oil stick on Plexiglas over framed acetate Plexiglas
20 × 26½ in. (50.8 × 67.31 cm)

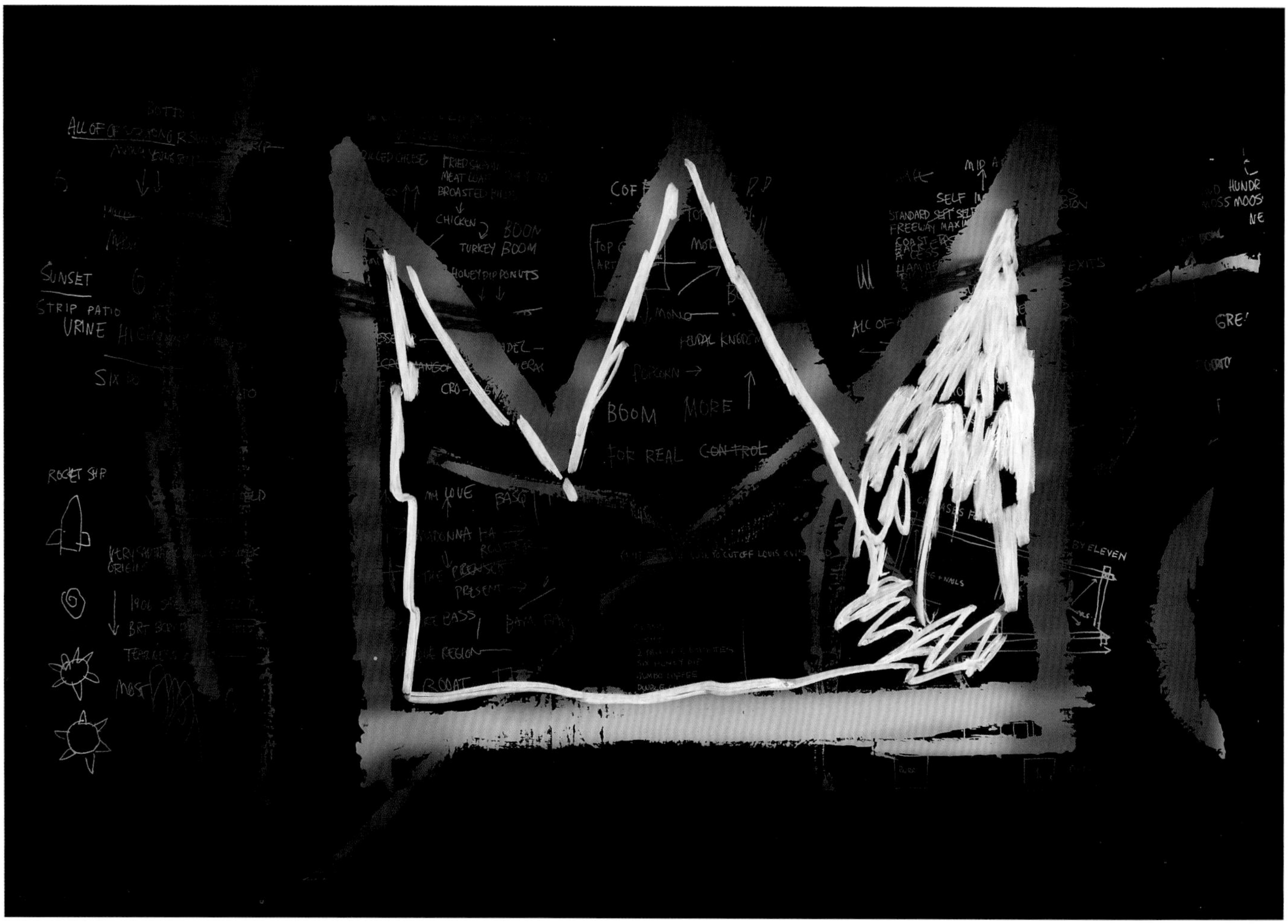

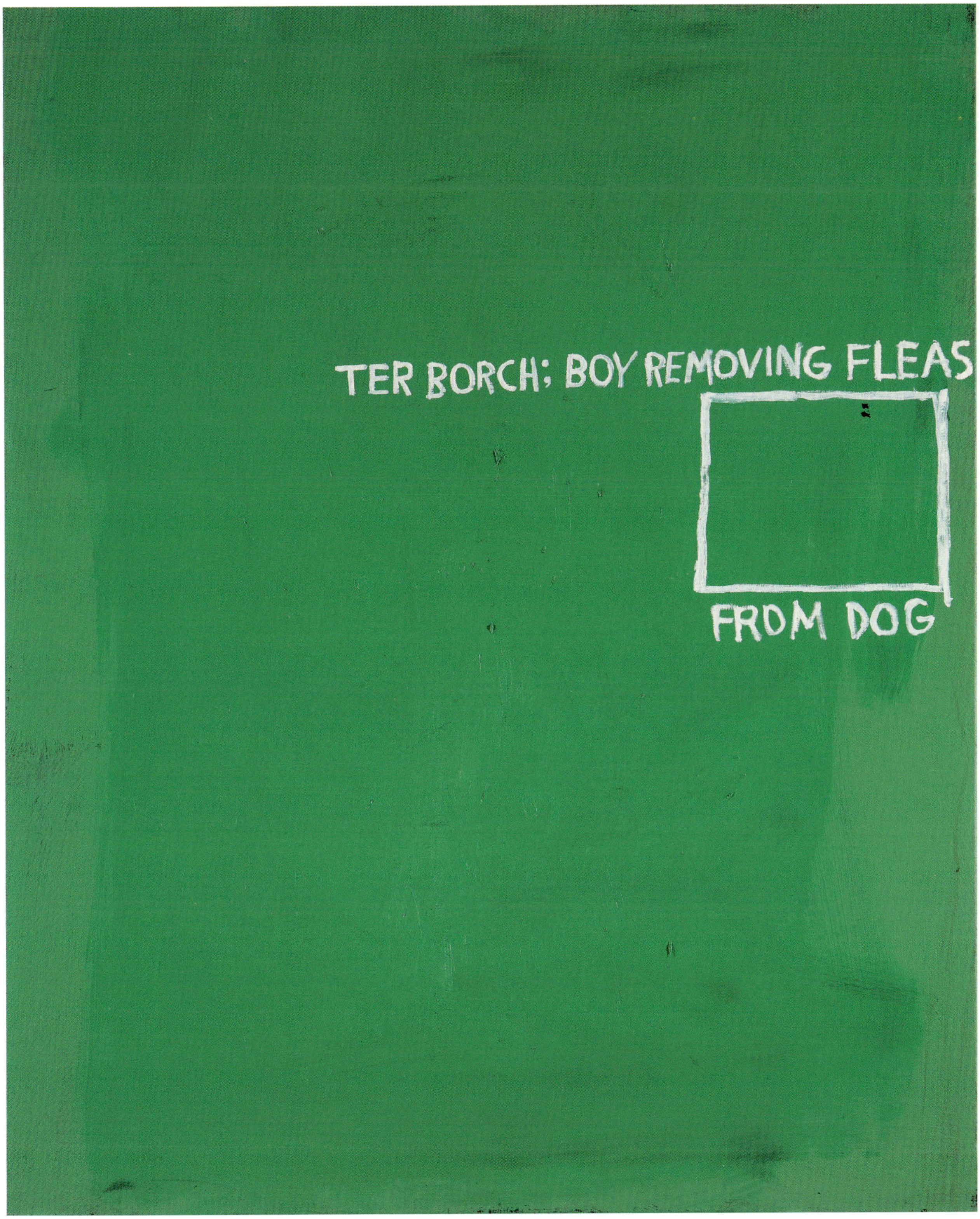

Untitled (Ter Borch: Boy Removing Fleas From Dog),
1984–88
Acrylic and oil stick on canvas
49½ × 39½ in.
(125.73 × 100.33 cm)

Jean-Michel loved to party, and from his late teens he was a denizen of the late night club scene in New York. From the Mudd Club (where he and his friends were referred to as the "baby crowd" because they were so young) and CBGB to the artist-favorite Area (known for its themed nights which were akin to a monumental art project) and the Palladium, where he was commissioned to make paintings for the VIP room, for Jean-Michel clubs were as much about partying as they were about connection—to the music he loved and the people who inspired him (and whom he in turn inspired).

In looking at these pictures and thinking back on this time in New York, it reminds one of the moments you walked into a dark room filled with pumping music and dancing people and everything crap just instantly fell away—and everyone would party the entire night in celebration of life! JEANINE AND LISANE

Jean-Michel at the Area Artists' Dinner at Mr Chow, New York, 1985
© BEN BUCHANAN

LATE NIGHT NEW YORK

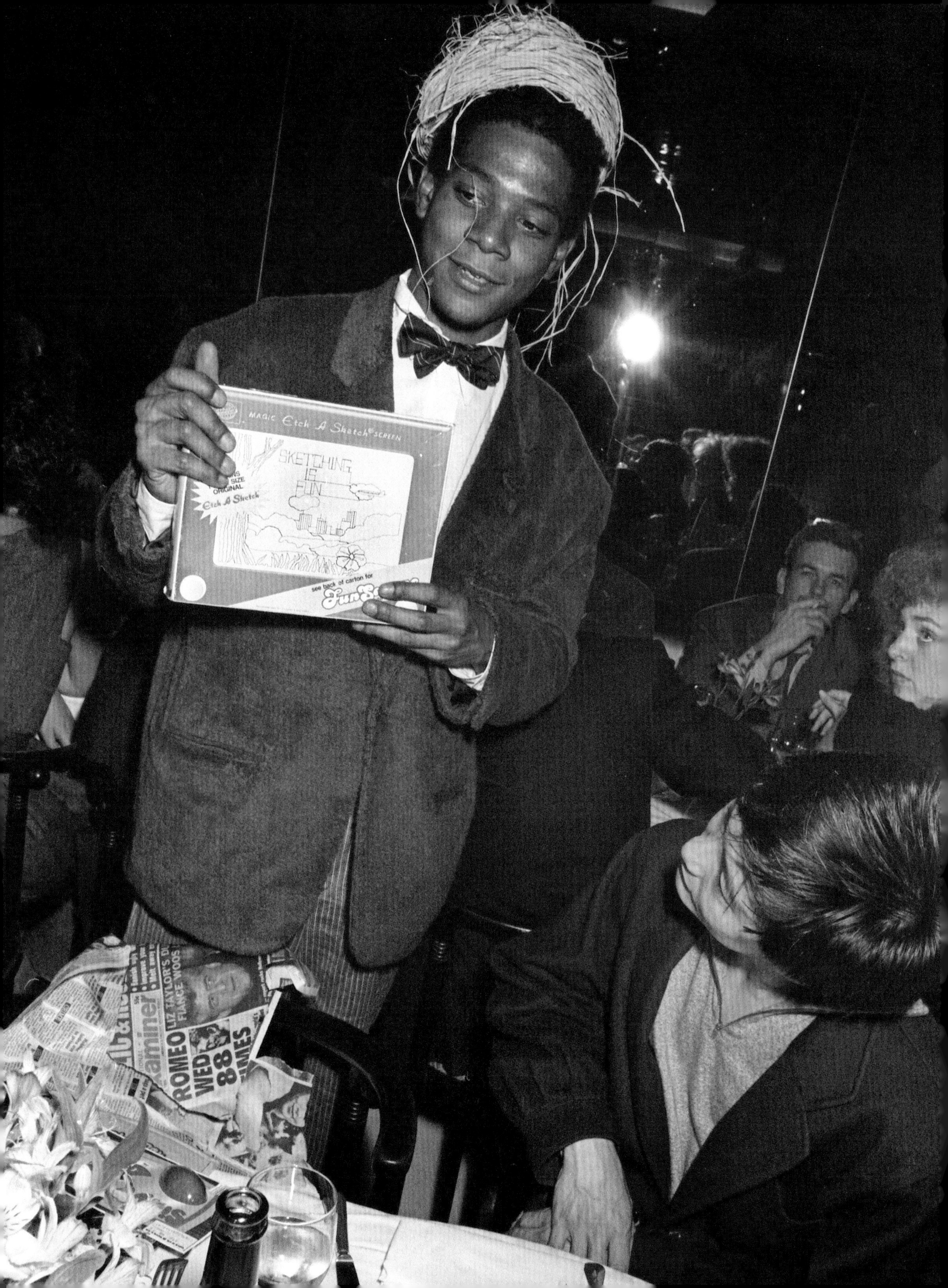

MAGIC Etch A Sketch® SCREEN
SKETCHING IS FUN
ORIGINAL
Etch A Sketch
see back of carton for
LIZ TAYLOR'S
FIANCE WOOS
ROMEO
WED
88
TIMES

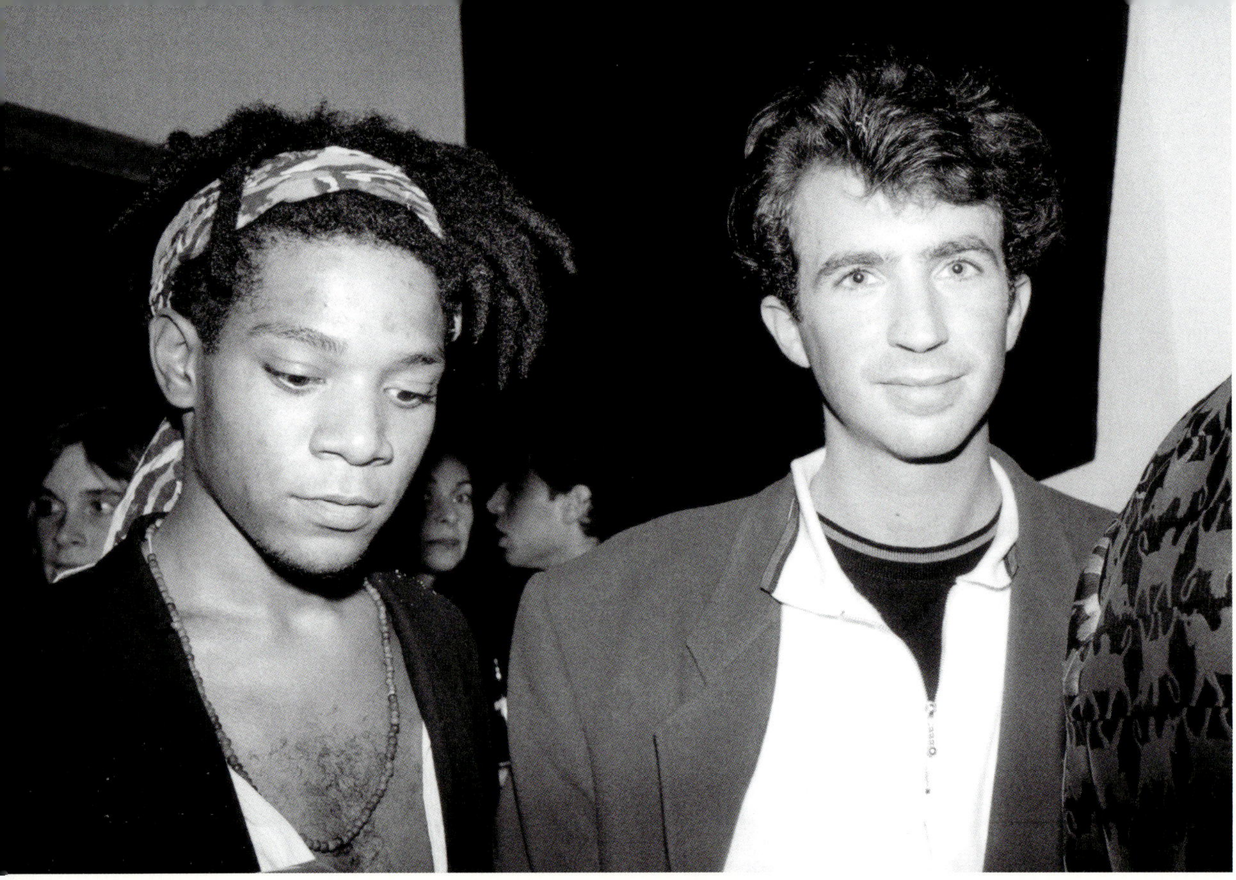

Jean-Michel with Eric Goode at Area, December 1985

OPPOSITE
Jean-Michel DJing at his joint birthday party with Eric Goode at Area, December 19, 1985

BELOW
Bird's nest hat made of straw by Stephen Jones for Comme des Garçons, spring/summer 1984. *Jean-Michel wore this hat at the Area Artists' Dinner, 1985.*

JEAN-MICHEL'S 25TH BIRTHDAY PARTY AT AREA

We Basquiats love to party. In 1985, Jean-Michel had a birthday party at Area, one of the most popular nightclubs at the time. Jean-Michel was DJing and our family was there: Papa, Nora, Lisane, my childhood friend Cherita, and our cousins Theresa and Reuben. We all danced and people-watched the entire night. JEANINE

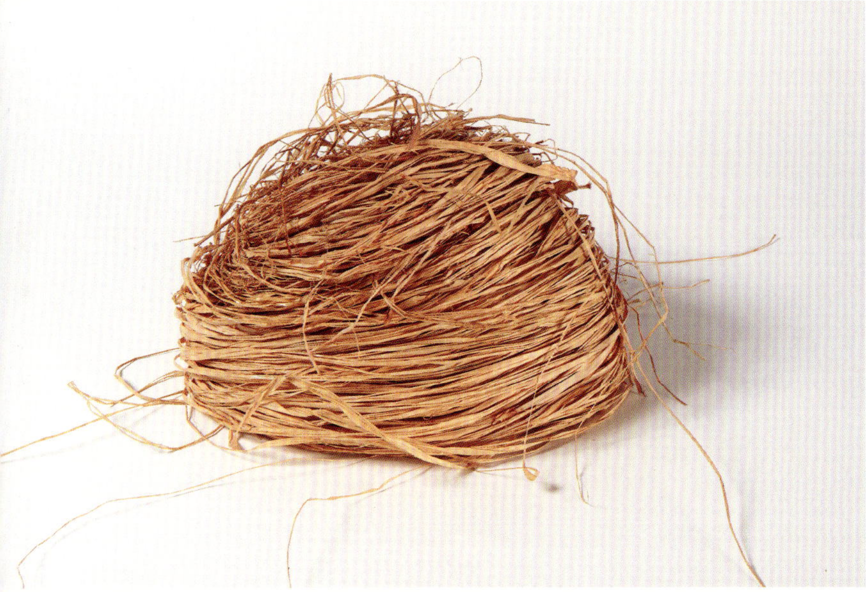

I remember being excited about the number of people who were there for him and how very theatrical and creative the party was. It was clearly a party for the "in" crowd, and I was thrilled to be there. It was a beautiful celebration in his honor and it felt profound. My father and Nora were there, Jeanine and I, and our cousins, along with Andy Warhol and Debbie Harry. Jean-Michel was partying, DJing, celebrating. I remember how impressed my father was; he was happy. It was badass—just a fabulous party.

There were models positioned throughout the party who were like statues. I remember trying to talk to them, to get them to say something or move. They wouldn't—they would not break character.

I'm still so happy that Jean-Michel was celebrated in such a grand way. LISANE

JEAN-MICHEL'S
CLUB PLAYLIST

"Adventures of Super Rhymes"
Jimmy Spicer

"Another One Bites the Dust"
Queen

"Apache"
The Sugarhill Gang

"Bad Girls"
Donna Summer

"Beat Bop"
Rammellzee, K-Rob

"Call Me"
Blondie

"Devil's Gun"
C.J. & Co.

"Dim All the Lights"
Donna Summer

"Do You Really Want to Hurt Me"
Culture Club

"Don't You Want Me"
The Human League

"Electric Avenue"
The Jamaican Reggae Band

"Everybody"
Madonna

"Flash Light"
Parliament Funkadelic

"Galaxy"
War

"Girls Just Want to Have Fun"
Cyndi Lauper

"The Glamorous Life"
Sheila E.

"Heart of Glass"
Blondie

"Hip Hop Be Bop"
Man Parrish

"Hot Stuff"
Donna Summer

"I Can't Wait"
Nu Shooz

"It's Yours"
T La Rock

"Jam on It"
Newcleus

"Karma Chameleon"
Culture Club

"Let's Dance"
David Bowie

"The Message"
Grandmaster Flash and the Furious Five

"99 Luftballons"
Nena

"Pass the Dutchie"
Musical Youth

"Planet Rock"
Afrika Bambaataa

"Pull Up to the Bumper"
Grace Jones

"Rapture"
Blondie

"Rock Box"
Run-D.M.C.

"Rumors"
Timex Social Club

"Shout"
Tears for Fears

"Situation"
Yazoo

"Slave to the Rhythm"
Grace Jones

"Somebody's Watching Me"
Rockwell

"Sucker M.C.'s"
Run-D.M.C.

"Sunset People"
Donna Summer

"Tainted Love"
Soft Cell

"Trans-Europe Express"
Kraftwerk

"Walk of Life"
Dire Straits

"Walk This Way"
Run-D.M.C. featuring Aerosmith

"Walking on Sunshine"
Rockers Revenge

"White Lines (Don't Do It)"
Grandmaster Flash

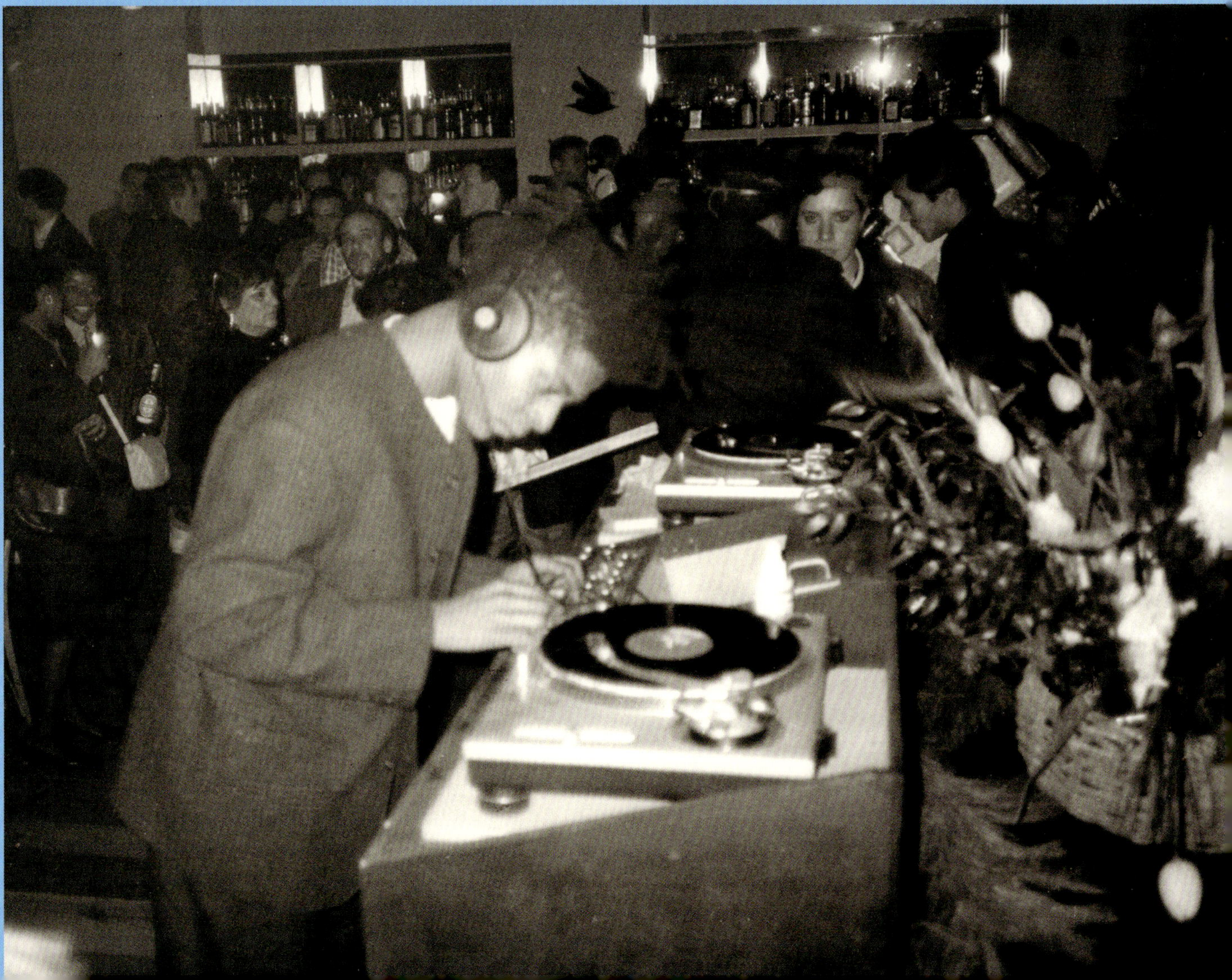

MEETING JEAN-MICHEL

Jean was one of the first people I met when I moved to New York City in 1978. I walked into the cafeteria of the School of Visual Arts (SVA) and he turned his gaze at me. He asked to see the portfolio I was carrying and then told me I would be famous. I've never met anyone with such an intensity. Soon after meeting, I went to the apartment in Chelsea where he was staying, which happened to be near my apartment. There he showed me a collage he had done of the Kennedy assassination with Jackie O. I was blown away—I couldn't believe the energy radiating from this early work. To this day, his vibrations emanate from each and every brushstroke. Very powerful and inspirational. KENNY SCHARF

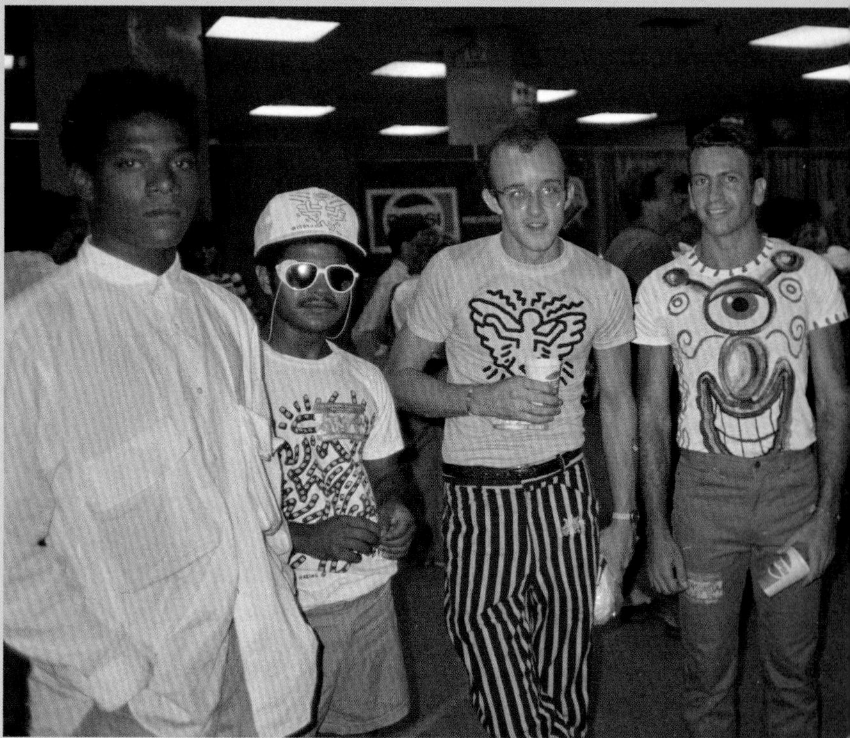

PARTYING

As a big brother, Jean-Michel was the coolest to hang out with. I would often go with him to The Odeon or Mr Chow, which were two of the hippest restaurants at the time. Or we would visit friends' homes. I vividly recall going to fashion designer Halston's apartment and meeting Liza Minnelli, Bianca Jagger, and one of the Hemingway sisters. JEANINE

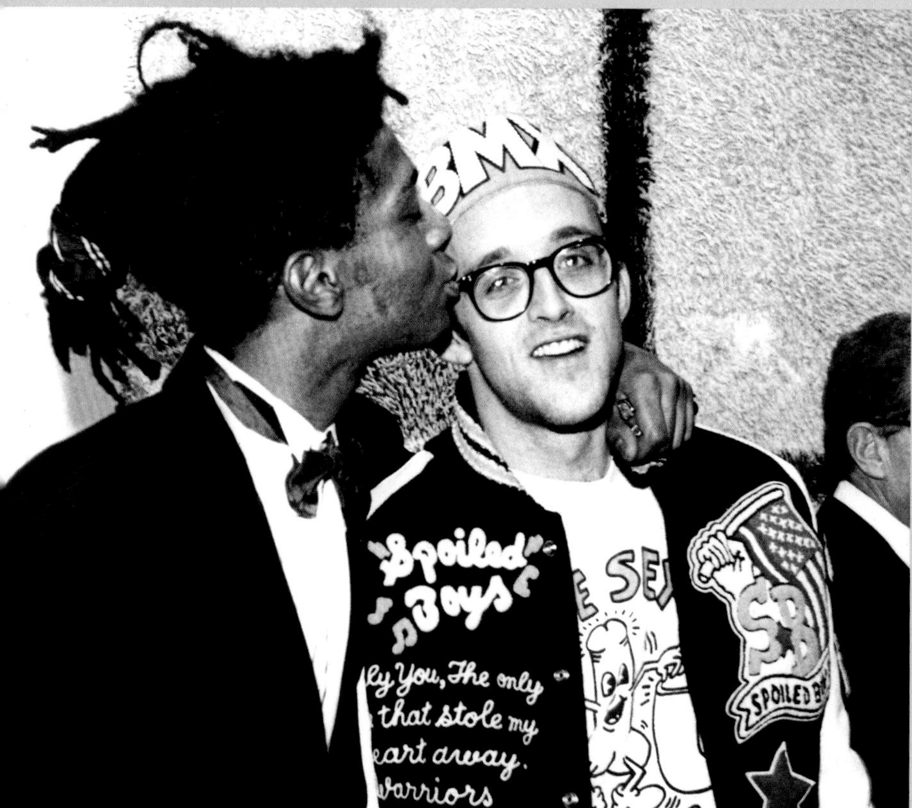

TOP
Jean-Michel, Little Angel, Keith Haring, and Kenny Scharf, 1984

LEFT
Jean-Michel and Keith Haring at Julian Schnabel's opening at the Whitney Museum of American Art, New York, 1987

RIGHT
Jean-Michel's shirt that he wore while DJing at Area

BOTTOM
Jean-Michel DJing at Area, 1985
© BEN BUCHANAN

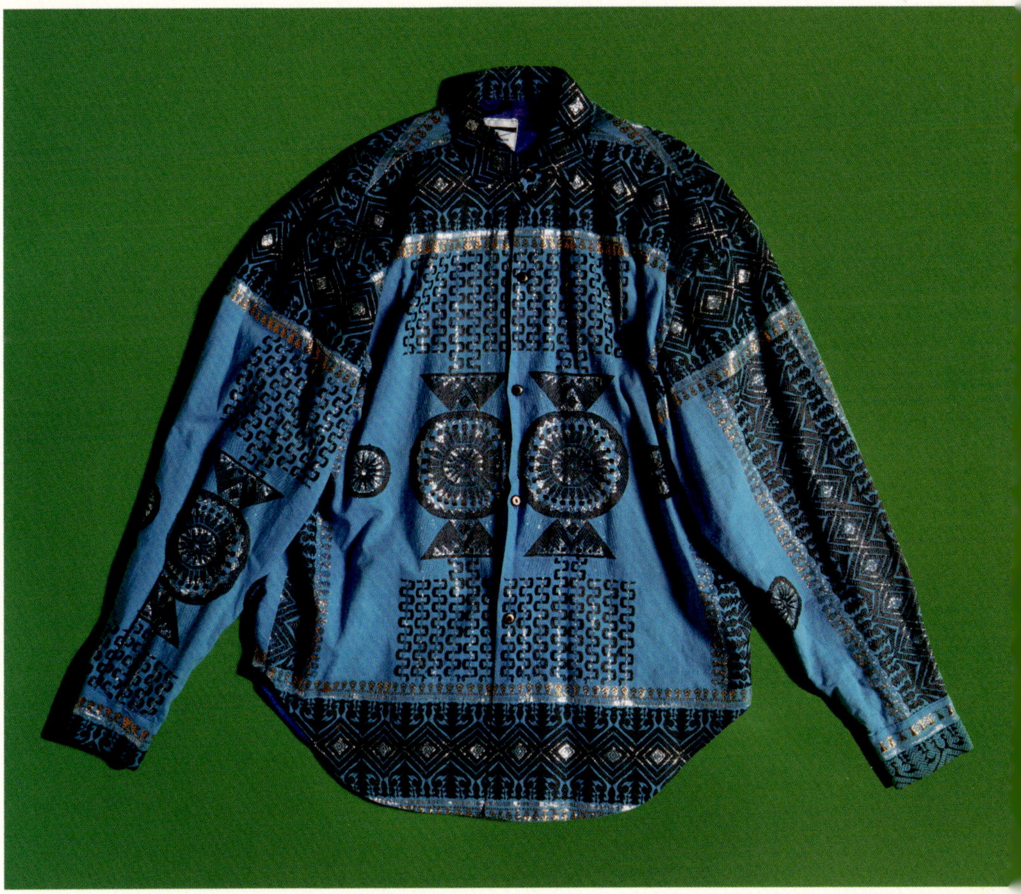

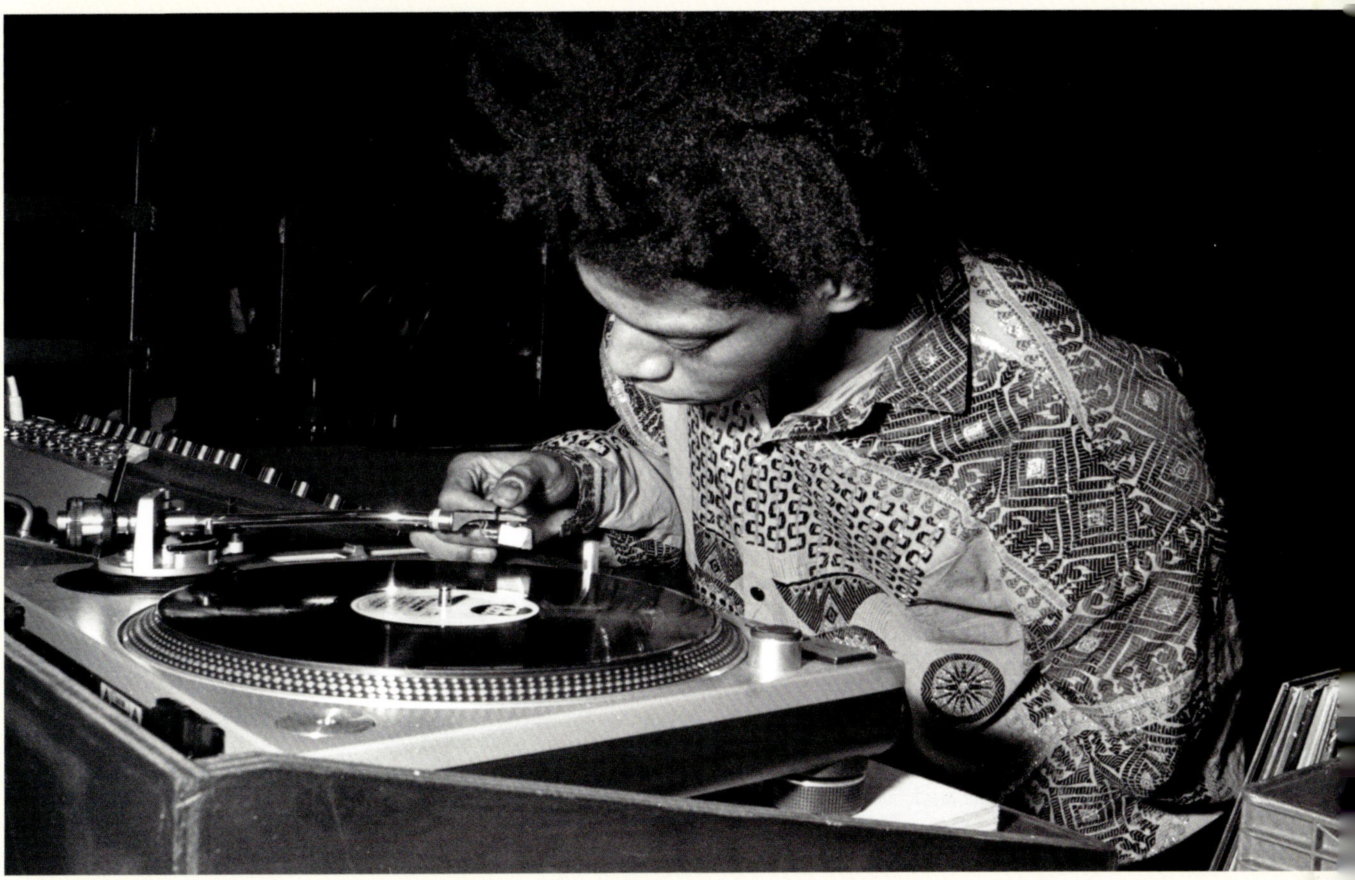

MEETING JEAN-MICHEL

Debbie Harry and Chris Stein of Blondie

We can't remember the very first time we met Jean-Michel, but we probably met him with Freddy [Braithwaite, aka Fab 5 Freddy] or Lee Quiñones [the graffiti artist]. Frequently he would be on that TV show we did with Glenn O'Brien called *TV Party*, and I probably started interacting with him then. He always said he would be on the show, but he would often just stay in the control room. There was a character generator in the camera and whatever you typed into it would appear on-screen in a very basic typewriter font. Jean would write phrases and strange inspirational sayings that he picked up. CHRIS STEIN

BUYING ONE OF JEAN-MICHEL'S FIRST PAINTINGS

I'm pretty sure I bought his first canvas because he had been painting on cardboard. I asked him to do a painting for me. He knew I was into militaria, so he did this painting of little stick figure army guys shooting cannons at each other. It was on a heavy piece of brown burlap canvas, very coarse. And famously, I gave him 200 bucks, and he went around telling people how much he had ripped me off. We sold it through Diego Cortez [the curator] a few years later for ten grand, long before Jean died, because we were broke. CHRIS STEIN

THE GREAT JONES STREET STUDIO

I always felt pretty close to Jean. I used to go to Great Jones Street and see his environment there all the time. That was amazing—it was great, terrific. He was just embedded and working all the time. When I told him I sold the painting I had bought, I asked him for another one. And he said, "I'm not gonna give you a $20,000 painting."

Andy [Warhol] would show up and he carried around a stack of $100 bills. He would just buy things from Jean on the spot—a couple of drawings or paintings and leave with them. Jean had a color Xerox machine in the studio, and he would do drawings and make multiples of them. CHRIS STEIN

FILM AND VIDEO

Jean was in Blondie's *Rapture* and *Atomic* videos. The story is, I guess, a little sensitive. The *Atomic* video was a postapocalyptic scene—specifically a postapocalyptic disco. Everybody's dancing around in this ruined warehouse, and the band is playing. Jean initially just came to the shoot with a bunch of other people from the Mudd Club to be one of the dancers in the audience. And he said, "I really want a bigger part." But there wasn't really much to go around because it was more like a performance video. As the video starts, a guy rides up on a horse, so we said, "Okay, Jean, you take the horse and lead it off." So he did that. After the shot was done, he came over to me and said, "You gave me the Black man role." He was annoyed about it, and it hadn't actually occurred to me when I asked him to take the horse. It was funny—I think Jean thought my being uncomfortable was funny. CHRIS STEIN

> Well, he was ornery, that's for sure, but he had a sensitive skin. That was his gift—his sensitivity. DEBBIE HARRY

WILLIAM S. BURROUGHS

I was friends with Burroughs back then, and I got one of his shotgun paintings from him—he would put a can of spray paint in front of a board and shoot it, which created a sort of Jackson Pollock effect. Jean saw the one I had and he really wanted one. When I went to visit Burroughs in Kansas, Jean made this elaborate sculpture, a really fantastic piece. I brought it in a paper shopping bag on the airplane to give to Burroughs and in return got one of the shotgun paintings for Jean. James Grauerholz, Burroughs's assistant for years, said they sold it for eighty grand. It was a really nice big piece.

One of the first times we met Burroughs was in December 1986 at the writer Victor Bockris's apartment. Jean was there. Burroughs was a great character and also another anarchist type and revolutionary rebel. Jean knew all about the Beat poets and all those references. CHRIS STEIN

> I think that Jean and Bill were able to understand each other because they both mumbled a lot. DEBBIE HARRY

DECEMBER 1986: DINNER WITH BURROUGHS

The event Chris and Debbie are referring to was a small dinner party I gave in my apartment at 106 Perry Street for William S. Burroughs (Bill), Allen Ginsberg, Debbie and Chris, and Richard Hell. I had invited Jean but he was busy. Chris, Debbie, James Grauerholz, and Bill had just come from the Factory. Bill had left Andy one of his shotgun paintings. Then he wondered if it might not have been appropriate. Chris called Vincent Fremont at the Factory who assured him not to worry—Andy took these things in stride. Richard Hell had to leave before dinner. As soon as dinner ended, I called Jean on the off-chance he was no longer engaged. He rushed over. As soon as he saw we had no dessert, he rushed back out to the local deli and bought a box of donuts and big tub of ice cream. He then threw together a concoction that he said was of his own making. It was kind of funny because just before he went to the deli, Jean and Bill had been talking about killing rats with poison donuts.

The conversation flowed throughout the evening, but it took on another level of dignity and hilarity with Jean's happy, energetic presence. VICTOR BOCKRIS

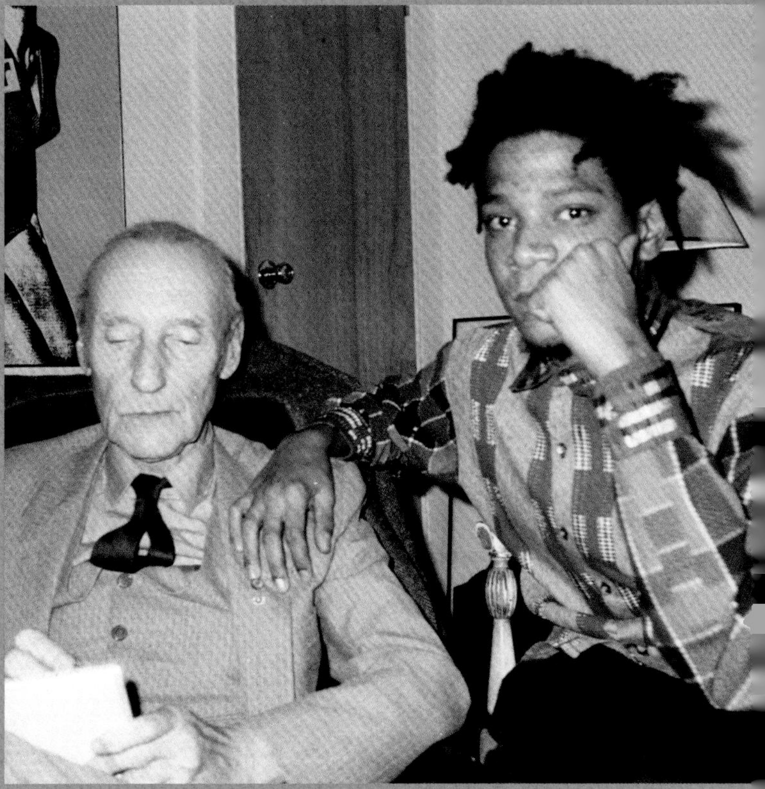

William S. Burroughs and Jean-Michel at dinner at the home of Victor Bockris, 106 Perry Street, New York, December 20, 1986

DOWNTOWN '81

Downtown '81 was a crazy screw-up. The film was funded by Rizzoli and they had to put the production on hold, because I think they got caught up in some crazy political bullshit in Italy. When they finally got the funding to finish, they had lost the audio track, so everybody had to redo their vocals. They brought in an actor to redo Jean's. But luckily the music was intact, and there are really great performances by Kid Creole and DNA. CHRIS STEIN

> We had to lip read the film. I think Glenn [O'Brien] hired a lip reader to write down what we were saying. It was crazy. DEBBIE HARRY

> Jean liked being on film, and I think that, had he stuck around, he might have actually been an actor or certainly done some acting. DEBBIE HARRY

JEAN-MICHEL'S ART

I always thought his work was great. We'd been exposed to a lot of work like that coming up in the downtown scene, you know, so maybe I took it for granted. I didn't quite see the impact it would have on the world in general. In the later years, I was more aware of how well thought-out and well-designed it all is. But I probably didn't appreciate it as much at the time. CHRIS STEIN

HANGING OUT WITH JEAN-MICHEL

We were at a restaurant with Iggy Pop and a bunch of people—it overlooked Times Square and I never remember what the hell it was called. Jean came in with a bucket of Kentucky Fried Chicken and he pulled out a big bag of weed and started rolling joints. He and Iggy got into a whole beef because he asked Jean to stop. The incident was so ironic because Iggy is a complete anarchist maniac. And for him to be standing up for the rule of law to Jean was totally crazy. CHRIS STEIN

> He was stealing the spotlight from Iggy. I felt that there was a bit of that, and Iggy was past that stage in his career and was annoyed by it. I think a lot of the things that Jean did were actually performance art. And that was totally in keeping with his art, his paintings, and his identity crisis. I really think that a lot of the time he was in public, it definitely was a performance. As with many of us, you know, we go out and we're performing who we are and who we think we are. He was being provocative on every level. DEBBIE HARRY

Jean would get into rifts with people over what sometimes seemed like imagined fights. I couldn't tell if they were real or if it was just more about him being performative and just acting like he was getting into a beef with somebody. CHRIS STEIN

> He was edgy. People would say, "He's looking for trouble," but he had a philosophy behind what he was doing and real emotional content. It was more like this ongoing train. I sort of felt like he was collecting things in this train. It's kind of a nice image. DEBBIE HARRY

> Jean would show up at different times with different people. I never really thought of him hanging with any one particular person. You would see him with Kenny [Scharf] sometimes or even with Glenn. And then sometimes with Freddy or Lee. I think that he had a lot of associates and a lot of people he hung around, but I also think that his personality tended to push people away initially. And that served him well, because, in the long run, he didn't have a lot of people that were trying to get at him, you know? DEBBIE HARRY

JEAN-MICHEL'S BAND GRAY

I think it was more like a noise band from what I can remember—it reminded me of the things that we used to do when we were doing Happenings in the '60s. It was great in that respect; I always liked that kind of madness. I sort of remember everybody screaming at each other. They would have had to be a little bit more organized and thematic for them to be able to carry on as a band. I don't think that they were the kind of artists who could work in connection with others. And I don't think of Jean as being able to collaborate as part of a band. DEBBIE HARRY

Jean was just dabbling—dabbling in different art forms. CHRIS STEIN

COACH X JEAN-MICHEL BASQUIAT

In 2020, the estate did a collaboration with the fashion brand Coach, and I got to walk in the runway show. I was able to hang out a tiny bit with the family. I think they're doing a respectable job with regard to his work—they are being honorable about it—and I think Coach handled it nicely. They're not mucking around with it and it's not really a kind of art that you could screw around with anyway. They're treating it in a very respectable way.
DEBBIE HARRY

Jean-Michel and Debbie Harry at dinner at the home of Victor Bockris, 106 Perry Street, New York, December 20, 1986
© VICTOR BOCKRIS

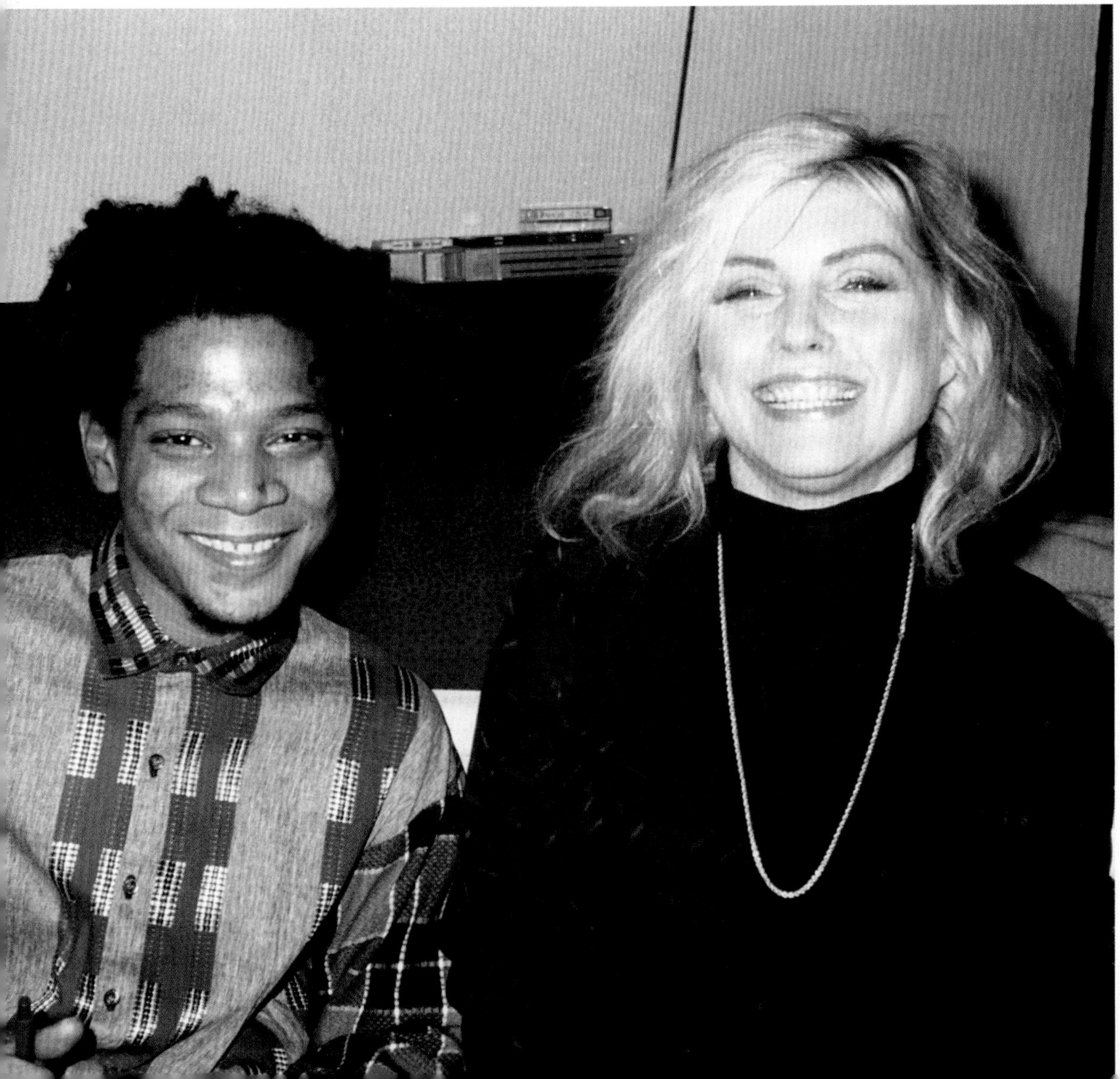

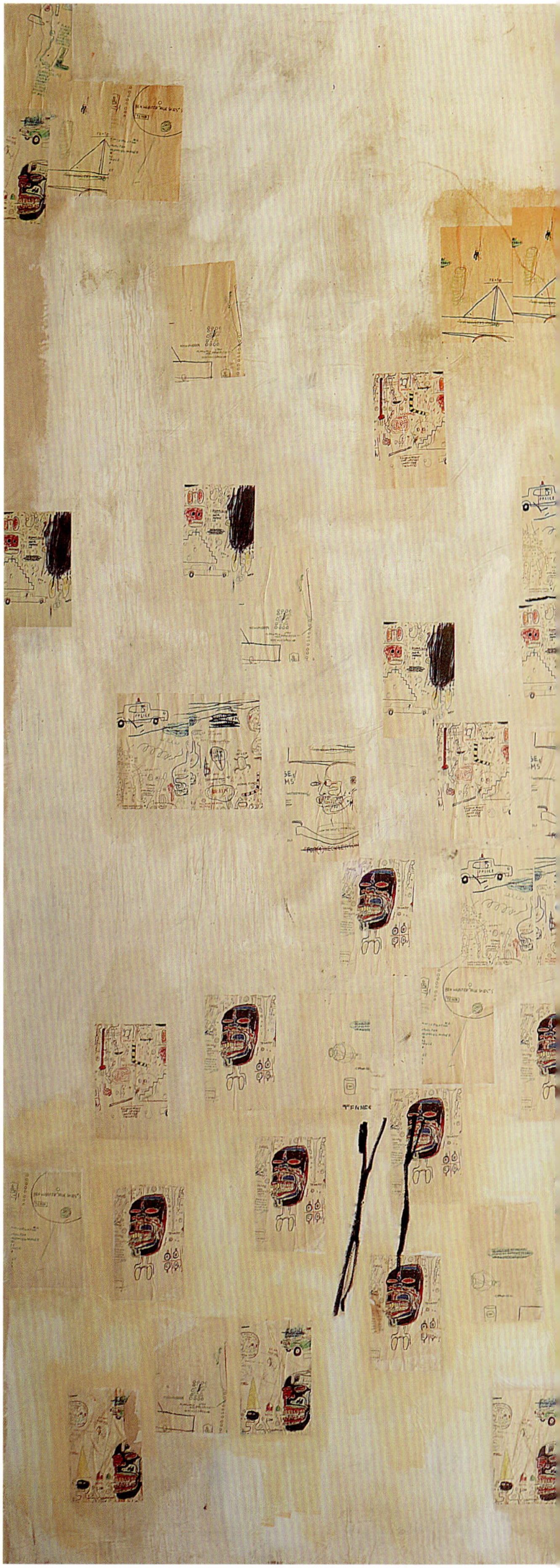

Untitled (Palladium), 1985
Acrylic on canvas
189¼ × 222 in.
(480.70 × 563.88 cm)

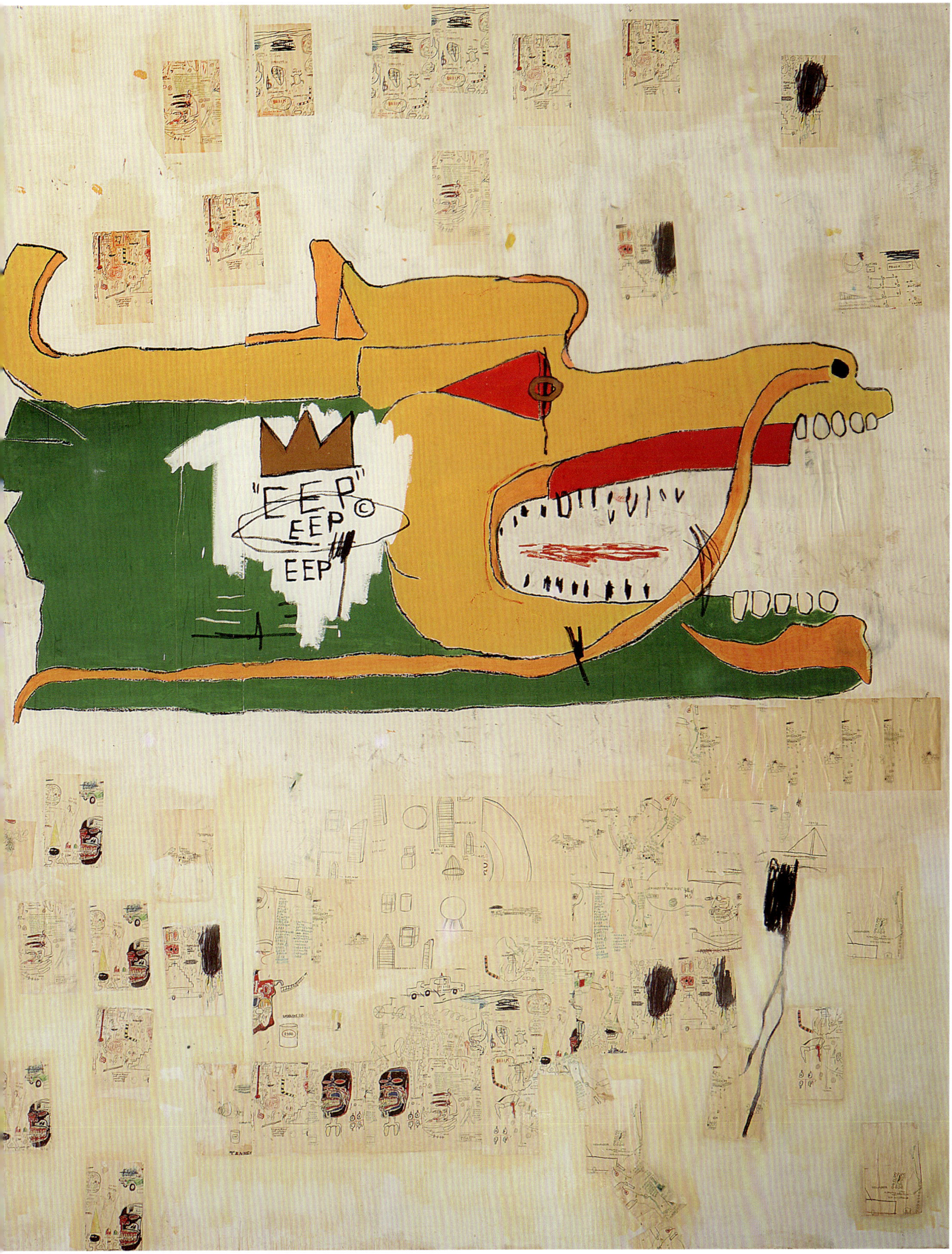
"EEP"©
EEP
EEP

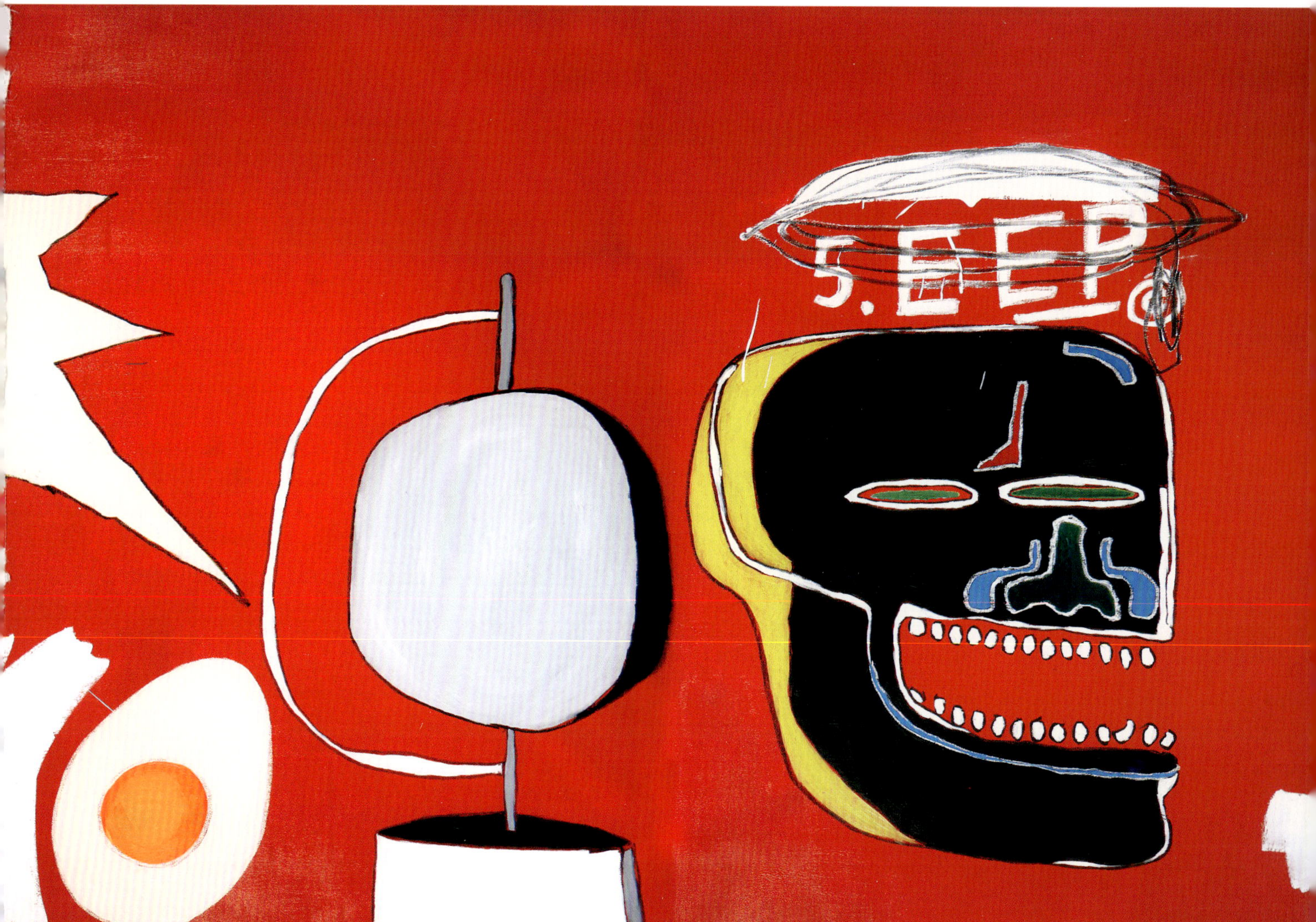

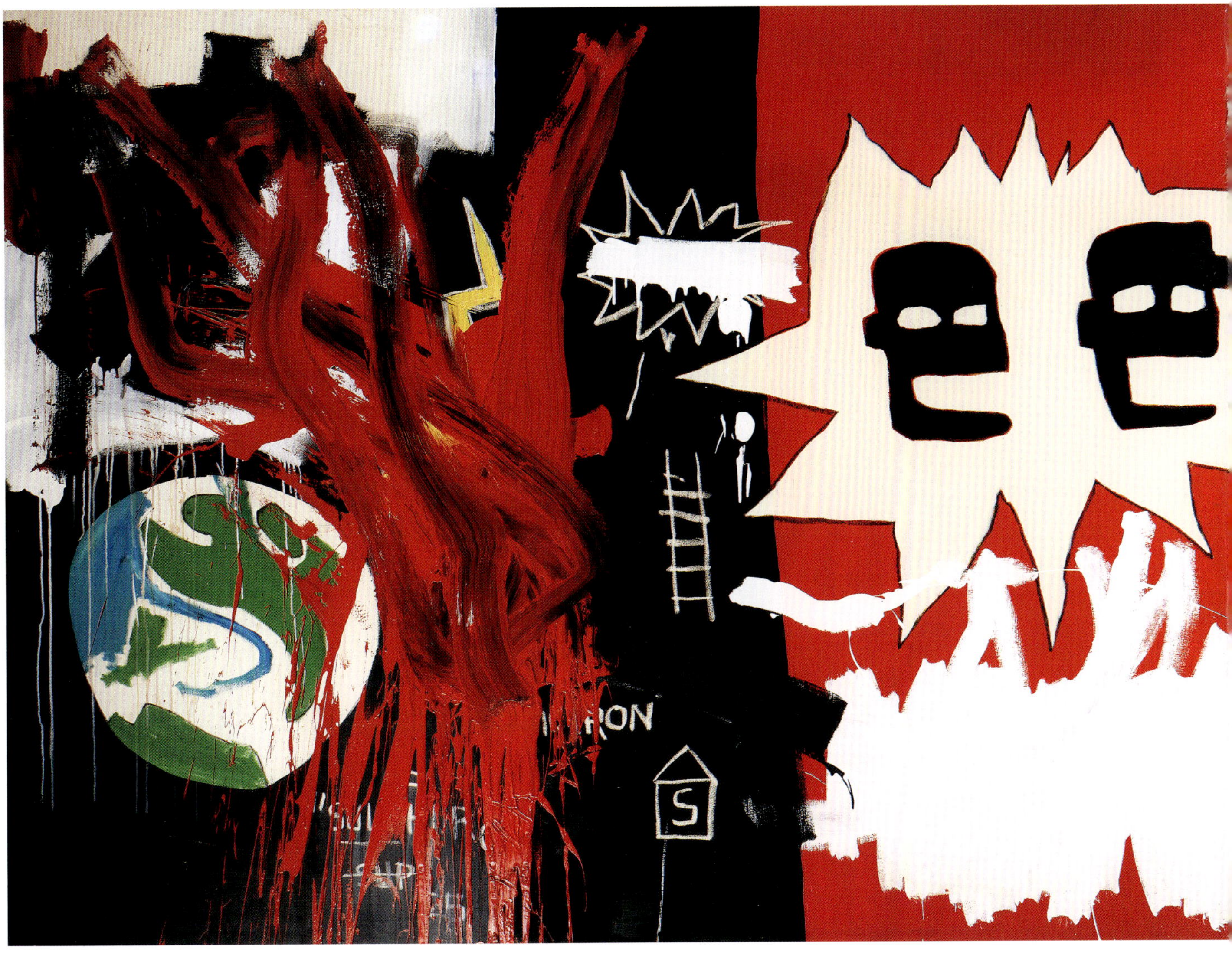
RON
S

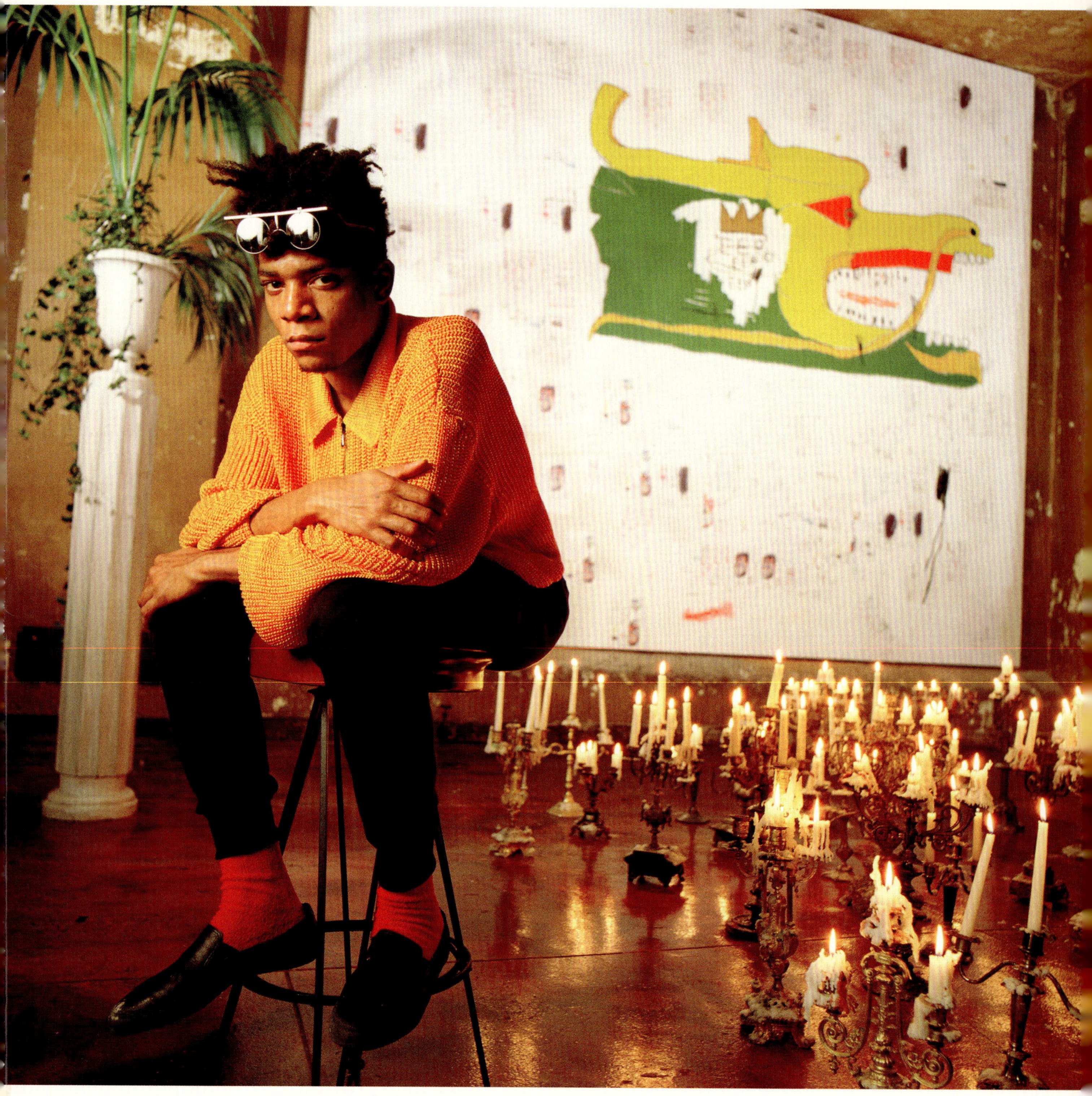

PALLADIUM

I went to the Palladium with Jean-Michel right before the opening so that he could check out how his paintings were hung in the upstairs VIP area. When I later attended one of the opening nights, Jean-Michel showed me around, and I remember standing on one of the balconies looking down at the dance floor. I didn't stay long because I was underage, but I got to experience the excitement of the Palladium and the legendary Michael Todd Room. JEANINE

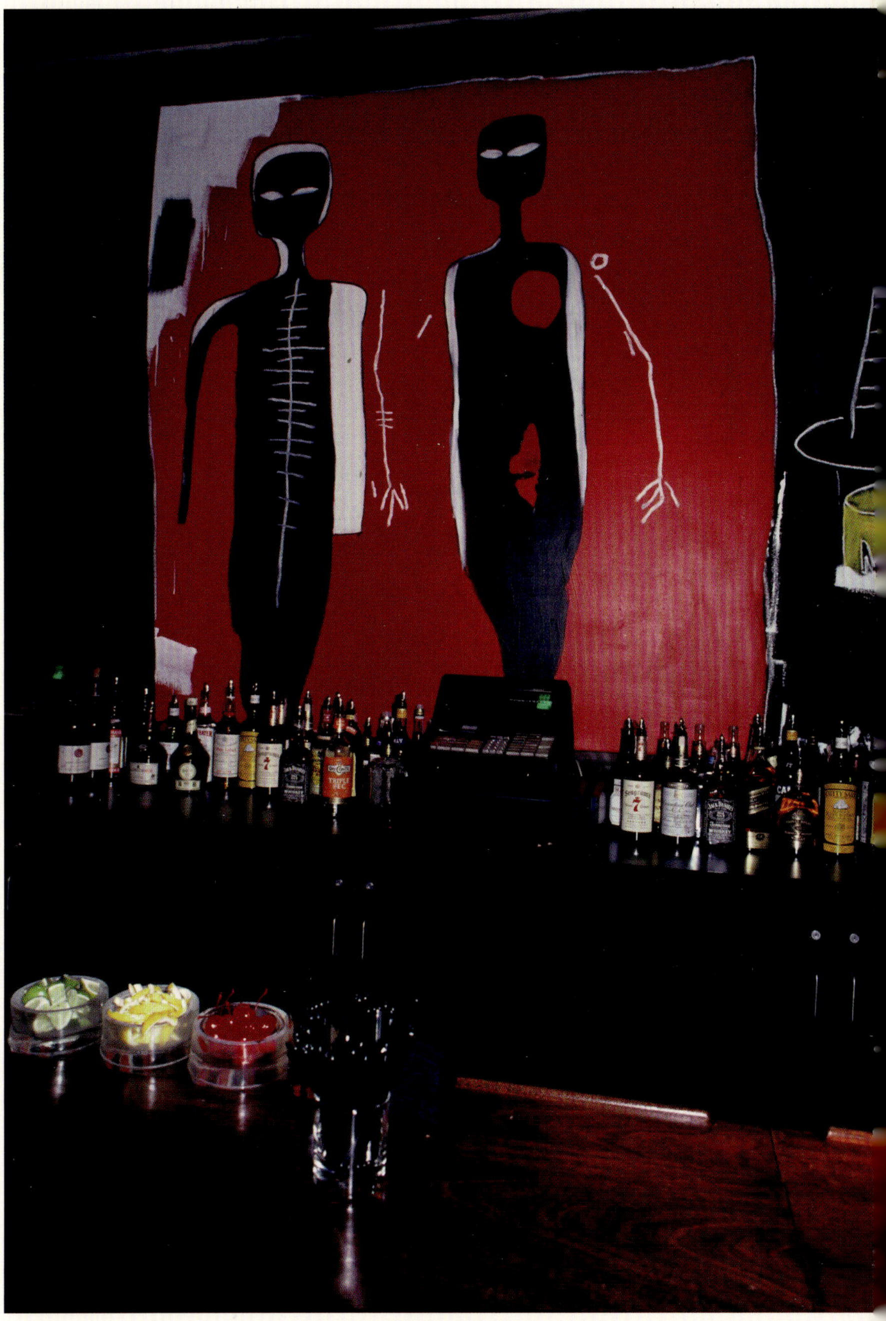

OPPOSITE
Jean-Michel with his painting *Untitled (Palladium)* in the Michael Todd Room, the VIP lounge, 1985
© BENNO FRIEDMAN

RIGHT
Jean-Michel's painting *Nu-Nile* installed in the Palladium's Michael Todd Room, 1985
© VOLKER HINZ

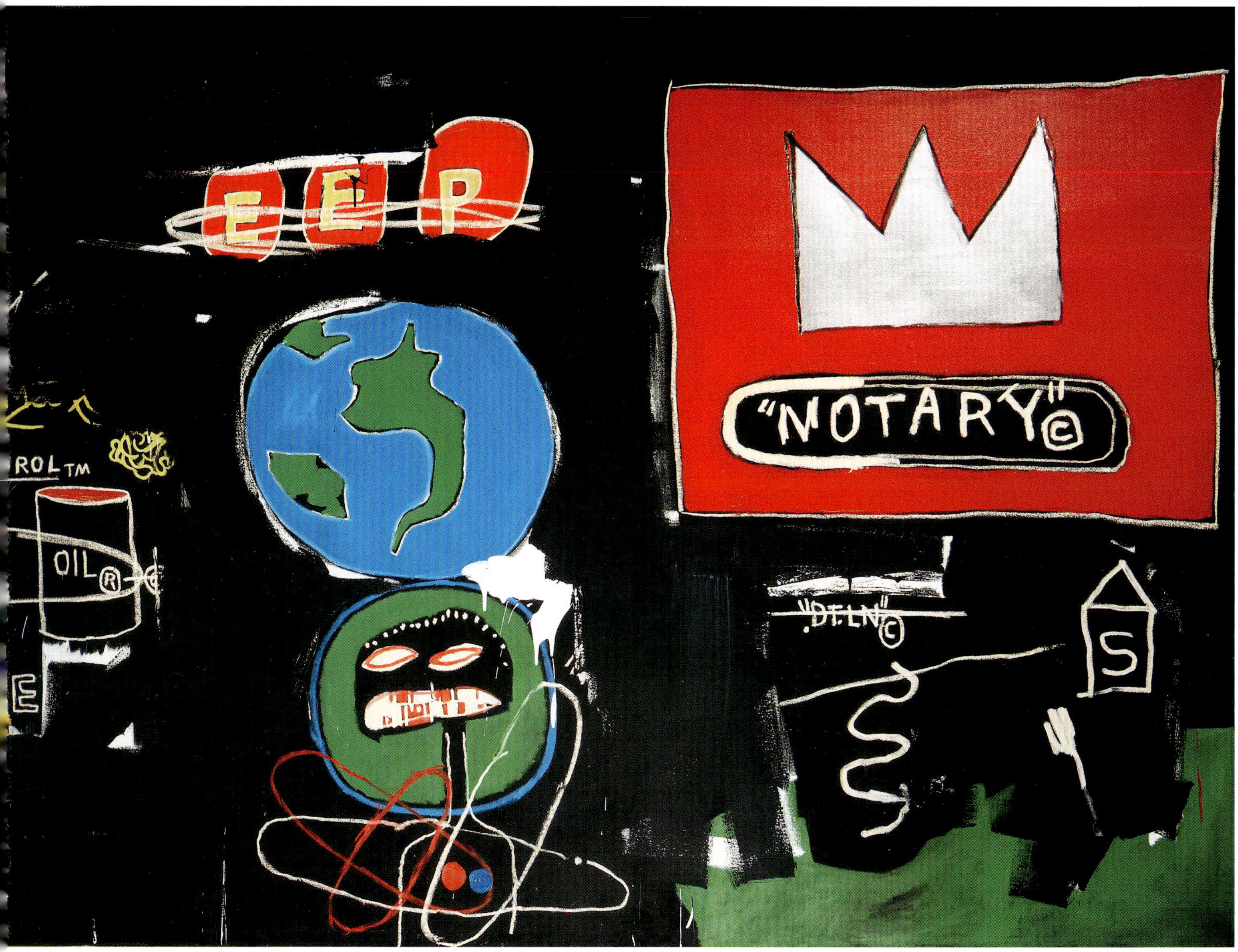

Nu-Nile, 1985
Acrylic and oil stick on canvas
101 ½ × 496 in.
(257.81 × 1,259.84 cm)

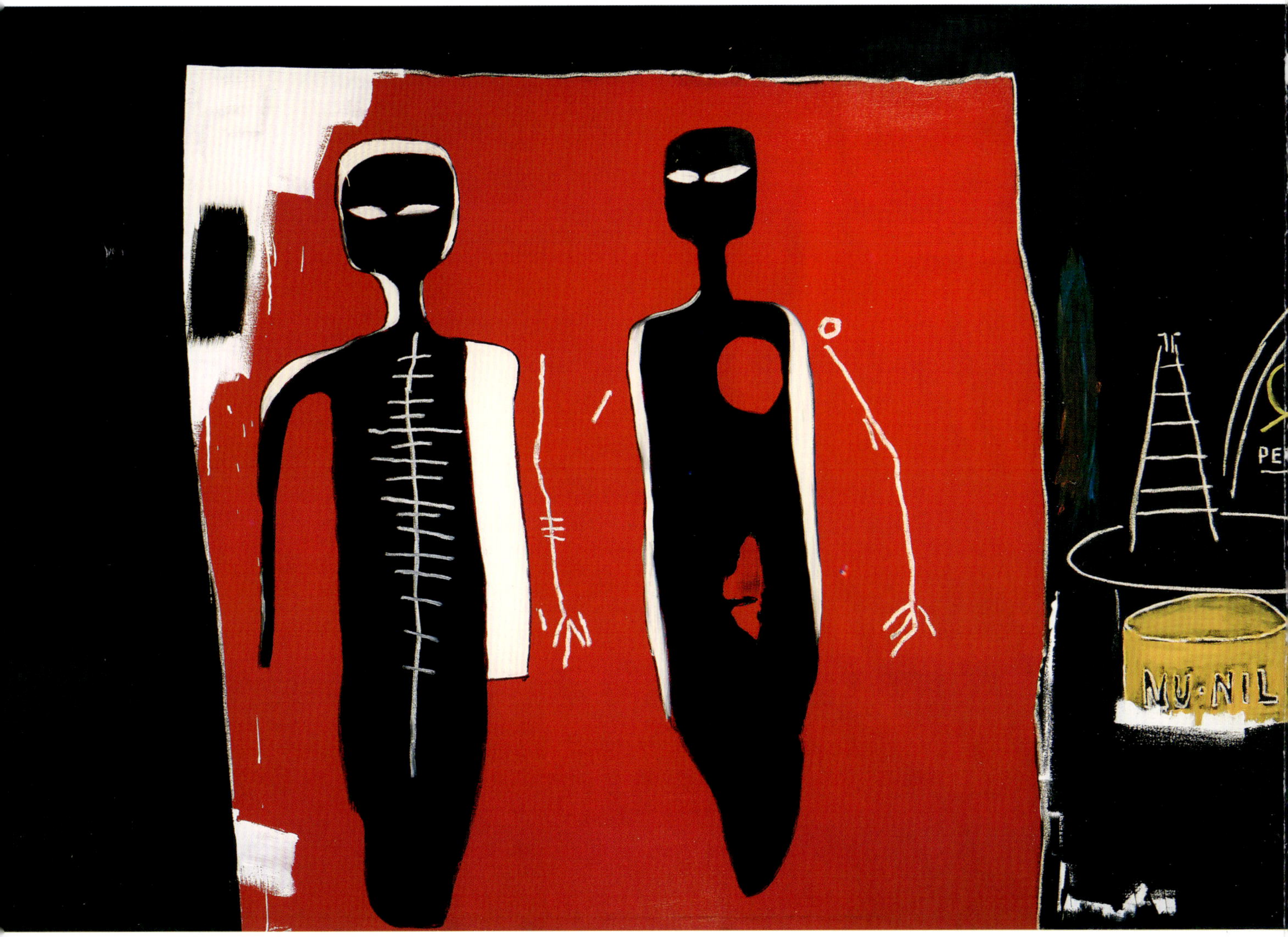
NU·NIL

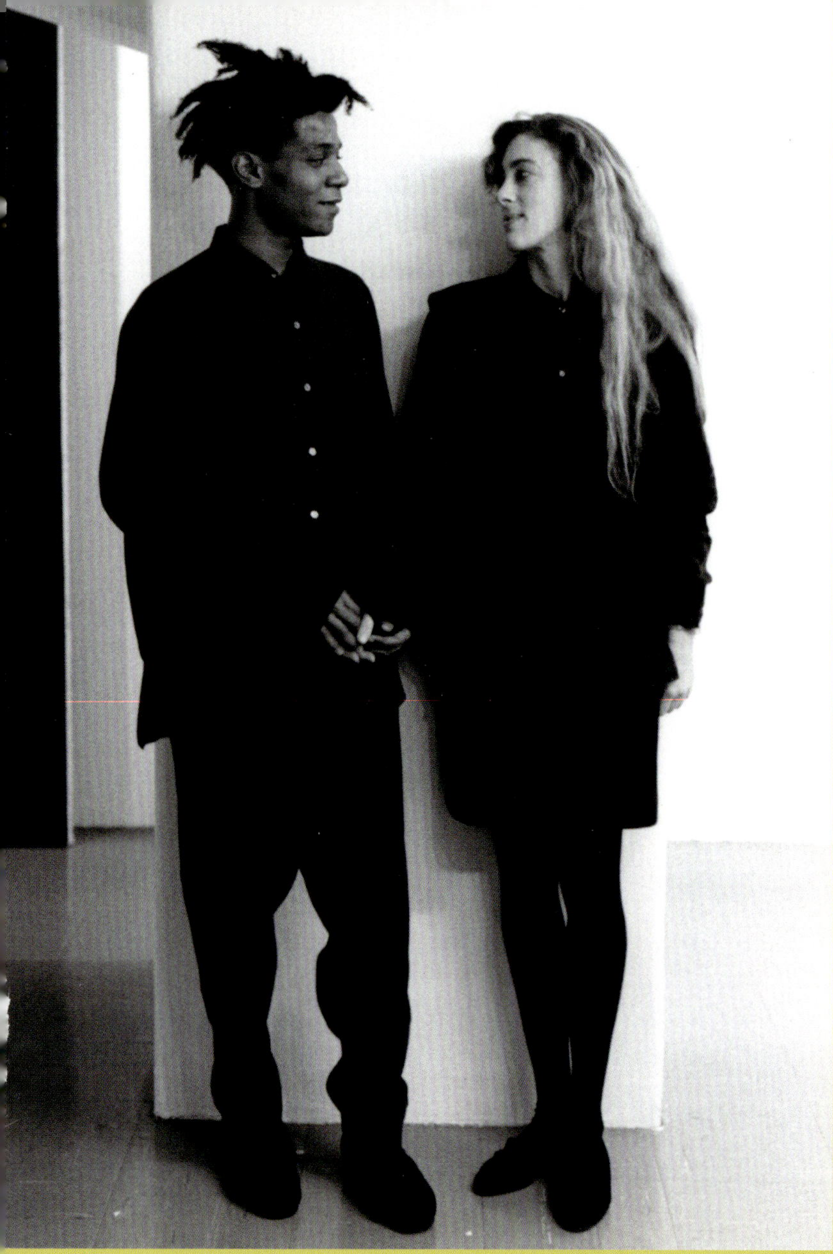

MEETING JEAN-MICHEL

I was standing near the entrance of the club one night and this cute guy came in with a group of friends and bought them all entrance tickets. I didn't know who he was, but I was impressed that he bought everyone tickets. Most downtown kids would try to get in for free—and they usually did! I brought him a bottle of champagne, and he told me his name was Jean-Michel. I still had no idea who he was. On our first date we went to see the movie *Witness* with my mother and sister. I picked him up in the club truck with the four of us squished into one seat. What a date!

JENNIFER GOODE
(QUOTED IN *AREA: 1983–1987*, 2013)

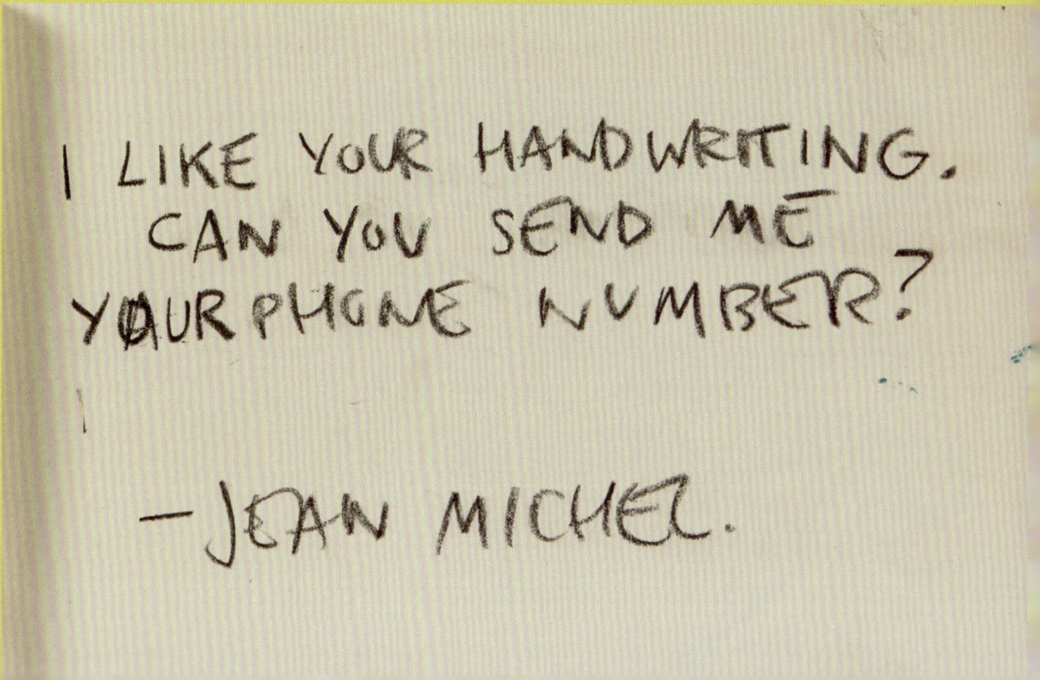

TOP
Jean-Michel and Jennifer Goode at Akira Ikeda Gallery, Tokyo, November 9, 1985
YOSHITAKA UCHIDA
© IKEDA GALLERY, JAPAN

RIGHT
Note found in Jean-Michel's studio

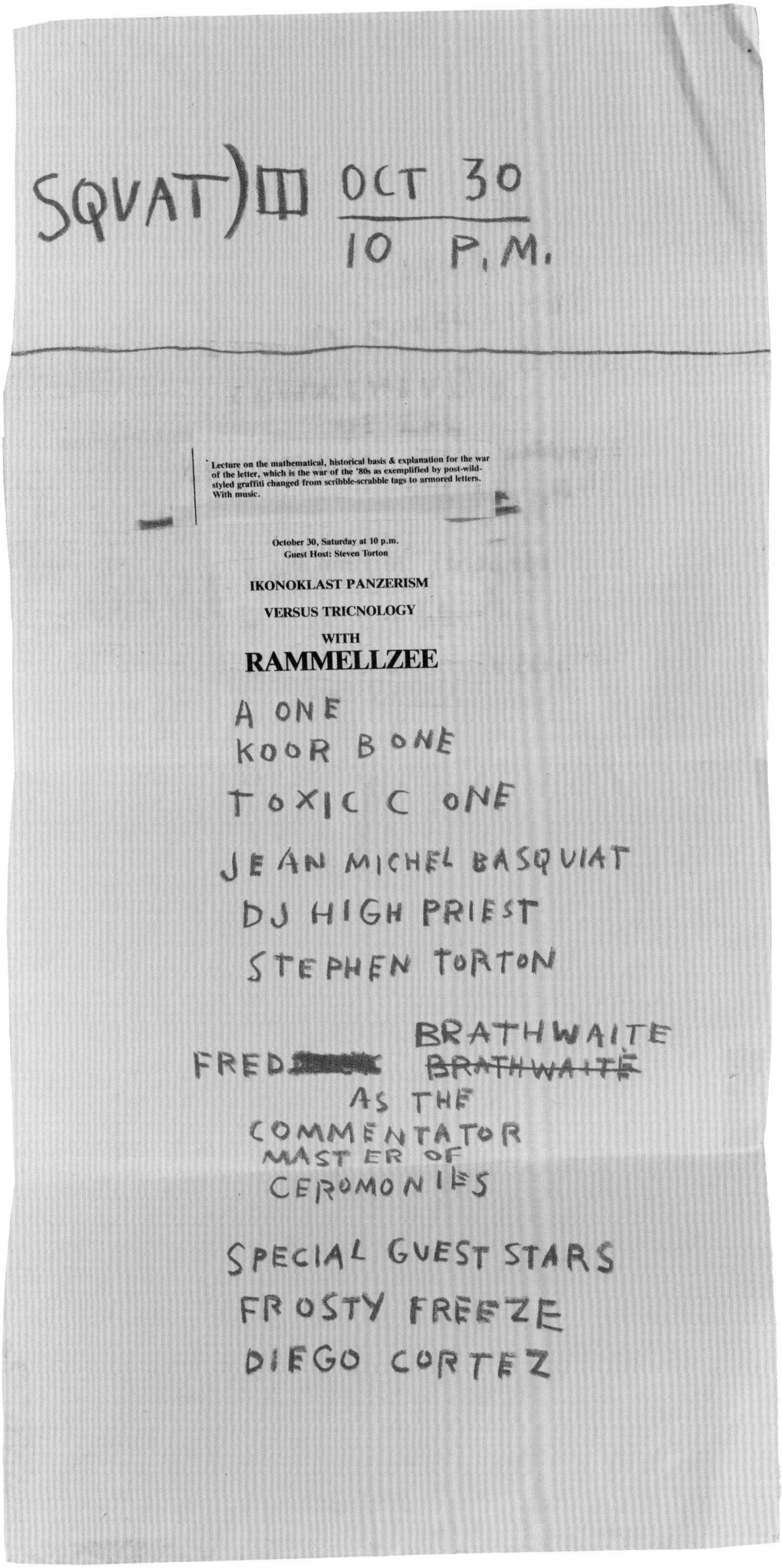

Poster featuring Jean-Michel's hand lettering for a one-night benefit at Squat Theatre, West 23rd Street, New York

Jean-Michel's many personal Black heroes can be found throughout his paintings and drawings. From jazz musicians and singers to sports heroes, they were immortalized in much of his work. Charlie Parker, the jazz legend, was a particular favorite of Jean-Michel's—my brother loved his music, which is apparent by the number of works he painted in Parker's memory. JEANINE

Untitled, n.d.
Crayon and oil stick on paper
17½ × 13¾ in. (44.45 × 32.93 cm)

ROYALTY

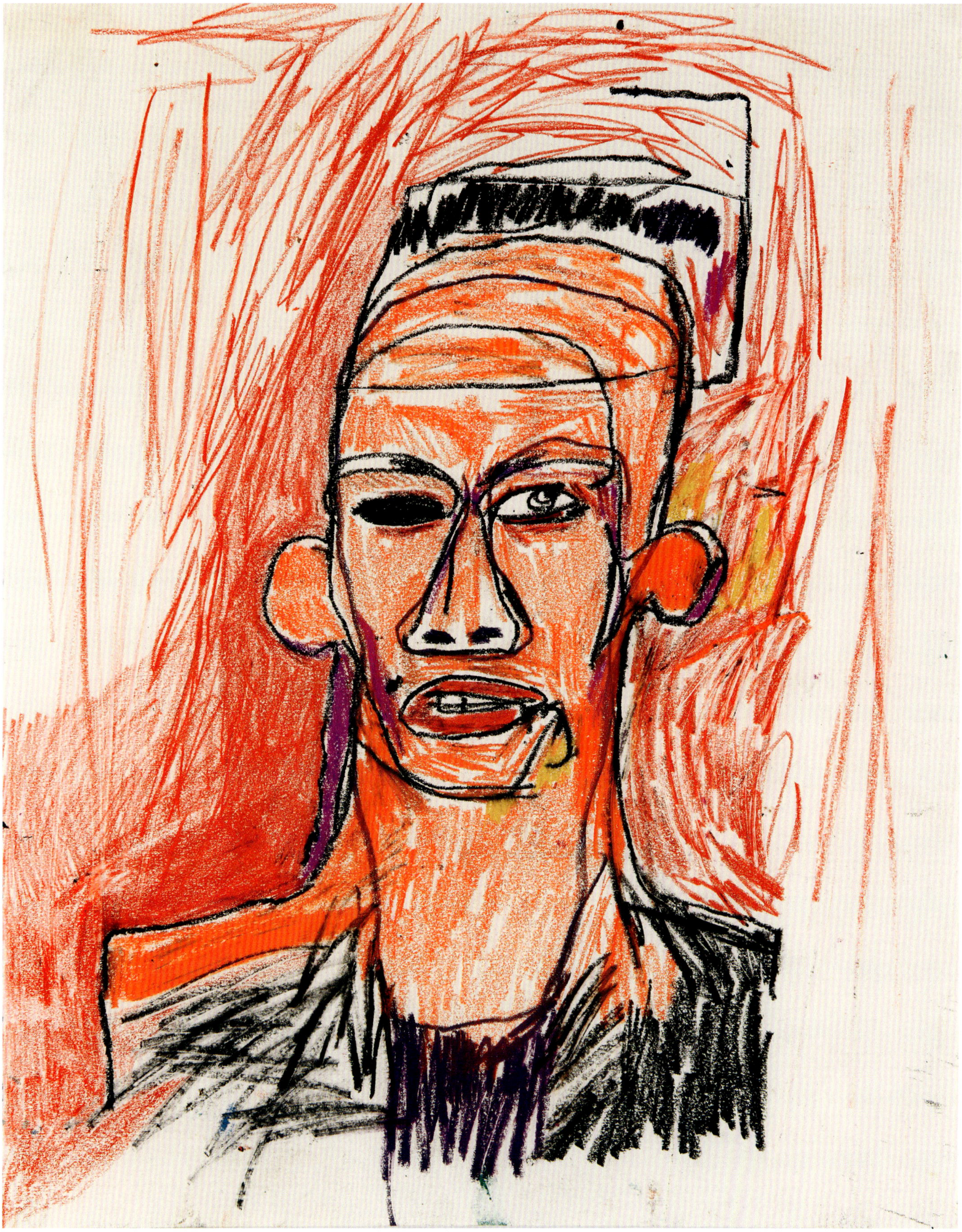

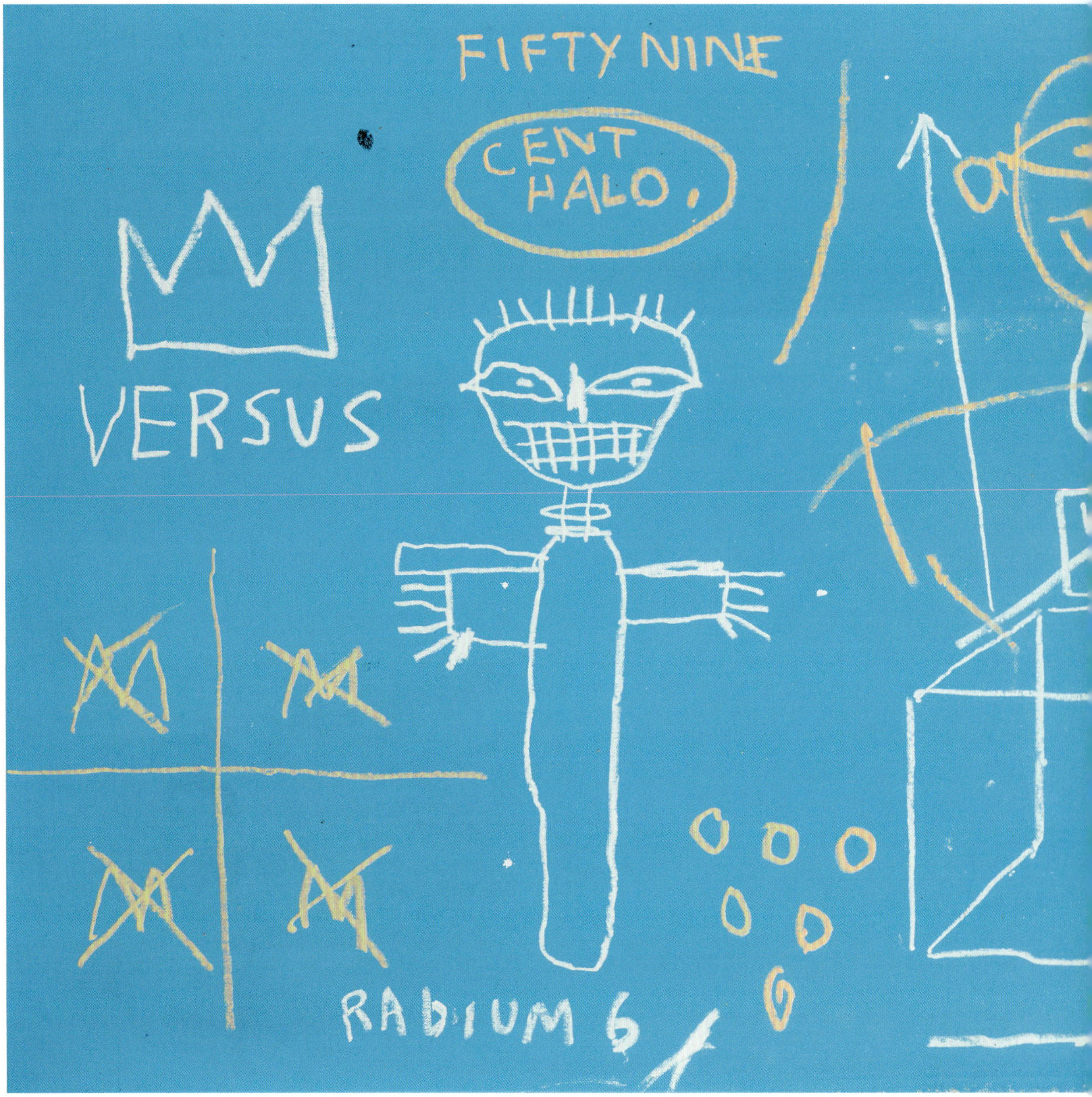

ROYALTY, HEROISM, AND THE STREETS

When asked what his subject matter was in a 1983 interview, Jean-Michel answered, "Royalty, heroism, and the streets." He was speaking to how he would like to see Black people portrayed in America. My brother was critical of how they were depicted on TV, in film, and in the arts, despite our tremendous contributions in those arenas and American culture generally. Black people were more often than not portrayed as the help, as thieves, gang members, pimps, prostitutes—either as something negative or insignificant. He painted his pantheon of Black heroes as royalty—that is why there are crowns throughout his work. And this treatment extends to paintings of street artists as well. Knowing Jean-Michel, it seems clear this was the message he was trying to convey. JEANINE

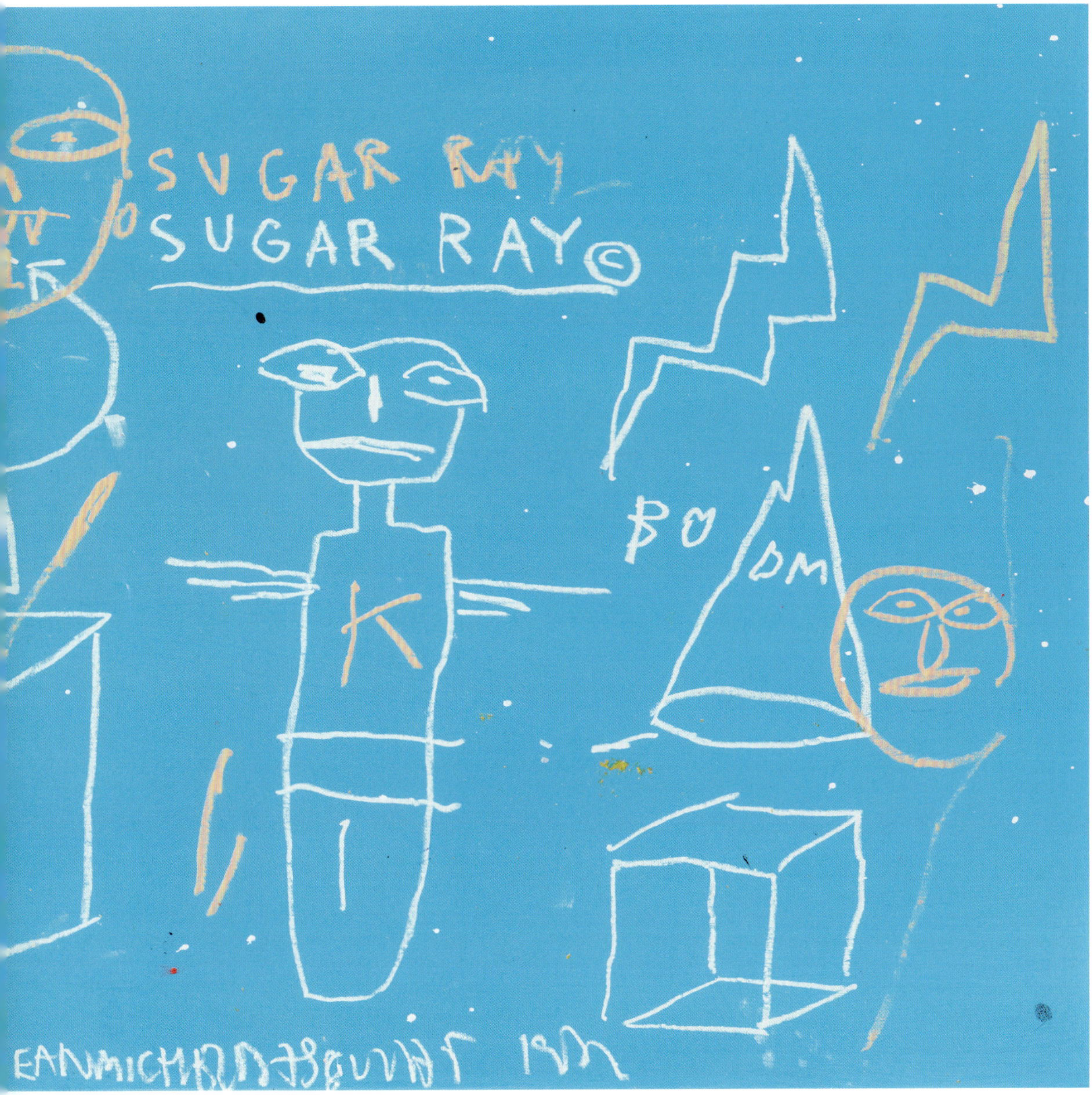

Untitled (Sugar Ray), 1982
Acrylic and oil stick on canvas
43 × 89½ in. (109.22 × 226.70 cm)

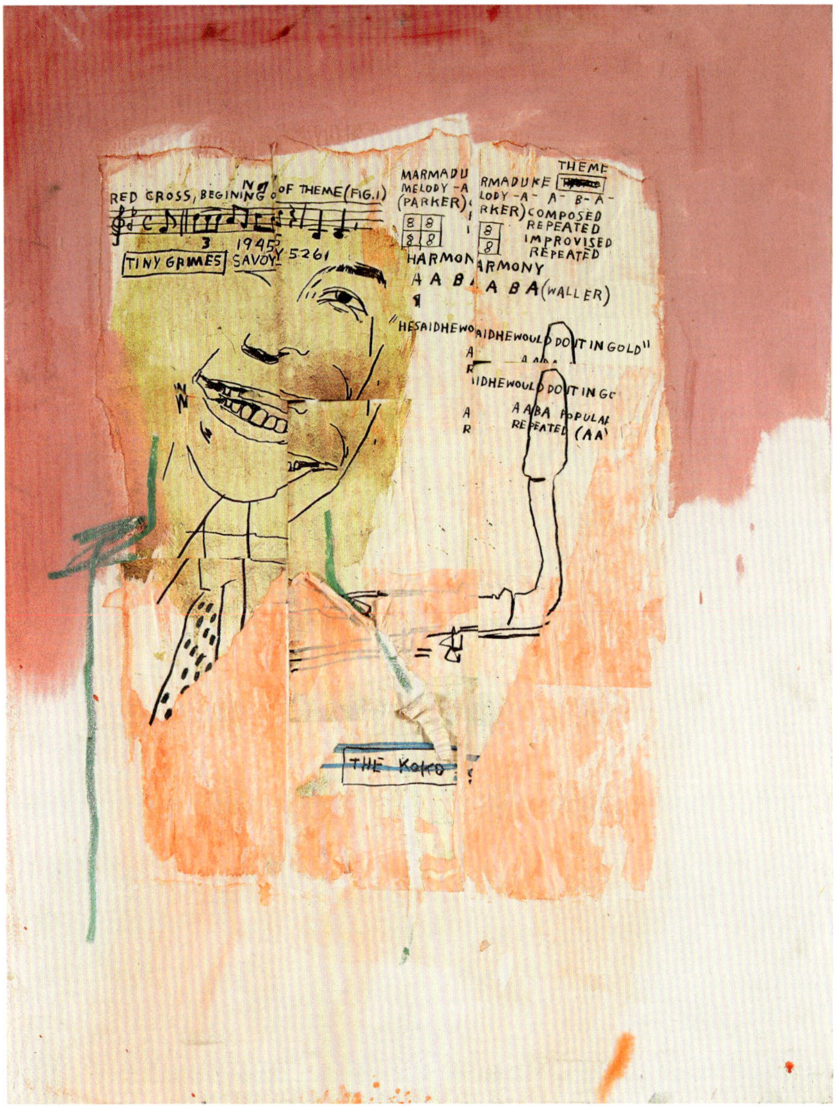

LEFT
Pink Parker, 1983
Acrylic, oil stick, and color copies on canvas
48 × 38 in. (121.92 × 96.52 cm)

OPPOSITE
Untitled (Tommy Potter), n.d.
Colored pencil, graphite, and ink on paper
14 × 9¼ in. (35.56 × 23.50 cm).
Charles Thomas Potter was a jazz double bass player best known for having been a member of Charlie Parker's "classic quintet" with Miles Davis between 1947 and 1950.

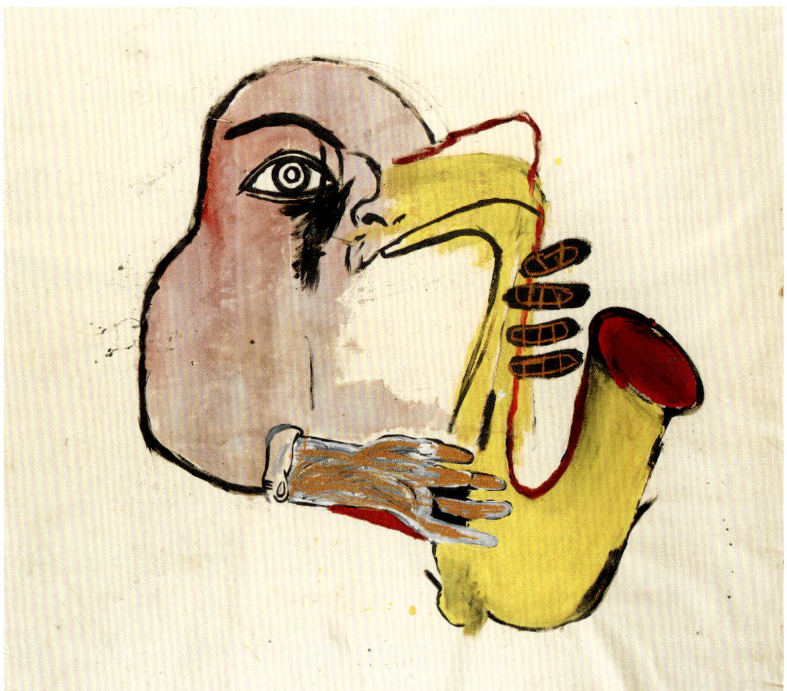

Untitled, n.d.
Acrylic and oil stick on canvas
83 × 93½ in.
(210.82 × 237.49 cm)

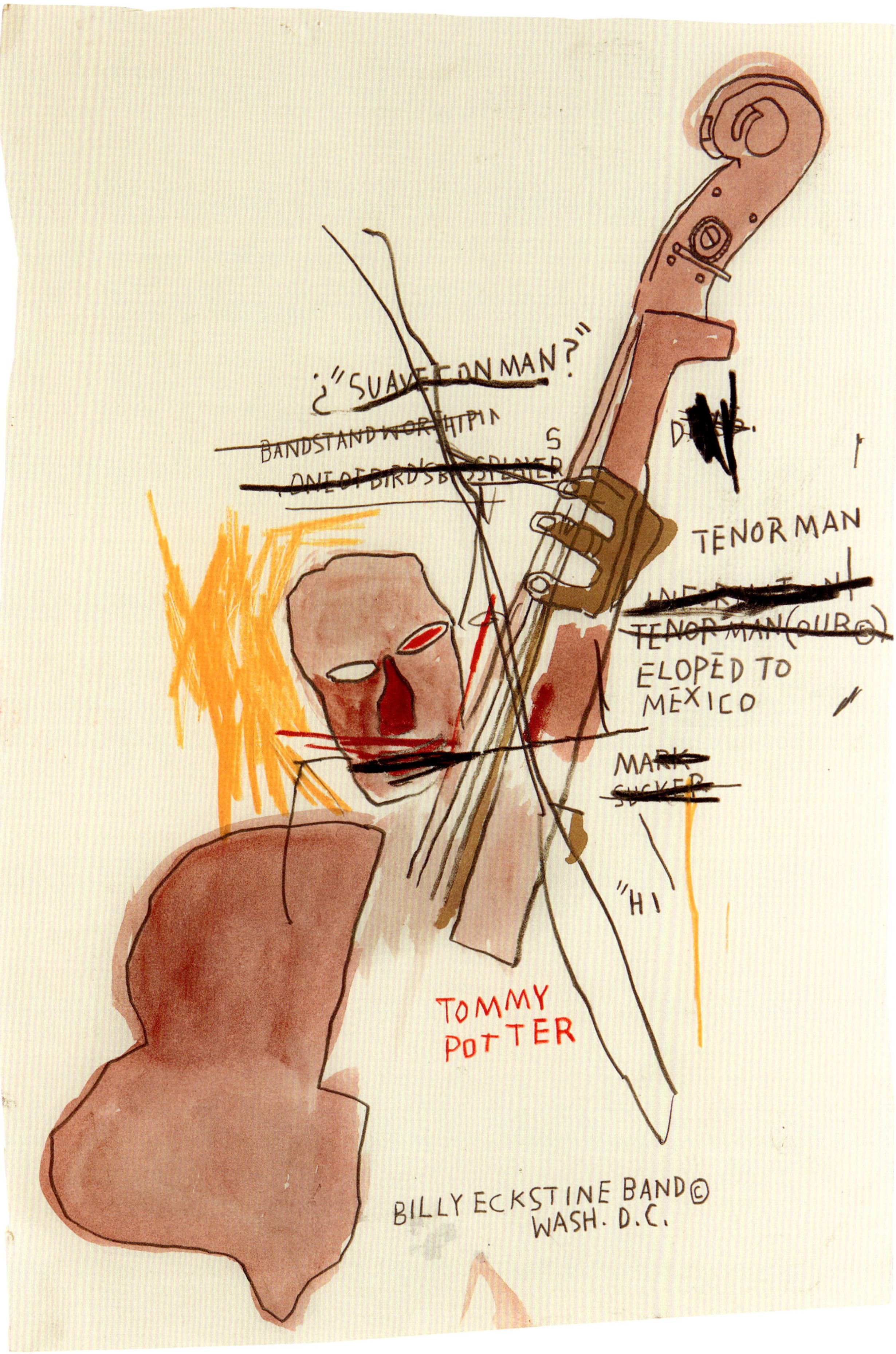
¿"SUAVE CON MAN?"
TENOR MAN
TENOR MAN (OUR©)
ELOPED TO
MEXICO
MARK
SUCKER
"HI
TOMMY
POTTER
BILLY ECKSTINE BAND©
WASH. D.C.

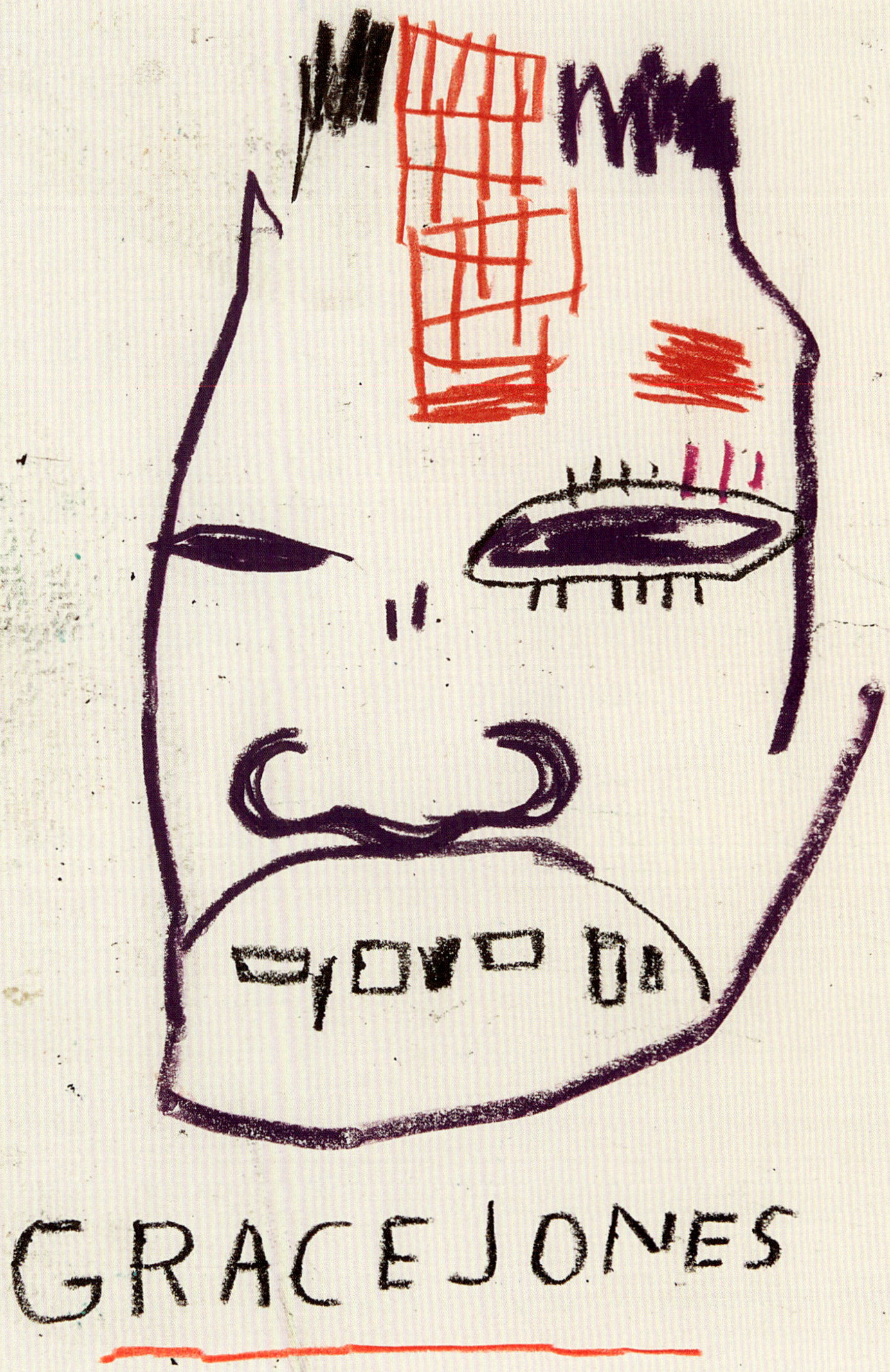
GRACEJONES

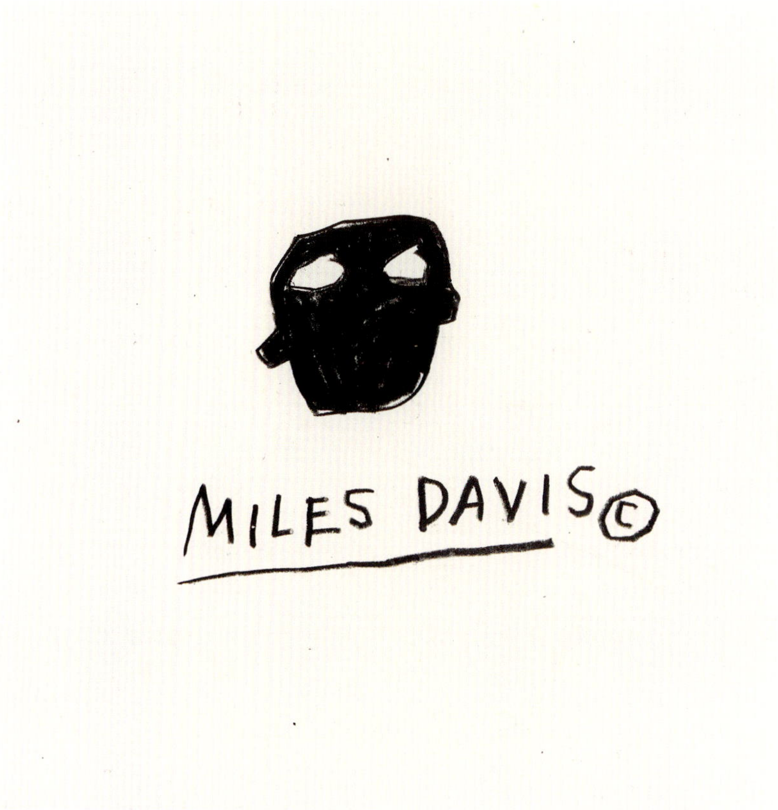

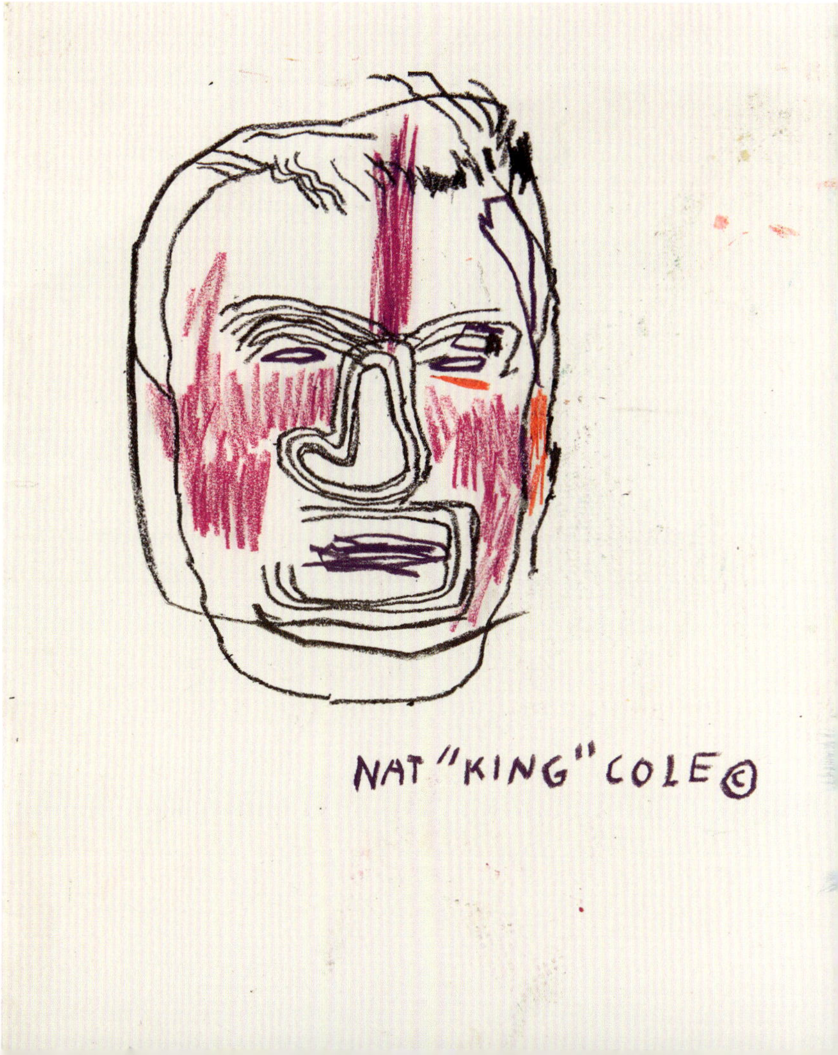

OPPOSITE
Untitled (Grace Jones), n.d.
Oil stick on paper
17½ × 13¾ in. (44.45 × 34.93 cm)

TOP
Untitled (Miles Davis), n.d.
Oil stick on paper
30 × 22¼ in. (76.2 × 56.52 cm)

RIGHT
Untitled (Nat King Cole), n.d.
Oil stick on paper
17½ × 13¾ in. (44.45 × 34.93 cm)

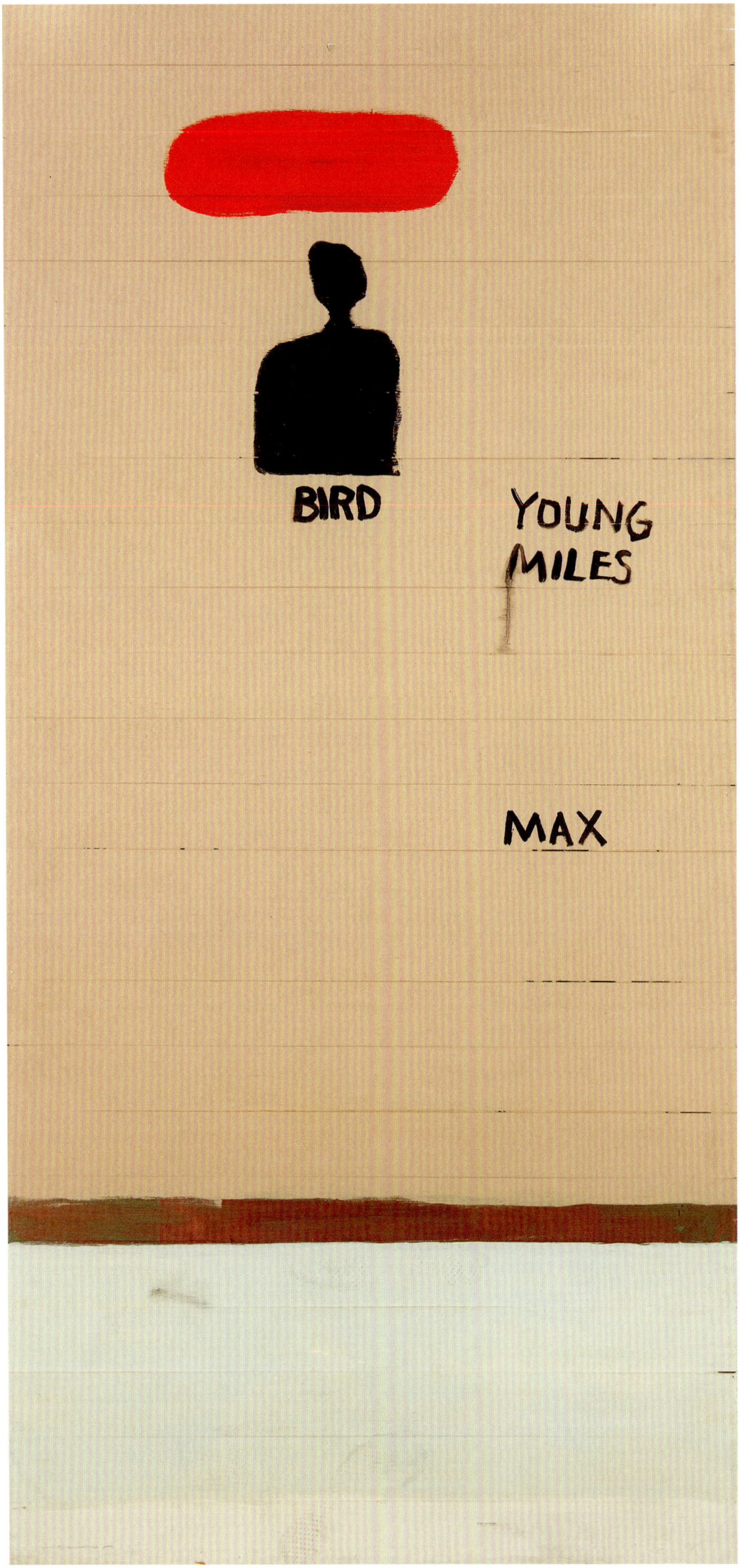

Untitled, n.d.
Acrylic on wood
85 × 39½ in. (215.9 × 100.33 cm)

Untitled (Bird), 1984–88
Acrylic and oil stick on wood
49½ × 47 in. (125.73 × 119.38 cm).
Jean-Michel greatly admired Charlie "Bird" Parker. He depicted him in many of his paintings and drawings, listened to his music, and read Bird*, the book about his life. He purchased cases of the book and gave them out to friends.*

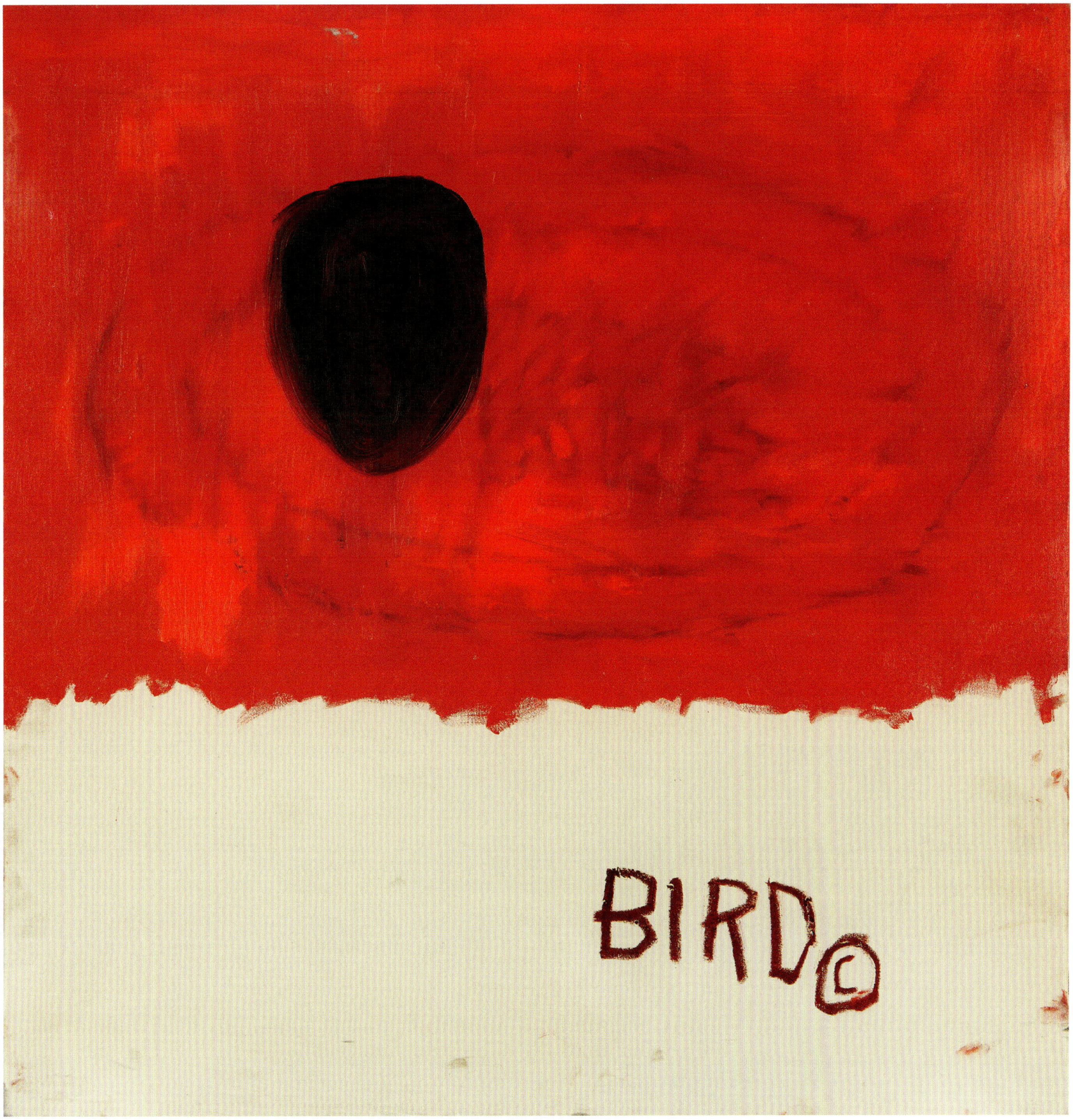

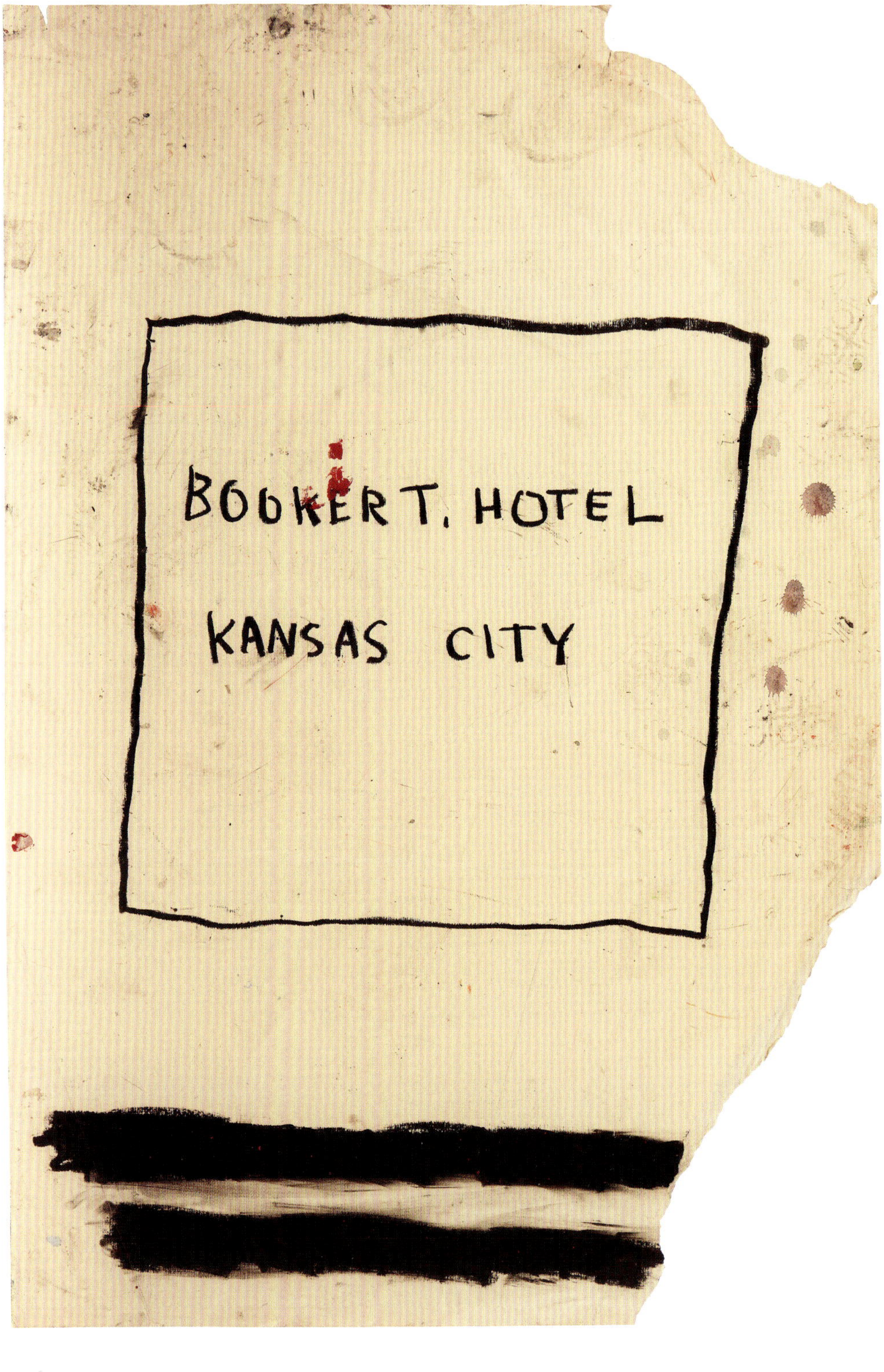

Untitled (Booker T. Hotel), n.d.
Oil stick on paper
40 × 26 in. (101.6 × 66.04 cm)

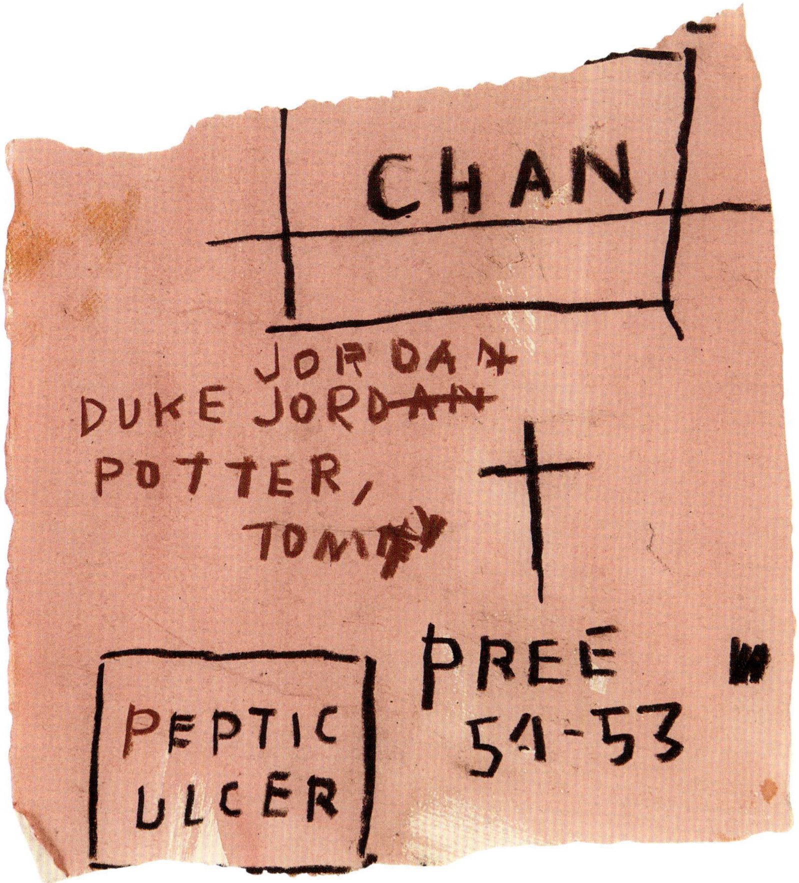

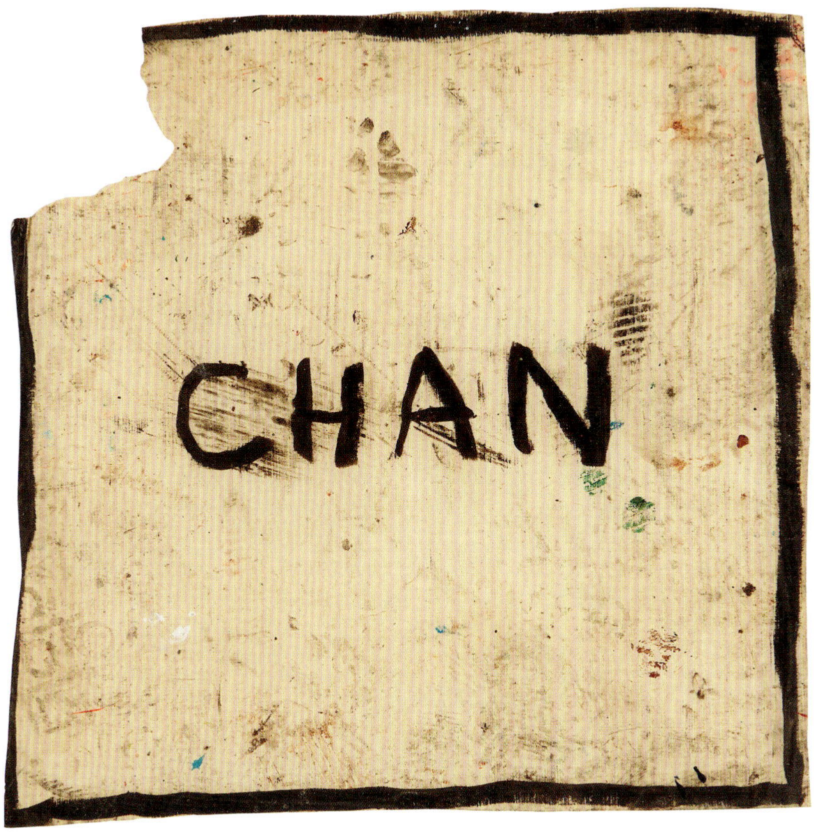

TOP
Untitled (Chan), n.d.
Charcoal, oil stick,
watercolor on paper
11 × 10 in. (27.94 × 25.4 cm)

RIGHT
Untitled (Chan), n.d.
Oil stick on paper
14 × 13¾ in. (35.56 × 34.93 cm)

BIRD THEORY
RAT ROOM © TM
"FREYTAG" ©
DISCH
COLE, MOUNT (MT.)
ELLIS
WHITE
SADIGHIAN

OPPOSITE
Untitled (Bird Theory), n.d.
Crayon on paper
30 × 22¼ in. (76.2 × 56.52 cm)

RIGHT
Untitled (For Lack Of), n.d.
Graphite on paper
3½ × 4¼ in. (8.89 × 10.80 cm).
Charlie Parker had a daughter named Pree. She died of a heart defect at two and a half years old.

BOTTOM
Untitled, n.d.
Oil stick on composition board
20 × 30 in. (50.8 × 76.2 cm)

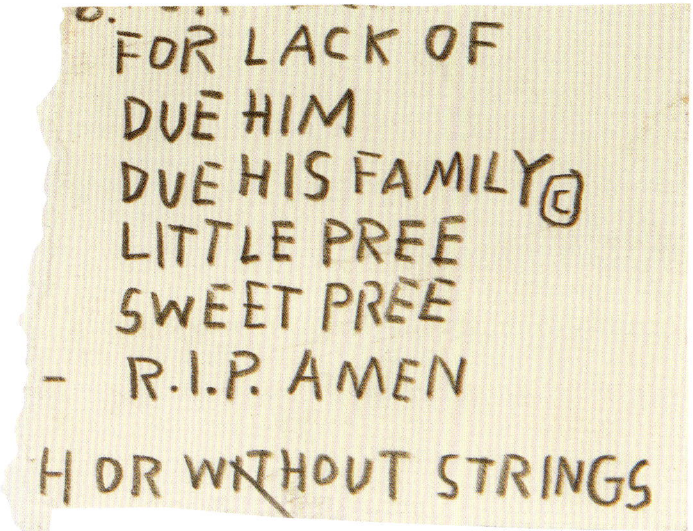

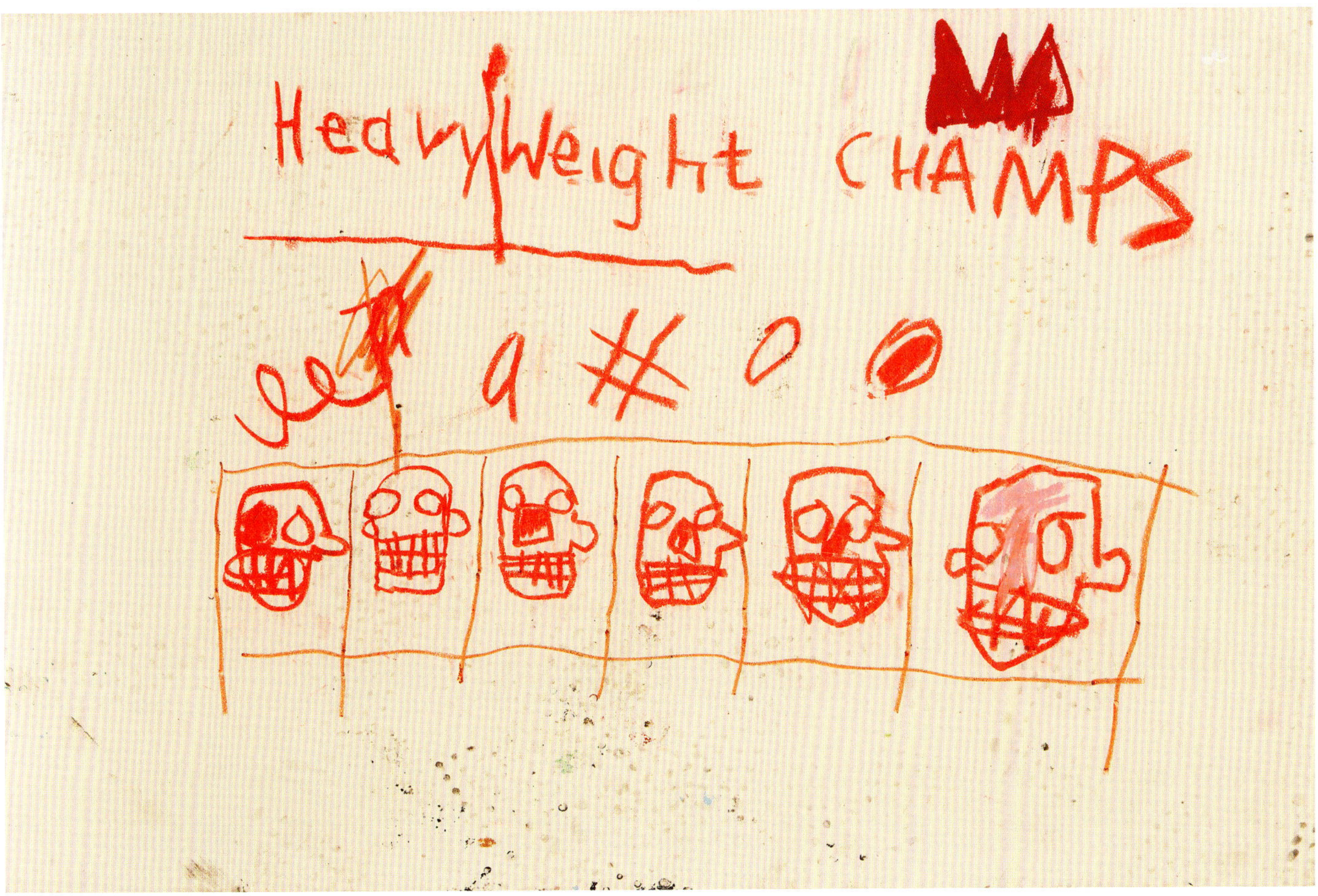

The Bond, Earle, Stanhope, 1983
Oil stick on canvas mounted
on wood supports
Triptych, 45¾ × 50 in. overall
(116.21 × 127 cm).
*Charlie Parker died at the
Stanhope Hotel.*

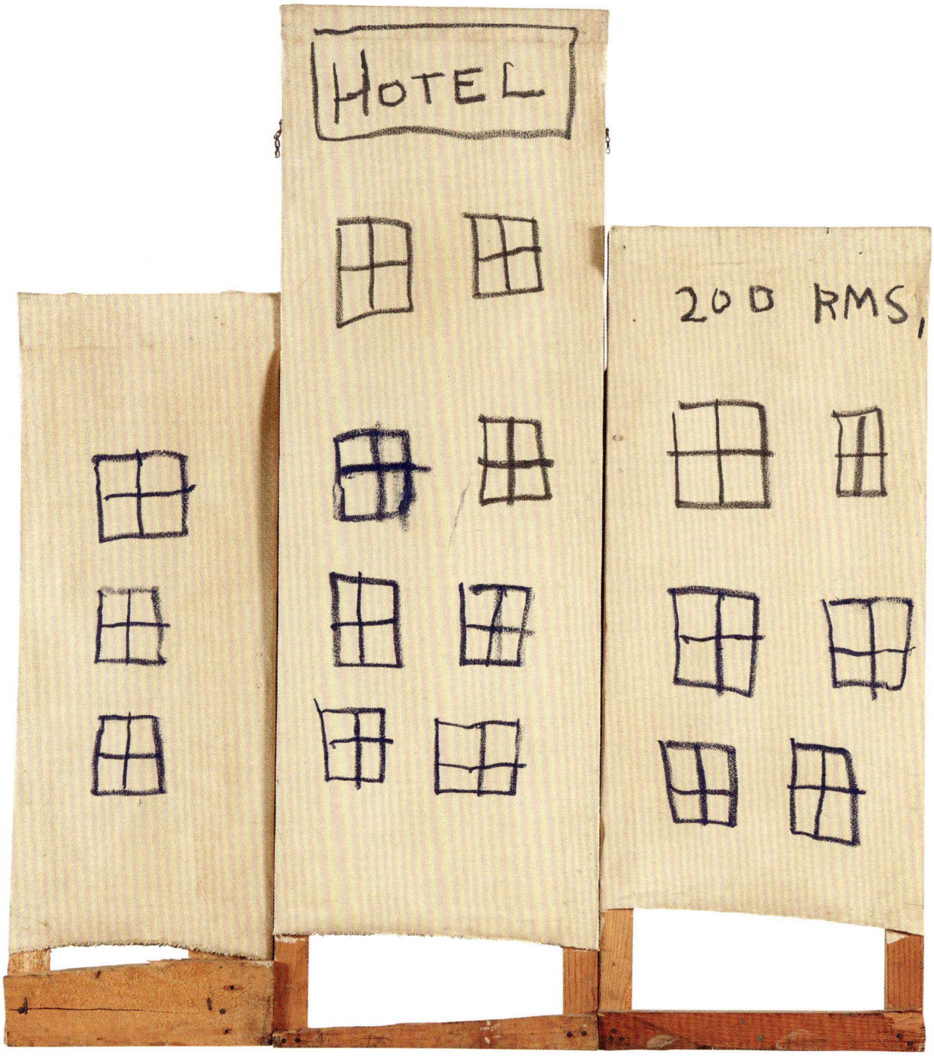

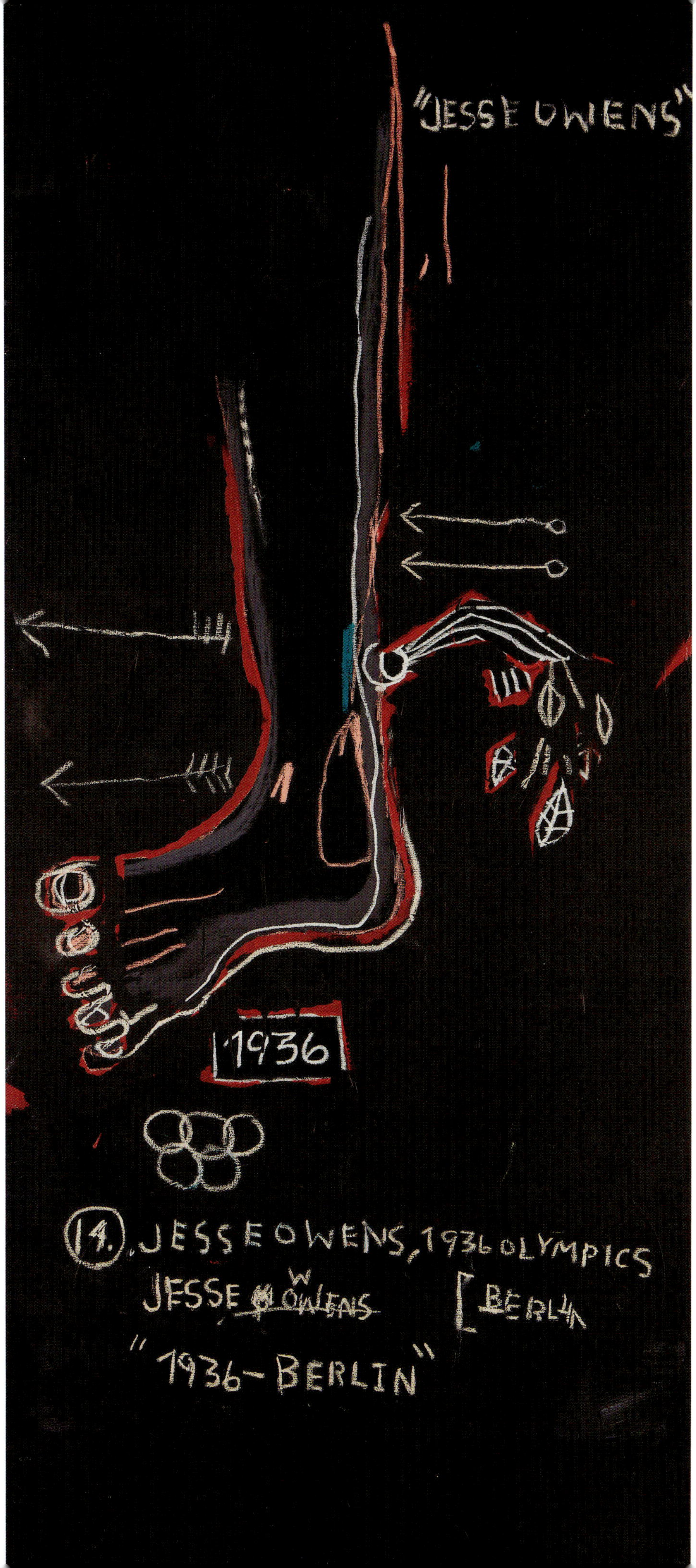

Dark Race Horse / Jesse Owens, 1983
Acrylic and oil stick on canvas
84 × 36 in. (213.36 × 91.44 cm)

Jean-Michel had a way of tugging at our coattails, reminding us to pay attention and dig a bit deeper to see what has been normalized and accepted within society. He held up a mirror to the hypocrisies and self-righteousness that are at the root of so much cultural discord, and he did it with a wry smile. He challenges our illusions, encouraging us to do better and to see more clearly.

The works featured in this chapter feel like a history lesson. Jean-Michel serves up power, race, science, war, and religion. Here we feature works such as *Jawbone of an Ass* (page 250) and *Untitled (Too Much Reign)* (page 256), and others that we found simple, direct, and deeply profound, like *Untitled (Those Who Dress Better Can Receeve Christ)* (page 255). LISANE

Untitled (Bird of God), n.d.
Acrylic, crayon, and masking tape with collage on paper
10½ × 8½ in. (26.67 × 21.59 cm)

THOSE WHO DRESS BETTER CAN RECEIVE CHRIST

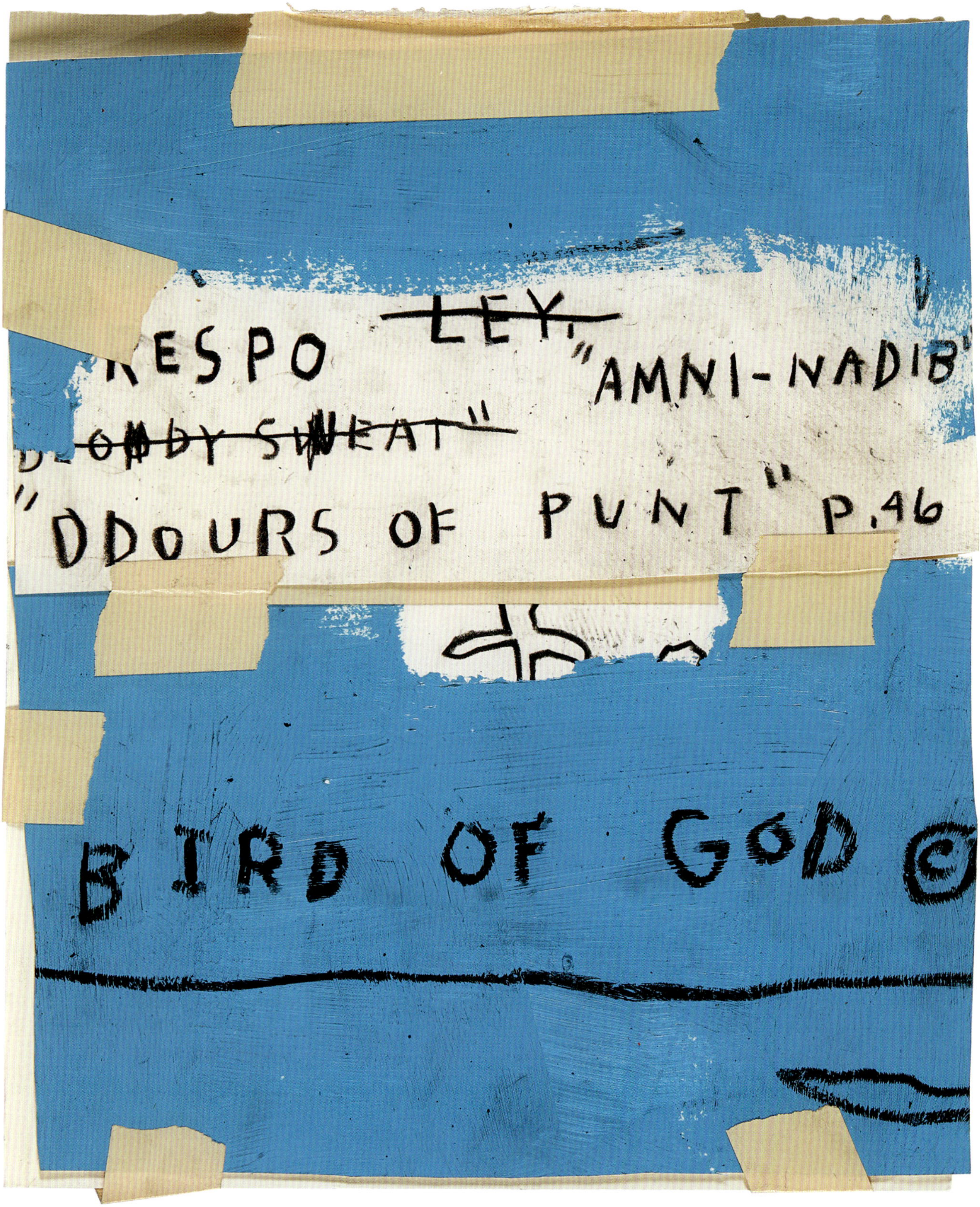
RESPO LEY "AMNI-NADIB"
"ODOURS OF PUNT" P.46
BIRD OF GOD ©

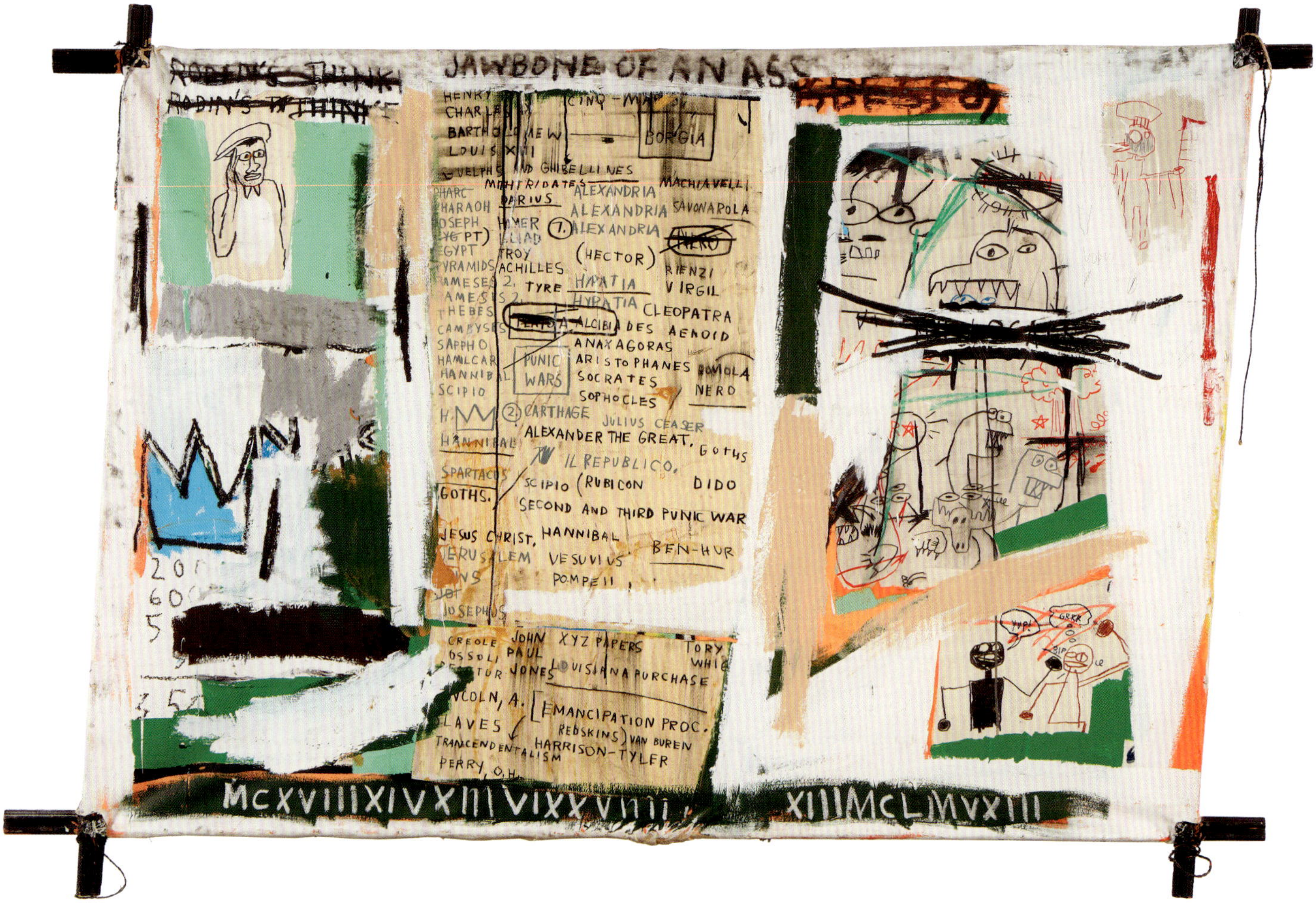

Jawbone of an Ass, 1982
Acrylic, oil stick, and paper
on canvas with string and
wood supports
60 × 84 in. (152.4 × 213.36 cm)

Three Quarters of Olympia Minus the Servant, 1982
Acrylic, oil stick, and Xerox collage on canvas
48 × 44½ in. (96.52 × 113.03 cm)

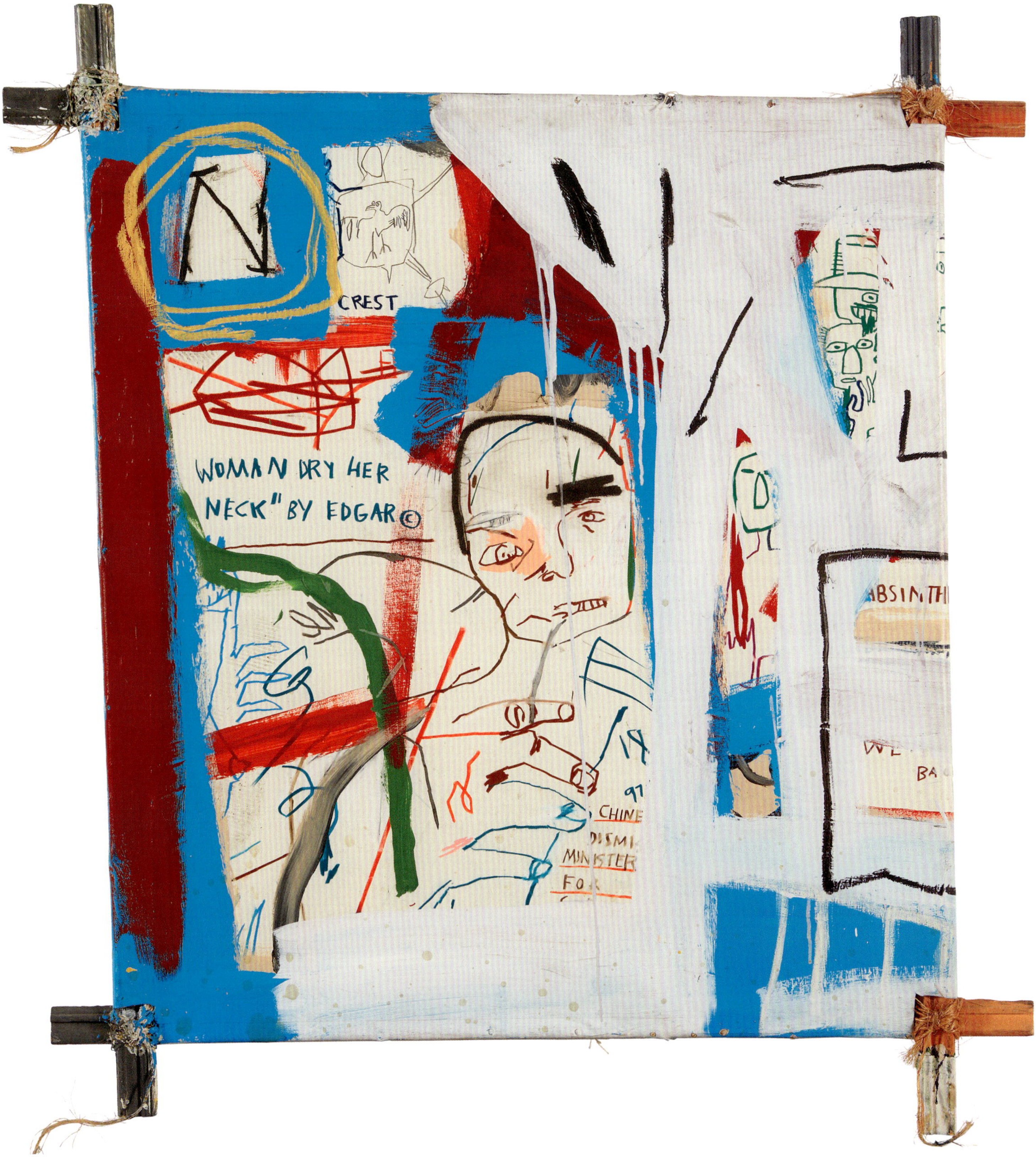

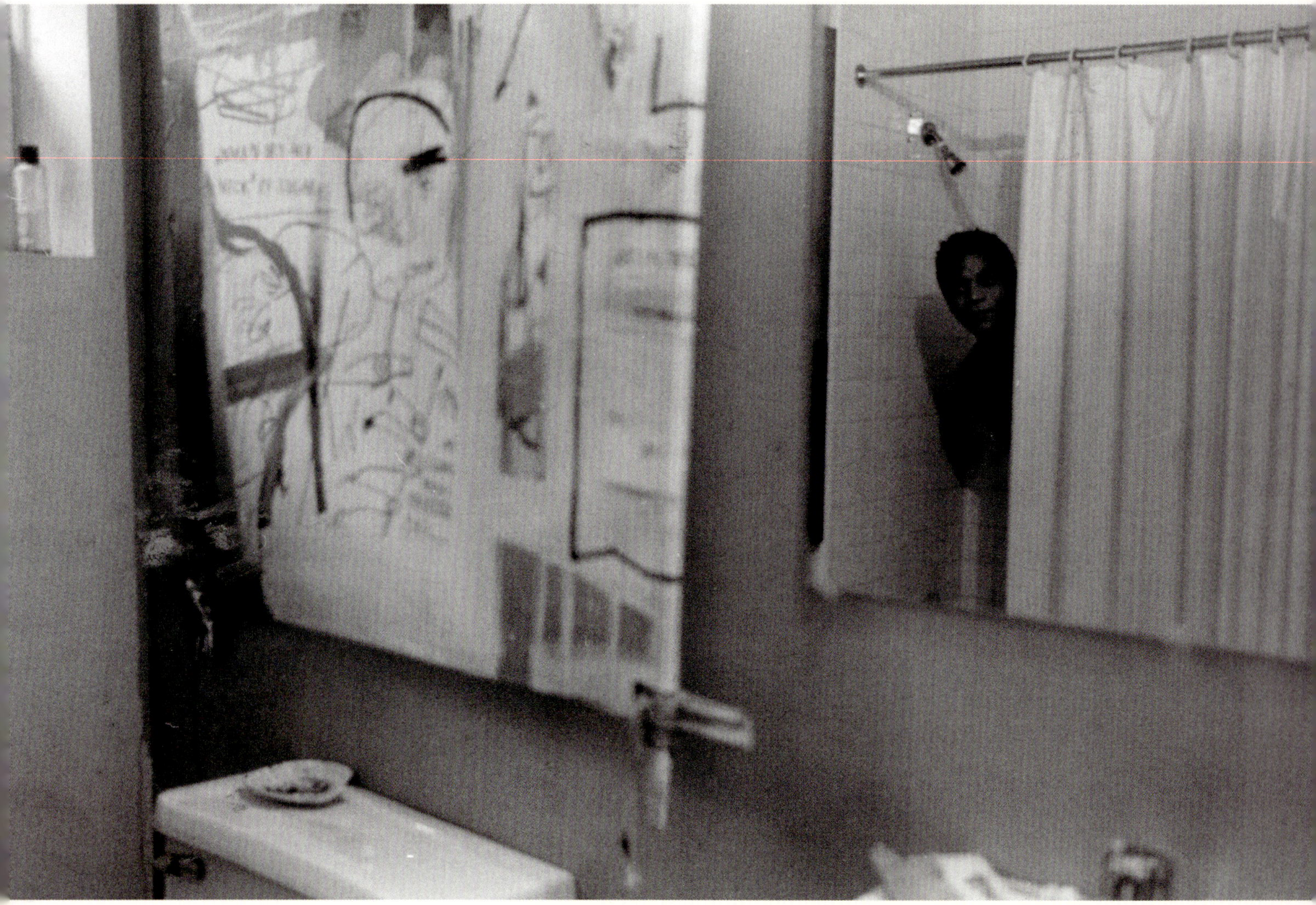

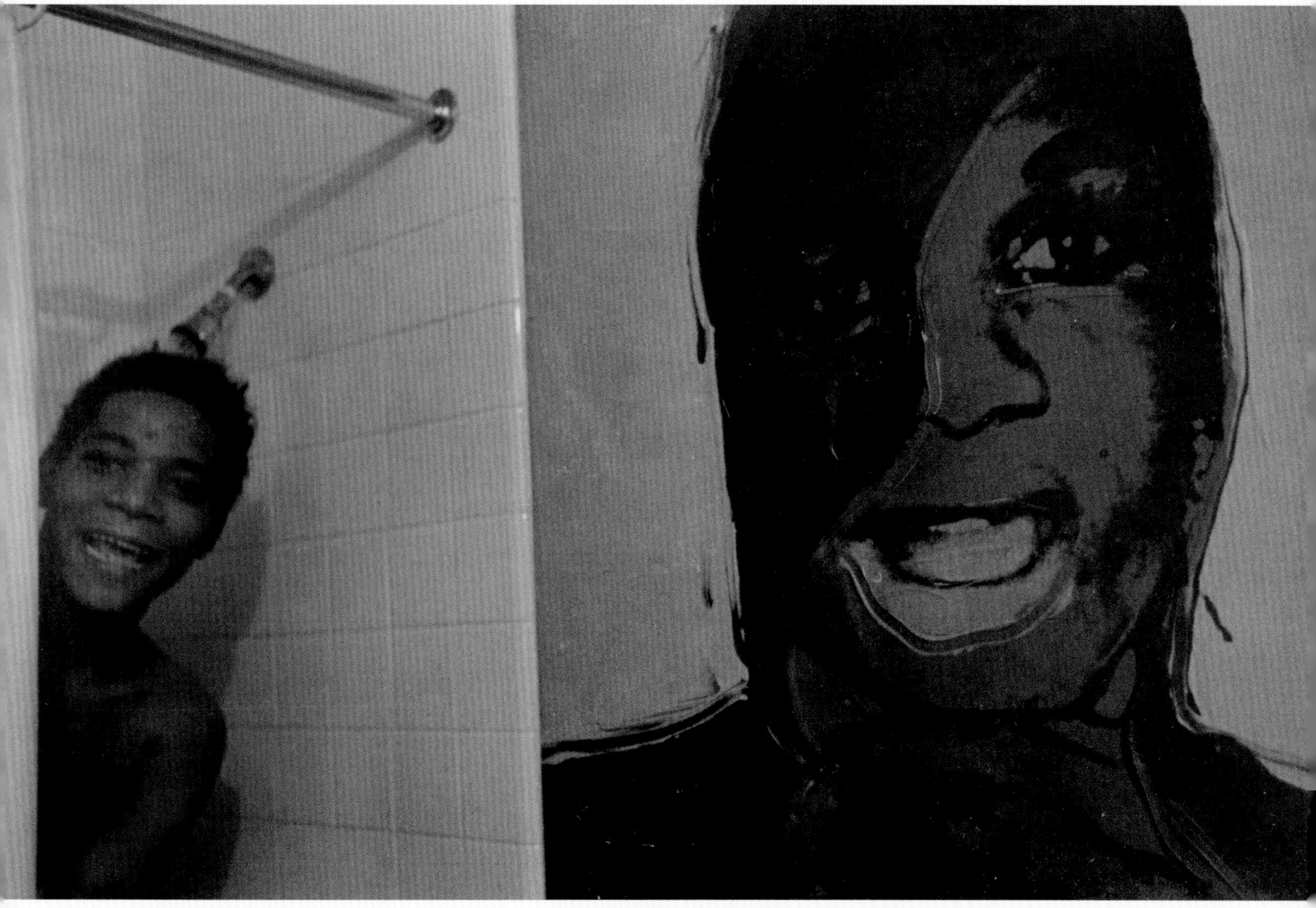

Jean-Michel in the shower with *Three Quarters of Olympia Minus the Servant* on the wall (opposite), ca. mid-1980s

Untitled (Titian), n.d.
Acrylic, crayon, masking tape,
and oil stick with collage
10½ × 8½ in. (26.67 × 21.59 cm)

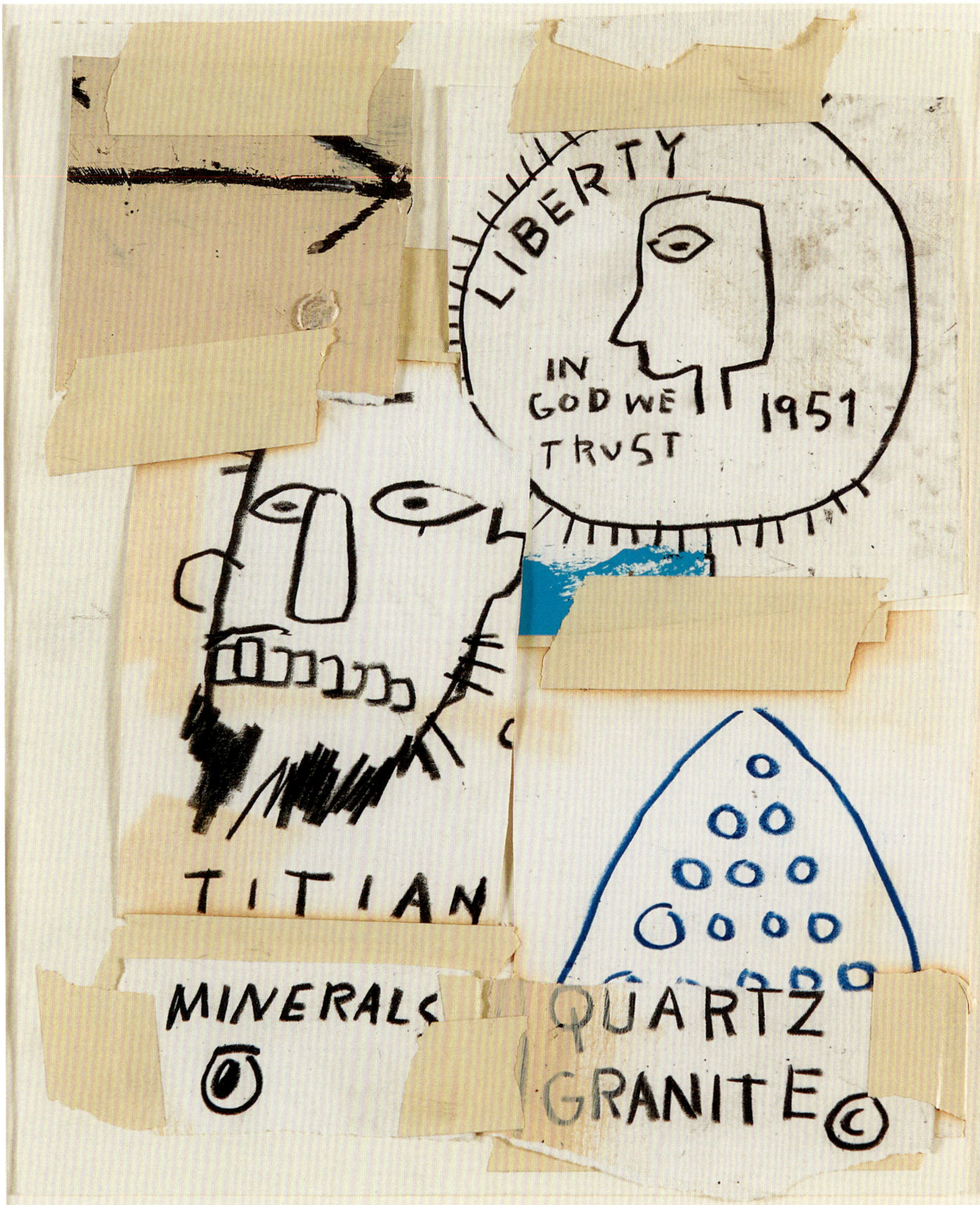

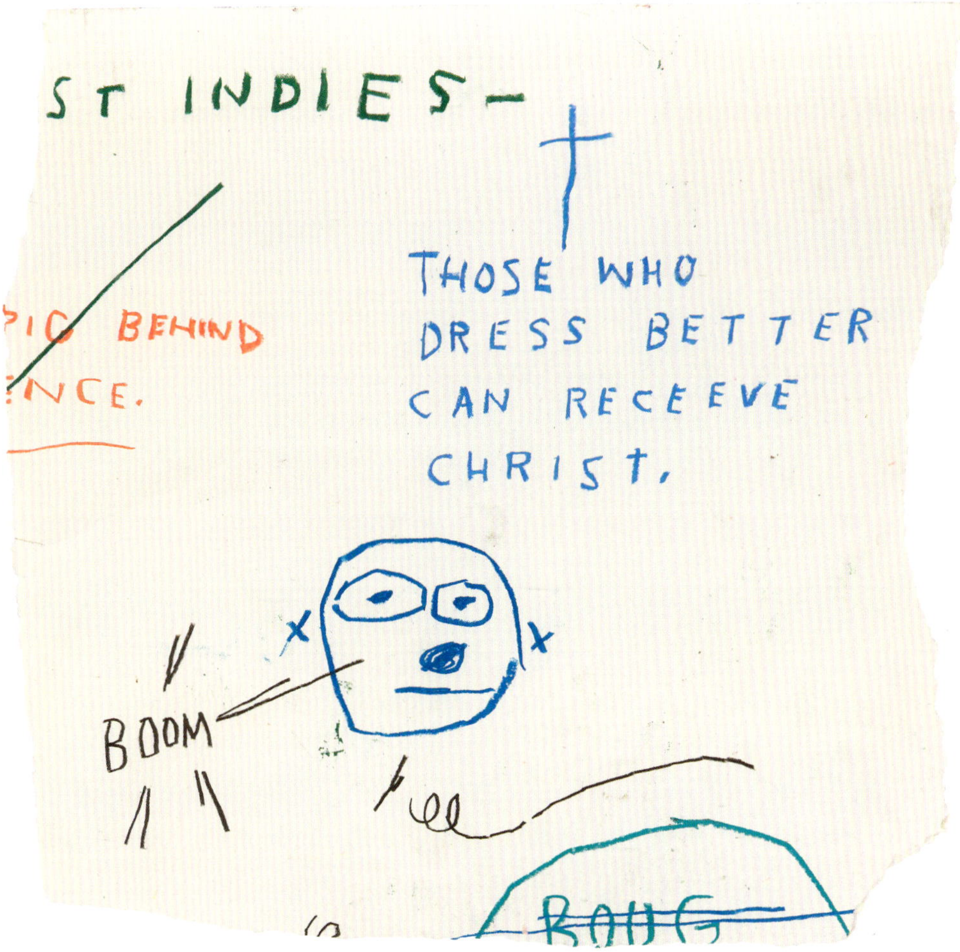

RIGHT
Untitled (Those Who Dress Better Can Receeve Christ), n.d.
Oil stick on paper
24 × 23 in. (60.96 × 58.42 cm).
Jean-Michel wasn't afraid to provoke thought and often did it through irony. LISANE

BOTTOM
Untitled (War Rations), n.d.
Colored pencil on paper
10 × 14 in. (25.4 × 35.56 cm).
We believe this drawing to reference Laika, the stray dog sent to orbit the Earth during a Soviet experiment in 1957. LISANE

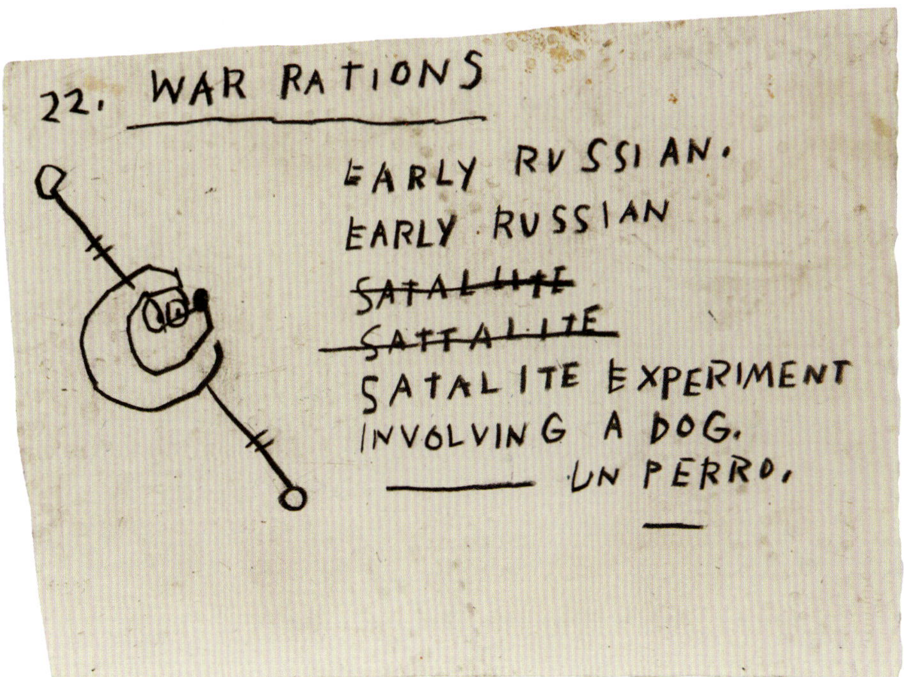

Untitled (Too Much Reign), n.d.
Crayon, graphite, and
oil stick on paper
13½ × 14¼ in.
(34.29 × 26.20 cm)

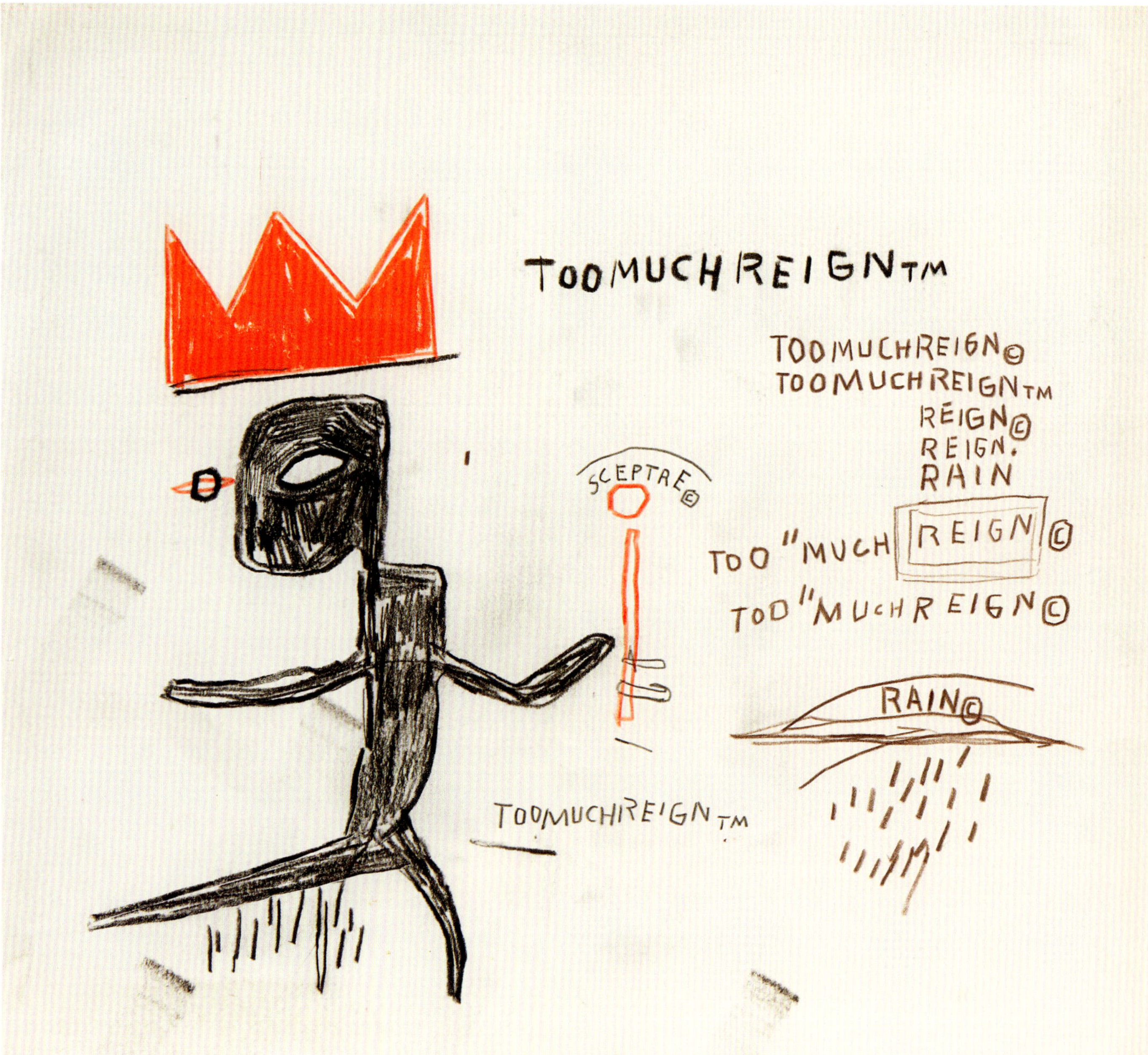

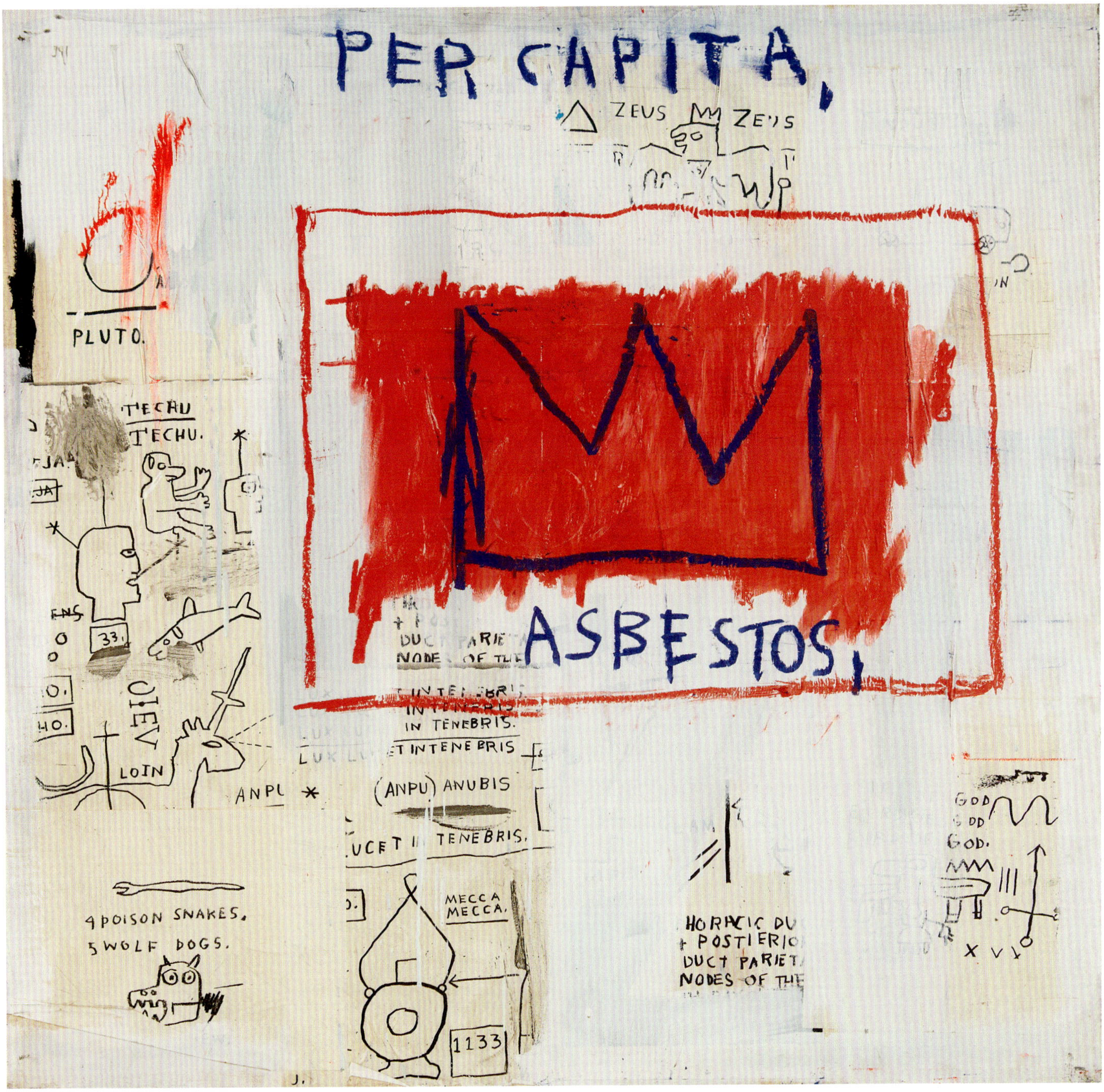

Untitled (Per Capita), 1983
Acrylic, oil stick, and Xerox
collage on aluminum
35 × 35 in. (88.9 × 88.9 cm)

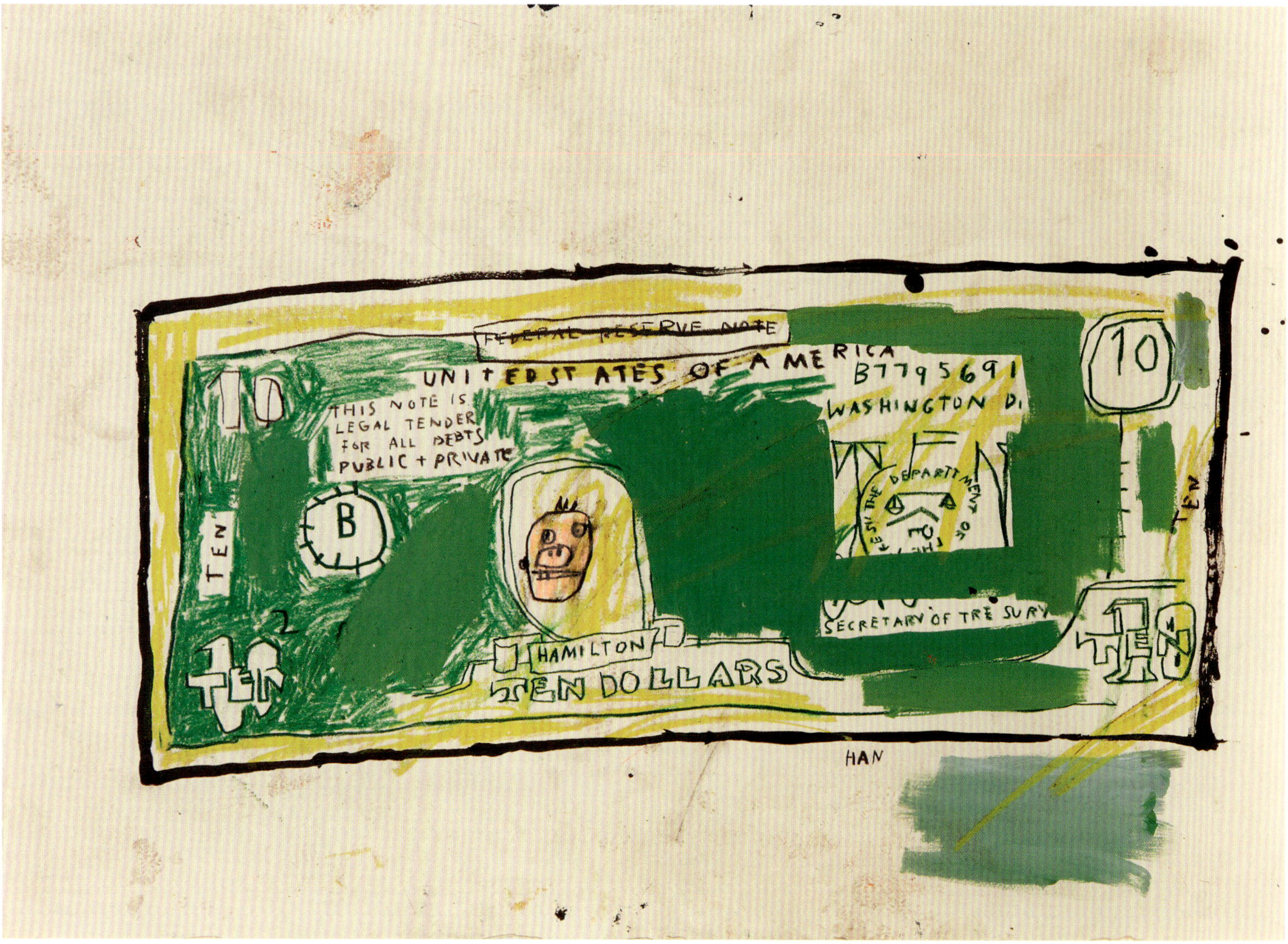

Untitled (Ten Dollars), n.d.
Acrylic, crayon, and oil stick
on paper
22¼ × 30 in. (56.52 × 76.2 cm)

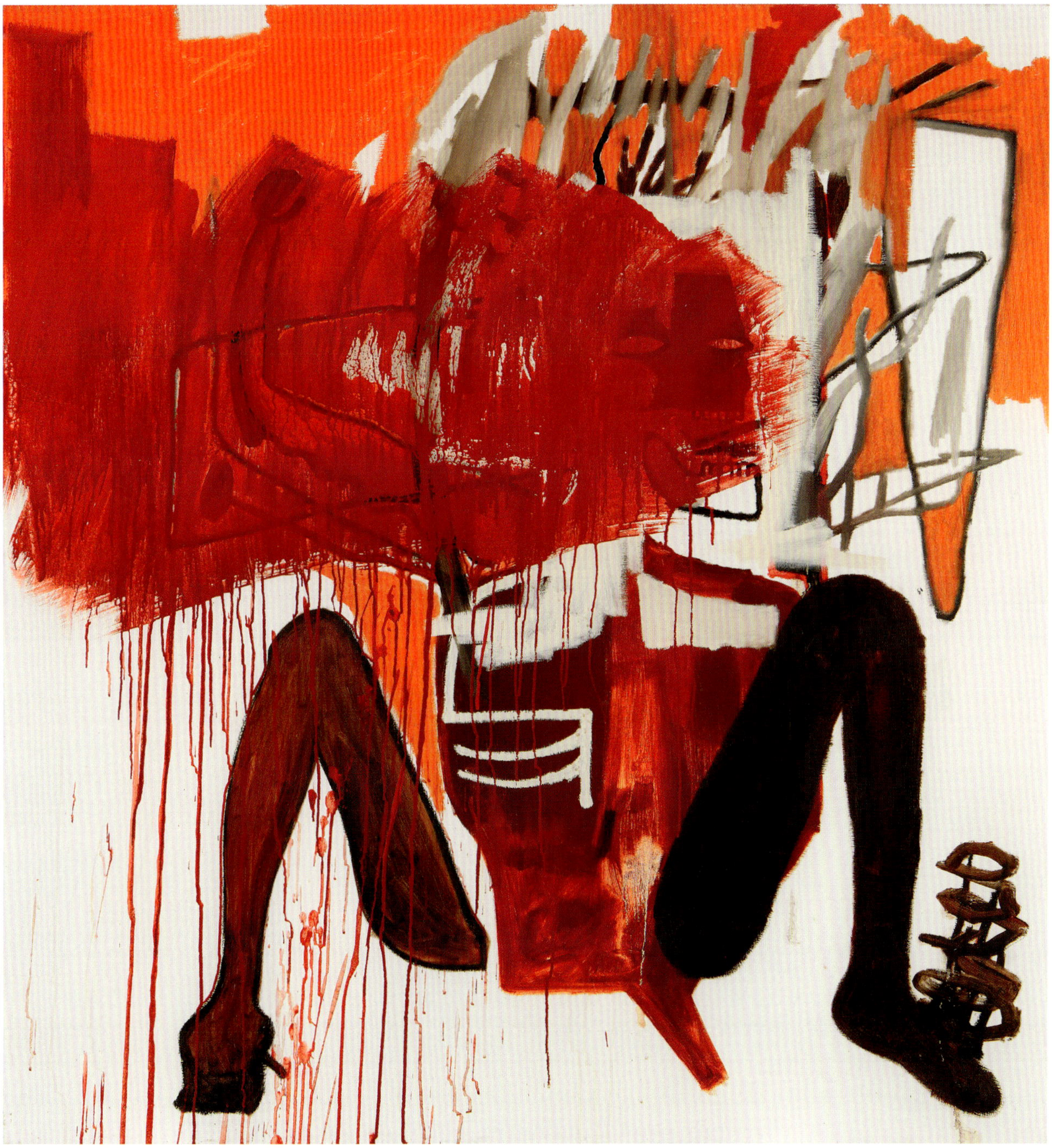

Untitled, 1984
Acrylic on canvas
65½ × 60 in. (166.37 × 152.4 cm)

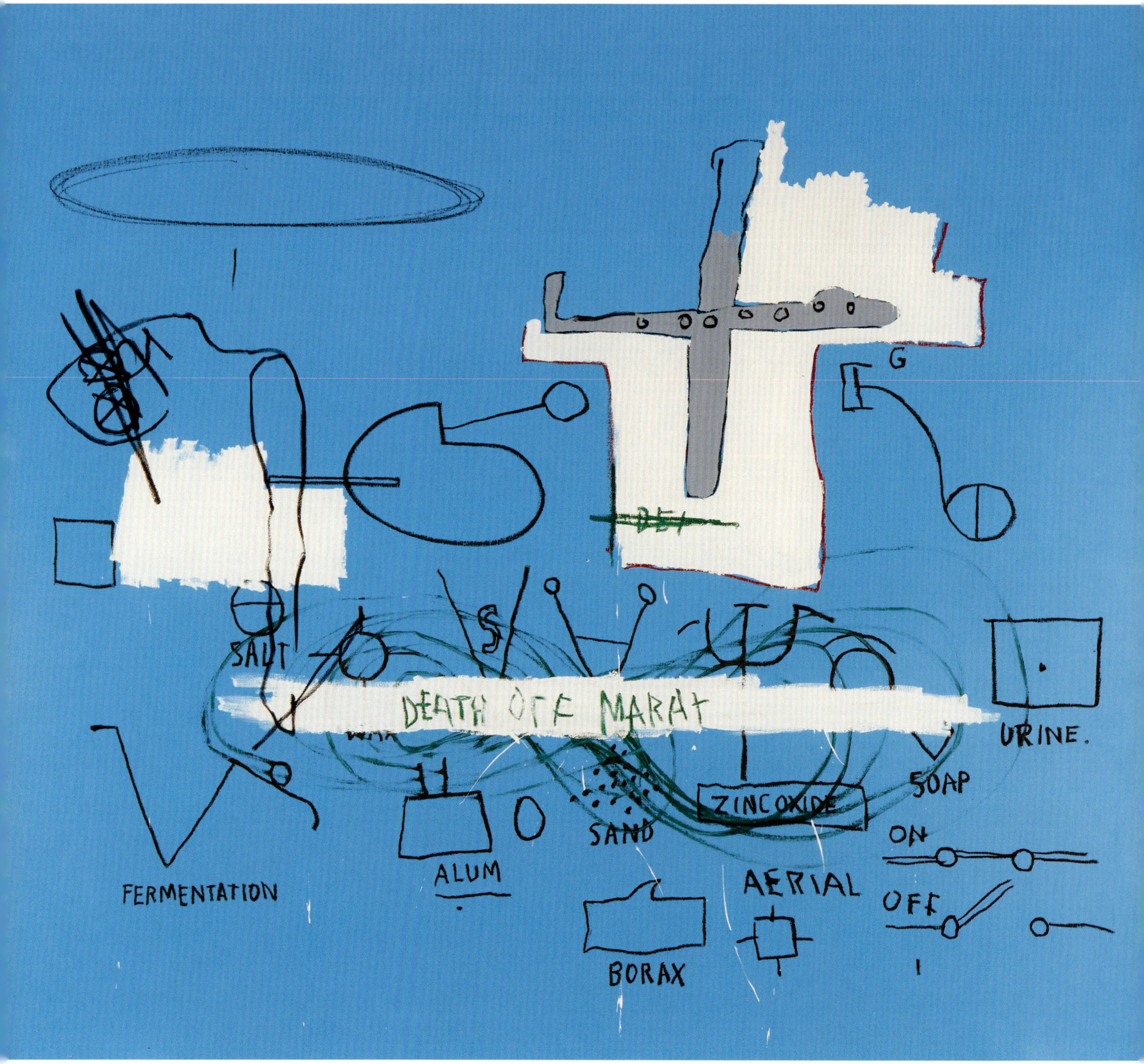

Kalik, 1988
Acrylic and oil stick on canvas
102 × 114 in. (259.08 × 289.56 cm)

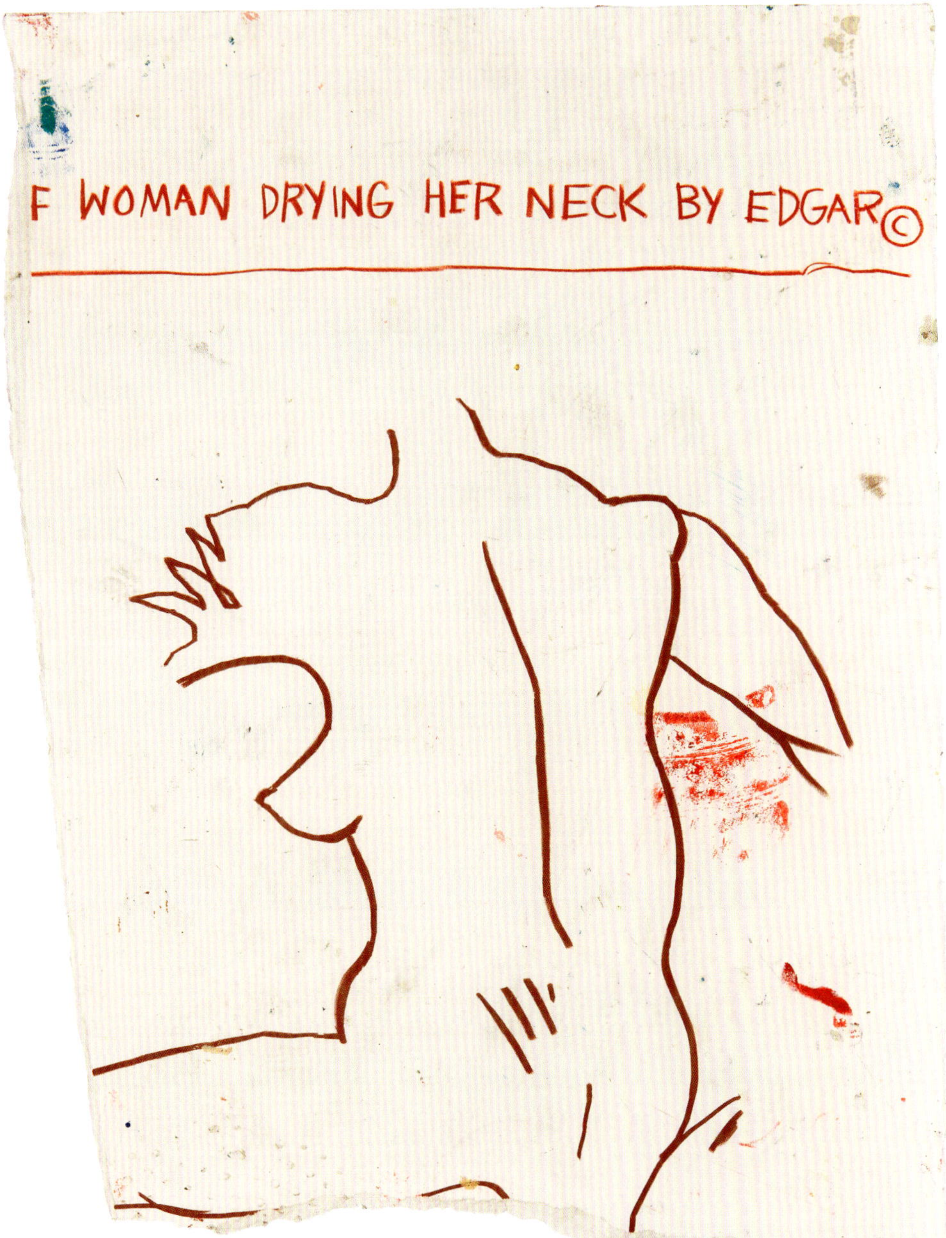

Untitled (Woman Drying Her Neck by Edgar), n.d.
Oil stick on paper
23 × 16 in. (58.42 × 40.64 cm)

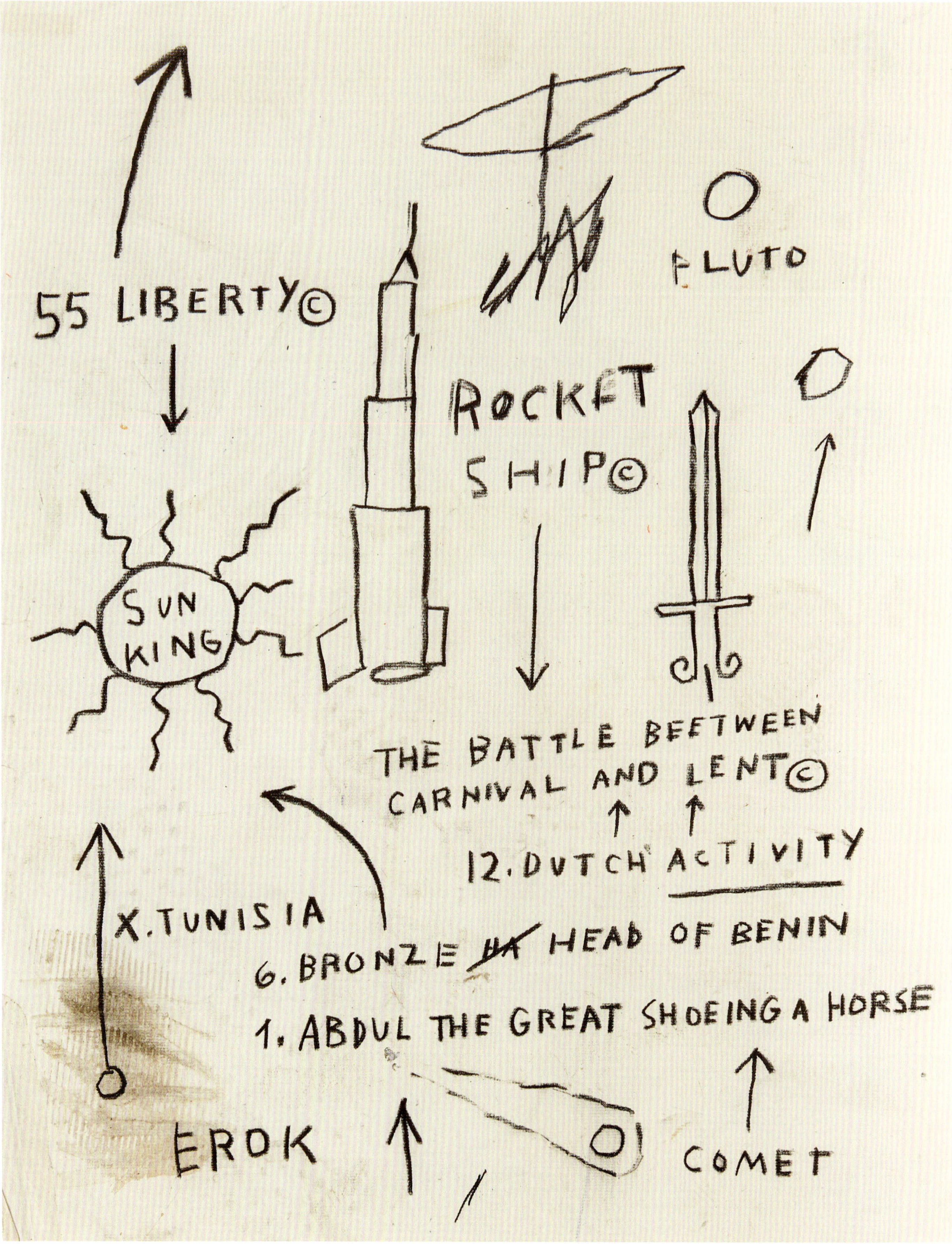
55 LIBERTY©
PLUTO
ROCKET
SHIP©
SUN
KING
THE BATTLE BEETWEEN
CARNIVAL AND LENT©
12. DUTCH ACTIVITY
X. TUNISIA
6. BRONZE ~~HA~~ HEAD OF BENIN
1. ABDUL THE GREAT SHOEING A HORSE
EROK
COMET

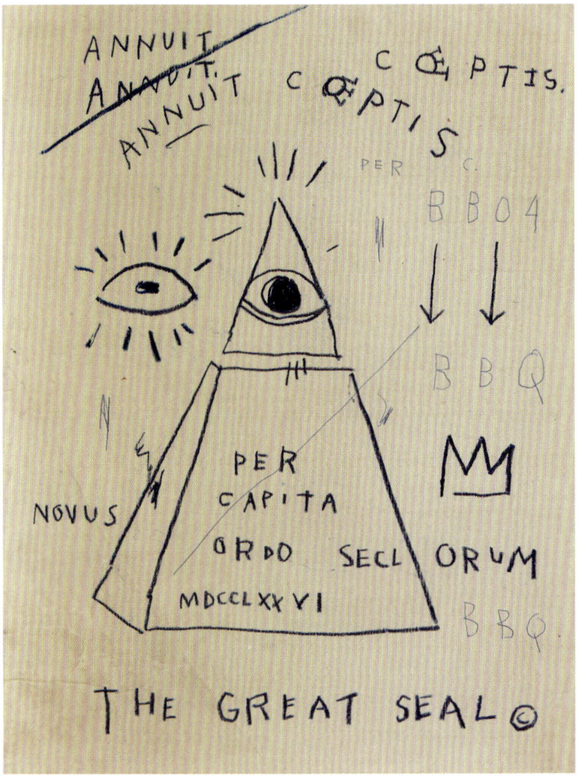

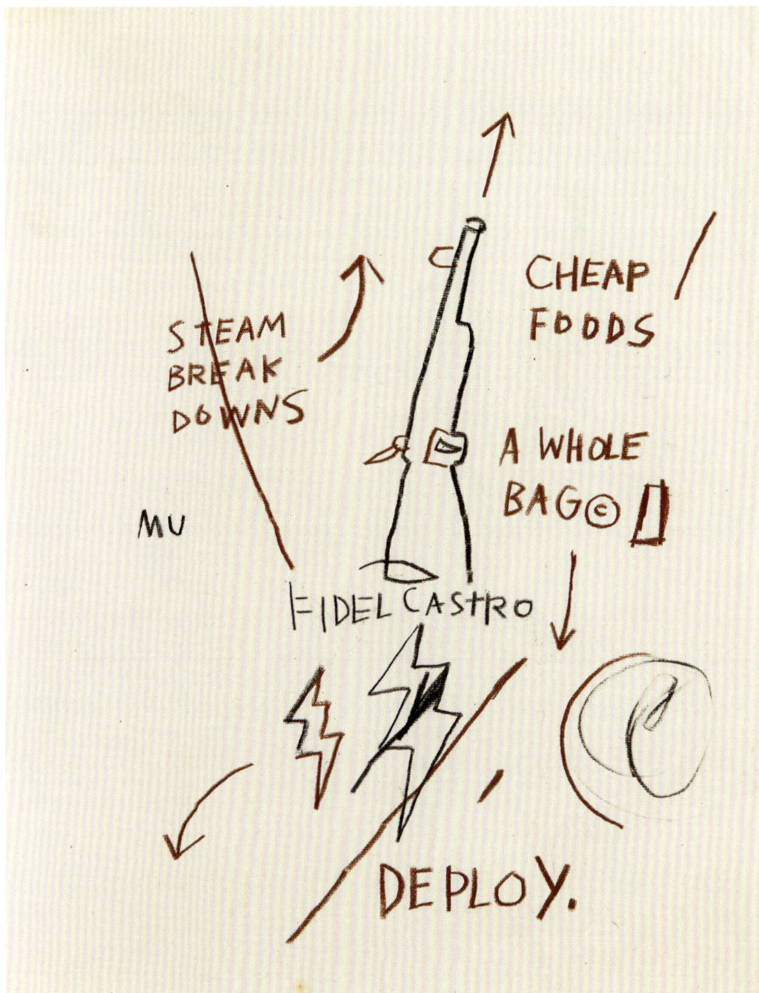

OPPOSITE
Untitled (55 Liberty), n.d.
Crayon on paper
26 × 18 in. (66.04 × 45.72 cm)

TOP
Untitled (Comics Code), n.d.
Oil stick on paper
26 × 19¼ in. (66.04 × 48.90 cm)

RIGHT
Untitled (A Whole Bag), n.d.
Oil stick on paper
24 × 18 in. (60.96 × 45.72 cm)

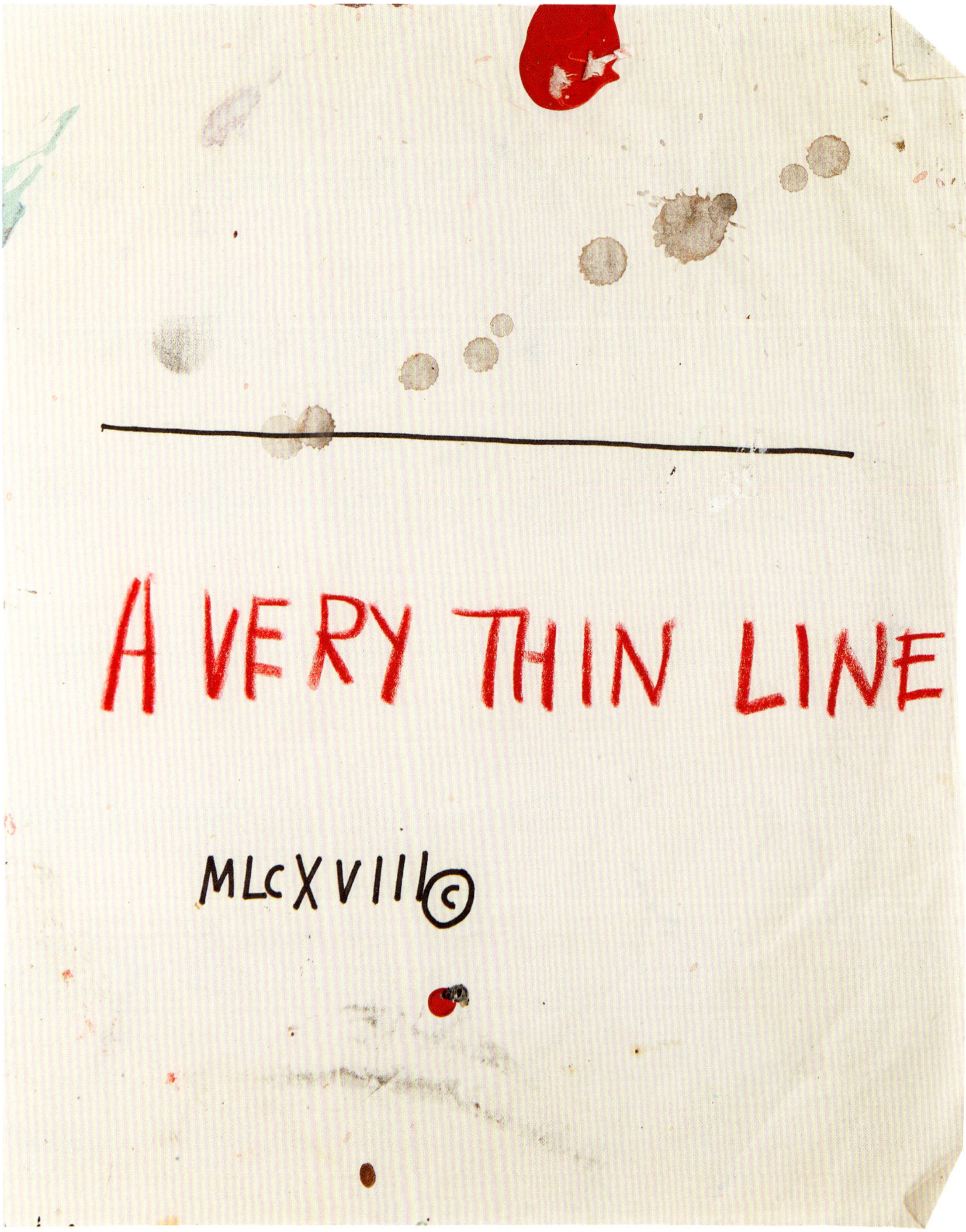

ABOVE
Untitled (A Very Thin Line), n.d.
Crayon and ink on paper
11 × 8½ in. (27.94 × 21.59 cm)

OPPOSITE
Untitled (Malcom X), n.d.
Oil stick on paper
24 × 18 in. (60.96 × 45.72 cm)

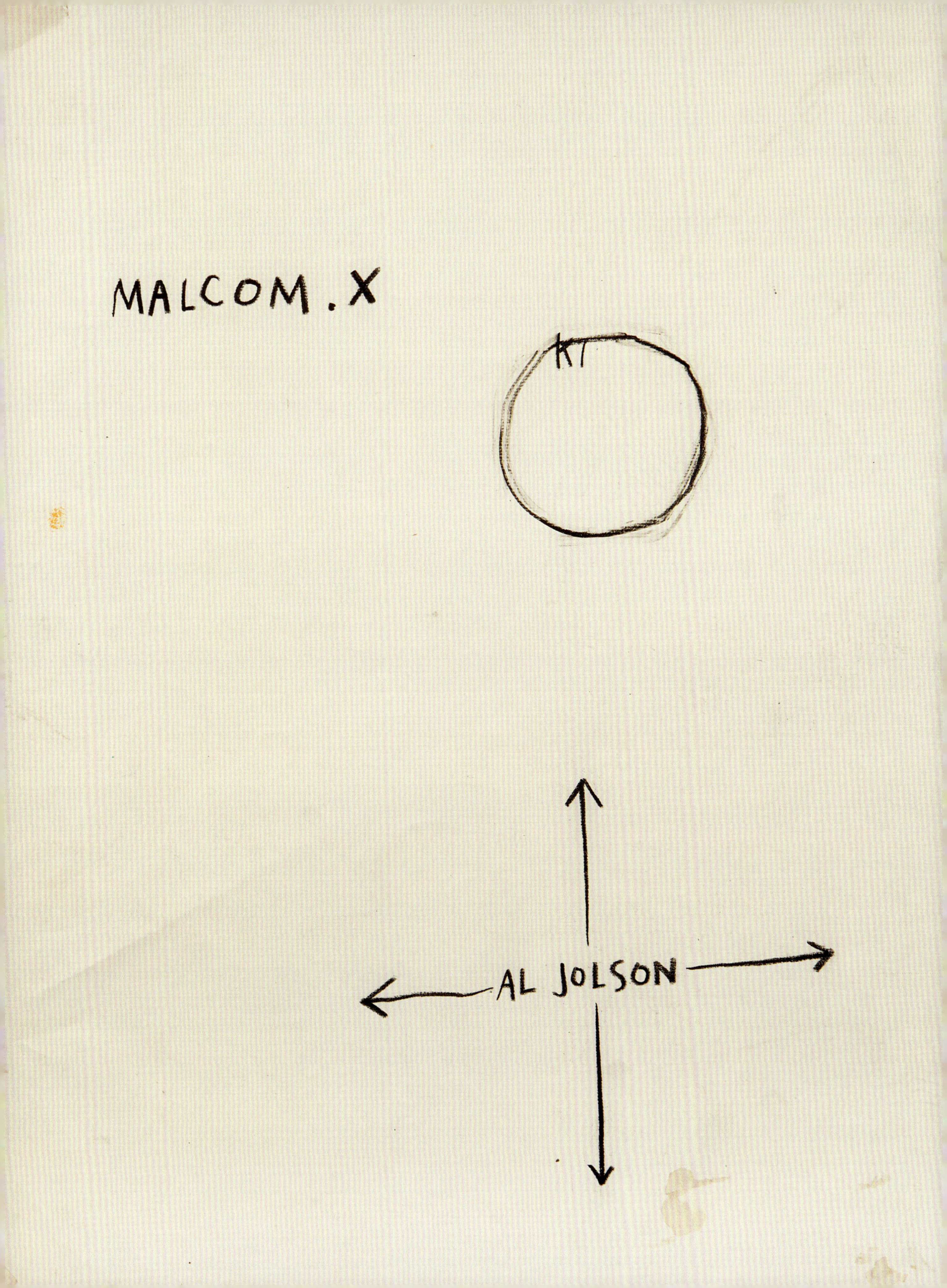
MALCOM .X
AL JOLSON

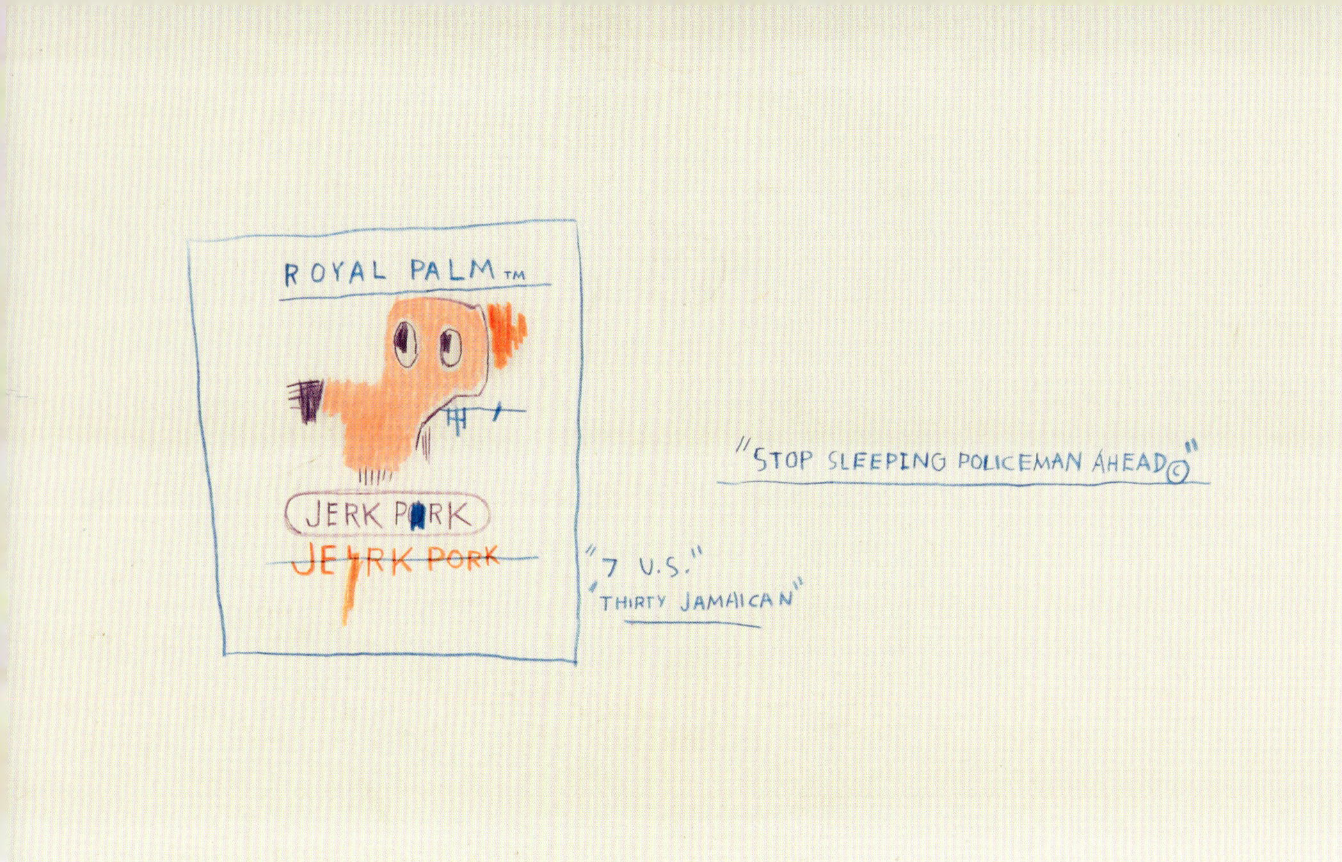

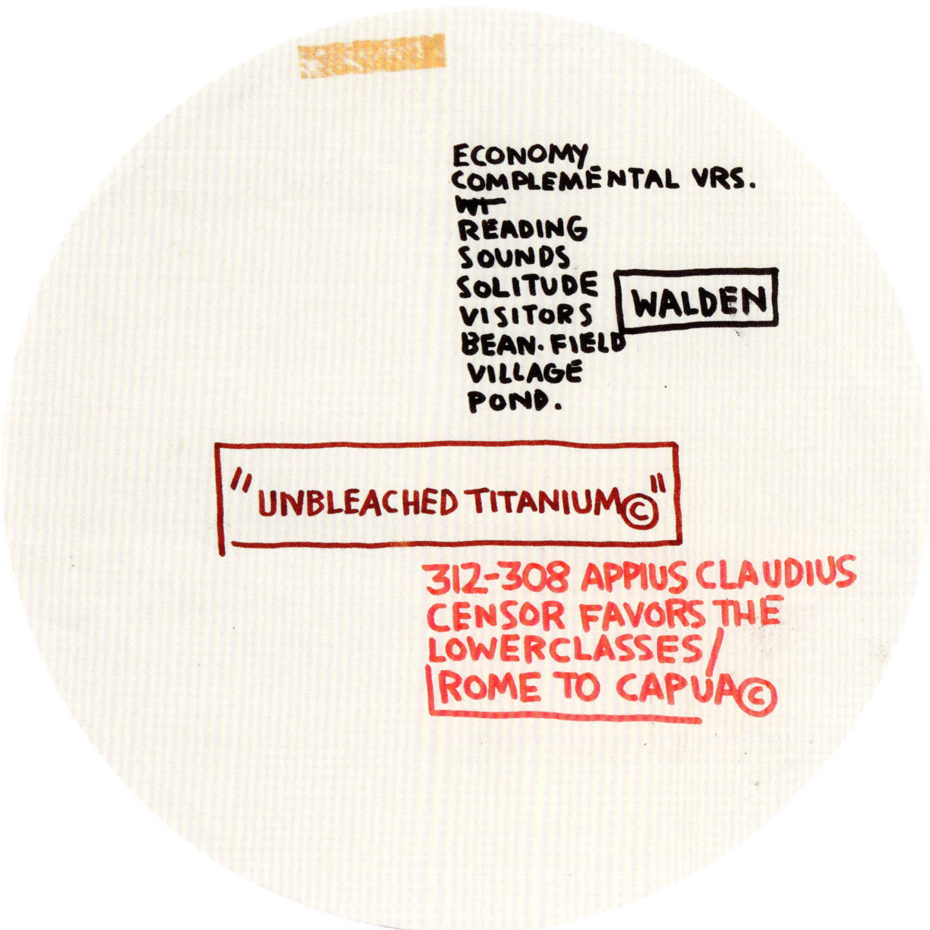

TOP
Untitled (Stop Sleeping Policeman Ahead), n.d.
Acrylic and crayon on paper
24 × 18 in. (60.96 × 45.72 cm)

LEFT
Untitled (Unbleached Titanium), n.d.
Ink on paper
Diameter 10¼ in. (26.04 cm)

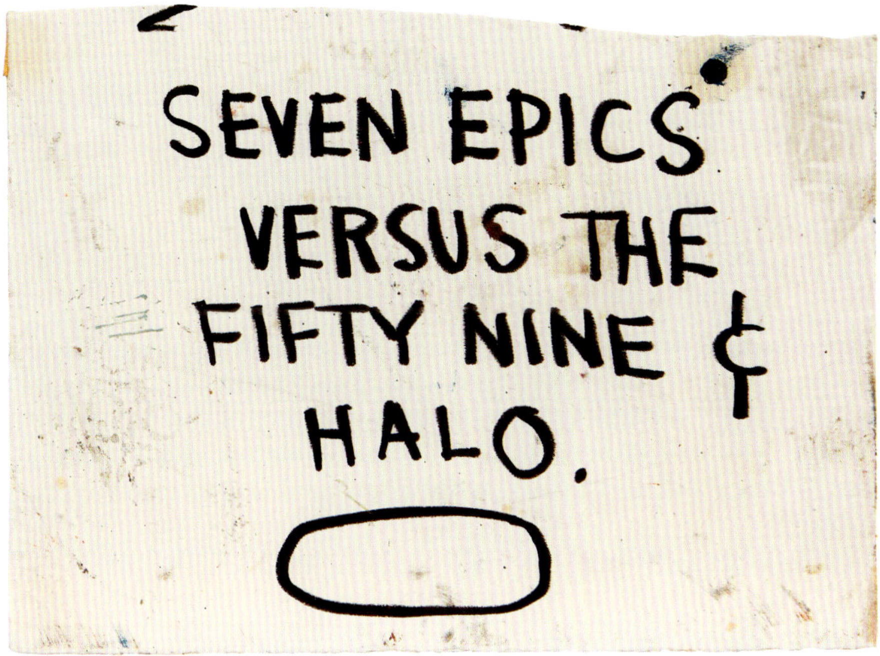

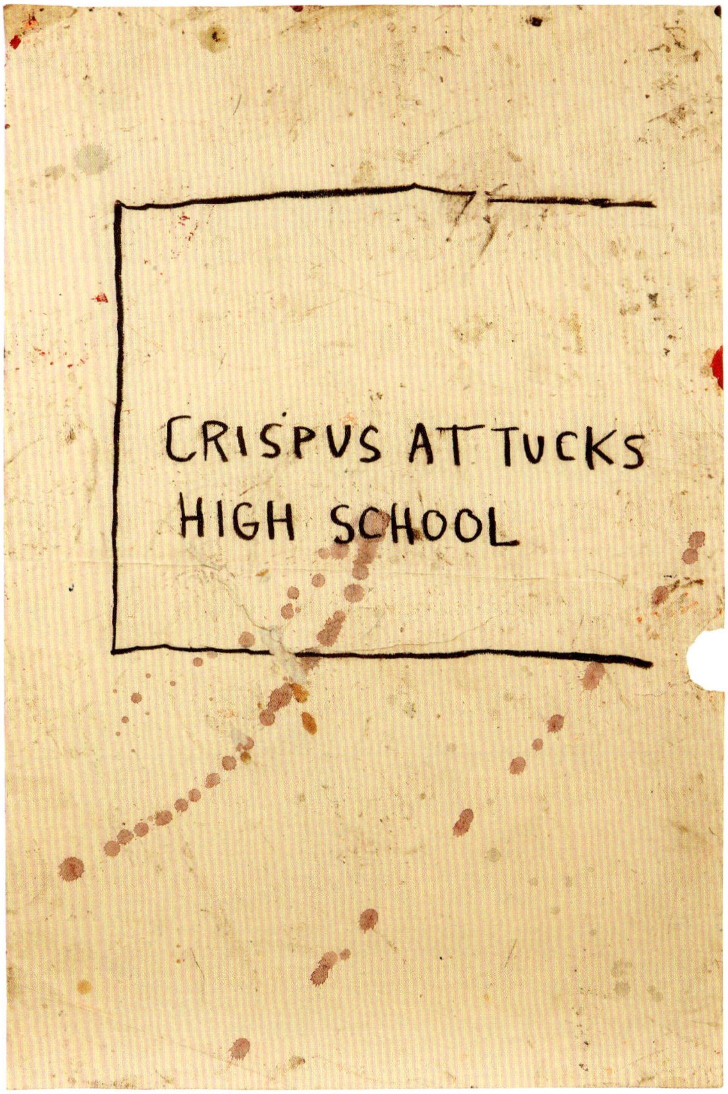

TOP
Untitled (Seven Epics), n.d.
Oil stick on paper
11 × 15 in. (27.94 × 38.1 cm)

LEFT
Crispus Attucks High School, n.d.
Oil stick on paper
40 × 26 in. (101.6 × 66.04 cm)

So much of what Jean-Michel created was both social study and subjective exploration. *Irony of Negro Policeman,* one of Jean-Michel's earliest and most important works, was painted in 1981. It remains as relevant today as it was forty years ago, as do works featured here addressing similar issues, such as *Jailbirds* (1983; opposite) and *Untitled (Edgar)* (pages 270–71). We continue to witness how little the needle has moved and how even more chaotic, destructive, and intractable racism is. *Irony of Negro Policeman* speaks as much to police brutality as it does to the ways that those who are underrepresented turn on each other to attempt to elevate their station in life. *Untitled (Edgar)* references *Four Studies of a Male Head*, an oil painting by Peter Paul Rubens from 1600 exploring the facial expressions of African men. In that work, Jean-Michel foregrounds the objectification of a Black man using part of his own birthdate (Jean-Michel was born on December 22, 1960) in the context of his identification within this culture as a "ARBLCKML2260," which is a numbering convention similar to those used to identify prisoners.

People often ask members of our family to opine on what Jean-Michel may have thought about certain topics, but one only needs to go to his work—Jean-Michel speaks quite clearly and loudly for himself. LISANE

IRONY OF NEGRO POLICEMAN

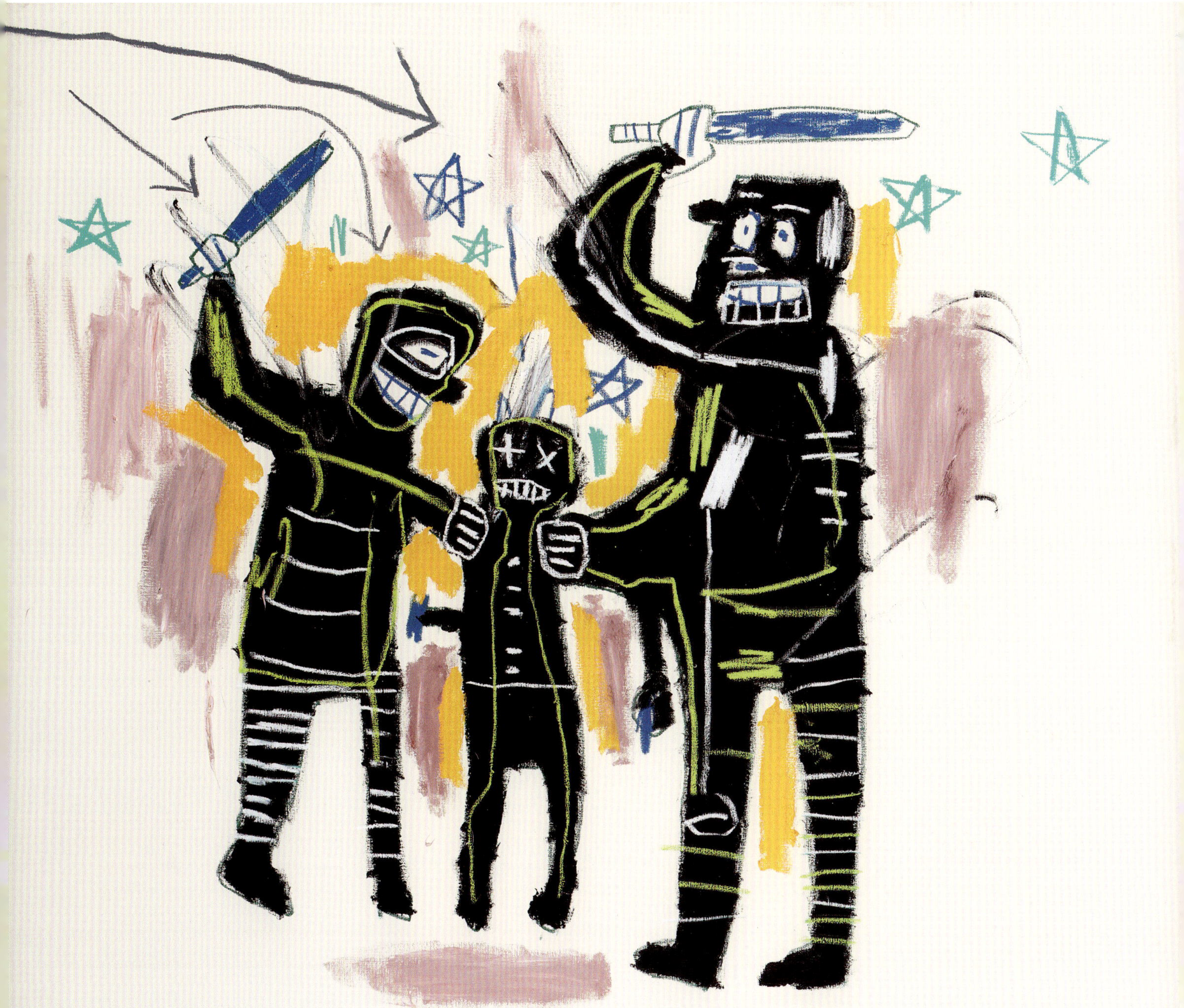

Jailbirds, 1983
Acrylic and oil stick on canvas
65 × 90½ in. (165.1 × 229.87 cm)

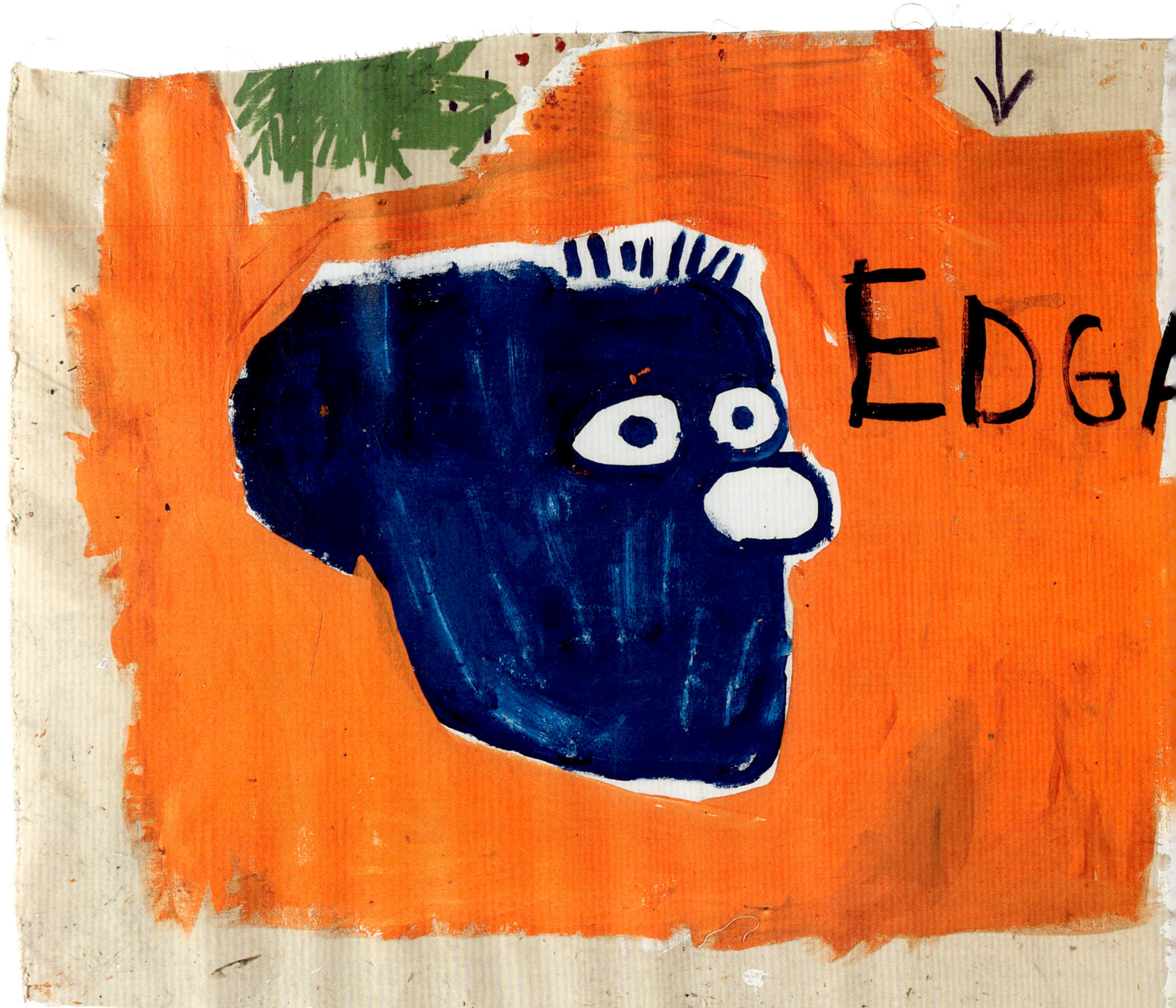
EDGA

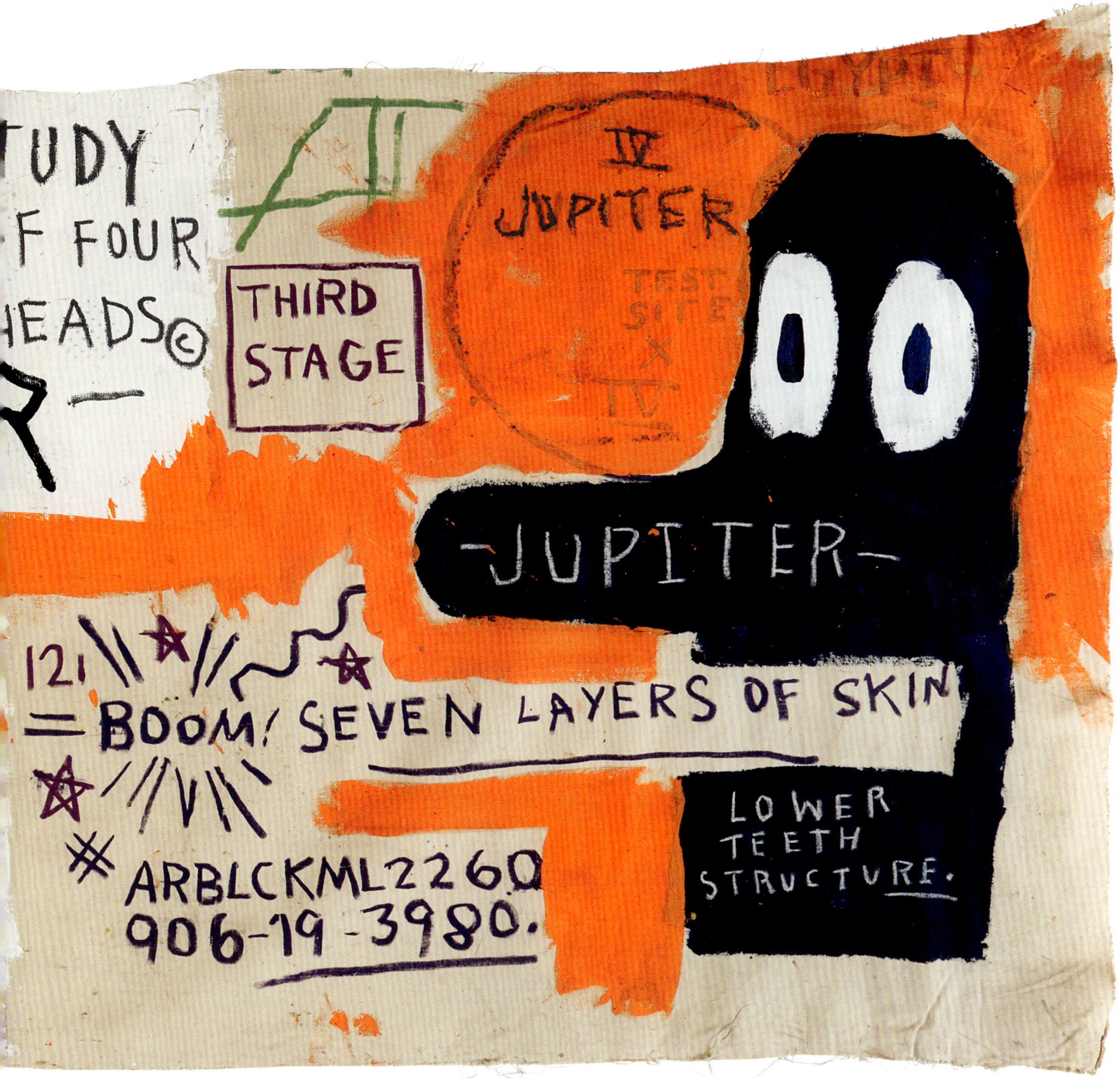

Untitled (Edgar), n.d.
Acrylic and oil stick on canvas
42 × 92 in. (106.68 × 233.68 cm)

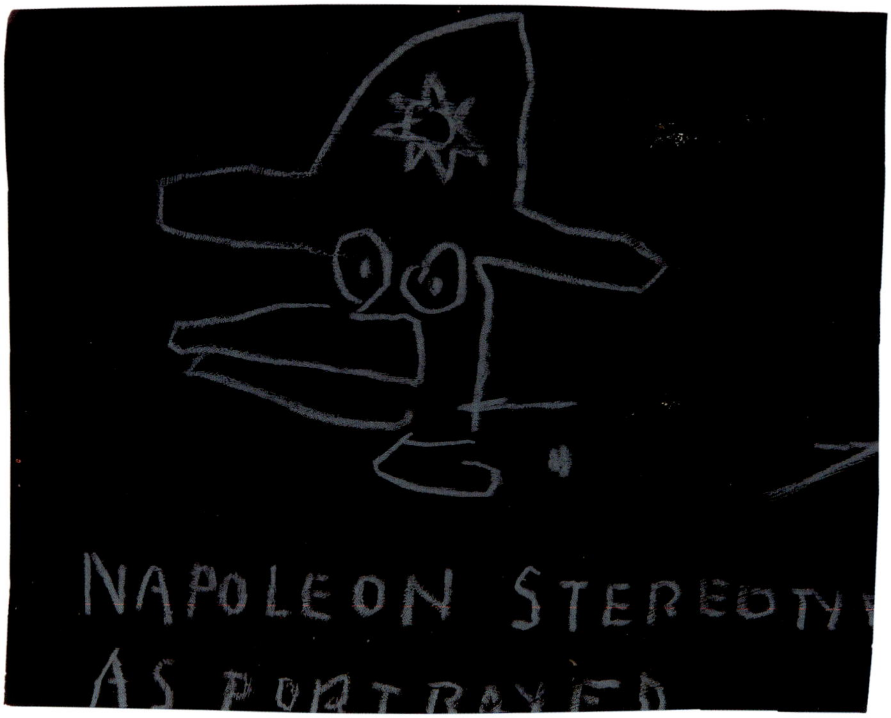

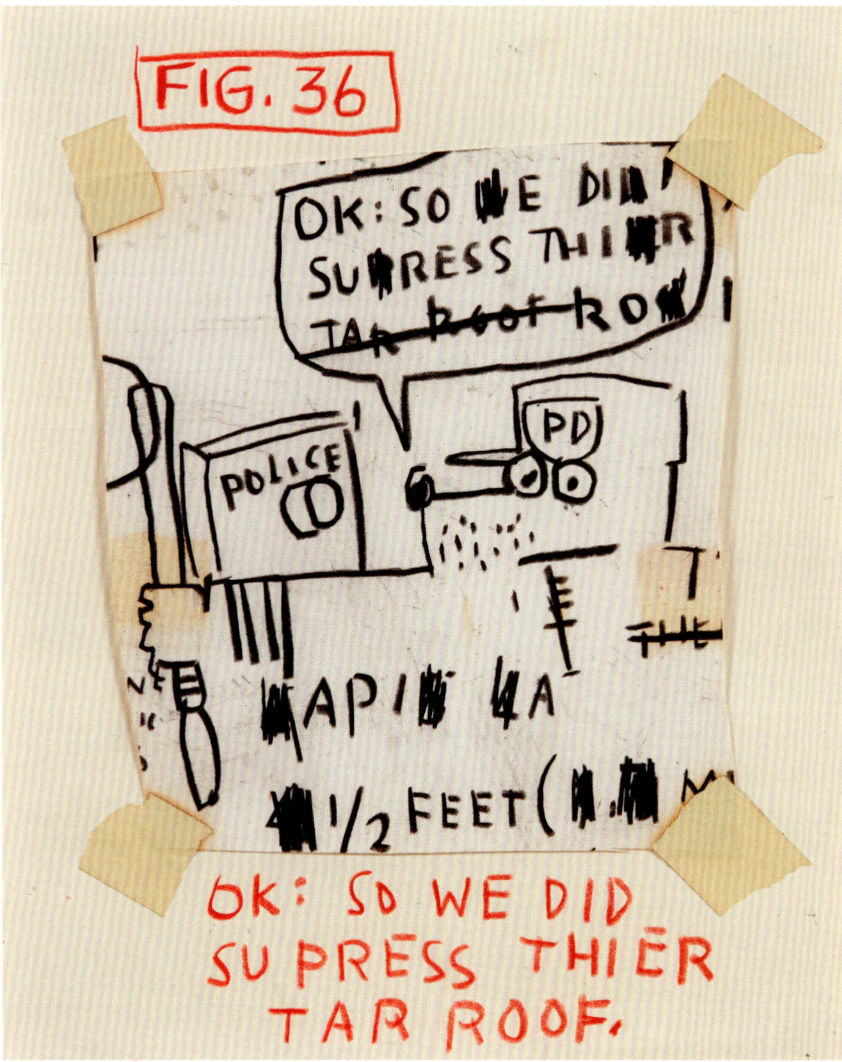

TOP
Untitled (Napoleon), n.d.
Acrylic and oil stick on paper
8¼ × 10 in. (20.96 × 25.4 cm)

LEFT
Untitled, n.d.
Crayon, masking tape, and
oil stick with collage on paper
10½ × 8½ in. (26.67 × 21.59 cm)

OPPOSITE
Untitled (Snakes), n.d.
Crayon, masking tape, and
oil stick with collage on paper
10½ × 8½ in. (26.67 × 21.59 cm)

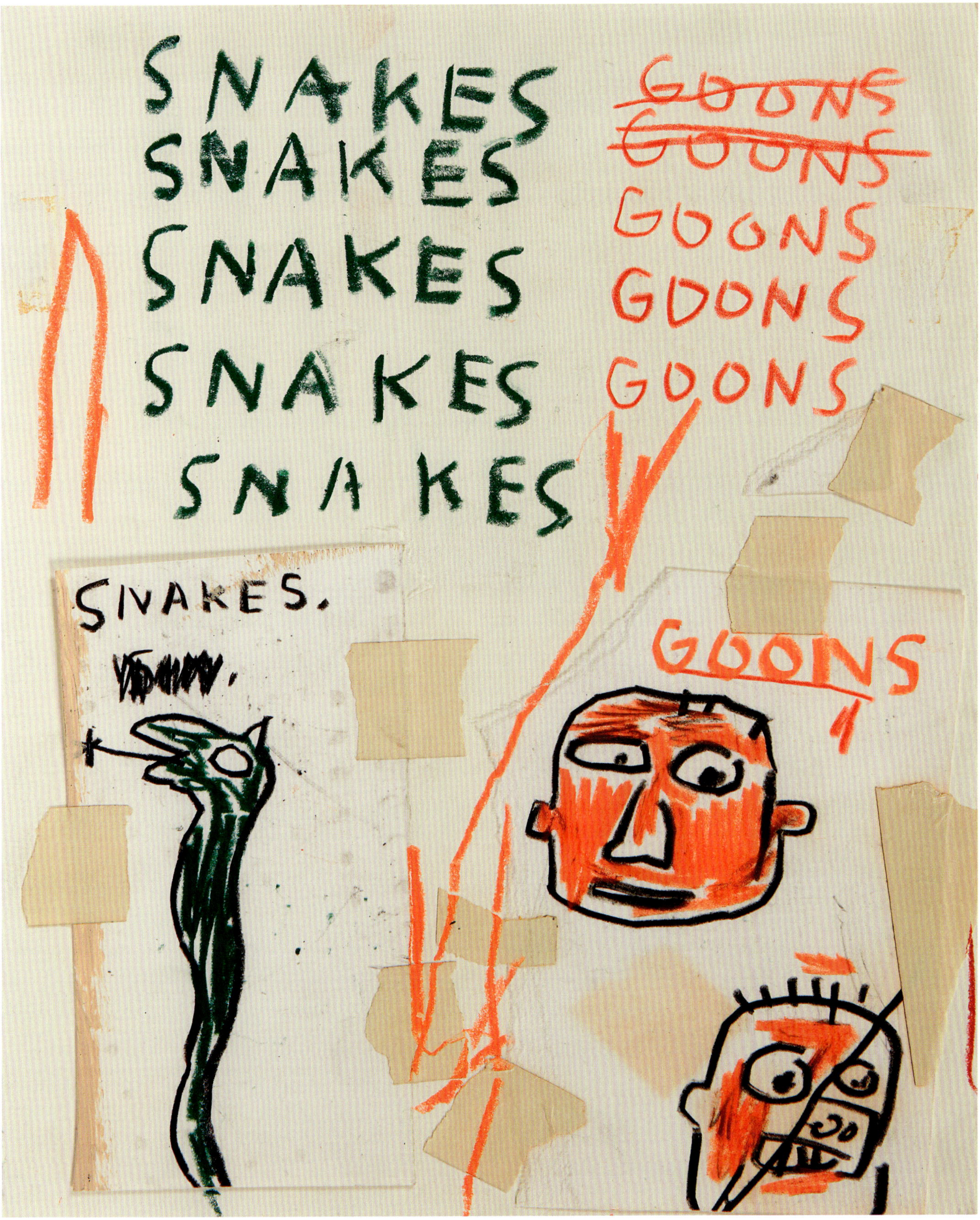
SNAKES
SNAKES
SNAKES
SNAKES
SNAKES
GOONS
GOONS
GOONS
GOONS
GOONS
SNAKES.
GOONS

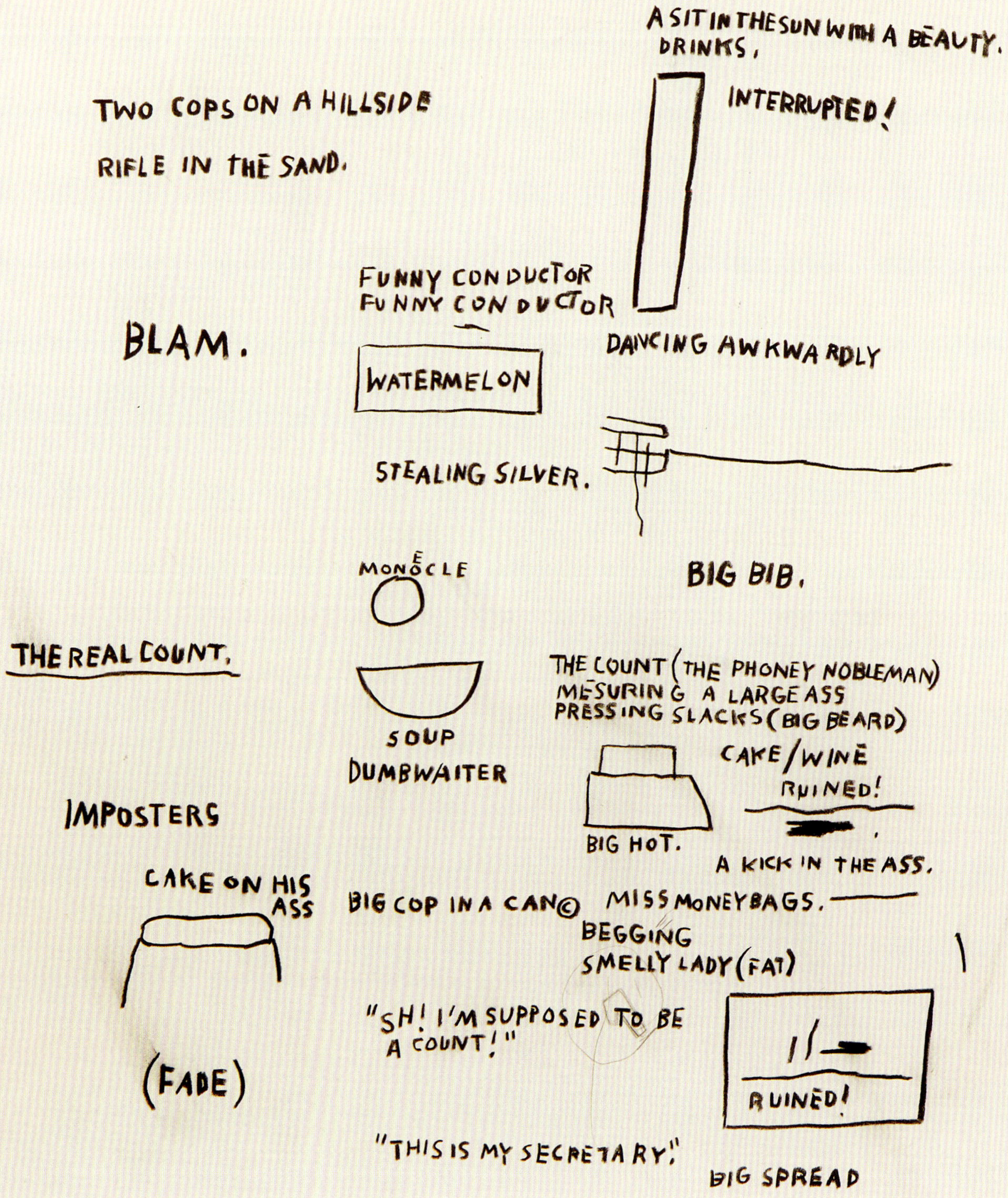
A SIT IN THE SUN WITH A BEAUTY.
DRINKS.
TWO COPS ON A HILLSIDE
RIFLE IN THE SAND.
INTERRUPTED!
FUNNY CONDUCTOR
FUNNY CONDUCTOR
BLAM.
WATERMELON
DANCING AWKWARDLY
STEALING SILVER.
MONOECLE
BIG BIB.
THE REAL COUNT.
THE COUNT (THE PHONEY NOBLEMAN)
MESURING A LARGE ASS
PRESSING SLACKS (BIG BEARD)
SOUP
DUMBWAITER
CAKE/WINE
RUINED!
IMPOSTERS
BIG HOT.
A KICK IN THE ASS.
CAKE ON HIS ASS
BIG COP IN A CAN©
MISS MONEYBAGS.
BEGGING
SMELLY LADY (FAT)
"SH! I'M SUPPOSED TO BE A COUNT!"
RUINED!
(FADE)
"THIS IS MY SECRETARY."
BIG SPREAD

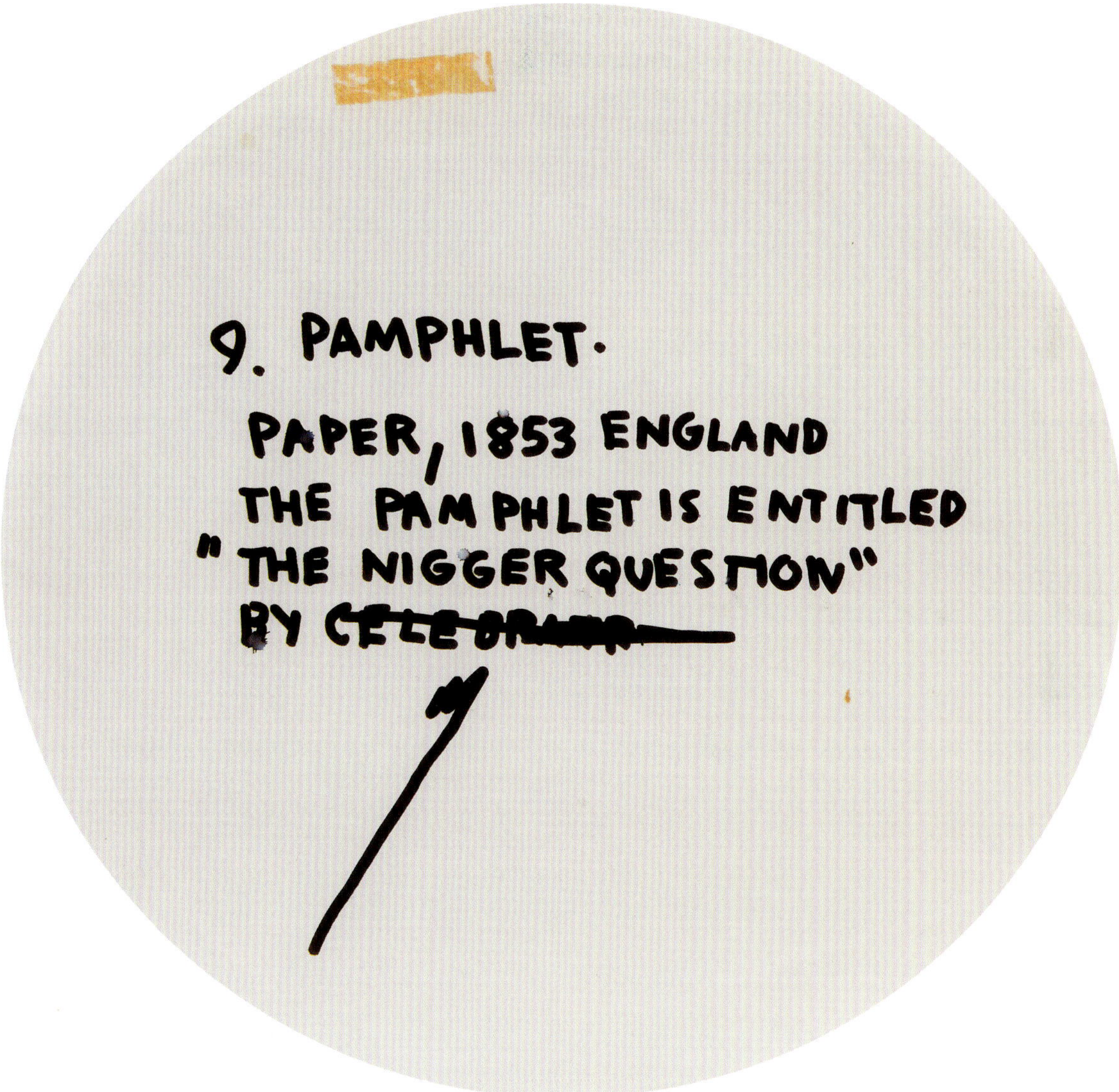

OPPOSITE
Untitled (Blam), n.d.
Crayon on paper
29½ × 42 in. (74.93 × 106.68 cm)

ABOVE
Untitled (Pamphlet), n.d.
Ink on paper
Diameter 10⅜ in. (26.35 cm)

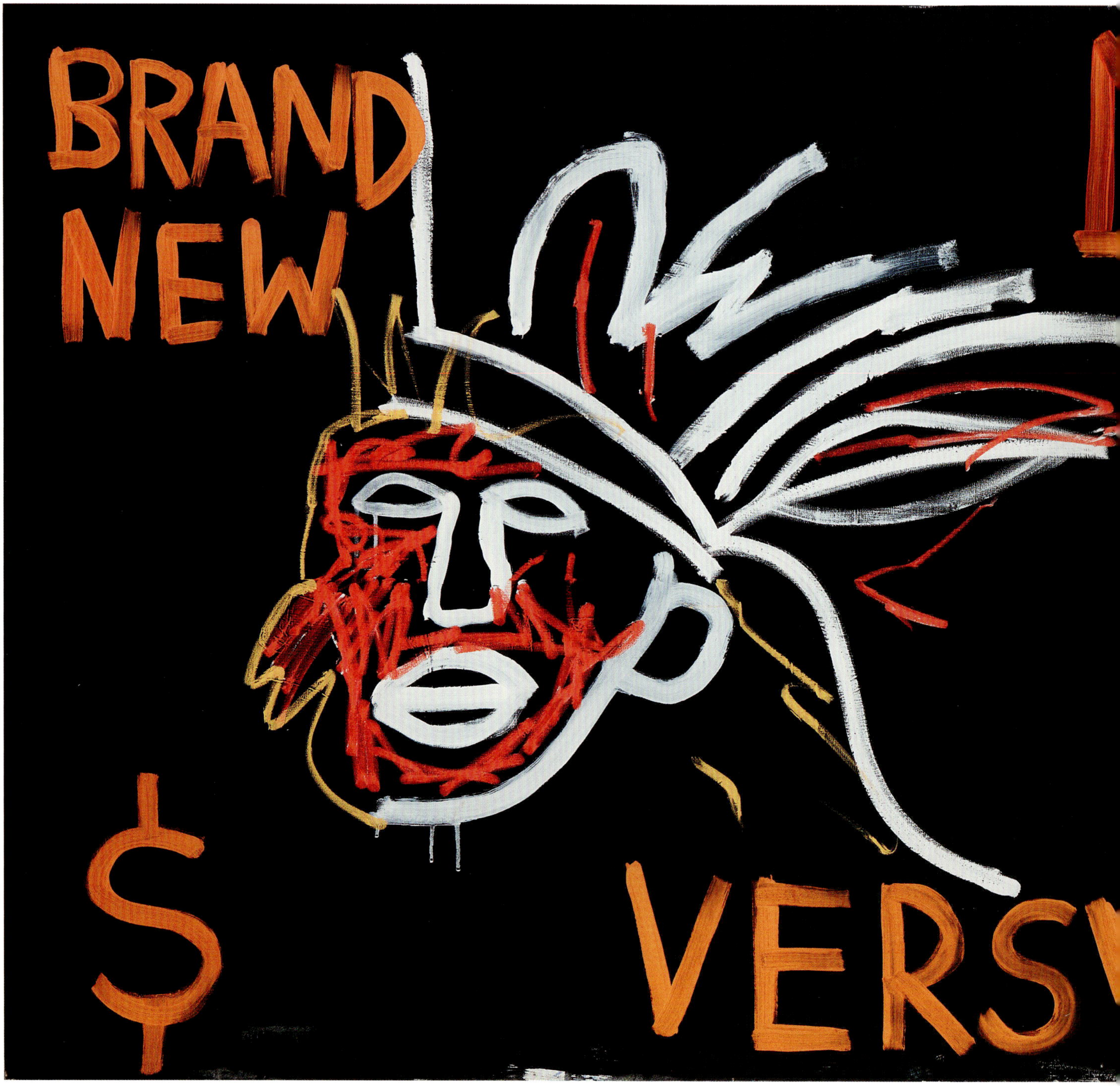
BRAND
NEW
$
VERS

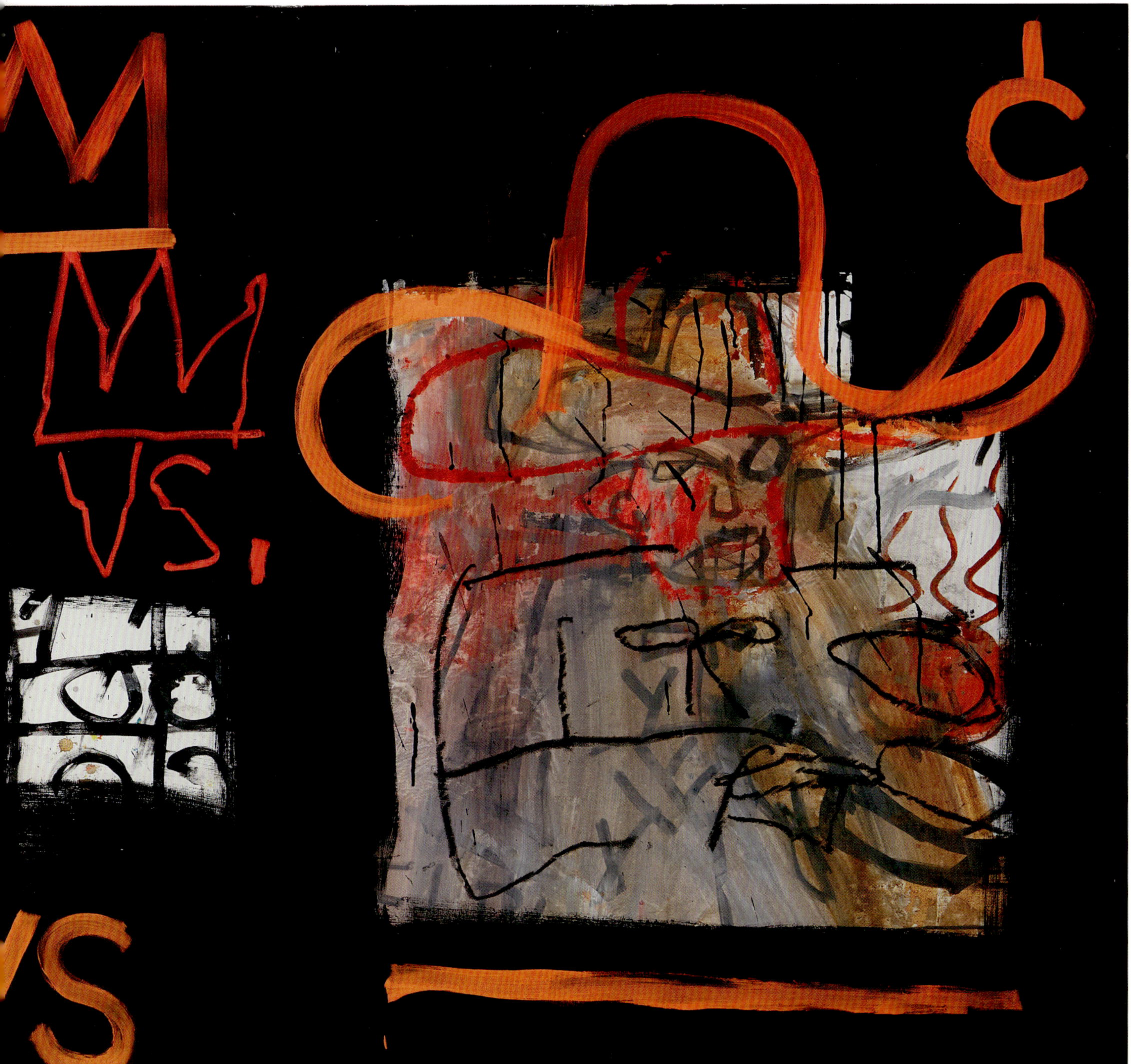

Untitled (Cowboy and Indian), 1982
Acrylic and oil stick on canvas
50 × 105 in. (127 × 266.7 cm)

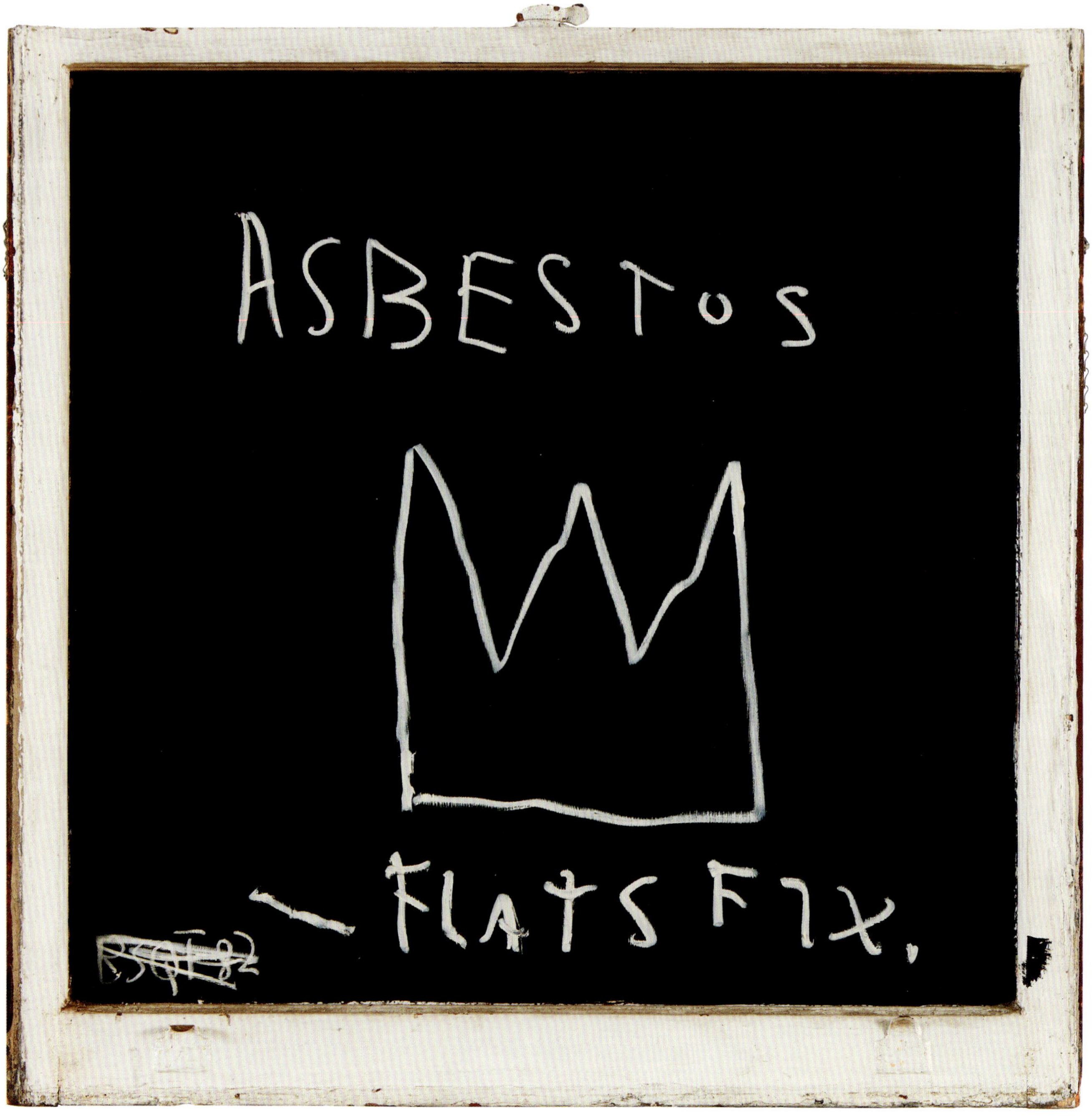

Untitled (Asbestos Flats Fix), 1982
Acrylic on glass in window frame
35 × 33½ in. (88.9 × 85.09 cm)

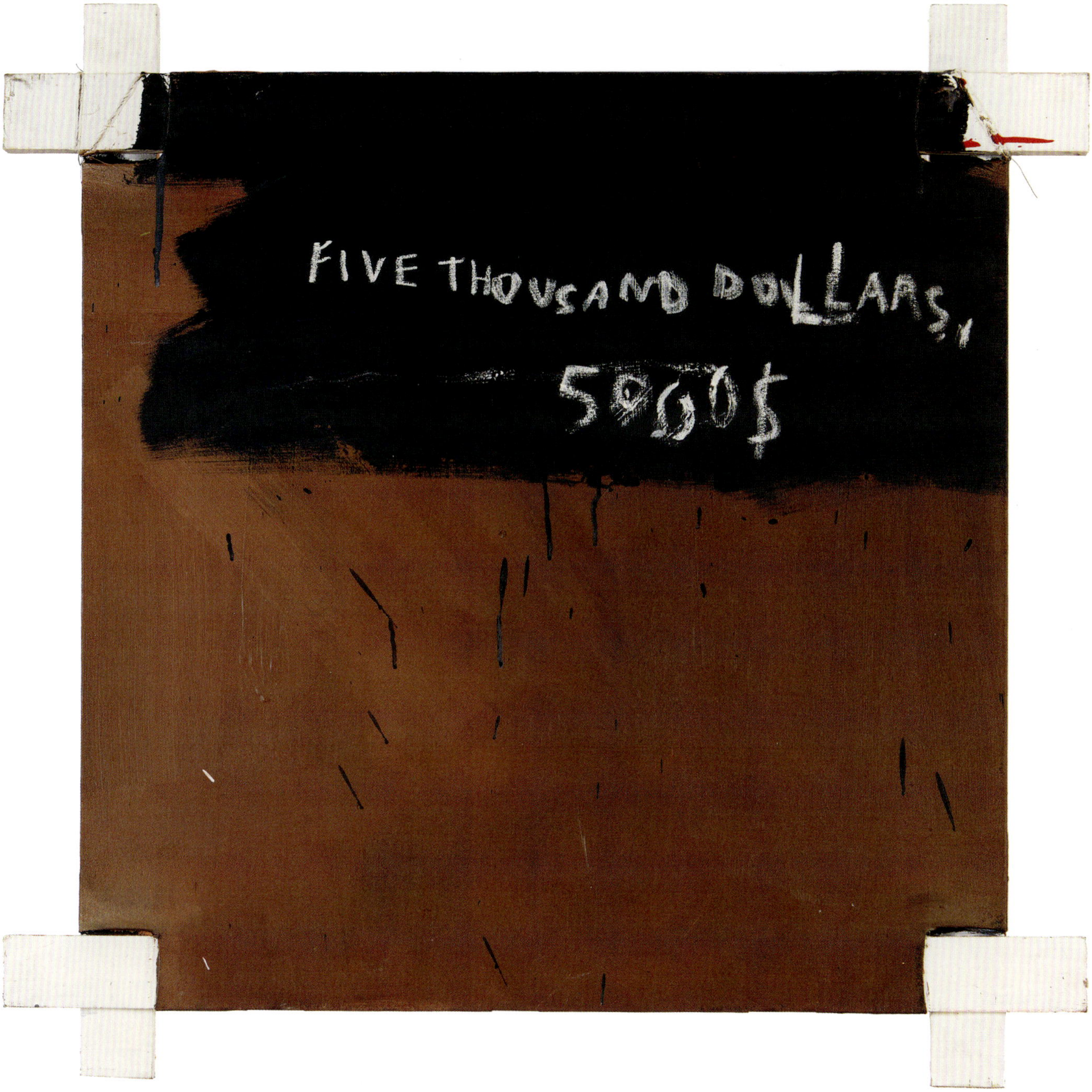

Untitled (Five Thousand Dollars), 1982
Acrylic and oil stick on canvas with wood supports
37 × 35¾ in. (93.98 × 90.81 cm)

JEAN-MICHEL'S PASSING

In his interview with Henry Geldzahler in 1983, the curator asked Jean-Michel, "If it was your last day on earth, what would you do?" And he responded, "I'd hang out with my mom and my girlfriend." This quote has stayed seared in my memory since his death.

The last two years of Jean-Michel's life were difficult, and it seemed clear he was going through a depression. We spoke and I visited him, but it was definitely more infrequent.

My brother was always aware of his Blackness as he navigated New York City, whether being racially profiled or chastised for how he dressed or wore his hair. He always had a hard time catching a cab as a Black man, so he resorted to riding a bike to get around the city. All of it wore him down.

I was 21 when Jean-Michel passed away. I'll never forget it—it was a Friday night. I was driving home from Lisane's apartment. My phone was ringing as I was walking in the door. My dad was on the line, "He's gone." "What?" "Jean-Michel, he's gone. He's dead." I can still hear myself screaming. I barely heard my father, but he said Jean-Michel had overdosed. That was the first death I had experienced of a close relative. It devastated me.

I went back to Lisane's house to decide how we were going to tell our mother. And at three in the morning, we woke her to say her son was gone.

Immediately after Jean-Michel died, my dad stepped in and took care of the funeral, emptied his apartment, met with attorneys, created the estate, and began his education: How to manage an artist's estate 101. JEANINE

MAMI

Our mother lost her son, and it was unimaginably painful for her. So much so that, in the beginning, she helped herself through the pain by imagining that Jean-Michel was simply away traveling. She never fully got over his death. What mother could? We talked about him often—we talked about him as a son and a brother, not as Jean-Michel the Artist. Years later, she started a journal that she wanted everyone in the family to contribute to. It was very important to her that we all remembered Jean-Michel and that our memories of him didn't get lost in the world's vision of him as an artist. This exhibition and book are a way of fulfilling and honoring her desire to keep our memories of him grounded in who he was to us. LISANE

My mother was deeply saddened by Jean-Michel's death. I don't think she ever got over it, and when it was her time, she was ready to go be with her son. As a parent, I can't imagine losing a child so young. We were all really thrown and didn't know how to process it. JEANINE

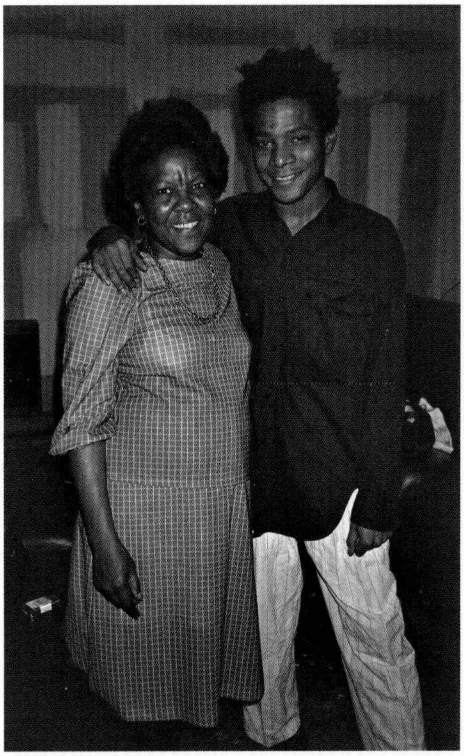

Matilde and Jean-Michel in his studio, June 1986

Jean-Michel's passing was surreal and shocking. It had been a few months since I'd seen him in person. I was a young mother living on my own at the time, and he was really enmeshed in his career and life as well. We spoke a few days before he died. He didn't sound like himself.

Jean-Michel was really struggling with things in his own life. He was grieving the loss of Andy. He was lonely, depressed, overwhelmed, and isolated. He just wasn't in a good place and couldn't get himself out of it. He was in pain.

Over the years, I've seen this kind of thing happen to men in their late twenties, where they start to consider these larger existential questions about who they are and why they're here and what matters. I know of many men at that age who go through this kind of funk unless they've developed some coping skills previously to help temper those feelings of uncertainty. Jean-Michel was starting to see the rewards of pursuing his dream and fulfilling the promise of his artistic gifts. Financially, he could see that the door had opened. He was sought after. He was traveling the world. He was able to give and share with others, which he loved because he was an extremely generous person. Yet there was still this emptiness, because he still had these unanswered questions about his life in spite of the accolades, the money, the attention, the friendships, the women. For him, there were still nagging questions: "What is all of this? Why haven't I resolved my childhood? What am I doing?" And then he loses Andy. He was experiencing uncertainty on top of grief, on top of loss, on top of isolation. It was a lot. There is a lesson in this. LISANE

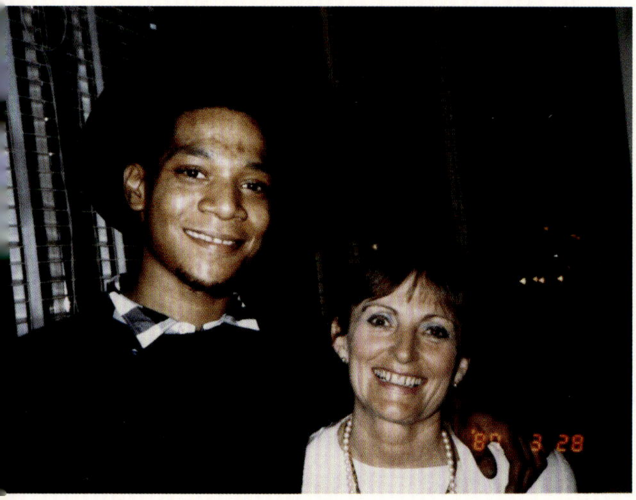

Jean-Michel and Nora at The Odeon, New York, 1987
PHOTO: GERARD BASQUIAT

It happened on a Friday. We used to go up to the country on Friday night after work, Gerard and I, and we went home to Brooklyn first to pick up the dog. I went into the house. Gerard stayed outside in the car because we couldn't park. When I was in the house, the phone rang. I almost didn't pick it up. It was a policeman at Jean-Michel's apartment calling to advise us. So, we went to Jean-Michel's apartment and there was already a crowd there. Jean-Michel had been taken to the hospital. I don't remember the exact details of whether he died immediately or whether he died in the hospital. But shortly afterward, we had to go to the medical examiner's office to identify the body. Gerard could not do it, so I did.

We had to vacate the apartment on Great Jones Street. The landlords wanted it as quickly as possible. The paintings were put into a warehouse, as well as the furniture, much of which was rented. NORA

PAPA

Jean-Michel's death was devastating for my father. No parent expects their child to pass away. Things moved so quickly in both his and Jean-Michel's lives but they were in the process of building a more adult relationship. Our father learned how to raise a son in a different country just as Jean-Michel learned how to fight for his dreams. They both fought for what they believed in and were getting to a place of better understanding and mutual respect—adult man to adult man. That journey was cut short, and for that and so many other reasons, our father never fully recovered from Jean-Michel's death. He lived and breathed it for the remainder of his life. LISANE

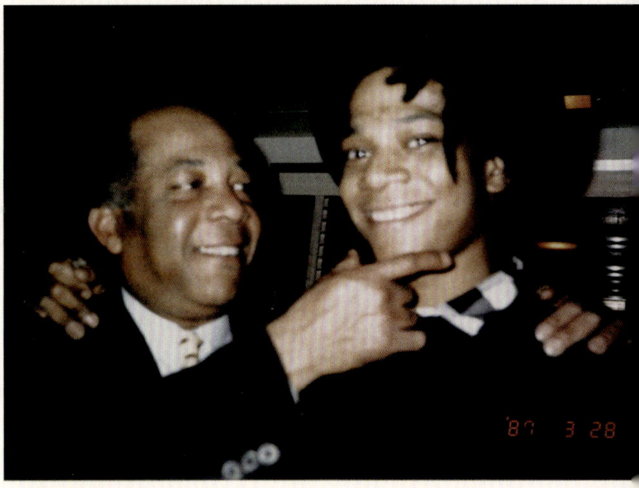

Gerard and Jean-Michel at The Odeon, New York, 1987
PHOTO: NORA FITZPATRICK

OUR FAMILY

Our parents hadn't been together for decades by the time Jean-Michel passed away, and for the remainder of their lives they both lived with a hole in their hearts from the loss of their son. No matter their personal relationship, Gerard and Matilde were 100 percent committed to us, their children. They saw the three of us as their full responsibility and both honored that role with all they had and with what they knew. They did so while they were together and continued that commitment after they separated. Each of them made incredible sacrifices, imparted values that we continue to benefit from, and neither shied away from making decisions they believed were in our best interests, even when they were tough.

When Jean-Michel passed away, time stopped for our family in some way. Our parents were completely blindsided by the loss of a son who never even reached the age of thirty. And we were unprepared for the horrific tragedy that surrounded his death. We stagnated as a family because once he passed away there was no possibility of resolving anything in our relationships anymore. All that remained was this enormous void and the unrelenting grief.

My brother's death took its toll on our family—excruciating for all of us collectively and individually. We lost a part of ourselves when he left this earth. The world continues to be very excited about Jean-Michel. He was incredible, and we are so very proud of what he did and for the impact his life and work has had on popular culture and the art world. What is important for everyone to understand, though, is that he was a son, and a brother, and a grandson, and a nephew, and a cousin, and a friend. He was all of that in *addition* to being a groundbreaking artist. LISANE

EULOGY

AUGUST 17, 1988

For many of us who lived downtown about nine to ten years ago, Jean-Michel Basquiat was already a presence in our lives before we had ever met him or even knew who he was. As the street poet SAMO, his unsettling phrases, a kind of surreal version of advertising slogans, and his distinctive signature seemed to be everywhere. This secret person left his unforgettable mark outside every new club, on the walls of every building where interesting art could be seen, or where especially interesting people were living.

Jean-Michel already had such a distinctive vision, such a sure hand, even as a teenager, that he could just draw a few lines or a make a few marks on the wall with a Magic Marker, and these images, however spare, were unforgettable, and they were uniquely his. There are very few artists who had such a force of personality, who could express their whole aesthetic just by drawing a few lines.

When you met Jean-Michel you understood why that line and signature were so powerful. He was a personality unlike any other—a remarkable breadth, intelligence, passion, sympathy, generosity. He was a person with such charisma and strength of character that just his look, a few terse comments, a few lines drawn on paper, could communicate so much.

Somehow Jean-Michel had managed to intuitively absorb most of modern art history before he was twenty. His first publicly exhibited works caused a sensation and were immediately compared to those of some of the great modern artists. But Jean-Michel's statement was uniquely his own. He invented a vocabulary, a sense of composition, a new way to use the medium of painting that captured the intensity and the disjointed quality of today's urban reality. Jean-Michel's statement summed up what was happening on TV, in the galleries, and on the streets, churning the languages of modern and pre-modern art to encompass a totally contemporary vision.

Jean-Michel was an artist in the broadest sense—not just a great painter but a great poet. Not, of course, a poet in the stereotyped romantic mode—penning verse about rolling hills and romantic reveries—but presenting an arresting portrait of contemporary consciousness. In the future, I think that the literary qualities of Jean-Michel's work will be admired as much as the visual qualities. I don't know of any modern artist who has merged the verbal and visual so effectively.

Jean-Michel accomplished enough in ten years to earn a place as one of the great artists of our time. It is perhaps a little strange to describe a person who many of us in the art world knew so well in elevated, historical terms. But Jean-Michel really was a genius—someone with truly remarkable qualities on all levels. I'll never forget his remarkable memory. He could astonish me by recalling off-hand comments that I had made four years before.

Jean-Michel was an extraordinary person not only for his remarkable talent and accomplishments; he was a remarkable personality as well. He was someone who was always his own man—who was always fighting to keep people from taking advantage of him. Someone with the force of will to get his own way, to play the game his way. And talking with friends of Jean-Michel over the last few days, we have all marveled over his incredible generosity. In a time when the traditional artist's custom of giving artwork as gifts has diminished, Jean-Michel gave away dozens if not hundreds of his works.

Andy Warhol told me a story about first getting to know Jean-Michel years ago, when he was about fifteen. Jean-Michel was selling printed T-shirts in Greenwich Village and went up to Andy Warhol's studio to try to borrow money to buy materials. Andy gave him about twenty-five dollars to get him to go away. One of the first things that Jean-Michel did when he started to make some money about five years later was to go visit Andy to pay him back.

Jean-Michel took a tough stance toward the world but at the same time was uncommonly warm and generous with his friends. We will long remember his engaging, almost innocent smile and his sense of humor, which was often directed at art dealers who were trying to take advantage of him. Last spring, he described to me how an art dealer whom he found unnecessarily cheap, was manipulated into picking up an enormous check for Jean-Michel and his friend in a fancy restaurant.

In an era when art is becoming almost a profession—like being a lawyer—when artists try to go to the right school, try to chat up the right people, Jean-Michel took his own path. He did it his way, not someone else's way. He will long be an inspiration to people, a demonstration that no matter where an artist starts, by force of personality and application, one can capture the attention of the world and reach thousands.

Many of us have very strong memories and will miss him badly. But in Jean-Michel's case, it's more than memories that will live on. He has left behind not just memories but a legend. I am sure that a hundred years from now and even beyond, people will still be astounded by his work. JEFFREY DEITCH

Originally published in Anna Palmqvist, ed.,
Jean-Michel Basquiat / Julian Schnabel.
Uddevalla, Sweden: Rooseum, 1989.

PLACE JEAN-MICHEL BASQUIAT

JEAN-MICHEL'S LEGACY

Jean-Michel's audience has changed dramatically since his passing. During his lifetime, and for some time after, his work was more appreciated in Europe and Asia than in the United States—and mostly within the art world. As he became more widely known outside of art circles because of TV, movies, fashion, and hip-hop music, a younger generation started to take notice. Hip-hop in particular has been influential in introducing his work to a younger audience of color, who were finally able to see an artist that looked like them and painted about issues that related to their lives.

Jean-Michel was definitely flawed—as we all are—and a deeply complex person and artist. As we have shared here the many stories of his life and our time with him, it is the incredible legacy and gift that he left through his art that will remain at the center of our work as a family on his behalf.

In writing about Jean-Michel's legacy, it's important that we speak about the profound contribution my dad made. When Jean-Michel died, my father was an executive in the corporate world. For a few years, he tried to manage both his job and the estate, but eventually it became too challenging. My dad ran the estate for over twenty-five years, ensuring the integrity of Jean-Michel's life's work and that the value of his paintings remained high. He also founded an authentication committee, which existed for nearly twenty years to certify works by Jean-Michel, further ensuring that the market for his work—and his legacy—was not compromised. While he focused on all of those duties, he was still a grieving father. Visiting Jean-Michel's exhibitions was very emotional for him, and he attended only a handful.

In the last twenty years, there have been quite a number of retrospectives at important institutions, in Paris, London, Bilbao, Toronto, and his hometown of Brooklyn. Lisane, Nora, and I have also been honored to accept several awards on his behalf. JEANINE

Jean-Michel's life and work speak to people from many different fields and ethnicities, because his work is like nothing you've ever seen before—it is truly groundbreaking in so many ways. The way he combined images with words captivates the audience, because you don't have to guess what was going on in his mind—the message was direct and powerful. The paintings show so much emotion, it's hard not to get drawn in. His references to Black people in history make the work particularly alluring to people of color.

To witness over the years how much his work has permeated mainstream culture has been awe-inspiring. In the TV special *A Celebration of American Creativity: In Performance at the White House*, there was a painting by Jean-Michel in the background. The program aired in January 2016, right after President Barack Obama's last Christmas as president. That was pretty amazing.

The most rewarding experience of managing Jean-Michel's legacy for me has been the personal interactions with his fans. Two moments that stand out are when a staff member at The Barbican Centre in London who was also an artist gave us one of his own artworks as a gift. I was so touched by that. And while we were at the Mori Arts Center in Japan, a group of young women came over to us. One was crying and expressed how Jean-Michel has inspired her since she was fifteen. Moments like those are incredibly special. JEANINE

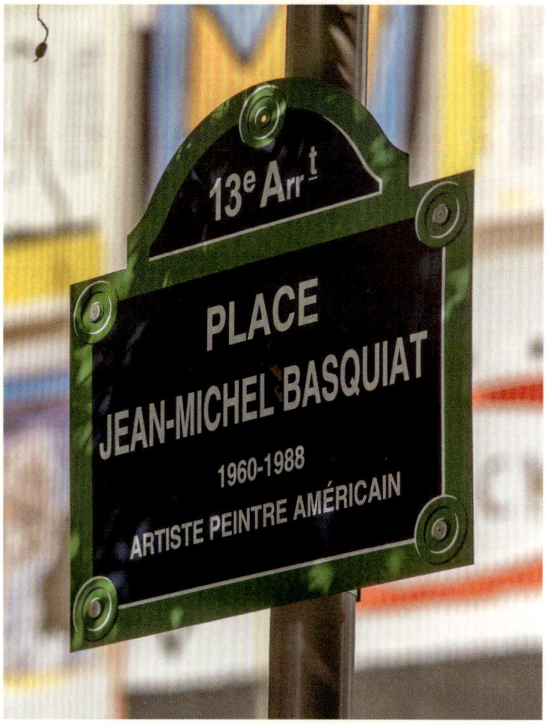

Place Jean-Michel Basquiat, Paris
PHOTO: © DUC TRUONG

EXCERPT FROM THE SPEECH FOR THE INAUGURATION OF PLACE JEAN-MICHEL BASQUIAT, PARIS

Naming a square is always a solemn, serious act, an act that must have meaning, and naming this square in the 13th arrondissement after Jean-Michel Basquiat makes a lot of sense. I believe that in the times we live in, which are not always simple, which can sometimes be a little worrying, we always need to come back to the meaning of the acts we perform.

This incredible artist, so young, who left so early but who, like all great geniuses, like all great creators, started from his fragility, from the fragility of life, from the fragility of reality to come and touch us, to come and touch this light that can be in each one of us. At the moment we met the work of Jean-Michel Basquiat, whatever our age, whatever our origin, we were touched. Yes, because he was a genius, and we met this genius through his work. And we see in this work someone who was not afraid to shake things up, but not simply for the pleasure of shaking things up or distressing people, but to push us to go further, to look perhaps at the deepest part in each of us. He was not afraid to ask questions. He was not afraid to provide answers. He was not afraid to say that life takes place in the streets, and that from the streets an expression and a way of speaking about what we live is invented. In the recent exhibition at the Musée d'art moderne de la Ville de Paris, we could very much understand the strength of his art and the strength of what made him move and express with this radicality—because he expressed with radicality—our weaknesses and our wounds.

When we name a square in someone's honor, it is there forever. And maybe in fifty years, in one hundred years, when children look up and see that this square is named after Jean-Michel Basquiat, maybe they will discover what we also discovered thanks to him: these wounds, these wounds from which light finally comes out, these wounds that allow us to live as long as we accept them, wounds that we must respond to with humanity—and humanity was very much the message of Jean-Michel Basquiat.

ANNE HIDALGO, MAYOR OF PARIS, SEPTEMBER 29, 2018

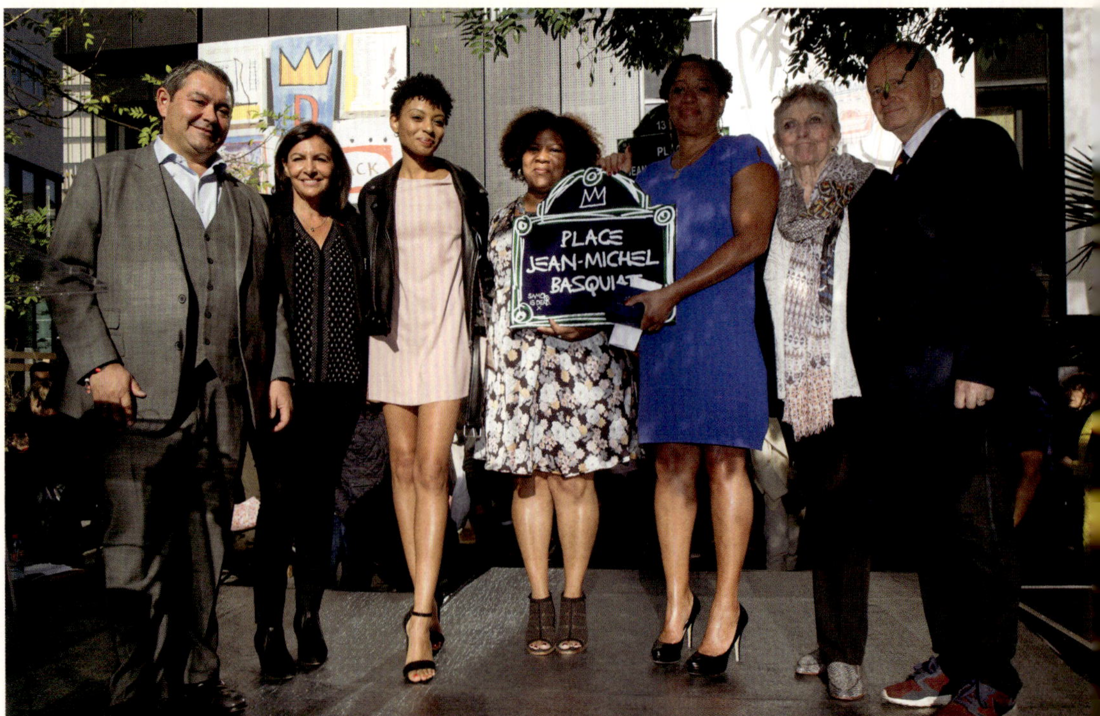

On September 29, 2018, the city of Paris celebrated the inauguration of a square built and named after Jean-Michel in the 13th arrondissement. Left to right: Jérôme Coumet, Anne Hidalgo, Jessica Kelly, Jeanine Heriveaux, Lisane Basquiat, Nora Fitzpatrick, and Christophe Girard

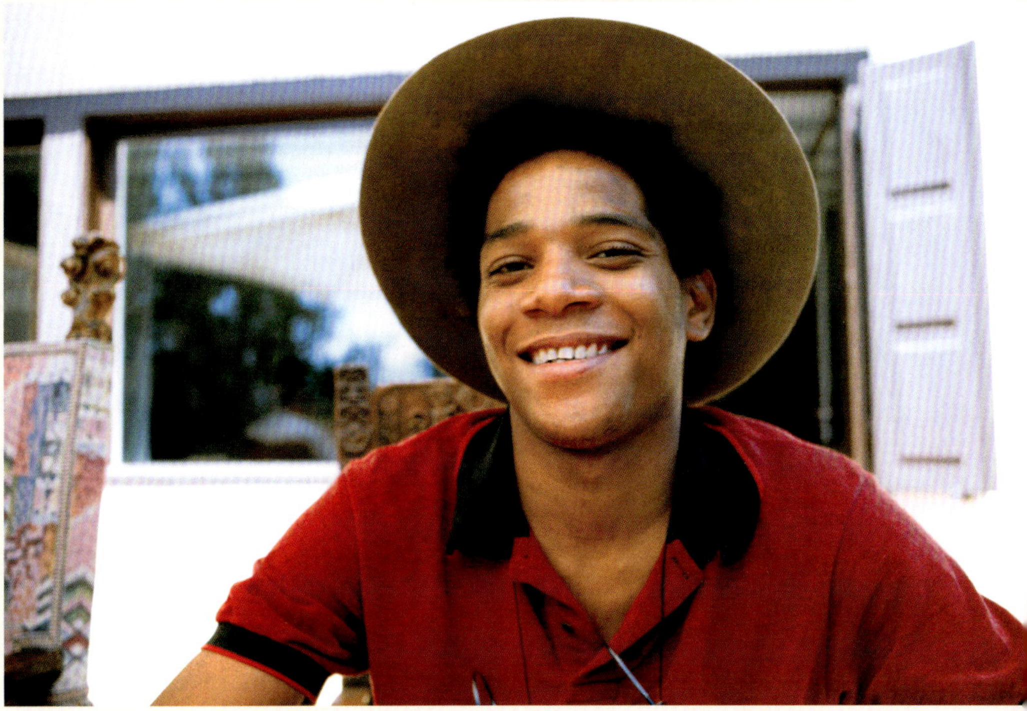

Jean-Michel in St. Moritz, Switzerland, 1983

First and foremost, I want visitors to the exhibition and those reading this book to be warmed, energized, and inspired to live their own dreams, whatever those might be. Just go for it! Secondly, I want them to know a little more about who Jean-Michel is and to better understand the social commentary that is such an important aspect of his work. Lastly, I want people to feel more deeply attuned to the fact that, no matter how famous or how much one has accomplished in their life, we are all simply human beings trying to find our way. I think that that is ultimately the message behind Jean-Michel's life—our shared humanity.

Like other figures who have had a profound and public impact on the world, Jean-Michel is often seen as larger-than-life, the embodiment of greatness, success, and mastery of his craft. Those are the outward expressions of a unique and courageous man who stood in the truth of his humanity and channeled his creativity brilliantly and authentically.

My hope is that this project helps viewers see how our brother lived, how hilarious, generous, and sharp he was, and how great a friend. I want people to see how his creativity translated into pranks, jokes, adventurousness, and true joy. Some people choose to focus on the depression and sadness that he experienced in the year leading to his death, and there is no doubt that this aspect of his life continues to resonate with so many. That was the essential dichotomy of his life—he enjoyed his life and accomplishments, and he also struggled.

I want my brother to be seen in full: for his humanity, his journey as an artist, and as a person who had his own identity and values. I want people to know that Jean-Michel was beautiful, sensitive, a deep thinker, hilarious (*really* funny!). He had an intense work ethic, spoke the truth, was "swagalicious," and loved fun and pleasure. He was also a brilliant pioneer, wise, deeply observant, a teacher, a star, and part of the "in crowd" that partied like crazy. He had difficulties like everyone else, but he produced an incredible body of work that continues to be powerfully relevant.

Jean-Michel has inspired generations of artists in the decades following his death. Please know that he busted his ass for that; it wasn't just women, drugs, and hanging out. Jean-Michel was deeply committed to his craft; he worked hard at it, and gave it his best, with integrity. He was smart—balancing keen business acumen and artistic genius. He fought hard for himself because he understood why he was here: to reshape the conversation and do Art his way, on his own terms, and to place his stake in the ground. He did just that—with style, generosity, grace, and magnificence.

Jean-Michel has a multipronged cultural legacy—he put at the center of his work the struggle that Black people, and Black men in particular, have in this country. He was a Black man whose roots gave him a different perspective with unique challenges of acculturation.

To Black people he is an inspiration because he spoke truth in the face of what we are subjected to: racism, classism, colonialism, capitalism, etc. He pulled no punches and was "in-your-face direct," completely unable to be anything but searingly honest and authentic. It is one of the most profound aspects of his long-lasting legacy.

To immigrants, especially those of the African diaspora and the Caribbean, and Haiti specifically, he represents hope, passion, and patriotism. People of the Caribbean living in the US don't always get that kind of consideration, especially not in art or culture. He blew past securing a piece of the American Dream. He blew past expectations and assumptions, and rejected any box at all. And he didn't just dream about these things, he did what he said he was going to do. Jean-Michel made it—he has earned our respect.

It is no secret that he was frustrated by assumptions about who he was, particularly in the rarefied art world. He was a dreadlocked chameleon of sorts, weaving in and out of environments and micro-communities—of other artists, musicians, friends, art world insiders, etc. The world was his classroom and lecture hall. LISANE

OPPOSITE TOP
Plaque honoring Jean-Michel, Brooklyn Botanic Garden, 2017.
On June 11, 2017, during the "Welcome Back to Brooklyn" ceremony, Jean-Michel was awarded an engraved paver along the Brooklyn Botanic Garden's Celebrity Path.

OPPOSITE BOTTOM LEFT
Key to the City honoring Jean-Michel, Brooklyn Botanic Garden, 2017
During the "Welcome Back to Brooklyn" ceremony, Jean-Michel was also awarded "Keys to Brooklyn."

OPPOSITE BOTTOM RIGHT
Asher B. Durand Award, Brooklyn Museum, 2015.
On April 15, 2015, the Brooklyn Artists Ball honored museum director Arnold Lehman along with Jean-Michel for being one of three artists with major exhibitions at the museum during Lehman's tenure.

I think that the art world was the arena where he could confront all the things that he was already thinking and saying about the world. He was also incredibly sensitive to and aware of the formula that the art world was using, and he intended to break through that. He wanted to bring life and energy and excitement to art, and make it accessible. He wanted to affect people, using art to speak about the world that we live in.

Though he experienced remarkable success during his lifetime, he didn't get the acknowledgment he felt he deserved. At the time, museums in particular didn't understand what a watershed his work represented—they would catch up to this fact eventually, but only after his death. I don't think he got the appropriate recognition—superstar recognition—though he did get some confirmation that he was on the right track.

Jean-Michel has inspired so many visual artists working in different media, not just painters. And that influence extends beyond fine art: We are now beginning to see the impact that Jean-Michel has had on popular culture—music, food, fashion. Our family is celebrating his influence on creative expression across so many fields and industries.

I want to celebrate the way he lived, and his dedication to listening to what was inside of him. His is a very powerful and inspirational story. LISANE

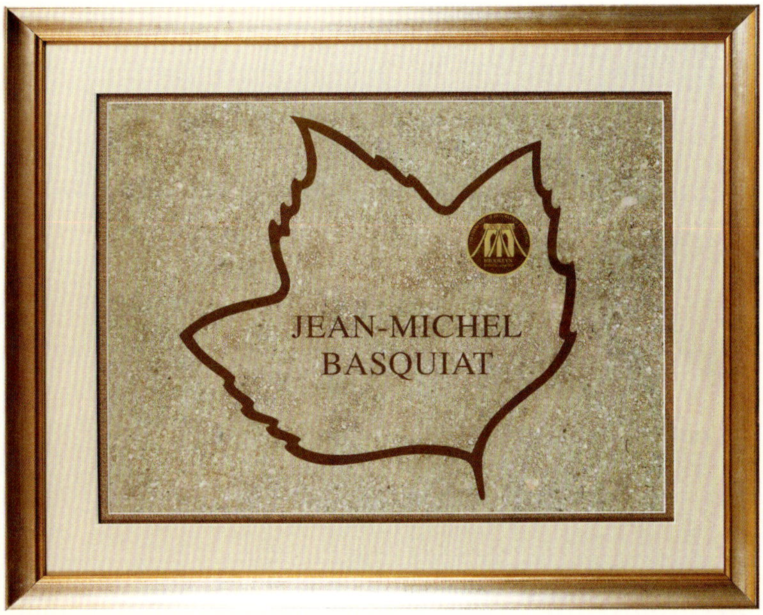
JEAN-MICHEL
BASQUIAT

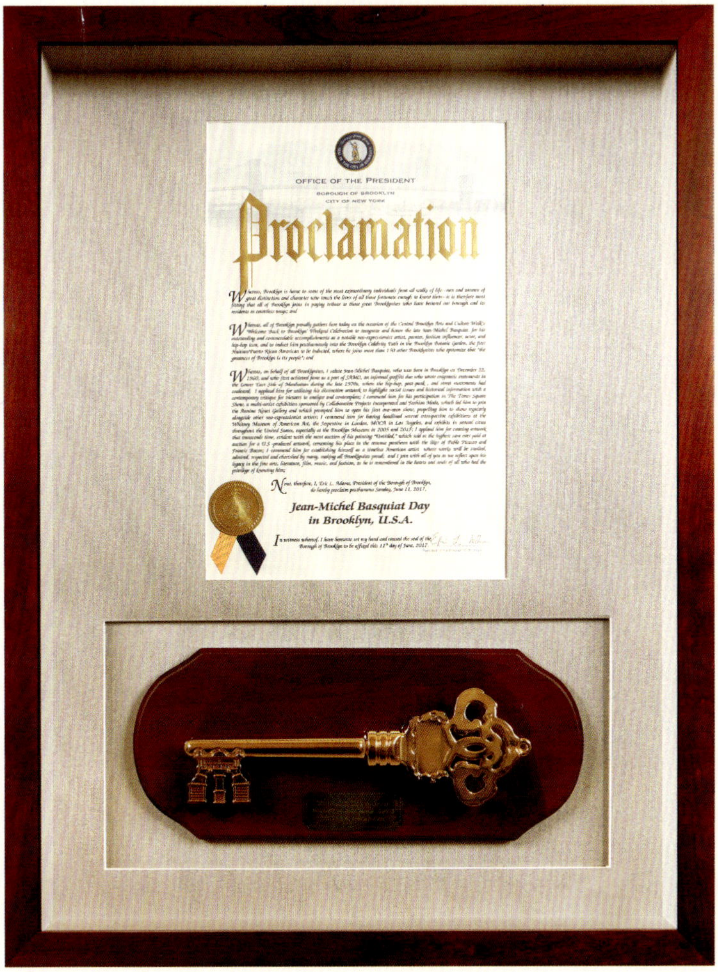
OFFICE OF THE PRESIDENT
BOROUGH OF BROOKLYN
CITY OF NEW YORK
Proclamation
Jean-Michel Basquiat Day
in Brooklyn, U.S.A.

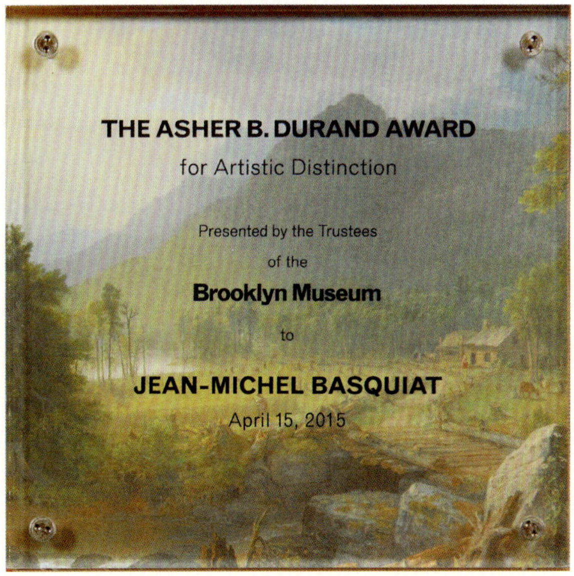
THE ASHER B. DURAND AWARD
for Artistic Distinction
Presented by the Trustees
of the
Brooklyn Museum
to
JEAN-MICHEL BASQUIAT
April 15, 2015

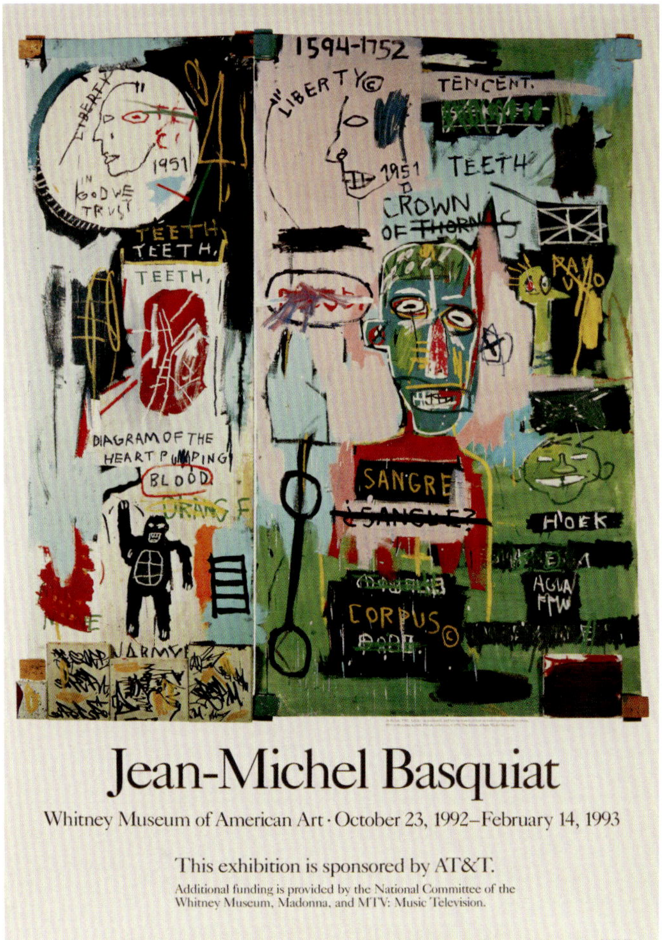

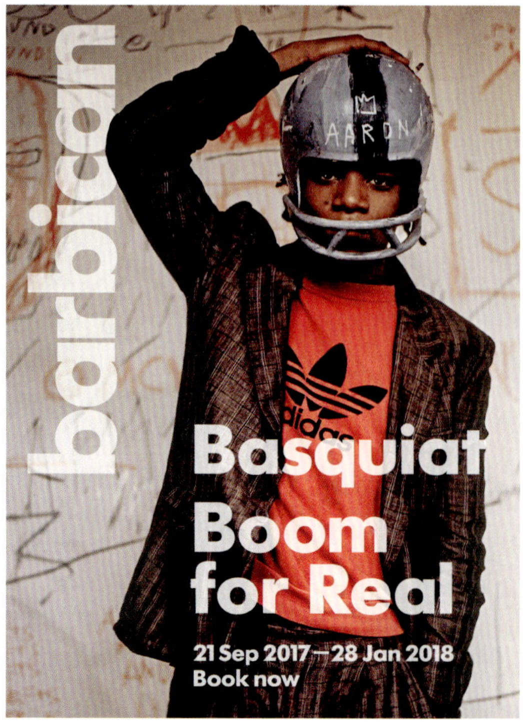

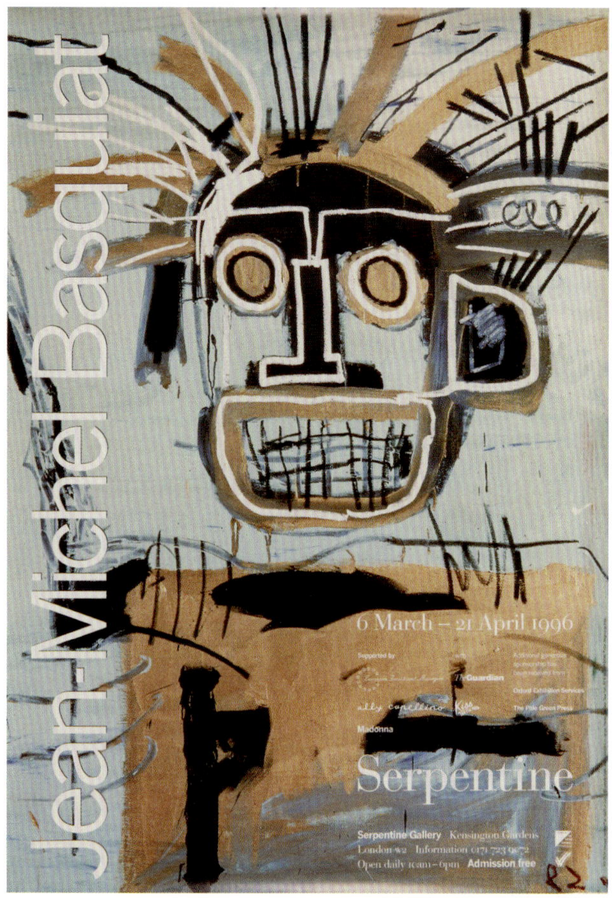

Posters for various posthumous exhibitions: Whitney Museum of American Art, New York, October 23, 1992–February 14, 1993; *Basquiat: Boom for Real*, The Barbican Centre, London, September 21, 2017–January 28, 2018; Serpentine Gallery, London, March 6–April 21, 1996

PHOTO IN BARBICAN POSTER: © EDO BERTOGLIO

THE ESTATE

Between the time of Jean-Michel's death and 1994, when the authentication committee was officially formed, Gerard was working towards establishing the estate. He was running things, and we were learning at the same time. We worked with Robert Miller Gallery. Eventually all the works were moved from Jean-Michel's warehouse to the gallery warehouse. Then we put together a team for the estate in those years. It took a while to find the right people. It was difficult because there weren't that many people who knew Jean-Michel's work at that time.

In 1988 we were introduced to the lawyer Michael Stout. We actually began putting together the authentication committee in 1992—it took a couple of years to get going. On October 5, 1995, we moved into our office on University Place. Before that, the committee met in different places, such as art dealer John Cheim's apartment or curator Diego Cortez's apartment.

Eventually, people began to realize that they couldn't sell or buy any work without having authentication done. It took some time for auction houses to request authentication, but finally they did—before they sold anything, a request would be submitted to the committee. Our work was starting to take hold. NORA

My dad managed the estate for several decades, and during that time, Lisane and I were able to have our own careers and raise our families. I've had the opportunity to live very privately. Since we have taken on the responsibility of running the estate after my father's death, I've had to come out of my shell a bit. JEANINE

We, as a family, are committed to ensuring that our decisions regarding Jean-Michel's work and legacy are always made through our understanding of what he would want. For me and Jeanine, it's a little different because our perspective as his sisters is different from the perspective of our parents. So, we always ask, "What would he want?" and that's not always an easy question to answer because Jean-Michel was twenty-seven when he passed. We are doing our best to translate what we think he would want into a different moment in time.

What is important is ensuring that Jean-Michel's legacy is respected, that his voice continues to be the one that tells his own story. That is the biggest challenge. It is a tremendous responsibility to be the steward of your brother's legacy. The heavy work is not what is entailed in caring for Jean-Michel's estate, it is responding to the ways that people want to own his voice. I think it's beautiful that so many people want to get into his head—they want to know what he had to say, they want to hear him. At times, they filter this through their own perspective, which sometimes distorts his voice. We are in the position to point them back to the words he set down on paper and canvas. I feel very honored and humbled to support him in this way. He was an amazing force in the world. Even thirty-four years later, it's overwhelming sometimes to think about. LISANE

Our dad passed away in 2013. He shared quite a bit about administering the estate and made sure that we were set up for success. We were always very close, and Papa, Nora, and I hung out quite a bit.

For Jeanine and me, our first priority was to learn as much as we could and keep the estate running while integrating this new role into our lives. Eventually we focused on opportunities that would extend Jean-Michel's reach and allow us to fund the estate's expenses without having to sell his work.

This has been an interesting journey for the two of us, and the rest of our family. It's a constant lesson in honoring who Jean-Michel was—Jean-Michel the person—and having each other's back. LISANE

JEAN-MICHEL'S NEW YORK

We wanted to provide a tour of the neighborhoods Jean-Michel grew up in and the places he frequented in New York and Brooklyn. While some no longer exist, others remain great places to visit. Our family shared many amazing experiences growing up around the Prospect Park area in Brooklyn that includes the Brooklyn Museum, Brooklyn Botanic Garden, Prospect Park, and the Brooklyn Public Library.
LISANE

Jean-Michel left an indelible mark on the city we grew up in, from the schools he attended to his favorite places as an adult, like The Odeon and Mr Chow or the downtown clubs where he DJ'd. JEANINE

1. BROOKLYN BOTANIC GARDEN
The family visited the Brooklyn Botanic Garden regularly.
455 FLATBUSH AVE., BROOKLYN

2. PROSPECT PARK LONG MEADOW
Jean-Michel often went to Prospect Park with his family as a child to picnic and play.
PROSPECT PARK WEST, BROOKLYN

3. WETSON'S
Wetson's was a fast-food chain that served hamburgers until 1975 and was frequented by the Basquiat family.
EMPIRE BLVD. AND FLATBUSH AVE., BROOKLYN

4. P.S. 6
43 SNYDER AVE., BROOKLYN

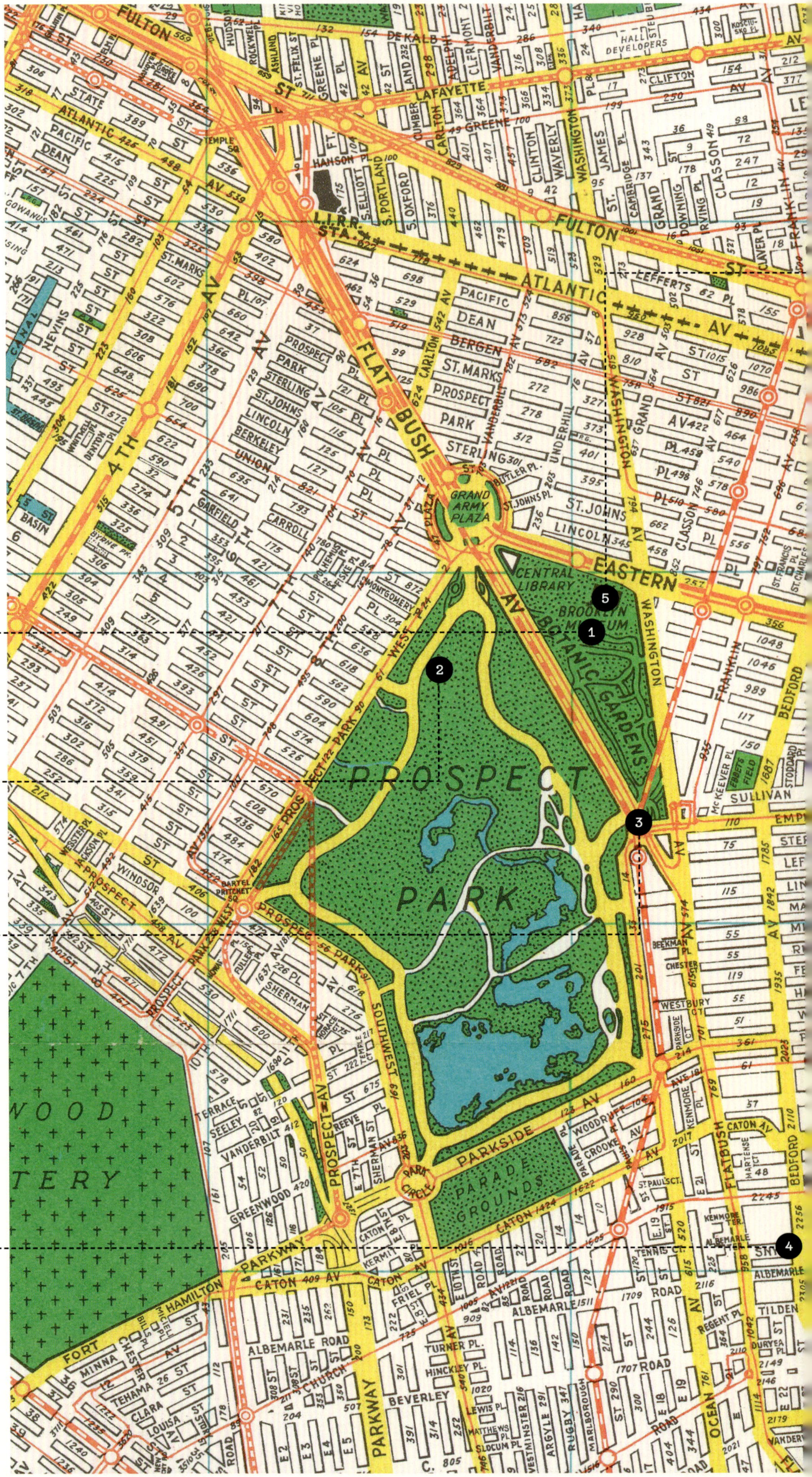

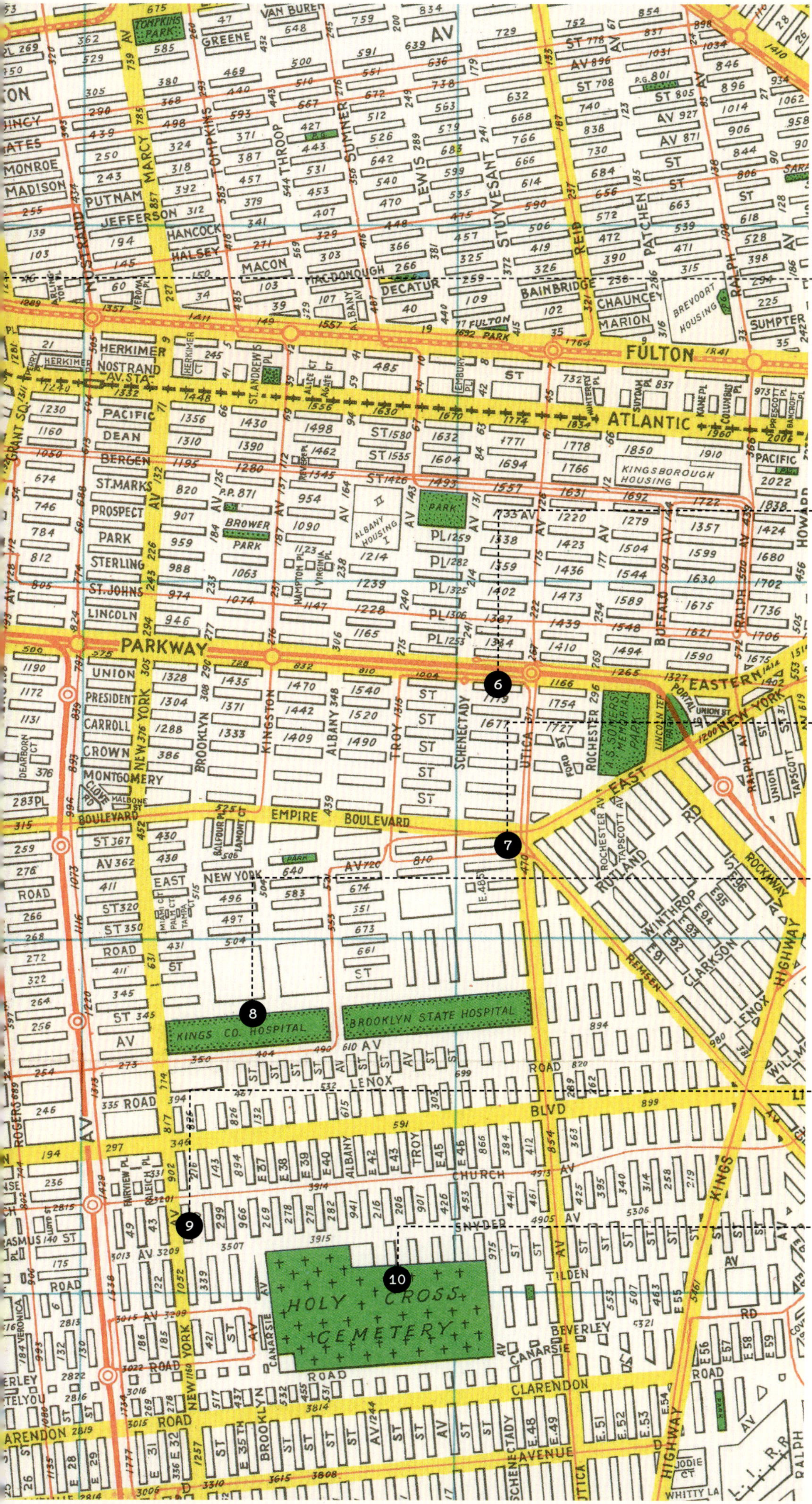

5. BROOKLYN MUSEUM

Matilde often took Jean-Michel to the Brooklyn Museum as a child. He had a junior membership.

200 EASTERN PKWY., BROOKLYN

6. BROOKLYN PUBLIC LIBRARY

The Basquiat children went to the public library often. They would ride their bikes to the library from their home in Boerum Hill, and have fun riding them up and down the long entrance steps.

1044 EASTERN PKWY., BROOKLYN

7. WHITE CASTLE

Gerard would pick up a sack of hamburgers after work as a treat for his children.

846 LEFFERTS AVE. AND UTICA AVE., BROOKLYN

8. KINGS COUNTY HOSPITAL

Jean-Michel was taken to Kings County Hospital after he was hit by a speeding car in 1968 outside the family's East Flatbush home. He was hospitalized for almost a month, after his spleen was removed.

451 CLARKSON AVE., BROOKLYN

9. P.S. 181

In 1971, Jean-Michel left Saint Ann's and began attending P.S. 181.

1023 NEW YORK AVE., BROOKLYN

10. HOLY CROSS CEMETERY

Gerard took Jean-Michel and, later, Lisane to the Cortelyou Rd. side of the cemetery to teach them how to ride bicycles. Jean-Michel and his friends would ride bikes alongside and in the cemetery later.

3620 TILDEN AVE., BROOKLYN

1. A&S DEPARTMENT STORE (FLAGSHIP STORE)
The Basquiat family frequented the department store, often shopping there for back-to-school clothes.
422 FULTON ST., BROOKLYN

2. BROOKLYN HEIGHTS PROMENADE
Montague Street in Brooklyn Heights was the urban equivalent of a small town main street for the Basquiat children as they grew up. Gerard would take them to Baskin-Robbins and then go to the promenade to eat it, play, talk, and look at the New York City skyline.
MONTAGUE ST. AND PIERREPONT PL., BROOKLYN

3. SAINT ANN'S SCHOOL
In 1967, Basquiat began attending Saint Ann's Catholic School, where he became friends with Mark Prozzo. Together, they created a children's book. He also competed in track events.
129 PIERREPONT ST., BROOKLYN

4. CITY-AS-SCHOOL HIGH SCHOOL
In 1976, Jean-Michel transferred to City-As-School, an alternative high school centered around hands-on learning. He became friends with Al Diaz, who was one of his early artistic collaborators.
59 SCHERMERHORN ST., BROOKLYN

5. I.S. 293, NATHAN HALE JUNIOR HIGH SCHOOL
All three Basquiat siblings attended I.S. 293.
284 BALTIC ST., BROOKLYN

6. LOEW'S METROPOLITAN THEATRE
Neighborhood movie theater that Jean-Michel and his sisters frequented. It was closed in the late 1970s and is currently the home of the Brooklyn Tabernacle evangelical church.
392 FULTON ST., BROOKLYN

7. P.S. 38
Jeanine and Lisane attended this school as children.
450 PACIFIC ST., BROOKLYN

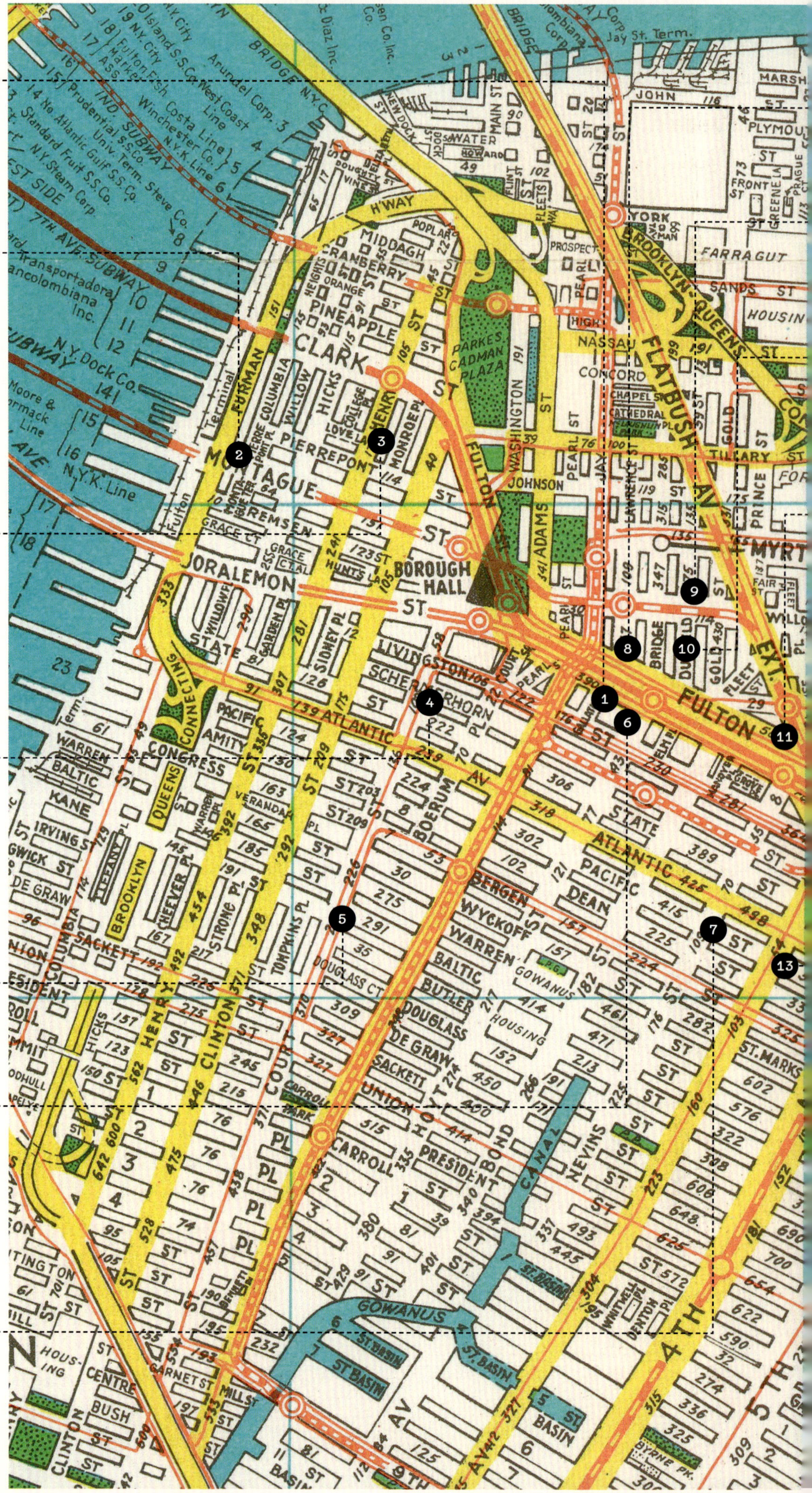

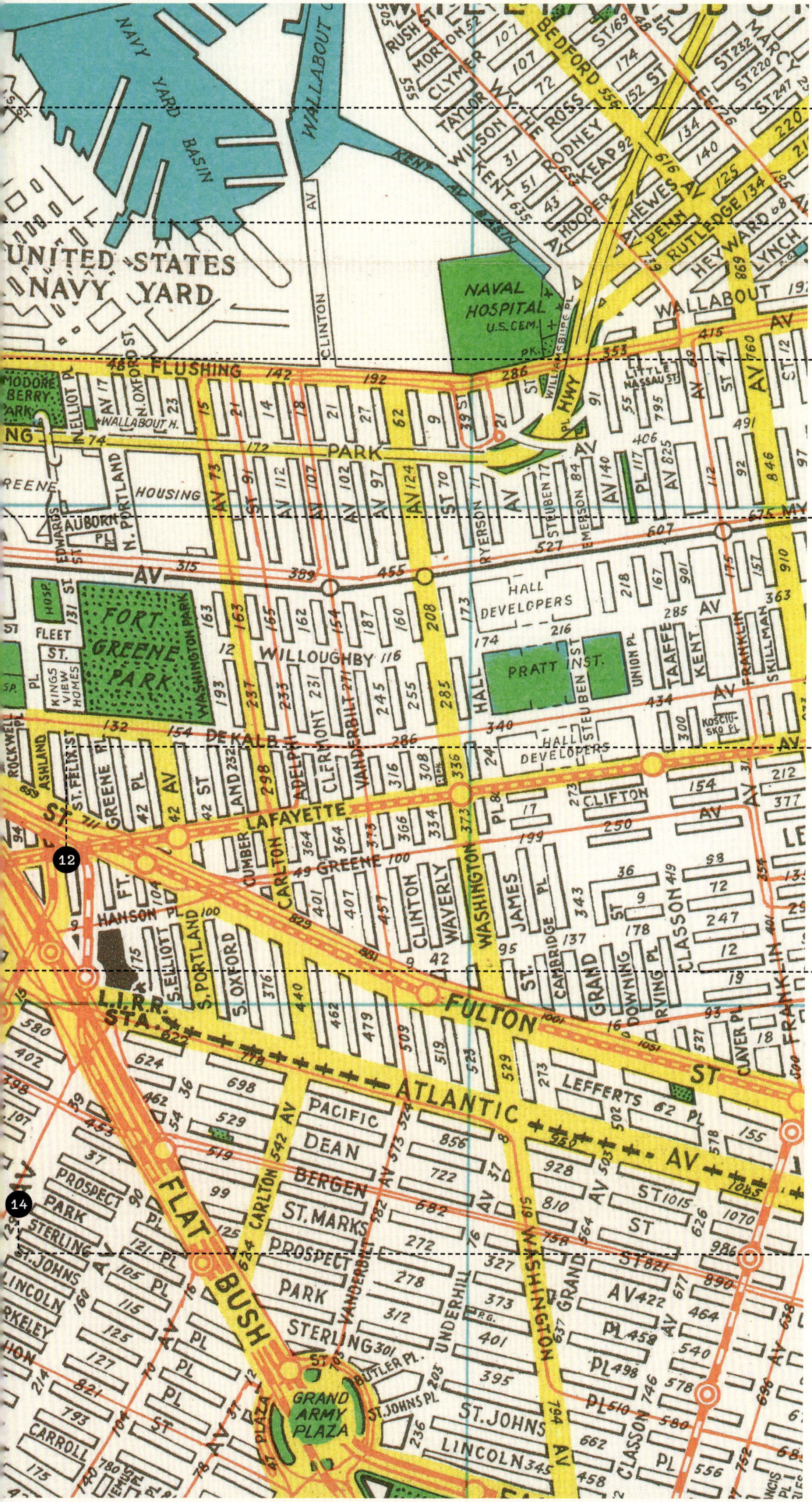

8. CHOCK FULL O' NUTS
Matilde took Jean-Michel and his sisters here for lunch.
451 FULTON ST., BROOKLYN

9. NEW YORK TELEPHONE COMPANY
Matilde worked at the telephone company as a posting clerk.
101 WILLOUGHBY ST., BROOKLYN

10. DUFFIELD THEATRE
The Duffield was a local movie theater that Jean-Michel and his sisters often went to.
249 DUFFIELD ST., BROOKLYN

11. WOOLWORTH'S
Jean-Michel, Lisane, and Jeanine frequented the store with their parents. Matilde took them to shop and have lunch as a treat.
408 FULTON ST., BROOKLYN

12. BROOKLYN ACADEMY OF MUSIC (BAM)
BAM was located close to the Basquiat family home in Boerum Hill. The family watched many programs there.
30 LAFAYETTE ST., BROOKLYN

13. BOERUM HILL FAMILY HOME
In 1972, Gerard moved into a brownstone in Boerum Hill with Jean-Michel and his sisters. They rented out the home when they moved to Puerto Rico in 1974 and resumed living there when they returned to New York in 1976. Jean-Michel left home for good in June 1978.
PACIFIC ST. AND THIRD AVE., BROOKLYN

14. PROSPECT HEIGHTS FAMILY HOME
Jean-Michel lived here with his parents and younger sister Lisane from the time of his birth until 1966.
BROOKLYN

1. GREEN-WOOD CEMETERY
Green-Wood Cemetery is the final resting place of Jean-Michel Basquiat.
500 25TH ST., BROOKLYN

2. EDWARD R. MURROW HIGH SCHOOL
Jean-Michel briefly attended Edward R. Murrow High School in 1976 after he lived in Puerto Rico with his father and two sisters and then returned to New York.
1600 AVE. L, BROOKLYN

3. BELT PKWY. NEAR VERRAZANO BRIDGE
Gerard would pick up White Castle and Kentucky Fried Chicken on a Friday night after work, and the family would go to the waterfront along the Belt Parkway and fly kites.
BROOKLYN

4. P.S. 101
2360 BENSON AVE., BROOKLYN

5. CONEY ISLAND
Jean-Michel and his sisters enjoyed visiting Coney Island with Matilde and riding the Cyclone.
BROOKLYN

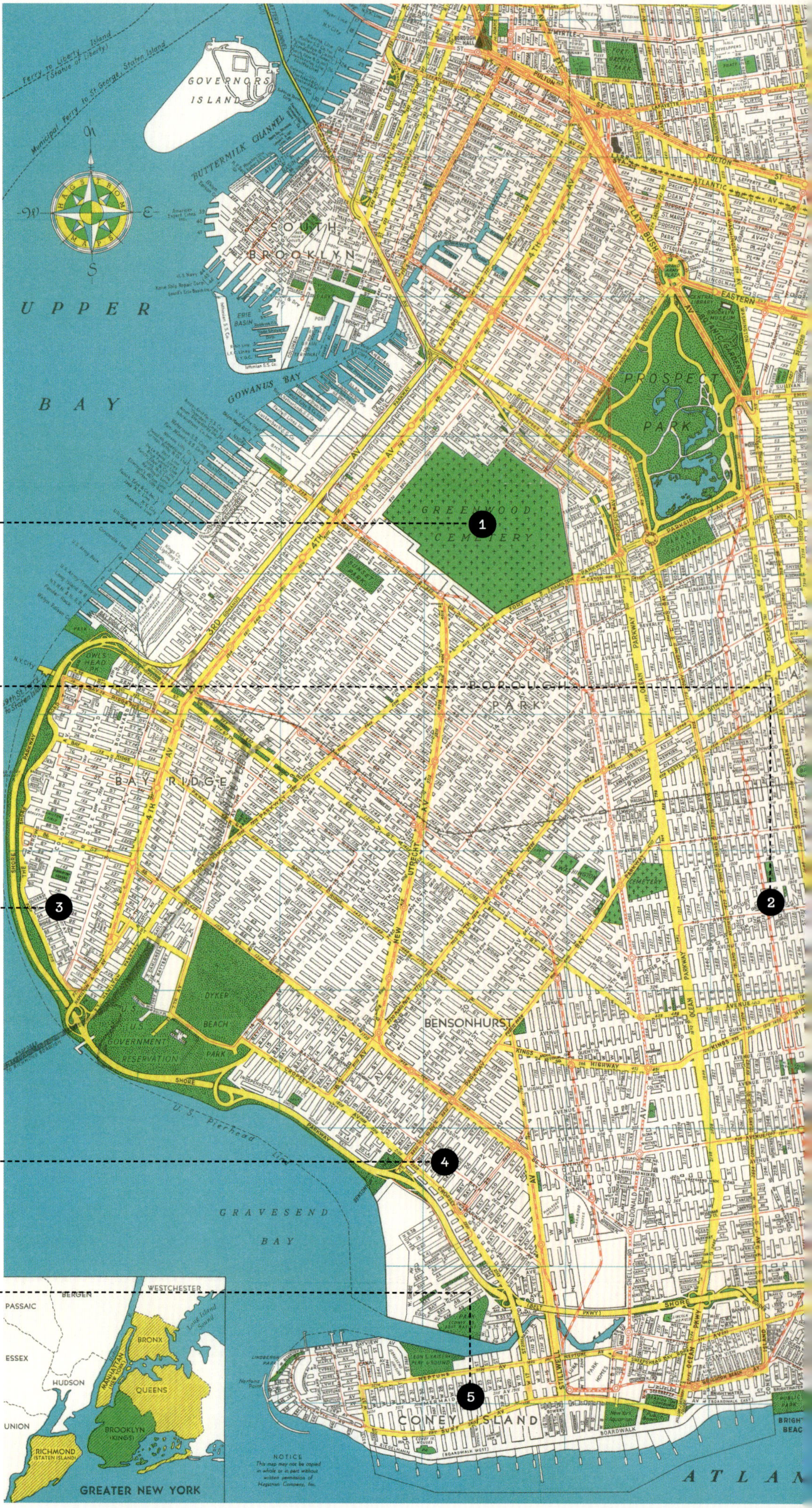

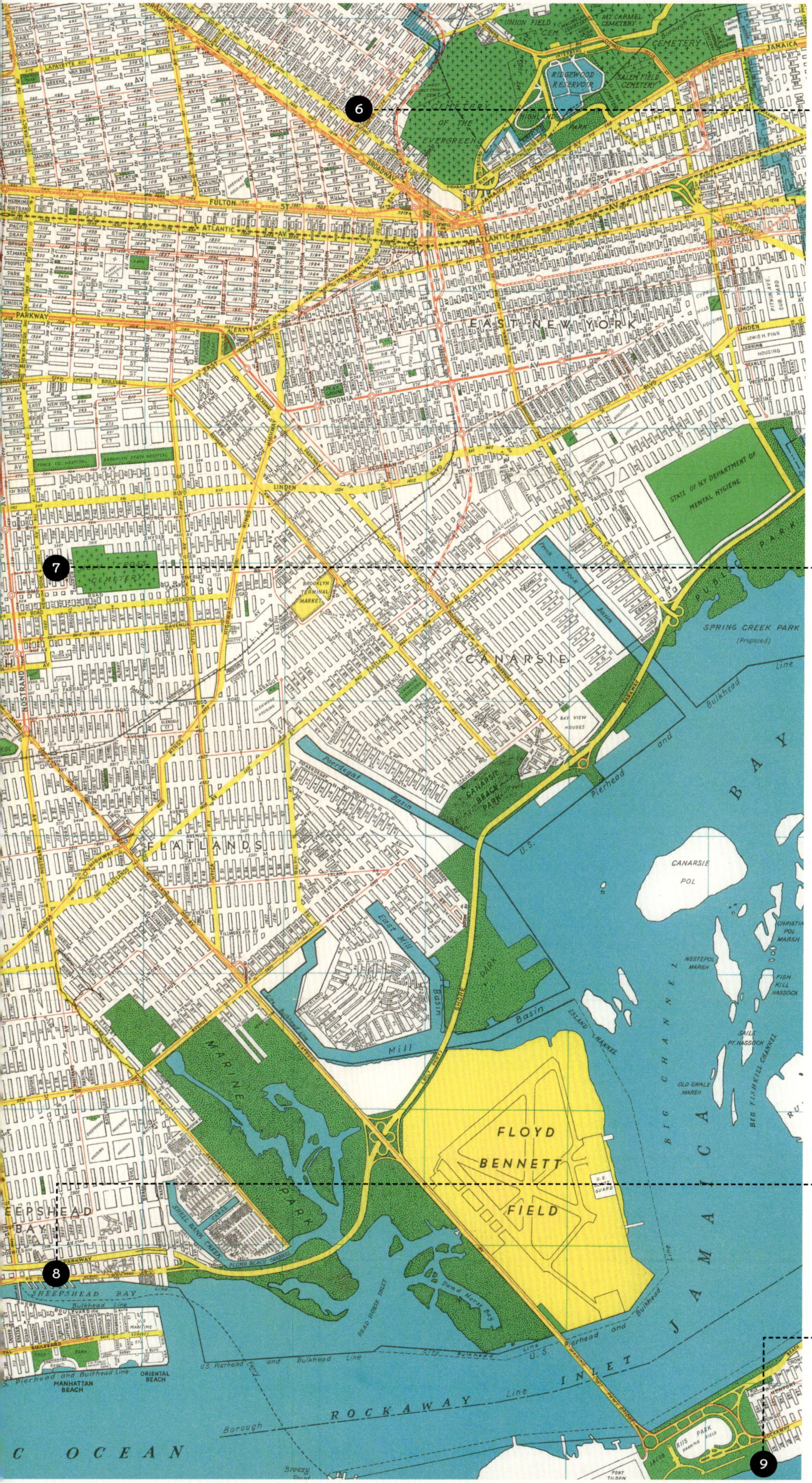

6. P.S. 45

84 SCHAEFER ST., BROOKLYN

7. EAST FLATBUSH FAMILY HOME

Jean-Michel moved to East Flatbush with his family in 1966. In 1968, Jean-Michel was in a car accident and hospitalized. He and his friends often frequented the corner store (E. 35th St. and Tilden Ave.) referred to by local children as "Mr. Ernie's."

E. 35TH ST., BROOKLYN

8. SHEEPSHEAD BAY PIERS

Gerard often took the family to Sheepshead Bay for lunch (clams, etc.) when they were younger.

SHEEPSHEAD BAY, BROOKLYN

9. RIIS BEACH

Matilde and Gerard would take their kids to the beach here.

JACOB RIIS PARK, BROOKLYN

CAMP ABELARD
Jean-Michel and his sister Lisane attended Camp Abelard sleepaway summer camp. Jeanine attended for one summer.
HUNTER, NY (NOT SHOWN ON MAP)

1. HURRAH
Hurrah was a popular nightclub that Jean-Michel went to with his friends.
36 W. 62ND ST., NEW YORK

2. MUSEUM OF MODERN ART
As a child, Jean-Michel visited MoMA with his mother, Matilde. Later on, Jean-Michel sold his postcards outside the museum. In May 1984, his work was included in *An International Survey of Recent Painting and Sculpture*.
11 W. 53RD ST., NEW YORK

3. *TIMES SQUARE SHOW* VACANT BUILDING
In June 1980, Jean-Michel's work was first publicly exhibited in the influential *Times Square Show*, organized by Colab (Collaborative Projects, Inc.).
W. 41ST ST. AND 7TH AVE., NEW YORK

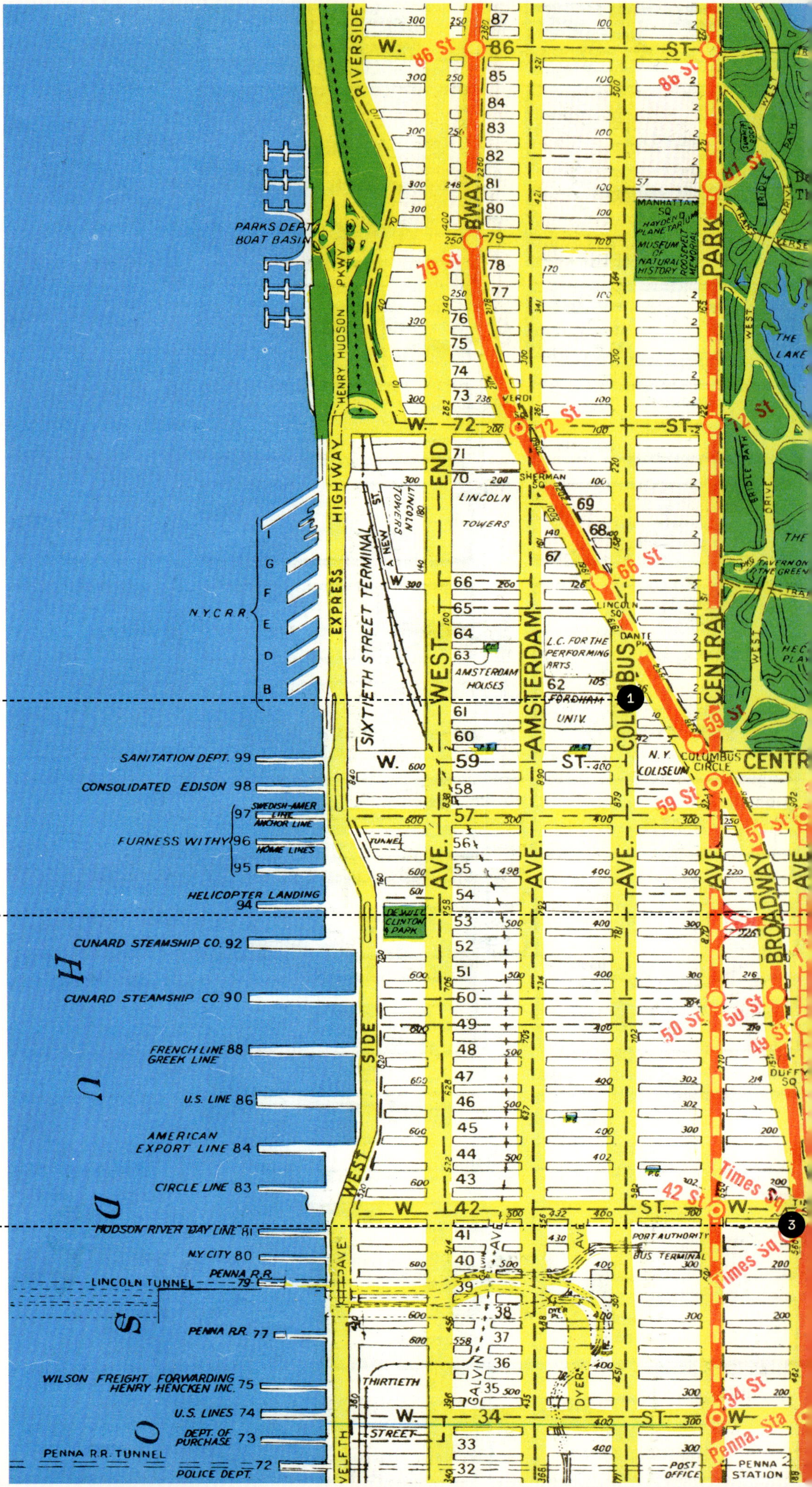

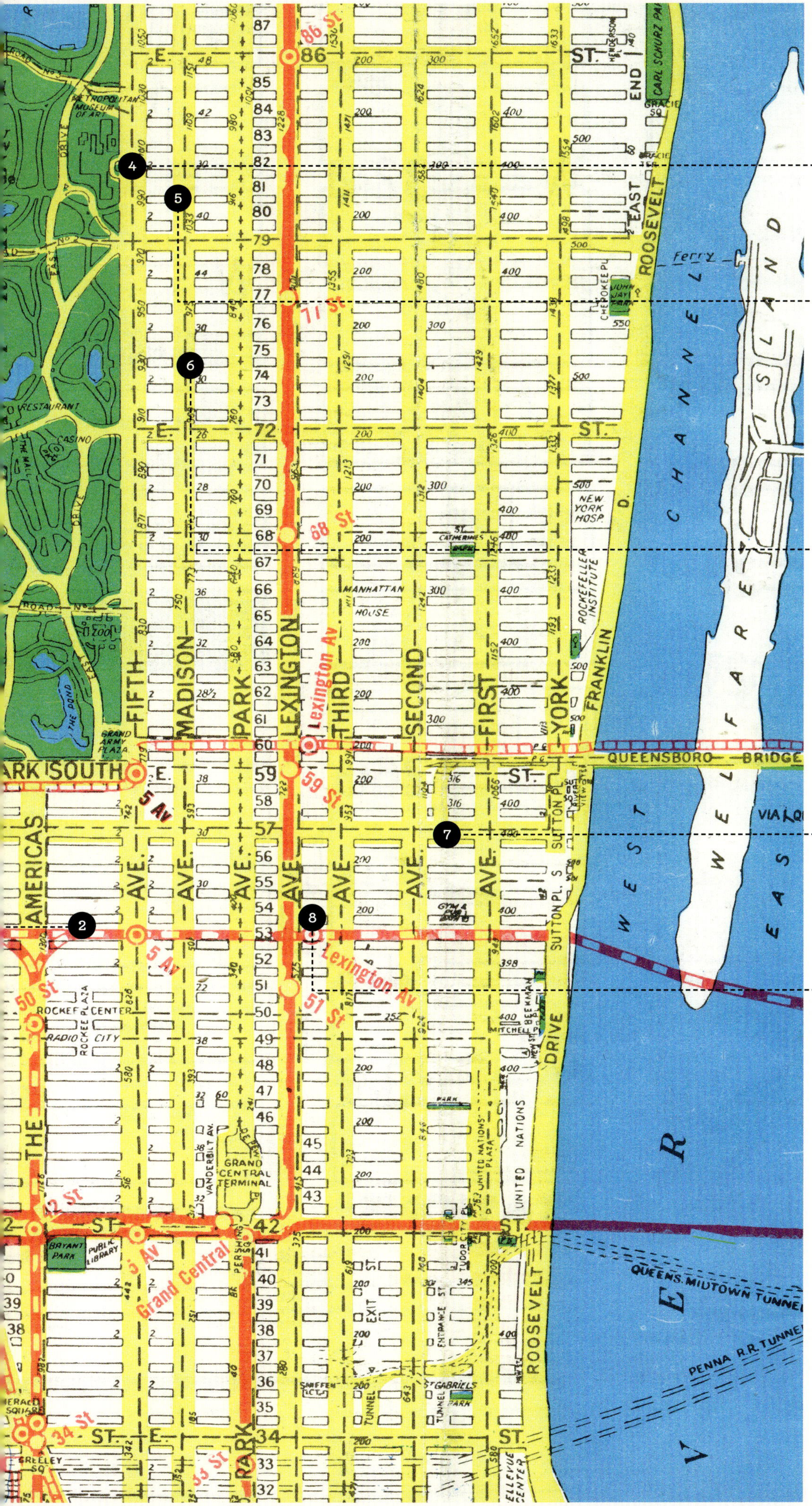

4. METROPOLITAN MUSEUM OF ART
The Met was another museum Jean-Michel enjoyed as a child.
1000 5TH AVE., NEW YORK

5. FRANK E. CAMPBELL FUNERAL CHAPEL
Jean-Michel passed away on August 12, 1988. On August 17, a private funeral for him was held at the Frank E. Campbell Funeral Chapel. Close friends and family attended, and art dealer Jeffrey Deitch gave the eulogy.
1076 MADISON AVE., NEW YORK

6. WHITNEY MUSEUM OF AMERICAN ART
Jean-Michel's work was included in the Whitney Biennial in 1983.
945 MADISON AVE. NEW YORK

7. MR CHOW
Jean-Michel dined at Mr Chow locations in both New York and Los Angeles.
324 E. 57TH ST., NEW YORK

8. ST. PETER'S CHURCH
On November 5, 1988, a memorial gathering was held for Jean-Michel at St. Peter's Church. Jean Michel's friends and admirers honored the artist by playing music and reciting poetry.
619 LEXINGTON AVE., NEW YORK

P.S. 1 INSTITUTE FOR ART AND URBAN RESOURCES
Jean-Michel's work was exhibited in the *New York / New Wave* show at P.S. 1, organized by Diego Cortez. His work attracted the attention of Emilio Mazzoli, Bruno Bischofberger, and Annina Nosei.
2225 JACKSON AVE., QUEENS
(NOT SHOWN ON MAP)

1. CABLE BUILDING, VREJ BAGHOOMIAN, INC.
In May 1987, Jean-Michel met Vrej Baghoomian through Tony Shafrazi. Baghoomian became Jean-Michel's art dealer.
611 BROADWAY, NEW YORK

2. ANNINA NOSEI GALLERY
In September 1981, Annina Nosei invited Jean-Michel to participate in *Public Address*, a group show that focused on socio-political content. Jean-Michel was given the entire rear gallery for his paintings. Nosei then became his primary dealer and offered him a space for his studio. In March 1982, Jean-Michel had his first solo exhibition at her gallery.
100 PRINCE ST., NEW YORK

3. AREA
Jean-Michel frequented Area nightclub. In 1984, he met Jennifer Goode, the sister of Area's owners, Eric and Christopher Goode. When Jean-Michel turned twenty-five, there was a joint birthday party for him and Eric for which he was the DJ.
157 HUDSON ST., NEW YORK

4. DAVE'S LUNCHEONETTE
Dave's Luncheonette was a restaurant that clubgoers often went to after partying at the Mudd Club. An employee at Dave's Luncheonette may have been the inspiration behind Jean-Michel's drawing *Untitled (Jimmy the Eggman)*.
508 BROADWAY, NEW YORK

5. DEAN & DELUCA
Jean-Michel frequented this gourmet food store.
560 BROADWAY, NEW YORK

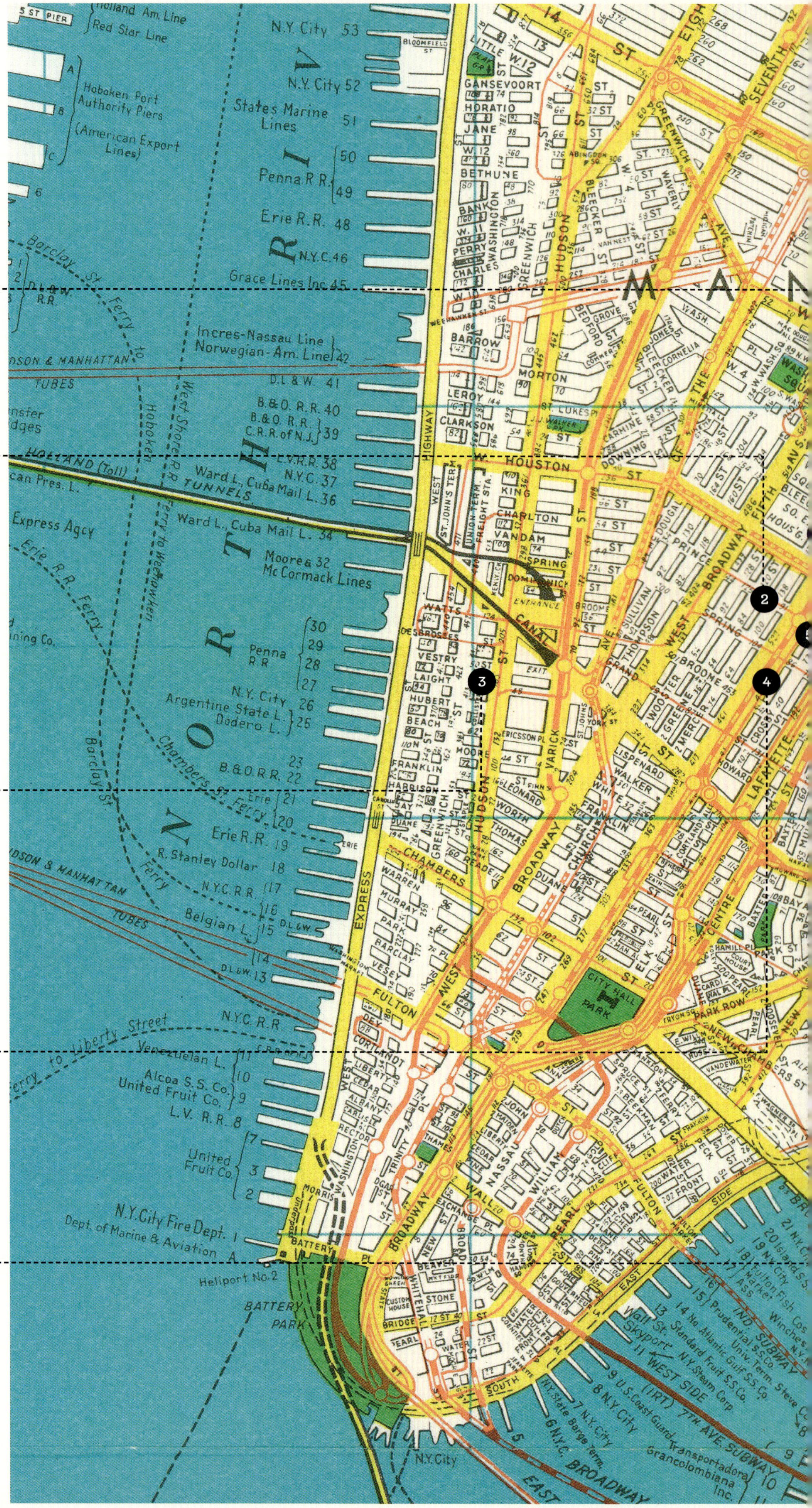

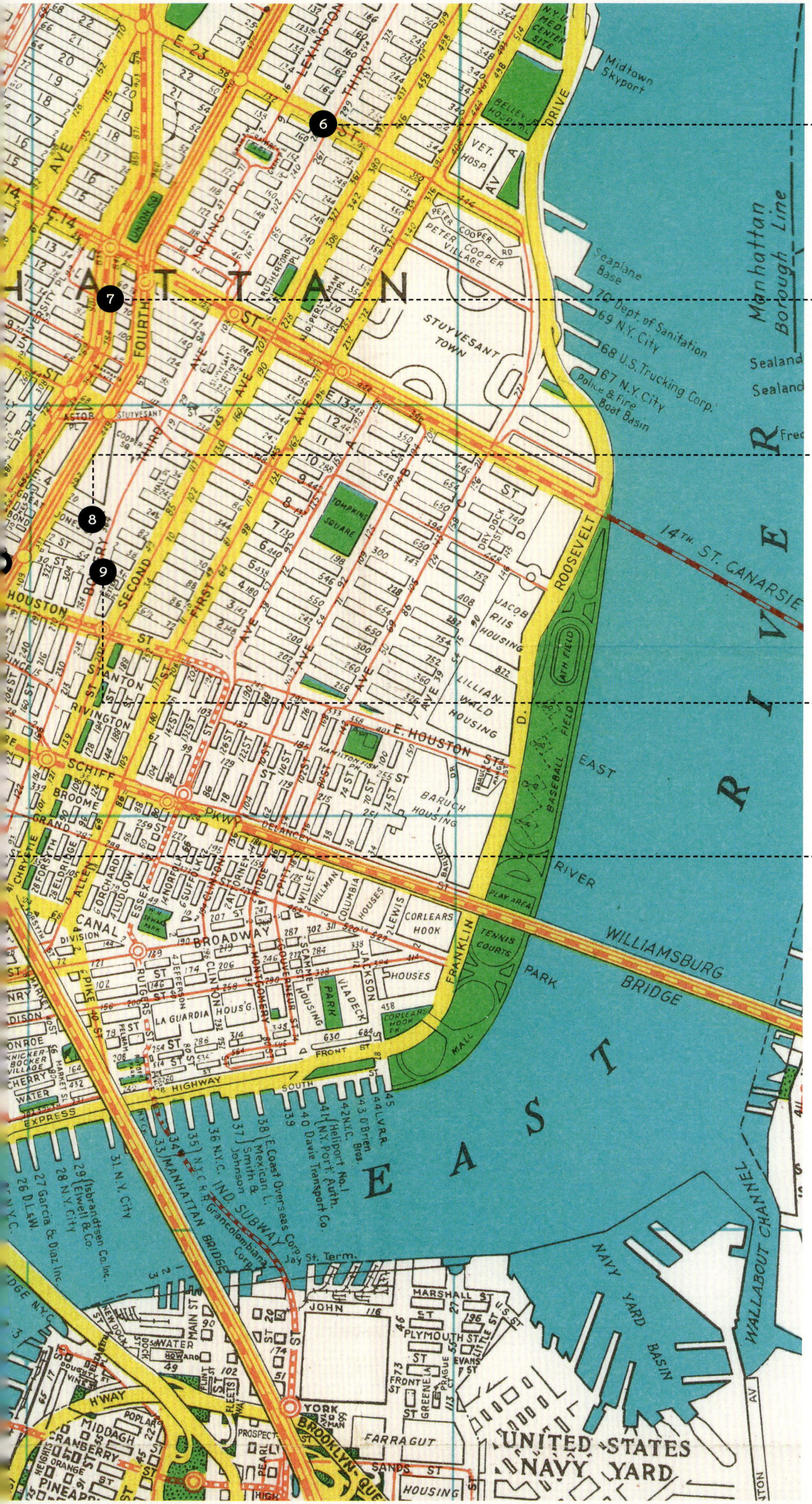

6. SCHOOL OF VISUAL ARTS
In the fall of 1979, Jean-Michel met Keith Haring and Kenny Scharf while wandering around the School of Visual Arts.
209 E. 23RD ST., NEW YORK

7. STRAND BOOK STORE
Jean-Michel read a lot of books and was constantly purchasing new ones to add to his library.
828 BROADWAY, NEW YORK

8. GREAT JONES ST. APARTMENT AND STUDIO
On August 15, 1983, Jean-Michel moved into 57 Great Jones St. He rented the space from Andy Warhol, who owned the building. Jean-Michel lived and worked in the apartment.
57 GREAT JONES ST., NEW YORK

9. CBGB
One of several downtown clubs Jean-Michel frequented.
315 BOWERY, NEW YORK, NY

10. CROSBY STREET LOFT
In January 1982, art dealer Annina Nosei arranged for Jean-Michel to move into an apartment on Crosby St. After his professional relationship with her ended in November 1982, Jean-Michel used his Crosby St. apartment as his studio.
151 CROSBY ST., NEW YORK

1. W.P.A. RESTAURANT

In 1978, while walking past W.P.A. Restaurant, Jean-Michel spotted Andy Warhol and curator Henry Geldzahler dining there. Jean-Michel approached them and Warhol purchased one of the artworks he was making on postcards; Geldzahler dismissed him as "too young."

152 SPRING ST., NEW YORK

2. MARY BOONE GALLERY

In March 1984, Jean-Michel became associated with Mary Boone Gallery. She was one of his primary dealers. Jean-Michel had solo exhibitions at the gallery in May 1984 and in March 1985.

420 W. BROADWAY, NEW YORK

3. TIER 3

Tier 3 was a club Jean-Michel frequented. He spray-painted a mural and also the DJ booth on the first floor of the club after a worker bought him spray paint.

W. BROADWAY AND WHITE ST., NEW YORK

4. THE ODEON

Jean-Michel often dined at The Odeon with his friends and family.

145 W. BROADWAY, NEW YORK

5. MUDD CLUB

Jean-Michel began to frequent the Mudd Club in 1978. At the clubs, he and his friends were known as the "baby crowd." In 1979, he met curator Diego Cortez there. Through Cortez, Jean-Michel got to know curator Henry Geldzahler, who became his friend and a collector of his work. When Jean-Michel announced that he was going to quit the band Gray, they played their last show at the Mudd Club on August 3, 1980. In February 1981, Jean-Michel was included in the *Lower Manhattan Drawing Show* at the club, organized by Keith Haring. In April 1981, he participated in *Beyond Words: Graffiti Based, Rooted, Inspired Works* at the Mudd Club.

77 WHITE ST., NEW YORK

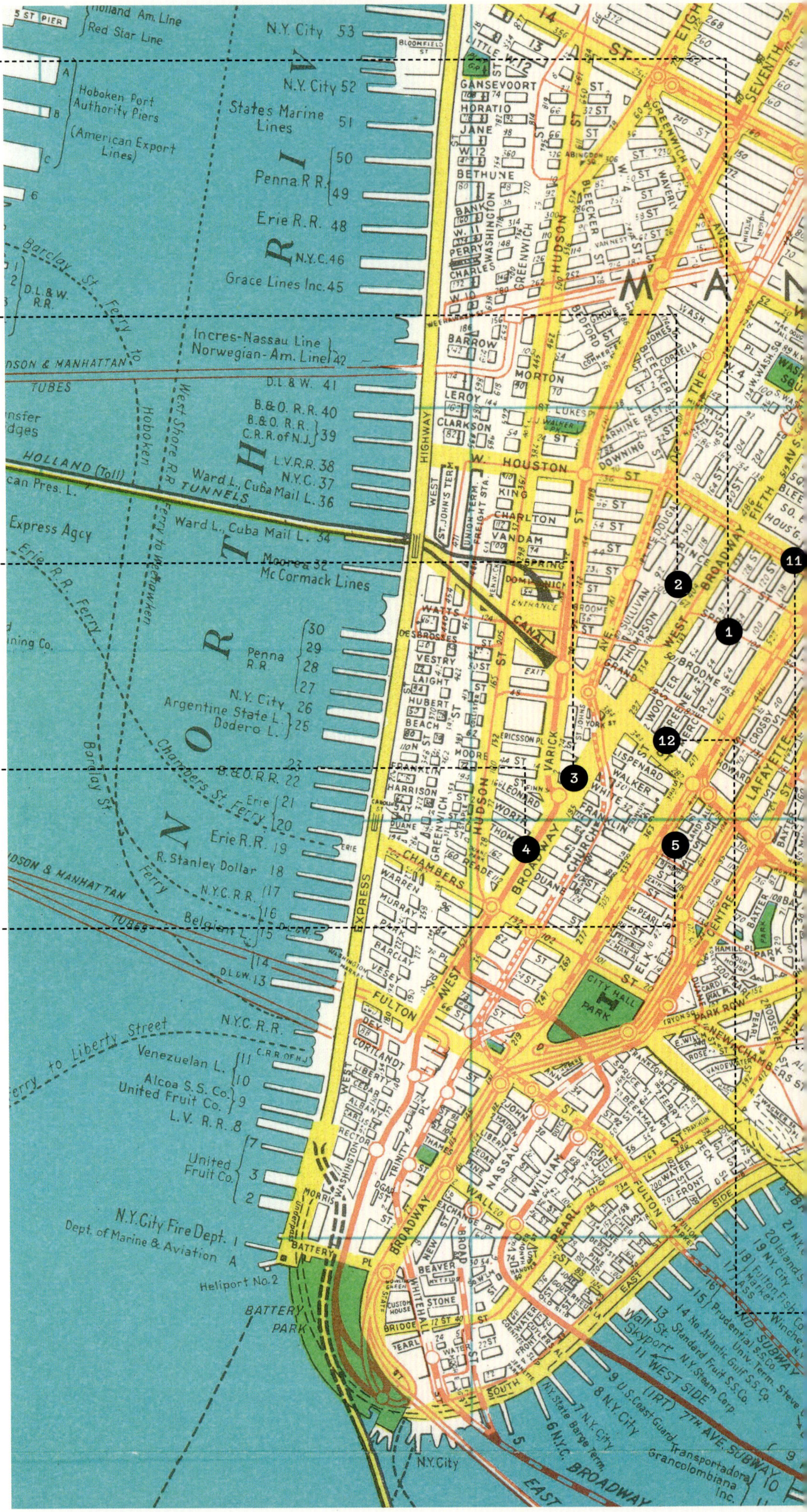

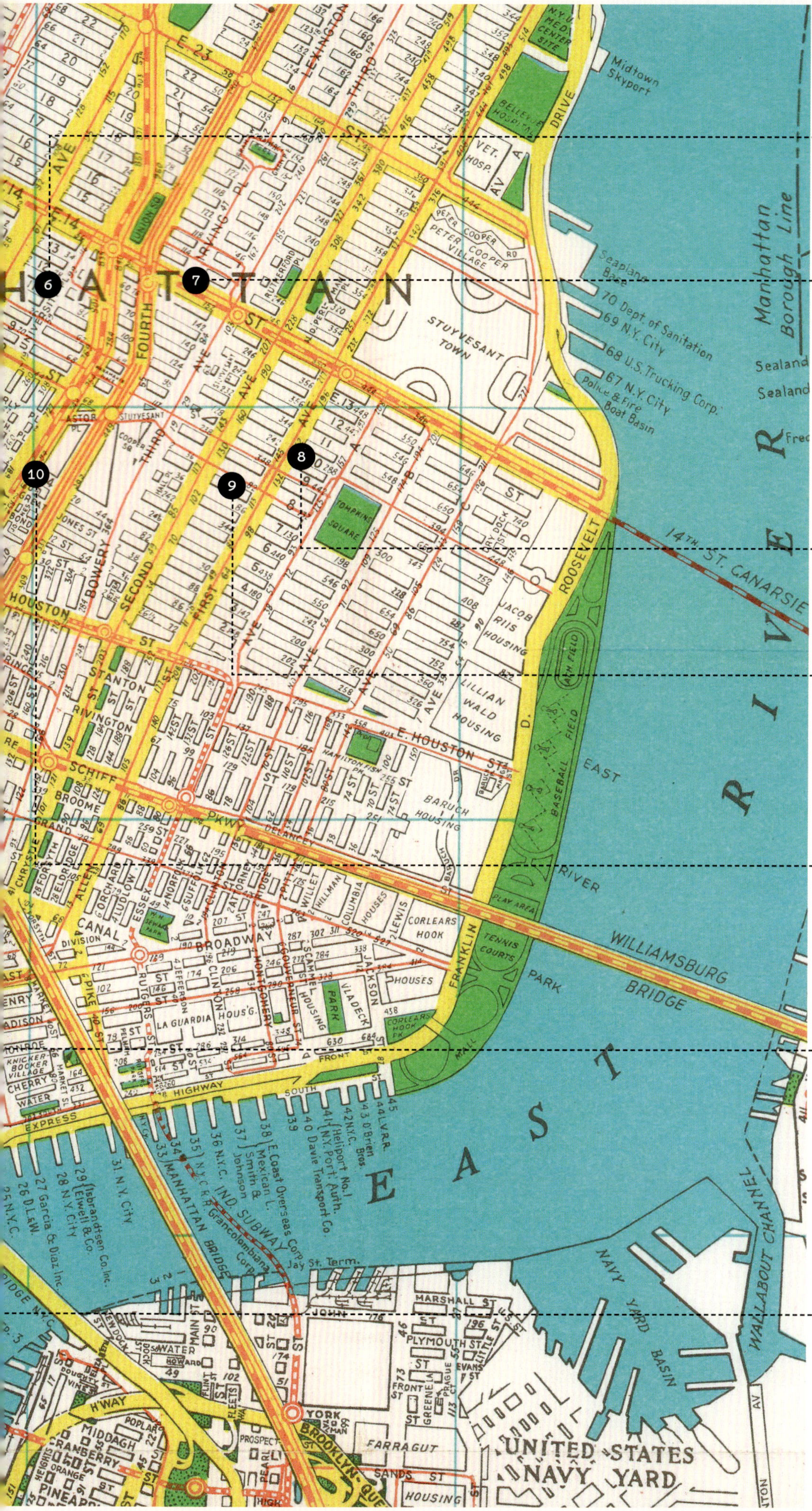

6. NEW VIDEO
Jean Michel frequented this store to purchase and rent videotapes.
90 UNIVERSITY PL., NEW YORK

7. PALLADIUM
In May 1985, Jean-Michel was commissioned to create two large paintings for Palladium, a nightclub opened by the owners of Studio 54. Other artists commissioned included Keith Haring, Francesco Clemente, and Kenny Scharf. His murals were in the Michael Todd Room, the VIP area of the club.
126 E. 14TH ST., NEW YORK

8. FUN GALLERY
In November 1982, Jean-Michel had a solo exhibition at Fun Gallery.
254 E. 10TH ST., NEW YORK

9. CLUB 57
One of the clubs Jean-Michel often went to with his friends. Keith Haring performed a eulogy for SAMO, Jean-Michel's graffiti tag, at Club 57 after he read, "SAMO is dead."
57 ST. MARK'S PL., NEW YORK

10. TOWER RECORDS
Jean-Michel enjoyed an array of music from different genres, including hip hop, jazz, and bebop. Tower Records was his go-to record store.
E. 4TH ST. AND BROADWAY, NEW YORK

11. TONY SHAFRAZI GALLERY
In September 1985, Jean-Michel and Andy Warhol debuted their collaborative works at Shafrazi's gallery. In May 1987, three large works on paper by Jean-Michel were exhibited there.
163 MERCER ST., NEW YORK

12. PEARL PAINT
Jean-Michel purchased art supplies from this store.
308 CANAL ST., NEW YORK

POSTHUMOUS EXHIBITION HISTORY

Jean-Michel Basquiat: Paintings, Gallery Schlesinger Limited, New York, November 1988.

Collaborations: Andy Warhol, Jean-Michel Basquiat, Mayor Rowan Gallery, Mayor Gallery, and David Grob Limited, London, England, November 21, 1988–January 21, 1989.

Jean-Michel Basquiat: Memorial Exhibition, Annina Nosei Gallery, New York, December 3, 1988–January 14, 1989.

The Enchanted in Contemporary Art. Warhol, Basquiat, and Clemente, The National Museum of Art Osaka, Osaka, Japan, January 7–18, 1989.

Words, Tony Shafrazi Gallery, New York, January 21–February 18, 1989.

Jean-Michel Basquiat / Julian Schnabel, Rooseum, Malmö, Sweden, April 8–May 28, 1989.

1979–1989: American, Italian, Mexican Art from the Collection of Francesco Pellizzi, Hofstra Museum, Hofstra University, Hempstead, New York, April 16–May 26, 1989. Traveled to Lehigh University Art Galleries, Ralph Wilson Gallery, Bethlehem, Pennsylvania, September 8–November 2, 1989.

The Chase Manhattan Bank Collection 1974–1989, Yokohama Museum of Art, Yokohama, Japan, June 18–October 1, 1989.

A Decade of American Drawing 1980–1989, Daniel Weinberg Gallery, Los Angeles, California, July 15–August 26, 1989.

Maîtres Modernes et Contemporains, Artis, Monte Carlo, Monaco, July 21–September 15, 1989.

The Blues Aesthetic: Black Culture and Modernism, Washington Project for the Arts, Washington, DC, September 14–December 9, 1989. Traveled to California Afro-American Museum, Los Angeles, California, January 12–March 4, 1990.

The Blues Aesthetic: Black Culture and Modernism, Duke University Museum of Art, Durham, North Carolina, March 23–May 20, 1990. Traveled to Blaffer Gallery, University of Houston, Houston, Texas, June 8–July 31, 1990; and the Studio Museum in Harlem, New York, September 16–December 30, 1990.

Jean-Michel Basquiat: Das zeichnerische Werk, Kestner-Gesellschaft, Hannover, West Germany, September 15–October 22, 1989.

Warhol-Basquiat: Collaborations, Didier Imbert Fine Arts, Paris, France, September 28–November 25, 1989.

Jean-Michel Basquiat, Vrej Baghoomian, Inc., New York, October 21–November 25, 1989.

Jean-Michel Basquiat: Peintures, sculptures, œuvres sur papier et dessins, Galerie Enrico Navarra, Paris, France, November 8–December 31, 1989.

Jean-Michel Basquiat, Dau al Set, Galeria d'Arte, Barcelona, Spain, November–December, 1989.

Selected Americans, Edward Totah Gallery, London, England, November 28–December 16, 1989.

Cross, Joseph Helman Gallery, New York, December 13, 1989–January 6, 1990.

Selected Works, The Greenberg Gallery, Saint Louis, Missouri, 1990.

Sélection Américaine, Galerie Hadrien-Thomas, Paris, France, January 10–February 24, 1990.

Jean-Michel Basquiat: Œuvres sur papier, Galerie Le Gall Peyroulet, Paris, France, January 23–March 3, 1990.

Par hasard: A Changing Installation of Recent Acquisitions, Douglas Drake Gallery, New York, February 3–24, 1990.

Drawings of the 80s from the Collection: A Century of American Drawings, Museum of Modern Art, New York, April 12–July 10, 1990.

Gesture & Signature, Michael Kohn Gallery, Santa Monica, California, May 12–June 10, 1990.

The Decade Show: Frameworks of Identity in the 1980s, Museum of Contemporary Hispanic Art, New Museum of Contemporary Art, and The Studio Museum in Harlem, New York, May 12–August 19, 1990.

Faces, Marc Richards Gallery, Los Angeles, California, June 29–July 28, 1990.

Summer—Works on Paper, Fay Gold Gallery, Atlanta, Georgia, June–August 1990.

Pharmakon '90, Nippon Convention Center, International Exhibition Hall, Tokyo, Japan, July 28–August 20, 1990.

The Last Decade: American Artists of the '80s, Tony Shafrazi Gallery, New York, September 15–October 27, 1990.

Basquiat, Galerie Fabien Boulakia, Paris, France, September 27–November 3, 1990.

Jean-Michel Basquiat and Andy Warhol, Ho-Am Gallery, Seoul, South Korea, October 1–31, 1990.

Language in Art, The Aldrich Contemporary Art Museum, Ridgefield, Connecticut, October 20, 1990–January 6, 1991.

Works on Paper, Cavaliero Fine Arts, New York, November 1–30, 1990.

Quickdraw: American Master Drawings Since 1959, Frank Bernaducci Gallery, New York, November 2–December 1, 1990.

Jean-Michel Basquiat: Drawings, Robert Miller Gallery, New York, November 3–December 1, 1990.

Keith Haring, Jean-Michel Basquiat: Paintings, Tony Shafrazi Gallery, New York, December 15, 1990–January 26, 1991.

The 1980s: A Selected View from the Whitney Museum of American Art, Whitney Museum of American Art, New York, January 16–March 24, 1991.

Jean-Michel Basquiat: Oil Paintings, Drawings, Etc., PS Gallery, Tokyo, Japan, March 4–May 17, 1991.

Words & #s, Museum of Contemporary Art, Wright State University, Dayton, Ohio, April 7–May 10, 1991.

An Aspect of Contemporary Art, Wilderness: Toward Their Own Nature, Setagaya Art Museum, Tokyo, Japan, April 2–May 6, 1991.

Selected Works, Enrico Navarra Gallery, New York, May 6–June 20, 1991.

Compassion and Protest: Recent Social and Political Art from the Eli Broad Family Foundation Collection, San Jose Museum of Art, San Jose, California, June 1–August 25, 1991.

Drawings Acquisitions, 1980–1991: Selections from the Permanent Collection of the Whitney Museum of American Art, Whitney Museum of American Art at Philip Morris, New York, June 12–September 5, 1991.

Portraits on Paper, Robert Miller Gallery, New York, June 25–August 2, 1991.

Mito y Magia en América: los Ochenta, Museo de Arte Contemporaneo de Monterrey, Monterrey, Mexico, June–September 1991.

Andy Warhol & Jean-Michel Basquiat, Sonje Museum of Contemporary Art, Kyongju, South Korea, September 14–October 20, 1991. Traveled to National Museum of Modern and Contemporary Art, Seoul, South Korea, November 1–30, 1991.

Art of the 1980s: Selections from the Collection of the Eli Broad Family Foundation, Duke University Museum of Art, Durham, North Carolina, September 20, 1991–January 5, 1992.

Devil on the Stairs: Looking Back on the Eighties, Institute of Contemporary Art, University of Pennsylvania, Philadelphia, October 4, 1991–January 5, 1992. Traveled to The Forum and Washington University Gallery of Art, Saint Louis, Missouri, February 1–March 22, 1992; and Newport Harbor Art Museum, Newport Beach, California, April 16–June 21, 1992.

Jean-Michel Basquiat. Œuvres sur papier, Galerie de Poche, Paris, France, December 5–28, 1991.

Domenikos Theotokopoulos: A Dialogue, Philippe Briet Gallery, New York, December 5, 1991–January 25, 1992.

A Passion for Art: Watercolors and Works on Paper, Tony Shafrazi Gallery, New York, December 7, 1991–January 25, 1992.

Works on Paper, Annina Nosei Gallery, New York, December 10, 1991–January 7, 1992.

American Artists of the 80s, Palazzo delle Albere, Museo Provinciale d'Arte Sezione Contemporanea, Trento, Italy, December 18, 1991–March 1, 1992.

Paris Connections: African American Artists in Paris, Bomani Gallery and Jernigan Wicker Fine Arts, San Francisco, California, January 14–February 29, 1992.

Yvon Lambert Collectionne, Musée d'Art Moderne, Villeneuve d'Ascq, France, January 18–April 20, 1992.

Jean-Michel Basquiat, Vrej Baghoomian, Inc., New York, February 8–March 7, 1992.

Allegories of Modernism: Contemporary Drawing, Museum of Modern Art, New York, February 16–May 5, 1992.

Jean-Michel Basquiat, Galerie Eric van de Weghe, Brussels, Belgium, April 9–May 23, 1992.

An Exhibition for Satyajit Ray, Philippe Briet Gallery, New York, April 11–May 16, 1992.

Passions and Cultures: Selected Works from the Rivendell Collection, 1967–1991, Richard and Marieluise Black Center for Curatorial Studies, Bard College, Annandale-on-Hudson, New York, April–October 1992.

The Power of the City / The City of Power, Whitney Museum of American Art, Downtown Branch, New York, May 20–July 10, 1992.

Ars Pro Domo: Zeitgenössische Kunst aus Kölner Privatbesitz, Gesellschaft für Modern Kunst am Museum Ludwig, Cologne, Germany, May 22–August 9, 1992.

Gifts and Acquisitions in Context, Whitney Museum of American Art, New York, May 22–September 20, 1992.

Jean-Michel Basquiat, Jonathan Borofsky, Richard Bosman, Kang So Lee, Terry Winters, Haenah-Kent Gallery, New York, June 6–July 10, 1992.

Jean-Michel Basquiat: Une Rétrospective, Musée Cantini, Marseille, France, July 4–September 20, 1992.

Le portrait dans l'art contemporain, Musée d'Art moderne et contemporain, Nice, France, July 3–September 27, 1992.

Le Cri et la raison, Espace de l'Art Contemporain, Château de Mousans-Sartoux, France, July 6–November 22, 1992.

Baziotes to Basquiat . . . and Beyond, Bellas Artes, Santa Fe, New Mexico, August 20–September 30, 1992.

X Mostra da Gravura, Curitaba / Mostra America, Fundacio Cultural de Curitaba / Museo de Gravura, Curitaba, Brazil, October 16–December 6, 1992.

Installation of "Nu-Nile" and Untitled (Palladium Painting), Metropolitan Museum of Art, New York, October 19, 1992–April 22, 1993.

Jean-Michel Basquiat, Whitney Museum of American Art, New York, October 23, 1992–February 14, 1993. Traveled to Des Moines Art Center, Des Moines, Iowa, May 22–August 15, 1993; The Menil Collection, Houston, Texas, March 12–May 9, 1993; and Montgomery Museum of Fine Arts, Montgomery, Alabama, November 18, 1993–January 9, 1994.

Jean-Michel Basquiat, Vrej Baghoomian, Inc., New York, March 11–May 9, 1993.

Dream Singers, Story Tellers: An African-American Presence, Fukui Fine Arts Museum, Fukui, Japan, November 6–December 2, 1992. Traveled to Tokushima Modern Art Museum, Tokushima, Japan, January 23–March 7, 1993; Otani Memorial Art Museum, Nishinomiya, Japan, April 10–May 9, 1993; and New Jersey State Museum, Trenton, New Jersey, August 7, 1993–March 20, 1994.

I Am the Enunciator, Thread Waxing Space, New York, January 9–February 27, 1993.

Extravagant: The Economy of Elegance, Tony Shafrazi Gallery, New York, January 30–February 27, 1993. Traveled to Russisches Kulturzentrum, Berlin, Germany, May 7–June 27, 1993.

Jean-Michel Basquiat, Alpha Cubic Gallery, Tokyo, Japan, March 1993.

The Theater of Refusal: Black Art and Mainstream Criticism, Fine Arts Gallery University of California, Irvine, California, April 8–May 12, 1993.

1982–1983: Ten Years After, Tony Shafrazi Gallery, New York, May 7–July 30, 1993.

Jean-Michel Basquiat, Galerie Sho Contemporary Art, Tokyo, Japan, May 11–June 6, 1993.

Jean-Michel Basquiat, Galerie Bruno Bischofberger, Zurich, Switzerland, June 10–September 11, 1993.

Jean-Michel Basquiat, Newport Harbor Art Museum, Newport Beach, California, July 10–September 12, 1993.

Jean-Michel Basquiat, FAE Musée d'Art Contemporain, Pully-Lausanne, Switzerland, July 10–November 7, 1993.

Et tous ils changent le monde, Biennale d'Art Contemporain de Lyon, Halle Tony Garnier, Lyon, France, September 3–October 13, 1993.

Jean-Michel Basquiat: Paintings, Tony Shafrazi Gallery, New York, November 20, 1993–January 8, 1994.

Jean-Michel Basquiat: Peinture, dessin, écriture, Musée-Galerie de la Seita, Paris, France, December 17, 1993–February 26, 1994.

Jean-Michel Basquiat, Galerie Delta, Rotterdam, the Netherlands, 1993.

The Herman and Harriet Kelley Collection of African American Art, San Antonio Museum of Art, San Antonio, Texas, February 4–April 3, 1994.

The Shaman as Artist / The Artist as Shaman, Aspen Art Museum, Aspen, Colorado, February 10–April 10, 1994.

Jean-Michel Basquiat, Henry Art Gallery, University of Washington, Seattle, Washington, February 18–April 28, 1994.

30 Years: Art in the Present Tense, The Aldrich Contemporary Art Museum, Ridgefield, Connecticut, May 15–September 18, 1994.

Against All Odds: The Healing Powers of Art, Ueno Royal Museum, Tokyo, Japan, June 17–25, 1994. Traveled to Hakone Open-Air Museum, Hakone, Japan, July 13–August 14, 1994.

Jean-Michel Basquiat: The Blue Ribbon Paintings, Mount Holyoke College Art Museum, South Hadley, Massachusetts, September 8–December 22, 1994. Traveled to Wadsworth Atheneum, Hartford, Connecticut, January–March 1995; The Andy Warhol Museum, Pittsburgh, Pennsylvania, April 12–September 17, 1995; and Museum of Contemporary Art, North Miami, Florida, October 15, 1995–December 8, 1996.

Jean-Michel Basquiat, Sandro Chia, Francesco Clemente, Enzo Cucchi, David Salle, Julian Schnabel, Akira Ikeda Gallery, Yokosuka, Japan, August 6–September 24, 1994.

Jean-Michel Basquiat, Johnson County Community College Gallery of Art, Overland Park, Kansas, September 11–October 18, 1994.

From Beyond the Pale: Art and Artists at the Edge of Consensus, Irish Museum of Modern Art, Dublin, Ireland, September 23, 1994–January 15, 1995.

Maîtres Modernes et Contemporains, Galerie Jérôme de Noirmont, Paris, France, October 6–December 6, 1994.

Jean-Michel Basquiat: Works in Black and White, Robert Miller Gallery, New York, November 14, 1994–January 7, 1995.

Jean-Michel Basquiat, Galerie Delta, Rotterdam, the Netherlands, 1994.

A New York Time: Drawings of the Eighties, Bruce Museum, Greenwich, Connecticut, January 22–April 23, 1995.

Two Cents: Works on Paper by Jean-Michel Basquiat and Poetry by Kevin Young, Centre Gallery, Miami-Dade Community College, Wolfson Campus, Miami, Florida, October 20, 1995–January 14, 1996. Traveled to Castellani Art Museum, Niagara University, New York, February 11–March 31, 1996; University of Memphis, Memphis, Tennessee, April 19–June 22, 1996; University of South Florida Art Museum, Tampa, Florida, July–August 1996; Otis Gallery, Otis College of Art and Design, Los Angeles, California, September–October 1996; and Austin Museum of Art, Austin, Texas, November–January 1997.

Passions privées, Musée d'Art Moderne de la Ville de Paris, Paris, France, December 19, 1995–March 24, 1996.

Collaborations: Basquiat, Clemente, Warhol, Kunsthalle Fridericianum, Kassel, Germany, February 4–May 5, 1996. Traveled to Museum Villa Stuck, Munich, Germany, July 25–September 29, 1996; and Castello di Rivoli, Turin, Italy, October 17, 1996–January 19, 1997.

Bodies and Heads: Drawings from the Estate of Jean-Michel Basquiat, Robert Miller Gallery, New York, February 6–March 9, 1996.

Jean-Michel Basquiat, Serpentine Gallery, London, England, March 6–April 21, 1996.

Jean-Michel Basquiat. Peintures, Galerie Enrico Navarra, Paris, France, April 2–June 12, 1996.

Jean-Michel Basquiat. Œuvres sur papier / Works on Paper, Galeries Lucien Durand-Enrico Navarra, Paris, France, May 3–June 15, 1996.

Jean-Michel Basquiat, Palacio Episcopal, Málaga, Junta de Andalucia, Andalusia, Spain, May 16–July 7, 1996.

Jean-Michel Basquiat, Galerie Bruno Bischofberger, Zurich, Switzerland, June 1–August 31, 1996.

Comme un Oiseau, Fondation Cartier pour l'art contemporain, Paris, France, June 19–October 13, 1996.

Thinking Print: Books to Billboards 1980–1995, Museum of Modern Art, New York, June 20–September 10, 1996.

Quelques impressions d'Afrique, Galerie Beaubourg, Vence, France, July 8–November 30, 1996.

Basquiat, Bruce Museum, Greenwich, Connecticut, August 4–September 8, 1996.

Bill Traylor, Philip Guston, Jean-Michel Basquiat, Gary Komarin, John McEnroe Gallery, New York, September 13–October 26, 1996.

Jean-Michel Basquiat: A TRIBUTE—Important Paintings, Drawings and Objects, Tony Shafrazi Gallery, New York, September 21–November 23, 1996.

Jean-Michel Basquiat, Galeria Luisa Strina, São Paulo, Brazil, October 29–November 20, 1996.

Jean-Michel Basquiat: 1980–1988, Quintana Gallery, Coral Gables, Florida, December 17, 1996–February 21, 1997.

35 Jaar: 1962–1997, Galerie Delta, Rotterdam, the Netherlands, January 8–February 8, 1997.

Jean-Michel Basquiat, Kaohsiung Museum of Fine Arts, Kaohsiung, Taiwan, China, January 26–April 27, 1997. Traveled to Taichung Museum, Taichung, Taiwan, China, May 4–June 4, 1997.

Andy Warhol & Jean-Michel Basquiat: Collaborations, Gagosian, New York, March 15–April 26, 1997.

35 Jaar: Delta Werken, Galerie Delta, Rotterdam, the Netherlands, March 22–June 15, 1997.

Jean-Michel Basquiat. Œuvres sur papier / Works on Paper, Musée Maillol-Fondation Dina Vierny, Paris, May 23–September 29, 1997.

In Your Face: Keith Haring, Jean-Michel Basquiat, Kenny Scharf, Malca Fine Art, New York, June 17–August 30, 1997.

Jean-Michel Basquiat, Gallery Hyundai, Seoul, South Korea, July 15–August 17, 1997.

King for a Decade: Jean-Michel Basquiat, Parco Museum, Tokyo, Japan, July 22–September 17, 1997.

Jean-Michel Basquiat, Art Beatus Gallery, Vancouver, Canada, September 10–October 14, 1997.

Jean-Michel Basquiat, Mitsukoshi Museum of Art, Tokyo, Japan, October 28–November 24, 1997.

Jean-Michel Basquiat, Galerie Sho, Tokyo, Japan, October 1–November 15, 1997.

American Graffiti, Chiostro del Bramante, Rome, Italy, October 3–December 8, 1997.

Jean-Michel Basquiat, Big Step Inc., Osaka, Japan, October 16–21, 1997.

Jean-Michel Basquiat. Obras sobre papel, Museo Nacional de Bellas Artes, Buenos Aires, Argentina, December 8, 1997–February 13, 1998.

Jean-Michel Basquiat: Paintings and Drawing 1980–1987, Gagosian, Los Angeles, California, February 12–March 14, 1998

30th Anniversary of Mr Chow: Portrait Collection, PaceWildenstein, Beverly Hills, California, February 14–28, 1998. Traveled to Mayor Gallery, London, England, October 27–November 18, 1998.

Jean-Michel Basquiat: obras sobre papeis, Museu de Arte Moderna, Recife, Brazil, April 1–May 31, 1998.

Œuvres sur papier et photographies. La Collection Yvon Lambert, Dialogue avec des artistes contemporains, Yokohama Museum of Art, Yokohama, Japan, April 11–June 21, 1998.

Jean-Michel Basquiat, MIMOCA (Marugame Genichiro Inokuma Museum of Contemporary Art), Marugame, Japan, April 18–May 31, 1998.

Jean-Michel Basquiat, Tony Shafrazi Gallery, New York, April 25–May 30, 1998.

Crossings: Kunst zum Hören und Sehen, Kunsthalle Wien, Vienna, Austria, May 29–September 13, 1998.

Jean-Michel Basquiat, Pinturas / Obras sobre papeis, Pinacoteca do Estado, São Paulo, Brazil, June 16–September 20, 1998.

Jean-Michel Basquiat, La Tête d'Obsidienne, Fort Napoléon, La Seyne-sur-Mer, France, June 26–August 14, 1998.

Au Fil du Trait—De Matisse à Basquiat, Carré d'Art, Nîmes, France, June 26–September 27, 1998.

L'intraçable frontière, Espace EDF Bazacle, Toulouse, France, July 3–19, 1998.

Portraits Obscured, Gagosian, New York, July 20–September 12, 1998.

Ensemble moderne: Das moderne Stilleben, Galerie Thaddaeus Ropac, Salzburg, Austria, July 25–August 31, 1989.

Basquiat + Haring + Scharf from the Leo Malca Collection, Kirin Plaza, Osaka, Japan, August 7–September 6, 1998.

Jean-Michel Basquiat: Témoignage, 1977–1988, Galerie Jérôme de Noirmont, Paris, France, October 2–November 27, 1998.

Jean-Michel Basquiat. 1980–1988, Galeria Maeght, Barcelona, Spain, October 27–November 28, 1998.

Azzedine Alaïa in the 20th Century, Groninger Museum, Groningen, the Netherlands, 1998.

Jean-Michel Basquiat, Kunst Haus Wien, Vienna, Austria, February 11–May 2, 1999.

Bad-Bad: That Is a Good Excuse, Staatliche Kunsthalle Baden-Baden, Baden-Baden, Germany, April 18–June 20, 1999.

Jean-Michel Basquiat, Centre Culturel L'Espal, Le Mans, France, April 29–June 15, 1999.

Other Narratives, Contemporary Arts Museum, Houston, Texas, May 15–July 4.

Jean-Michel Basquiat, Civico Museo Revoltella, Trieste, Italy, May 15–September 15, 1999.

Basquiat a Venezia, Fondazione Bevilacqua La Masa, Venice, Italy, June 9–October 30, 1999.

48 Esposizione Internazionale d'Arte, La Biennale de Venezia, Venice, Italy, June 13–November 17, 1999.

Jean-Michel Basquiat, Werke auf papier / Works on Paper, Stadtgalerie, Klagenfurt, Austria, June 18–September 26, 1999.

Basquiat, Galleria Dante Vecchiato, Forte dei Marmi, Italy, July 10–August 5, 1999. Traveled to Galleria Dante Vecchiato, Cortina d'Ampezzo, Padua, Italy, August 6–29, 1999.

20 Years / 20 Artists, Aspen Art Museum, Aspen, Colorado, August 5–September 26, 1999.

Making Choices, Museum of Modern Art, New York, March 16–September 26, 2000.

Jean-Michel Basquiat, Galerie Sho Contemporary Art, Tokyo, September 1–October 14, 2000.

Piecing It Together: A Visual Journal, San Jose Museum of Art, San Jose, California, September 26, 1999–January 9, 2000.

The American Century: Art and Culture, 1900–2000. Part 2, 1950–2000, Whitney Museum of American Art, New York, September 26, 1999–February 13, 2000.

Jean-Michel Basquiat, Keith Haring, Kenny Scharf, Galerie Delta, Rotterdam, the Netherlands, October 30–November 20, 1999.

Pittura dura: Dal Graffitismo alla Street Art, Palazzo Bricherasio, Turin, Italy, November 24, 1999–January 30, 2000.

Portrait Collection of Mr Chow, Galerie Enrico Navarra, Paris, France, December 1, 1999–January 10, 2000.

Jean-Michel Basquiat, Stephen Lacey Gallery, London, England, February 16–March 18, 2000.

Haiti: Anges et Démons, Halle Saint-Pierre, Paris, France, March 20–June 30, 2000.

Off White, Tony Shafrazi Gallery, New York, May 18–June 12, 2000.

Around 1984: A Look at Art in the Eighties, MoMA PS1, New York, May 21–September 30, 2000.

Et l'art se met au monde, Institut d'Art Contemporain, Lyon, France, June 23–October 29, 2000.

Le Nu au XXe siècle, Fondation Maeght, Saint-Paul, France, July 4–October 30, 2000.

Jazz and Visual Improvisations, Katonah Museum of Art, Katonah, New York, January 21–April 15, 2001.

Mythic Proportions: Painting in the 1980s, Museum of Contemporary Art, North Miami, Florida, February 16–May 13, 2001.

Group Exhibition: Basquiat, Boetti, Fontana, Nauman, Ruscha, Warhol, Van de Weghe, New York, April 2–29, 2001.

Jasper Johns to Jeff Koons: Four Decades of Art from the Broad Collections, Los Angeles County Museum of Art, California, October 7, 2001–January 6, 2002. Traveled to Corcoran Gallery of Art, Washington, DC, March 16–June 3, 2002; Museum of Fine Arts, Boston, Massachusetts, July 28–October 20, 2002; and Museo Guggenheim Bilbao, Bilbao, Spain, February 15–September 7, 2003.

Jean-Michel Basquiat—The Mugrabi Collection, Museum Würth, Künzelsau, Germany, September 2001–June 2002.

Naked since 1950, C & M Arts, New York, October 11–December 8, 2001.

One Planet Under a Groove: Hip Hop and Contemporary Art, Bronx Museum of the Arts, New York, October 26, 2001–March 3, 2002. Traveled to Walker Art Center, Minneapolis, Minnesota, July 14–October 13, 2002; Spelman College Museum of Art, Atlanta, Georgia, spring 2003; and Villa Stuck, Munich, Germany, October 18, 2003–January 11, 2004.

Warhol-Basquiat-Clemente. Obras en colaboración, Museo Nacional Centro de Arte Reina Sofía, Madrid, Spain, February 5–April 24, 2002.

Accrochage d'hiver: Photographies contemporaines, Galerie Jérôme de Noirmont, Paris, France, February 8–March 14, 2002.

New York Expression, Bergen Kunstmuseum, Bergen, Norway, February 15–April 28, 2002.

Les Jeux dans l'art du XXème siècle, Le Bellevue, Biarritz, France, June 22–October 3, 2002. Traveled to Palacio de Montemuzo La Lonja, Zaragoza, Spain, October 29, 2002–January 6, 2003.

In the Spirit of Martin: The Living Legacy of Dr. Martin Luther King, Jr., Bass Museum of Art, Miami Beach, Florida, September 6–November 10, 2002.

Exhibition of Andy Warhol and Jean-Michel Basquiat: Rare Collections, Galerie Sho Contemporary Art, Tokyo, Japan, October 21–December 21, 2002.

Talking Pieces: Text und Bild in der zeitgenössischen Kunst, Museum Morsbroich, Leverkusen, Germany, January 26–April 20, 2003.

Splat Boom Pow! The Influence of Comics in Contemporary Art, Contemporary Arts Museum, Houston, Texas, April 12–June 29, 2003. Traveled to Institute of Contemporary Art, Boston, Massachusetts, September 17, 2003–January 4, 2004; and Wexner Center for the Arts, Columbus, Ohio, January 31–April 30, 2004.

Pittura/Painting: Rauschenberg to Murakami, 1964–2003, Museo Correr, Venice, Italy, June 15–November 2, 2003.

Jean-Michel Basquiat: histoire d'une œuvre, Musée Maillol, Paris, France, June 27–October 23, 2003.

Raymond Saunders / Jean-Michel Basquiat, Galerie Sho Contemporary Art, Tokyo, Japan, September–November 2003.

Fantasme fantasque, Galerie Jérôme de Noirmont, Paris, France, October 8–13, 2003.

Fire Under the Ashes: From Picasso to Basquiat, Jan Krugier Gallery, New York, November 6, 2003–January 6, 2004. Traveled to Ditesheim & Cie, Geneva, Switzerland, April 29–July 31, 2004; and Institut Valencià d'Art Modern, Valencià, Spain, May 5–August 28, 2005.

Andy Warhol–Tom Wesselmann–Jean-Michel Basquiat, Stella Art Galley, Moscow, Russia, November 28, 2003–January 31, 2004.

Los Años 80, Galeria Guereta, Madrid, Spain, January 8–February 10, 2004.

Drawings, Gagosian, London, England, January 29–April 17, 2004.

African American Artists of the 20th Century: Selections from the Permanent Collection, Castellani Art Museum, Niagara University, Niagara Falls, New York, March 1–May 31, 2004.

MoMA at El Museo: Latin American and Caribbean Art from the Collection of the Museum of Modern Art, El Museo del Barrio, New York, March 5–July 25, 2004.

Moi! Autoportraits du XXe siècle, Musée du Luxembourg, Paris, France, March 31–July 25, 2004.

Picasso, Bacon, Basquiat, Tony Shafrazi Gallery, New York, May 8–July 30, 2004.

Takes & Outtakes: From the Andy Warhol Museum, Ronald Feldman Gallery, New York, June 10–July 30, 2004.

Jean-Michel Basquiat, Museo del Palacio de Bellas Artes, Mexico City, Mexico, October 5–December 19, 2004.

Pop Art & Co. The Berardo Collection, Bunkamura Museum of Art, Tokyo, Japan, November 6–December 26, 2004. Traveled to Daimaru Museum Umeda, Osaka, Japan, January 19–February 6, 2005; The Museum of Modern Art, Gunma, Japan, February 19–March 27, 2005; The Museum of Art, Kochi, Japan, April 3–May 22, 2005; Hiroshima City Museum of Contemporary Art, Hiroshima, Japan, May 29–July 10, 2005; Hokkaido Museum of Modern Art, Sapporo, Japan, July 26–August 28, 2005; and Nagoya City Art Museum, Nagoya, Japan, September 10–October 30, 2005.

Basquiat, Brooklyn Museum, New York, March 11–June 5, 2005.

In Word Only, Cheim & Read, New York, February 17–March 26, 2005.

Jean-Michel Basquiat, Museo d'Arte Moderna, Lugano, Switzerland, March 20–June 14, 2005.

Basquiat, Museum of Contemporary Art, Los Angeles, California, July 17–October 10, 2005

Drawing from the Modern, 1975–2005, Museum of Modern Art, New York, September 14, 2005–January 9, 2006.

Basquiat "Heads," Van de Weghe, New York, March 10–May 12, 2006.

Jean-Michel Basquiat 1981: The Studio of the Street, Deitch Projects, New York, May 4–May 27, 2006.

Full House: Views of the Whitney's Collection at 75, Whitney Museum of American Art, New York, June 29–September 23, 2006.

The Jean-Michel Basquiat Show, Fondazione La Triennale di Milano, Milan, Italy, September 19, 2006–January 28, 2007.

Jean-Michel Basquiat, Kukje Gallery, Seoul, South Korea, October 12–November 12, 2006.

Basquiat: An Anthology for Puerto Rico, Museo de Arte de Puerto Rico, Santurce, Puerto Rico, October 21, 2006–January 7, 2007.

Jean-Michel Basquiat Works on Paper, Van de Weghe, New York, May 4–June 8, 2007.

Glossolalia: Languages of Drawing, Museum of Modern Art, New York, March 26–July 7, 2008.

Andy Warhol, Jean-Michel Basquiat and Collaboration Paintings, Van de Weghe, New York, May 7–June 7, 2008.

Jean-Michel Basquiat: To Repel Ghosts, Fundación Marcelino Botín, Santander, Spain, July 11–September 14, 2008.

Jean-Michel Basquiat: To Repel Ghosts, Fondazione Memmo, Rome, Italy, October 2, 2008–February 1, 2009.

Jean-Michel Basquiat, Van de Weghe, New York, November 7–December 19, 2008.

The Jazz Century, Museo di arte moderna e contemporanea de Trento e Rovereto, Rovereto, Italy, November 15, 2008–February 15, 2009. Traveled to Musée du quai Branly, Paris, France, March 10–June 28, 2009; and Centre de Cultura Contemporània de Barcelona, Barcelona, Spain, July 21–October 18, 2009.

30 Americans, Rubell Family Collection, Miami, Florida, December 3, 2008–May 30, 2009. Traveled to North Carolina Museum of Art, Raleigh, North Carolina, March 20–September 4, 2011; Corcoran Gallery of Art, Washington, DC, October 1, 2011–February 12, 2012; Chrysler Museum of Art, Norfolk, Virginia, March 16–July 15, 2012; Milwaukee Art Museum, Milwaukee, Wisconsin, June 14–September 8, 2013; Frist Center for the Visual Arts, Nashville, Tennessee, October 11, 2013–January 12, 2014; Contemporary Arts Center, New Orleans, Louisiana, February 8–June 15, 2014; Arkansas Arts Center, Little Rock, Arkansas, April 9–June 21, 2015; Detroit Institute of Arts, Detroit, Michigan, October 18, 2015–January 18, 2016; Cincinnati Art Museum, Cincinnati, Ohio, March 19–August 28, 2016; Tacoma Museum of Art, Tacoma, Washington, September 24–January 15, 2017; McNay Art Museum, San Antonio, Texas, February 8–May 6, 2018; Juliet Art Museum, Charleston, West Virginia, May 12–August 19, 2018; Tucson Museum of Art, Tucson, Arizona, October 5, 2018–January 13, 2019; Joslyn Art Museum, Omaha, Nebraska, February 2–May 5, 2019; Nelson-Atkins Museum of Art, Kansas City, Missouri, June 1–August 25, 2019; Barnes Foundation, Philadelphia, Pennsylvania, October 27, 2019–January 12, 2020; Honolulu Museum of Art, Honolulu, Hawaii, February 22–June 21, 2020; Albuquerque Museum, Albuquerque, New Mexico, October 3, 2020–January 3, 2021; Arlington Museum of Art, Arlington, Texas, May 29–August 30, 2021; and Columbia Museum of Art, Columbia, South Carolina, September 25, 2021–January 17, 2022.

USA Collected Visions, Bronx Museum of the Arts, New York, March 5–May 10, 2009.

Looking at Music: Side 2, Museum of Modern Art, New York, June 10–November 30, 2009.

Art of Jean-Michel Basquiat, Makoto Saito, and Andy Warhol, Galerie Sho Contemporary Art, Tokyo, Japan, July 27–August 29, 2009.

A Tribute to Ron Warren, Mary Boone Gallery, New York, September 12–October 24, 2009.

Andy Warhol: The Last Decade, Milwaukee Art Museum, Milwaukee, Wisconsin, September 26, 2009–January 3, 2010. Traveled to Modern Art Museum of Fort Worth, Fort Worth, Texas, February 14–May 16, 2010; and Brooklyn Museum, New York, June 18–September 12, 2010.

We Want Miles—Miles Davis: Jazz Face to Face with Its Legend, Musée de la Musique / Cité de la Musique, Paris, France, October 16, 2009–January 17, 2010. Traveled to Montreal Museum of Fine Arts, Montreal, Canada, April 30–August 29, 2010.

Jean-Michel Basquiat: Large Drawings, Stellan Holm Gallery, New York, November 3–December 5, 2009.

MOCA's First Thirty Years, Museum of Contemporary Art, Los Angeles, California, November 15, 2009–May 3, 2010.

Basquiat/Warhol, Bowdoin College Museum of Art, Brunswick, Maine, January 12–April 4, 2010.

Big Paper Winter, Woodward Gallery, New York, January 16–February 27, 2010.

Afro Modern: Journeys through the Black Atlantic, Tate Liverpool, Liverpool, England, January 29–April 25, 2010.

C'est la vie! Vanités de Caravage à Damien Hirst, Musée Maillol, Paris, France, February 3–June 28, 2010.

Crash, Gagosian, London, England, February 11–April 1, 2010.

Your History Is Not Our History, Haunch of Venison, New York, March 5–May 1, 2010.

Miró / Dubuffet / Basquiat, Nassau County Museum of Art, Roslyn Harbor, New York, March 13–May 23, 2010.

Now's the Time, Black Rat Projects, London, England, April 22–May 20, 2010.

Jean-Michel Basquiat, Fondation Beyeler, Basel, Switzerland, May 9–September 5, 2010. Traveled to Musée d'Art Moderne de la Ville de Paris, Paris, France, October 15, 2010–January 30, 2011.

Street and Studio: From Basquiat to Séripop, Kunsthalle Wien, Vienna, Austria, June 25–October 10, 2010.

Flash in Naples (title of work exhibited), Nevada Museum of Art, Reno, Nevada, July 13–November 28, 2010.

Basquiat / Terada / Mapplethorpe, Robert Miller Gallery, New York, September 23–October 30, 2010.

Jean-Michel Basquiat, Galerie Pascal Lansberg, Paris, France, October 23–December 4, 2010.

The 80s Revisited: The Bischofberger Collection, Kunsthalle Bielefeld, Bielefeld, Germany, March 13–June 19, 2011.

Art in the Streets, The Geffen Contemporary at the Museum of Contemporary Art, Los Angeles, California, April 17–August 8, 2011.

Sketchbook for Arto, AS IF Gallery, New York, May 7–28, 2011.

Made in Italy, Gagosian, Rome, Italy, May 27–June 19, 2011.

Graffiti New York 80s, Galerie Jérôme de Noirmont, Paris, France, May 27–July 20, 2011.

The Street Art Show, Opera Gallery, London, England, June 17–30, 2011.

Club 57 and Friends, Dorian Gray Gallery, New York, September 8–October 9, 2011.

Warhol: Headlines, The National Gallery of Art, Washington, DC,

September 25, 2011–January 2, 2012. Traveled to Museum für Moderne Kunst, Frankfurt, Germany, February 11–May 13, 2012; Galleria nazionale d'arte moderna, Rome, Italy, June 11–September 9, 2012; and The Andy Warhol Museum, Pittsburgh, Pennsylvania, October 14, 2012–January 6, 2013.

Ménage à Trois: Warhol, Basquiat, Clemente, Bundeskunsthalle, Bonn, Germany, February 10–May 20, 2012.

This Will Have Been: Art, Love & Politics in the 1980s, Museum of Contemporary Art, Chicago, Illinois, February 11–June 3, 2012.

This Will Have Been: Art, Love & Politics in the 1980s, Walker Art Center, Minneapolis, Minnesota, June 30–September 30, 2012. Traveled to Institute of Contemporary Art, Boston, Massachusetts, November 15, 2012–March 3, 2013.

Motion and Emotion: Contemporary Art from Gerhard Richter to Chakaia Booker, Bowdoin College Museum of Art, Brunswick, Maine, February 16–June 3, 2012.

Micro Mania, Gagosian, Paris, France, April 18–May 31, 2012.

Picasso/Basquiat, Van de Weghe, New York, April 29–May 30, 2012.

Caribbean: Crossroads of the World, El Museo del Barrio, New York, June 12, 2012–January 6, 2013.

Jean-Michel Basquiat and Andy Warhol: Olympic Rings, Gagosian, London, England, June 19–August 11, 2012.

The Masterpieces of the Yvon Lambert Donation, Collection Lambert Avignon, Avignon, France, July 7–November 11, 2012.

Times Square Show Revisited, Hunter College Art Galleries, New York, September 14–December 8, 2012.

Self-Portrait, Louisiana Museum of Contemporary Art, Humlebæk, Denmark, September 14, 2012–January 13, 2013.

Refocus: Art of the 1980s, Museum of Contemporary Art, Jacksonville, Florida, September 15, 2012–January 6, 2013.

In Extremis: Death and Life in 21st-Century Haitian Art, Fowler Museum at UCLA, Los Angeles, California, September 16, 2012–January 20, 2013.

Regarding Warhol: Sixty Artists, Fifty Years, Metropolitan Museum of Art, New York, September 18–December 31, 2012.

Blues for Smoke, Museum of Contemporary Art, Los Angeles, California, October 21, 2012–January 7, 2013. Traveled to Whitney Museum of American Art, New York, February 7–April 28, 2013.

Masterpieces from the Berardo Collection, Gary Nader Art Centre, Miami, Florida, December 5–9, 2012.

Don't Be Shy, Don't Hold Back, San Francisco Museum of Modern Art, San Francisco, California, December 8, 2012–June 2, 2013.

Jean-Michel Basquiat, Gagosian, New York, February 7–April 6, 2013.

Jean-Michel Basquiat, Kukje Gallery, Seoul, South Korea, February 14–March 31, 2013.

Selections from the Permanent Collection, Museum of Contemporary Art, Los Angeles, California, March 3, 2013–January 27, 2014.

I, You, We, Whitney Museum of American Art, New York, April 25–September 1, 2013.

Man Made: Jean-Michel Basquiat, S|2 Gallery (Sotheby's), New York, May 2–June 9, 2013.

Textures: The Written Word in Contemporary Art, ACA Galleries, New York, May 4–June 15, 2013.

Jean-Michel Basquiat, Gagosian, Hong Kong, China, May 21–August 10, 2013.

Calligraphiti 1984–2013, Leila Heller Gallery, New York, September 5–October 5, 2013.

Jean-Michel Basquiat: Paintings and Drawings, Galerie Bruno Bischofberger, Zurich, Switzerland, June 3–September 13, 2013.

Adventures of Truth—Painting and Philosophy: A Narrative, Fondation Maeght, Saint Paul de Vence, France, June 29–November 11, 2013.

30 Years, Galerie Thaddaeus Ropac, Salzburg, Austria, July 24–August 28, 2013.

Time Machine: Jean-Michel Basquiat, Fred Tomaselli, Jackson Pollock, Jeppe Hein, Galerie Sho Contemporary Art, Tokyo, Japan, August 1–September 15, 2013.

Navigating Art Languages: The James M. Shelton, Jr. Collection, El Paso Museum of Art, El Paso, Texas, September 20, 2013–February 3, 2014.

Warhol/Basquiat, Kunstforum, Vienna, Austria, October 16, 2013–February 2, 2014.

Stranger than Fiction: Art of Our Time, Museum of Modern Art, New York, February 1–May 5, 2014

Look at Me: Portraiture from Manet to the Present, Leila Heller Gallery, New York, May 8–August 29, 2014.

The House, Faggionato Fine Art, London, England, June 12–August 15, 2014.

Shaping a Collection: Five Decades of Gifts, Whitney Museum of American Art, New York, July 17, 2014–October 19, 2014.

Poetics of the Gesture: Schiele, Twombly, Basquiat, Nahmad Contemporary, New York, May 2–June 14, 2014.

Jean-Michel Basquiat Drawing: Work from the Schorr Family Collection, Acquavella Galleries, New York, April 30–June 12, 2014.

Basquiat and the Bayou, Prospect.3 Triennial, Ogden Museum of Art, New Orleans, October 25, 2014–January 25, 2015.

Post Pop: East Meets West, Saatchi Gallery, London, England, November 26, 2014–February 23, 2015.

Jean-Michel Basquiat: Now's the Time, Art Gallery of Ontario, Toronto, Canada, February 2–May 10, 2015. Traveled to Guggenheim Museum Bilbao, Bilbao, Spain, July 3–November 1, 2015.

A Strong Sweet Smell of Incense: A Portrait of Robert Fraser, Pace, London, England, February 6–March 28, 2015.

Pressionism: Masterpieces of Graffiti on Canvas from Basquiat to Bando, Pinacothèque, Paris, France, March 12–September 13, 2015.

Michael Chow: Voice for My Father, Power Station of Art, Shanghai, China, April 2015–June 28, 2015. Traveled to The Andy Warhol Museum, Pittsburgh, Pennsylvania, February 13–May 8, 2016.

Basquiat: The Unknown Notebooks, Brooklyn Museum, New York, April 3–August 23, 2015. Traveled to Pérez Art Museum Miami, Miami, Florida, August 12–October 16, 2016.

I Like It Like This, S|2 Gallery (Sotheby's), New York, April 28–June 12, 2015.

America Is Hard to See, Whitney Museum of American Art, New York, May 1–September 25, 2015.

Collecting Contemporary, 1960–2015: Selections from the Schorr Collection, Princeton University Art Museum, Princeton, New Jersey, June 27–September 20, 2015.

I Got Rhythm: Art and Jazz Since 1920, Kunstmuseum Stuttgart, Stuttgart, Germany, October 10, 2015–March 6, 2016.

Second Wave: Aesthetics of the 80s in Today's Contemporary Art, Sweeney Art Gallery at UCR / California Museum of Photography, Riverside, California, November 14, 2015–March 19, 2015.

Human Interest: Portraits from the Whitney's Collection, Whitney Museum of American Art, New York, April 2, 2016–April 2, 2017.

Words Are All We Have: Paintings by Jean-Michel Basquiat, Nahmad Contemporary, New York, May 2–June 18, 2016.

Enduring Homage: Portraits of a Patron, Fresno Art Museum, Fresno, California, May 20–August 28, 2016.

Basquiat, Dubuffet, Soulages . . . A Private Collection, Fondation de l'Hermitage, Lausanne, Switzerland, July 24–October 30, 2016.

Fast Forward: Painting from the 1980s, Whitney Museum of American Art, New York, January 27–May 14, 2017.

Basquiat Before Basquiat: East 12th Street, 1979–1980, Museum of Contemporary Art Denver, Denver, Colorado, February 11–May 7, 2017. Traveled to Cranbrook Art Museum, Bloomfield Hills, Michigan, November 17, 2017–March 11, 2018.

Animal Farm, The Brant Foundation Art Study Center, Greenwich, Connecticut, May 14–October 1, 2017.

Basquiat: Boom for Real, Barbican, London, England, September 21, 2017–January 28, 2018. Traveled to Schirn Kunsthalle Frankfurt, Frankfurt, Germany, February 16–May 27, 2018.

Club 57: Film, Performance, and Art in the East Village, 1978–1983, Museum of Modern Art, New York, October 31, 2017–April 8, 2018.

One Basquiat, Brooklyn Museum, New York, January 28–March 11, 2018.

Zeitgeist: The Art Scene of Teenage Basquiat, Howl! Happening: An Arturo Vega Project, New York, May 13–June 10, 2018.

Sea of Desire, Fondation Carmignac, Porquerolles, France, June 2–November 4, 2018

Jean-Michel Basquiat, Fondation Louis Vuitton, Paris, France, October 3, 2018–January 14, 2019.

Jean-Michel Basquiat, Galerie Pascal Lansberg, Paris, France, October 5–November 5, 2018.

Salm Modern #1: Dimensions of Dialogue, National Gallery Prague, Prague, Czech Republic, December 2, 2018–December 1, 2019.

Jean-Michel Basquiat, The Brant Foundation Art Study Center, New York, March 6–May 14, 2019.

Jean-Michel Basquiat | Xerox, Nahmad Contemporary, New York, March 12–May 31, 2019.

Visions of the Self: Rembrandt and Now, Gagosian, London, England, April 12–May 18, 2019.

Forever Young: 10 Years of the Museum Brandhorst, Museum Brandhorst, Munich, Germany, May 24–July 19, 2019.

Basquiat X Warhol, The School, Jack Shainman Gallery, Kinderhook, New York, June 1–September 7, 2019.

Basquiat's "Defacement": The Untold Story, Guggenheim Museum, New York, June 21–November 6, 2019.

Jean-Michel Basquiat: Works on Paper, Château La Coste, Le Puy-Sainte-Réparade, France, August 11–October 13, 2019

Jean-Michel Basquiat: Made in Japan, Mori Arts Center Gallery, Tokyo, Japan, September 21–November 17, 2019.

Third Dimension: Works from The Brant Foundation, The Brant Foundation Art Study Center, New York, November 13, 2019–September 3, 2020.

Keith Haring | Jean-Michel Basquiat: Crossing Lines, National Gallery of Victoria, Melbourne, Australia, December 1, 2019–April 13, 2020.

Around Day's End: Downtown New York, 1970–1986, Whitney Museum of American Art, New York, September 3–November 1, 2020.

Writing the Future: Basquiat and the Hip Hop Generation, Museum of Fine Arts, Boston, Massachusetts, October 18, 2020–July 25, 2021.

Africa Reborn, Musée du quai Branly, Paris, France, February 9–July 11, 2021.

Grief and Grievance: Art and Mourning in America, New Museum, New York, February 17–June 6, 2021.

The World Stage: Contemporary Art from the Collections of Jordan D. Schnitzer and His Family Foundation, Boise Art Museum, Boise, Idaho, March 6–July 11, 2021.

Galerie de Portraits, Galerie Le Minotaure, Paris, France, March 13–May 15, 2021.

Impressionist, Modern, and Postwar Masters, Acquavella Galleries, Palm Beach, Florida, April 1–May 28, 2021.

Go back to the future, EAC, Espace de l'Art Concret, Mouans-Sartoux, France, April 3, 2021–April 3, 2022.

Spring Contemporary, Maddox Gallery, London, England, April 11–May 20, 2021.

1988, Artworks from the Collection Lambert, Collection Lambert, Avignon, France, May 19–September 5, 2021.

Warhol and Basquiat in Focus: Works from the Permanent Collection, Andy Warhol Museum, Pittsburgh, Pennsylvania, June 7–September 20, 2021.

Call & Response: Collecting African American Art, Munson-Williams-Proctor Arts Institute, Utica, New York, June 19–November 28, 2021.

Basquiat, Van de Weghe, East Hampton, New York, June 25–August 25, 2021.

Word Play, David Benrimon Fine Art, New York, July 15–August 21, 2021.

Hey! Did you know that Art does not exist . . ., Tel Aviv Museum of Art, Tel Aviv, Israel, July 27, 2021–January 7, 2022.

Jean-Michel Basquiat: King Pleasure©, Starrett-Lehigh Building, New York, April 9–December 2022

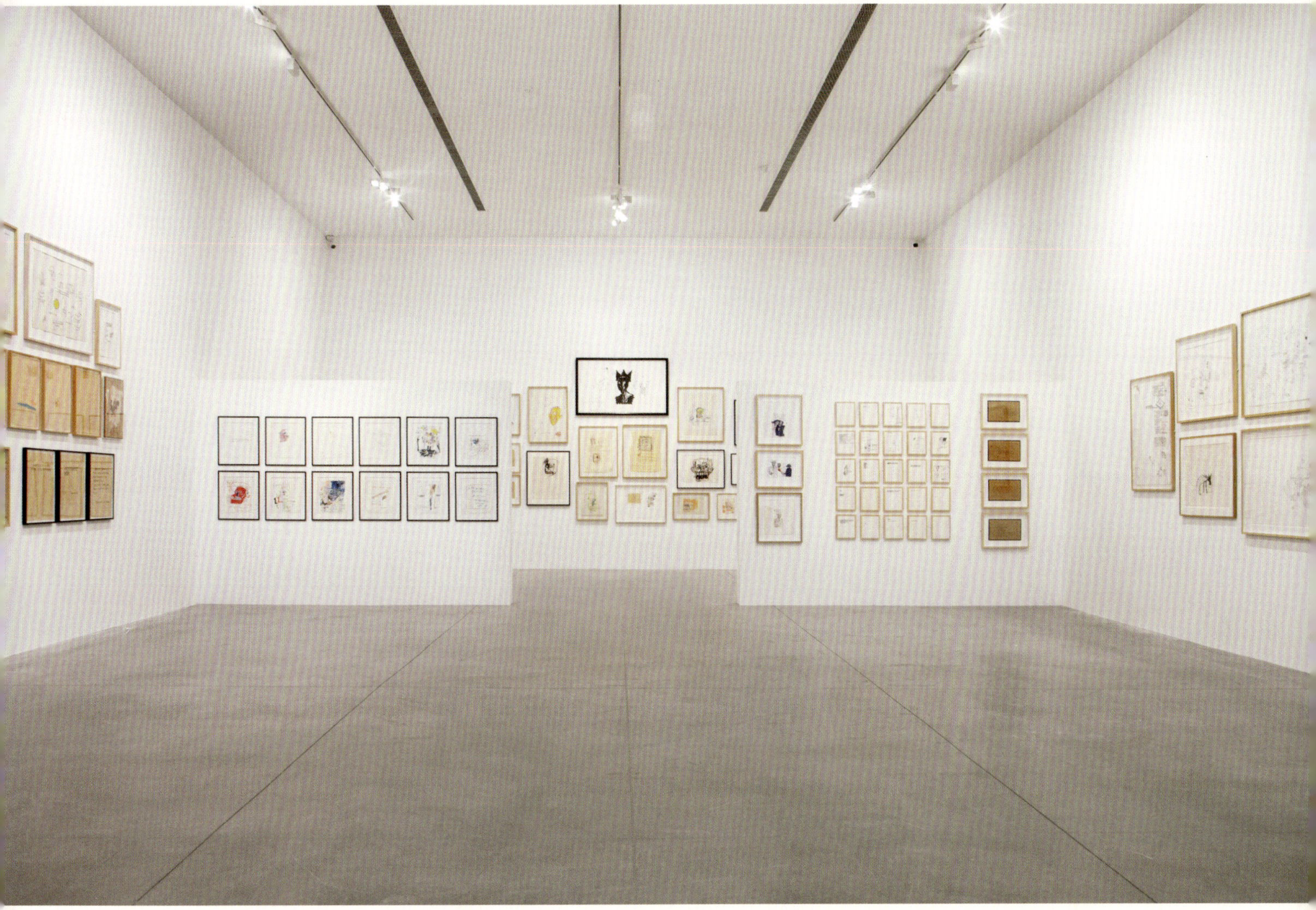

Installation views (with family and friends below), *Jean-Michel Basquiat: Works on Paper*, Château La Coste, Le Puy-Sainte-Réparade, France, 2019

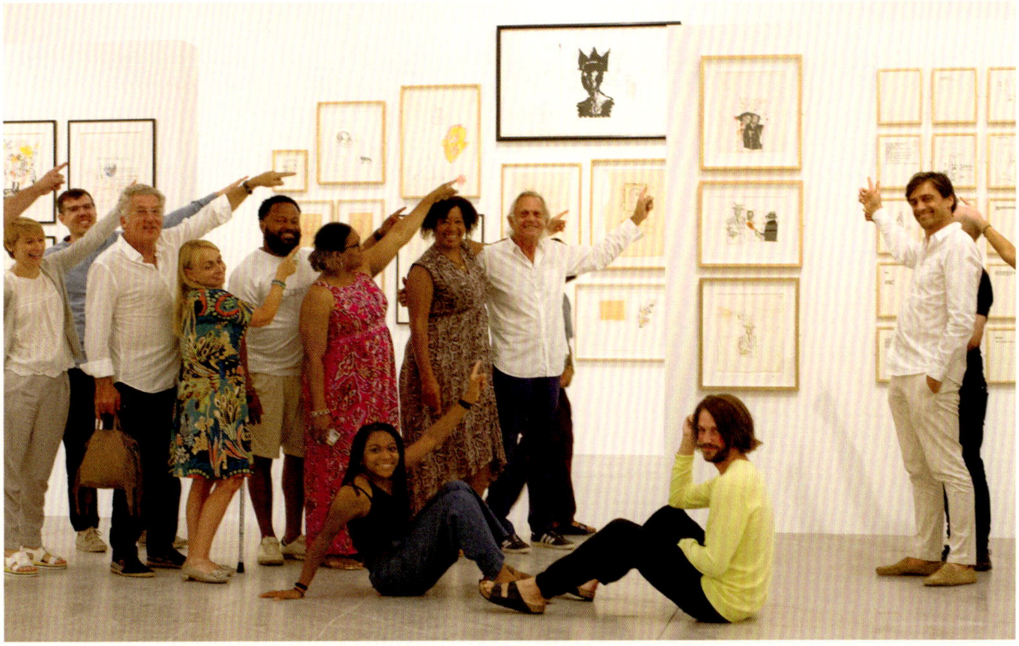

ABOUT THE AUTHORS AND CONTRIBUTORS

Lisane Basquiat is Jean-Michel's younger sister, and she has co-administered the Estate of Jean-Michel Basquiat since the passing of their father in 2013. She is the founder of Shaping Freedom, the owner of Hera Hub Carlsbad, and co-owner of Hera Hub San Marcos. Her ownership of the latter two enterprises are in honor of her mother, Matilde Basquiat.

Jeanine Heriveaux is Jean-Michel's youngest sister and the co-administrator of the Estate of Jean-Michel Basquiat.

Nora Fitzpatrick was the life partner of the late Gerard Basquiat for nearly forty years. She retired from United Airlines in 1992 to work alongside Gerard on the Estate of Jean-Michel Basquiat until his passing in 2013. Today, she continues to work with the artist's sisters Jeanine and Lisane in support of Jean-Michel's legacy.

Victor Bockris is a US-based author who has written books and articles on artists and musicians including William S. Burroughs, Lou Reed, and Andy Warhol.

Jeffrey Deitch has been involved with modern and contemporary art for more than forty years as a curator, advisor, and dealer.

Jennifer Goode is the sister of Eric Goode, the founder of Area nightclub. Jennifer worked in Area's art department, and she was Jean-Michel's girlfriend from 1984–87.

Debbie Harry is a singer-songwriter and actress and best known as the lead singer/co-founder of the group Blondie.

Anne Hidalgo has been the mayor of Paris, France, since 2014.

Annina Nosei is an art dealer and gallerist who has represented and exhibited a wide variety of artists including Barbara Kruger and Robert Longo. She was Jean-Michel's first art dealer.

Kenny Scharf is an American painter and was an important member of the downtown art scene of the 1980s alongside Keith Haring and Jean-Michel.

Johanne Shepley Siff is a luxury and fashion brand advisor. Previously she was the US brand manager for Comme de Garçons where she first met Jean-Michel.

Chris Stein is a musician, songwriter, and guitarist and co-founder of the group Blondie.

ACKNOWLEDGMENTS

We remain appreciative of the scholarship done by critics, art historians, and curators during the past thirty-four years. These catalogues and monographs have ensured a deeper understanding of Jean-Michel's work and his invaluable contribution to art history.

This is *not* an academic publication. This catalogue and the accompanying exhibition are, first and foremost, a gift that we offer in homage to the legacy and life of our brother, The Artist, Jean-Michel Basquiat. This project has facilitated another step in our family's healing from the inconceivable tragedy and loss that befell us in August 1988.

Little did we know that a conversation back in 2017 about the importance of showing Jean-Michel's work would lead to one of the most rewarding, reflective, and profound projects of our lifetimes: sharing our personal perspective on Jean-Michel's life and his journey from childhood to man and ultimately Artist.

We very quickly discovered that what we envisioned was both incredibly exciting and a huge undertaking that we could not do alone. The exhibition *Jean-Michel Basquiat: King Pleasure*© and this publication are the result of extraordinary teamwork by a talented, passionate, and supportive group of individuals who helped bring our vision to fruition. This was the dream team, each and every person playing an important role in a final product we are so very proud of.

We are so grateful for our brother who made his dream come alive and left such an incredible body of work for the world to see in perpetuity. There will never be enough words to thank Jean-Michel for who he was and how he showed up.

We thank our father, Gerard Basquiat, for dedicating so much of his life to his children and for tirelessly fighting to ensure that Jean-Michel's work and sacrifice was valued and respected. Nora, thank you for being an unconditional partner and friend to our father, especially as he navigated the unimaginable and uncharted.

We remain forever grateful to our mother, Matilde Basquiat, for her gentleness, compassion, grace, and never-ending generosity of spirit.

We acknowledge and appreciate the generous financial support of our sponsors: Spotify, with special thanks to Alia Calhoun, Andrea Fernandes, and Rasheed Habler; and Phillips, in particular Scott Nussbaum and Amy Ivy. (A special note of appreciation to you, Scott, for the myriad ways that you have shown up for our family over the years—with kindness, grace, and compassion.) And thank you to Vice, especially Kim Persse and Emma Crouchen.

We also acknowledge the exhibition team, all of whom have demonstrated a profound dedication to excellence. Thank you.

To Producer and Project Manager, ISG Productions, Ileen Gallagher: Ileen, your "badassery" is remarkable and you are amazing! You quickly understood what we intended to accomplish, and you brought it—every day immersing yourself in the vision for this project with passion, dedication, an incredible work ethic, and a drive for outstanding results. We respect, salute, and appreciate you. Thank you for a challenging job so well done. Your diligence is astounding. To Exhibition Assistant Sophie Culton, thank you for your support and for keeping us on track with your close attention to so many of the details.

To our exhibition design team, Adjaye Associates: Thank you Sir David Adjaye OBE for understanding our vision from our very first exchange. A warm thank you to the team of Marc McQuade, Abraham Murrell, and Morgan Mpungose for your creativity, outside-the-box thinking, flexibility, and collaborative support. Brilliantly done!

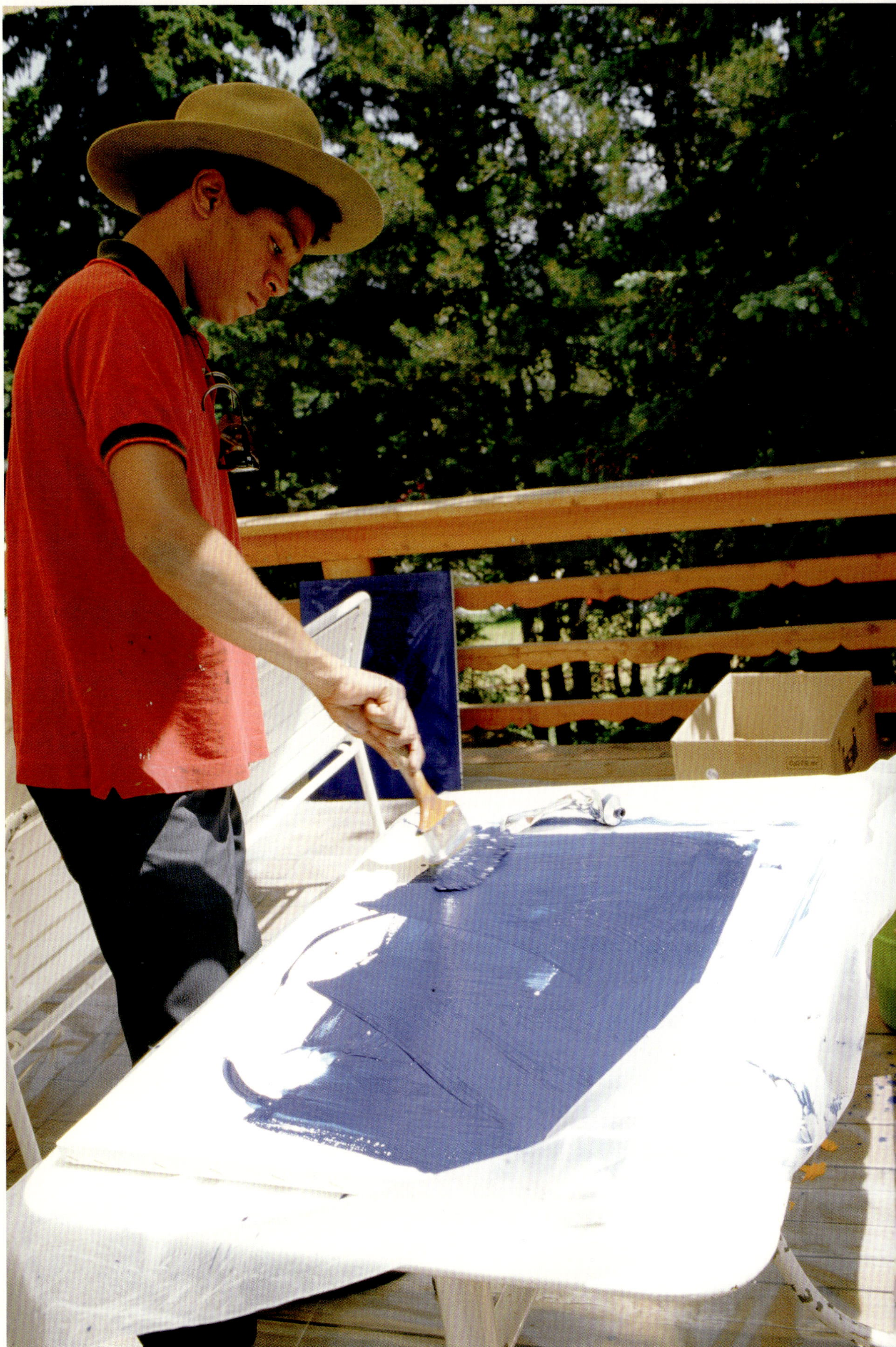

Jean-Michel painting in St. Moritz, Switzerland, 1983 © LEE JAFFE

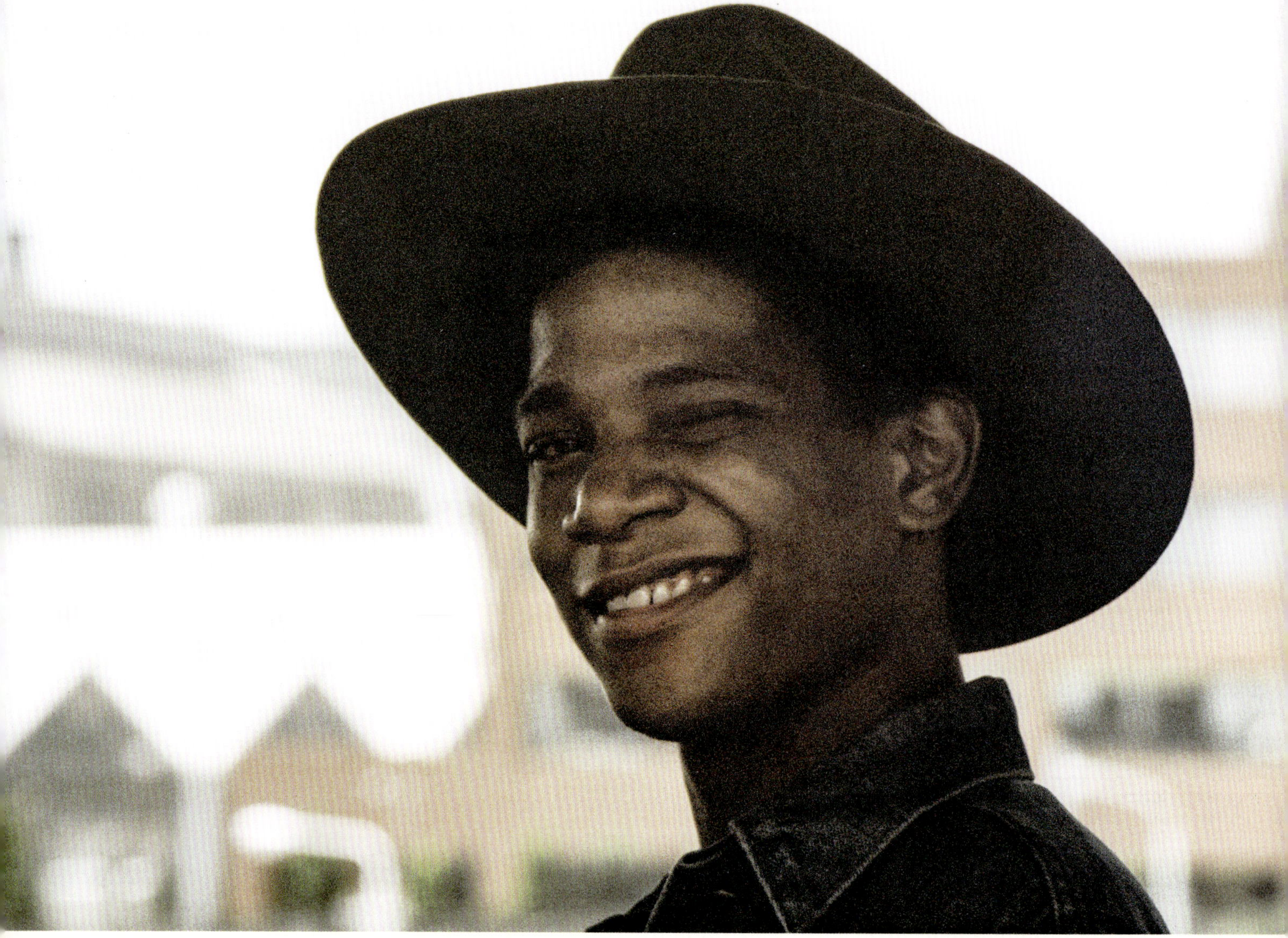

Jean-Michel in Tokyo, 1983

Thanks to our graphic design team at Pentagram: J. Abbott Miller, Yoon-Young Chai, and Michelle Brown. You are meticulous in your creation of beautiful things. We thank you for your attention to detail, your openness to ideas, and your passion and enthusiasm.

To our audio-visual designers FRAY Studio: Finn Ross, Adam Young, and Carolyn Downing. Thank you for your creative approach to the video content in the exhibition.

Thanks to David Harvey for the design of the audio-visual systems and to Suzanne Tillotson, Whitney Mire, and Zoe Grosshandler for the beautiful lighting design.

To our fabrication team at Digifab: Peter Brown, Bob McNulty, Michael Mochari, Matt Hutchinson, Neil Allen, and John Tompkins. Thanks for your extraordinary care and craft in the execution of the exhibition.

To management at Superblue: Marcy Davis, Marc Glimcher, and Mollie Dent-Brocklehurst and the team for your incredible operational support and marketing efforts. To Marcy, you are an amazing team player. Your perseverance to do what it took to get the job done is appreciated. We never saw you sweat, even when we knew you were juggling a million little details. Thank you to Eric Van Speights, Shantelle Rodriquez, Brandon Grom, Joyann Anello, Pat Elifritz, Kathleen Forde, Holly Campbell, and Maria Vogel for your passion, perseverance, and teamwork. It's been a pleasure.

Our public relations team at Girlie Action: Felice Ecker, Aleix Martinez, Carter Lou McElroy, Rosie Boyd, and David Elkin. Thank you to Felice. You are great at what you do—a fantastic collaborator, well-connected, and a warm supporter and cheerleader. We felt completely set up for success and so deeply appreciate all that you did.

Video interviews produced and directed by Goldfin Productions: Thank you, Sophia Loren Heriveaux, for an amazing job. We appreciate how dedicated you are to your craft, your ever-present professionalism, and grace under fire. We also appreciate your comfortable and warm interviewing style.

Director of Photography, Leo Gallagher. Thank you, Leo. We really appreciate the warmth of your style and your ability to follow direction to produce a clear cinematic vision with an attention to detail. We also appreciate that you are a team player and a great advocate for the team above and below.

To the interview film crew: Thank you so much to Naomi Crohn, Emma Weinswig, Julia Kupiec, Allison Cavanaugh, Estevan Falcon, Allie Iacono, Joji Baratelli, Sam Stephan Rice, Riede Dervey, Jeremy Herron, Lucy Smith Williams, Max Guillen, Richard Robles, Josh Sheehan, Daniel Muller, Paolina Weber, Ben Chesneau, Philip Kim, Young Ho Kim, Mia Varrone, Jahmal Mayers, Aidan Erbter, and Kachi Nwanonyiri for a job so well done!

To the interviewees: Thank you to Noelle Heriveaux, Sophia Loren Heriveaux, Jolie Heriveaux, Jessica Kelly, Joseph Basquiat, Hervey Heriveaux, David Stark, Jim Cinque, Reuben Andrades Jr., Steven O'Hara, Annina Nosei, Johanne Shepley Siff, and Steven Worthy. We are so grateful for your generosity and willingness to share your stories and perspectives, even in the midst of the pandemic.

And our general thanks:

The Artestar team, led by its founder and our dear family friend David Stark. Thank you, Sara Citarella, Ted Beckstead, Alex de Ronde, and Natalie Bryt, for always having our back. We adore you. Karrie Goldberg, and JP Duran at Kage Konsulting; and Reed Zukerman at RxR. We are so grateful to have found such an ideal space as the Starrett-Lehigh Building. A warm thank you to Elizabeth Ellis and Harry Fisher-Jones at AEA for helping to ground things at the onset. Thank you, Neil Davis, for being an awesome team player and for your enthusiasm. To Thomas Manzi, Debbie Harry, and Chris Stein, thank you for your generosity and great interviews. Thank you, Miranda Penn Turin, for an amazing and surreal experience and great pics. We love your energy and spirit and team. Thank you to Phillip Morrison, Kim White, and Karen Miller.

Thank you to Christina Burns of Rome Pays Off for your flexibility, creative eye, attention to detail, and for always having our best interests in mind. To the Enrico Navarra Gallery, thank you for so many things and for being friends in so many ways. To Isabel Venero at Rizzoli Electa, you are amazing and filled with "badassery." It's been such a pleasure working with you. We appreciate your great ideas, flexibility, and your commitment to and passion for the subject matter. And thanks to Charles Miers, Publisher of Rizzoli, and Margaret Chace, Associate Publisher of Rizzoli Electa, for your initial enthusiasm for the project. Jennifer Goode, thank you for sharing your photos and filling in some gaps. Thank you, Christina Bischofberger for lending photos. Thank you, always, to Frank Minieri for your flexibility, warmth, and for always welcoming us. Others who generously provided locations for video interviews include Comme des Garçons, New York, and Joanne Heyler and Dominque Clayton at The Broad. Thank you, Eleanor Nairne, Fred Hoffman, Jeffrey Deitch, and Sharon Matt Atkins for your generosity and your passion and commitment to the subject matter. Thank you, dear Jim Cinque, for always having our back and our family's best interests at heart. Thanks to Isabelle Hochberg, who provided valuable research assistance.

Film project: Thank you to the entire team for your generous support and vision for getting this project on the screen. We appreciate you. Thanks to Katherine Oliver, Lindsey Firestone, Ashley Stachowski, Bloomberg Philanthropies; Quinn Wilson and your collaborators Anthony Konigbagbe and Emi Stewart have shown such heart and dedication—you are the perfect team to tell our story.

Photographers: Thank you, Lizzie Himmel, Ben Buchanan, Volker Hinz Estate, George Hirose, Christopher Makos, Valerie Shaff, Donna Van Der Zee, George DuBose, Stellan Holm, Jean Kallina, Muna Tseng Dance Project Inc., Edo Bertoglio, Beth Phillips, Georges Courrèges, Victor Bockris, Lee Jaffe, Yoshitaka Uchida, Michael Nagle, and The Andy Warhol Foundation for the Visual Arts for allowing us to use your beautiful photos of our brother.

A special thank you to Bonnie Morrison for your professionalism, efficiency, and rigor in photographing the body of work and ephemera contained within the exhibition and this catalogue. Thank you, Jessica Kelly and Noelle Hervieux for spending months ensuring that the works and ephemera were photographed and catalogued.

There will never be room enough to acknowledge each and every person that has supported Jean-Michel, either through the development of this project, by remaining a fan of his incredible body of work, or by contributing to his becoming one of the greatest artists of our time. Please know that we thank you, appreciate you, and remain humble and in awe of how profoundly Jean-Michel has touched the lives and minds of so many.

Lastly, thank you to our respective and collective Basquiat, Heriveaux, and Kelly families. We love you and are deeply appreciative of all you've done to ensure that we felt supported, loved, and encouraged during the intense time of bringing our vision for *Jean-Michel Basquiat: King Pleasure*© to life. XO

Thank you. Thank you.
Thank you.

LISANE BASQUIAT,
JEANINE HERIVEAUX, AND
NORA FITZPATRICK, EXECUTIVE
PRODUCERS AND CURATORS

We'd like to also acknowledge the passing of our dear family friend and a passionate admirer of Jean-Michel, Enrico Navarra, who passed away in July 2020 during the curation of this exhibition.

Published on the occasion of the exhibition *Jean-Michel Basquiat: King Pleasure©*: Starrett-Lehigh Building, New York, NY: April 9–December 2022.

First published in the United States of America in 2022 by Rizzoli Electa, A Division of Rizzoli International Publications, Inc.
300 Park Avenue South
New York, NY 10010
www.rizzoliusa.com

FOR RIZZOLI ELECTA
Publisher: Charles Miers
Editor: Isabel Venero
Production Manager: Kaija Markoe
Designer: J. Abbott Miller and Yoon-Young Chai, Pentagram

FOR ISG PRODUCTIONS
Editor and Producer: Ileen Gallagher
Project Coordinator: Sophie Culton

Printed in China

2024 2025 2026 2027 /
10 9 8 7 6 5 4 3

ISBN (hardcover): 978-0-8478-7187-2
ISBN (paperback): 978-0-8478-7195-7
Library of Congress Control Number: 2021951127

Visit us online:
Facebook.com/RizzoliNewYork
Twitter: @Rizzoli_Books
Instagram.com/RizzoliBooks
Pinterest.com/RizzoliBooks
Youtube.com/user/RizzoliNY

Front cover:
James Van Der Zee,
Jean-Michel Basquiat, 1983
© James Van Der Zee Archive, The Metropolitan Museum of Art

Back cover:
Untitled, n.d.
Oil stick on paper
16 × 13 in. (40.64 × 33.66 cm)

Front endpaper (hardcover):
"Andy Warhol" notebook, detail of interior cover, n.d.
Graphite, colored pencil, ink, and oil stick on paper
14 ¾ × 12 ¾ in. (37.47 × 32.39 cm)

Back endpaper (hardcover):
"Andy Warhol" notebook, n.d.
14 ¾ × 12 ¾ in. (37.47 × 32.39 cm)

MIX
Paper | Supporting responsible forestry
FSC® C008047
www.fsc.org

Proud Sponsor

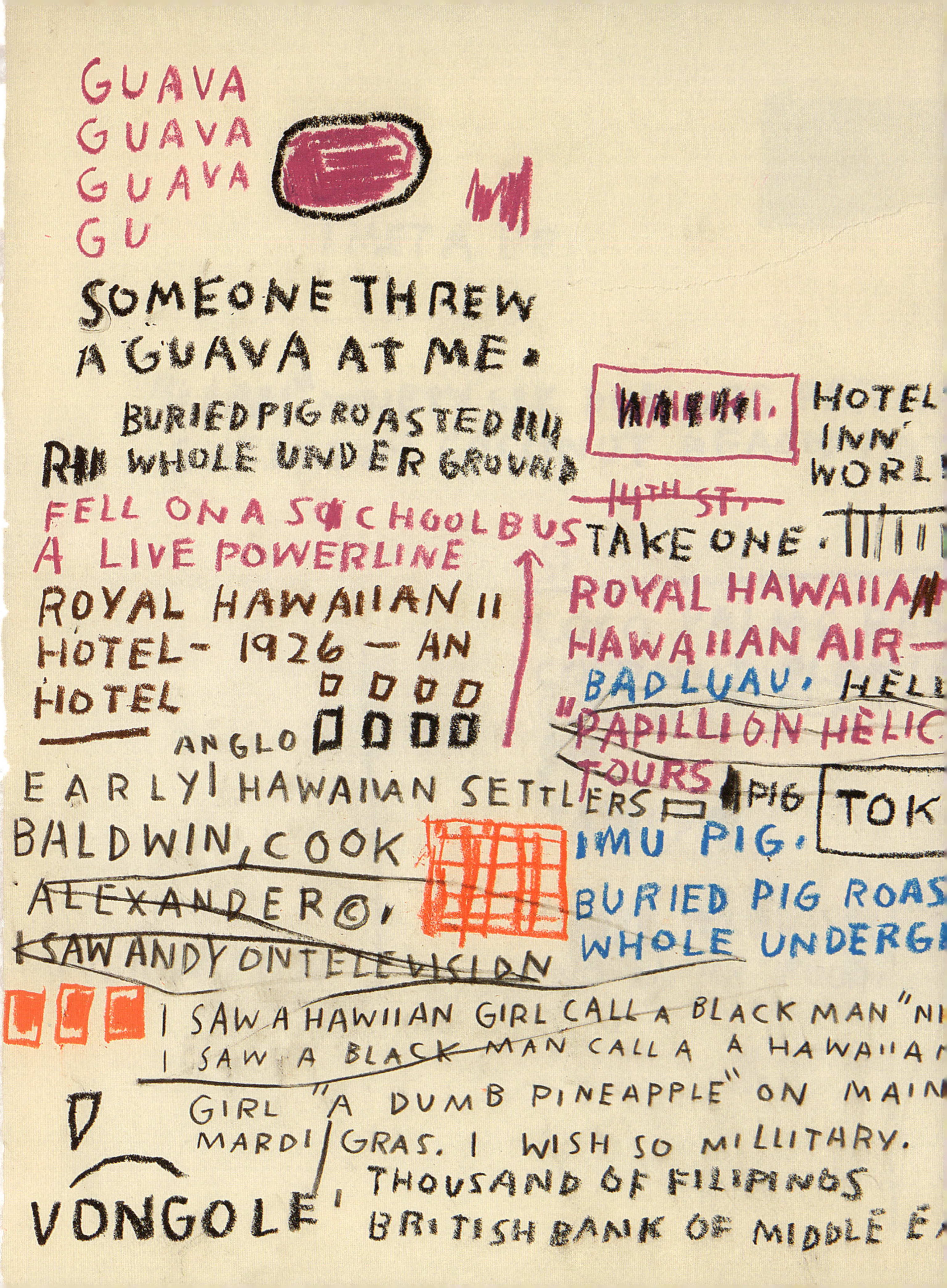
GUAVA
GUAVA
GUAVA
GU
SOMEONE THREW
A GUAVA AT ME.
BURIED PIG ROASTED
WHOLE UNDER GROUND
FELL ON A SCHOOLBUS
A LIVE POWERLINE
ROYAL HAWAIIAN
HOTEL - 1926 - AN
HOTEL
ANGLO
EARLY HAWAIIAN SETTLERS
BALDWIN, COOK
ALEXANDER©.
I SAW ANDY ON TELEVISION
HOTEL
INN
WORL
14TH ST.
TAKE ONE.
ROYAL HAWAIIA
HAWAIIAN AIR—
BAD LUAU. HEL
"PAPILLION HELIC
TOURS
PIG
TOK
IMU PIG.
BURIED PIG ROAS
WHOLE UNDERG
I SAW A HAWIIAN GIRL CALL A BLACK MAN "N
I SAW A BLACK MAN CALL A A HAWAIIA
GIRL "A DUMB PINEAPPLE" ON MAIN
MARDI GRAS. I WISH SO MILLITARY.
THOUSAND OF FILIPINOS
BRITISH BANK OF MIDDLE E
VONGOLE